T0213940

Lecture Notes in Computer Science 12209

Founding Editors

Gerhard Goos
Karlsruhe Institute of Technology, Karlsruhe, Germany
Juris Hartmanis
Cornell University, Ithaca, NY, USA

Editorial Board Members

Elisa Bertino
Purdue University, West Lafayette, IN, USA
Wen Gao
Peking University, Beijing, China
Bernhard Steffen
TU Dortmund University, Dortmund, Germany
Gerhard Woeginger
RWTH Aachen, Aachen, Germany
Moti Yung
Columbia University, New York, NY, USA

More information about this series at http://www.springer.com/series/7409

Qin Gao · Jia Zhou (Eds.)

Human Aspects of IT for the Aged Population

Technology and Society

6th International Conference, ITAP 2020
Held as Part of the 22nd HCI International Conference, HCII 2020
Copenhagen, Denmark, July 19–24, 2020
Proceedings, Part III

 Springer

Editors
Qin Gao
Tsinghua University
Beijing, China

Jia Zhou
Chongqing University
Chongqing, China

ISSN 0302-9743   ISSN 1611-3349   (electronic)
Lecture Notes in Computer Science
ISBN 978-3-030-50231-7   ISBN 978-3-030-50232-4   (eBook)
https://doi.org/10.1007/978-3-030-50232-4

LNCS Sublibrary: SL3 – Information Systems and Applications, incl. Internet/Web, and HCI

© Springer Nature Switzerland AG 2020
This work is subject to copyright. All rights are reserved by the Publisher, whether the whole or part of the material is concerned, specifically the rights of translation, reprinting, reuse of illustrations, recitation, broadcasting, reproduction on microfilms or in any other physical way, and transmission or information storage and retrieval, electronic adaptation, computer software, or by similar or dissimilar methodology now known or hereafter developed.
The use of general descriptive names, registered names, trademarks, service marks, etc. in this publication does not imply, even in the absence of a specific statement, that such names are exempt from the relevant protective laws and regulations and therefore free for general use.
The publisher, the authors and the editors are safe to assume that the advice and information in this book are believed to be true and accurate at the date of publication. Neither the publisher nor the authors or the editors give a warranty, expressed or implied, with respect to the material contained herein or for any errors or omissions that may have been made. The publisher remains neutral with regard to jurisdictional claims in published maps and institutional affiliations.

This Springer imprint is published by the registered company Springer Nature Switzerland AG
The registered company address is: Gewerbestrasse 11, 6330 Cham, Switzerland

Foreword

The 22nd International Conference on Human-Computer Interaction, HCI International 2020 (HCII 2020), was planned to be held at the AC Bella Sky Hotel and Bella Center, Copenhagen, Denmark, during July 19–24, 2020. Due to the COVID-19 coronavirus pandemic and the resolution of the Danish government not to allow events larger than 500 people to be hosted until September 1, 2020, HCII 2020 had to be held virtually. It incorporated the 21 thematic areas and affiliated conferences listed on the following page.

A total of 6,326 individuals from academia, research institutes, industry, and governmental agencies from 97 countries submitted contributions, and 1,439 papers and 238 posters were included in the conference proceedings. These contributions address the latest research and development efforts and highlight the human aspects of design and use of computing systems. The contributions thoroughly cover the entire field of human-computer interaction, addressing major advances in knowledge and effective use of computers in a variety of application areas. The volumes constituting the full set of the conference proceedings are listed in the following pages.

The HCI International (HCII) conference also offers the option of "late-breaking work" which applies both for papers and posters and the corresponding volume(s) of the proceedings will be published just after the conference. Full papers will be included in the "HCII 2020 - Late Breaking Papers" volume of the proceedings to be published in the Springer LNCS series, while poster extended abstracts will be included as short papers in the "HCII 2020 - Late Breaking Posters" volume to be published in the Springer CCIS series.

I would like to thank the program board chairs and the members of the program boards of all thematic areas and affiliated conferences for their contribution to the highest scientific quality and the overall success of the HCI International 2020 conference.

This conference would not have been possible without the continuous and unwavering support and advice of the founder, Conference General Chair Emeritus and Conference Scientific Advisor Prof. Gavriel Salvendy. For his outstanding efforts, I would like to express my appreciation to the communications chair and editor of HCI International News, Dr. Abbas Moallem.

July 2020   Constantine Stephanidis

HCI International 2020 Thematic Areas
and Affiliated Conferences

Thematic areas:

- HCI 2020: Human-Computer Interaction
- HIMI 2020: Human Interface and the Management of Information

Affiliated conferences:

- EPCE: 17th International Conference on Engineering Psychology and Cognitive Ergonomics
- UAHCI: 14th International Conference on Universal Access in Human-Computer Interaction
- VAMR: 12th International Conference on Virtual, Augmented and Mixed Reality
- CCD: 12th International Conference on Cross-Cultural Design
- SCSM: 12th International Conference on Social Computing and Social Media
- AC: 14th International Conference on Augmented Cognition
- DHM: 11th International Conference on Digital Human Modeling and Applications in Health, Safety, Ergonomics and Risk Management
- DUXU: 9th International Conference on Design, User Experience and Usability
- DAPI: 8th International Conference on Distributed, Ambient and Pervasive Interactions
- HCIBGO: 7th International Conference on HCI in Business, Government and Organizations
- LCT: 7th International Conference on Learning and Collaboration Technologies
- ITAP: 6th International Conference on Human Aspects of IT for the Aged Population
- HCI-CPT: Second International Conference on HCI for Cybersecurity, Privacy and Trust
- HCI-Games: Second International Conference on HCI in Games
- MobiTAS: Second International Conference on HCI in Mobility, Transport and Automotive Systems
- AIS: Second International Conference on Adaptive Instructional Systems
- C&C: 8th International Conference on Culture and Computing
- MOBILE: First International Conference on Design, Operation and Evaluation of Mobile Communications
- AI-HCI: First International Conference on Artificial Intelligence in HCI

Conference Proceedings Volumes Full List

1. LNCS 12181, Human-Computer Interaction: Design and User Experience (Part I), edited by Masaaki Kurosu
2. LNCS 12182, Human-Computer Interaction: Multimodal and Natural Interaction (Part II), edited by Masaaki Kurosu
3. LNCS 12183, Human-Computer Interaction: Human Values and Quality of Life (Part III), edited by Masaaki Kurosu
4. LNCS 12184, Human Interface and the Management of Information: Designing Information (Part I), edited by Sakae Yamamoto and Hirohiko Mori
5. LNCS 12185, Human Interface and the Management of Information: Interacting with Information (Part II), edited by Sakae Yamamoto and Hirohiko Mori
6. LNAI 12186, Engineering Psychology and Cognitive Ergonomics: Mental Workload, Human Physiology, and Human Energy (Part I), edited by Don Harris and Wen-Chin Li
7. LNAI 12187, Engineering Psychology and Cognitive Ergonomics: Cognition and Design (Part II), edited by Don Harris and Wen-Chin Li
8. LNCS 12188, Universal Access in Human-Computer Interaction: Design Approaches and Supporting Technologies (Part I), edited by Margherita Antona and Constantine Stephanidis
9. LNCS 12189, Universal Access in Human-Computer Interaction: Applications and Practice (Part II), edited by Margherita Antona and Constantine Stephanidis
10. LNCS 12190, Virtual, Augmented and Mixed Reality: Design and Interaction (Part I), edited by Jessie Y. C. Chen and Gino Fragomeni
11. LNCS 12191, Virtual, Augmented and Mixed Reality: Industrial and Everyday Life Applications (Part II), edited by Jessie Y. C. Chen and Gino Fragomeni
12. LNCS 12192, Cross-Cultural Design: User Experience of Products, Services, and Intelligent Environments (Part I), edited by P. L. Patrick Rau
13. LNCS 12193, Cross-Cultural Design: Applications in Health, Learning, Communication, and Creativity (Part II), edited by P. L. Patrick Rau
14. LNCS 12194, Social Computing and Social Media: Design, Ethics, User Behavior, and Social Network Analysis (Part I), edited by Gabriele Meiselwitz
15. LNCS 12195, Social Computing and Social Media: Participation, User Experience, Consumer Experience, and Applications of Social Computing (Part II), edited by Gabriele Meiselwitz
16. LNAI 12196, Augmented Cognition: Theoretical and Technological Approaches (Part I), edited by Dylan D. Schmorrow and Cali M. Fidopiastis
17. LNAI 12197, Augmented Cognition: Human Cognition and Behaviour (Part II), edited by Dylan D. Schmorrow and Cali M. Fidopiastis

38. CCIS 1224, HCI International 2020 Posters - Part I, edited by Constantine Stephanidis and Margherita Antona
39. CCIS 1225, HCI International 2020 Posters - Part II, edited by Constantine Stephanidis and Margherita Antona
40. CCIS 1226, HCI International 2020 Posters - Part III, edited by Constantine Stephanidis and Margherita Antona

http://2020.hci.international/proceedings

6th International Conference on Human Aspects of IT for the Aged Population (ITAP 2020)

Program Board Chairs: Qin Gao, Tsinghua University, China, and Jia Zhou, Chongqing University, China

- Inês Amaral, Portugal
- Ning An, China
- Venkatesh Balasubramanian, India
- Alex Chaparro, USA
- Honglin Chen, China
- Jessie Chin, USA
- José Coelho, Portugal
- Francesca Comunello, Italy
- Hua Dong, UK
- Katharine Hunter-Zaworski, USA
- Hirokazu Kato, Japan
- Jiunn-Woei Lian, Taiwan
- Chi-Hung Lo, Taiwan
- Eugène Loos, The Netherlands
- Brandon Pitts, USA
- Jing Qiu, China
- Peter Rasche, Germany
- Marie Sjölinder, Sweden
- Wang-Chin Tsai, Taiwan
- Ana Isabel Veloso, Portugal
- Konstantinos Votis, Greece
- Yuxiang (Chris) Zhao, China
- Junhong Zhou, USA
- Martina Ziefle, Germany

The full list with the Program Board Chairs and the members of the Program Boards of all thematic areas and affiliated conferences is available online at:

http://www.hci.international/board-members-2020.php

HCI International 2021

The 23rd International Conference on Human-Computer Interaction, HCI International 2021 (HCII 2021), will be held jointly with the affiliated conferences in Washington DC, USA, at the Washington Hilton Hotel, July 24–29, 2021. It will cover a broad spectrum of themes related to Human-Computer Interaction (HCI), including theoretical issues, methods, tools, processes, and case studies in HCI design, as well as novel interaction techniques, interfaces, and applications. The proceedings will be published by Springer. More information will be available on the conference website: http://2021.hci.international/.

General Chair
Prof. Constantine Stephanidis
University of Crete and ICS-FORTH
Heraklion, Crete, Greece
Email: general_chair@hcii2021.org

http://2021.hci.international/

Contents – Part III

Technology Acceptance and Societal Impact

Aging and Social Media

Mapping Intergenerational Masculinities on Instagram

Inês Amaral[1,2]([envelope]), Sofia José Santos[3,4], and Maria José Brites[5]

[1] Faculdade de Letras da Universidade de Coimbra, Coimbra, Portugal
ines.amaral@uc.pt
[2] Centro de Estudos de Comunicação e Sociedade da Universidade do Minho, Braga, Portugal
[3] Faculdade de Economia da Universidade de Coimbra, Coimbra, Portugal
sjs@ces.uc.pt
[4] Centro de Estudos Sociais da Universidade de Coimbra, Coimbra, Portugal
[5] Universidade Lusófona/CICANT, Porto, Portugal
mariajosebrites@ulp.pt

Abstract. Gender identities and roles do not stand alone but rather evolve while intersecting with other traits, namely age, resulting in cross and hybrid (gender and age) identities. Media are one of the pivotal formative spaces where audiences learn role models and the way they should express and behave: Therefore, media environments influence the way one perceives and understands age and gender identities as well as expresses them publicly. Media also promote (inter)generational contexts given that different age groups organize their technological experience in their own specific ways and interact with different other generations. This article explores how masculinities are represented in the digital realm, shedding light on intergenerational dynamics and collective hashtag narratives. Specifically, this article will analyse collective narratives on Instagram through a hashtag stream, focusing specifically on representations of masculinities and how different generations interact and represent how to be, behave and express as "a man".

Keywords: Generations · Ageing · Masculinities · Gender identities · Collective narratives

1 Introduction

As gender is a social construction, gender identities and roles are not immanent nor immutable [1]. Masculinities and femininities represent, thus, culturally and socially constructed ideals of what a boy/man and a girl/woman should be, express themselves and behave. These have been built within patriarchy and on a relational and binary basis [2, 3]. Although there is a prevailing conception of what it means to be a boy/man and a girl/woman, femininities and masculinities are multiple (depending on context, ideology, experiences, and sense of self) and, at times, even contradictory [2, 4]. As an identitarian element, gender identities and roles do not stand alone but evolve while intersecting with other traits or social categories, such as class, race and age. In point of

© Springer Nature Switzerland AG 2020
Q. Gao and J. Zhou (Eds.): HCII 2020, LNCS 12209, pp. 3–16, 2020.
https://doi.org/10.1007/978-3-030-50232-4_1

fact, the expression of gender identities is also anchored upon a generational sense of belonging. To be an "old man" (as hegemonically conceived, see Sect. 1.1) might entail features "young adults" are not allowed to have. According to Mannheim [5], there is a continuing character of generational changes that broadens the notion of a 'generational situation'. In the same line of reasoning, Corsten proposes the notion of a "we sense" [6] in order to summarize historical and social experiences that are lived individually or collectively, enabling the identification of subjects with various generational groups.

The media are one of the key formative spaces where boys and girls, and men and women learn how to be, express themselves, and behave in terms of gender identities [8]. Likewise, media environments can emerge as (inter)generational contexts given that different age groups organize their technological experience in their own specific ways. In fact, media experiences take place within people's cultural environments [9], an idea that is associated with belonging to a group. Historical and social experiences refer to the concept of 'we-sense' [6] and allow the identification of a specific subject with particular groups. Images contribute substantially to the creation of the we-sense, as people can have a concrete sense of specific experiences even if they existed before they were born, thus serving as a memory of unlived narratives, or happened elsewhere, thus creating expectations or fears.

If this mass media power concerning the formation of identities has been rendered consensual [3, 6, 7], the digital realm has not been an exception. Similar life experiences and cultural backgrounds induce identical appropriations of digital media, which, in turn, might generate the notion of a generational identity [5]. It follows that the different generations experience a social and technological change in an intergenerational logic. Social media allows the sharing of images that build intergenerational narratives. In computer-mediated communication platforms, connectivity patterns exist that metamorphose digital culture, enabling the identification of content-based social networks and conversation-based social networks. Social networks based on semantic indexing of content allow the analysis of content systems, interactions and social representations based on micro conversations from a perspective of distributed production of identity expressions.

Age and gender categories correlate with differences in social power, status, and access to resources. In this sense, both categories fall into power relations systems that shape all other social hierarchies [10]. Richardson [11] argues that "gender is socially and spatially (re)created and (re)organised in different ways by different generations". An intergenerational approach to masculinities allows for an understanding of everyday practices over generations of men from an intersection perspective. Intergenerationality is one of the elements to consider in social relations given that "masculinities are formed relationally with and against femininities, but also with and against other masculinities" [11].

This article aims to explore how digital collective narratives represent masculinities, shedding light on intergenerational dynamics. The research question that guides this study is: How do digital collective narratives represent masculinities, and how do those representations reflect intergenerational identities and relations? How can digital collective narratives portray male intergenerational relations? To answer this question, we will analyse collective narratives on Instagram through a hashtag stream, focusing specifically on representations of masculinities and how different generations interact and represent how to be, behave and express as a man.

1.1 Age and Gender: Intersecting Masculinities and Ageing

Masculinity is usually understood as a set of features that characterise and provide guidance on how boys and men should be, express themselves and behave. Although there is a hegemonic understanding of masculinity, Connel sheds light on the need to acknowledge the existence of 'multiple masculinities' [4, 12], namely hegemonic, complicit, subordinate, and marginal or subaltern masculinities, which are structured in relation to a specific patriarchal gender hierarchy [13].

The concept of 'hegemonic masculinity' refers to specific attributes - e.g. rationality, toughness, leadership, strength - and cultural dynamics through which men claim and perpetuate a position of power in the existing gender hierarchy [4, 13]. It is, thus, a normative proposal which represents an ideal to which men and boys should look up, offering guidance on how boys and men should be, think, feel, express themselves and behave [2, 3]. Men who adopt attributes commensurate with the ideal of hegemonic masculinity can assert their (alleged) superiority over women (and non-hegemonic men) and consolidate their general position of domination over them [14]. According to Connell [10], 'complicit masculinities' are characterized by an identification with the practices of hegemonic masculinity, seeking the benefits of the patriarchy [10]. Whereas "hegemonic masculinity" is not statistical, but rather normative [2, 4]; complicit masculinities can become statistically prominent.

In turn, the notion of subaltern masculinity emerges from an unequal relationship that is established between hegemonic masculinities and those who do not conform to them [15, 16]. In fact, "men who do not fit the paradigm of hegemonic masculinity and who show characteristics understood as "feminine" (e.g. sensitivity, fear, emotion, subordination, and passivity) are invariably ridiculed and viewed as inferior" [7, 14]. As Januário explains, the practices of subordination and domination include open and direct violence but also other less visible forms of violence, such as economic and social discrimination [16]. As masculinities and femininities are relational and defined on a binary basis, the "symbolic in subordinate masculinity approaches the symbolic of femininity" [17].

A growing body of literature has focused on 'toxic masculinities' [18] and 'hybrid masculinities' [19]. The concept of toxic masculinity depicts regressive male traits that fuel the need and legitimacy of (unjustified) violence and domination, subscribing not seldom times misogynist and homophobic ideologies [14, 18]. Finally, 'hybrid masculinities' can be defined as incorporation of identity elements that are associated with various marginalized and subordinated masculinities, as well as the performance of femininities and privileged male gender identities [19]. Bridges and Pascoe argue that "hybrid masculinities [which] may place discursive (though not meaningful) distance between certain groups of men and hegemonic masculinity, are often undertaken with an understanding of White, heterosexual masculinity as less meaningful than other (more marginalized or subordinated) forms of masculinity, and fortify social and symbolic boundaries and inequalities" [19].

The configurations of practices and behaviours are socially constructed [1] and therefore cannot be perceived and interpreted as static. The cultural diversity of the meanings of masculinity and femininity [17] is associated with a geographic diversity [19], as well as the idea that the practices and behaviours change as a function of space and time [10].

1.2 Identities, Collective Narratives and Online Engagement

Identity is the essence of being and ensures a sense of continuity in individuals, groups and society itself, even if in constant (re)construction [20]. It derives from the socialization process and summarizes existential pathways that are in permanent (re)adaptation and (re)invention, requiring thus (re)negotiation.

The Internet is often seen is a space for participatory and collective culture, identity formation in online environments is one of the central points of cyberculture research [20]. However, it can also be seen as a platform where the worst of offline is shared and represented. This comes as no surprise since the internet is a social network [21]. The social networking argument goes back to the idea of a networked society built on a fragmented collective identity that uses the network to bind to other subjects with similar attributes or preferences. Just like it happens offline, cyberspace is a repository of "narratives created by its inhabitants that remind us who we are, it is life as lived and reproduced in pixels and virtual texts" [22]. As such, for Turkle [23] "the Internet has become a significant social laboratory for (…) shap[ing] and creat[ing] ourselves". However, as Pierre Lévy [24] argues, it is important to demystify the theory that tends to see offline and online as opposites and not as interconnected realms. In fact, "real" and "virtual" are not antagonistic spaces but rather influence each other. Thus, the construction of online identity is influenced by elements that are external to the virtual realm and one may say imported from offline. On the other hand, the user experiences with the space of a given social network directly interfere with the construction of the self. Immersive experiences in virtual environments allow the user integration in space and the network, as a social sphere, actively, providing new relationships and social practices based on the premise of an integrated element in the community.

Contemporary socio-technical spheres are embodied in large-scale action networks and are becoming prominent in the various dimensions of society [20]. These networks enhance organised and institutionalised collective actions as a consequence of new modes of expression [25–27]. The digital age promotes individualised forms of individual and political action, challenging the nature of collective action [28]. 'Digital network action' depends on the intersection between personal action and social media networks [25].

Cyberspace enhances the shared social construction that materialises in platforms in which communication flows and debate is promoted, as Dahlberg [29] points out. Platforms such as Twitter, Instagram or Facebook are tools that support collective identity by facilitating communication channels.

Older people are not a homogeneous group that is isolated from the digital context [30–32]. Social representations anchored to the idea of old age, such as 'dependence' and 'useless', fill the social imaginary that the media perpetuate [3, 33]. However, digital platforms tend to bring generations together [34–36].

Collective narrative processes in digital enhance intergenerational relations. Content indexing is a digital practice with various appropriations. "The functional significance of hashtags resides in the archival cataloguing of topics and discussions generated by users which can underpin the emergence of social worlds and allow them to function in the new media environment" [37]. There is an individual culture of network participation, which is reflected in the sense of belonging, identity and group through code appropriation and semantic indexing [20]. Also, through a hashtag structure, online media are able to visibly aggregate individual testimonies and expressions into a networked collective narrative, allowing the dissemination [38] of specific understandings of particular identities, namely gender and age.

2 Method

This article aims to map and analyse the expression of an intergenerational masculinity identity in collective narratives, through content semantically indexed in the photo-sharing service Instagram. "How do digital collective narratives represent masculinities, and how do those representations reflect intergenerational identities and relations?" is the research question that guides this paper. The study relies on collective narrative processes around the hashtag #fashiongrandpas, which we understand as one expression that aggregates intergenerational representations of masculinities.

Considering the assumption of media affordances [39] and "moulding forces" on social practices [40], computational methods were used to extract data within a medium-specific approach [41]. The dataset was collected through the tool Instagram Scraper and consists of randomly selected 1068 media items published between 2011-12-18 and 2019-11-23. The time period of the sample comprehends the time span from the first time the hashtag has been used on Instagram until the day when the data was retrieved through Instagram Scraper. Data was collected from the public stream of Instagram by the semantic indexation to the hashtag. The media items are mostly photos (n = 1052, 98.5%). Video content published with the hashtag #fashiongrandpas is only residual (n = 16, 1.5%).

The methodological approach is a quantitative content analysis to map the intergenerational male identity collective expressions. The main goals of this study are to 1). Identify the most common hashtags used with #fashiongrandpas; 2). Map the dominant discourses about the hashtag in analysis; 3). Analyse most engaged media items correlating these with the dominant discourses.

3 Results and Discussion

The #fashiongrandpas hashtag is mobilised in posts by people of various generations, predominantly among older adults and adults profiles about everyday life. In younger generations, the hashtag is used by profiles whose central topic is fashion. The use of the hashtag for several generations refers to the symbolic capital that #fashiongrandpas entails as an umbrella for the identity expression of multiple masculinities. Most users identify themselves or can be identified as man.

The ten most common co-hashtags published between 2011-12-18 and 2019-11-23 are presented in Table 1. Hashtags are used to anchor content to collective narrative processes. The results show three predominant modes of appropriation of semantic indexing: 1). Indexing of fashion content; 2). Use of common hashtags on Instagram to index content to streamings with more users; 3). Including soft porn content by indexing the hashtag #fashiongrandpas.

Table 1. Top 10 co-hashtags.

Hashtags	Frequency
#style	222
#fashion	216
#menswear	163
#instadaily	114
#instamood	108
#followme	107
#samatized	105
#budapestsam	104
#nofilter	103
#lifeassam	103

The use of hashtags mobilises different types of social capital. Indexing content aggregates individuals into disaggregated streaming microstructures, enhancing the mobilisation of social capital distinctly from the macrostructures [20, 42]. Through content analysis, we have isolated five social practices [20] as described in Table 2.

Table 2. Social appropriations in the use of hashtags.

Appropriation	Social practice
Content publishing	Content publishing; conversation through the publication of content; posting content mentioning other users; content posting with mention of the user himself/herself
Conversation	Conversation with other users by publishing content; posting content mentioning other users; content with self-referencing
Meta conversation	Reproduction of content from other users; reproduction of content from other users with mentioned sources; meta-conversation with content added by the reproducing user; reproducing content from other users with mentions of other actors
Multiple indexing	Posting content, conversation through content, or reproducing the content that is indexed to more than one hashtag
Self-referencing	Posting content with self-references to the author; reproduction of user's own content with his/her mention

Table 2 presents the sociability modalities observed, considering them as a result of an adaptation to the new spatiotemporal conditions. The observed practices refer to flows where information circulates, and social connections are established. Following Gurvitch [43], we consider that appropriations of media affordances and semantic indexing are embodied in spontaneous and organized sociability. We found that there are practices that translate the identification of users with the stream #fashiongrandpas. The practices of self-referencing, multiple indexing, and isolated publication of non-interacting content all fit into organised sociability and are the most common. Conceptually, it is also possible to consider that social practices of content publishing, conversation and meta-conversation are forms of spontaneous sociability.

Social capital is directly related to the concept of network culture because it is established through social ties that bond individuals. Social capital is defined by Bourdieu [44] as being generated by social relations and requiring actors' effort for sociability and investment. Bravo and Bertolini [45] developed a multidimensional perspective based on five dimensions: 1). relational social capital (relationships that are established between individuals); 2). cognitive social capital (relationship with knowledge transmission and acquisition); 3). normative social capital (rules that must be followed by a particular social group); 4). social capital of trust in the social environment (the level of confidence that individuals accredit in a given social context); 5). institutional social capital (the institution in which the group is inserted).

In the context of self-interest theories [46], social capital stems from social dynamics that occur through the appropriation of platforms and their affordances. Recuero [42] states that the concept of social capital refers to the set of resources that exist in the relationships between individuals and that result from belonging to a system. Zago and Batista [47] argue that social capital is a central process and founder of the social dynamics, which result from social structures. Therefore, "cooperation between individuals makes possible not only the emergence of collective actions by generating social capital based on common interest and the pursuit of reputation but the emergence of life in society".

Adapting Bravo and Bertolini's proposal [45] to the instantaneity of the digital context, Table 3 presents a categorisation of appropriations of media's affordances and semantic indexing. These are concretised in social practices that result from sociability modalities and generate social capital. The social capital dimension of trust in the social environment was not operationalised. We consider that it was not possible to assess the mobilisation of this type of social capital without a qualitative content analysis.

Table 3. Social capital mobilised through the appropriations in the use of hashtags.

Appropriation	Social capital
Content publishing	Cognitive social capital
Conversation	Relational social capital
Meta conversation	Institutional social capital
Multiple indexing	Normative social capital

The results show that the media items analysed include cognitive social capital (content publishing), relational social capital (conversation), institutional social capital (meta-conversations). We also consider that the use of multiple hashtags reveals the presence of normative social capital [47].

We identified 3500 hashtags used simultaneously with #fashiongrandpas in the analysed posts, published between 2011-12-18 and 2019-11-23. Then we categorised those that appeared more than 50 times in the sample. This parameter resulted in a small dataset of 45 hashtags which we then further analysed and created ten categories of hashtags (Table 4).

Table 4. Categories of co-hashtags.

Category	Hashtags	Use frequency
Beauty	#samtheagency ($n = 77$), #handsome ($n = 57$)	134
Fashion	#style ($n = 222$), #fashion ($n = 216$), #menswear ($n = 163$), #swag ($n = 100$), #mensfashion ($n = 95$), #streetstyle ($n = 83$), #beardedmodel ($n = 78$), #streetfashion ($n = 68$), #malemodel ($n = 63$), #streetwear ($n = 57$), #outfitoftheday ($n = 51$), #menfashion ($n = 50$),	**1246**
Toxic masculinities	#oldgoat ($n = 85$), #realmen ($n = 86$)	171
Hybrid masculinities	weeerk ($n = 66$)	66
Instagram	#instadaily ($n = 114$), #instamood ($n = 108$), #followme ($n = 107$), #nofilter ($n = 103$), #follow ($n = 101$), #webstagram ($n = 97$), #instagood ($n = 87$), #inspiration ($n = 63$)	**780**
Hegemonic masculinities	#menstyle ($n = 71$), #bearded ($n = 69$), #beardedmen ($n = 68$), #beardporn ($n = 67$), #beardlife ($n = 61$), #beard ($n = 57$), #beards ($n = 56$)	**449**
Vintage style	#crackedactor ($n = 73$), #vintage ($n = 52$)	125
Photo	#portrait ($n = 71$), #streetphotography ($n = 57$), #ootd ($n = 56$), #selfie ($n = 51$)	**235**
Places	#nyc ($n = 101$)	101
Soft-porn	#samatized ($n = 105$), #budapestsam ($n = 104$), #hegivesgoodface ($n = 103$), #lifeassam ($n = 103$), #youwontforgetmyface ($n = 91$), #hotdaddy ($n = 63$), #madeinhungary ($n = 55$)	**624**

#fashiongrandpas streaming is associated with fashion issues but also with an intergenerational approach to male identity. The categories of co-hashtags show that the dominant discourses are about fashion, soft-porn and hegemonic masculinities. Instagram, photo and places are instrumental categories in which hashtags are used to index the content to multiple streams. The sixth category corresponds to discourses on toxic masculinities. There is also the presence of discourses on hybrid masculinities, specifically transgender. The beauty and vintage categories are connected to fashion and can be assumed as sub-categories. In fact, the vintage category is associated with nostalgic publications, retrieving concepts of masculinity from the past and featuring replicas of the multiple and hybrid masculinities assumed by David Bowie.

The engagement with the content analysed through the indicator 'like' has an average of 256.81 likes per post, with a total of 274 268 likes (Table 5).

Table 5. Number of likes (categorised into quartiles).

Likes	n	%
<=50	394	36.9
51–100	138	12.9
100–150	94	8.8
>151	442	41.4
Total	**1068**	**100.0**

The engagement generated concerning the comment indicator is reduced. Most posts have less than five comments (58.2%), and only 10.4% have more than 20 comments (Table 6).

Table 6. Comments on posts (categorised into quartiles).

Comments	n	%
<=5	625	58.5
5–10	179	16.8
11–20	153	14.3
>21	111	10.4
Total	**1068**	**100.0**

Posts with greater engagement through 'likes' portray older men being the predominant descriptor is fashion (Table 7). The data show that intergenerational and cross-generational content is the most prominent of the sample in terms of engagement. There is also a diversity of themes.

Table 7. Hashtags in the captions of the top ten posts according to likes.

Likes	Hashtags	Descriptor	Generation depicted
2299	#relationshipgoals, #levelten, #stayfresh, #fashiongrandpas, #notfashiondads, #originalhipsters, #badassmc, #love, #celebration	Love	Old adults
2156	#preach, #fashiongrandpas, #ifeellikeabadasstoday, #thursdayrulez	Old age	Old adults
1900	#halloween, #fashiongrandpa, #up!!, #icant, #toomuchcute, #littlebowtie, #fashiongrandpas	Kids	Children
1594	#waytogo, #cuba, #havana, #local, #localsonly, #fashiongrandpas, #stunning, #chipper, #cigars, #gentleman, #killingit, #swagfordays	Fashion	Young old adults
1567	#mondays, #fashiongrandpas	Fashion	Old adults
1553	#vsfashionshow, #yeahright, #fashiongrandpas, #repost	Sport	Old adults
1543	#bae, #beardonfleek, #fashiongrandpas, #hiphiphooray, #complexgrandpas, #whoisthisman, #letsgrabacoffee	Fashion	Young old adults
1499	#fashiongrandpasstrong, #fashiongrandpas, #backtoback, #showsomelove, #argyle, #swag	Fashion	Old adults
1460	#heartbreakers, #beyoncegotnothingonthesefashiongrandpas, #fashiongrandpas, #runshit	Old age	Old adults
1405	#fashiongrandpas	Family	Intergenerational

There are three matching posts in the top ten likes and comments that portray seniors and kids. Their descriptors are love, kids and sports. In the posts with the most comments (Table 8), there are three that ridicule senior citizens. These are young adult publications.

This study argues that content categorised as fashion, beauty, hegemonic masculinities, toxic masculinities, and hybrid masculinities is mostly cross-generational. Intersections between adults and old adults are common in discourses on hegemonic and toxic masculinities. The contents of the vintage category are markedly generational, published by young users. Men of different generations post soft-porn content.

Table 8. Hashtags in the captions of the top ten posts according to comments.

Comments	Hashtags	Descriptor	Generation depicted
217	#relationshipgoals, #levelten, #stayfresh, #fashiongrandpas, #notfashiondads, #originalhipsters, #badassmc, #love, #celebration	Love	Old adults
191	#plaid, #sunny, #florida, #cool, #learningthisdance, #swag, #stepup, #fashiongrandpas	Ridicule	Old adults
187	#bae, #beardonfleek, #fashiongrandpas, #hiphiphooray, #complexgrandpas, #whoisthisman, #letsgrabacoffee	Fashion	Young old adults
153	#preach, #fashiongrandpas, #ifeellikeabadasstoday, #thursdayrulez	Older people	Old adults
153	#halloween, #fashiongrandpa, #up!!, #icant, #toomuchcute, #littlebowtie, #fashiongrandpas	Kids	Children
119	#vsfashionshow, #yeahright, #fashiongrandpas, #repost	Sport	Old adults
111	#fashiongrandpas, #onedayonly, #unlessyoureafashiongrandpa, #merightnow, #squeeze, #relationshipgoals, #relationshipreality, #meandbae, #truelove	Manhood	Old adults
108	#fashiongrandpas, #applause, #legend, #mrjehovas, #legendseverywhere, #boombox, #nothomeless, #justfeelslikeit, #highkick, #societycantkeepup	Performance	Old adults
104	#heartbreakers, #repost, #amiright, #fashiongrandpa, #fashiongrandpas, #elite, #wewelcomeyou	Ridicule	Old adults
99	#tokyo, #fashiongrandpas, #fur, #red, #boss, #plaid, #dukeoftokyo, #prancing, #og, #pimpdaddy, #myspiritanimal, #trustnobitch, #getoutofthewaybasics	Ridicule	Old adults

4 Conclusions and Limitations

This paper aimed to analyse the expression of an intergenerational male identity in collective narratives, in order to answer the research question: "How do digital collective narratives represent masculinities, and how do those representations reflect intergenerational identities and relations?".

The analysis shows that online representations of male identities tend to perpetuate hegemonic masculinity. Therefore, power relations are perpetuated in images that anchor discourses of heteronormativity that tend to confirm a man's ideal. How men should be and behave is presented as an aggregating element of male group identity. Fashion, beauty, manhood and soft-porn as aggregating elements, the expressions of being a man are shared in the analysed stream. The complexity and multiplicity of masculinities arise in dissonant discourses as they are not consistent with a single identity. Hybrid masculinities exist in the stream because they share the aggregating hashtag but mobilise different ideas and concepts from being a man.

Multiple masculinities are present in the sample analysed. From an intergenerational perspective and with a unique group identity, hashtags are mobilised to create identity ties that derive from different types of social capital [45].

Considering that masculinities form relationally with and against femininities as well as with and against other masculinities [11], we found differences in the appropriation of the hashtag for different purposes. There are traces of hegemonic masculinities in power relations, especially ridiculing old adults as opposed to strong young men. It is also verified that hybrid masculinities assume an intersectional character, considering class and race. However, this issue is not considered in the discourses that fall into the other categories.

Given that the use of a hashtag is a form of content indexing and thus a statement, we consider that the 1068 posts analysed are 'digital network action' [25] that promote ideologies in collective narrative processes. With traits of hegemonic masculinity but also common of manhood, the men portrayed in the contents of this streaming refers to the ideal of group identity. The fashion and beauty discourses emphasise a collective identity: white, heterosexual and financially healthy man.

The main limitations of this study are related to the quantitative approach. Future research will focus on qualitative content analysis of posts and comments, as well as analysis of post-tag and co-tag networks.

5   Implications for Future Studies

The results of this study show that the dominant masculinity discourses on Instagram perpetuate hegemonic masculinities anchored upon heteronormativity. However, we note that there is no single intergenerational male identity. The results shed light on the complexity of 'multiple masculinities' [4, 12] in the collective process of narratives analysed. Hegemonic masculinities, toxic masculinities, and hybrid masculinities are cross-generational. Future studies should take the theory of intersectionality as a theoretical framework and consider mixed methodologies furthering qualitative analysis to complement the quantitative perspective.

Moreover, future studies on digital collective narratives of masculinity should endeavour to identify whether the data reveals a connective action logic [25] by analysing co-hashtag networks from a cross-platform perspective [48]. Hashtag co-occurrence networks enable to observe indirect connections in order to explore associations, related actors and content (visual and textual). Furthermore, it is possible to identify if there are intersections between masculinity discourses on different platforms, promoted by connective actions. This methodological approach also makes it possible to identify the dominant voices, central actors, network patterns, community building, as well as the discourses mobilised as ties between communities.

Acknowledgments. This article was financed by national Portuguese funds through FCT (Fundação para a Ciência e a Tecnologia) in the framework of the project "(De)Coding Masculinities: Towards an enhanced understanding of media's role in shaping perceptions of masculinities in Portugal" (Reference PTDC/COM-CSS/31740/2017).

References

1. Lorber, J., Farrell, S.A.: The Social Construction of Gender. Sage, Newbury Park (1991)
2. Connell, R.W., Messerschmidt, J.W.: Hegemonic masculinity: rethinking the concept. Gender Soc. **19**(6), 829–859 (2005)
3. Amaral, I., Santos, S.J., Daniel, F., Filipe, F.: (In)visibilities of men and aging in the media: discourses from Germany and Portugal. In: Zhou, J., Salvendy, G. (eds.) HCII 2019. LNCS, vol. 11593, pp. 20–32. Springer, Cham (2019). https://doi.org/10.1007/978-3-030-22015-0_2
4. Carrigan, T., Connell, B., Lee, J.: Toward a new sociology of masculinity. Theory Soc. **14**(5), 551–604 (1985)
5. Mannheim, K.: The problem of generation. In: Mannheim, K. (ed.) Essays on the Sociology of Knowledge, pp. 276–320. Routledge & Kegan Pau, London (1952)
6. Corsten, M.: The time of generations. Time Soc. **8**(2–3), 249–272 (1999)
7. Boni, F.: Framing media masculinities: men's lifestyle magazines and the biopolitics of the male body. Eur. J. Commun. **17**(4), 465–478 (2002)
8. Katz, J., Earp, J.: Tough Guise: Violence, Media & the Crisis in Masculinity. Media Education Foundation (1999)
9. Colombo, F., Fortunati, F.: Broadband Society and Generational Changes. Peter Lang, Frankfurt am Main (2011)
10. Connell, R.W.: Masculinities, 2nd edn. University of California Press, Berkeley (2005)
11. Richardson, M.J.: Embodied intergenerationality: family position, place and masculinity. Gender Place Cult. **22**(2), 157–171 (2015)
12. Connell, R.W.: Masculinities. University of California Press, Berkeley (1995)
13. Hopkins, P., Noble, G.: Masculinities in place: situated identities, relations and intersectionality. Soc. Cult. Geogr. **10**(8), 811–819 (2009)
14. Santos, S.J.: Entre o papel de espelho e o de produtor da realidade: os media e a (des) codificação de masculinidades. In: Atas do Seminário Internacional "Media e violência sexual: da investigação à comunicação", pp. 139–158. CES, Coimbra (2018)
15. Kimmel, M.S.: A produção simultânea de masculinidades hegemônicas e subalternas. Horizontes Antropológicos **4**(9), 103–117 (1998)
16. Januário, S.B.: Masculinidades em (re) construção: Gênero, Corpo e Publicidade. LabCom. IFP, Covilhã (2016)
17. Gardiner, J.K.: Masculinity Studies and Feminist Theory. Columbia University Press, New York (2002)
18. Kupers, T.A.: Toxic masculinity as a barrier to mental health treatment in prison. J. Clin. Psychol. **61**(6), 713–724 (2005)
19. Bridges, T., Pascoe, C.J.: Hybrid masculinities: new directions in the sociology of men and masculinities. Sociol. Compass **8**(3), 246–258 (2014)
20. Amaral, I.: Redes Sociais na Internet: Sociabilidades Emergentes. LabCom Books, Covilhã (2015)
21. Cavanagh, A.: Sociology in the Age of the Internet. Tata McGraw-Hill Education, New York (2010)
22. Fernback, J.: The individual within the collective: virtual ideology and the realization of collective principles. In: Jones, S. (ed.) Virtual Culture: Identity & Communication in Cybersociety, pp. 36–54. Sage Publications, London, Thousand Oaks, New Delhi (1997)

23. Turkle, S.: A vida no ecrã. A identidade na era da Internet. Relógio d'Água, Lisboa (1997)
24. Lévy, P.: O que é o virtual. Quarteto Editora, Coimbra (2001)
25. Bennett, W.L., Segerberg, A.: The logic of connective action: digital media and the personalization of contentious politics. Inf. Commun. Soc. **15**(5), 739–768 (2012)
26. Murru, M.F., Amaral, I., Brites, M.J., Seddighi, G.: Bridging the gap between micro and macro forms of engagement: three emerging trends in research on audience participation. In: Das, R., Ytre-Arne, B. (eds.) The Future of Audiences, pp. 161–177. Springer, Cham (2018). https://doi.org/10.1007/978-3-319-75638-7_9
27. Kavada, A.: Social movements and political agency in the digital age: a communication approach. Media Commun. **4**(4), 8–12 (2016)
28. Bimber, B.: Three prompts for collective action in the context of digital media. Political Commun. **34**(1), 6–20 (2017)
29. Dahlberg, L.: Democracy via cyberspace: mapping the rhetorics and practices of three prominent camps. New Media Soc. **3**(2), 157–177 (2001)
30. Amaral, I.: Senior citizens and the internet. In: Merskin, D. (ed.) The SAGE International Encyclopedia of Mass Media and Society, pp. 1549–1551. Sage Publications, Thousand Oaks (2020)
31. Loos, E.: Generational use of new media and the (ir)relevance of age. In: Colombo, F., Fortunati, L. (eds.) Broadband Society and Generational Changes, pp. 259–273. Peter Lang, Berlin (2011)
32. Loos, E.: Senior citizens: digital immigrants in their own country? Observatorio (OBS*) **6**(1), 01–023 (2012)
33. Daniel, F., Antunes, A., Amaral, I.: Representações sociais da velhice. Análise Psicológica **33**(3), 291–301 (2015)
34. Bolin, G., Skogerbø, E.: Age, generation and the media. Northern Lights **11**, 3–14 (2013)
35. Amaral, I., Brites, M.J.: Trends on the digital uses and generations. In: Proceedings of INTED2019 Conference, INTED, Valencia, pp. 5109–5115 (2019)
36. Loos, E., Haddon, L., Mante-Meijer, E.: Generational Use of New Media. Routledge, London and New York (2016)
37. Lamont, M., Ross, A.S.: Deconstructing embedded meaning within cyclists' Instagram discourse: #fromwhereiride. Ann. Leis. Res. 1–25 (2019)
38. Clark-Parsons, R.: "I SEE YOU, I BELIEVE YOU, I STAND WITH YOU": #MeToo and the performance of networked feminist visibility. Feminist Media Stud. 1–19 (2019)
39. Bucher, T., Helmond, A.: The affordances of social media platforms. In: The SAGE Handbook of Social Media, pp. 223–253 (2017)
40. Hepp, A.: Cultures of Mediatization. Wiley, Hoboken (2013)
41. Rogers, R.: Digital Methods. MIT Press, Cambridge (2013)
42. Recuero, R.: Redes sociais na internet. Sulina, Porto Alegre (2009)
43. Gurvitch, G.: A vocação actual da Sociologia. Cosmos, Lisboa (1986)
44. Bourdieu, P.: O poder simbólico. Difel, Lisboa (2001)
45. Bertolini, S., Bravo, G.: Social Capital, a Multidimensional Concept (2004). https://pdfs.sem anticscholar.org/ab8d/2ed286d0c225b47fca4785cef2dd1dc7fac6.pdf. Accessed 16 Dec 2019
46. Monge, P., Contractor, N.: Emergence of communication networks. In: Jablin, F., Putnam, L. (eds.) Handbook of Organizational Communication, pp. 440–502. Sage, Thousand Oaks (1999)
47. Zago, G., Batista, J.: Manifestações coletivas no ciberespaço: cooperação, capital social e redes sociais. In: Actas do Simpósio Nacional da ABCIBER, São Paulo, vol. 1 (2008)
48. Omena, J.J., Amaral, I.: Sistema de leitura de redes digitais multiplataforma. In: Omena, J.J. (ed.) Métodos Digitais: Teoria-Prática-Crítica, pp. 121–140. iNOVA Media Lab – ICNOVA, Lisboa (2019)

Ageism and Media Generations in the Croatian Post-socialist Context

Antonija Čuvalo[(⊠)]

Faculty of Political Science, University of Zagreb, Zagreb, Croatia
Antonija.cuvalo@fpzg.hr

Abstract. The paper discusses the concepts of ageism and media generations. The concept of media generations gains increased attention within media studies with the increase in rhythm of social changes driven at least partly by the development of communication and media technologies. The starting point here is that ageism is implied in the bulk of research on the generational differences in media use. Alternative approach is proposed in order to overcome ageism when analysing media use and its implications for the individuals of different age. The alternative is based on the concepts of media generations, generation units and media repertoires. Media repertories [1–3] here serve as an indicator of media generation units on the societal level [4]. Such an approach allows for the shared intergenerational media practices, recognizing also intragenerational diversity and the contemporary complex high choce media environment. This approach is open for the application of the multi-method research strategies. Examples of the analysis of the media generation presented here are from the article by Antonija Čuvalo and Zrinjka Peruško [5] on media generations in Croatia and Dina Vozab's [6]. The main argument of this article is that the practice-based definition of media generation units through their media repertoire is more useful than dividing the generations by the decade of birth.

Keywords: Media generations · Ageism · Media repertoires · Youth · Elders · Post-socialist · Croatia

1 Introduction

The concept of media generations is gaining greater attention among media and communication scholars which is parallel to the increase in the rhythm of social changes which could be at least partly driven by technological development [7]. Media scholars [7–10] argue for usefulness of the concept of media generation for better understanding of changes in media environment and socio-cultural changes brought with the development of communication technologies [43]. The basic assumption here is that emergence of specific media and communication technology plays "a significant role in common experiences of different age groups during their formative years" [11]. There are numerous studies of media use of youth in the West, therefore, other age groups, especially older people were rarely in the focus of interest [5, 12, 13].

© Springer Nature Switzerland AG 2020
Q. Gao and J. Zhou (Eds.): HCII 2020, LNCS 12209, pp. 17–28, 2020.
https://doi.org/10.1007/978-3-030-50232-4_2

Unfortunately, we don't know much about the way how specific socio-political, economic and cultural contexts of the socialist and post-socialist experience shaped generational identities of Croatian media generations. Croatia, the current presidential EU country is also the youngest EU. The country shares 100 years of common history with Slovenia which is also a member of EU (since 201), and together with Serbia, Macedonia, (EU candidate), Montenegro, and Bosnia and Herzegovina, they share almost 50 years of socialist experience within Socialist Federal Republic of Yugoslavia. Only a few very recent quantitative studies try to examine different media generations in Croatia: Dina Vozab's article on generational newsmedia repertoires [6] and Antonija Čuvalo and Zrinjka Peruško's [5] study on generational media repertoires. Outside of region that once shared the same political and economic framework within socialist Yugoslavia several studies address "different generation's relations with the media" in the context of the transformation from communism to capitalism and the democracy, like Kalmus, Masso and Laurstin [11] study of Estonian media generations.

The aim of the paper is to discuss two approaches to media generations based on the studies by Antonija Čuvalo and Zrinjka Peruško's [5] and Dina Vozab's [6] article on the newsmedia repertoires. The important question here is related to the gaps between different media generations produced by different media experiences of different generations 11, see also Gumpert and Cathcart 1985]. Nevertheless, the Čuvalo and Peruško's study [5] show that different age generations share the practice of media use represented through their media repertoire [1, 3].

2 Theoretical Background

Increased attention among media and communication scholars in the concept of generation parallels the increase in the rhythm of social changes and technological development [7]. Media scholars [7–10; and others] argue for usefulness of the concept of media generation for better understanding of changes in media environment and socio-cultural changes brought with the development of communication technologies [5]. The basic assumption here is that emergence of specific media and communication technology plays "a significant role in com-mon experiences of different age groups during their formative years" [11].

2.1 Ageism and Media Use

The term ageism is often used to describe our stereotypical perception of older people and our actions toward older people based on this perception [14]. Robert N. Butler's original definition of is more general and defines it as "prejudice by one age group against another age group" [15] which is manifested in behaviour, organisational practices and policies also generates self-fulfilling prophecies regarding discriminated age groups. Butler [15] argues that usually middle-aged generation discriminate against younger and older generations, "because middle-age generation is group is responsible for the welfare of the younger and older age groups, which are seen as dependent" [14]. Though age-related prejudice could be positive or negative, they tend to carry negative connotations, and its discriminatory effects are like sexism and racism. Ageism is not only present in intergenerational relations but can be traced in the age group's self-perception [14]. Age stereotypes and age discrimination are usually taken as mutually inter-twined [14], yet Voss, Bodner and Rothermund [16] argue for the dismantlement of these two concepts. Clary Krekula, Pirjo Nikander, and Monika Wilińska [17] state that age is socially constructed "in interaction with other categorizations, such as gender, class, race and ethnicity". For example, gendered ageism often refers to the subordinate position of older women. Age with categories like gender, class, race and others serve as "an intersection of power relations" [17].

Regarding media use different kinds of ageism could be traced in relation to young people, middle-aged generation and the older generation in usually simplified constructions of young (and elders) as homogenous undifferentiated groups [13]. More attention is given to young people and their habits and styles of media use. Andrea Rosales and Mireia Fernández-Ardèvol [18] identify some instances of ageism in big data approaches. They show how "biased samples and biased tools tend to exclude the habits, interests and values of older people from algorithms and studies, which contributes to reinforcing structural ageism." [18]. Only a few studies aimed to compare young users with older age groups [21]. Recently, more attention is given to the role of digital communication technologies in intergenerational and intragenerational relations [12, 19, 20]. Colombo, Aroldi and Carlo [20] challenge construction of digital disconnection of elders as their technological incompetence or low literacy and offer more generational, social and cultural explanation of their resistance to "the pressure to be always connected and tech-no-enthusiasts" and as their "claim" of "the freedom to choose their degree of digital inclusion". Youngs also try to keep distinction against elders through their social media practices [9]. Furthermore, narratives of young as media and technologically savvy digital generation are challenged by the study of Fortunati et al. [21], which shows that second digital generation (digital natives) loses position of technological pioneers in comparison with older generation which was according the authors the first digital generation (Generation X). Implicit ageism in media use research focused on users' age tend to neglect differences in social, economic, cultural within the same birth cohort, i.e. between the different generational units. Furthermore, similar socio-cultural position and shared life conditions between individuals of different age can make them closer in terms of their media generational identity than between the individuals of the same age but different socio-economic and cultural position. Media repertoires [1, 3], styles and practices of media use thus serve as cues for social distinction [Bourdieu, 1984] or power relations which are more complicated than those based on the class exclusively and involve intersection of social categories like age, gender, class, race, ethnicity.

2.2 Ageism and Media Use

Since the 1980s and especially since the beginning of the 21st century, with the rapid change of media landscape, we are facing with the growing interest in the concept of generations in general public and academic discourse [22, 23]. The concept of generations was developed by German sociologist Karl Mannheim in 1920s and elaborated in his essay "The Problem of Generations" [24]. Mannheim argues that the concept is useful for the understanding of the process of social change. Generations are understood as the drivers of social change. Mannheim's conceptualization of generations comprise two elements: a) birth cohort of people whose shared characteristic is the pure fact that they are born about the same time and within the same historical, geographical and cultural context (generation-as-location) and b) common generational identity based on the shared experience of the same extraordinary and traumatic historical events (generation-as-actuality). An important moment in Mannheim's theory on generations is the first contact with objects and events [25]. Novelties, innovations, revolutions, everything new has the deepest impact on young people in formative age, who have not had similar experiences than on the older generations. For Mannheim, formative years between seventh and twenty-fifth year are the most important for forming relatively stable relationship toward specific and similar object, event, or phenomena [10]. Following this argument, early experience and growing up with new technology or media potentially creates specific generational experience and identity [7, 9, 26, 27] and shape habits, style and practice of media use in adulthood [13, 25]. Specific media generation represents an outcome of the experience of growing up in the specific media environment while new media generation emerges with the expansion of new communication technology [22] and the change in the space of technological affordances [4]. American media scholars Gary Gumpert and Robert Cathcart [28] first used the term media generations. Media generations emerge with electronic media which temporalities (compression, increase, shortened lifespan) enabled the formation of specific generational identity [9]. Television is often considered as significant for forming the baby boom generation born after World War I, which is the first media and multimedia generation [10]. Generation X refers to the generation born between the television and the internet generation, while those borne after the end of the 1970s are usually taken as the first digital generation.

Mannheim's concept of generations recognizes the differences in socio-economic location defining the different generation units within the same biologically defined generations. Applied on the media generations, generational units also imply differences in access to a specific technology.

Goran Bolin distinguishes between media generations by kinship and synchronic generational relations between "peers born around same time" [22]. Generations by kinship (family generations) are diachronic, they are represented in family albums, family videos, family stories, through family memories on the Facebook, and its members share a limited amount of experiences. Though, generations are at the same time drivers of the change but also of intergenerational continuities, interchange and commonalities [13, 29–31]. Studies by Ingrid Volkmer [32] and Goran Bolin [25] deal with the role of media in shaping memories and experiences Recent research in media nostalgia points to the intergenerational characteristics of the contemporary media consumption in the context of hybrid media ecosystem [19]. Later is often neglected in favour of former. Bolin [2017:3] argues that generations help us to explain societal changes by bridging "objectivist and subjectivist analytical position". The generational approach is also useful for solving agency/structure problem in social sciences because it implies that perceptions and experiences are context-dependent recognizing also impact of the shared perceptions and experiences on the structural conditions. Seriously taken and well-theorised, the concept of a generation can be a useful tool for studying social and cultural change [22]. Yet, the relevance of generations end specifically media generations for cultural change is still not empirically confirmed nor theoretically elaborated. Only few studies test generational hypothesis [4, 10, 11, 13]. Also, there are no many cross-cultural studies on media generations [33, 34].

Nevertheless, studies show differences between generations which were growing before and after the emergence of commercial television and before and after the spread of mobile phones [13]. Generational media cultures have been analysed in term of their media or technological repertoires (e.g. Pew Research Center), differences in media use, use of time and space, use of the linguistic and narratives [9]. Some authors identified generational differences in political apathy, news avoidance [35]. Unfortunately, these and similar studies easy fall into the trap of determinism and neglect socio-cultural heterogeneity among the biologically defined generation. Focus is usually on the new(est) media, while other media from the specific media landscape are often neglected. Since the 2010s, scholars acknowledged importance of examining the multimedia use [1, 3, 36–39]. Uwe Hasebrink and Hanna Domeyer [1] define media repertoires as relatively stable patterns of media use or, in other words, "the entirety of media that a person regularly uses". The concept of media repertoires implies a) user-centred perspective (asks which media a person uses), the entirety of media regularly combined by an individual, c) relationality, or meaningful (from users' perspective) inner structure of media repertoires. Starting from the users' perspective, media repertoires can be defined on a different level: media types, genres, topics, or specific brand or product. Furthermore, Hasebrink and Domeyer's [1] definition of media repertoires contributes "to bridging the conceptual and methodological gap between different threads of research on media use" providing the framework for the combining quantitative and qualitative methods.

Steffen Leppa, Stefan Weinzerl and Anne-Kathrin Hoklas [4] suggest that the "analysis of culturally meaningful media generation units may be achieved by 'quantitative' media repertoire studies on the societal level" combined with qualitative method for the interpretation of "the underlying orientation patterns". They applied latent class analysis for the identification of German audio media repertoires. Media repertoires are here regarded as the result of the media generation process driven by the substantial changes in the media environment. Media repertoires as the relatively stable dispositions have certain durability against changes in the technological environment or life circumstances [4]. Platform and content abundance [40] combined with the cross-platform convergence and attention scarcity [41] lead to increased fragmentation and polarization of media audiences in terms of their media repertoires [42]. Generational patterns of this fragmentation and/or polarization and their effect on the political attitudes, election behaviour, social capital and other social phenomena are still under-researched themes. Furthermore, generational patterns of distinction through cultural practices and its social effects should also be addressed theoretically concerning class to better understand social stratification in the context of deep mediatization [43].

3   Media Repertoires as the Indicators of the Media Generations: The Croatian Case

The application of the analysis of media generations through media repertoires could be a helpful tool for avoiding ageism implied in audience research which is dealing with the media habits of the users of different age. Apart from avoiding ageism, the generational approach should also recognize differences in the historical trajectories of the specific geographic areas in order to avoid decontextualized generalizations on generations [45]. Post-socialist European countries have been an under-researched region in terms of its media generations. Only a few studies from the SEE and CEE region focus on this issue [46]. The following section describes the specific socialist and post-socialist context within which Croatian media generations developed. Results on media generations are presented with two recent studies [5, 6]. These two studies represent two different approaches to the analysis of media generations with inherent (dis)advantages in terms ageism implied.

3.1 Socialist and Post-socialist Media Landscape in Croatia

Croatia is an independent country since the 8th of October 1991 and EU member from the 1st of July 2013. Before its independency, since the year 1918, the country was a part of two Yugoslavia's [47] with Slovenia, Bosnia and Herzegovina, Serbia (with Kosovo and Vojvodina), Macedonia and Montenegro. Media generations within this context were shaped in a different way than its Western and Eastern European cotemporaries from the Warshaw Pact. Within the context of socialist Yugoslavia (1945–1991) Croatia developed its media system and mass media market [48]. The socialist period was marked by the rise of television followed by the emergence of mass media audiences and market orientation of press media within the framework of self-management socialism during the 1960s. In the 1970s, Yugoslav socialist culture faced with the proliferation of the alternative youth print media [49], punk and new wave music, black wave film (crni talas), alternative youth radio, beginning of the pluralization and liberalization of media and society parallel with the system crisis during the 1980s. Unlike other socialist countries that were part of the Eastern Block under the SSSR, Yugoslavia was a member of European Broadcasting Union (EBU) and participated in the Eurovision contest since 1961.

The early 1990s were marked by the breakup of Yugoslavia, the fall of socialism, Croatia's independence, the transition to democracy and capitalism in the context of war (1992–1995). The 21st century started with the political consolidation, further liberalization, privatization of broadcast media, commercialization, the spread of mobile telephony and digital media. Further mediatization [44] in the next decade was marked with the increase in penetration of smartphones and social media. The transformation from socialist to liberal democracy and capitalism involved transformation of the media system and changes in practices of media professionals and audiences. The breakup of socialism leads to break up with the past on the individual and societal level and opened a space for creation of the new or revision of old historical narratives via oral family histories or public (re)construction through media or education [50].

Croatian media system today cluster with the countries of Mediterranean with [51, 52] the lower newspaper circulation, higher political parallelism and lower professionalization of journalism, lower or medium quality of public service television [53]. The unanswered question here is how this specific historical trajectory shapes Croatian media generations. Two studies presented in the following section try to reconstruct generational media repertoires and identify generational patterns of media use.

3.2 Croatian Media Generations Through Their Media Repertoires

Media generations in Croatia and the wider region that was once part of Yugoslavia are still undisclosed. We still do not know how the experiences of socialist media, of the breakup of Yugoslavia and transition shaped audiences practices and generational patterns of media use. Though audience research in Croatia exist since the beginning of television system and mass press [5] there are not many theoretically elaborated studies of audience practices and experience. Generational approach is completely absent from the Croatian media and communication research. Recently, two studies aim to fill this gap. First one is Čuvalo and Peruško's [5] study of the generational media repertoires based on the nationally representative stratified sample (N = 800) fort the population aged 18+ and second is Dina Vozab's [6] analysis of generational news repertoires. Both studies started from Karl Mannheim's theory of generations, but they used different strategies to define media generations. The main argument of this article is that the practice-based definition of media generations through their media repertoire is more useful than dividing the generations by the decade of birth.

Čuvalo and Peruško [5] operationalize media generations as "relatively persistent, typical media repertoires" [1, 3], generationally related and shared in a certain amount. Relationship of the specific repertoire with certain generational cohort is not strong but fuzzy [4]. Similar relationship occurs regarding the social location or specific communication technology. Shape and share of different repertoires thus can "be interpreted as causal trace of the long term process of cultural change" and is a result of the intersection of generational and ontogenetic processes with the life cycle trajectories [4]. The method used for identifying generational media repertoires was latent class analysis with covariates. The main postulate here is generation units are "loosely coupled with actual cohorts and socio-demographic" and with "the historical advent of single media technologies" [4]. Latent class analysis is a probabilistic method of classification "able to discover hidden latent dependencies within complex multivariate data sets" and sort observational data "into the classes of the most similar patterns" [4]. Data set came from the nationally representative sample (N = 800) stratified according to the region, size of the settlement, age and gender generated four classes of media users.

Two sets of indicators measured media use. First set of indicators measured use of media on the different platforms with the question: "Did you yesterday...1) watched TV on the TV set, 2) watched TV on mobile phone, 3) watched TV on the computer, 4) listen radio on the radio set, 5) listen the radio on the mobile phone, 6) listen the radio on the computer, 7) read printed newspapers, 8) read newspapers on mobile phone, 9) read newspapers on the computer, 10) rad the printed book. Second set of indicators measured online use by the question: "Did you yesterday ...1) read online news, 2) read and write emails, 3) download the music, films, or podcasts, 4) play online games, 5) visit social media, 6) visit chat rooms, 7) read discussions on forums and blogs, 8) visit pages related to your hobbies or interests?"

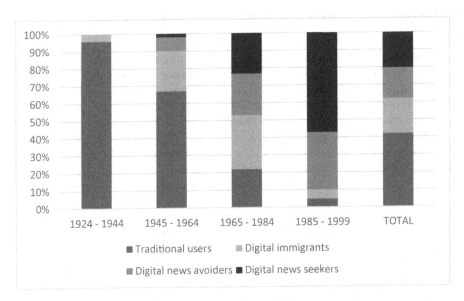

Fig. 1. The share of media generation units within different birth cohorts and on total sample.

Extracted latent classes represent four media generation units with the respective media repertoires on the Croatian market: class of traditional media users, a class called "digital immigrants", class of "digitally oriented news avoiders" and a class of "digitally oriented news seekers". The share of different media generation units within different birth cohorts is presented in Fig. 1. The class of traditional users has the highest share (41, 33%) and is highly dependent on TV. All respondents born between 1924 and 1942 share this repertoire, and this is the only media repertoire identified within this cohort. This is the most prevailing repertoire till the generation born in mid of 1960s. The repertoire of digital immigrants emerged among those born after 1941 and is the most usual repertoire for those born from the second part of the 1960s till the end of 1980s. Digital immigrants are less dependent on TV than traditional users and less dependent on social media than digitally oriented users. Their characteristic is that they read newspapers on the computer more than the other three repertoires, they also more often read print newspapers. Digital media repertoires appeared first among people born at the end of the 1940s, first appeared repertoire of digitally-oriented news avoiders, then repertoire of digitally-oriented news avoiders. For both types of digitally-oriented users, TV is a weaker indicator of class membership than in "older" media repertoires. Digital news seekers use more social media than news avoiders, and they do not read online news. Generally, digital repertoires of users on the Croatian market were relatively undiversified and straightforward, focused mostly on social media use and/or online news. However, digital news seekers have the most diverse media repertoire and the most diverse online repertoire.

Among cohorts born at the end of the 1940s till those born at the end of 1999, we have present all four identified repertoires thus we discuss four different generational units (in terms of their repertoire) within these cohorts. Among those born after 1997, we traced only digital repertoires with almost equal shares.

Among traditional media users, more respondents did not finish primary school and who live in smaller towns (less than 2.000 inhabitants) than among digital immigrants and digital users. Digital immigrants and digital news seekers live mostly in the big cities (more than 100.000 inhabitants). Digital news seekers have the highest education level.

Dina Vozab's [6] analysis of the generational news repertoires is based on the data from Reuters Digital News Survey. The survey was conducted online on the sample representative for internet users in Croatia (N = 2010). Vozab's approach to media generation was somewhat different than applied by Čuvalo and Peruško [5] because she predefined media generations as four successive birth cohorts: 1) Dutifulls born before 1946; 2) Boomers, born between 1946 and 1964; 3) Generation X, born between 1965 and 1983 and 4) Millennials, born after 1983. Vozab analyzed differences in patterns of news consumption by means of ANOVA test. Millennials use less television and digital-born news than older generations, but they do not read less fewer print newspapers. Millennials and Generation X thus differ in their online repertoires. Secondly, Vozab identified five news repertoires by using the latent class analysis: minimalists, digital-born users, traditionalists, commercial media users and eclectics. Repertoires differ on the axis digital vs traditional media and the wider/narrower range of sources used. The predefined categorization of media generation was used as covariate for latent classes. The analysis shows differences between generations in relation to traditional media and online born news.

4 Discussion and Conclusion

Presented studies discern some problems within media and communication studies that arise when we try to apply a generational approach to media use. Both approaches presented here have its own (dis)advantages. An important question here is how to define media generation. Vozab's [6] approach based on the arbitrary or theoretically informed division between the successive birth cohorts is more often applied within media and communication research. This paper argues for the practice-based definition of media generations which relies on the shared practice of media use represented by the specific media repertoires. The main assumption is that the specific media repertoires could be interpreted as causal traces of the long-term process of cultural and technological change in interplay with generational and life cycle trajectories. However, it also reveals the changes in the media landscape and even the disappearance of some media repertoires within the youngest age cohort. Assumed relationship of media repertoires with actual cohorts, life cycle trajectory, specific socio-demographics and advent of certain media technology is loose and more open for changes between these categories. Thus, practice-based approach is more open for intra-generational differences, inter-generational similarities which helps us to avoid ageism because it discerns intergenerationally shared practices.

What is missing here is a qualitative insight into the sense-making process concerning media repertoires and generational self-identification. Without a qualitative part, we do not know what does the same or similar media repertoires mean for different birth cohorts which grew up in different historical context? We also do not know how the process of the transition from socialism to post-socialist context shaped related media practices of older and younger generations. Also, it is important to find out does the same media repertoire traced within different cohorts indicate their intergenerationally and does this mean that this is the basis for some shared generational identities? Future studies would benefit from mixed method approach. The productive possible way is to combine and triangulate practice-based strategy of defining media generations based on the quantitative study with qualitative methods like documentary method [Lepa, Hoklas and Weinzierl, 2014], media diaries and card sorting [2].

References

1. Hasebrink, U., Domeyer, H.: Media repertoires as patterns of behaviour and as meaningful practices: a multimethod approach to media use in converging media environments. Participations J. Audience Reception Stud. **9**(2), 757–779 (2012)
2. Hasebrink, U., Hepp, A.: How to research cross-media practices? Investigating media repertoires and media ensembles. Convergende: Int. J. Res. New Media Technol. **23**(4), 362–377 (2017)
3. Hasebrink, U., Popp, J.: Media repertoires as a result of selective media use: a conceptual approach to the analysis of patterns of exposure. Eur. J. Commun. Res. **31**(3), 11–28 (2006)
4. Leppa, S., Weinzierl, S., Hoklas, A.M.: Discovering and interpreting audio media generation units: a typological-praxeological approach to the mediatization of everyday music listening. Participations J. Audience Reception Stud. **11**(2), 207–238 (2014)
5. Čuvalo, A., Peruško, Z.: Ritmovi medijskih generacija u Hrvatskoj: istraživanje medijskih generacija iz sociološke perspective. Revija za sociologiju **47**(3), 271–302 (2017)
6. Vozab, D.: Generational patterns of digital news consumption: from traditionalists to millennial minimalists. Medijske studije **10**(20), 107–126 (2019)
7. Aroldi, P., Colombo, F.: Questioning 'digital global generations: a critical approach. Northern Lights **11**(1), 175–190 (2013)
8. Bolin, G.: The rhythm of ages: analyzing mediatization through the lens of generations across cultures. Int. J. Commun. **10**(1), 5252–5269 (2016)
9. Vittadini, N., Siibak, A., Reifova, I., Bilandzic, H.: Generations and media: the social construction of generational identity and differences. In: Carpentier, N., Schroder, K.C., Hallet, L. (eds.) Audience Transformations: Shifting Audience Positions in Late Modernity, pp. 65–81. Routledge, New York (2014)
10. Bolin, G., Weslund, O.: Mobile generations: the role of mobile technology in the shaping of Swedish media generations. Int. J. Commun. **3**(1), 108–124 (2009)
11. Kalmuss, V., Masso, A., Laurstin, M.: Preferences in media use and perception of intergenerational differences among age groups in Estonia: a cultural approach to media generations. Northern Lights **11**, 15–34 (2013)
12. Bolin, G., Skogerbo, E.: Age, generations and the media. Northern Lights **11**(1), 3–14 (2013)
13. Westlund, O., Weibull, L.: Generation, life course and news media use in Sweden 1986–2011. Northern Lights **11**, 147–173 (2013)
14. Ayalon, L., Tesch-Römer, C. (eds.): Contemporary Perspectives on Ageism. Springer, Cham (2018). https://doi.org/10.1007/978-3-319-73820-8
15. Butler, R.N.: Ageism: a foreward. J. Soc. Issues **36**(2), 8–11 (1980)
16. Voss, P., Bodner, E., Rothermund, K.: Ageism: The relationship between age stereotypes and age discrimination. In: Ayalon, L., Tesch-Römer, C. (eds.) Contemporary Perspectives on Ageism, pp. 11–31. Springer, Cham (2018). https://doi.org/10.1007/978-3-319-73820-8_2

17. Krekula, C., Nikander, P., Wilińska, M.: Multiple marginalizations based on age: gendered ageism and beyond. In: Ayalon, L., Tesch-Römer, C. (eds.) Contemporary Perspectives on Ageism, pp. 33–50. Springer, Cham (2018). https://doi.org/10.1007/978-3-319-73820-8_3
18. Rosales, A., Fernández-Ardevol, M.: Structural ageism in big data approaches. Nordicom Rev. 40(1), 51–64 (2019)
19. Amaral, I., Brites, M.J.: Trends on digital uses and generations. In: Proceedings of INTED 2019 Conference, 11th–13th March, Valencia, Spain (2019)
20. Colombo, F., Aroldi, P., Carlo, S.: I use it correctly!: the use of ICTs among Italian grandmothers in a generational perspective. Hum. Technol. 14(3), 343–365 (2018)
21. Fortunatti, L., Taipale, S., de Luca, F.: Digital generations, but not as we know them. Convergence Int. J. Res. New Media Technol. Online 25(1), 1–18 (2017)
22. Bolin, G.: Media Generations: Experience, Identity and Mediatised Social Change. Routledge, London and New York (2017)
23. Osgerby, B.: Youth Media. Routledge, London (2004)
24. Mannheim, K.: Essays on the Sociology of Knowledge. Routledge & K. Paul, London (1952)
25. Bolin, G.: Media generations: objective and subjective media landscapes and nostalgia among generations of media users. Participations J. Audience Reception Stud. 11(2), 108–131 (2014)
26. Buckingham, D., Willet, R. (eds.): Digital Generations: Children Young People and New Media. Lawrence Erlbaum, Mahwah (2006)
27. Colombo, F.: The long wave of generations. In: Fortunatti, L., Gebhardt, J., Vincent, J. (eds.) Participation in Broadband Society, vol. 5, pp. 19–36. Peter Lang, Frankfut am Main (2011)
28. Gumpert, G., Cathcart, R.: Media grammars, generations, and media gaps. Crit. Stud. Mass Commun. 2(1), 23–35 (1985)
29. Siibak, A., Tamme, V.: Who introduced granny to Facebook?': an exploration of everyday family interactions in web-based communication environments. Northern Lights 11(1), 71–89 (2013)
30. Livingstone, S., Haddon, L.: EU Kids Online: final report 2009. EU Kids Online, Deliverable D6.5. EU Kids Online Network, London (2009)
31. Mesch, G.S.: Family relations and the internet: Exploring a family boundaries approach. J. Fam. Commun. 6(2), 119–138 (2006)
32. Volkmer, I. (ed.): News in Public Memory: An International Study of Media Memories Across Generations. Blackwell, New York (2006)
33. Aroldi, P., Ponte, C.: Adolescents of the 1960s and 1970 s: an Italian-Portuguese comparison between two generations of audiences. Cyberpsychology J. Psychosoc. Res. Cyberspace. 6(2) (2012). https://doi.org/10.5817/CP2012-2-3
34. Nimrod, G., Adoni, H., Nossek, H.: The internet as cultural forum: a European perspective. Int. J. Commun. 9(1), 321–343 (2015)
35. Bennet, S.E., Craig, S.C., Radmacher, E.W. (eds.): After the Boom: The Politics of Generaton X. Rowman and Littlefield, Lanham (1997)
36. Hasebrink, U., Hepp, A.: How to research cross-media practices? Investigating media repertoires and media ensembles. Convergende Int. J. Res. New Media Technol. 23(4), 362–377 (2017). https://doi.org/10.1177/1354856517700384
37. Kim, S.J.: A repertoire approach to cross-platform media use behaviour. New Media Soc. 18(3), 353–372 (2014)
38. Bjur, J., Schröder, K.C., Hasebrink, U., Courtois, C.: Cross-Media Use-Unfolding Complexities in Contemporary Audiencehood. Audience Transformations. Shifting Audience Positions in Late Modernity. Routledge, New York (2013)
39. Schröder, K.C.: Audiences are inherently cross-media: audience studies and the cross-media challenge. CM Commun. Media 18, 5–28 (2011)
40. Napoli, P.: Audience Economics: Media Institutions and the Audience Marketplace. Columbia University Press, New York (2003)

41. Ksiazek, T.B.: Repertoires of media use across platforms: Understanding patterns of audience. duplication through network analysis. In: Proceedings of the 59th Annual Conference of the International Communication Association. Chicago, IL (2009)
42. Lindell, J., Hovden, J.F.: Distinctions in the media welfare state: audience fragmentation in post-egalitarian Sweden. Media Cult. Soc. **40**(5), 639–655 (2017)
43. Couldry, N., Hepp, A.: The Mediated Construction of Reality. Polity Press, Cambridge (2017)
44. Egri, C.P., Ralston, D.A.: Generation cohorts and personal values: a comparison of China and the United States. Organ. Sci. **15**(2), 210–220 (2004)
45. Volčić, Z.: Yugo-Nostalgia: cultural memory and media in the former Yugoslavia. Crit. Stud. Media Commun. **24**(1), 21–38 (2007)
46. Ramet, S.P.: Three Yugoslavias: State building and Legitmation 1918–2005. Indiana University Press, Bloomington (2006)
47. Peruško, Z., Vozab, D., Čuvalo, A.: Comparing Post-Socialist Media Systems: The Case of Southeast Europe. Routledge, Europe (2020)
48. Zubak, N.: The Yugoslav Youth Press (1968–1980). Student Movements, Youth Subcultures and Alternative Communist Media. Srednja Europa, Zagreb (2018)
49. Blanuša, N.: Drugi svjetski rat kao transgeneracijska trauma: sablast prošlosti među mladima u Hrvatskoj. In: Ilišin, V., Gvozdanović, A., Potočnik, D. (eds.) Demokratski potencijali mladih u Hrvatskoj, pp. 125–144. Insititut za društvena istraživanja u Zagrebu, Centar za demokraciju i pravo Miko Tripalo/nl, Zagreb (2015)
50. Peruško, Z.: Historical institutionalist approach in comparative media systems research: the case of post-Yugoslavia. Javnost Public **23**(3), 255–272 (2016)
51. Peruško, Z., Vozab, D., Čuvalo, A.: Digital mediascapes, institutional frameworks, and audience practices across Europe. Int. J. Commun. **9**(1), 342–364 (2015)
52. Hallin, D., Mancini, P.: Comparing Media Systems. Three Models of Media and Politics. Cambridge University Press, Cambridge (2004)

"You Don't Need Instagram, It's for Young People": Intergenerational Relationships and ICTs Learning Among Older Adults

Simone Carlo[✉] and Francesco Bonifacio

Università Cattolica del Sacro Cuore, Milan, Italy
{simone.carlo,francesco.bonifacio}@unicatt.it

Abstract. The present research focuses on the problems connected to digital literacy for the elderly and on moments of intergenerational learning. The paper presents the main results of an ethnographic research carried out for a course on the risks related to the unintentional use of ICTs. The course took place in March 2019, involving 60 seniors as attendees and 25 students from a secondary school in a small town in the north of Italy as lecturers. The research seems to remark the importance of the context where the encounters between younger and older people take place. Overall, our observations do not indicate that intergenerational learning is useless per se, nor they suggest that it is not successful at all. The joining of different generations always raises symbolic challenges in terms of social recognition. What appears clear from our observations is that placing an intergenerational training in a classroom is not sufficient in itself to transform young students in teachers. It neither puts older people in the correct disposition to feel like students again.

Keywords: Aging and social media · Aging and technology acceptance · Generational differences in IT use · Training the elderly in the use of IT

1 Introduction

The use of digital media continues to grow among the over-65s in the Western world [1], therefore attracting the interest of academic research. Researchers focused on the role of the traditional dimensions of inequality (e.g. economic and educational) within the elderly on one hand, and on the specificities of their use of ICTs (Information Communication Technologies and the related the digital skills) on the other [2]. These latter studies in particular, often tend to problematize the dimension of formal and informal digital learning by the elderly [3–6]. Within this debate, both in academic literature [7] and in public discourses on policies [8], the urgency to encourage moments of intergenerational exchange based on the use of ICTs has emerged.

As a consequence, the present research concentrates on the elderly's digital literacy, with a special attention to instances of intergenerational learning. More specifically, the paper presents the main results of an ethnographic research carried out on the occasion of a course focused on the risks related to the non-conscious use of ICTs. The course

© Springer Nature Switzerland AG 2020
Q. Gao and J. Zhou (Eds.): HCII 2020, LNCS 12209, pp. 29–41, 2020.
https://doi.org/10.1007/978-3-030-50232-4_3

took place in March 2019, involving 60 seniors as attendees and 25 students from a secondary school in a small town in the north of Italy as lecturers. Moments of frontal teaching alternated with moments of assistance in the performance of some activities.

The research, conducted in March 2019, included the submission of 60 question-naires to the senior participants, 2 participant-observation sessions and a series of short group interviews with both the elderly and the young ones. Only the results from the interviews and the ethnographic observations are here illustrated, choosing to postpone the questionnaires' results to future publications.

Our study was aimed to answer two large research questions:

- RQ1: How is the relationship between different generations and ICTs incorporated and enacted during formal occasions of digital learning?
- RQ2: How do older and younger people acknowledge the inversion in the role of "mentor" that is traditionally anchored to ideas of age and experience?

2 Background: The Digitalisation of the Elderly in Italy

Italy is a super-aged country: more than one fifth of the population is over 65 and projec-tions see a progressive aging of the population, due to both increasing life expectancy and decreasing birth rate [9]. At the same time, the Italian society is also a highly unevenly-digitalised one, with the number of elderly Internet users ranking among the lowest in Europe. In 2017 the percentage Internet users among seniors (aged over 65) was 25,8% [10]: a very low figure compared to the rest of Europe, where the average in the 28 EU countries (including also the poorest countries in Eastern Europe) is 38,5%, while Western European countries range well above 40% of connected elderly people (Fig. 1).

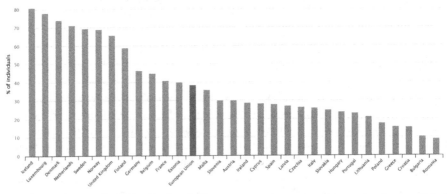

Fig. 1. Percentage of individuals using the Internet every day or almost every day, for a period of 3 months. Source: Eurostat, 2017

If Italians over 65 are therefore among those who less use Internet in Europe, at the same time the younger generations prove to be highly digitalised: 89,4% of people under the age of 24 in Italy use the Internet regularly, in line with the European average of 92,2%.

These data show that in Italy the digital generational gap is very strong [11], with a (increasingly) radical difference between media used by young people (mainly the Internet) and media used by the elderly (mainly TV).

In terms of literacy of the elderly, therefore, Italy seems to suffer a delay of about ten years compared to more digitalised countries. It is particularly urgent nowadays to address the factors that hinder the adoption of ICTs by Italian senior citizens and to understand the role played by ICTs, in order to provide cultural and relational resources useful to support active aging and a better quality life for older people [12].

In this context Italian private and public institutions, both at the local and national level, have been committed to spread digital culture among the population over 65, often with mixed results: even in the field of policy and research on the elderly and ICTs, Italy stays behind in comparison to other more digitalised countries [8].

ICTs is certainly a tool to ensure active aging, a greater well-being and a better quality of life for older people [13]. However, as we will see in this article, in some cases Italian (and European) public discourses and policies would seem to force the adoption of digital technologies by older people, in spite of the fact that researches have not yet effectively demonstrated in which contexts ICTs can actually produce the expected benefits in the life of the elderly [14]. In this sense, it seems appropriate to combine a reflection on the factors (individual and social) that contribute to either hinder or support the diffusion of the Internet and computers among the elderly, with an assessment of risks and opportunities in the use of digital media as perceived by the over 65 [15].

3 The Role of Digital Media in the Daily Life of the Italian Elderly: Uses and Skills

As pointed out in the previous section, the presence and use of digital media involves only part of the Italian elderly. In 2013–2015 a multidisciplinary group based at the Università Cattolica (Italy) carried out a research on a representative sample of Italian seniors aged 65–74. In data processing OssCom - Università Cattolica's media and communication research centre - focused on the sub-sample of older internet users to better understand the uses and skills of the so-called "digital young elderly". The research shows [16] that only 17.5% of individuals own a personal laptop they use, and the number decreases to 16.7% when it comes to a pc. While the diffusion of computers is still limited, the data on the spreading of smartphones are more encouraging: the diffusion of mobile phones among the elderly exceeds 70%, but less than 10% of the elderly are used to regularly surf the Internet using them. The data on technological equipment become more interesting when correlated to age (discriminating between two age-related sub-cohorts: 65–69 and 70–74) and gender. It is clear, in particular, that men aged 65–69 year possess and use computers and the Internet significantly more than women and older individuals. Beyond a deeper problem of gender inequality, this gap can be facilitated by different working condition: according to the OssCom questionnaire, over 20% of males over 65 (against 7% of women) work at least occasionally, so it is possible that some of these work activities involve the use of a PC. Furthermore, the younger age group (65–69 years) has grown in a more digitalised labour market than the older one (70–74 years), thus generating over the years a greater propensity to possession and use of communication technologies: 49.8% of older users say they have learned to use the PC at work. 45% of the elderly who presently use a computer have started doing so before the age of 50, 28.2% between 50 and 59 years old, 19.1% between 60 and 64 years of age. Only 9.1% of users are "new" ICTs users (they started using computers after the age of 64), with a significant difference between males and females: new male users are only 6.8%, against 12.8% of women.

These data indicate that the elderly who normally use PC and Internet have a consolidated background of use behind them. They are not "natives" of the digital world, but rather long-term "immigrants" [17] who, in their approach to the evolution of the *new* IT and ICTs world, could bring with them skills, attitudes and resistances influenced by their own history as users. Conversely, the number of new senior users is relatively low with an interesting percentage of women who in the last few years, if not months, are starting to learn to use ICTs, basically starting directly via the use of smartphones.

The world of ICTs senior users appears to be far from one-dimensional; it seems to be composed by layers and waves of users who come to the PC, tablet, Internet and Web 2.0 from pre-formed paths of profoundly different ICTs adoptions and skills.

4   The Relationship Between Generations: Intergenerational Learning Processes

In this section we will deal with the issue of relations between generations and in particular with how the learning processes using digital media fit into the relational processes between different generations.

As explained above, the use of digital media is increasing in the over-65 population range of the Western world, even though in policies and public debate the elderly are still considered as a segment of the population showing learning difficulties in the use of ICTs.

Academic research has long been committed to study the relationship between ICTs and the elderly, focusing in particular on the reasons for the lack of use of ICTs within the older population [4], on the dimension of formal and informal learning by the elderly [5] and on the contexts (work, family, school) where the elderly acquire their digital skills.

The above mentioned research [16] even wanted to investigate the possible relationships in place between the elderly and the youth, aiming to understand the dynamics at play in intergenerational exchange, family use and domestication of ICTs.

Our quantitative data indicate that the possession and use of ICTs is more likely to accompany an old age condition characterised by good levels of physical activity, a large number of friends, a low perception of one's age and a propensity for intergenerational relationships.

It significantly emerges from the qualitative part of the research that the biographies of adoption allow us to understand different uses of ICTs: beyond the biological age, also the personal, working, family and generational dimensions all influence older adults' paths towards technology domestication. The study shows how the elderly started to learn and use ICTs since the '90s, thanks to their work relations (intra-generational dimension), and to their private relations with their children and grandchildren (intergenerational dimension).

In particular, several researches have underlined the importance, in digital literacy processes, of "informal and family" intergenerational exchanges taking place between the elderly and young people as a support to active aging [12]. They help to fit into the need for "new" solidarity relations between different generations based on the mutual exchange of resources (and skills) [18], but also to weave new ties between young and old generations in the presence of intergenerational fracture [19].

Similarly, the urgency to encourage moments of intergenerational exchange based on ICTs often surfaces in public speeches and policies.

From a comparative research carried out in 2015 on the analysis of Italian and British digital inclusion policy documents for the elderly [8], it emerged that the reference to intergenerational learning processes is fundamental, particularly in Italy:

- The intergenerational dimension is considered a push for the elderly to access digital contents
- Social media are presented as essential and useful tools for communicating with children and grandchildren
- Learning how to use the Internet and computers is an opportunity to learn the same language spoken by the younger generations.
- Learning to use ICTs in courses taught by children is an opportunity to improve the relationship with the youth.

In several revised Italian documents, when it comes to teaching the intergenerational approach is supported through the promotion of intergenerational digital literacy courses. The "intergenerational rhetoric" [20] is quite recurrent in Computer and Internet learning courses where young people train the elderly.

Said documents often use the terms of "digital native" and "digital immigrants", and stress the importance of intergenerational relations as (family and social) moments during which seniors learn how to use computers.

The employment of the younger generations (in particular secondary school or university students) as formal or informal teachers appears in various political documents and it seems to be one of the main trends in the digital inclusion policies for the elderly in Italy, especially if compared with European Nordic Country [8]. Furthermore, most of the documents we have analysed promote schools and senior centres as places to organise courses. In particular, secondary schools seem to represent the right location where older people could learn to use ICTs in a "back to school" sort of way.

If the 'intergenerational-divides' framing of ageing population really stands out in the digital inclusion policies in Italy, then how do field programmes of digital literacy based on the intergenerational exchange really work?

Starting from these reflections, this article aims to focus on the digital literacy processes of the elderly and more specifically on learning moments and intergenerational relationships. In this regard, over the next section we will present the first evidence of an ethnographic research carried out on the occasion of a course focused on the risks related to the non-conscious use of ICTs.

5   The Case Study

Public and private projects that promote a greater dialogue between generations through the help of ICTs are significantly emerging, especially in Italy [8]. While promoters often foster the importance of such forms of digital learning, social research may contribute to the existing debate by observing them in action and questioning what kind of relational processes are involved.

In order to pursue this goal, we identified a digital literacy course directed to senior citizens. The project took place in a sparsely populated area in the north of Italy and it was promoted by a group of local associations. This initiative claimed to encourage a conscious use of ICTs among older adults by enlisting the help of younger secondary school students. The idea was to raise the attendees' awareness of risks connected to ICTs use, hence the whole project consisted of both informative and laboratory meetings. During the former, older adults attended psychologists' and police officers' lectures focused on risks prevention. In occasion of laboratory meetings instead, they usually spent an afternoon practicing on their smartphone with the help of their young educators. This type of encounters were meant to implement older adults' confidence with ICTs: the presence of young people was meant to help them solve every-day practical difficulties by using smartphones and other digital devices. In this vein, the initiative was intentionally set in the young tutors' school to metaphorically "bring older adults back to school" in order to improve their ICTs use. The laboratory consisted of a huge room where younger and older people were divided in groups. Each older adult was randomly assigned to a young tutor and, due to the former's higher number, some tutors supervised two older adults at once.

5.1   Sample, Research Objects and Methods

The course was designed to enrol over 65 people and students from secondary school. In the end 60 senior students submitted an application (40 women and 20 men, with an average age of 73 years old) and 25 young mentor (15 boys and 10 girls, with an average age of 16 years old) were involved. All senior participants except for one were retirees. Our interest was not directly focused on evaluating older adults digital learning accomplishments. Given to its brevity (only two encounters were scheduled between young and older people) the initiative was merely suitable for elaborating inferences about the course's success in terms of digital skills achieved by older adults. Actually, this was not even the goal pursued by the project promoters; they more generally aimed to raise senior citizens' awareness about the risks related to ICTs use with the help of a younger generation supposedly more confident with such tools.

Our attention was therefore directed to critically observe the relational dynamics underlying the on-going learning processes. Despite common public encouragement, linking two distant generations in order to enhance older adults' confidence with ICTs entails some concerns. In this case, we meant to study how ideas about ICTs may vary between different generations, and how such discrepancies may become visible during an encounter between the two groups, hence affecting the digital learning processes. Such concerns seemed even more important due to the mere functional nature of the relationship between younger and older people, which was strictly limited to the time allotted for the meetings.

Another critical aspect was the *reverse mentoring* rhetoric underlying the course's purpose [5]. According to that, younger people are supposed to be able to teach something to older adults just because of their age; however such process is not inherently linear. On the contrary, the inversion of social roles may be better understood as a negotiation between two different social identities. It is therefore an inter-subjective process unfolding during situated encounter between social actors (in this case the young and the elderly). As social researchers, we believe that these relational dynamics should be empirically questioned in order to address the efficacy of such ways of learning. Our research intended to broadly observe the way in which the social identities of members of both generations as ICTs users were negotiated during the meetings. Special attention was paid to how younger and older people were (re)presented by the course promoters. Our study was then aimed to answer two large research questions:

- How is the relationship between different generations and ICTs incorporated and enacted during formal occasions of digital learning?
- How do older and younger people acknowledge the inversion in the role of "mentor" that is traditionally anchored to ideas of age and experience?

From a methodological point of view, in order to grasp such aspects during the encounters in action we conducted ethnographic observations that, given the initiative's brevity, may as well be regarded as exploratory. Their heuristic efficacy is of course limited to this course's contingency. We were introduced as researchers by the promoters during the opening meeting with senior participants. Despite the further clarification of our role during the events, our presence still seemed ambiguous sometimes. This was perhaps caused by our age (definitely closer to the younger people's), as we were occasionally addressed as if we were tutors by the older adults. Therefore, it often happened that the seniors shared with us their ideas and doubts in relation to the use of the smartphone and to the ongoing training activity. Also, some of the younger students approached us as confidants when they did not feel equipped to deal with the mentoring sessions. In both cases we did not deny the help, and such instances ended up being also fruitful to our research interests. They became true moments of sharing that enabled us to converse with older adults and to grasp understandings that would have inevitably remained invisible to a mere non-intrusive observation. During the activities, older adults were sometimes asked to better explain any ambiguous statements that we reckoned could potentially be relevant to our research goals. Moreover, we conducted short group interviews at the end of both training sessions in order to collectively clarify our considerations. Yet, the majority of findings and statements reported in this paper are related to ethnographic notes. During the encounters, we took note of people's words and we also recorded the entire sessions in order to avoid relevant omissions during the following phase of analysis. After the first ethnographic session, our notes were analysed and transformed in concepts to be analytically used in the second session. All the statements present in this paper were translated to English by the authors.

5.2   The Representations of Generational Identities in Terms of ICTs Use

Our observations indicate that the detrimental dichotomy between digital natives and digital immigrants [17] appears to be naturalised and deeply incorporated in discourses. Already during the opening meeting, the project's promoters defined young students as *"guardians"* or *"digital natives"*, able to take care of a *"problematic parterre"*, meaning the elderly (course promoter, F). The shared awareness of a significant generational digital divide emerged also from conversations between older students and younger tutors. Two statements pronounced by two of the tutors working close to each other during the activity stood as particularly emblematic. Asked by their older students about the difference between Facebook and Instagram, the first guy answered:

The difference is…well…as young people we don't use Facebook, basically it is used by older people (young tutor, M).

The second further confirmed:

Yes, Instagram is used by young people, while Facebook is for old ones (young tutor, M).

Consistently with that, another tutor answered to her older student's enquiry about WhatsApp stories:

Well, nothing, WhatsApp stories are just not important. They are stuff for young people (young tutor, F).

This divide rhetoric was significantly recurring during both meetings. In another symbolic case, a guy replied to his older mentee's curiosity about a gaming App by simply stating: *"you don't need this App, it's useless"*. All these conversation fragments are symbolically explanatory of the persistence of such techno-deterministic stereotypes. Despite social research's attempt to demystify them, they are still part of people's common sense, in both younger and older generations. These kinds of stereotypes do not only link older people and low digital skills but, more importantly, they deterministically attribute specific uses and o older adults, depicting them as *older users*, as opposed to younger ones. Similarly, young people's rhetoric seems to assume that the elderly do not need to learn what they want to know, but essentially what it is supposedly necessary in their everyday life (according to common sense).

Eventually, said prior understanding of older adults' digital needs often ends up bracketing uses only related to entertainment reasons [21], excluding gaming and "light" activities [22]. Such findings were particularly arising when young people lacked to ask the seniors about their specific interests and needs, *de facto* considering older adults as a monolithic category.

Conversely, when training activities followed an interlocutory phase, older adults were observed to offer unpredicted answers about their interests. It is the case of a woman asking for instructions on how to consult the Facebook page of a radio she used to listen to. In another case, an old lady expressed the wish to learn how to use Google Maps in order to geographically locate her sons' houses. These cases show how ICTs (both softwares and devices) cannot be considered as discrete and abstract entities, nor can be studied or taught as such. The use of ICTs holds its place in people's everyday life, needs and practices. For example, the above mentioned instance would suggest that the woman connected a meaningful use of Facebook to part of her everyday routine such is listening to the radio.

Even though they differ from the stereotypical view of ICTs usage among older adults, these uses emerged as subjectively meaningful. During our ethnographic work we clearly noted that when young tutors let older adults express themselves, practices entailing a possibly meaningful use of ICTs were more easily identified. Yet, this does not seem to be only a matter of needs. For instance, the Google Maps example suggests older adults' ability to originally answer to a commonly acknowledged age-related need as an element enhancing *social connectedness*. When interests are shared beforehand, the training processes also seem to be more successful at least in terms of the participants' involvement and curiosity. Case in point, once the lady understood how to check her favourite radio's Facebook page, she asked her tutor to keep exploring other Facebook functionalities.

The ability to properly use technical language also emerges as a place with inherent symbolic divisions between generations. Some of the younger tutors acknowledged the older adults' difficulties to understand apparently innocuous terms such as *profile* and *account,* confirming what had already surfaced during the first ethnographic session. Although possibly motivated by a certain naïve lack of care in young people, the use of technical language was sometimes observed to strengthen older adults' perceived distance from young people and to discourage ICTs adoption on their part. For instance, when they did not request any further explanation, ending up bored and gradually losing interest in the training itself.

5.3 Drawing the Profile of a Resistant Elderly

Together with outlining such incorporation of the dichotomous digital divide within practices and oral communication, our observations also draw the profile of a critical older adult. The strategy of *reverse mentoring* characterising such initiative means to reverse the commonly-acknowledged image of the relationship between young and old people, based on the idea that the former are supposed to look after the latter, given their greater experience and knowledge. However, our observations suggest some forms of resistance among older adults. In particular, two examples seem particularly emblematic. In the first case, a man asked by his young tutor about his Facebook skills replied:

Right or wrong, everybody can use those things [social media]. *Technically, they are not that hard to use. It is not like studying Latin as I did in my time. They are intentionally designed to be easy to use. The very problem is that you are giving the property of your information to someone unknown. You just don't know who stands behind the door* (old man, M).

In another case, a man with a high cultural and economic capital (a retired bank director) stated to his young tutor in relation to the use of Facebook:

I worked for thirty years in a bank; I was also in charge of coding tasks. Using digital media does not seem that hard to me. […] Rather, I was wondering if it would have been more useful for you guys to attend a course on domestic finance…. (old man, M)

Despite the difference between the form of speech used by the two men (the second one more gentle and dissimulating than the first), both their statements were meant to undermine the importance of digital knowledge, and indirectly the value of young tutors' teaching itself. In both cases older adults also tried to relativize the hardship of achieving digital skills by comparing them with other fields knowledge (Latin and coding). In the first example, the old man warns against privacy risks related to the use of social media, remarking the stereotype of *naïve* and superficial young people. In the second case, the man stresses the lack of young individuals' knowledge in terms of domestic finance, remarking its importance as a concrete matter for people in their everyday life. Both examples may be considered as discursive traces of the symbolic struggle potentially emerging during the encounter between generations. Older adults were observed to challenge the label of *mentors* implicitly attributed to young people and based only on their familiarity with ICTs. This symbolic resistance inherently channelled their traditional roles as *educators*, given the vast knowledge and experience they hold. There is a final noteworthy aspect specifically related to digital risks: as conveyed by previous examples, young and older people have a different sensitivity about digital risks. It is evident in the ingenuity showed in the words of a guy helping his old student to create a Facebook profile: *"don't bother putting your phone number in there; we are going to delete the account later"*. On the contrary, older adults appear to be more concerned: their worries still seem to be deeply linked to their overall media consumption, especially TV. During the final focus group, a senior participant expressed his frustration because he had not learnt yet how to recognise dangerous internet sources. He said:

they [referring to television media] *scared us about the internet so much that now I feel unsafe to even turning the computer on. So now please teach us how to understand what is good and what is wrong* (old man, M).

6   Conclusion, Limitations and Implications for Future Research

Our research has focused on the elderly's digital literacy processes and, in particular, on the moments of learning within intergenerational relationships.

- RQ1: How is the relationship between different generations and ICTs incorporated and enacted during formal occasions of digital learning?

The role of intergenerational communication seems to have a great impact on the appropriation of digital media among the elderly [19]. From this point of view, the possibility of connecting with family members, especially the younger ones, is perceived by the elderly as an important incentive to go online [23], thus strengthening intergenerational relations [24]. Nevertheless, evident criticalities emerge from the observation of situated learning processes, in particular where intergenerational relations are instrumentally and exclusively constructed with the purpose of activating such processes.

In fact, if social speeches tend to produce normative approaches and stereotypes around the appropriate use of digital technologies with respect to age and gender [25], older users tend to reaffirm through daily experience their ability to use technologies according to their needs, and even critically distancing themselves from the use that other generations do of ICTs [14].

Finally, a generational sensitivity about the dimension of risks related to the use of ICTs (in particular those related to privacy issues) has been detected. The elderly sometimes seemed disoriented by young people's carelessness in sharing their personal information on the Internet, an instance that clashes with the information about internet-related dangers that senior citizens retain from mass-media.

- RQ2: How do older and younger people acknowledge the inversion in the role of "mentor" that is traditionally anchored to ideas of age and experience? This research contributed to observe that:

– A course based on the importance of reversing the intergenerational relationship in the field of digital learning [5], eventually tended to question the traditional "immigrant-native" regulatory image [26, 27]. Such image usually depicts young people as the custodians of digital knowledge, and the elderly as weak subjects who need to be alphabetised on the "correct" use of the related media. As a consequence, learning activities sometimes risked enhancing the generational distance between old and young participants. This occurred mainly on a symbolic level, as well as through the different use made by young and old people of the "technical" language connected to the Internet and ICTs.

Participants often encountered a certain difficulty accepting the inversion of the classical teacher-student roles, with young people teaching the elderly. In some cases the effect turned out to be a dissimulated but effective refusal to learn on the elderly's part, in an attempt to reaffirm their traditional "status" as mentors.

Our previous researches confirm that ICTs are important tools in order to build relationships between family members belonging to different generations and create opportunities to show (in a more or less explicit way) the love and intimacy existing between people of different ages [14, 16]. More struggles emerge when relationships limited in time and merely functional to the training in play. On this note, the present research seems to remark the importance of the context where the encounters between younger and older people take place. Overall, our observations do not indicate that intergenerational learning is useless *per se*, nor they suggest that it is not successful *at all*. As we briefly showed through some examples, the joining of different generations always raises symbolic challenges in terms of social recognition. What appears clear from our observations is that placing an intergenerational training in a classroom is not sufficient in itself to transform young students in teachers. It neither puts older people in the correct disposition to feel like students again.

Acknowledgments. This research is a pilot project within the wider international project HARVEST - eHealth and Aging in Rural Areas: Transforming Everyday Life, Digital Competences, and Technology. Harvest is funded by Joint Programming Initiative (JPI) "More Years, Better Lives" (Third Call). The third Joint Transnational Call, launched in December 2016, is entitled "Ageing and Place in a digitising world", Joint Programming Initiative "More Years, Better Lives" (JPI MYBL) is supported by J-Age II. J-Age II is funded by Horizon2020, the EU Framework Programme for Research and Innovation, under Grant Agreement nr 643850. International Coordinator: Simon Lindgren - Umeå University (Sweden). Italian coordinator: Fausto Colombo – Università Cattolica del Sacro Cuore (Italy).

References

1. Standard Eurobarometer. Media use in the European Union (2017). for more recent percentages. https://ec.europa.eu/commfrontoffice/publicopinion/index.cfm/ResultDoc/download/DocumentKy/82786
2. Loos, E., Haddon, H., Mante-Meijer, E. (eds.): Generational Use of New Media. Ashgate, Farnham (2012)
3. Czaja, S.J., et al.: Factors influencing use of an e-health website in a community sample of older adults. J. Am. Med. Inform. Assoc. **20**, 277–284 (2013)
4. Hunsaker, A., Hargittai, E.: A review of Internet use among older adults. New Media Soc. **20**(10), 3937–3954 (2018)
5. Breck, B.M., Dennis, C.B., Leedahl, S.N.: Implementing reverse mentoring to address social isolation among older adults. J. Gerontol. Soc. Work **61**, 513–525 (2018)
6. Kim, J., Gray, J.: Qualitative evaluation of an intervention program for sustained internet use among low-income older adults. Ageing Int. **41**(3), 240–253 (2015). https://doi.org/10.1007/s12126-015-9235-1
7. Neves, B.B., Amaro, F., Fonseca, J.R.S.: Coming of (old) age in the digital age: ICTs usage and non-usage among older adults. Sociol. Res. Online **18**, 22–35 (2013)
8. Sourbati, M., Carlo, S.: The mutuality of age and technology in digital divide policy. In: Partnership for Progress on the Digital Divide 2015 International Conference, Scottsdale (Phoenx), Arizona, USA, 21–22 October 2015 (2015)
9. ISTAT: Rapporto annuale 2017, La situazione del Paese (2017). http://www.istat.it/it/archivio/199318
10. European Commission: Europe's Digital Progress, report 2017 (2017). https://ec.europa.eu/digital-single-market/en/european-digital-progress-report
11. CENSIS 15° Rapporto Censis sulla comunicazione (2018). http://www.censis.it/comunicazione/15%C2%B0-rapporto-censis-sulla-comunicazione
12. Rossi, G., Boccacin, L., Bramanti, D., Meda, S.G.: Active ageing: intergenerational relationships and social generativity. Stud. Health Technol. Inform. **203**, 57–68 (2014)
13. Sourbati, M.: On older people, internet access and electronic service delivery: a study of sheltered homes. In: Loos, E., Haddon, L., Mante-Meijer, E. (eds.) The Social Dynamics of Information and Communication Technology, pp. 95–104. Ashgate, Aldershot (2008)
14. Colombo, F., Aroldi, P., Carlo, S.: "I use it correctly!": the use of ICTs among Italian grandmothers in a generational perspective. Hum. Technol. **14**, 343–365 (2018). https://doi.org/10.17011/ht/urn.201811224837
15. Carlo, S., Vergani, M.: Risk and benefit perceptions: resistance, adoption and uses of ICT among the Italian elderly. In: Zhou, J., Salvendy, G. (eds.) ITAP 2016. LNCS, vol. 9754, pp. 155–166. Springer, Cham (2016). https://doi.org/10.1007/978-3-319-39943-0_15
16. Aroldi, P., Carlo, S., Colombo, F.: New elders, old divides: ICTs, inequalities and well being amongst young elderly Italians. Comunicar **23**(45), 47–55 (2015). peer reviewed
17. Prensky, M.: Digital natives, digital immigrants. Horizon **5**, 1–6 (2001)
18. Bramanti, D.: Scambi tra famiglie e prosocialità intergenerazionale. In: Scabini, E., Rossi, G. (eds.) La famiglia prosociale, pp. 157–180. Vita e Pensiero, Milano (2002)
19. Carlo, S., Rebelo, C.: Technology: a bridge or a wall? The inter(intra)generational use of ICTs among Italian grandmothers. In: Zhou, J., Salvendy, G. (eds.) ITAP 2018. LNCS, vol. 10926, pp. 446–464. Springer, Cham (2018). https://doi.org/10.1007/978-3-319-92034-4_34
20. Lüscher, K., et al.: Generations, intergenerational relationships, generational policy: a multilingual compendium, Universität Konst. Rocznik Andragogiczny **22**, 459 (2016). https://doi.org/10.12775/ra.2015.032

21. Buse, C.E.: When you retire, does everything become leisure? Information and communication technology use and the work/leisure boundary in retirement. New Media Soc. **7**, 1143–1161 (2009)
22. Nimrod, G.: The internet as a resource in older adult leisure. Int. J. Disabil. Hum. Dev. **8**(3), 207–214 (2008)
23. Ivan, L., Hebblethwaite, S.: Grannies on the net: grandmothers' experiences of Facebook in family communication. Revista Română de Comunicare şi Relaţii Publice **18**(1), 11–25 (2016)
24. Fernández-Ardèvol, M., Sawchuk, K., Grenier, L.: Maintaining connections: octo- and nonagenarians on digital 'use and non-use'. Nordicom Rev. **38**(1), 39–51 (2017). https://doi.org/10.1515/nor-2017-0396
25. Comunello, F., Fernández-Ardèvol, M., Mulargia, S., Belotti, F.: Women, youth and everything else: age-based and gendered stereotypes in relation to digital technology among elderly Italian mobile phone users. Media Cult. Soc. **39**(6), 798–815 (2017)
26. Loos, E.: Senior citizens: digital immigrants in their own country? Observatorio **6**(1), 1–23 (2012)
27. Bennett, S., Maton, K., Kervin, L.: The 'digital natives' debate: a critical review of the evidence. Br. J. Edu. Technol. **39**(5), 775–786 (2008)

Young and Elderly Fashion Influencers

Manuela Farinosi[✉] [iD] and Leopoldina Fortunati [iD]

University of Udine, Via delle Scienze, 206, 33100 Udine, Italy
{manuela.farinosi,leopoldina.fortunati}@uniud.it

Abstract. The aim of this paper is to analyse a new phenomenon that has emerged in the fashion system: the advent of female fashion influencers over 70. To outline all the novelties this brings with it, we produced a comparison between elderly and young fashion influencers along the evolution of the fashion system in the last decade. We considered both the first wave of fashion blogging (2012–15) populated by young fashion bloggers and the second wave (2015–19) in which we considered especially elderly fashion influencers. At the operational level, we selected the four fashion bloggers who were most followed on Facebook in 2011 in Italy: Chiara Ferragni (theblondesalad.com), Veronica Ferraro (thefashionfruit.com), Nicoletta Reggio (scentofobsession.com), and Irene Colzi (ireneccloset.com). Regarding old women, in 2019 we selected the top 20 elderly influencers over 70, identified using Instagram's search feature to detect age-related trends (i.e., using hashtags such as #over70 or #advancedstyle). While the four young fashion influencers are Italian, for the older fashion influencers we needed to select English-speaking women from across the globe, as this phenomenon is still just beginning in Italy. We applied qualitative and quantitative methods to capture bloggers' online strategies and activities for two weeks at both the discursive and visual levels. The results show that while young fashion influencers have been incorporated into the fashion system, fashion influencers over 70 are still producing an important discourse for women, the elderly, and the whole society, although the initial attempts on the part of fashion houses to colonize them are emerging.

Keywords: Ageing · Fashion · Blogger · Influencer · Feminism · Young women · Elderly women · Elderly

1 How the Increasing Weight of Intermediation Suffocates Any Creative Initiative from Grassroots in the Fashion Field

The aim of this paper is to explore a new phenomenon that has emerged in the fashion system—the birth of female fashion influencers over 70. To properly analyse this phenomenon and outline all the novelties this brings with it, we produced a comparison between elderly and young fashion influencers along the evolution of the fashion system in the last decade. We are not new to this topic; we previously conducted a study on the first phase of young fashion bloggers in Italy and China (Fortunati et al. 2017). Since then, we have continued to observe and study the fashion sphere online.

© Springer Nature Switzerland AG 2020
Q. Gao and J. Zhou (Eds.): HCII 2020, LNCS 12209, pp. 42–57, 2020.
https://doi.org/10.1007/978-3-030-50232-4_4

Here, we begin by analysing how grassroots fashion storytelling has developed in recent years, from fashion bloggers to the appearance of a new breed of PR-driven media producer—the influencers. We argue that only by historicizing the phenomenon of grassroots fashion narratives is it possible to make sense of its real social dynamics despite the rhetoric that still surrounds it even in the scientific literature. The research we present here tries to shed light on the evolution of this contemporary phenomenon and investigate how the Internet and particularly informational and social platforms have enabled fashion consumers, so far anonymous and recipient social subjects, not only to become producers (Bruns 2008) but also to get a leading role in fashion online.

The phenomenon of fashion bloggers began to take off online in 2007 and evolved at a remarkable pace, with many amateurs (mainly women) who started creating blogs to express their points of view on fashion (finally the users began to talk back in the fashion system!) and to convey fashion in words and images by taking existing genres and combining them into new formats (Rocamora 2012). Since their appearance, these blogs have subverted the rigid hierarchy that existed in the fashion world where communication was only top-down, and they have established themselves as a central platform for the creation and circulation of fashion-related news, information, and discussion. In more recent times, they have also implemented multi-platform strategies based on the adoption of social channels such as Instagram, Facebook, YouTube, and so on.

The phenomenon of fashion blogging has added a lot to the fashion narrative in terms of grassroots fashion storytelling by generating a set of disintermediation processes and the subversion of traditional communication flows existing in the fashion system. In the first instance, fashion blogs allowing regular people to become part of the international fashion conversation were hailed by fashion scholars for "democratizing style" (Allen 2009; Pham 2011; Fortunati and Farinosi 2014). Even the mainstream media has described the fashion blogosphere as a space for expressing democratic engagement where women who do not fit into the stereotyped feminine fashion model (thin, tall, and rich) can enjoy a powerful form of self-expression (Khamis and Munt 2010).

In this first wave of studies on the fashion blogosphere, three main tropes were formulated. The first was the equality trope (Duffy 2013), which was based on (and strengthened by) a larger discourse about the power of the Internet to democratize communication and foster collaboration. According to Duffy (2013), the fashion blogosphere offered users an alternative to mainstream fashion media and opened up spaces antithetical to the rigorously patrolled fashion world in which users could finally talk about fashion, their experiences on fashion, their tastes, and their desires (Pham 2011). From simple receivers of fashion communication and proposals on the part of firms, users became producers of a grassroots discourse on fashion.

The second was the authenticity trope in which fashion blogs were overwhelmingly seen as producers of a discourse on fashion, which was more adhering to the taste, style, and practices of use by people than the content of mainstream magazines. The bloggers' use of casual, immediate language and the prevalence of street fashion photography were perceived as showing a customer intimacy that differentiated them from more traditional market relationships. According to Marwick (2013), authenticity was the key to attracting followers. She claimed that the online image that bloggers created of themselves was an important factor in successful blogging. Readers were looking for an accessible person they could identify with instead of the unattainable top models.

The third, equally pushed by this first wave of studies, was the counterculture trope, concerning amateur content creators (Bruns 2008). Fashion blogs were seen as contributing substantially to overcoming the traditional hierarchical structure of the fashion system and reshaping traditional sources of cultural and media production (i.e., women's magazines).

In this first phase, fashion bloggers expressed a double strategy. On one hand, they aimed at creating a bottom-up fashion communication as an alternative to the one offered by glossy magazines and a more genuine, spontaneous, and experiential narration of fashion. On the other hand, they tried to create a communication that re-introduced the intermediation between fashion houses and their public/customers that in a first moment was skipped, this time set up by themselves. Although in this phase blogs and social platforms played an important role in bridging the gap between the directive world of the fashion system and the lived experience of fashion with its new counterculture and agency of fashion consumers, overall they have received little scholarly attention (Berry 2010; Khamis and Munt 2010; Palmgren 2010).

Furthermore, the evolution of fashion blogs and social platforms has started a second wave with respect to which these three tropes proved unable to provide an effective framework to understand its nuanced cultures and political economies. The dividing line in fashion blogosphere history concerns the fact that, at a certain point in time, the fashion industry started to pay more attention to the most popular fashion bloggers and to court them, thus marking an evolution of the blog itself. The second wave of fashion blogs can be named the "colonization" period by fashion firms, which began to consider them as a powerful, additional market tool. Fashion firms began to send to the most popular of these bloggers free samples of the designer pieces that they had mentioned in their posts, and some of them got paid for working as brand ambassadors, for wearing and publishing a brand name product on their Instagram account, or for attending fashion shows and reporting in real-time their opinions of runway trends. Moreover, advertising agencies started to place advertising inserts in these blogs. Both the number of fashion blogs and the number of fashion media mentions of fashion blogs have grown considerably since then, and fashion blogs have increasingly become a part of mainstream fashion communication. A little at a time, fashion bloggers have been accepted and incorporated (though with many reservations) into the fashion system, becoming a further source of advertisement to both designers and fashion retail stores and a highly profitable digital media business.

The marketization of fashion blogs meant for fashion amateurs to enter into the fashion business. From a personal diary kept spontaneously by a fashion lover, these blogs became a sophisticated communication and marketing tool. Money availability was invested by many fashion bloggers in strengthening the digital infrastructure of their blogs. In addition to the blog, they increasingly adopted a multi-platform strategy in which visual channels (e.g., Instagram) take over.

At the same time, the role of their owners (the fashion bloggers) changed from that of simple fashion lovers to communication professionals or semi-professionals; bloggers became digital influencers.

The influencers must be understood as persons (especially women) able to dictate new trends and move their fans or followers in certain directions. Fashion influences have become micro- and meso-celebrities (Abidin 2016; Pedroni 2016), as through the new platforms they were able to attract the attention of millions of followers, more or less truthful. Nowadays, influencer marketing is increasing its importance and popularity within the fashion industry and is becoming an important element in advertising. Even those who have never read a specialized magazine can access important features of the fashion system, at no cost and in real time, thanks to fashion bloggers and the rapid "viralization" of their content spreading throughout the internet.

Fashion influencers have the merit to have diminished the distance between fashion companies and the public, making the contact between the two parties less complex. At the same time, as we mentioned, the set of initial disintermediation processes has been replaced by a series of new re-intermediation practices that have seen the appearance behind the scenes of various specialized agencies, managers, and web-marketing experts who mediate between bloggers and the fashion houses and direct the blogger in the implementation of best strategies and the correct use of tools offered by the web.

The structure of this paper is as follows. In the next section, we explore the second phase of fashion bloggers, which is their transformation into fashion influencers and the advent of a new figure—the fashion influencer over 70. Then we describe the methodology of our research, and in the following section we present our results. In the final section, we illustrate and discuss the comparison between younger and older fashion influencers. Some reflections on the limits of our research conclude this article.

2   Fashion Influencers: An Evolving Field

The evolution in the field of online fashion has also marked the birth of fashion influencers over 70, which represents a significant novelty for fashion, for women, and for the world of the elderly. This rapidly growing phenomenon is also confirmed by the data provided by an influencer marketing agency according in which the top 10 senior influencers on Instagram had seen a 24% increase in followers from September 2017 to the end of 2018 (Harvey 2019).

This is a novelty for fashion because, thanks to fashion influencers over 70, the fashion system has been stimulated to elaborate a language and style adapted to women of this age, overcoming the cultural limits that have characterized the fashion sphere in an era based on the myth of eternal youth. In doing so, it could begin to cover a segment of the market that was underpowered by the cultural and social limits of fashion itself, which has addressed mainly young consumers at least in recent decades. Despite the growing number and economic well-being of older people (higher compared to the past), only in recent times have apparel companies and the fashion system begun to look at this market segment as attractive and promising (Kohlbacher et al. 2011). This lack of attention toward older women has been attributed to several factors, from the negative stereotypes associated with ageing to businesses' fears that their products will become associated with senility (Lee 1997; Long 1998; Tunaley et al. 1999) to marketers' comfort with long-standing promotional strategies developed when young consumers were in the majority (Corlett 1998). Thomas and Wolfe (1995) suggest that focusing on the product needs and preferences of young (rather than old) consumers probably is linked also to the fact that the majority of people employed in product promotion are themselves young. The inattention to this consumer segment has resulted not only in lost revenues for business and lost consumption and service opportunities for the elderly but also a lack of narratives regarding body and beauty at a certain age, covering women of this age with a veil of invisibility. Now, however, faced with the phenomenon of influencers over 70, both designers and advertisers have begun to become aware of this more mature market and the opportunities in terms of business that this opens to fashion industries. A sign of this more widespread awareness is indicated by the fact that the British agency GreyModels, which specializes in mature models, is receiving more and more requests from fashion houses. Especially those houses that use strategies in line with the tendency to resort to such models for the presentation of the collections or that present collections addressing the needs of this section of the population are particularly interested to revolutionize the world of catwalks (Huffington Post 2015).

Influencers over 70 represent a significant novelty also for women, because this phenomenon has opened the opportunity to create and experiment with a vision of the beauty of their bodies outside the box of traditional stereotypes. Older fashion influencers succeed in being of great support for the social and political elaboration of a positive and free image of women at every age and for the strengthening of women's power in general. Nowadays, visual culture is saturated with pictures of youth and bodily perfection (Featherstone 1995), and old bodies are viewed as a disruption to the visual field, as something considered unwelcome and undesirable (Hepworth 2000). Even the visual representations of age and ageing often tend to systematically devalue and erase age (Twigg 2013). Providing a helpful overview of feminist scholarship on the cultural invisibility of older women, Meagher writes: "in order to learn to look at old women in new ways, they need to be wrenched from [...] cultural invisibility. Old women must become a part of our visual culture, present in popular visual culture and in art" (2014: 142). Nowadays, the increasing adoption of digital media by women over 70 and the spread of grassroots fashion communication are subverting the dominant paradigm and proving that "old" can be different from what it used to be in the past and that online influence is not exclusive to people of a younger age. The grey "models" who are smashing myths and stereotypes around ageing, beauty, and society's expectations are receiving big attention for their online content, not only from women in their peer group but also from younger female (and male) followers.

Influencers over 70 represent a significant novelty for the elderly because older women for the first time through social platforms and the use of new media have been able to independently create content and share it online, narrating their everyday lives in first-person and therefore outside the stereotypes that surround the world of senior citizens at every level. Ageism, understood as the set of discriminations addressed against the elderly, is a social phenomenon that has been articulated in various directions, from body shaming to the political and social disvalue that marks the third age to the invisibility of the elderly in mainstream content (Minichiello et al. 2000).

Influencers over 70 could emerge because in reality, the elderly demographic and social situation has changed importantly in post-industrialized countries. Nowadays, the aged population in most countries and regions in the world is experiencing growth in number and proportion. According to an extensive study conducted by the United Nation (2017), this growth is projected to accelerate in the coming decades. Considering that the number of people aged 60 years or over was 962 million in 2017, more than twice as large as in 1980 when there were 382 million, it is expected to double again by 2050, when it is projected to reach nearly 2.1 billion (United Nation 2017).[1]

For this reason, population ageing is supposed to become one of the most important social transformations of the 21st century, with challenges and implications for nearly all sectors including labour, the demand for goods and services, financial markets, transportation infrastructure, and communication technology (i.e., the Internet and mobile phones).

In addition, it is also noteworthy that although the mainstream media "maintain the discourse that older adults are technologically inept and digitally illiterate" (Schreurs et al. 2017: 361), recent studies do not support this stereotype. As highlighted for example by the research of Hargittai and Dobransky, many "older adults below 65 years of age [...] are still using the Internet in their work life" and that "those 65–79, though many are retired, [...] have experienced the diffusion of the online world into their daily work and home lives" (2017: 207).

Moreover, the percentage of older adults who use social media has dramatically increased in recent years (Hutto et al. 2015; Anderson and Perrin 2017). Older adults are quickly becoming more familiar with social networking technologies and use them to find news and information, connect with friends and family, and share their experiences. A study done by PEW in the US notes that 34% of Americans over 65 today use social networking sites like Facebook or Twitter (Anderson and Perrin 2017). Hutto et al. report that "among older adults, social media users tend to be younger seniors, female, educated with higher income, have higher confidence in technology and more positive attitudes of ICT, mostly access social media technology from their home computers, and typically desire to stay connected with family as their primary goal" (2015: 85).

Although the scientific literature on the extremely recent phenomenon of old fashion influencers is still scarce (with some exceptions; see Cereda 2017 and McGrath 2018), evidence of the emergence of older influencers as a fashionable and popular issue can be found in print media. To shed more light on the topic, it is necessary to consider the cultural context and the characteristics of the blogs and their owners in order to understand whether this trend represents a way of constructing new, less normative corporealities by older women or whether it represents a moment of effervescence to strengthen an already consolidated diktat by fashion firms.

3 Aim, Method, and Sample

The aim of this contribution is to investigate at an intergenerational level the phenomenon of women's grassroots fashion online storytelling from a sociological perspective. This research situates itself in the second phase of fashion grassroots initiatives online, which has seen the advent of fashion influencers. In particular, we focus on a subpopulation of fashion bloggers and Instagram users that is constituted by women producing fashion

---

[1] https://population.un.org/ProfilesOfAgeing2017/index.html.

and general lifestyle content, and we propose an analysis of how the cultural trajectory of these younger and older women has developed online. To show the evolution of these trajectories online, we report data related to both the first and the second phases to highlight the shift from fashion bloggers to fashion influencers. Through this research design, we are able to produce a comparison between the first and second phases and between younger and older influencers. Our research questions are: RQ1) In which terms do influencers change the relationship between women and fashion with respect to fashion bloggers? RQ2) How do elderly influencers change fashion communication compared to younger ones? RQ3) What kinds of content and visual storytelling do they use to produce and convey their messages on social media platforms such as Instagram in comparison with younger ones?

Regarding young women, we selected the four fashion bloggers who were most followed on Facebook in 2012 in Italy: Chiara Ferragni (theblondesalad.com), Veronica Ferraro (thefashionfruit.com), Nicoletta Reggio (scentofobsession.com), and Irene Colzi (ireneccloset.com), starting from the second phase of fashion blogging (Table 1). Applying qualitative and quantitative methods, in 2015 we analysed the bloggers' online strategies and activities for two weeks at both a discursive and visual level (Goffman 1959; Ball and Smith 1992). We monitored not only their blogs but also their social media practices. In addition, we conducted a qualitative analysis of the content they produced and shared online. Moreover, we applied virtual ethnography (Hine 2015) to study their practices through their different social media accounts (Facebook, Twitter, Instagram, and YouTube) in three different years (2012, 2015, and 2019), which illustrates the evolution of this phenomenon. We report below the data regarding young fashion influencers in 2012 because they illustrate the situation in the first phase of this phenomenon.

Table 1. The four most popular Italian fashion blogs in 2012 including their number of followers on Instagram, Facebook, Twitter, and YouTube in 2012.

	Instagram	Facebook	Twitter	YouTube
	2012	2012	2012	2012
Theblondesalad	383,901	230,196	115,049	10.913
Thefashionfruit	9,878	22,366	12,044	N.A.
Scentofobsession	4,846	13,404	3,513	N.A.
Ireneccloset	4,744	12,654	4,606	N.A.

Regarding old women, in 2019 we selected the top 20 elderly influencers over 70 using Instagram's search feature to detect age-related trends (i.e., using hashtags such as #over70 or #advancedstyle). Some elderly influencers create, publish, and curate their own content; others are filmed by family members who manage the various tasks necessary to convey their public images online. While for the young fashion influencers we could count on a sufficient presence of young fashion bloggers in the Italian digital context, which has always been the context we have studied, for the older fashion influencers we needed to refer to a more international sample, given that in Italy this phenomenon is still in the beginning. In Italy, older women's social condition at the moment is less politically problematized and contested than at the international level (e.g., US or Canada). Thus, we selected 20 English-speaking women from across the globe (see Table 2). We adopted an approach similar to that used for the younger ones, monitoring for two weeks through unobtrusive observation their online practices and activities (i.e., posting, captioning, commenting, replying, hashtagging, and username tagging) and carrying out a quasi-quantitative research study aiming to explore their attitudes in using new media, their communication strategies, and the relationships they build and manage with their followers. Although some of the women have a presence on multiple social media platforms, we chose to focus on the most content-rich and widely used—Instagram and blogs.

Table 2. The 20 elderly influencers analysed, their number of followers, the number of those they follow, the country where they live, and the links to their websites in 2019.

Influencer	Followers	Following	Country	Link
Helen Ruth Elam Van Winkle (baddiewinkle)	3,839,033	108	USA	https://www.instagram.com/baddiewinkle/
Iris Apfel	1,291,258	42	USA	https://www.instagram.com/iris.apfel/
Lyn Slater (iconaccidental)	663,125	897	USA	https://www.instagram.com/iconaccidental/
Maye Musk	242,713	165	Canada	https://www.instagram.com/mayemusk/
Sarah Jane Adams (saramaijewels)	182,374	0	UK	https://www.instagram.com/saramaijewels/
Moonlin0106	99,656	6	China	https://www.instagram.com/moonlin0106/
Beth Djalali (styleatcertainage)	84,037	507	USA	https://www.instagram.com/styleatacertainage/
Licia Fertz (buongiorno nonna)	61,395	311	Italy	https://www.instagram.com/liciafertz/
Jan Correll (silver_isthenewblonde)	53,186	2,327	N/A	https://www.instagram.com/silver_isthenewblonde/
Eileen Smith	50,834	278	Ireland	https://www.instagram.com/eileenstylequeen/
Judith Boyd (Style Crone)	48,366	1,100	USA	https://www.instagram.com/stylecrone/
Dorrie Jacobson (seniorstylebible)	43,894	1,102	USA	https://www.instagram.com/seniorstylebible/
Jenny Kee	37,717	222	Australia	https://www.instagram.com/jennykeeoz/
Patricia Fox (purely patricia)	36,384	436	USA	https://www.instagram.com/purelypatricia/
Drusilla Foer	35,102	470	Italy	https://www.instagram.com/drusillafoer/
Tziporah Salamon	31,336	556	Israel	https://www.instagram.com/tziporahsalamon/
Magda Llohis de Gutierrez (magdalife57)	20,716	522	Spain	https://www.instagram.com/magdalife57/
Patti (notdeadyetstyle)	16,779	1,379	N/A	https://www.instagram.com/notdeadyetstyle/
Jan de Villeneuve	16,302	973	UK	https://www.instagram.com/jandevilleneuve/
Ilona Royce Smithkin	12,937	31	USA	https://www.instagram.com/ilonaroycesmithkin/

To overcome ethical and methodological challenges posed by social media research, all of the blogs and social accounts studied are public.

At the operational level, given that online self-presentation takes place through the construction of profiles and through interaction with other users, we focused our attention on the profiles and interactions of our sample of fashion influencers, and we examined self-representation strategies evident within the visual and textual content of posts. In addition to unobtrusive observation of activities on Instagram and blogs, we collected and categorized data related to 1) online presence across the different online platforms (i.e., Instagram, Facebook, YouTube, personal blogs), 2) their Instagram profile (i.e., bio, number of followers, number of following), and 3) a selection of 20 photos for each influencer (a total of 400 pictures) and the associated captions, number of likes, numbers of comments, and comment texts. In doing so, we took into account both personal identity cues (posting a profile picture, writing a short bio, selecting hashtags, replying to comments left by followers, etc.) and social identity cues (followers, likes, comments left by followers, and hashtags that express group affiliation; Baym 2010).

4   Findings

In the present paper, there is not enough space to report all the data produced for this research, and thus we report a subset of the results obtained. In this section, we illustrate the data that can give an idea of the main characteristics of these fashion sites and to situate the data about young influencers and those related to older influencers in two separate subsections.

4.1   Young Influencers

The first finding that emerged from the analysis of young fashion influencers was that the multi-platform strategy adopted by fashion bloggers at the end of the first phase (2012) was strengthened in the second phase of their evolution to become fashion influencers (2015 up to 2019; see Table 3). They have tended to use an array of social platforms to cover their everyday life and the events to which they were invited and/or they promoted. Activating several platforms increased the number of their followers and acknowledgements from other bloggers, advertisers, and even the mainstream press. In short, once a blogger acquires a large audience through repeated displays of good taste, this audience begins to attract the interest of the fashion system. This, in turn, provides the blogger with greater social and economic resources, further augmenting her or his audience (McQuarrie et al. 2013).

A second finding (see Table 3) shows the magnitude of the increase in the fashion blogging phenomenon in the last few years, and as the readership of fashion blogs has grown, so has their influence on the fashion industry. An enormous increase in followers from 2015 to 2019 occurred across all the social media platforms we considered.

Table 3. The increasing number of social media followers of the four most popular Italian fashion bloggers from 2012 to 2015 and from 2015 to 2019.

	Instagram			Facebook			Twitter			YouTube		
	2012	2015	2019	2012	2015	2019	2012	2015	2019	2012	2015	2019
The blonde salad	383,901	3,779,597	17,800,000	230,196	1,061,260	1,230,617	115,049	241,828	408.219	10.913	46.933	138.000
The fashion fruit	9,878	197,457	979	22,366	1,988,277	2,494,241	12,044	26,359	30.166	N.A.	277	3.090
Scentofobsession	4,846	110,53	419	13,404	146,129	361,738	3,513	12,395	11.935	N.A.	713	685
Ireneccloset	4,744	81,794	285	12,654	329,497	357,041	4,606	14,227	17.910	N.A.	2.658	75.100

For comparison reasons, we again report in the table data related to 2012 to show at a glance the scope of the increase in the numbers of followers.

The third finding shows that the colonization and commercialization of the fashion blogosphere, which began at the end of the fashion blogger season, continue to grow relentlessly and become even stronger on the part of fashion houses. Very often, the outfits presented by these bloggers are quite expensive and often given for free by high fashion companies like Dior, Louis Vuitton, and Hermes, or by e-commerce websites such as Asos, Zalando, and LuisaViaRoma. What is different from before is that now bloggers do not even make the effort to talk and discuss about fashion with their followers and come up with new ideas, personalized styles, or trends to recommend; they merely act as the ambassadors of more or less high-end fashion brands. Numerous posts are witness to the bloggers' attendance at fashion shows and fashion weeks in major world cities (New York, London, Paris, Milan, Tokyo), at the openings of new shops, nightlife events, and new product launches. Influencers are able to participate in these events thanks to the invitation of mainstream brands who pay for everything (such as flights and hotels) in exchange for a little advertising on their blogs and social accounts aimed at a specific target market—fashion lovers. Fashion democratization, authenticity, and counterculture—the three main arguments developed in the first phase of fashion blogging—are now a pale memory. The followers have been reduced simply to lookers, and again the right to talk about fashion by people has been put aside. The hope that had moved a million people to raise their voices on elegance, style, and fashion has once again been ignored by the fashion establishment that has completely embedded young influencers in the system.

The close, colonizing relationship that has developed over time between young fashion influencers and the mainstream system emerges not only from the analysis of the content of blog posts but also from the analysis of the brands mentioned or worn by fashion bloggers and from the links to products they report at the end of their posts regarding everyday outfits.

The colonization and commercialization of their online spaces have happened because a large number of companies has started to promote their clothing through fashion influencers, engaging in a kind of competition. In particular, it is possible to identify at least four types of engagement with brands on the part of fashion influencers. They receive gifts and products for free and then create their outfits using the clothes given to them. They practice affiliated marketing, which consists of linking the products on a post to an online shop, and when the reader purchases a product, the influencer receives a percentage of the amount that the reader has spent. They display banners or different kinds of advertisements in their blog. They organize giveaways or contests for their followers, donating samples, clothes, or accessories received from companies. Furthermore, they can in many cases become sponsored by brands, which send them samples in the form of clothes or accessories. These practices have quickly compromised the so-called "creative autonomy" of bloggers and have led to a continuous negotiation between creativity and commerce, transforming blogs and social media profiles, in many cases, into market-driven entities.

The fourth finding is that the rigid hierarchy historically present in the mainstream fashion system is now re-emerging in fashion blogs. Under the apparent, more democratic structure of communication between influencers and followers, the same power mechanisms that had characterized the pre-internet fashion system are being restored in the relationship between influencers and followers, thanks also to the hierarchical structure of social networks (it suffices to think of term "follower").

Finally, the fifth finding is that, contrary to what had emerged in 2012, when textual communication was used more frequently by fashion bloggers than visual communication, now with fashion influencers, posts tend to use almost exclusively visual communication, reducing communication with their followers only to the presentation of their pictures of everyday outfits. Consequently, the space dedicated to the textual content is increasingly reduced and over time almost tends to disappear.

4.2 Elderly Influencers: "Silver Is the New Blonde"

The subtitle of this paragraph takes up the name of one of the Instagram accounts analysed, that of Jan Correll (username: silveristhenewblonde). We found it particularly suitable because Jan has even been named one of "the glamorous grandmas of Instagram" in a June 2018 New York Times article.[2] Furthermore, albeit in a completely involuntary way, this title overturns the best known title of the blog, "The blonde salad" by Chiara Ferragni, proving that "silver" is not what it used to be and that Instagram is not just for young people.

The first finding that emerged from the content analysis of the visual materials related to elderly influencers suggests that they tend to adopt more personal and authentic styles compared to many younger ones. These women usually play with their image and propose outfits from a registry that demonstrate their courage to clear the third-age stereotypes with elegance, irony, and a touch of cheek. Married or single, working or not, make-up or natural, minimalist, hippie and most often grandmothers, they seem to scream to the world that they exist. They do it with boldness, delicacy, and intelligence. In general, the material they produce revolves around perennial style, ageless active, bold beauty, and positive ageing. As Lyn Slater pointed out during an interview for New York Times: "I'm not 20. I don't want to be 20, but I'm really freaking cool. That's what I think about when I'm posting a photo." They aim to promote an optimistic version of later life and an acceptance-oriented attitude toward ageing counters and to prove that beauty, style, and success know no age. In doing so, these women are simultaneously reflecting and contributing to a gradual shift in the common perception of ageing.

As to the second result, it emerged that elderly influencers often tend to dismiss age stereotyping with humour. Photo captions are often straightforward and thought-provoking and sometimes characterized by anti-ageism sentiments. For example, Helen Winkle, the most popular influencer on our list, wrote in her Instagram bio, "Stealing ur man since 1928!!" Sarah Jane Adams coined the hashtag #mywrinklesaremystripes after a makeup artist asked if she would like her wrinkles covered. Magda Llohis de Gutierrez wrote in her bio, "Age is an illusion. People call me a fashionista, I call myself

---

[2] https://www.nytimes.com/2018/06/20/style/instagram-grandmas.html.

an artist." Lyn Slater, a university lecturer turned fashion influencer, wrote in a caption, "Nothing like a few wrinkles to make life more interesting. Heading out."

The third finding highlights that, in the case of fashion influencers over 70, textual content still plays a dominant role, and sometimes the photos represent just the chance to discuss topics of specific interest for their age group. Often the elderly influencers are not only focused on style, fashion, beauty, and what suits mature women but also on personal interests and daily activities. Occasionally their feeds feature posts related to fitness and health, mainly dealing with issues of interest to mature women such as menopause. From this perspective, although they also adopt a multi-platform communication strategy, unlike their younger colleagues, the blog still has a fundamental role precisely because it gives them the space necessary to deepen the topics covered and to offer diverse, personal, and innovative perspectives on age and ageing. It is possible to identify various types of blogs managed by senior influencers ranging from simple advice on how to combine outfits to not resign to the time passing (e.g., Not Dead Yet Style) to those who have made the discourse on fashion a tool for redemption or recreation of one's life (e.g., Style Crone or Accidental Icon) and those who offer a gallery of strictly over-age street styles (e.g., Style at Certain Age). On one hand, the initial situation of fashion bloggers re-appears here. On the other hand, in the case of elderly fashion influencers, there is an addition: the production of freer, more political, and deeper content.

The fourth result shows that fashion influencers over 70 can be seen as a phenomenon that is important also at intergenerational level. This emerges in particular from the analysis of the comments left by followers under the photos. We observed that the accounts analysed receive numerous (sometimes hundreds of) comments on each post, which affirm their sharing of the expressed content. The vast majority of comments from their followers are characterized by a positive connotation, and often younger women demonstrate a sort of a "wish-I'd-been-there" mentality about their posts. It is interesting to note that young women are the main followers of older influencers. This is testified also by Sarah Jane Adams, who reported during an interview: "The insights of my Instagram page reveal that 75% of my followers are women between the ages of 25 and 34 around the world. I believe that what interests them is my attitude to life and daily interactions rather than my clothes since I have always dressed for myself and not to follow a fashion."[3] Many individuals who commented on the pictures shared online by these influencers use terms like "inspirational," "empowering," and "encouraging" to describe how they perceived these women, or they leave posts saying "How can we be like you?" or "I want to get older like you." Comments generally offer compliments and include emojis, icons that range from decorative to emotive. The particularly positive climate created by this type of comments is emphasized further by Instagram's automatic comment moderation feature that filters out comments that might be inappropriate, offensive, or bullying.

Finally, the fifth finding shows that in the case of older fashion influencers, a series of intermediate actors are also emerging. Sensing a considerable interest toward them from the market, they have started to co-opt them into agencies created ad hoc. After all, the interest of the fashion and beauty industry in making use of the image of elderly men and women is part of a broader contemporary trend, namely that of inclusion, aiming to

---

[3] https://d.repubblica.it/moda/2018/03/22/news/fashion_blogger_anziane_su_instagram_lyn_sla ter_iconaccidental_saramaijewels-3900472/.

propose aesthetic models capable of representing the multiplicity of the population in terms of gender, ethnicity, body shape, age, and so on. It will be interesting to see how elderly influencers will react to these attempts by fashion houses to co-opt them into the system. The attempt at colonization is already underway; it is a question of whether the wisdom of these women will win or whether fashion houses will find a way to empty them of their content and to ferry them—like they did with young influencers—into the world of the fashion system.

5 Discussion and Final Remarks

Let us pick up again our three research questions and analyse whether our results are able to answer to them. As to our first research question, "In which terms do influencers change the relationship between women and fashion with respect to fashion bloggers?"—our data suggest that fashion influencers, in a certain sense, have betrayed the "mission" they had expressed in the first phase of fashion bloggers. This mission consisted in taking charge of the genuine, grassroots interest and agency that had characterized the first phase of fashion blogging by contributing to the democratization of the discourse on fashion, the authenticity of the content produced in the fashion blogs, and the attempt to generate an alternative culture of fashion, not stiffened and aimed only at profit from the fashion houses.

As to our second research question, "How do elderly influencers change fashion communication compared to younger ones?"—our data suggest that elderly influencers are revitalizing fashion communication, on one hand by recreating in the content they produce the values expressed in the beginning by fashion bloggers, and on the other hand by introducing new elements into their discourse that are more political and more radically connected to social change.

As to our third research question, "What kinds of content and visual storytelling do they use to produce and convey their messages in a social media platform such as Instagram in comparison with younger ones?"—our data show that elderly influencers are more textual and less visual than young influencers and much less colonized by advertising agencies and fashion houses.

Considering the design of this research, which is based on the comparison between young and old fashion bloggers, our study shows that the strategy of historicizing the phenomenon of fashion blogging and of comparing young and elderly fashion influencers has been important because this has helped us to understand that the features of this phenomenon in the second wave have radically changed. While in the first wave the tropes were centred on equality, counterculture, and authenticity, in the second wave the main characteristics have become technological diversification, commercialization, and a preference for visual communication. Instead of democratizing and simplifying the fashion system, they have contributed in the second phase to make it even more hierarchical and complex. Especially young fashion influencers now represent another level of intermediation between fashion houses and customers.

Over this short period of time, the discourse on fashion emerging from the blogosphere has changed substantially. The result is that nowadays fashion influencers tend to appropriate (rather than resist) fashion system infrastructures and traditional media industry logics. They have become increasingly popular and achieved a pivotal role in promoting and driving new fashion trends, but at the same time they have also become an integral part of the fashion industry (Bruzzi and Gibson 2013). However, the fashion system has lost the opportunity to cultivate a real and fruitful relation with its customers.

This study has contributed to investigating a new topic, that of elderly influencers, and to exploring their practices on social media. Unlike their younger colleagues, whose images are now controlled by other people, the older ones still tend to control their self-representation and the performances of their identity, even if the first signs of a possible re-intermediation by the agencies begin to appear on the scene. As pointed out by Suzie Shaw, managing director at social media and influencer agency We Are Social: "No doubt there are fewer influencers over 50 than [those] in their 20s, but those that are there are gaining real traction because they more faithfully represent their audience than mainstream media, and they are also more authentic and relatable" (Brown 2019).

The secret is just the critical discourse that these women have opened with their blogs. It is a discourse that is very important and that was lacking in the landscape of both the feminist movement and the elderly movement. Elderly fashion influencers are extremely positive and beneficial for older women in general but also for society as a whole. The women we analysed are challenging negative age stereotypes and propose both visually and rhetorically an image of older women capable of recovering freedom from outdated social roles, encouraging their followers to "learn to look at women in new ways" (Meagher 2014: 142). Moreover, they reject the idea that to age means automatically to become invisible within society (the invisibility myth), subverting shop-worn notions of what "old" looks and feels like, and offering an alternative vision as well as a strategy for how social media can provide connectivity, community, and support. We believe that it will be easy for the fashion system to colonize this bulwark of women's subjectivity and agency.

Finally, this study has important limitations, the most macroscopic of which is that the selection of the groups of women we studied does not enable us to generalize our results to the population of reference, which is that of young and elderly fashion influencers. The online media practices of these bloggers deserve to be studied further and with more solid procedures from a statistical point of view and with semi-structured interviews with the main protagonists of this revolution.

References

Abidin, C.: Visibility labour: engaging with influencers' fashion brands and #OOTD advertorial campaigns on Instagram. Media Int. Australia **161**(1), 86–100 (2016)

Allen, C.: Style Surfing changing parameters of fashion communication: where have they gone? In: 1st Global Conference: Fashion Exploring Critical Issues, Mansfield College, Oxford, 25–27 September 2009 (2009)

Anderson, M., Perrin, A.: Tech adoption climbs among older adults. PEW Research Center (2017). https://www.pewresearch.org/internet/wp-content/uploads/sites/9/2017/05/PI_2017.05.17_Older-Americans-Tech_FINAL.pdf

Ball, M.S., Smith, G.W.H.: Analyzing Visual Data. Sage, London (1992)

Baym, N.: Personal Connections in the Digital Age. Polity, Cambridge (2010)

Berry, J.: Flâneurs of fashion 2.0. Scan J. **8**(2) (2010) http://scan.net.au/scan/journal/display.php?journal_id=152

Brown, A.: The rise of the over-50 fashion influencer. The Sidney Morning Herald, 3 March 2019. https://www.smh.com.au/lifestyle/fashion/the-rise-of-the-over-50-fashion-influe ncer-20190228-p510uw.html

Bruns, A.: Blogs, Wikipedia, Second Life, and Beyond. From Production to Produsage. Peter Lang, New York (2008)

Bruzzi, S., Gibson, P.C.: Fashion Cultures Revisited: Theories, Explorations and Analysis. Routledge, London (2013)

Cereda, A.: Digital fashions beyond age. Piano b: Arti e culture visive **2**(2), 23–42 (2017)

Corlett, C.: Shattering the stereotypes of the 50+ shopper: marketing. Vital Speeches Day **64**, 478–480 (1998)

Duffy, B.E.: 'Regular people with a passion for fashion': authenticity, community, and other social media myths. Paper presented at the Internet Research 14.0, Denver, USA, 23–26 October (2013)

Featherstone, M.: The boy in consumer culture. In: Featherstone, M., Hepworth, M., Turner, B. (eds.) The Body, Social Process and Cultural Theory, pp. 170–196. Sage, London (1995)

Fortunati, L., Farinosi, M., Nie, Y.: Exploring grassroots fashion storytelling: an analysis of the practices and strategies of Italian and Chinese bloggers. In: Motta, G., Biagini, A. (eds.) Fashion through History: Costumes, Symbols, Communication, pp. 154–166. Cambridge Scholars Publishing, Cambridge (2017)

Fortunati, L., Farinosi, M.: Influence of the web and Italian Dress Practices. In: Berg Encyclopedia of World Dress and Fashion, vol. 10. Global Perspectives, Online Exclusives (2014). http://dx. doi.org/10.2752/BEWDF/EDch10611

Goffman, E.: The Presentation of Self in Everyday Life. Penguin, Harmondsworth (1959)

Hargittai, E., Dobransky, K.: Old dogs, new clicks: digital inequality in skills and uses among older adults. Can. J. Commun. **42**(2), 195–212 (2017)

Harvey, L.: The rise of the 'granfluencer'. Meet the seniors who are better at social media than you. BBC 30 May 2019 (2019). https://www.bbc.co.uk/bbcthree/article/d6e8fb6f-b92f-4952- ae3c-62bc5974ce6f

Hepworth, M.: Stories of Ageing. Open University Press, Buckingham (2000)

Hine, C.: Ethnography for the Internet: Embedded, Embodied and Everyday. Bloomsbury Academic, London (2015)

Huffington Post: L'agenzia per modelle mature Grey Models sta rivoluzionando la moda e le copertine dei femminili, Huff Post, 22 October (2015). https://www.huffingtonpost.it/2015/10/ 22/modelle-mature-grey-model_n_8357386.html

Hutto, C.J., et al.: Social media gerontology: understanding social media usage among older adults. Web Intell. **13**, 69–87 (2015)

ISTAT: Anziani.Stat. Dati e indicatori sull'invecchiamento della popolazione in Italia. Aspetti della vita quotidiana. Internet – Persone di 55 anni e più (2019). http://dati-anziani.istat.it/

Khamis, S., Munt, A.: The three CS of fashion media today: convergence, creativity & control. SCAN J. Media Arts Cult. **8**(2). (2010). http://scan.net.au/scan/journal/display.php?journal_i d=155

Kohlbacher, F., Hersatt, C., Schweisfurth, T.: Product development for the silver market. In: Kohlbacher, F., Herstatt, C. (eds.) The Silver Market Phenomenon. Marketing and Innovation in the Aging Society, pp. 3–13. Springer, London (2011). https://doi.org/10.1007/978-3-642- 14338-0_1

Lee, R.: The youth bias in advertising. Am. Demographics **19**, 46–50 (1997)

Long, N.: Broken down by age and sex: exploring the ways we approach the elderly consumer. J. Res. Market Res. Soc. **40**, 73–91 (1998)

Marwick, A.E.: 'They're really profound women, they're entrepreneurs': conceptions of authenticity in fashion blogging. Paper Presented at the 7th International Conference on Weblogs and Social Media (ICWSM), Cambridge, MA, 8 July (2013)

McGrath, L.: Achieving visibility: midlife and older women's practices on Instagram and blogs. LiCS **6**(2), 94–116 (2018)

McQuarrie, E.F., Miller, J., Phillips, B.J.: The megaphone effect: taste and audience in fashion blogging. J. Consum. Res. **40**, 136–158 (2013)

Meagher, M.: Against the invisibility of old age: Cindy Sherman, Suzy Lake, and Martha Wilson. Feminist Stud. **40**(1), 101–143 (2014)

Minichiello, V., Browne, J., Kendig, H.: Perceptions and consequences of ageism: views of older people. Ageing Soc. **20**(3), 253–278 (2000)

Palmgren, A.: Posing my identity. Today's outfit, identity and gender in Swedish Blogs. Observatorio (OBS*) J. **4**(2), 19–34 (2010)

Pedroni, M.: Meso-celebrities, fashion and the media: how digital influencers struggle for visibility. Film Fashion Consumption **5**(1), 103–121 (2016)

Pham, M.T.: Blog Ambition: Fashion, Feelings, And The Political Economy Of The Digital Raced Body. Camera Obscura **26**(176), 1–37 (2011)

Rocamora, A.: Hypertextuality and remediation in the fashion media. Journalism Pract. **6**(1), 92–106 (2012)

Schreurs, K., Quan-Haase, A., Martin, K.: Problematizing the digital literacy paradox in the context of older adults' ICT use: aging, media discourse, and self-determination. Can. J. Commun. **42**(2), 359–377 (2017)

Thomas, V., Wolfe, D.B.: Why won't television grow up? Am. Demographics **17**, 24–27 (1995)

Tunaley, J., Walsh, S., Nicolson, P.: I'm not bad for my age: the meaning of body size and eating in the lives of older women. Ageing Soc. **19**, 741–759 (1999)

Twigg, J.: Fashion and Age: Dress, the Body and Later Life. Bloomsbury Academic, London (2013)

United Nations: World Population Prospects: the 2017 Revision (2017). https://population.un.org/wpp/

Methods Matter: Assessment of the Characteristics of a Sample to Analyze Digital Practices and Social Connectedness in Later Life

Mireia Fernández-Ardèvol[✉], Andrea Rosales, and Francisca Morey

Internet Interdisciplinary Institute (IN3), Universitat Oberta de Catalunya, Barcelona, Catalonia, Spain
{mfernandezar,arosalescl}@uoc.edu, xiscamorey6@gmail.com

Abstract. The purpose of the article is to assess the characteristics of the actual dataset obtained in an online-based research project interested in the digitization of later life in four countries by comparing it to the planned sample. It aims is to make visible the consequences of usual constraints –technical or not, and common uncritical assumptions to contribute to fighting unnoticed forms of ageism in the area. Compared to the online adult population, the collected sample shows imbalances that must be taken into account in the analysis of the results: there are more men than women, they are younger and better educated than the average online population. The characteristics of the individuals who effectively participated in the research project reflect the existing digital divide, which remains of particular relevance among the older age groups of the population. We do argue that empirical research on digital practices, being it conducted through online channels or not, must clearly state the age range of the sample and acknowledge the limitations in reaching the older old. It is critical to follow such a strategy to avoid generalizations that, in fact, disregard the older old and, therefore, contribute to reinforce ageism.

Keywords: Research design · Sample assessment · Methodological reflection · Digital practices · Mixed methods · Later life · Older adults · Ageism

1 Introduction

More often than not, quantitative papers succinctly explain the challenges encountered during fieldwork, as they keep to the point of discussing the results based on the data obtained. The method tends to be appropriately explained, but the analysis of the divergences vis-à-vis the ideal procedure of data collection is rarely the object of discussion as there is no room for, and no interest in, explaining the failures. Yet, managing a research project is also managing deviations from thorough plans [e.g., 1]. This paper describes the main issues faced in a mixed-methods project [2] and assesses the characteristics of the actual sample obtained, as well as its similarities and discrepancies with regards to the target population.

© Springer Nature Switzerland AG 2020
Q. Gao and J. Zhou (Eds.): HCII 2020, LNCS 12209, pp. 58–68, 2020.
https://doi.org/10.1007/978-3-030-50232-4_5

Our experience in researching the digital practices of the older population has obstinately demonstrated how challenging it could be accessing good quality, reliable data able to represent the diversity of the old age [3, 4]. We do argue, first of all, that if it is difficult to reach a given population, we should not try to hide it, but we must make it clear so improvements can be made in future research. And secondly, that there is a need for transparency in evaluating the strengths and weaknesses of online quantitative samples for high-quality analyses–as argued among others by [5]. To overcome such issues, this paper aims at critically reflecting on the consequences of such problems going beyond discussions of data validity usual in positivist approaches. We do attach to the idea that data are not innocent [e.g., 6]. As Penissat and Rowell [7] summarize, despite the apparent scientific objectivity of statistical measurements, they are not politically or socially neutral but have transformative effects that are made obvious by selection and categorization. Selection, here, refers to the selected individuals that are actually included in quantitative research, while categorization refers to the way information is organized from collection to delivery to users. Those processes simplify the reality and produce new inquiry objects that shape the way the society is able to look at the world. Under this perspective, the current paper is interested in delimiting what we are able, and not able, to analyze when the focus is on the digital practices in later life. By doing this exercise, we aim at producing stronger results that will not be generalized beyond what is technically correct [8]. In this sense, the paper contributes to the literature on ageism by discussing the consequences that given social groups remain inaccessible or invisible for particular methods of research. This is the case of the older old when the interest is on their digital practices from a quantitative perspective, which contribute to reinforce ageism [as argued by 9, 10 in the case of big data analyses]. This kind of aged-based discrimination, more subtle than explicit [11], appears to sustain ageist attitudes in a particular social practice [12] –quantitative research– that, in turn, shape the way academia, decision makers, policy makers and the society in general are able to look at given social phenomena.

The research interest of the project we assess here is on how mobile digital practices relate to perceived social connectedness among older adults aged 55–79 years old. The particular focus is on smartphone practices, and the selected countries are Canada, the Netherlands, Spain, and Sweden. They constitute relevant contexts for a comparative analysis of digitization of later life as different levels of Internet diffusion and smartphone usage have shaped the local digital practices differently. Finally, the research project's particular goal is to conduct a comparative analysis of how different groups use smartphones in diverse ways to theorize digitization in later life, with a specific interest in the role of digital communication in the perception of social connectedness. It was part of a larger project, 'BConnect@Home: Being Connected at Home - Making use of digital devices in later life' [13], which investigates fundamental changes in the contemporary experience of later life, at the intersection of digital infrastructures, place and the experience of "being connected."

This paper builds on a previous discussion of the research design and the selected methods [14] that justified the relevance of the project, the analytical framework, the research design and its limitations, and the *a priori* practical considerations we took into account in response to the challenges we identified. Also, it described key practicalities as the securing of ethical clearance in the four participant countries or the way participants consented to participate. In what follows, we will reproduce relevant contents for the discussion, while we invite the reader to check [14] for further details.

2 Designed Sample and Actual Sample Introduction

The aimed universe of study corresponds to online older adults aged 55 to 79-year-old living in Canada, the Netherlands, Spain, and Sweden. The project focuses on cohorts [15, 16] born between 1939 and 1963, a group that spans a period of 25 years. While the project is interested in the third age [17], part of the older adults in this research does not belong to this category as they are younger. However, by considering younger ages, it is possible to understand the differences between cohorts to have a more focused perspective on the intersection of digitization and ageing [18]. The upper threshold on age, in this case, 79 years old, responds to technical limitations of online-based research, as companies that manage online panels do not expect to be able to reach older old individuals, whose levels of internet access tend to be comparatively lower [for instance, see 19]. The aimed sample was 150 individuals per country, adding a total of 600 participants. Fieldwork, planned for early 2019, followed a sequential mixed-method approach [1] of three steps. First, the tracking of the smartphone activity gathered participants' activity for four weeks–28 days. Second, an online survey addressed to the same participants. Finally, the last instrument of data gathering was a qualitative interview with 10% of the total participants. Designed to be deployed simultaneously in the four countries, delays in bureaucratic aspects of the project caused different fieldwork schedules (see Table 1). Canada and Spain followed quite similar schedules. There, the 4-week smartphone logs collection started in late-February, the online survey ran mostly in April, and the qualitative interviews were conducted in June and July. Sweden follows in the completion of fieldwork, which ran between April and November. Finally, in the Netherlands data collection initiated in mid-March and qualitative interviews finished in January 2020.

For data collection, we hired a marketing research company with access to an online panel of consumers through local partners in each country. The company provided the software for smartphone tracking and online survey in all the countries. To avoid some of the biases of snow-ball techniques, and as usual in non-probabilistic online sampling, quotas of gender and age guided the selection of participants [8].

Fieldwork faced some issues and, as Table 1 reports, the expected number of participants was not reached for the quantitative analysis. We applied the usual procedures of data cleaning to the tracked logs and the online survey. First, the nature of the tracking process, which allows the collection of by-product data, made necessary the cleaning of the collected dataset, a process not necessary with the survey. Besides, some participants in the survey were discarded due to the incompleteness of the logs' dataset evaluated at the individual level. Five participants did not pass the control for outliers (z-score test, [20]). Also, 52 participants did not meet the completeness criteria. We discarded individuals tracked during three or fewer days, as we set a threshold of a minimum of 10% days observed out of the planned 28 days of observed activities. The final number of valid participants in the tracking is 444, meaning that the actual sample size for the

Table 1. Fieldwork: planned and actual number of participants, by country

	Canada	Netherlands	Spain	Sweden	*TOTAL*
Tracking of smartphone activity (planned: 150/country; length: 4 weeks)					
Data collection	Feb/26–Mar/25	Mar/15–Jun/6	Feb/26–Mar/25	Apr/24–May/21	*Feb–Jun 2019*
Participants	126	131	138	115	*510*
Valid participants	119	105	125	95	*444*
% over planned	79%	70%	83%	63%	*76%*
Online survey (planned: 150/country; length: 12 min on average)					
Data collection	Mar/31–Apr/8	Jun/28–Jul/13	Apr/9–Apr/12	Jun/7–Jun/26	*Mar–Jul 2019*
Participants (= valid participants)	126	114	151	121	*512*
% over planned	84%	76%	101%	81%	*85%*
Tracking and survey combined (planned: 150/country)					
Valid participants	119	91	125	95	*430*
% over planned	79%	61%	83%	63%	*70%*
Qualitative interview (goal: 15/country; length: 45 min on average)					
Data collection	Jun/17–Jul/16	Nov/13–Jan/20	Jun/24–Jul/22	Oct/7–Nov/20	*Jun 2019–Jan 2020*
Participants (= valid participants)	15	15	15	15	*60*
% over planned	100%	100%	100%	100%	*100%*

tracking consider alone represents the 76% of the planned sample. The total number of valid observations ascends to 1.3 million of logs corresponding to almost 3,800 different apps.

Second, the design of the online questionnaire provided a dataset with no issues in terms of outliers or completeness, and all the collected responses were valid. They add up to 512 participants, which represent 85% of the planned sample. Finally, as the valid cases in the tracking did not necessarily correspond to the valid cases in the survey, the sample with valid observations coming from both the tracking and the survey reached a total of 430 participants (70% of the planned sample). The percentage of valid observations varied per country, with higher ratios in Canada and Spain in front of lower proportions in the Netherlands and Sweden. Finally, the issue of statistical representativeness does not affect the qualitative part of the fieldwork [e.g., 21] because the semi-structured interviews aimed to provide a richer analytical interpretation of the data collected using the tracking and the online survey [1].

The mixed-method approach might have also been affected by the fact that online panelists appear to show limited levels of willingness to perform more than one task [22]. Given the low response ratios, it is relevant to compare the sample characteristics to the target population for a more nuanced interpretation of the results, as done in the next section.

3   Comparison Between the Sample and the Target Population

3.1   Socio-Demographic Characteristics of the Sample

Table 2 gathers basic socio-demographics of the sample and, in the case of the three EU countries, compares it against the general population and the online population of older adults. The last available data from Eurostat refers to 2018 [19, 23, 24]. The two older age groups correspond to individuals aged 55–64 and 65–74. Even though the age range, 55–74, is different from our study, 55–79, we do consider that comparison is viable and relevant, as it provides enough insights on data distribution despite it is not perfect. Contrastingly, we decided not to include the comparison against the official data of the Canadian population because age ranges for the two older age groups are 45–64 and 65+, significantly different from those in our study [25]. We focus on valid observations of the survey to illustrate the differences. We could also include a comparison against the sample of valid cases of the tracking and the survey, but we do not for the sake of briefness and simplicity.

The age-based digital divide is the cause of the socio-demographic differences between the general population and the online population in Table 3. Such differences increase with age [26–30] despite adoption rates in old age are growing at a fast pace, particularly among younger older adults [31–34]. Also, country-level data for the older age groups in the studied countries confirm that the digital divide is higher among women than men, except Sweden, and that it closes as the educational level increases (see Table 4).

The age-based digital divide would be one of the dimensions able to explain the particular socio-demographic characteristics of the samples. In the case of the EU countries, it becomes evident that the samples reproduce the imbalance in age, gender, and educational level, as there are more young older adults, more men, and they hold higher educational levels than in the online population. We do consider that such imbalance also reflects the active technical involvement required from participants to be part of the study, as they had to install a tracking software on their smartphone to track their digital activities during four weeks before receiving the invitation to respond the online survey [14].

Table 2. Basic socio-demographic characteristics. Samples in the four countries, and general and online population of the three EU countries[a]

%	Gender		Age		Educational level[b]		
	Men	Women	55–64	65–74/9[a]	Low	Medium	High
Canada							
Sample (N = 126)	58	42	62	38	1	15	84
Netherlands							
Sample (N = 114)	64	36	60	40	1	56	43
General pop.	50	50	55	45	38	37	26
Online pop.	50	50	57	43	34	39	27
Spain							
Sample (N = 151)	56	44	66	34	15	50	36
General pop.	48	52	57	43	62	17	21
Online pop.	50	50	67	33	44	23	32
Sweden							
Sample (N = 121)	67	33	36	64	7	31	62
General pop.	50	50	51	49	24	45	31
Online pop.	48	52	54	46	20	46	34

[a] *Sample data corresponds to valid observations in the online survey and refer to individuals aged 55 to 79 (year 2019). General and online population refer to Internet usage in the last 3 months among individuals aged 55 to 74 years old (year 2018).*
Country-level data sources: Eurostat [19, 23, 24] and own elaboration.
[b] *Educational level: Low = Less than primary, primary and lower secondary education (levels 0–2, ISCED); Medium = Upper secondary and post-secondary non-tertiary education (levels 3 and 4, ISCED); High = Tertiary education (levels 5–8, ISCED). On Individuals - internet use [isoc_ci_ifp_iu], labels are: low, medium and high formal education*

Table 3. Internet users (%). Total population and older age groups. Year 2018.

%	Total population[a]	55–64	65–74	75+
Netherlands[1]	95	93	87	..
Spain[1]	86	76	49	17
Sweden[1]	92	93	83	..
	Total population[b]	45–64	65 and over	
Canada[2]	91	94	71	

.. Not available.
[a] Total refers to the population aged 16 to 74.
[1] Individuals who accessed the internet in the last 3 months [19].
[b] Total refers to the population aged 15 and over.
[2] Individuals who used the internet last month [25].

Table 4. Internet use in later life (%), by gender and educational level. Year 2018.

%	Internet users	Of whom...				
	55–74 years old	Female	Male	Low education	Medium education	High education
Netherlands[a]	90	89	91	81	96	97
Spain[a]	64	62	67	45	87	95
Sweden[a]	88	90	85	75	90	95
	65+ years old	Female	Male	Low education	Medium education	High education
Canada[b]	71	68	75	54	81	91

[a]Individuals who accessed the internet in the last 3 months [19]. Educational level refers to formal education: ISCED 0–2 (Low), ISCED 3–4 (Medium), and ISCED 5–8 (High)
[b]Individuals who used the internet last month [25]. Educational level: Low = High school or less; Medium = College, trade school or some university; High = Bachelor's degree or higher.

3.2 Instruments for Data Collection

Beyond the age-based digital divide, which is clearly affecting the access to older participants and excludes them from digital-based research [9, 10] and the characteristics of the sample, two other issues should be taken into account. They can be considered limitations in the instruments for data collection. First is the language of the data collection tools. Second is the constraint of the tracking software in different smartphones' operating systems. We discuss them in what follows, even though we do not evaluate the biases they produce.

Regarding language, the instruments were translated into one local language in each country, which was the language each local team decided to use to communicate with participants [14]: in Canada, English, Dutch in the Netherlands, Spanish in Spain, and Swedish in Sweden. Selecting one language per country excludes individuals speaking other languages or those who do not feel comfortable or skilled in using that language, which includes immigrant citizens and citizens who speak either non-official languages or minority languages–recognized or not in each country. In Canada, for instance, there are two official languages, English and French, and differentiated linguistic areas of indigenous peoples [36]. The percentage of the population with English knowledge is 85% [37]. Besides, in the Netherlands, Spain and Sweden, there is one official language at country level that is know by the vast majority of the population, together with recognized national, regional or minority languages [38–40]. We must acknowledge the language limitations of the collected data, particularly in Canada but not only. We must also recognize that resource limitations are common, not only in terms of budget but also in terms of the knowledge limitations of the local research teams to work in all the languages spoken in the participant countries.

Regarding the tracking software, we planned to collect data from both Android and iOS smartphones. However, technical conditions made it only possible to collect data from Android devices [see 14]. The effect on data is different as the two operating systems have varying degrees of popularity in each country (see Table 5). In Spain (73%), the Netherlands (60%), and Sweden (51%), Android is estimated to be the most used operating system, whereas this is not the case in Canada (49%) [35]. A possible dimension to analyze would be the different socio-demographics of Android and iOS users, but we have no access to such data. The Android market is more diverse in terms of costs, as several brands rely on this operation system, in front of iOS that only operates on Apple devices. As Apple products target a higher power purchase market, there might have been a bias towards lower-income users particularly in Canada and Sweden. However, to be taken into account is that participants in the sample are already more educated than the average older adult who regularly go online so including Apple users would increase the participation of even higher-income older adults in the study.

Table 5. Market share: Android and iOS. Year 2019.

%	Canada	Netherlands	Spain	Sweden
Android	49	60	73	51
iOS	51	40	27	49

Source: Device Atlas, 2019 [35]. Data focus exclusively on Android and iOS systems and do not consider other operating systems available in the market. As for the information provided in the source, "statistics are based on mobile web traffic from Q2 2019, to a global network of partner websites using the DeviceAtlas device detection platform" [35].

4   Conclusion

The purpose of the article is to assess the characteristics of the actual dataset obtained in an online-based research project interested in the digitization of later life in four countries by comparing it to the planned sample. It aims to make visible the consequences of common constraints, being them technical or not, and common uncritical assumptions to contribute to fighting unnoticed forms of ageism in the area.

The research interest is on how mobile digital practices relate to perceived social connectedness among older adults aged 55–79 years old. The particular focus is on smartphone practices, and the selected countries are Canada, the Netherlands, Spain, and Sweden. They constitute relevant contexts for a comparative analysis of digitization of later life as different levels of Internet diffusion and smartphone usage have shaped the local digital practices differently.

We can conclude that the sample meets the conditions to reach the goal of the research project, which is to conduct a comparative analysis of how different groups use smartphones differently to theorize digitization in later life, with particular interest on the role of digital communication in the perception of social connectedness. However, any generalization towards the online adult population in the selected countries would be a methodological mistake and would help increasing the invisibility of the older age groups. The main issues are the characteristics of the sample–due to the difficulty of reaching the targeted population, and the limitations in the instruments for data collection.

Compared to the online adult population, the collected sample shows imbalances in gender, age, and educational levels. In general, there are more men than women; they are younger and better educated than the average online population in each country. The characteristics of the individuals who effectively participated in the research project reflect the existing digital divide, which remains of particular relevance among the older age groups of the population. The level of (technical) engagement required by the study, which included the necessary installation of a tracking app during four weeks, might have accentuated the bias towards more skilled or, at least, more intensive digital users together with the fact that participants were expected to participate in at least two different tasks [22].

The exercise we conducted is useful at different levels. First, at an internal level, to grant the validity of the analysis to be undertaken. A clear understanding of the characteristics of the sample allows a more nuanced evaluation of the result, and better recommendations to decision-makers, either in public or in the private sectors. Second, at a more general methodological level, to provide evidence of the challenges of having good quality data in online-based research on older people. While we already defined a maximum threshold in age, 79 years old, in anticipation of problems to reach the oldest age groups, the collection of data faced several issues, most of them apparently related to the participants' age.

Finally, the exercise this paper conducts helps to build more solid reflections on research practices that, in unperceived ways, appear to be contributing to ageism [9]. Notably, it is essential to determine and clearly communicate the age range and acknowledge the limitations in reaching the older old. Due to expected issues in accessing the older segments of the population, we already defined an upper age threshold in 79 years old. The analytical implications are that conclusions should not be extended beyond the characteristics of the sample. We, as researchers, must claim better access to online older adults and work towards it. Both when data collection is implemented by the research team or by a private, marketing research company. Deciding who actually collects the data has implications at different levels, some of them discussed here. However, regardless of who collects the data, researchers should be transparent in the limitations of their data and must avoid pretending that actual samples do include the older old when they do not. It is not possible to reach a good knowledge of the digitization of the old age without high quality, empirical evidence that includes both the younger and the older old age groups.

Acknowledgments. The research project BConnect@Home (https://www.jp-demographic.eu/wp-content/uploads/2017/01/BCONNECT_2017_conf2018_brochure.pdf.) is funded by the JTP 2017 - JPI More Years, Better Lives (Grant Agreement 363850), and the Spanish funding body is the Ministry of Science, Innovation, and Universities (MINECO, ref. PCI-2017-080). MINECO also supported the first two authors with personal grants ref. CAS19/00041 (Fernández-Ardèvol), and IJCI-2017-32162 (Rosales).

References

1. Creswell, J.W.: Research Design: Qualitative, Quantitative, and Mixed Methods Approaches. Sage, Thousand Oaks, CA (2014)
2. Spicer, N.: Combining qualitative and quantitative methods. In: Seale, C. (ed.) Researching Society and Culture (2nd edition), pp. 293–303. SAGE Publications, London (2004)
3. Rosales, A., Fernández-Ardèvol, M.: Beyond WhatsApp: older people and smartphones. Rom. J. Commun. Public Relations. **18**, 27–47 (2016). https://doi.org/10.21018/rjcpr.2016.1.200
4. Rosales, A., Fernández-Ardèvol, M., Ferran-Ferrer, N.: Long-term appropriation of smart-watches among a group of older people. In: Zhou, J., Salvendy, G. (eds.) ITAP 2018. LNCS, vol. 10926, pp. 135–148. Springer, Cham (2018). https://doi.org/10.1007/978-3-319-92034-4_11
5. Revilla, M.: Impact of the mode of data collection on the quality of answers to survey questions depending on respondent characteristics. BMS Bull. Sociol. Methodol. Bull. Methodol. Sociol. **116**, 44–60 (2012). https://doi.org/10.1177/0759106312456510
6. Koro-Ljungberg, M., MacLure, M., Ulmer, J.: Data, Data ++, data, and some problematics. In: Denzin, N.K., Lincoln, Y.S. (eds.) The SAGE Handbook of Qualitative Research, 5th edn., pp. 462–484. SAGE, Los Angeles (2017)
7. Penissat, E., Rowell, J.: The creation of a european socio-economic classification: limits of expert-driven statistical integration. J. Eur. Integr. **37**, 281–297 (2015). https://doi.org/10.1080/07036337.2014.990140
8. Ochoa, C., Porcar, J.M.: Modeling the effect of quota sampling on online fieldwork efficiency: an analysis of the connection between uncertainty and sample usage. Int. J. Mark. Res. **60**, 484–501 (2018). https://doi.org/10.1177/1470785318779545
9. Rosales, A., Fernández-Ardèvol, M.: Structural ageism in big data approaches. Nord. Rev. **40**, 51–64 (2019). https://doi.org/10.2478/nor-2019-0013.51
10. Hargittai, E.: Potential biases in big data: omitted voices on social media. Soc. Sci. Comput. Rev. **38**, 10–24 (2020). https://doi.org/10.1177/0894439318788322
11. Ayalon, L., Tesch-Römer, C. (eds.): Contemporary Perspectives on Ageism. Springer Open, Cham (2018). https://doi.org/10.1007/978-3-319-73820-8
12. AGE Platform Europe: AGE Platform Europe Position on Structural Ageism, Brussels, Belgium (2016)
13. BCONNECT@HOME: BCONNECT@HOME: Being Connected at Home – Making use of digital devices in later life. https://www.jp-demographic.eu/wp-content/uploads/2017/01/BCONNECT_2017_conf2018_brochure.pdf
14. Fernández-Ardèvol, M., et al.: Methodological strategies to understand smartphone practices for social connectedness in later life. In: Zhou, J., Salvendy, G. (eds.) HCII 2019. LNCS, vol. 11593, pp. 46–64. Springer, Cham (2019). https://doi.org/10.1007/978-3-030-22015-0_4
15. Alwin, D.F., McCammon, R.J.: Generations, cohorts, and social change. In: Mortimer, J.T., Shanahan, M.J. (eds.) Handbook of the Life Course, pp. 23–50. Kluwer Academic Publishers, New York (2003)
16. Bristow, J.: The Sociology of Generations: New Directions and Challenges. Palgrave Macmillan, London (2016)
17. Moen, P., Spencer, D.: Converging divergences in age, gender, health, and well-being. In: Binstock, R.H., George, L.K., Cutler, S.J., Hendricks, J., Schulz, J.H. (eds.) Handbook of Aging and the Social Sciences, pp. 127–144. Elsevier, Amsterdam (2006)
18. Gilleard, C., Higgs, P., Hyde, M., Wiggins, R., Blane, D.: Class, cohort, and consumption: the British experience of the third age. J. Gerontol. Ser. B. **60**, S305–S310 (2005). https://doi.org/10.1093/geronb/60.6.S305

19. Eurostat: Individuals Internet use in the last 3 months [isoc_ci_ifp_iu] (2018). Last update: 03 July 2019. http://appsso.eurostat.ec.europa.eu/nui/show.do?dataset=isoc_ci_ifp_iu&lang=en

20. Tabachnick, B.G., Fidell, L.S.: Using Multivariate Statistics. Pearson Education, Boston (2007)

21. Morse, J.: Reframing rigor in qualitative inquiry. In: Denzin, N.K., Lincoln, Y.S. (eds.) The SAGE Handbook of Qualitative Research, 5th edn, pp. 796–817. SAGE, Los Angeles (2017)

22. Revilla, M., Couper, M.P., Ochoa, C.: Willingness of online panelists to perform additional tasks. Methods Data Anal. **13**, 29 (2019). https://doi.org/10.12758/mda.2018.01

23. Eurostat: Population on 1 January by age group and sex [demo_pjangroup] (2018). Last update 06 June 2019. https://appsso.eurostat.ec.europa.eu/nui/show.do?dataset=demo_pjan group&lang=en

24. Eurostat: Population by educational attainment level, sex and age (%) [edat_lfs_9903] 2018. Last update 11 December 2019. https://appsso.eurostat.ec.europa.eu/nui/show.do?dataset= edat_lfs_9903&lang=en

25. Statistics Canada: Internet use and intensity of use per week by gender, age group and highest certificate, diploma or degree completed (2018). https://doi.org/10.25318/2210008201-eng. https://www150.statcan.gc.ca/t1/tbl1/en/tv.action?pid=2210008201

26. Friemel, T.N.: The digital divide has grown old: determinants of a digital divide among seniors. New Media Soc. **18**, 313–331 (2016). https://doi.org/10.1177/1461444814538648

27. Neves, B.B., Amaro, F., Fonseca, J.R.S.: Coming of (Old) age in the digital age: ICT usage and non-usage among older adults. Sociol. Res. Online. **18**, 1–14 (2013). https://doi.org/10. 5153/sro.2998

28. Bergström, A.: Digital equality and the uptake of digital applications among seniors of different age. Nord. Rev. **38**, 79–91 (2017). https://doi.org/10.1515/nor-2017-0398

29. König, R., Seifert, A., Doh, M.: Internet use among older Europeans: an analysis based on SHARE data. Univers. Access Inf. Soc. **17**, 621–633 (2018). https://doi.org/10.1007/s10209-018-0609-5

30. Schlomann, A., Seifert, A., Woopen, C., Rietz, C.: Use of information and communication technology (ICT) devices among the oldest-old : loneliness, anomie, and autonomy, vol. XX, pp. 1–10 (2020). https://doi.org/10.1093/geroni/igz050

31. Anderson, M., Perrin, A.: Tech Adoption Climbs Among Older Adults. Pew Research Center, Washington, DC (2017)

32. Eurostat: Individuals who accessed the internet in the last 12 months (isoc_ci_ifp_iu) [data explorer]

33. Statistics Canada: Life in the fast lane: How are Canadians managing? (2016). https://www 150.statcan.gc.ca/n1/daily-quotidien/171114/dq171114a-eng.htm

34. International Telecommunication Union: World Telecommunication/ICT Indicators Database. ITU, Geneva (2017)

35. Device Atlas: Android v iOS market share 2019, 9 September 2019. https://deviceatlas.com/blog/android-v-ios-market-share

36. Canada. https://en.wikipedia.org/wiki/Canada

37. Statistics Canada: Canada [Country] and Canada [Country] (table). Census Profile. 2016 Census. Statistics Canada Catalogue no. 98-316-X2016001. Ottawa. Released November 29, 2017., https://www12.statcan.gc.ca/census-recensement/2016/dp-pd/prof/index.cfm? Lang=E

38. Netherlands. https://en.wikipedia.org/wiki/Netherlands

39. Spain. https://en.wikipedia.org/wiki/Spain

40. Sweden. https://en.wikipedia.org/wiki/Sweden

Consuming Fake News: A Matter of Age? The Perception of Political Fake News Stories in Facebook Ads

Eugène Loos[1(✉)] and Jordy Nijenhuis[2]

[1] Utrecht University, Bijlhouwerstraat 6, 3511 ZC Utrecht, The Netherlands
e.f.loos@uu.nl
[2] Impact Consultancy, Amsterdamsestraatweg 959A, 3555 HR Utrecht, The Netherlands
jordy@dtbg.nl

Abstract. Social media are increasingly being used by young and old as a source of information. Fake news is also on the rise. The role played by age in the consumption of fake news on social media, however, is unclear. This paper explores the generational differences in the consumption of fake news, first by discussing previous empirical studies in this field and then on the basis of an empirical study carried out between the beginning of February 2018 and the end of June of 2018. In that empirical study, 14 political fake news articles (e.g., relating to Brexit and Donald Trump) were disseminated in the form of advertisements on Facebook. User interaction with the fake content was tracked in order to analyze the number of users in the age groups 13–17, 18–24, 25–34, 35–44, 45–54, 55–64, 65+. The results of the empirical study show that the articles had a higher reach amongst the older age groups, as well as that many people likely took the headlines at face value without clicking on the link. The number of emotional responses posted by the pro-Brexit and pro-Trump groups was greater than those posted by the pro-remain and anti-Trump groups. All of the posts were permitted to run as advertisements on Facebook despite Facebook's efforts to limit the spread of fake news on their platform. In the final section, conclusions are drawn, limitations described and implications for future research are outlined.

Keywords: Fake news · Social media · Facebook · Age · Generations · Disinformation · Misinformation

1 Introduction

Looking up information about medical treatments, comparing programs of political parties at election time, browsing reviews to find a good restaurant: these are just a few examples from everyday life showing how often we rely on being able to find reliable information. In the past, we depended on family members, friends, neighbors and traditional media such as radio, television and printed versions of newspapers for such information. In today's digitized society, a host of new media are available, providing information about any topic we wish. Yet how can we be sure that the information we

© Springer Nature Switzerland AG 2020
Q. Gao and J. Zhou (Eds.): HCII 2020, LNCS 12209, pp. 69–88, 2020.
https://doi.org/10.1007/978-3-030-50232-4_6

read online can be trusted, so that we find the right treatment, the right politician to represent us or the right place to have a good dinner at a fair price in a nearby restaurant?

The problem of information credibility is nothing new [1–7]. As Obadă (2019) [7, p. 148] states: "Fake news is not a new phenomenon [8, 9] because the partisan press has always peddled biased opinions and stories lacking factual basis" [9]. New technologies, from the telegraph in the 19th century to contemporary social media algorithms, have led to the proliferation of fake news [8]. For example, Gelfert (2018) [8] refers to an article that appeared in the Arena journal written by J. B. Montgomery-McGovern in 1898, entitled "An important phase of gutter journalism: Faking", to outline the challenges of fake news in the 19th century. In his article, Montgomery-McGovern (1898) complains about "fake journalism", considered to be "the most sensational stories" published by news organizations (1898, 240), and he explains the "stand-for" technique used by "fakers" to deceive: they recruited a reputable member of the community (e.g., a doctor, dentist, architect, or other professional or business man) who, against payment, would corroborate the fake story.

Though the problem of news credibility is from time immemorial, the role of traditional information gatekeepers such as doctors, news agencies and restaurant critics has been diminished. Media displacement [10] has brought about the rise of social media networks, allowing everybody to post and read unfiltered information on social media networks such as Facebook and Twitter 24/7. Obadă (2019) [7, p. 148] states: "Gelfert (2018) [8] considers nowadays fake news creators eliminated the "middle-men" and address the readers directly, by sharing the sensational stories on social media." This leads to an increased risk of fake news, which has been defined by Aldwairi and Alwahedi (2018) [11, p. 215] as "fictitious articles deliberately fabricated to deceive readers". Commercial gain (profit through clickbaits or to make a competitor look bad), power (winning elections) are just some of the reasons for the production and distribution of fake news.

This is a dangerous development for our civil society, constituting as it does a threat to access to reliable information as a 'primary good' Rawls (1993) [12], as referred to by Van den Hoven (1994, p. 369) [13]. Bovens (2002) [14] and Bovens and Loos (2002) [15] even suggest that the equal right of access to information should be considered a basic right of all citizens, comparable to the classic (human) rights (see also De Jong and Rizvi, 2008 [16]). The European Commission states that "the exposure of citizens to large scale disinformation, including misleading or outright false information, is a major challenge for Europe. The Commission is working to implement a clear, comprehensive and broad set of actions to tackle the spread and impact of online disinformation in Europe and ensure the protection of European values and democratic systems." Humprecht et al. (2018) [17] analyzed how the content of fake news differ across Western democracies. They conclude: "(…) the current study (…) compares online disinformation republished by fact checkers from four Western democracies (the US, the UK, Germany, and Austria). The findings reveal significant differences between English-speaking and German-speaking countries. In the US and the UK, the largest shares of partisan disinformation are found, while in Germany and Austria sensationalist stories prevail. Moreover, in English-speaking countries, disinformation frequently attacks political actors, whereas in German-speaking countries, immigrants are most frequently targeted. Across all of the countries, topics of false stories strongly mirror national news agendas." If we want to guarantee the right of access to reliable digital information for all citizens, it is important to be aware of the role generational differences could play.

Though age-related limitations such as declining vision, hearing, cognition, and visual-motor functions may affect the use of ICT devices by older old people [18], the enhanced user friendliness of such devices (e.g., iPads) have, at the same time, made them accessible to this same age group. Moreover, compared to a decade ago, older people today are also more familiar with the new media, which has led to more ICT and internet experience [19–22]. Perceived benefits [23] by seeing examples of use by younger people may have also increased older adults' new media use and probably also convinced many older laggards [24] to start using ICT devices. Whatever the reason, the fact remains that over the past years, the number of older people using new media has clearly been on the rise in western societies. A survey conducted by Pew Research Center [25] revealed that in the USA in 2017 "roughly two-thirds of those ages 65 and older go online and a record share now own smartphones – although many seniors remain relatively divorced from digital life". Statistics from the EU show that 51% of people aged 55 and older used the internet at least once a week in 2017 [26, p. 16].

Older people's social media use has also grown in recent years. According to the results of a Pew Research Center survey conducted from January 8 to February 7, 2019 in the USA, 46% of people aged 60+ used Facebook in 2018. Despite this rise in social media use, the social media adoption rate among adults aged 60+ is still relatively low compared to other age groups (18–29: 79%, 30–49: 79%, 50–64: 68%) [27]. Further discussion of this topic is beyond the scope of this paper; we refer to Quinn [23], for a clear overview of studies presenting possible explanations. We also refer to Holt et al. [28, p. 31], who performed a four-wave panel study conducted during the 2010 Swedish national election campaign that found that "although younger people pay less attention to political news in traditional media than older people, they simultaneously are more frequent users of social media for political purposes."

Social media allow us to connect and share information with others, but it appears that social media users are increasingly shielding themselves from opinions which differ from their own. Ofcom's Adults: Media use and attitudes report 2019 shows that "compared to 2017, social media users are less likely to say they see views they disagree with; a quarter say they 'rarely' see views on social media they disagree with (vs. 18% in 2017). As such, more social media users say they 'rarely' see views they disagree with (24%) than say they 'often' see views they disagree with (17%)" [29, p. 9]. And the Reuters Institute digital news report 2017 states that "only a quarter (24%) of our respondents think social media do a good job in separating fact from fiction, compared to 40% for the news media. Our qualitative data suggest that users feel the combination of a lack of rules and viral algorithms are encouraging low quality and 'fake news' to spread quickly" [30, p. 8].

The vulnerability to fake news often focuses on younger people (e.g., [31–33]), as the following quote also illustrates: "(…) the [European] Commission will encourage fact-checkers and civil society organizations to provide educational material to schools and educators and include targeted initiatives on disinformation online in the #SaferInternet4EU Campaign" [34].

As we have made clear in this section, it is important that all citizens, regardless of their age, have access to reliable digital information, and that we gain insight into the vulnerability of older adults to fake news on social media. In this paper, therefore, we address the role of age in the susceptibility to fake news and will explore the following research question: What is the role of age in fake news consumption on social media? To that end, we will not only discuss previous empirical studies in this field but also present an empirical study carried out by ourselves, in which we disseminated 14 political fake news articles (e.g., relating to Brexit and Donald Trump) in the form of advertisements on Facebook. We then tracked the number of users consuming fake news in the age groups 13–17, 18–24, 25–34, 35–44, 45–54, 55–64, 65+ consumed Fake News. The methods results are presented in Sects. 3 and 4. In the final section, conclusions are drawn, limitations described and implications for future research outlined.

2 Fake News on Social Media

2.1 Introduction

While a detailed discussion of the dynamics of fake news on social media is beyond the scope of this article, we nonetheless refer to a number of empirical studies providing background information in order to set a context for our topic: the role of age in fake news consumption on social media.

Allcott et al. (2019) [35, p. 1] offer a clear view on trends in the diffusion of what they call misinformation on social media: "In recent years, there has been widespread concern that misinformation on social media is damaging societies and democratic institutions. In response, social media platforms have announced actions to limit the spread of false content. We measure trends in the diffusion of content from 569 Fake News websites and 9540 Fake News stories on Facebook and Twitter between January 2015 and July 2018. User interactions with false content rose steadily on both Facebook and Twitter through the end of 2016. Since then, however, interactions with false content have fallen sharply on Facebook while continuing to rise on Twitter, with the ratio of Facebook engagements to Twitter shares decreasing by 60%. In comparison, interactions with other news, business, or culture sites have followed similar trends on both platforms. Our results suggest that the relative magnitude of the misinformation problem on Facebook has declined since its peak."

For a current state-of-the-art study on fake news *detection*, we recommend Mosinzova et al. (2019) [36]. More information about the *consumption* of news via Facebook can be found in the work of Flintham et al. (2018) [37] and Quintanilha et al. (2019) [38]. Resende et al. (2019) [39] provide insight into the characteristics of shared textual (mis)information in WhatsApp groups, while Meinert et al. (2019) [40] outline the development of fake news in the communication on social media platforms.

For more information on the role of fake news in journalism we refer to Waisbord (2018) [41]. Good examples of empirical studies focusing on fake news during the 2016 US presidential elections, are those conducted by Allcott and Gentzkow (2017) [42], Bakir and McStay (2018) [43], Guo and Vargo (2018) [44] and Guess et al. (2018, 2019)

[45, 46]. Mehta and Guzmán (2018) [47, p. 111] analyzed news media discourses around those same elections by looking at their use of quantitative visual rhetoric (persuasive multimodal moves that draw on quantification through visual, spatial, and textual manipulation). Pierri et al. (2019) [48] analyzed the role of Twitter in Italian disinformation spreading during the European elections, Morstatter et al. (2018) [49] present a Twitter analysis of the 2017 German federal election in which they also address fake news, while Broersma and Graham (2012) [50] analyzed the role to Tweets as a news source during the 2010 British and Dutch elections. Dutton et al. [51, p. 5] conducted an online survey of Internet users in seven nations: Britain, France, Germany, Italy, Poland, Spain, and the US, to examine how Internet users "use search, social media, and other important media to get information about political candidates, issues, and politics generally, as well as what difference it makes for individuals participating in democratic processes." Finally, Fedeli (2018) [52] focuses on the phenomenon of fake news in the context of travel and tourism.

2.2 Generational Differences

Neither in the edited volume Detecting Fake News on social media [53] nor in The Handbook of Research on Deception, Fake News, and Misinformation Online [54] nor in the Reuters Institute digital news report 2017 [30] is any attention paid to generational differences relating to the *consumption* of fake news. A google scholar search (01.02.2020) using the key words 'social media' AND 'Fake News' AND 'generation' OR 'Age' OR 'young' OR 'old' also failed to return any hits for scientific papers on this topic.

While handbooks, manuals, reports and empirical studies offering insight into the role that age differences play in the consumption of fake news on social media would appear to be unavailable, a limited number of reports have been published that shed some light on the topic, albeit in relation to *only one specific age group* (mainly younger people).

In Net Children Go Mobile: The UK Report, Livingstone et al. [55, p. 30] showed that in 2013, 61% of the UK respondents aged 11+ reported that they compare websites to decide whether information is true. It should be noted that these finding are based on self-reported data that might or might not reflect real behavior, and that they relate to websites in general and not to social network sites specifically.

Marchi (2012) [56, p. 257] used individual interviews and focus groups with 61 US high schoolers aged 14 to 19 to explore how teenagers view news, and found that "teens gravitate toward fake news, "snarky" talk radio, and opinionated current events shows more than official news, and do so not because they are disinterested in news, but because these kinds of sites often offer more substantive discussions of the news and its implications." This is another example of a study based on self-reported data.

A report released in 2016 by the Stanford History Education Group [57, 58] focused on students' capability to judge the credibility of information. It described how several online tasks were administered to 7,804 students in middle school through college to reason about information found on the internet, and particularly on social media sites. The main conclusion regarding their social media use was: "Our 'digital natives' may be able to flit between Facebook and Twitter while simultaneously uploading a selfie to

Instagram and texting a friend. But when it comes to evaluating information that flows to social media channels, they are easily duped" [57, p. 4].

Another empirical study [59, p. 407], which focused on university students in Spain (Andalusia) yielded the following: "In order to ascertain the degree of credibility that young users in Andalucía give to information, this study presents the results of the evaluation of online news by university students pursuing degrees in communication and education (N = 188), using the CRAAP test. The data reveal differences in gender and degree program in the credibility assigned to the news. The conclusion is that university students have difficulty differentiating the veracity of the sources, in line with previous studies, with fake news earning higher ratings than real news."

Gottfried and Shearer (2016) [60] report that in the US, 62% of adults get their news from social media and that about one third say they trust the information they get from social media 'some' or 'a lot'. Once again, these findings are based on self-reported statements.

Regarding the role of generational differences in the *dissemination* of fake news, we found one recent study by Guess et al. [46, p. 1], who write that they examined the individual-level characteristics associated with sharing false articles during the 2016 U.S. presidential campaign. "To do so, we uniquely link an original survey with respondents' sharing activity as recorded in Facebook profile data. First and foremost, we find that sharing this content was a relatively rare activity. Conservatives were more likely to share articles from fake news domains, which in 2016 were largely pro-Trump in orientation, than liberals or moderates. We also find a strong age effect, which persists after controlling for partisanship and ideology: On average, users over 65 shared nearly seven times as many articles from fake news domains as the youngest age group."

Finally, we refer to an original empirical study conducted by Roozenbeek and Van der Linden [61] who developed a game drawing on "an inoculation metaphor, where preemptively exposing, warning, and familiarizing people with the strategies used in the production of fake news helps confer cognitive immunity when exposed to real misinformation. We conducted a large-scale evaluation of the game with N = 15,000 participants in a pre-post gameplay design. We provide initial evidence that people's ability to spot and resist misinformation improves after gameplay, irrespective of education, age, political ideology, and cognitive style. (…) There was a significant difference for age so that older players adjusted their reliability ratings somewhat less (…), although the standardized difference was so small that it can be considered negligible."

As the findings of the empirical studies discussed in this section demonstrate, there is a lack of research into the role of age regarding the consumption of Fake News on social media. We therefore decided to conduct an empirical study ourselves, with the aim of generating more insight into this field.

3   Materials and Methods

To gain a better understanding of the generational dynamics in the online consumption of fake news and the perception of fake news by its audiences (e.g., [62]), the second author of this paper created, together with a Belgian fact checker (see acknowledgements), a fake news website of their own. We copied the approach of 'real' fake news websites and chose Facebook as the social media platform to disseminate the stories. Facebook offers page owners insights into their audiences and makes it possible to analyze who that audience is. Moreover, Facebook is the platform of choice for many fake news websites because it offers the opportunity to create targeted advertisements and increase their post reach by 'boosting' the posts, enabling larger audiences to be reached. We launched a fake news website, that closely mimicked 'real' fake news websites, making use of click-bait styled articles featuring the same type of language and tactics as 'real' fake news websites (e.g. playing into preexistent biases, sparking outrage, making absurd claims). We used a simple Wordpress website and a Facebook account to disseminate our articles, just as fake news websites do. The only difference with 'real' fake news was that our posted articles contained a surprise message about fake news for readers actually clicking on the link (see Appendix 1 and 2 for the text of the post).

Our posts followed the usual structure: a clickbait headline with a clear image was posted on Facebook; users clicking on the link were redirected to our website where they could read the first paragraph/introduction of the article with the made-up news. In the middle of the article, a question was asked (or we stopped halfway through a sentence), which was first followed by a few blank lines or an image and then came the surprise message aimed at educating users about fake news.

Facebook offers page users the opportunity to 'boost' posts, which is basically a feature that turns Facebook posts into online advertisements. This can be used to reach a greater audience, and to appear on the timeline of people who do not follow the page the article is published on. The feature also includes a menu with specific audience targeting options based on demographic information like location, age, gender and interests.

We posted 14 political fake news articles (see below for more information) and used €50 per article to create the advertisements, which we targeted at different audiences. All of our audiences were based in the UK and/or the USA and included people who had shown interest in the topic of the article (i.e., the political articles were targeted at people who, according to Facebook, were 'Likely to engage with political content' (conservative)', 'Likely to engage with political content (liberal)' or 'Likely to engage with political content (moderate)'. The age group option was set to 13–17, 18–24, 25–34, 35–44, 45–54, 55–64, 65+.

Once the advertisements were created and approved by an automated Facebook tool, the ads ran for seven days. During these seven days, the Facebook algorithms showed the advertisements to different audiences (based on non-specified demographics to avoid any bias) in an effort to maximize the reach for the dedicated budget. The articles were not published on different pages or platforms, but were written in as 'clickbaity' style as possible, after which we let the Facebook algorithm do the work for us. Facebooks algorithms tend to include previous user behavior and current engagement with similar content in order to optimize the reach (appearances on peoples timelines) of each advertisement.

Regarding the content of the articles, we observed the following ethical guidelines: No use of racism, hate speech or real conspiracies. Use vague language so people can fill in the blanks ('they', 'experts', etc.). Don't show ads on the website. Don't use spam tactics, such as bought likes and fake profiles. Show a surprise educational message about fake news once people click on the link.

For the topics of our fake news Facebook posts we decided to write articles playing into the biases of two groups within a polarized debate. The following two examples illustrate this approach: 1. We posted an article on the Big Ben, the famous British monument, reporting that it would allegedly be moved from London to Brussels because of Brexit. We expected this news to antagonize both the remain camp (it's the fault of Brexit) and the Brexit camp (it's the fault of Brussels). 2. Our posted article on Donald Trump's Wall, who allegedly had to pay royalties to China for using the words 'the wall'. We expected this to spark outrage amongst his supporters, and glee amongst his opponents.

We hoped to discover whether age was a factor in the extent to which these political groups became outraged by this political fake news, without even clicking on the link or doing some simple fact-checking. We come back to these two cases in Sect. 4 (see also Appendix 1 and 2).

These two posted articles were part of a total of 14 articles bearing, in no particular order, the following headlines: 'BREAKING: Plans revealed to skip National anthem during superbowl!!'; 'Is Valentine's Day a communist holiday?!'; 'Horrific! Can You See Why This Local Pedophile Got Exactly What He Deserved?'; 'Experts: Trump must pay royalties to Chinese government for the 'Wall'.'; 'Big Ben to be moved to Brussels because of Brexit?!'; 'Breaking: Reservation of Proud Native Tribe Declares Independence!'; 'Huge Cambridge Analytica Data Leak! Is Your Data Affected?'; 'Tables Turned: Personal info of every US company leaked!!'; 'JUST IN: You Won't Believe Who Is Scrambling In Full Panic Mode After The Shocking Truth Is Revealed'; 'Experts: Blocking Website Visitors For GDPR Reasons Is Illegal Under GDPR'; 'BREAKING: this celebrity just got arrested for domestic violence!!'; 'Russian influence suspected in 2018 FIFA World Cup!!'; 'New Treatment Kills Cancer Cells From 500 Yards Away'; and 'Campaign to save the Pacific Northwest tree octopus is gaining momentum'.

We spent 700 euros to boost these articles, while using different topics in order to diversify our audiences as much as possible. Strikingly, Facebook permitted all of the posts to be turned into advertisements. We collected our data with the help of the Facebook 'insights' tool, and Facebook's 'ad center' in the period from the beginning of February 2018 to the end of June of 2018.

4   Results

We reached 119,982 people with the 14 articles we posted, 41.2% of whom were women and 58.8% men. A mere 12.7% of those reached actually clicked on the link to our website, while the rest only saw the headline of the article on Facebook. In other words, 87.3% did not have the opportunity to read our surprise educational message about fake news. We reached the following age groups (following Facebook's age segmentation based on the following age-groups): 13–17: 5,293 (4.4%), 18–24: 6,856 (5.7%), 25–34: 14,265 (11.9%), 35–44: 15,928 (13.3%), 45–54: 22,051 (18.4%), 55–64: 29,603 (24.7%), 65+: 25,736 (21.5%).

Figure 1 shows that persons of all ages consumed the 14 posted articles. This is an important finding, as intervention programs such as the #SaferInternet4EU Campaign by the European Commission [34] (see also Sect. 1) are specifically targeted at schools.

Media literacy programs in primary and secondary education are often mentioned as a way to combat fake news (e.g., [31–33]), but Fig. 1 clearly demonstrates the need to target older people as well.

Age Groups

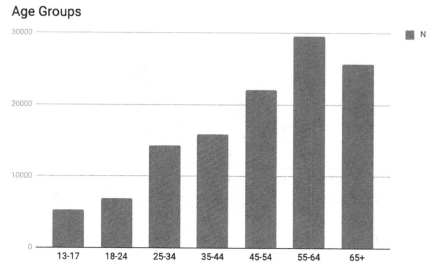

Fig. 1. Fake news consumption by age group (N) for all 14 posted articles

The headlines triggered many emotions and drew much comment in the comment section below the post on Facebook (see Appendix 1 and 2 for some examples). A closer look at two of our more popular and antagonizing posts reveals more about the Facebook audience these attracted.

Our posted article on the Big Ben (see also Appendix 1) reached 11,094 people (women: 29.3%, men: 70.7%), and collected 178 comments directly on the post. Of these, 12.92% had read the article and got the joke, 19.22% responded emotionally with a pro-Brexit stance; 3.37% responded emotionally with an anti-Brexit stance; 24.73% responded emotionally without a clear political affiliation; 28.56% responded with skepticism, and 10.67% responded in other ways. Figure 2 shows that the posted articles had a higher reach amongst older age groups than the younger ones, which could be due to the type of news (political).

Interestingly, while this post failed completely to reach the two youngest age groups, we found that all the other age groups consumed the news of this post (Fig. 2 and Table 1).

Our posted article on Donald Trumps' Wall (see also Appendix 2, Fig. 3 and Table 2) reached 7,500 people (women: 29.8%, men: 70.2%), and got 108 comments. Of these, 12.04% had read the article and got the joke; 20.37% responded emotionally with a pro-Trump stance; 5.56% responded emotionally with an anti-Trump stance; 12.96% responded emotionally without a clear political affiliation; 44.44% responded with skepticism; and 4.63% responded in other ways.

Age Groups

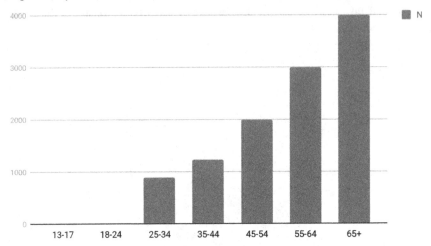

Fig. 2. Fake news consumption by age group (N) for the posted article on the Big Ben

Table 1. Fake news consumption by age group (%) for the post on the Big Ben

13–17: 0%
18–24: 0%
25–34: 8%
35–44: 11%
45–54: 18%
55–64: 27%
65+: 36%

Table 2. Fake news consumption by age group (%) for the post on Donald Trump's

Wall
13–17: 0%
18–24: 3%
25–34: 8%
35–44: 11%
45–54: 19%
55–64: 31%
65+: 28%

As Fig. 3 shows, the youngest age group was wholly uninterested, and the 18-24-year-olds in this audience were only barely interested in this post. However, the other age groups were clearly interested in the news of this post.

Age Groups

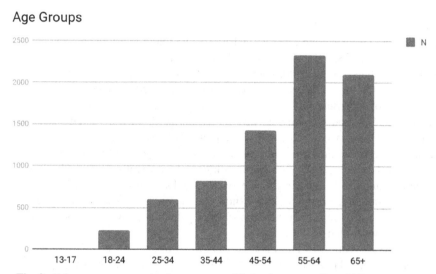

Fig. 3. Fake news consumption by age group (N) for the post on Donald Trump's Wall

Hence these two items proved to act as emotional triggers for people, who were then happy to broadcast their political views even without clicking on the link to read the entire article (see also Appendix 1 and 2). Of those who commented, only 12.04% and 12.92% had clearly read the article and understood that it was meant as a lesson on Fake News. Some 28.56% and 44.44% respectively displayed an instinctive skepticism without elaborating on a lesson having been learned. They may very well have therefore not clicked on the link as they disbelieved the headline of the article to begin with. Those responding emotionally (whether with anger, insults or with satisfaction at the news) showed no indication of having learned any lesson or of having understood the purpose of the article. They are likely not to have clicked on the article for further reading and simply to have taken the headline at face value. Of those with emotional responses, 19.22% were pro-Brexit and 20.37% pro-Trump versus 3.37% who were anti-Brexit and 5.56% anti-Trump. This might imply that the pro-Brexit and pro-Trump groups are both more likely to believe and actively comment on fake news and are more easily emotionally triggered.

5   Conclusions, Limitations and Implications for Future Research

This paper focused on the following research question: What is the role of age in fake news consumption on social media? Our review of previous empirical studies in this field showed that prior to this study, generational differences had not yet been studied in relation to this topic. A limited number of empirical studies had collected data on the way younger people consumed this kind of news. The overall conclusion was that the media literacy of the young in relation to fake news is not yet very well developed. Or, in the words of Wineburg and McGrew (2016) [58]: "Our "digital natives" may be able to flit between Facebook and Twitter while simultaneously uploading a selfie to Instagram and texting a friend. But when it comes to evaluating information that flows to social media channels, they are easily duped. (SHEG, 2016, p. 4) [57]." The one study (conducted by Gottfried and Shearer, 2016 [60]) we found that looked at older adults reports that in the US, 62% of adults get their news from social media, and that about one third *say* they trust the information they get from social media 'some' or 'a lot'. These findings, it should be noted, are based on self-reported statements.

The lack of empirical studies comparing the extent to which different generations consume fake news on social media was the reason for conducting an empirical study aimed at providing insight into such generational differences. We posted 14 political fake news articles containing a surprise educational message about fake news, as advertisements on Facebook. User interaction with the fake content was tracked in order to analyze the number of users in the age groups 13–17, 18–24, 25–34, 35–44, 45–54, 55–64, 65+. Figure 1, 2 and 3 in Sect. 4 show that the posted articles had a higher reach amongst older age groups than the younger ones, which could well be due to the kind of political news posted.

While the algorithms of Facebook are somewhat of a 'black box', using the same tactics and articles should produce a similar reach of these fake news pages amongst these age groups. Whether the algorithm pushed these stories based on previous behavior of the target audience or because the level of engagement was higher amongst the older age groups is not important for the end result; the fact remains that the stories had a higher reach amongst older age groups.

This is an important finding, as intervention programs such as the #SaferInternet4EU Campaign [34] by the European Commission (see also Sect. 1) are targeted at schools, while our empirical study shows that we also need to target people who are older.

Also noteworthy is the fact that only 12.7% of the people our posts reached actually clicked on the link. Given the number of emotional responses, it seems likely that many persons took the headlines at face value. Of the people who responded emotionally, those in both the pro-Brexit and pro-Trump groups were more likely to believe and actively comment on fake news, and were more easily emotionally triggered.

A limitation of our study is that we do not know whether, in a real life situation, people would have distributed the post to others. Future empirical studies should address this point (for example by conducting a controlled experiment) and should also include the role of gender, educational level and nationality. In addition, other types of articles than political fake news articles alone should be posted: age groups could differ in their preferences regarding types of articles. The Facebook advertisement tool allowed all of the articles to be published, but under the new regulations introduced after we conducted our study, this is no longer likely to be the case. The set-up of the present empirical study could be used as a guideline for the design of future evidence-based empirical studies to gain more insight into the generational dynamics of fake news consumption on social media, the audience's perception and the effectiveness of Facebook's tools in combatting fake news. Another limitation is that we did not track the interactions of the audiences with the website. A tracking tool based on cookies or the 'Facebook Pixel' could have helped to learn more about who actually clicked on the headlines to find out more. For future studies we would recommend implementing tracking tools on the website to identify the role of age in source verification (fact-checking). A more thorough analysis (with the inclusion of a variety of age groups) of the comments is also recommended, as, due to privacy restrictions, this was not possible on a public Facebook page.

Acknowledgements. We would like to thank Belgian fact-checker Maarten Schenk, who created the Fake News website together with the second author of this paper, which made it possible to disseminate the fake news stories on Facebook. This paper is part of the research project BConnect@Home (https://www.jp-demographic.eu/wp-content/uploads/2017/01/BCONNECT_ 2017_conf2018_brochure.pdf), funded by the JTP 2017 - JPI More Years, Better Lives (Grant Agreement 363850) - the Netherlands, ZONMW (Project 9003037411).

Appendix 1

Fake News Post on the Big Ben

Since the EU paid for the current renovation of the Big Ben tower in London some people are claiming that the tower should be moved to Brussels. The UK has voted to leave the European Union and is scheduled to depart on Friday 29 March, 2019. The UK and EU have provisionally agreed on the three "divorce" issues of how much the UK owes the EU, what happens to the Northern Ireland border and what happens to UK citizens living elsewhere in the EU and EU citizens living in the UK. Talks are now moving on to future relations, and the Big Ben tower in London could become part of those talks. 80% of the funding for the renovation of the tower is contributed by the EU and now people want their money back!

Which people, you might ask..

Well.. None!!

Because this article is Fake!

It is written to show you how easy it is to create false headlines, and how dangerous they are. Websites that post click-baity headlines often fill their pages with ads, and are making a shitload of money. These headlines often include outrageous claims which are not supported by evidence. By clicking on unfounded sensational news you contribute to the spreading of fake news. The only thing we can do is undermining their business model!

So next time you see a headline like ours? Think twice about clicking on the link!

Target Audience for Advertisement (Facebook Options)

Living in: United Kingdom

Age: 13-65+

People who match: Interests: Theresa May, Big Ben, Boris Johnson, London or UNILAD and Politics: Likely to engage with political content (conservative) or Likely to engage with political content (liberal).

Facebook Results (Some Examples)

- Headline: 'Big Ben to be moved to Brussels because of Brexit?!'
- Persons reached: 11.094 persons (women: 29,3%, men: 70,7%)
- 355 reactions (104 likes, 1 love, 226 haha, 4 wow, 20 angry)
- 206 comments (178 on post, 28 on shares)
- 47 shares
- 1.515 Post clicks (redirects to website) = 13.66%.

178 Comments Directly on Post (Including Some Examples)
Read the article and got the joke: **23** (12.92%)

- "If you read it. It says that it fake news. Made up to see how things spread on the internet."
- "Amazing comments on here. Does anyone actually read the full article these days? Or are you all happy just to read a headline and get angry?"

Emotional pro-Brexit: **35** (19.66%)

- "Teresa may is giving the EU all our other assets and freedoms they may as well have this to"
- "Might as well as the bells will be in the way of the call of prayer 5 times a day . . One they cleared out free speech"

Emotional anti-Brexit: **6** (3.37%)

- "Can you imagine the look on brexiters faces if this had to happen? Would be comedy moment of the century."
- "Aww crying Brexiters really perk up my day…"

Emotional without clear affiliation: **44** (24.73%)

- "O fuck off"
- "Yep & take all the corrupt pigs in the troth with it, weak government, no morals all on the take, time to sort em out!"

Skeptical: **51** (28.65%)

- "yeah sure"
- "Sounds like April fool"

Other: **19** (10.67%)

– Reply to friend: "With you I'm always right "

– "And apparently we are going to have to keep the maroon Passports as we cannot make blue ones in the UK!!!"

Appendix 2

Fake News Post on Donald Trump's Wall

Experts claim that Donald J. Trump has to pay royalties to the Chinese government for the 'Wall'.

President Donald Trump has set in motion his plan to build an "impenetrable, physical, tall, powerful, beautiful, southern border wall" between the US and Mexico. This border is about 1,900 miles (3,100 km) long and traverses all sorts of terrain. But what he does not know, is that the collection of fortifications known as the 'Great Wall of China' has exclusive rights on the term "Wall".

In Chinese histories, the term "Long Wall(s)" (長城)appears in Sima Qian's Records of the Grand Historian, where it referred to both the separate great walls built between and north of the Warring States and to the more unified construction of the First Emperor. The longer Chinese name "Ten-Thousand Mile Long Wall" (萬里長城)came from Sima Qian's description of it in the Records, though he did not name the walls as such. The ad 493 Book of Song quotes the frontier general Tan Daoji referring to "the long wall of 10,000 miles" Because of the wall's association with the First Emperor's supposed tyranny, the Chinese dynasties after Qin usually avoided referring to their own additions to the wall by the name "Long Wall".

The current English name evolved from accounts of "the Chinese wall" from early modern European travelers. By the 19th century, "The Great Wall of China" had become standard in English, French, and German, although other European languages continued to refer to it as "the Chinese wall". Since then a copyright has been imposed on Wall-like structures by the Chinese government. And now they are preparing a lawsuit against Donald Trump.

They'll see him in court!

The court date has been set for never.. Because, this article is a lot of bogus. We wrote this article to show you how easy it is to make people believe in wild stories.. You probably clicked on this link because you thought it was funny, it made you angry or sparked your interest.

We are sorry to break it to you, but articles that are too crazy to believe, are probably not true!

Keep that in mind next time you see a headline like ours;-)

Target Audience for Advertisement (Facebook Options)

Living in: United States
    Age: 13–65+

People who match: Politics: Likely to engage with political content (conservative), Likely to engage with political content (liberal) or Likely to engage with political content (moderate).

Facebook Results (Some Examples)

- Headline: 'Experts claim that Donald J. Trump has to pay royalties to the Chinese government for the 'Wall'. They'll see him in court!'
- Persons reached: 7.500 people (women: 29.8%, men: 70,2%)
- 355 reactions (189 likes, 11 love, 344 haha, 10 wow, 1 sad, 28 angry)
- 118 comments (108 on post, 10 on shares)
- 121 shares
- 491 Post clicks (redirects to website) = 6.55%.

108 Comments Directly on the Post (Including Some Examples)
Read the article and got the joke: **13** (12.04%)

- "Yeah. Good joke"

- "It's nothing Other than a humorous joke "

Emotional pro-Trump: **22** (20.37%)

- "Maybe we can hire Chinese labor to build the wall that Mexico is going to build."
- "Oh my! Liberals will try anything to make our President look bad! Give it up already!"

Emotional anti-Trump: **6** (5.56%)

- "Good luck! He filed Bankruptcy on the million his Dad lent him. Never paid Daddy back either. His Attorneys will handle it."
- "Trump sucks on all levels."

Emotional without clear affiliation: **14** (12.96%)

- "BULLSHIT, NOTTA going to happen."
- "STOP YOUR BULL. CHINA DIDN'T INVENT WALLS."

Skeptical: **48** (44.44%)

- "Fake all the way. America doesn't pay China for any wall. Only total idiots would believe this"
- "I guess I will also have to pay there is a "wall" in my backyard and the one inside "

Other: **5** (4.63%)

- "[Tag of a friend]"
- "[GIF]".

References

1. Carey, K.M.: Fake News: How Propaganda Influenced the 2016 Election, a Historical Comparison to 1930's Germany. Marzenhale Publishing, Snow Hill (2017)
2. Swart, J., Peters, C., Broersma, M.: Shedding light on the dark social: the connective role of news and journalism in social media communities. New Media Soc. **20**(11), 4329–4345 (2018)
3. Van der Horst, H.: Nepnieuws. Een wereld van desinformatie [Fake news: a world of disinformation]. Scriptum, Schiedam (2018)
4. Edgerly, S., Mourão, R.R., Thorson, E., Tham, S.M.: When do audiences verify? How perceptions about message and source influence audience verification of news headlines. Journal. Mass Commun. Q. **97**, 52–71 (2019). https://doi.org/10.1177/1077699019864680
5. Goyanes, M.: Antecedents of incidental news exposure: the role of media preference, use and trust. Journal. Pract. **39**, 1–16 (2019)
6. Mustăţea, M., Balaban, D.C.: News sharing on social media platforms. Theoretical approaches: In: Iancu, I., Balaban, D.C., Hosu, I. (eds.) Communication. Strategic Perspectives, pp. 66–80. Babeş-Bolyai University Cluj-Napoca PR Trend International Conference, Accent, Cluj-Napoca, Romania, 26th–27th February 2018 (2019)
7. Obadă, R.: Sharing fake news about brands on social media: a new conceptual model based on flow theory argumentum. J. Semin. Discursive Log. Argum. Theory Rhetor. **17**(2), 144–166 (2019)
8. Gelfert, A.: Fake News: A Definition. Informal Log. **38**(1), 84–117 (2018)
9. McGonagle, T.: Fake news: false fears or real concerns? Neth. Q. Hum. Rights **35**(4), 203–209 (2017)
10. Nimrod, G.: Older audiences in the digital media environment. Inf. Commun. Soc. **20**(2), 233–249 (2017)
11. Aldwairi, M., Alwahedi, A.: Detecting fake news in social media networks. Procedia Comput. Sci. **141**, 215–222 (2018)
12. Rawls, J.: Political Liberalism. Columbian University Press, New York (1993)
13. Van den Hoven, M.J.: Towards ethical principles for designing politico-administrative information systems. Inf. Public Sect. **3**(3/4), 353–373 (1994)
14. Bovens, M.A.P.: Information rights. Citizenship in the information society. J. Polit. Philos. **10**(9), 317–341 (2002)
15. Bovens, M.A.P., Loos, E.F.: The digital constitutional state: democracy and law in the information society. Inf. Polity **7**(4), 185–197 (2002)
16. De Jong, J., Rizvi, G.: The State of Access. Success and Failure of Democracies to Create Equal Opportunities. Brookings Institution Press, Washington (2008)
17. Humprecht, E.: Where 'fake news' flourishes: a comparison across four western democracies. Inf. Commun. Soc. **22**(13), 1973–1988 (2019)
18. Loos, E.F., Romano Bergstrom, J.: Older adults. In: Romano Bergstrom, J., Schall, A.J. (eds.) Eye Tracking in User Experience Design, pp. 313–329. Elsevier, Amsterdam (2014)
19. Loos, E.: In search of information on websites: a question of age? In: Stephanidis, C. (ed.) UAHCI 2011. LNCS, vol. 6766, pp. 196–204. Springer, Heidelberg (2011). https://doi.org/10.1007/978-3-642-21663-3_21

20. Hill, R., Dickinson, A., Arnott, J., Gregor, P., McIver, L.: Older Users' Eye Movements: Experience Counts, CHI 2011, Vancouver, British Colombia, Canada, 7–12 May (2011)
21. Loos, E.F.: Senior citizens: digital immigrants in their own country? Observatorio (OBS*) J. **6**(1), 1–23 (2012)
22. Loos, E.F.: De oudere: een digitale immigrant in eigen land? Een terreinverkenning naar toegankelijke informatievoorziening. [oratie] Older people: digital immigrants in their own country? Exploring accessible information delivery [inaugural lecture]. Boom/Lemma, Den Haag (2010)
23. Quinn, K.: Older adults and social media. In: Nixon, P.G., Rawal, R., Funk, A. (eds.) Digital Media Usage Across the Life Course, pp. 132–145. Routledge, Abingdon (2016)
24. Rogers, E.M.: Diffusion of Innovations. Free Press, New York (2003)
25. PEW: Tech Adoption Climbs Among Older Adults, 17 May 2017. https://www.pewinternet.org/2017/05/17/tech-adoption-climbs-among-older-adults/
26. Standard Eurobarometer: Media use in the European Union (2017). https://www.google.com/url?sa=t&rct=j&q=&esrc=s&source=web&cd=1&ved=2ahUKEwicu-fIrtziAhUFJ1AKHZRPBbUQFjAAegQIAxAC&url=https%3A%2F%2Fec.europa.eu%2Fcommfrontoffice%2Fpublicopinion%2Findex.cfm%2FResultDoc%2Fdownload%2FDocumentKy%2F82786&usg=AOvVaw17UrDp_hb6W7jBAMXEa6Ic
27. PEW: Share of U.S. adults using social media, including Facebook, is mostly unchanged since 2018, 10 April 2019. https://www.pewresearch.org/fact-tank/2019/04/10/share-of-u-s-adults-using-social-media-including-facebook-is-mostly-unchanged-since-2018/
28. Holt, K., Shehata, A., Strömbäck, J., Ljungberg, E.: Age and the effects of news media attention and social media use on political interest and participation: do social media function as leveller? Eur. J. Commun. **28**(1), 19–34 (2013)
29. Ofcom: Adults: media use and attitudes report 2019 (2019). https://www.ofcom.org.uk/__data/assets/pdf_file/0021/149124/adults-media-use-and-attitudes-report.pdf
30. Newman, N., Fletcher, R., Kalogeropoulos, A., Levy, D., Nielsen, R.K.: Reuters institute digital news report 2017 (2017)
31. Leu, D.J., et al.: Defining online reading comprehension: using think aloud verbal protocols to refine a preliminary model of Internet reading comprehension processes. In: Alvermann (Chair), D. (ed.) 21st Century Literacy: What is It, How do Students Get It, and How do We Know if They have It (2007)
32. Loos, E.F., Ivan, L., Leu, D.: "Save the Pacific northwest tree octopus": a hoax revisited. Or: how vulnerable are school children to fake news? Inf. Learn. Sci. **119**(9, 10), 514–528 (2018)
33. Pilgrim, J., Vasinda, S., Bledsoe, C., Martinez, E.: Critical thinking is critical: octopuses, online sources, and reliability reasoning. Read. Teach. **73**(1), 85–93 (2019)
34. European Commission: Tackling online disinformation. https://ec.europa.eu/digital-single-market/en/tackling-online-disinformation. Accessed 08 Aug 2019
35. Allcott, H., Gentzkow, M., Yu, C.: Trends in the diffusion of misinformation on social media. Res. Polit. **6**(2) (2019). https://doi.org/10.1177/2053168019848554
36. Mosinzova, V., Fabian, B., Ermakova, T., Baumann, A.: Fake news, conspiracies and myth debunking in social media-a literature survey across disciplines, 3 February 2019
37. Flintham, M., Karner, C., Bachour, K., Creswick, H., Gupta, N., Moran, S.: Falling for fake news: investigating the consumption of news via social media. In: Proceedings of the 2018 CHI Conference on Human Factors in Computing Systems, p. 376. ACM, April 2018
38. Quintanilha, T.L., Silva, M.T.D., Lapa, T.: Fake news and its impact on trust in the news. Using the Portuguese case to establish lines of differentiation. Commun. Soc. **32**(3), 17–33 (2019)
39. Resende, G., Melo, P., Reis, J.C., Vasconcelos, M., Almeida, J.M., Benevenuto, F.: Analyzing Textual (Mis) Information Shared in WhatsApp Groups (2019, preprint)

40. Meinert, J., Mirbabaie, M., Dungs, S., Aker, A.: Is it really fake? – towards an understanding of fake news in social media communication. In: Meiselwitz, G. (ed.) SCSM 2018. LNCS, vol. 10913, pp. 484–497. Springer, Cham (2018). https://doi.org/10.1007/978-3-319-91521-0_35

41. Waisbord, S.: Truth is what happens to news: on journalism, fake news, and post-truth. Journal. Stud. 19(13), 1866–1878 (2018)

42. Allcott, H., Gentzkow, M.: Social media and fake news in the 2016 election. J. Econ. Perspect. 31(2), 211–236 (2017)

43. Bakir, V., McStay, A.: Fake news and the economy of emotions: problems, causes, solutions. Digit. J. 6(2), 154–175 (2018)

44. Guo, L., Vargo, C.: "Fake news" and emerging online media ecosystem: an integrated intermedia agenda-setting analysis of the 2016 US presidential election. Commun. Res. 47, 178–200 (2018). https://doi.org/10.1177/0093650218777177

45. Guess, A., Nyhan, B., Reifler, J.: Selective exposure to misinformation: evidence from the consumption of fake news during the 2016 US presidential campaign. European Research Council, p. 9 (2018)

46. Guess, A., Nagler, J., Tucker, J.: Less than you think: prevalence and predictors of fake news dissemination on Facebook. Sci. Adv. 5(1), eaau4586 (2019)

47. Mehta, R., Guzmán, L.D.: Fake or visual trickery? Understanding the quantitative visual rhetoric in the news. J. Media Lit. Educ. 10(2), 104–122 (2018)

48. Pierri, F., Artoni, A., Ceri, S.: Investigating Italian disinformation spreading on Twitter in the context of 2019 European elections. arXiv preprint arXiv:1907.08170 (2019)

49. Morstatter, F., Shao, Y., Galstyan, A., Karunasekera, S.: From alt-right to alt-rechts: Twitter analysis of the 2017 German federal election. In: Companion Proceedings of the Web Conference 2018, pp. 621–628. International World Wide Web Conferences Steering Committee, April 2018

50. Broersma, M., Graham, T.: Social media as beat: tweets as a news source during the 2010 British and Dutch elections. Journal. Pract. 6(3), 403–419 (2012)

51. Dutton, W.H., Reisdorf, B., Dubois, E., Blank, G.: Search and politics: the uses and impacts of search in Britain, France, Germany, Italy, Poland, Spain, and the United States (2017)

52. Fedeli, G.: Fake news' meets tourism: a proposed research agenda. Ann. Tourism Res. 80 (2019)

53. Shu, K., Liu, H.: Detecting Fake News on Social Media. Morgan & Claypool, Williston (2019)

54. Chiluwa, I.E., Samoilenko, S.A.: Handbook of Research on Deception, Fake News, and Misinformation Online. IGI Global, Hershey (2019)

55. Livingstone, S., Haddon, L., Vincent, J., Mascheroni, G., Ólafsson, K.: Net children go mobile: the UK report (2014). http://eprints.lse.ac.uk/59098/

56. Marchi, R.: With Facebook, blogs, and fake news, teens reject journalistic "objectivity". J. Commun. Inq. 36(3), 246–262 (2012)

57. SHEG (Stanford History Education Group): Evaluating information: the cornerstone of civic online reasoning. Research Report (2016). www.sheg.tandford.edu

58. Wineburg, S., McGrew, S.: Why students can't Google their way to the truth. Educ. Week 36(11), 22–28 (2016)

59. Herrero-Diz, P., Conde-Jiménez, J., Tapia-Frade, A., Varona-Aramburu, D.: The credibility of online news: an evaluation of the information by university students/La credibilidad de las noticias en Internet: una evaluación de la información por estudiantes universitarios. Cultura y Educ. 31(2), 407–435 (2019)

60. Gottfried, J., Shearer, E.: News use across social media platforms 2016. Pew Research Center, 26 May 2016. http://www.journalism.org/2016/05/26/

61. Roozenbeek, J., Van der Linden, S.: Fake news game confers psychological resistance against online misinformation. Palgrave Commun. **5**(1), 12 (2019)
62. Tandoc Jr., E.C., Ling, R., Westlund, O., Duffy, A., Goh, D., Zheng Wei, L.: Audiences' acts of authentication in the age of fake news: a conceptual framework. New Media Soc. **20**(8), 2745–2763 (2018)

Masculinities and Ageing: Deconstructing Online Representations Among Portuguese Speaking Users

Sofia José Santos[1,2](✉), Inês Amaral[3,4], and Maria José Brites[5]

[1] Faculdade de Economia da Universidade de Coimbra, Coimbra, Portugal
[2] Centro de Estudos Sociais da Universidade de Coimbra, Coimbra, Portugal
sjs@ces.uc.pt
[3] Faculdade de Letras da Universidade de Coimbra, Coimbra, Portugal
ines.amaral@uc.pt
[4] Centro de Estudos de Comunicação e Sociedade da Universidade do Minho, Braga, Portugal
[5] Universidade Lusófona/CICANT, Porto, Portugal
mariajosebrites@ulp.pt

Abstract. Media and social media perform a pivotal role in the construction of social reality and shared meaning. As social representations, gender and age identities are included in those dynamics, per se and interacting with each other. This article aims to analyse the complexity, non-linearity and hybridity of representations of men and age within today's digital realm. Stemming from an intersectional and feminist approach, this article explores how Twitter users represent older men in their posts, assessing whether these representations promote or hinder respectful ageing relationships and gender equality. How do Portuguese-speaking online users' representations of men and masculinities interact with age and ageism? To put the analysis forward, data were extracted from Twitter and analysed through quantitative and qualitative content analysis. Data showed that intersection between masculinities and age among Portuguese speaking twitter users is low concerning the number of times that "men" and "old" are used in the same tweet text. However, data also showed that when patriarchal discourses intersect with ageism, they tend to perpetuate stereotypes, hindering egalitarian relationships concerning age and gender.

Keywords: Masculinities · Ageism · Twitter · Online

1 Introduction

Social representations result from broader socialization processes within which the media perform a pivotal role. Within today's media ecosystem, social media have been increasingly used for people to individually express themselves, share experiences, and engage with others while at the same time promoting collective action. Gender and age identities as social representations are included in this social dynamic, both *per se* and through interacting with each other. In fact, representations of gender and age

© Springer Nature Switzerland AG 2020
Q. Gao and J. Zhou (Eds.): HCII 2020, LNCS 12209, pp. 89–100, 2020.
https://doi.org/10.1007/978-3-030-50232-4_7

often go hand in hand, reinforcing or weakening, through an intersectional logic, particular forms of power and, thus, empowering or disempowering specific subjects. As many other forms of discrimination, patriarchy and ageism do not operate detached from each other nor in isolation from other hierarchical social categories [1], such as class or race, but rather intersect with them creating complex variable-geometry positions within wider hierarchical structures through which one moves and is moved, influencing perceptions of oneself and of others. Gender-wise, increasing age has been traditionally perceived as a paramount source of power for men. As men get older, there are a number of characteristics hegemonically attributed to being a "real man" - such as leadership, rationality, experience, protection - that potentially increase. As Hearn clarifies, traditionally "'maleness' and 'age (dness)'" have been "mutually reinforcing and reaffirming as means to power" [2]. However, as notions of masculinity have been openly understood in its complexity, particularly with men performing more and more domestic and caregiving roles and show greater concern and interest in their own physical appearance and health, a linear connection between maleness and agedness might be challenged. The combination of emerging normative frameworks, such as "lookism, and fitnessism, further supported by ideals of consumerism, means that our future understanding and the scope of gendered ageism continues to unfold" [3].

This article understand masculinities as multiple [2, 3], and stems from Hearn's understanding of 'the ageing of men', which does not entail "the chronological process by which men are assumed to become older", but rather "the ways in which 'men' are constructed as meanings through and by reference to 'age'" [2]. I.e., it includes both the social construction of what it means to be, express and behave like a "real man" but also "the construction of men's experience through the lens of age" [2].

The study intends to explore, through an intersectional and feminist approach, how online social media users have been representing older men in their posts, shedding light on how these representations promote or hinder gender-equitable and respectful ageing relations. To do so, it seeks to answer the following research question: How do Portuguese-speaking online users' representations of men and masculinities interact with age and ageism? To put this study forward, data were extracted from Twitter in the form of tweets using Node XL. We collected textual data from Twitter feeds using the search terms 'homem' (man, in English) and 'velho' (old, in English), focusing on time-lapse 19th august 2019 - 19th November 2019, and deleting accounts with less than 100 followers. We have grouped tweets according to specific categories and selected the three most shared tweets in each category to analyse through content analysis. Understanding ageism and patriarchy as both hierarchical social structures and sociocultural practices based on socially legitimated orders/systems of privilege and discrimination, this article draws attention to the importance of the sociocultural context and the dynamics involved in the creation and reproduction of social reality, including social inequalities, with a particular focus on the digital realm.

2   Intersecting Patriarchy and Ageism

Intersectional analysis stems from a central premise "that all social categories (race, gender, class, and more) are experienced in relationship to and constituted by other social categories" [4], allowing to uproot and understand, in an intersectional perspective, crossing dynamics between identity, agency and power [4]. It "addresses the manner in which racism, patriarchy, class oppression and other discriminatory systems create inequalities that structure the relative positions of women, races, ethnicities, classes and the like" [5]. Although some authors have limited their analyses to the main axis of intersectional study, namely race, gender and class, others have broadened their scope of analysis, introducing new categories and addressing different forms of inequality and hierarchies of power [4], namely age. As Hearn and Melechi state [6], to discuss men and masculinities is to discuss age whether in explicit or implicit terms. In fact, age has been traditionally involved in the social construction of what it means to be a man "both in the distinction of men from young men and boys, and in the construction of particular types of men" [2].

Masculinities and femininities represent a culturally imagined (and discursively and semiotically conveyed) ideal of what it means to be and behave like a boy/man and a girl/woman [7]. As a social construct, masculinities and femininities have been developed based upon shifting realities concerning time and space, but consistently constructed within generalised patriarchal structures, and built upon an essentialist and binary lens [7]. To talk about masculinities and patriarchy does not necessarily mean to talk about men, but rather to map and unveil gender relations, specifically the privileged position of men within a broader and hierarchical gender order [8, 9]. In point of fact, patriarchy represents and reflects the institutionalization of male domination in a gendered hierarchy that is legitimised - and, thus, accepted - by the hegemonic culture [10]. Within the patriarchal system, power dynamics and asymmetric relationships between the different subjects are not only established between men and women but also among men themselves [9]. At the centre of the construction and maintenance of patriarchy lies the concept of "hegemonic masculinity" [9]. Hegemonic masculinity represents a culturally imagined ideal of what it means to be, to express and to behave "like a man", and goes in line with notions of rationality, leadership, courage, endurance, strength, heteronormativity, and sexual drive [12, 13]. Accordingly, men who adopt traits consistent with the hegemonic ideal of masculinity affirms their alleged superiority over women and men who fall short of this pattern, consolidating their general position of domination [14]. Representing a reference upon which men are identified and categorized in relative terms, hegemonic masculinity is not the standard and most common behaviour of boys and men but it constitutes an ideal that informs and provides guidance to men and boys (and women and girls) concerning behaviours, choices, aspirations, and expectations [7, 14]. Men who adopt traits consistent with the ideal of hegemonic masculinity traditionally affirm their claimed superiority over women, rendering increasingly solid their general position of domination [14]. Likewise, men who have characteristics traditionally understood as "feminine" (such as sensitivity, caring, fear, emotion, and/or passivity), are ridiculed and perceived as inferior, feeling, hence, ostracized, inferior or even rendered insignificant or marginalized [15]. Hegemonic masculinity incorporates, thus, the legitimacy of patriarchy itself [11].

Just as patriarchy is an unequal and oppressive system, so is ageism. Ageism is a system of social oppression and inequality that is based upon the understanding of age as a pivotal signifier concerning subjects, ranking them considering what is conceived as more and less desired ages [19]. Perceptions and representations of age entail both stable and fluid meanings, combining traditional understandings and dynamic trends, which complexify the frameworks upon which 'age' can be perceived and constructed in society. Socialization, social context and political understandings are, thus, implicated in the social construction of 'age' [3, 16–19].

Understood as "political and discursive location" and a "cultural and social construct" [19], age "comes with an easily accessible and ready-to-use arsenal of culture-specific beliefs and norms" [19] which are permanently being renegotiated. Representations of *ageing* and *being old* are, thus, a social depiction that is based upon traditional understandings of age, while adapting to the context that structures meaning and that attributes specific significances to be a specific age. Nowadays, age in the West is often considered as a time of a certain decadence, in the sense of losing body and mind abilities and also professional vitality [18]. Taking cue on this understanding, ageism as a form of discrimination put forward on the grounds of age renders older people more vulnerable. In spite of the fact that there are several indicators of positive representations of *ageism* and *getting older* [18], they are seldom able to successfully challenge dominant forms of conceiving to be, express and behave "like a man" as hegemonically understood [2].

2.1 Patriarchy, Ageism and Variable Geometry

Ageism and patriarchy are two interacting power structures which, based upon socially constructed imaginaries and symbolic representations, produce and reflect hierarchies and, subsequently, positions and relations of privilege, vulnerability, and discrimination among the different subjects [20]. Whereas ageism discriminates people on the grounds of age, patriarchy privileges men aligned with the ideal of "hegemonic masculinity" [9].

Concerning power, age and masculinities have been traditionally perceived as mutually reinforcing [2] and older men have been recognised "as part of the hegemonic ideology" [23]. However, the implication of age in the construction of maleness (as hegemonically conceived) is not a linear one, and patriarchy and ageism may intersect differently depending on one's own circumstance, purpose and agenda, leading to differentiated positions of vulnerability or domination. Just like gender is socially "(re)created and (re)organised in different ways by different generations" [22], age defines expectations concerning each person's gender, reinforcing specific subjects while diminishing others within established dominant hierarchies [6].

Within patriarchy, as men age, characteristics that are hegemonically attributed to men, such as dexterity and physical and sexual strength, for example, might decrease, making specific men see their power (or the perception of their power) to decrease. On the other hand, within patriarchy, as men get closer to seniority, the possibility of satisfactorily fulfilling the expectations of being a safe economic provider and a leader with solid knowledge and experience - attributes that go in line with what is hegemonically perceived as being "a real man" - increases. Also, as nowadays men in the West show greater concern towards their own physical appearance and health [3], existing conceptions on the intersection of age and masculinities might be challenged [2, 3].

As patriarchy and ageism interact with one another, privilege and discrimination involve everyone - men and women, and girls and boys - differently [3, 19]. This highlights the fact that "discourses of gender and ageing have a political character: they define relations between different groups of people, establish a power structure and play a determining role in assigning certain societal spaces to individuals" [24]. In fact, and as Krekula argues, the "construction of a norm and of its deviants represents an issue of power" [21].

3   Gender and Ageing on Social Media

The relationship between discourse, and age and gender identity is mutually reinforcing. By means of the construction and dissemination of discourses, gender (and age) performances emerge and are, in turn, discursively rendered legitimate [25]. Within the discursive realm, social media have been increasingly used, on a daily basis, for people to express themselves and engage with others, most times in an individual "disclosure logic" [26]. At the same time, the digital environment is identified as a public space that promotes collective action [27]. Bimber [28] argues that the digital media ecosystem is, in itself, an element of change in the context of collective action and, consequently, an element of change concerning the social representations that shape and reconfigure the ever-changing public space. Chadwick's [29] theory of media hybridism is consistent with Bimber's argument which states that the digital allows the "collapse of boundaries between types of media and the processes of adaptation and mutual adjustment between actors involved in power struggles through political communication" [28].

As new media emerge, there is a new space for aggression and resistance and for enhanced new forms of network activism. In fact, the digital revolution is contributing to refocus, or at least to enlarge, the angle and, thus, to reconsider the lens through which one defines and redefines the form society looks at both gender and old people. Discourses that reproduce patriarchal and ageist structures in the new digital ecosystem normalise and generalise collective social representations that often fit as violence, like the usage of hate speech to validate gender-based violence and age stereotypes in distinct dimensions. On the other hand, older citizens might resist to ageism through social media, contesting - by means of discourse or practice - hegemonic narratives of their inability to use technology [30]. Considering intergenerational use of media, new media can be pivotal exploring "the general dynamics of the generation-building processes and the roles played in them by the media" [31]. The digital provides the plurality of geographically dispersed generations a potential for connection, and while 'generational units' are still anchored upon their own specific contexts [32], the online environment facilitates the strengthening of ties, including cross-generational ones, and a re-configuration of the generational identity" [33]. At the same time, social media "allow people to gather for social, cultural, and civic purposes, and they help people connect with a world beyond their close friends and family" [34]. Concerning age, Comunello and colleagues point out what they coin as "generational semantics", which are semantic that "are produced by senior citizens to interpret their own relationship with ICT deals with the perception of both personal abilities and socially expected performances and might be shaped by their own perception of age and ageing" [35]. The digital age allows, hence, the blurring of barriers between different generations that interact through and with technologies, enhancing the narrowing of intergenerational relationships and new forms of sociability, which are anchored to generational contexts [36].

Digital platforms tend to facilitate also an interesting relation between different generations [36–38]. On one hand, digital literacy skills can reinforce active ageing [39–41] and open more diverse and positive perspectives concerning ageing and the world. On the other hand, there are representations in the digital landscape that give continuity to age stereotypes associated with ageism and patriarchal structures [42].

4   Method

Quantitative and qualitative content analyses were used to put forward the proposed study. Computational methods were used to extract data within a medium-specific approach [43]. Data were selected and extracted from Twitter in the form of tweets using the network analysis and visualization software NodeXL. We collected textual data from Twitter feeds using the search terms "homem" and "velho" (in English: "man" and "old"). We went through the data mining process of data cleaning, focusing on time-lapse 19th August 2019 to 19th November 2019, and deleting accounts with less than 100 followers. We have grouped the remaining 4231 tweets from 3621 users according to four specific categories (Table 1).

Through an intersectional and feminist approach, this study aims to explore how online social media users have been representing older men to identify if these representations promote or hinder gender-equitable and respectful ageing relations. Therefore, the research question that guides this study is: How do Portuguese-speaking online users' representations of men and masculinities interact with age and ageism?

Table 1. Codebook used in the analysis.

Category	Description
Intersecting age and masculinities subscribing to patriarchy and/or ageism	Tweets whose message intersects age and masculinities engaging with patriarchal and/or ageist imaginaries
Intersecting age and masculinities not subscribing to patriarchy nor ageism	Tweets whose message intersect age and masculinities, and do not engage with patriarchy and/or ageist imaginaries
Complexity and non-linearity	Tweets whose message intersect age and masculinities and may contest and subscribe to patriarchy and/or contest and subscribe to ageism
Other	Tweets whose message does not relate to any of the above or was unclear

5 Results and Discussion

Results show that most of the coded texts (84,58%) fall into the category of 'Other' as the majority of the sample tweets included "man" and "old" but did not intersect age and masculinities in their message (Table 2). Most of them refer men and masculinities but whenever the term "old" was used, it was used as an informal/slang interjection. The other categories, although representing a smaller universe concerning the sample (13,6%), are the ones selected to put forward our qualitative analysis. Within these 13,6% which intersected age and masculinities in their messages, 5,29% subscribed to patriarchy and/or ageism, whereas 6,31% did not subscribe to patriarchy and ageism and 2% included messages which may contest and subscribe to patriarchy and/or contest and subscribe to ageism, shedding light on the nonlinearity of the intersection between ageism and patriarchy.

Table 2. The number of tweets according to macro selected categories.

Number of category	Category	Number of tweets	Frequency ($N = 4231$)
1	Intersecting age and masculinities subscribing to patriarchy and/or ageism	**224**	**5,29%**
2	Intersecting age and masculinities not subscribing to patriarchy and/or ageism	**267**	**6,31%**
3	Complexity and non-linearity	**85**	**2%**
4	Other	**3655**	**84,58%**

We grouped tweets according to specific categories (Table 2) and selected the three most shared tweets in each category to analyse through qualitative content analysis in order to unearth social power structures and relations as well as their underpinning imaginaries which are validated and constituted through language as discourse [44]. Within this analytical selection, only four tweets reached more than 100 retweets. These fall into the categories of "Intersecting age and masculinities subscribing to patriarchy and/or ageism" and "Intersecting age and masculinities not subscribing to patriarchy and/or ageism" (Table 3).

Table 3. Three most shared tweets within the three selected categories

Category	Tweet	Retweets
1	"Me: I wanted a sugar daddy; any old men. Old man: Hi! Me: https://t.co/UhlmvOSrBs" [the hyperlink takes the reader to a vine with a young woman running away]	18259
1	Nobody lives on money, man has to have sense. Do you want to parade with a beautiful woman and contribute with nothing? Be selfish and stay with the rich old man, who only has money to offer. If you are not like that, do nothing more than the obligation to help the woman who is with you!	1251
1	My mother has a friend who only has relationships with old men. Her nickname: pussy de Melo nursing home	27
2	Cristiano Ronaldo after turning 30, and playing for the Portugal team: 👕 46 games ⚽ 47 goals THIS MAN IS JUST LIKE WINE: THE OLDER, THE BETTER! PT 🏆 https://t.co/fp91KK3Uz7 [the hyperlink takes the reader to a photo of Cristiano holding a football cup]	226
2	In the approved list, you will find men and women, old and new, single and married, who "only study" and who work, who makes the question before or after, who are rich and poor. The list is heterogeneous. The common point is that everyone studied. So, stop looking at others and do your part	197
2	Older and more experienced men are so good that I have no idea why I keep wasting my time with new blood	47
3	Then the classics return with a single crowd and then you can't complain about this savagery, a bunch of old bearded men fighting among themselves over the football team, what a shame !!! https://t.co/cF8VxdLJes [the hyperlink takes the reader to a video depicting the described scene on a stadium]	6
3	Men will never know what it is like to go out in the street in shorts and have to hear jokes from a bunch of disgusting old men	3
3	I HATE old men, those who are old enough to be my grandfather, who keep looking at me in the middle of the street, and say "pssst", ah f*** you, do "pssst" to your hand mother f****[a]	2

[a]This tweet was edited in order to sidestep offensive language.

In terms of representations of men and masculinities and the way these interact with age and ageism, we have identified three main representations (Table 3). The first one represents men as the "sugar daddy" figure, i.e., a rich older man who offers expensive or extravagant gifts to a much younger woman as a repay for her company or sexual favours. The second one is the idea that individual attributes, such as age, gender, class are not relevant and should not be taken into account. The third one represents men as wicked, harassing and violent. Accordingly, men behave this way as they lack empathy and had never been in the woman's place to understand what it feels like when one's being harassed. These representations also go in line with the idea that these attitudes might be reinforced with age. However, if older men are represented as holding these characteristics in a more evident way, they are also represented as ridiculous since older men are understood as less attractive and less strong but, regardless of those ageing traits, they behave as if they continue at their peak concerning maleness.

6 Conclusions and Limitations

This study intended to explore, through an intersectional and feminist approach, how online social media users have been representing older men in their posts, with the intent to shed light on how these representations promote or hinder gender-equitable and respectful ageing relations. To do so, it sought to answer the following research question: How do Portuguese-speaking online users' representations of men and masculinities interact with age and ageism? Data showed that intersection between masculinities and age among Portuguese speaking twitter users is low concerning the number of times that "men" and "old" are used in the same tweet text. Also, the tweets whose message intersects masculinity and age tend to be equally divided between those that subscribe to patriarchy and ageism and those that do not subscribe (or even implicitly contest) to these systems of social oppression and inequality, shedding light on the fact that both discourses - discriminatory and equalitarian - circulate in the same proportion.

However, as patriarchy and ageism are embedded and pervasive in today's societies, usage of patriarchal and ageist imaginaries surpasses - concerning absorption and validation - in a more effortless way counter-narratives concerning these two systems or the representations they entail. Also, taking into account the rise of the #metoo or #timesup feminist movements which have opened the floor to public discussions and growing awareness on harmful masculinities, representations concerning patriarchy might be produced in a more conscious way that the ones of ageism, which have not had the same political visibility as patriarchy. Data also show that the interaction between patriarchy and age is not necessarily an interaction that mutually reinforces both systems - patriarchy and ageism. In fact, young women holding a subordinate position within patriarchy, and in face of harassment perpetrated by older men - contest patriarchy by recovering ageist imaginaries as, within ageism, they occupy a privileged position vis-à-vis the dominant normative standards. In this context, older men are constructed as meanings by reference not to age per se, but to age in what concerns hegemonic masculinity. This sheds light on the fact that subaltern subjects in a given system can regain power concerning other subjects who occupy a privileged position within that same system through using the imagery of other oppression systems in which the positions of power are reversed.

The main limitations of this study are related to content analysis and the delimitation of the sample by language. Future research will focus on a critical discourse analysis of tweets and retweets, as well as analysis of co-tag networks in order to identify who are the dominant voices and how do the leading hashtags contribute to the construction of discourses and social representations on masculinities and ageing.

The results of this study show that the patriarchal discourses intersect with ageism, perpetuating stereotypes. However, we note that the interaction between patriarchy and ageism is not mutually reinforcing. Future studies should take connective action logic

[45] as a theoretical framework and consider mixed methodologies. Moreover, future studies should also encompass samples of tweets in different languages.

Acknowledgments. This article was financed by national Portuguese funds through FCT (Fundação para a Ciência e a Tecnologia) in the framework of the project "(De)Coding Masculinities: Towards an enhanced understanding of media's role in shaping perceptions of masculinities in Portugal" (Reference PTDC/COM-CSS/31740/2017).

References

1. Laws, G.: Understanding ageism: lessons from feminism and postmodernism. Gerontologist **35**(1), 112–118 (1995)
2. Hearn, J.: Imaging the aging of men. In Featherstone, M., Wernick, A. (eds.) Images of Aging: Cultural Representations of Later Life, pp-97–114. Routledge, London (2005 [1995])
3. Krekula, C., Nikander, P., Wilińska, M.: Multiple marginalizations based on age: gendered ageism and beyond. In: Ayalon, L., Tesch-Römer, C. (eds.) Contemporary Perspectives on Ageism. IPA, vol. 19, pp. 33–50. Springer, Cham (2018). https://doi.org/10.1007/978-3-319-73820-8_3
4. Davis, K., Zarkov, D.: Retrospective on intersectionality. Eur. J. Women's Stud. **13**(3), 1–8 (2017)
5. Center for Women's Global Leadership: A Women's Human Rights Approach to the World Conference Against Racism. http://www.cwgl.rutgers.edu/globalcenter/policy/gcpospaper.html. Accessed 21 Jan 2020
6. Hearn, J., Melechi, A.: The Transatlantic Gaze: Masculinities, Youth and the American Imaginary.age, Thousand Oaks (1992)
7. Connell, R.W., Messerschmidt, J.W.: Hegemonic masculinity: rethinking the concept. Gender Soc. **19**(6), 829–859 (2005)
8. Connell, R.W.: Masculinities, 2nd edn. University of California Press, Berkeley (1995)
9. Connell, R.W.: Masculinities, 2nd edn. University of California Press, Berkeley (2005)
10. Galtung, J.: Peace by Peaceful Means: Peace and Conflict, Development and Civilization, vol. 14. Sage, Thousand Oaks (1996)
11. Januário, S.B.: Masculinidades em (re) construção: Gênero, Corpo e Publicidade. LabCom. IFP, Covilhã (2016)
12. Femiano, S., Nickerson, M.: How do media images of men affect our lives? http://www.medialit.org/reading_room/article39.html. Accessed 21 Jan 2020
13. Katz, J., Earp, J.: Tough Guise: Violence, Media & the Crisis in Masculinity. Media Education Foundation, Northampton (1999)
14. Heilman, B., Barker, G., Harrison, A.: The Man Box: A Study on Being a Young Man in the US, UK, and Mexico. Promundo, London (2017)
15. Boni, F.: Framing media masculinities: men's lifestyle magazines and the biopolitics of the male body. Eur. J. Commun. **17**(4), 465–478 (2002)
16. Itzin, C., Phillipson, C.: Age Barriers at Work. METRA, London (1993)
17. Itzin, C., Phillipson, C.: Gendered ageism: a double jeopardy for women in organisations. In: Itzin, C., Phillipson, C. (eds.) Gender, Culture and Organisational Change. Putting Theory Into Practice, pp. 84–94. Routledge, London (1995)
18. Daniel, F., Antunes, A., Amaral, I.: Representações sociais da velhice. Análise. Psicológica **33**(3), 291–301 (2015)

19. Wilińska, M., de Hontheim, A., Anbäcken, E.-M.: Ageism in a cross-cultural perspective: reflections from the research field. In: Ayalon, L., Tesch-Römer, C. (eds.) Contemporary Perspectives on Ageism. IPA, vol. 19, pp. 425–440. Springer, Cham (2018). https://doi.org/10.1007/978-3-319-73820-8_26

20. Barrett, A.E., Naiman-Sessions, M.: 'It's our turn to play': performance of girlhood as a collective response to gendered ageism. Ageing Soc. **36**(04), 764–784 (2015)

21. Krekula, C.: The intersection of age and gender: reworking gender theory and social gerontology. Curr. Sociol. **55**(2), 155–171 (2007)

22. Richardson, M.J.: Embodied intergenerationality: family position, place and masculinity. Gender Place Cult. **22**(2), 157–171 (2015)

23. Amaral, I., Santos, S.J., Daniel, F., Filipe, F.: (In)visibilities of men and aging in the media: discourses from Germany and Portugal. In: Zhou, J., Salvendy, G. (eds.) HCII 2019. LNCS, vol. 11593, pp. 20–32. Springer, Cham (2019). https://doi.org/10.1007/978-3-030-22015-0_2

24. Wilińska, M.: Because women will always be women and men are just getting older: intersecting discourses of ageing and gender. Current Soc. **58**(6), 879–896 (2010)

25. Butler, J.: Gender Trouble: Feminism and the Subversion of Identity. Routledge, New York (1990)

26. Wills, D., Reeves, S.: Facebook as a political weapon: information in social networks. Br. Polit. **4**(2), 265–281 (2009)

27. Loader, B.D.: Social movements and new media. Sociol. Compass **2**(6), 1920–1933 (2008)

28. Bimber, B.: Three prompts for collective action in the context of digital media. Polit. Commun. **34**(1), 6–20 (2017)

29. Chadwick, A.: The Hybrid Media System: Politics and Power. Oxford University Press, Oxford (2017)

30. Trentham, B., Sokoloff, S., Tsang, A., Neysmith, S.: Social media and senior citizen advocacy: an inclusive tool to resist ageism? Polit. Groups Identities **3**(3), 558–571 (2015)

31. Aroldi, P.: Generational belonging between media audiences and ICT users. In: Colombo, F., Fortunati, L. (eds.) Broadband Society and Generational Changes, pp. 51–68. Peter Lang, Frankfurt am Main (2011)

32. Aroldi, P., Colombo, F.: Questioning 'digital global generations'. A critical approach. In: Northern Lights: Film & Media Studies Yearbook, vol. 11, no. 1, pp. 175–190 (2013)

33. Napoli, A.: Social media use and generational identity: issues and consequences on peer-to-peer and cross-generational relationships - an empirical study. Particip. J. Audience Recept. Stud. **11**(2), 182–206 (2014)

34. boyd, D.: Social network sites as networked publics: affordances, dynamics, and implications. In: Papacharissi, Z. (ed.) A Networked Self: Identity, Community, and Culture in Social Network Sites, pp. 39–58, Routledge, New York (2011)

35. Comunello, F., Fernández Ardèvol, M., Mulargia, S., Belotti, F.: Women, youth and everything else: age-based and gendered stereotypes in relation to digital technology among elderly Italian mobile phone users. Media Cult. Soc. **39**(6), 798–815 (2017)

36. Amaral, I., Brites, M.J.: Trends on the digital uses and generations. In: Proceedings of INTED2019 Conference, pp. 5109–5115. INTED, Valencia (2019)

37. Loos, E., Haddon, L., Mante-Meijer, E.: Generational Use of New Media. Routledge, London and New York (2016)

38. Amaral, I., Daniel, F.: The use of social media among senior citizens in Portugal: active ageing through an intergeneration approach. In: Zhou, J., Salvendy, G. (eds.) ITAP 2018. LNCS, vol. 10926, pp. 422–434. Springer, Cham (2018). https://doi.org/10.1007/978-3-319-92034-4_32

39. Abad Alcalá, L.: Media literacy for older people facing the digital divide: the e-inclusion programmes design. Comunicar **22**(1), 173–180 (2014)

40. Loureiro, A., Barbas, M.: Active ageing – enhancing digital literacies in elderly citizens. In: Zaphiris, P., Ioannou, A. (eds.) LCT 2014. LNCS, vol. 8524, pp. 450–459. Springer, Cham (2014). https://doi.org/10.1007/978-3-319-07485-6_44
41. Schäffer, B.: The digital literacy of seniors. Res. Comp. Int. Educ. 2(1), 29–42 (2007)
42. Amaral, I., Santos, S.J., Brites, M.J.: Mapping Intergenerational Masculinities on Instagram (in press)
43. Rogers, R.: Digital Methods. MIT Press, Cambridge (2013)
44. Fairclough, N.: Media Discourse. Edward Arnold, London (1995)
45. Bennett, W.L., Segerberg, A.: The logic of connective action: digital media and the personalization of contentious politics. Inf. Commun. Soc. 15(5), 739–768 (2012)

Intergenerational Social Media Use: Expectations of Adults and Elder Users

Nicoletta Vittadini[✉]

Università Cattolica del Sacro Cuore, Largo Gemelli, 1, 20123 Milan, Italy
nicoletta.vittadini@unicatt.it

Abstract. Since their origins, social media have been used by people belonging to different generations. The paper will describe how different generations use social media and is based on a review of literature and research projects. Observing social media users from a generational point of view allows to understand the different imaginations, interpretations of the platforms that each generation has developed and which often translate into different uses and processes of mutual adaptation. Furthermore, the generational post of view allows to understand how social media are used as a stage on which different generational identities are expressed and challenged through new forms of generational narratives. Narratives that allow generations to co-built each other through mutual representations.

Keywords: Social media · Generations · Narratives · Age cohorts

1 Introduction

Since their origins, social media has been used by people of different age cohorts.

Also in the auroral phase of their development, social media used mainly by teenagers (*LiveJournal* spread mainly among American teenagers) coexist with platforms used by young adults (*Friendster* in its first development phase) and by adults belonging to ethnic-cultural communities (*Blackplanet, AsianAvenue* and *MiGente*).

The success among the teenagers and young people of *MySpace*, in the following years, and the birth of *Facebook* in a youthful context such as that of the university campuses, contributed to the construction of an image of social media as a platform used above all by young people. Several studies have addressed the relationship between adolescents, young people and social media with respect to the motivations and practices of use [11], to the processes of building the identity [12, 17], to the risks and opportunities associated with self-expression and the disclosure of one's intimacy [13, 25].

In the expansion phase of social media (2003–2006), the success of *Twitter* and *Linkedin*, the birth of *Reddit*, a news sharing platform, the appropriation of *Flickr* by photography enthusiasts of all age groups - just to name a few examples - testify to a progressive expansion of users towards more adult age groups.

Starting from the expansion phase [40] social media are used by people who belong to different age cohorts that communicate, meet and sometimes collide through mediated conversations.

© Springer Nature Switzerland AG 2020
Q. Gao and J. Zhou (Eds.): HCII 2020, LNCS 12209, pp. 101–113, 2020.
https://doi.org/10.1007/978-3-030-50232-4_8

The co-presence of different age cohorts is particularly evident in countries where the appropriation of social media took place a little later in time.

In Italy, for example, social media began to be significant from 2007 [31]. *Twitter* begins to spread to a small circle of techno-fans more than teenagers [32]. Users are predominantly adults and immediately include public and information-related personalities (in 2007 it was the first twitter of a politician: Walter Veltroni). *Facebook* reaches the first million users in 2008 and among these, there is a more mature age group than in other geographical contexts. Among the 31 million active users on Facebook in Italy, the most represented age cohorts are, in fact, those between 25 and 44 with an increasing presence (in addition to young people) also of users among 45 and 54 years [43].

This does not mean that Italian teenagers and young people do not use social media. *Instagram*, in 2019, has an audience for more than half under 35 years with a prevalence of the range between 19 and 24 years [16]. Even in countries where the use of social media continues to be a privilege by the younger cohort of the population, such as in the United States, the co-presence of users belonging to different age groups is a matter of fact. According to the data released in 2019 by the Pew Research Center [33] even if the age group that uses the most social media remains that between 18 and 29 years (90%) users between 30 and 49 years have definitely grown (82%) and over 65 are 40%.

The presence of different age cohorts among network users has some significant implications.

The most immediate is that users are going through different phases of the life cycle (who is a student, who is a young worker, who has just built their own family and has young children etc.) characterized by different information and relationship needs.

The second is that users belong to different generations from a cultural point of view.

Observing social media users from a generational point of view allows us to understand the different imaginations, interpretations of the platforms that each generation has developed and which often translate into different uses and processes of mutual adaptation.

2 The Usefulness of the Concept of Generation

The term generation has often been associated with the use of media and, in recent years, with that of digital technologies.

An obvious example is the expression "digital generation" or "net generation" [39] which often occurs in social, public and private discourses, to indicate young people born and raised with digital media and the psychological and behavioral dispositions they share. The assumption is that some technological innovations determine the attitudes and behaviors of a particular age cohort.

The technologies have also been considered responsible for the changes that occur between one generation and another.

For example, Marc Prensky when distinguishing between digital natives and digital immigrants [35] states that the advent and the diffusion of digital technologies have been an element of discontinuity so radical as to produce a generational change. Those who have not experienced discontinuity, but who have always lived surrounded by technology, are defined (by analogy with the learning of language and culture) digital natives. They are opposed to immigrants, forced by the advent of digital technologies to learn a new language and culture.

The generational approach to social media, however, can help understand even more.

First what happens when different generations use the same platforms, bringing with them different imagery, expectations and uses. Second how several generations use social media to tell each other their identity and, therefore, build their identity towards each other.

Belonging to a generation, therefore, is something more complex than being born in the same years and being in a similar stage of life. The definition of this complexity starts from Karl Mannheim, who first systematized the concept of generation in the context of sociological studies [26].

According to Mannheim, a generation is formed when people who occupy the same historical position share a generational link thanks to three processes: they share the same experiences, are identified as a generation and identify themselves as a generation [10, 26]. Sharing the same experiences means that in the crucial years of their training (identifiable between the ages of 16 and 25) individuals belonging to the same generation share some common experiences. This may be the collapse of the Twin Towers in New York which constitutes an event shared generationally by those who were going through the training phase in 2001. Or again of the fall of the Berlin wall in 1989 when the members of the so-called Generation X were going through their training phase.

Not only dramatic events contribute to the formation of a generation. The media landscape that each generation experiences in the formative years (which is the way it comes in contact with world events) also contributes to forming the generation; as well as many other experiences related to daily life (the forms of meeting with others, fun and so on).

Sharing the same experiences would not be enough, however, to form a generation capable of being recognized and recognizable. Mannheim writes in fact "Not the fact of being born at the same time chronologically, of becoming young, adults and old at the same time constitutes the common place in the social space, but the possibility linked to it to participate in the same events and contents of life and above all, to be exposed to the same ways of stratifying consciousness" [26]. Mannheim specifies the concept of "stratification of consciousness" defining it as that set of principles of interpretation that allow the individual to face new events and sensations in a way largely predetermined by the generational group [26]. It is, therefore, a "background of homogeneous philosophical, social and cultural guidelines" for a generation [23].

These principles of interpretation and action have also been recognized as similar to the habitus described by Bourdieu as a set of values, ideals, constellations of tastes and sensitivities [10] that characterizes a social group. Or even to a Gestalt: a peculiar way of perceiving, interpreting and evaluating historical and cultural phenomena [1].

So a generation elaborates, starting from the experiences it shares (at different levels), principles of interpretation and evaluation of world events, values and ideals, together with tastes and preferences that constitute its cultural identity [18]. Corsten [15] uses the expression "generational semantics" that can be defined as a set of themes, interpretative models, evaluation principles and linguistic tools through which shared experience is transformed into discourse in the context of forms of daily interaction.

Cultural identity and generational semantics are the elements that make one generation recognizable from the others. For example, a generation after the war, or a generation of Baby Boomers, or a Generation X, or Millennials each characterized by its own cultural identity.

The construction of the cultural identity of a generation does not end, then, with the training phase, but continues through what generations narrate about themselves in a process that has been defined as generationing and which we can translate as "formation of a generation" [37, 38, 41].

The process of forming a generation would not be complete if there were not one last fundamental step for its definition and for its very existence: the fact that its own members identify themselves as a generation.

A generation exists, if there is also a sense of conscious and shared belonging that has been defined as generational we sense [14, 15]. This belonging is basically built through two processes: the storytelling of a generation and the construction of a generational collective memory. We find literary and cinematographic examples of generational narration [30], for example, Generation X by Douglas Coupland, obviously for the X generation. On the level of collective memory, on the other hand, acts the mutual confirmation through commemorative rituals (inside and outside the media) of the events that characterized the training phase.

The cultural approach to generations described is not a deterministic approach in which technological innovations determine the formation and forms of a generation. Rather, it is an approach in which people interpret the generation, contribute to modeling it and also to form individual generational units within it (the expression is always from Mannheim) which particularly outline the common characteristics of a generation. This differentiation may depend on the place where you live or have lived (near or far from the development of great historical events, as may be the case with the years of terrorism in Italy seen differently in large cities or small towns). Or it can depend on the socio-cultural conditions in which the training phase was carried out.

Which are the forms of the relationship between social media and generations?

As mentioned at the beginning of the paper, social media are now used by people belonging to different generations. For some generations, they have contributed in an essential way to connote the media landscape in which the years of training took place, the way in which they learned the news of the important events. For the other generations, they have been a medium to be imagined and used starting from a generational approach already formed and therefore conceived, used and imagined starting from different cultural identities.

Finally, for everyone, they are a tool through which to talk about oneself, continue to build the generational we sense and observe and tell other generations.

We'll focus on the second and third level: how different generations imagine and use social media starting from a generational approach and how social media can be a stage to perform generational identities.

3   The Generational Appropriation of Social Media

Social media, in their current configuration, are characterized by the coexistence of several generations. Each of them uses social media starting from a different generational semantics that includes a different approach to the media and technological innovation.

The studies on generations, in fact, have highlighted how generational belonging contributes to shape media-related processes of meaning construction (in this process the meaning attributed to media technologies, as well as their contents, must be included). According to Mannheim all media experiences will be oriented by the media grammar learned in the training phase so that each new medium that an individual will encounter will be read through the grammar of what might be called the "native media" [26].

More specifically "the media technologies (as well as their contents) encountered during the years of youth training can be considered the media that will form the subsequent media experiences" [10]. "The early acquisition of the awareness of a particular medium continues to shape the worldview of individuals even when, later on, they acquire awareness of new media" [20].

People belonging to different generations imagine, interpret and use social media starting from different "spaces of possibilities" that depend on the media grammars they learned first.

The type of medium that characterized the training phase was used to distinguish several media generations: the radio generation; the generation of black and white television; the generation of the Internet. We can also talk about media generations not in relation to a single medium, but in relation to the influence of the totality of the media landscape that they experienced in the training phase. For example a generation of the mass media, a digital generation and an intermediate generation called intermediate or buffer generation [28] grown with the mass media but which has gradually incorporated digital media [22].

Moreover, it is possible to identify some specific characteristics of the attitude towards the media of different generations. Characteristics that help to define the attitude that the same generation has towards the new media that it encounters in its biographical experience [42].

In this regard, we consider the following generations that didn't grow up with social media[1]:

- Post-war generation made up of subjects born between 1940 and 1952 who went through the training phase between the 1950s and 1960s.
- Generation of baby boomers made up of subjects born between 1953 and 1965 who went through the training phase between the sixties and seventies.

---

[1] Since the distinction between generations is affected by the cultural context in which they were formed, we take up the distinction relating to Italian generations proposed by Aroldi [2] in the volume Media e generations in Italian society. The only variation is that the term Neo will not be used for the generation born between the mid-sixties and the end of the seventies, but that of Generation X. The choice of the term Neo, in fact, is linked to the particular experiences that this generation he lived with respect to the evolution of the Italian television system. Although crucial in defining generations of television users, it seemed more appropriate to adopt a broader definition in this context.

- Generation X composed of subjects born between 1966 and 1978 and who went through their training phase between the eighties and nineties.

These different generations encountered, in their training phase, different types of media and experience a fresh contact with different technologies and media repertoires.

Each generation then had the opportunity to meet digital media in a different phase of its biographical pathway and associated with distinct values[2].

Both of these aspects have helped to mark their path towards social media.

The post-war generation, for example, in its training phase, experienced a fresh contact with the television medium, with vinyl records as a home entertainment tool and with the telephone in the home. In the media landscape, radio is present, as well as printed paper, but it is now naturalized media. The media repertoires that are included in the generational memories are concentrated on television programs and theater, films and actors [36].

The post-war generation has experienced a relationship with the media characterized by the presence of public institutions, national broadcasters, responsible for the production and distribution of information, educational and entertainment content. This generation experienced the advent of digital technologies in the 1980s as a transformation linked to professional activities. An innovation-driven from above, if not imposed, and characterized by specific careers. An innovation that has changed some professional routines and that has been associated with the perception of a state of perennial youth and acceptance of innovation [6].

Therefore, technological innovation is perceived as a necessary discontinuity and to which it is necessary (even if not natural) to adapt also in order not to be excluded from intergenerational relationships with which they do not want to perceive discontinuity [4].

Even in the relationship with social media, this generational semantics is reproduced by pushing the adoption of technological innovations in order not to remain excluded from intergenerational communication, but with a focus on social media as a place of relationship with institutions, as a public and collective space, as an opportunity to find information and news.

The generation of boomers in its training phase has experimented with fresh contact with some innovations related to the television medium: the advent of color and the multiplication of broadcasters (especially radio). From the point of view of routines, they are the first generation for which television is a familiar element, an integral part of the home and which contributes to organizing daily activities by offering fixed and recurring appointments [3].

The television became more personalized, for example through the presence of programs for children and teenagers. The media repertoires that belong to their generational

---

[2] These observations refer to the Italian context and are not applicable to the global scenario, but only to European countries where media innovations have had similar timelines. However, the following analysis can be replicable in different countries according with the different media innovation timeline.

memories are often characterized by the presence of events and programs aimed explicitly at them as targets [3], as well as being characterized by a sense of social, political and cultural belonging [4].

The popularization of audio recording tools has promoted a production activity aimed at entertainment and shared in order to build and maintain social networks. Examples are the recording of audio cassettes containing personalized musical repertoires (taken from radio programming). The ability to produce videos is also more generalized, albeit at an amateur level, and thus the creation of mimeographs often linked to political activity [4]. In its training phase, the boomers generation also experimented with fresh contact with video games and interactivity.

Boomers experience the opportunity to be productive and interactive, and they closely link productivity with belonging (often exhibited) or with building social networks.

The generation of boomers places digital technologies in the wake of innovation that characterized the media in their training period in which videogames, music recording tools appeared and associates them with sharing practices and shared cultural consumption that has characterized their peer groups. Digital media entered directly into their homes without necessarily passing through professional spaces first [6] and often saw technologies in their nascent phase [4].

So the contact with technological innovations is not traumatic for boomers, indeed is perceived as necessary [27] and is perceived as the meeting with new expressive tools aimed at self-realization or at entertainment [6]. They often perceive themselves as pioneers in the use of digital technologies [4].

The relationship of boomers with social media is marked by what has been experienced in their training phase. Social media are perceived as platforms where they have to be and are perceived as a medium for content searching and consumption (for example, information provided by institutional sources), but also of production. Their productivity is often linked to the performance of a cultural, political belonging, largely related to the public social dimension. The exchange of information and content referred to the private sphere is largely characterized by the construction of social, local, cultural memberships and the construction and maintenance of social networks that support them.

Productivity and public dimension, exchange and private dimension are therefore characteristics through which this generation imagines social media.

Generation X has experimented in its training phase the fresh contact with the multiplicity of channels and broadcasters, the birth of thematic broadcasters (such as music TV channels), the marketing of television production and distribution with the consequent important role covered by advertising communication [4]. The relationship with the television medium is, therefore, experienced above all through the possibility of enjoying forms of entertainment less and less linked to culture and information. Furthermore, these are increasingly personalized forms of use through the use of video recorders and the first DVD players.

In their generational media repertoires, cartoons for Japanese-made kids dominate, the TV series and significantly the brands conveyed by advertising communication and considered an element of generational identification [36].

Generation X also experiences fresh contact with technological innovation in its training phase through the spread of personal computers, the Internet, the development of web 1.0 and search engines. Generation X is, therefore, the first that has experimented - with the internet - the reconfiguration of the perception of space and of the relationships between geographical and social distances [7].

It is also the first generation that has experimented with the use of mobile media through the walkman and the first mobile phones. This use is associated with the idea of individual possession of the media reproduction devices and their portability (the audio tape player to listen to music) as well as the medium (the recorded cassette). Overall, this is a generation that has been able to experience digital innovation as an introjected and naturalized aspect of everyday life [4]. It incorporated personalization, portability and connection as natural media elements. For this generation, social media is an innovation that presents many elements of continuity with those already naturalized in the daily experience; for example, the use of the computer to connect to their networks, access to applications and services.

The particular configuration of the media space during the phase of their formation promotes the use of social media as an entertainment tool and also the construction of their profile has a strong hedonic component. Social media are used as a tool to use and share media content. Personalization in building the network of friends as well as in accessing ones favorite sources of information is a dominant element in the perception of the added value of social media (my friends, my sources and so on).

The possibility of receiving individual and customized answers from the institutions or sources of information within social media constitutes another important aspect for Generation X. Finally, the presence of brands within the platforms is not only naturalized, but also is sought as the possibility of establishing a personal, interactive and direct relationship.

The research results presented allows us to describe how three different imaginaries of the same platforms are present, which we could synthetically describe as:

- for the post-war generation, social media are platforms whose adoption is compulsory and which allow access to information and content conveyed by institutional subjects or communication between peers in a public space;
- for boomers, social media are platforms whose adoption is in line with being pioneers of the use of digital technologies. Social media allow the production of contents and their exchange within the networks in order to share a generational political, cultural or local belonging;
- for Generation X, social networks are platforms whose adoption is natural and which allow access to (entertainment) contents and personalized social networks or to maintain direct and personal relationships with institutions, brands or associations that fall within their sphere of interest.

Within these general positions, there are always forms of appropriation and use of different social media according to the different generational units.

4 Social Media as a Stage: The Generational We Sense

In describing the formation of the generations, it has been said that a generation exists if there is a conscious sense of belonging and shared generational we sense [2–15].

It has also been said that this sense of belonging is built through the self-narrative of a generation and the construction of a generational collective memory. The media play an essential role in building this sense of generational belonging since they are the tools through which the narratives of shared experience, of common generational semantics, are conveyed [15]. These narratives support the construction of a generational awareness since they provide people belonging to the same generation with stories in which to recognize themselves individually and as part of a wider social subject.

The diffusion of generational narratives through the media is not only functional to the consolidation of the identity of a generation but also has the function of allowing the mutual recognition of generations [1]. That is, the media narratives that describe a generation mean that other generations can recognize it, give it an identity and possibly define itself by difference.

Finally, the media are also the tool through which collective memory is consolidated. Precisely for this reason, Eyerman and Turner [19] speak of it as one of the elements through which generations institutionalize themselves and Aroldi and Colombo affirm "generations are built through the institutionalization of their collective memory through shared ritual narratives" [5].

The different generations, forming and consolidating themselves in contact with different media systems, have (or privilege) different tools to build their own generational narratives. For example, the generation of Boomers has entrusted the public expression of their generational narratives (elaborated internally through word of mouth) to the press, cinema and television through informants or cultural leaders who have produced generational discourses from within the media system.

However, as the process of we sense building continues throughout the lifetime of generations, these can also use new tools to build narratives or to consolidate collective memory.

We observe, therefore, a double level of interaction between the media and generations: generations have privileged narrative models linked to the media world that they have experienced in the training phase and, simultaneously, digital media can host narratives of different generations. Generations can also use social media to build generational narratives or to consolidate collective memory.

As Papacharissi says, social media offer the generations structures of the story: "textures, shades, models of speech and narrative modalities" and "each artifact tells a story. Each generation has stories to tell. The stories we tell help us build meanings along the way" [29].

Social media are spaces characterized by widespread productivity. Each user is able to produce, share and contribute to the construction of conversations. As Boccia Artieri [9] states, they are spaces characterized by the mass social production of contents. Generational contents are self-produced by a multiplicity of subjects belonging to different generations who do not have the status of privileged subjects with respect to the media system (such as writers or directors) who take on the burden of telling a story.

Social media makes generational narratives more similar to a flow of word of mouth within generations mediated by the widespread production of content. This flow, before the spread of social media, was still present and constituted a sort of preparatory path with respect to the construction of the narratives, which did not acquire a media visibility. It was a sort of background of generational narratives. Through social media, this preparatory flow acquires immediate social visibility. Even if, as Kortti [24] says, social media offer symbolic spaces in which even generational leaders and elites can make themselves visible to define their own generation.

Generational narratives circulate within social media in the form of generational content (fragments made up of single posts, shares, user-generated contents) that can be recomposed. The specificity of social media also lies in the form of these narratives. As Boccia Artieri states, they are "generational narratives made of conversations" [8] that do not often translate into a closed-form of story, but remain widespread in the discursive flows of users and, when they consolidate, take the form of page or group or hashtag [29].

Generational narratives are co-constructed according to the production logic that characterizes social media, in which different people belonging to the same generation and who perform different functions (ordinary people, journalists, project managers, institutions) contribute to the construction of the generational narration.

The sharing of images, audiovisual texts and fragments that have a symbolic value for a generation are also part of these conversations. Social media make available very large archives of fragments (images, videos) of media products and user-generated content that can be reused in the context of building a generational narrative. These are fragments that describe the generation or that are taken as a symbol by a generation. Self-narrations and hetero-narrations are mixed in a sharing activity that contributes, as part of an overall exchange logic, to the consolidation of relations between members of the same generation.

The size of the archives available to users (for example, through YouTube) gives persistence and searchability [11] to the elements of generational memory. The elements of generational memory can be easily found within a sort of database of the collective imagination [27]. In this database, however, fragments of the imagination of different generations are present, offering access to mixed repertoires that belong to different generations and can be mixed in the context of stories in which the same memorial elements converge with different symbolic values [1]. The same media products, in some cases, are re-contextualized in the memories of different generations who may have enjoyed them through different channels: television, cinema but also downloading or streaming online. Even the memories related to historical events can be re-contextualized in different generational narratives thanks to memes or collective forms of remembrance that are updated in online communication.

Generational narratives that are co-constructed online through the production of content or the sharing of fragments and which stabilize in the form of the hashtag pages, therefore, combine generational and intergenerational repertoires.

Social media can host different generational narratives that help define by difference the generations. They mix narratives of generations about themselves and narrations of generations about other generations (older or younger) [1, 21]. Thus different generational identities can be expressed and challenged, co-built each other through mutual representations and the production of social discourses [18, p. 8]. It is above all the most institutionalized generations, such as the post war or boomers, who are looking for an intergenerational audience to tell. Often these stories are triggered by the sharing of fragments of memory of collective biographical experiences (concert tickets, school photos etc.) [27].

5   Conclusion

The relationship between social media and generations goes beyond a simple defining mechanism, as in the case of the expression "digital natives" or "net generation".

It is not possible to imagine social media as a purely generational medium. Social media enable intra and intergenerational communication. People belonging to different generations communicate with each other and with younger or older people.

Above all, however, each generation ends up imagining and appropriating social media on the basis of its own generational semantics, its own system of expectations, values, practices that were formed and consolidated during their formation. Thus, more institutional approaches are combined with more playful approaches, communication activities perceived as public and others perceived as private. On this topic, future research projects may lead to a greater awareness of the richness of perspectives that coexist inside the social platforms.

Finally, social media are an additional stage on which perform generational narratives. Fundamental stories for building the self-consciousness of belonging to a generation. These are streams of conversations that consolidate in the form of the hashtag or the page. They are co-built both because they collect fragments produced by multiple people, and because they integrate media fragments and user-generated contents. They are inter-generational because they allow different generations to tell each other, to be told and to be defined as such by identity or difference.

References

1. Aroldi, P.: Generational belonging between media audiences and ICT users. In: Colombo, F., Fortunati, L. (eds.) Broadband Society and Generational Changes, pp. 51–67. Peter Lang, Frankfurt (2011)
2. Aroldi, P.: Ripensare il rapporto tra media e generazioni: concetti, indicatori, modelli. In: Colombo, F., Boccia, Artieri G., Del Grosso Destreri, L., Pasquali, F., Sorice, M. (eds.) Media e generazioni nella società italiana, pp. 33–64. FrancoAngeli, Milano (2012)
3. Aroldi, P.: Ricezione televisiva ed esperienze generazionali. Il caso dei boomer italiani. In: Garofalo, D., Roghi, V. (eds.) Televisione. Storia immaginario memoria, pp. 185–201. Rubbettino Editore, Soveria Mannelli (2015)
4. Aroldi, P., Colombo, F. (eds.): Successi culturali e pubblici generazionali. RTI, Milano (2007)
5. Aroldi, P., Colombo, F.: Questioning "digital global generations". A critical approach. In: Northern Lights: Film and Media Studies Yearbook, vol. 11, pp. 175–190 (2013)
6. Aroldi, P., Ponte, C.: Adolescents of the 1960s and 1970s: an Italian-Portuguese comparison between two generations of audiences. Cyberpsychol. J. Psychos. Res. Cyberspace 6(2), (2012). https://cyberpsychology.eu/article/view/4268/3307
7. Beck, U., Beck-Gernsheim, E.: Global generations and the trap of methodological nationalism for a cosmopolitan turn in the sociology of youth and generation. Eur. Sociol. Rev. 25(1), 25–36 (2008)

8. Boccia Artieri, G.: Generational "we sense" in the networked space. User generated representation of the youngest generation. In: Colombo, F., Fortunati, L. (eds.) Broadband Society and Generational Changes, pp. 109–120. Peter Lang, Frankfurth (2011)

9. Boccia Artieri, G.: Stati di Connessione: pubblici, cittadini e consumatori nella (social) network society. Franco Angeli, Milano (2012)

10. Bolin, G.: Media Generations. Routledge, Abingdon (2017)

11. Boyd, D.: Why youth (love) social network sites; the role of networked publics in teenage social life. In: Buckingham, D. (ed.) Youth Identity and Digital Media, pp. 119–142. MIT Press, Cambridge (2008)

12. Boyd, D., Heer, J.: Profiles as conversation: networked identity performance on Friendster. In: Proceedings of the 39th Annual Hawaii International Conference on System Sciences HICSS 2006 (2006)

13. Boyd, D., Marwick, A.: Social privacy in networked publics: teens' attitudes, practices, and strategies. In: A Decade in Internet Time: Symposium on the Dynamics of the Internet and Society, Berkley (CA), 2 September (2011). https://ssrn.com/abstract=1925128

14. Bude, H.: Die Wir-Schicht der Generation. Berliner Journal für Soziologie 7, 197–204 (1997)

15. Corsten, M.: The time of generations. Time Soc. 8(2), 249–272 (1999)

16. Cosenza, V.: Osservatorio social media. https://vincos.it/osservatorio-facebook/. Accessed 15 Jan 2020

17. Davis, J.: Architecture of the personal interactive homepage: constructing the self through MySpace. New Media Soc. 12(7), 1103–1119 (2010)

18. Edmunds, J., Turner, B.S.: Generations, Culture and Society. Open University Press, Buckingham and Philadelphia (2002)

19. Eyerman, R., Turner, B.S.: Outline of a Theory of Generations. Eur. J. Soc. Theory 1(1), 91–106 (1998)

20. Gumpert, G., Cathcart, R.: Media grammars, generations, and media gaps. Crit. Stud. Mass Commun. 2(1), 23–35 (1985)

21. Hartmann, M.: The Web Generation: the (de)construction of users, morals and consumption. SMIT-VUB, Free University of Brussels (2003)

22. Hepp, A., Berg, M., Roitsch, C.: Mediatized worlds of communitization: young people as localists, centrists, multi-localists and pluralists. In: Hepp, A., Krotz, F. (eds.) Mediatized Worlds: Culture and Society in a Media Age, pp. 174–203. Palgrave Macmillan, Basingstoke (2014)

23. Jaeger, H.: Generations in history. Reflections on a controversial concept. Hist. Theory 24(3), 273–292 (1985)

24. Kortti, J.: The problem of generation and media history. In: Colombo, F., Fortunati, L. (eds.) Broadband Society and Generational Changes, pp. 69–94. Peter Lang, Frankfurt (2011)

25. Livingstone, S.: Taking risky opportunities in youthful content creation: teenagers' use of social networking sites for intimacy, privacy and self-expression. New Media Soc. 10(3), 393–411 (2008)

26. Mannheim, K.: Das Problem der Generationen. Kölner Vierteljahreshefte für Soziologie 7(2), 157–185 (1928)

27. Napoli, A.: Social media use and generational identity: issues and consequences on peer-to-peer and cross-generational relationships–an empirical study. Particip. J. Audience Recept. Stud. 11(2), 182–206 (2014)

28. Opermann, S.: Understanding changing news media use: generations and their media vocabulary. In: Northern Lights: Film & Media Studies Yearbook, vol. 11, no. 1, pp. 123–146 (2013)

29. Papacharissi, Z.: Affective Publics: Sentiment, Technology, and Politics. Oxford University Press, Oxford (2015)

30. Pasquali, F.: Ritorno al Futuro, generazioni letterarie e racconti di generazione. Media e immaginario letterario dagli anni Ottanta a oggi (e viceversa). In: Colombo, F., Boccia Artieri, G., Del Grosso Destrieri, L., Pasquali, F., Sorice, M. (eds.) Media e generazioni nella società italiana, pp. 143–162. Franco Angeli, Milano (2012)
31. Pasquali, F., Scifo, B., Vittadini, N.: From modems to social media and from mobiles to smartphones. The history of digital communications in Italy. In: Colombo, F. (ed.) Media and Communication in Italy: Historical and Theoretical Perspectives, pp. 241–255. Vita e Pensiero, Milano (2019)
32. Peeters, B.: First State of the Italian Twittosphere. Twitterfacts, 7 May (2017). http://twitterfacts.blogspot.com/2007/05/first-state-of-italian-twitosphere.html. Accessed 30 Jan 2020
33. Pew Research Center: Social Media Fact Sheet, 12 June (2019). https://www.pewresearch.org/internet/fact-sheet/social-media/. Accessed 30 Jan 2020
34. Pilcher, J.: Mannheim's sociology of generations: an undervalued legacy. Br. J. Sociol. **45**, 481–495 (1994)
35. Prensky, M.: Digital natives, digital immigrants part 1. Horizon **9**(5), 1–6 (2001)
36. Rossi, L., Stefanelli, M.: I Media per raccontarsi e raccontarsela: L'indagine empirica tra vissuti e discorsi. In: Colombo, F., Boccia Artieri, G., Del Grosso Destreri, L., Pasquali, F., Sorice, M. (eds.) Media e generazioni nella società italiana, pp. 71–99. Franco Angeli, Milano (2012)
37. Siibak, A., Vittadini, N.: Editorial: introducing four empirical examples of the "generationing" process. Cyberpsychol. J. Psychosoc. Res. Cyberspace **6**(2) (2012). https://cyberpsychology.eu/article/view/4269/3308. Accessed 30 Jan 2020
38. Siibak, A., Vittadini, N., Nimrod, G.: Generations as media audiences: an introduction. Participations **2**, 100–107 (2014)
39. Tapscott, D.: Growing Up Digital: The Rise of the Net Generation. McGraw-Hill, New York (1998)
40. Vittadini, N.: Social media studies. I social media alla soglia della maturità. Franco Angeli, Milano (2018)
41. Vittadini, N., Siibak, A., Reifova, I., Bilandzic, H.: Generations and media: the social construction of generational identity and differences. In: Carpentier, N., Schrøder, K.C., Hallet, L. (eds.) Audience Transformations. Shifting Audience Positions in Late Modernity, pp. 65–81. Routledge, New York (2013)
42. Volkmer, I. (ed.): News in Public Memory. An International Study of Media Memories across Generations. Peter Lang, New York (2006)
43. We Are Social: Digital in 2097: in Italia e nel mondo (2019). https://wearesocial.com/it/blog/2019/01/digital-in-2019-in-italia-e-nel-mondo. Accessed 30 Jan 2020

Addressing Fear and Lack of Knowledge of Older Adults Regarding Social Network Sites

Torben Volkmann[✉], Isabella Miller, and Nicole Jochems

Institut für Multimediale und Interaktive Systeme,
Universität zu Lübeck, Lübeck, Germany
{volkmann,imiller,jochems}@imis.uni-luebeck.de

Abstract. Information and communication technologies (ICT) are shaping the world we live, collecting evermore user data. This development does not stop when it comes older adults, who often feel uncertainty and discomfort when using digital technology, although ICT could promote active aging and independence if done right. In this paper, the results of two workshops are presented which analyse and promote solutions to the problems and fears regarding Social Network Sites. We could show that lack of knowledge, especially regarding technical terms, fear regarding data privacy and uncertainty regarding computer usage were main hurdles to technology adoption. The results were used to develop a prototype which received high UEQ scores among older adults. The evaluation demonstrated that small interface changes can make a great difference in a system's perception, that benefits of use could best be provided by using actual examples and revealed a dilemma in need for data. Furthermore, we found that older adults are suspicious when providing data but like the personalization they get, when exposing them.

Keywords: Technology adoption · Older adults · Onboarding · Social network site

1 Introduction

Information and communication technologies are changing the way we consume and communicate. Previous content consumers become producers, reversing the information sovereignty. At the same time, more and more data of the users are exposed – an effect that does not stop at older adults and opens up a whole new problem space. Thus, older adults often feel uncertainty and discomfort when using digital technology. On the other hand, information and communication technology, if done right, can promote active aging and independence. Especially online engagement is associated with positive well-being among older adults, such as less depression [5,5,14], reduced loneliness and improved overall psychological well-being [25]. Research suggests that the importance of maintaining social ties is of great significance because aging often is linked to cognitive decline,

© Springer Nature Switzerland AG 2020
Q. Gao and J. Zhou (Eds.): HCII 2020, LNCS 12209, pp. 114–130, 2020.
https://doi.org/10.1007/978-3-030-50232-4_9

depression and isolation. Frequent social interactions enhance the sense of well-being and thus are essential for maintaining older adults' quality of life [16, 17]. Low technology adoption of older adults is an aspect that prevents these effects from occurring at large scale. One particular reason is that they miss the opportunity to socially connect with younger generations who increasingly rely on social media to socialize [9].

A particular challenge for system developers is the diversity of the user group which is manifested into diverse mental status, needs and preferences. Especially in a late stage of life they are formed by various surroundings in which they work and live and the diverse experience knowledge [20]. Therefore, we have to involve older adults during all stages of technology development to promote usability and meet requirements of the user group [17].

In this paper, we address the challenge of fear and lack of knowledge regarding social network sites using the example of Historytelling (HT). HT is a Social Networking Site (SNS), offering older adults the possibility to document and share personal life stories and categorize them regarding their historical, temporal and local context. We already examined challenges regarding the registration process in HT and developed guidelines in this regard [31], but found that it is also imperative to examine the first contact with a system. Therefore, the user group is involved during the analysis, design and evaluation to assess fears and problems in use with technology, develop solutions for these fears and problems and to evaluate a developed solution. Thus, 2 workshops with 7 older adults were conducted to analyse problems and fears regarding SNS, to elaborate solutions together with them and to evaluate the current state of onboarding in HT. These results were used to develop a revised prototype which was tested by 11 older adults.

1.1 Older Adults and Technology Adoption

Technology adoption "concerns the decision about technology selection, purchasing and commitment to use" [20]. Technology acceptance models such as the TAM [11] predict the probability of technology adoption. Especially perceived ease of use and perceived usefulness are measured variables in this regard [15]. Technology adoption stays low among older adults and several barriers to widespread technology adoption have been identified [7,10,15]. (1) Technology is ageist. Digital technologies, such as the Internet, smartphones and computers are designed by and for younger populations and thus limit the possibility of comfortable usage among older adults [10]. (2) There is a gap between what younger people believe about older people's real needs and desires. [10]. (3) Often, the provided technologies are not attractive, motivating or appealing to an older audience [15]. Other reasons for low technology adoption may be (4) challenging access to technology and high costs, (5) physical limitations and resulting usability issues or (6) a generally negative attitude towards digital technology [8,15]. (7) Nonetheless, often a perceived lack of usefulness is the main reason for technology adoption, not perceived affordability and difficulty in use [15].

Literature shows that technology can provide great benefits in well being for older adults, especially when used for communication purposes. One key desire is to be included in family interaction and can be used as a trigger for technology adoption. Studies show that many older adults used Skype to keep in touch with young relatives [2, 21, 23].

The low level of technology adoption among older adults, despite many potential benefits, makes it imperative to involve the user group in the development process of products older adults can benefit from early on, in order to mitigate the listed behavior and create technology that meets the needs of older adults. Approaches to improving technology adoption are suggested, for example by [20].

1.2   Older Adults and Social Network Sites

Social Network Sites (SNS) can be defined as "web-based services that allow individuals to (1) construct a public or semi-public profile within a bounded system, (2) articulate a list of other users with whom they share a connection, and (3) view and traverse their list of connections and those made by others within the system." [4]. SNS have the potential to enhance and sustain social ties by exchanging life events or daily updates through multimedia content [1, 9, 16]. Although SNS promise to confront loneliness and social isolation, especially in later stages of life, SNS adoption stays low among older adults missing an opportunity to strengthen their social ties and risk becoming more isolated. [1, 7, 9]. One dilemma is that SNS are developed for a specific age group below the age of 50. Contrary, SNS developed specifically for older adults exclude the younger generations [3, 16]. One key aspect for SNS adoption among older adults is to maintain online and offline relationships with their family and close friends. Thus, they are able to communicate without time and location constraints and therefore foster change of social relationships [1, 3]. Main obstacles for SNS use are anxiety of privacy and identity theft, but also usability issues, design complexity and discomfort to reveal too much personal information [1, 7, 16, 31].

One possibility to enhance the SNS adoption is the usage of technology acceptance models and the improvement of the perceived usefulness and trust, because many older adults nurture the desire to communicate with friends and family and maintain their relationships. Thus, younger and older user groups have to be involved during the development process to enhance the usability and accessibility of the system. Using technology that older adults already use has been proved to be particularly successful. The interface should be adapted and personalized regarding the needs and expectations of the users [1, 7, 9].

1.3   Historytelling

Historytelling (HT) is a social network site, offering older adults the possibility to document and share personal life stories and categorize them regarding their historical, temporal and local context. For development, it sets the focus on the participatory design [29]. It aims to compensate age-related deficits and addresses the strengths of older adults such as life-experience, but also notes the importance of integrating younger generations. Thus, HT seeks to foster social participation and connectedness with others, lifelong learning and reminiscing about the own history and thus, supports positive well-being. In order for older adults to use HT, we have to give them a strong reason to use the system to alleviate the fear of new technologies, the internet, and social media while at the same time providing us with their personal data, such as their personal life stories. From early on, especially older adults participated in the development of HT, even determining a road map and functionality [30]. Thus, HT offers the opportunity to share stories across generations to keep on- and offline connections between friends and family. In an component based development approach, different user interfaces have been developed to turn preliminary ideas into reality (see Fig. 1). An important aspect from the beginning was the question how to get older adults to use HT.

First research regarding fear and lack of knowledge in technology resulted in insights to the registration process and have already been published [31]. Another important factor, however, is the onboarding process, in which registration is one aspect, but communication of benefits, offering guidance on first visit, conversion and re-engagement also come into play [6]. Therefore, it is necessary to find out what fears and problems older adults have when using SNS and how these can be countered.

1.4   Participatory Design with Older Adults

Participatory design (PD) describes a mindset democratizing the design process and integrating various stakeholders into all phases of product development [18]. It can be defined as "a process of investigating, understanding, reflecting upon, establishing, developing and supporting mutual learning between multiple participants in collective 'reflection-in-action'" where participants fill the role as users and designers [29]. The designers aim is to learn about the users' situation, whereas users aim to describe their goals and to learn appropriate technological means to obtain them [29]. For example, PD with older adults in particular can improve their safety, quality of life and promote usability [12,19,24]. In the right environment and with the right people with shared goals but different skills and knowledge, creative and collaborative activities can flourish [20]. Therefore, new or adapted methods have to be developed in the phase of analysis, design and evaluation tailored to working with older adults [14,22]. There are several guidelines on how to work with older adults focusing either on the method itself or on the overall development process [10,28].

2   Workshop on Identification of Fears

Two workshops with 2 female and 5 male older adults aged from 61 to 72 (M = 64.7, SD = 4.2) were conducted to identify fears and lack of knowledge regarding SNS in general and in the context of HT specifically and gather suggestions for

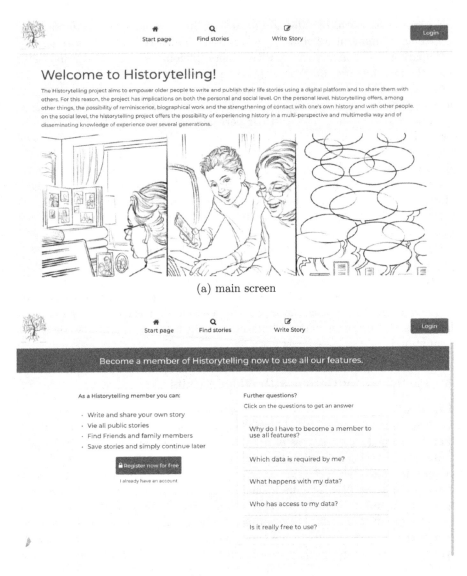

(a) main screen

(b) welcome screen

Fig. 1. User interface of Historytelling, translated from German

improvement. The first workshop was attended by 4 older adults, in the second workshop 3 older adults participated.

The workshops consisted of 3 phases. First, demographic data of the participants were gathered. Then, the participants were encouraged to reflect on their fears in SNS, to write them down and discuss them among the participants. In the last phase, the current state of HT was evaluated focusing on the onboarding process using the User Experience Questionnaire (UEQ) [26] and unmet requirements regarding fear were written down and discussed. Additionally, suggestions for improvement were collected.

2.1 Results

The results of the workshops are presented in the following. First, the demographic data regarding computer and SNS usage are presented in Table 1. Then fears and challenges regarding lack of knowledge of the participants and suggested improvements are listed for SNS in general. For an overview see Table 2. Finally, the fears and suggestions of improvement for HT are presented. For an overview see Table 3.

Demographic Data. All participants used computers at least on a regular basis. Their main usage were banking, mailing and browsing but participants also used the computer to do online shopping, consume the news or playing computer games such as solitaire. SNS were generally known but there was no usage among the participants.

Table 1. Computer and SNS usage among participants

ID	Frequency of computer usage	Type of usage	Social network usage
1	Daily	i.e. browsing, e-commerce, banking	None
2	Regularly	Browsing, banking, mailing, gaming	None
3	Regularly	Browsing, banking, mailing	None
4	Daily	Browsing, banking, mailing	None
5	Daily	Browsing, banking, mailing, ecommerce, gaming	None
6	Daily	Browsing, banking, mailing, ecommerce, news	None
7	Daily	Gaming	None

Fear in SNS in General. The participants identified a total of 6 problem areas, which were ranked and discussed among the participants (see Table 2).

(1) Especially unfamiliar technical terms and (2) lack of knowledge in technology lead to great insecurity and thus were seen as great barriers for technology adoption. (3) Data privacy is an important aspect for the participants. Particularly they do not like the idea of passing on their data to unknown third parties. (4) Thus, the older adults are reluctant to share their email address to protect themselves from spam mails, so that they do not accidentally buy products on

the internet. (5) Participants are in fear of "bandits of the internet". (6) They report to get information about this topic from TV or news paper which further fuel the fears of the participants. (7) Additionally, there is a general uncertainty in the use of technology, especially regarding mouse and keyboard handling.

After issue collecting, the participants were asked to make suggestions to improve the current situation. They wrote down 6 suggestions. These were, again, discussed and rated afterwards (see Table 2).

(1) As the most important point, they stated that unknown technical terms should be avoided and substituted by more understandable terms or at least should be explained. (2) The gain of registration should be explicit. One idea the participants discussed was that this can be achieved by using example postings. (3) The usage of provided user data should be clearly declared and only necessary data for SNS usage should be mandatory. An incremental, context sensitive disclosure of data could be envisaged. (4) Also, by providing more vague data the participants would feel more comfortable, such as providing only an age but not a full date of birth. (5) Participants can imagine to get help by step-by-step instructions by the system, for example to register successfully on a website. They stated that they are usually happy to receive help from experienced people. (6) Lastly, they suggested to add a possibility to unsubscribe to spam mails.

Table 2. Fear and problems regarding SNS as well as suggestions; 3 rating points per participant (N = 7)

Fear/problem	Rating points	Suggestions	Rating points
Unknown technical terms	6	Explain technical terms	7
Lack of knowledge regarding new technologies	6	Add examples	6
Data privacy	5	Clarify data usage and privacy	5
"Bandits of the internet"	2	Using vague user data	2
Warnings about the internet in other media	1	Take the user by the hand	1
General insecurity at computer usage	1	Button for disabling spam mails	0
Fear of spam mails	0		

Fears and Challenges of Historytelling. The UEQ questionnaire scored best in terms of perspicuity and efficiency, but also novelty and dependability were rated positive. The attractiveness and stimulation was rated neutral (see Table 4).

The participants identified 4 problem areas regarding the onboarding of HT which were ranked and discussed among the participants (see Table 3). Besides general fears in using computers and social networks, (1) the participants noted the usage of unknown technical terms within the initial information text. (2) Again, fears regarding data privacy were pointed out although information were provided, but participants did not notice them. (3) It was mentioned that there is a fear of embarrassment, especially when a shared personal story is not well received. (4) Lastly, the provided information text was too long, so that they had to read it multiple times to understand it.

Table 3. Fears and problems regarding HT as well as suggestions; 1 rating points per participant for fear/problem, 3 rating points per participant for suggestions (N = 7)

Fear/problem	Sticky dots	Suggestion	Rating points
Unknown technical terms	4	Clear definitions/usage of easy terms	5
Data privacy	3	Stories as examples	5
Fear of embarrassment	0	Better bait phrase	4
Information text too long	0	Using video to explain functionality	4
		Short descriptions	2
		Sample story writing	1
		Pictures for explanation	0

After collecting issues, the participants were advised to brainstorm system improvements to HT. They collected 7 suggestions. These were, again, discussed and rated afterwards (see Table 3). (1) To avoid unknown technical terms, the participants suggested using easier terms or to explain them. (2) To lease the fear of being embarrassed by sharing stories, they wanted to read examples of other stories in order to get a first impression and learn from them. (3) Participants called for one catchphrase, which also was called "bait phrase" by the participants. (4) For longer texts and explanations are hard to grasp, the older adults suggested using explanatory videos (7) or pictures instead. (5) Also, shorter explanations in form of keywords would be helpful in this regard. (6) Additionally, they stated that they would like to try out the story creation process before registering on HT.

Table 4. UEQ results of the preliminary onboarding interface tested within the workshop. The scale ranges from −3 to 3.

Scale	Mean	Variance
Attractiveness	0.38	0.38
Perspicuity	1.29	0.38
Efficiency	1.21	0.07
Dependability	0.86	0.08
Stimulation	0.75	0.67
Novelty	0.93	0.20

3   Prototype Development

Based on the results of the workshops, a web prototype consisting of two different screens was developed in three iterations and integrated into HT. The new main screen shows a welcome message combined with a picture and HT's slogan. Below, there is information about the usage scenario of HT. After that, there is an overview of public stories inside a slideshow. Also, functionality to write a new story was added, to show all public stories and to switch to the other new site with one click. See the appendix for screenshots.

The second improvement is an updated welcome screen, which consists of a revised version of information regarding system's usage and data privacy and reasons why to register.

4   Evaluation

The developed prototype was tested by 11 older women aged from 60 to 79 years (M = 68.2, SD = 6.0) during an evaluation with an exploratory setting. The goal was to evaluate the initial experience of HT without prior knowledge in a determined time frame to observe if all relevant information are found, seen and interpreted right. Additionally, it should be determined whether the presented information convinced the participants to register on HT.

4.1   Procedure

For evaluation purposes 11 older adults were invited to the university to participate in a workshop regarding HT. One part of this workshop was the evaluation of the developed interface. The evaluation took place in a computer pool with all older adults at once (see Fig. 2).

During the workshop, demographic data regarding the affinity for technology (ATI) [13] and computer literacy (CLS) [27] was collected.

Participants had 15 min to explore the onboarding process of HT and no specific task was provided. The screens were recording during the evaluation.

Afterwards, the User Experience Questionnaire (UEQ) and additional a self-constructed questionnaire to evaluate specific interface elements, the usability and fear of the system and intention to use HT were provided. The completion of the questionnaires was followed by a short discussion.

4.2   Results

The participants scored 3.2 on the Affinity for Technology Interaction Scale (SD = 1.4) on a scale from 1 to 6. The evaluation regarding computer literacy resulted in a score of 14.1 (SD = 5.0) on a scale from 0 to 26. They were using computers for 10 to 30 years (M = 18.7), 6 h per week on average, mostly for mailing, online banking and internet browsing.

Fig. 2. Evaluation setting in the computer pool

The UEQ was completely filled in 7 out of 11 times. All items were rated positively, with highest scores for stimulation and attractiveness. See Table 5 for more detailed results.

The self-constructed questionnaire showed that the onboarding interface and the usage of unknown technical terms and amount of text was convenient. The main page provided necessary information regarding the purpose of the system, but transparency of positive aspects of registration need to be improved. The invitation page stated clearly which data is needed for registration and how the data will be used. Also, they stated that they are unsure whether they would use the system in the future if they had access to it (See Table 6).

In the free texts and positive and negative aspects were collected. Participants mentioned the interface's clarity and usability, the general idea of HT while they particularly emphasized different aspects of the concept of telling their own individual stories as positive aspect and disliked the major rule stories about the war played, and commented on the lack of groupings functionality to cluster stories. Additionally, they stated it was unclear, which data that was entered while signing up will be handled as private information and what will be available to other users.

The analysis of the screen recordings showed that only one participant switched to the invitation screen, which provides information concerning data privacy and data usage. Most of the time was used to read through the information about HT and to read the provided stories. 4 out of 11 persons started to write her own personal story.

Table 5. UEQ results of the revised prototype, split into completed and incomplete questionnaires. The scale ranges from −3 to 3.

Scale	Complete (N = 7)		Incomplete (N = 4)	
	Mean	Variance	Mean	Variance
Attractiveness	1.62	0.40	2.02	0.58
Perspicuity	1.61	0.60	1.86	0.70
Efficiency	1.50	0.44	1.93	0.69
Dependability	1.36	0.48	1.76	0.69
Stimulation	2.07	0.18	2.23	0.21
Novelty	1.21	0.61	1.07	0.90

Table 6. Evaluation results of the self-constructed questionnaire. N = 11, N = 10 for question 3 and 7; The scale ranges from 1 to 6.

ID	Statement	M	SD
1	The system was easy to use	5.00	0.89
2	The system does what it should do without problems	4.91	0.94
3	Dealing with the system does not require much mental effort from me	4.90	0.88
4	The main page contains unknown technical terms	4.27	1.42
5	The main page contains too much text	4.91	0.54
6	I know what I can do with the system	5.00	1.18
7	I know why I should become a member of the system	3.70	1.70
8	It became apparent, which data will be needed for a membership	4.00	1.84
9	It became apparent, how my data will be further processed	3.91	1.81
10	If the system development would be completed, I intent to become a member	3.82	1.25
11	When I have access to the system, I predict I will use it	4.19	0.87

5   Discussion

In this paper we could show that lack of knowledge, especially regarding technical terms, fear regarding data privacy and uncertainty regarding computer usage were main hurdles to technology adoption among our participants. Therefore, we created a digital prototype in an iterative development process based on literature and suggestions of our participants. We could show that small changes in the interface can make a major difference in perception of Historytelling (HT). These findings emphasize the importance of integrating older adults from early on in a development process to accommodate to the needs of the user group but also underline that selection and correct application of user interface components and is crucial.

The evaluation also showed a dilemma regarding the need for data. Provided information, such as stimulus material and informational texts, should be personalized to meet the taste of every individual user. On the other hand, older adults are suspicious if they do not know why specific data is needed from them. Thus, it will be important to emphasize why and how data is used, for example by using an context sensitive data input. Additionally, these information could be used to fulfil the wish for shorter explanatory texts of some participants and thus provide adaptive interfaces. This result also suggests that systems should provide functionality even without prior registration and make the registration an optional step after the initial use which is an entire different approach most SNS use.

Another important aspect is providing stories in HT. The evaluation shows that providing stories for the public is of great importance for getting older adults to use HT. Participants in the study spent a long time reading the provided stories, although they stated that they did not like the war themed topics afterwards. The reading of stories even inspired some of the participants in a short time to write their own personal story.

6   Conclusion and Outlook

In this paper, an onboarding process for Historytelling (HT) was developed, focusing on countering fear and technology related lack of knowledge of older adults. Therefore, two workshops were conducted to gather problems regarding social network sites and HT and develop solutions together. Fears and problems of Social Network Sites (SNS) were mostly found regarding unknown technical terms, lack of knowledge regarding new technology and fear in terms of data privacy. The developed prototype was evaluated in an exploratory manner by 11 older women, which showed that the user experience improved in contrast to the prior interface.

During the evaluation, the participants focused on reading the provided public stories after they saw them on the prototype and started writing their own stories after a short familiarization phase. Since most of the stories in HT were war themed and they are of such an importance, more diverse stories with various topics should be considered in the future. Therefore, data from the users is needed to provide personalized stories. This data should be collected in context so that older adults are not repelled by providing too much information.

Appendix

New onboarding user interface of Historytelling, based on user feedback, translated from German.

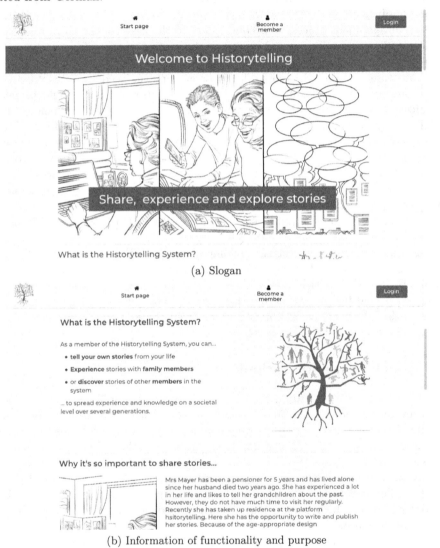

(a) Slogan

(b) Information of functionality and purpose

(c) Provided public stories

(d) Welcome screen

References

1. Arfaa, J., Wang, Y.K.: A usability study on elder adults utilizing social networking sites. In: Marcus, A. (ed.) DUXU 2014. LNCS, vol. 8518, pp. 50–61. Springer, Cham (2014). https://doi.org/10.1007/978-3-319-07626-3_5
2. Baez, M., Nielek, R., Casati, F., Wierzbicki, A.: Technologies for promoting social participation in later life. In: Neves, B.B., Vetere, F. (eds.) Ageing and Digital Technology, pp. 285–306. Springer, Singapore (2019). https://doi.org/10.1007/978-981-13-3693-5_17

3. Bell, C., Fausset, C., Farmer, S., Nguyen, J., Harley, L., Fain, W.B.: Examining social media use among older adults. In: Proceedings of the 24th ACM Conference on Hypertext and Social Media, HT 2013, pp. 158–163. Association for Computing Machinery, New York (2013). https://doi.org/10.1145/2481492.2481509

4. Boyd, D.M., Ellison, N.B.: Social network sites: definition, history, and scholarship. J. Comput. Mediat. Commun. **13**(1), 210–230 (2007). https://doi.org/10.1111/j.1083-6101.2007.00393.x

5. Brewer, R., Piper, A.M.: "Tell it like it really is": a case of online content creation and sharing among older adult bloggers. In: Proceedings of the 2016 CHI Conference on Human Factors in Computing Systems, CHI 2016, pp. 5529–5542. Association for Computing Machinery, New York (2016). https://doi.org/10.1145/2858036.2858379

6. Cascaes Cardoso, M.: The onboarding effect: leveraging user engagement and retention in crowdsourcing platforms. In: Proceedings of the 2017 CHI Conference Extended Abstracts on Human Factors in Computing Systems, CHI EA 2017, pp. 263–267. Association for Computing Machinery, New York (2017). https://doi.org/10.1145/3027063.3027128

7. Coelho, J., Rito, F., Luz, N., Duarte, C.: Prototyping TV and tablet Facebook interfaces for older adults. In: Abascal, J., Barbosa, S., Fetter, M., Gross, T., Palanque, P., Winckler, M. (eds.) INTERACT 2015. LNCS, vol. 9296, pp. 110–128. Springer, Cham (2015). https://doi.org/10.1007/978-3-319-22701-6_9

8. Coleman, G.W., Gibson, L., Hanson, V.L., Bobrowicz, A., McKay, A.: Engaging the disengaged: how do we design technology for digitally excluded older adults? In: Proceedings of the 8th ACM Conference on Designing Interactive Systems, DIS 2010, pp. 175–178. ACM, New York (2010). https://doi.org/10.1145/1858171.1858202

9. Cornejo, R., Tentori, M., Favela, J.: Enriching in-person encounters through social media: a study on family connectedness for the elderly. Int. J. Hum.-Comput. Stud. **71**(9), 889–899 (2013). https://doi.org/10.1016/j.ijhcs.2013.04.001

10. Davidson, J.L., Jensen, C.: Participatory design with older adults: an analysis of creativity in the design of mobile healthcare applications. In: Proceedings of the 9th ACM Conference on Creativity & Cognition, Sydney, Australia, pp. 114–123. Association for Computing Machinery (2013). https://doi.org/10.1145/2466627.2466652

11. Davis, F.D.: Perceived usefulness, perceived ease of use, and user acceptance of information technology. MIS Q. **13**(3), 319–340 (1989)

12. Demirbilek, O., Demirkan, H.: Universal product design involving elderly users: a participatory design model. Appl. Ergon. **35**(4), 361–370 (2004). https://doi.org/10.1016/j.apergo.2004.03.003

13. Franke, T., Attig, C., Wessel, D.: A personal resource for technology interaction: development and validation of the affinity for technology interaction (ATI) scale. Int. J. Hum.-Comput. Interact. **35**(6), 456–467 (2019). https://doi.org/10.1080/10447318.2018.1456150

14. Franz, R.L., Munteanu, C., Neves, B.B., Baecker, R.: Time to retire old methodologies? Reflecting on conducting usability evaluations with older adults. In: Proceedings of the 17th International Conference on Human-Computer Interaction with Mobile Devices and Services Adjunct, MobileHCI 2015, pp. 912–915. ACM, New York (2015). https://doi.org/10.1145/2786567.2794303

15. Gibson, L., Forbes, P., Hanson, V.: What can the 'ash cloud' tell us about older adults' technology adoption. In: Proceedings of the 12th International ACM SIGACCESS Conference on Computers and Accessibility, ASSETS 2010, pp. 301–302. ACM, New York (2010). https://doi.org/10.1145/1878803.1878881

16. Gibson, L., Moncur, W., Forbes, P., Arnott, J., Martin, C., Bhachu, A.S.: Designing social networking sites for older adults. In: Proceedings of the 24th BCS Interaction Specialist Group Conference, BCS 2010, pp. 186–194. BCS Learning & Development Ltd., Swindon, GBR (2010)

17. Harley, D.A., Kurniawan, S.H., Fitzpatrick, G., Vetere, F.: Age matters: bridging the generation gap through technology-mediated interaction. In: CHI 2009 Extended Abstracts on Human Factors in Computing Systems, CHI EA 2009, pp. 4799–4802. ACM, New York (2009). https://doi.org/10.1145/1520340.1520744

18. Harrington, C.N., Wilcox, L., Connelly, K., Rogers, W., Sanford, J.: Designing health and fitness apps with older adults: examining the value of experience-based co-design. In: Proceedings of the 12th EAI International Conference on Pervasive Computing Technologies for Healthcare - PervasiveHealth 2018. ACM Press, New York (2018). https://doi.org/10.1145/3240925.3240929

19. Lindsay, S., Jackson, D., Schofield, G., Olivier, P.: Engaging older people using participatory design. In: Proceedings of the SIGCHI Conference on Human Factors in Computing Systems, CHI 2012, pp. 1199–1208. ACM, New York (2012). https://doi.org/10.1145/2207676.2208570

20. Lu, Y., et al.: Can technology adoption for older adults be co-created? Gerontechnology 16(3), 151–159 (2017). https://doi.org/10.4017/gt.2017.16.3.004.00

21. Melenhorst, A.S., Rogers, W.A., Caylor, E.C.: The use of communication technologies by older adults: exploring the benefits from the user's perspective. Proc. Hum. Factors Ergon. Soc. Annu. Meet. 45(3), 221–225 (2001). https://doi.org/10.1177/154193120104500305

22. Muller, M.J.: Participatory Design: The Third Space in HCI, pp. 1051–1068. L. Erlbaum Associates, Inc., Hillsdale (2002)

23. Neves, B.B., Franz, R.L., Munteanu, C., Baecker, R., Ngo, M.: "My hand doesn't listen to me!": adoption and evaluation of a communication technology for the 'oldest old'. In: Proceedings of the 33rd Annual ACM Conference on Human Factors in Computing Systems, CHI 2015, pp. 1593–1602. ACM, New York (2015). https://doi.org/10.1145/2702123.2702430

24. Newell, A.F.: Design and the Digital Divide: Insights from 40 Years in Computer Support for Older and Disabled People. Morgan & Claypool, San Rafael (2011)

25. Norval, C.: Understanding the incentives of older adults' participation on social networking sites. In: ACM SIGACCESS Accessibility and Computing, pp. 25–29 (2012)

26. Schrepp, M., Hinderks, A., Thomaschewski, J.: Construction of a benchmark for the user experience questionnaire (UEQ). Int. J. Interact. Multimed. Artif. Intell. 4(4), 40–44 (2017). https://doi.org/10.9781/ijimai.2017.445

27. Sengpiel, M., Dittberner, D.: The computer literacy scale (CLS) for older adults-development and validation. In: Mensch & Computer, pp. 7–16 (2008)

28. Sengpiel, M., Volkmann, T., Jochems, N.: Considering older adults throughout the development process-the HCD+ approach. In: Proceedings of the Human Factors and Ergonomics Society Europe Chapter 2018 Annual Conference (2019). http://hfes-europe.org

29. Simonsen, J., Robertson, T. (eds.): Routledge International Handbook of Participatory Design, 0 edn. Routledge (2012). https://doi.org/10.4324/9780203108543

30. Volkmann, T., Sengpiel, M., Jochems, N.: Historytelling: a website for the elderly a human-centered design approach. In: Proceedings of the 9th Nordic Conference on Human-Computer Interaction, NordiCHI 2016. Association for Computing Machinery, New York (2016). https://doi.org/10.1145/2971485.2996735
31. Volkmann, T., Sengpiel, M., Jochems, N.: Altersgerechte gestaltung eines registrierungsprozesses für das historytelling-projekt. In: Dachselt, R., Weber, G. (eds.) Mensch und Computer 2018 - Tagungsband. Gesellschaft für Informatik e.V., Bonn (2018). https://doi.org/10.18420/muc2018-mci-0358

The Effect of Social Media Use on Older Adults' Loneliness-The Moderating Role of Self-disclosure

Xiaoting Xu[1]([⊠]) [iD], Yuxiang (Chris) Zhao[2] [iD], and Qinghua Zhu[1] [iD]

[1] Nanjing University, Nanjing 210023, China
xxt9337@163.com
[2] Nanjing University of Science and Technology, Nanjing 210094, China

Abstract. With the gradual deepening of the aging degree, older adults' loneliness seriously affects their physical and mental health. Social media as the main source of online social networking that can compensate for social impoverishment, hence have the great enthusiasm for older adults. However, relevant research on the influence of older adults' loneliness is not thorough enough, especially in the Chinese background. Therefore, this study selects the representative social media-WeChat, to explore its influence on older adults' loneliness. Firstly, we put forward hypotheses and models by reviewing existing researches. Then use questionnaire survey to obtain relevant data. Through stratified regression, the result shows that: (1) compared with users who do not use WeChat, WeChat use can alleviate loneliness. (2) We did not find a direct connection between the regular use of WeChat and older adults' loneliness, but we found that when the older adults are good at self-disclosure in WeChat, regular use of WeChat can alleviate loneliness. This study can help us better understand the impact of social media on older adults' loneliness, and guide relevant institutions to intervene and regulate loneliness for older adults in practice.

Keywords: Social media · Loneliness · Self-disclosure · Older adult · WeChat

1 Introduction

In a recent report, '2019 world population outlook : priorities', the department of economic and social affairs of the United Nations (UNDESA) said that the world's population is ageing and this divide will continue to develop, some countries are already facing severe ageing [1]. According to the national bureau of statistics (NBS), there were 249 million people aged 60 or above in China by the end of 2018, accounting for 17.9% of the total population [2]. China has consequently become an aging society. The aging of the population has brought many challenges to social development, such as social burden, family pension difficulties, prominent health needs, amongst others. In order to cope with the expansion of the elderly population, we should not only pay attention to physical health but also their mental health. Nevertheless, with the decline of physical

© Springer Nature Switzerland AG 2020
Q. Gao and J. Zhou (Eds.): HCII 2020, LNCS 12209, pp. 131–145, 2020.
https://doi.org/10.1007/978-3-030-50232-4_10

function and the loss of social environments, most older adults are facing a certain degree of loneliness [3, 4].

Loneliness refers to a subjective feeling state of being alone, separated or apart from others, and has been deemed as an imbalance between desired social contacts and actual social contacts [5, 6]. There are many adverse effects on the physical and mental health of older adults, such as increased stress, decreasing happiness, depression and even suicide [7, 8]. In recent years, a series of studies have attempted to evaluate the effectiveness of interventions aimed at older adults' loneliness [9–11]. With the development of information technology and the influence of loneliness and isolation, the older adults begin to venture into the Internet world, especially social media. According to the US census, people over the age of 65 will soon be the largest group of internet users; they hope that social media can reduce loneliness and improve digital literacy [12]. The influence of social media on the loneliness of older adults has become the focus of scholars, and subsequent studies found that loneliness always comes as an involuntary negative feeling related to lack of social networks and lonely people rely on media to compensate [11, 13]. However, studies on the relationship between social media and loneliness are inconsistent at present. Some scholars believe that the use of social media plays a positive role in relieving loneliness. For example, Kraut et al. [14] thought that lonely people are more willing to resort to social media in order to make up for the lack of social skills in face-to-face communication. Vally and D'Souza [15] found that students who did not use social media clearly showed a decline in satisfaction, an increase in negative affective emotions, and an increase in loneliness. Pittman and Reich [16] believed that users could promote intimacy in relationships and thus alleviate loneliness by using Instagram and Snapchat. In particular, users can often browse and interact with each other, and loneliness will be significantly reduced [17]. Some studies have taken the opposite results, suggesting that the use of social media can deepen loneliness and exert adverse effects. Such as Wright et al. [18] who believed that addiction to Facebook could lead to depression and seriously affect physical and mental health. The more time an individual spends on social networks, the less satisfied and the more stressed they become [19]. Wang et al. [20] verified the positive correlation between Facebook use and severe loneliness through empirical analysis. Additionally, some scholars believe that there is no direct connection between the use of social media and loneliness, Kathrin et al. [21] found no influence between smartphone use and stress and loneliness through continuous tracking of users' smartphone use. Through interviews, Aarts [22] found that although older people have a positive attitude towards social media use, they do not believe that social media can alleviate loneliness, and the use of social media has no connection with loneliness.

For such inconsistent conclusions, some scholars believe that differences in individual self-disclosure may regulate the relationship between social media and loneliness. For example, Ko and Kuo [23] found that self-disclosure can regulate the relationship between blogging use and subjective well-being. Chen and Li [24] found that self-disclosure can regulate the relationship between mobile social media and psychological well-being. Other studies on the moderating effects of self-disclosure on social media and loneliness draw similar conclusions [21, 25, 26]. Besides, the loneliness of older adults is also influenced by gender, age, educational and marital status [21, 27, 28]. Throughout existing research, we found studies focused on western societies (Facebook, Twitter), relevant research linking social media and loneliness of older adults in

Chinese backgrounds, is not yet mature. Therefore, we chose the representative social media - WeChat, to explore its influence on the loneliness of older adults while taking self-disclosure as the moderating role, trying to find the effectiveness of social media on the older adults' loneliness intervention.

2   Research Hypotheses

2.1   Social Media Use and Loneliness

Many researchers have confirmed that social media use can alleviate loneliness. Initially, Davis and Kraus [29] put forward the compensation hypothesis that states, persons with greater loneliness will be more likely to utilize mass media to compensate for social impoverishment. Quan-Haase and Young [30] believed that Facebook could give an insight into a person's whole social status, lonely people are more likely to use Facebook to compensate for the lack of offline relationships [31]. Twitter has also been shown to promote social interaction that can have a direct impact on one's psychological well-being [32, 33]. Older adults consider that social media can provide social support [34], using social media can be gratifying [35]. Lee and Ma [36] found that users pursuing socializing were more likely to share news on social media platforms such as Facebook and Twitter. This was particularly true on image-based platforms (e.g., Instagram, Snapchat) that offer a more intimate feel, so loneliness can be alleviated [16].

In addition, Thomas et al. [37] predicted the factors related to loneliness; the results show a negative correlation between social media use and loneliness, that means social media use can reduce loneliness. Notably, more intimate relationship on social media will have a negative association with the slope of loneliness [38]. Just as Valkenburg and Peter [39] found that spending more time communicating with friends online can improve the quality of friendship and thus reduce loneliness. All these studies have proved that social media plays a positive role in alleviating loneliness. Due to the decline of physical function, older adults suffer from a lack of social environment and feel isolated. Compared with the non-use of social media group, the use of social media can make up for the deficiency of offline social communication. Regular use can better maintain social relationship, facilitate, and enrich life, and relieve loneliness to a degree. Therefore, the following hypotheses are proposed:

Hypothesis 1: Social media can alleviate older adults' loneliness.
Hypothesis 1a: Social media use can alleviate loneliness compared to older adults who do not use social media
Hypothesis 1b: Regular use of social media can alleviate older adults' loneliness.

2.2   The Moderating Role of Self-disclosure

Self-disclosure refers to the action of revealing, communicating or sharing personal information to others, that is the expression of individual initiative [23, 40, 41]. This concept plays a central role in the development and maintenance of family, friends, and romantic partners, and relationships in general [42, 43], and consequently can have a direct impact on mental health [21]. We found that loneliness was associated with a perceived lack of self-disclosure [44, 45]. Scholars hold that self-disclosure can arouse social support, help individuals relieve stress, decrease depressive symptoms and heightened life satisfaction [26]. Vaclavikova and Dikaczova [46] studied 132 Facebook users, and the results identify a positive correlation between feelings of loneliness and self-disclosure. Wei et al. [25] found that self-disclosure can mediate the association between attachment avoidance and feelings of loneliness. Zhang [26] highlighted that self-disclosure can moderate the relation between stressful life events and life satisfaction. Besides this, self-disclosure plays a moderating role in smartphone use and stress, loneliness. For those users who prefer self-disclosure, regular use of smartphones can relieve loneliness and reduce pressure. Conversely, those users who are unwilling to make self-disclosures, regular use of smartphones will lead to increased pressure and loneliness [21]. Many other studies all have demonstrated the moderating effect of self-disclosure [23, 24]. Therefore, we believe that users who are willing to disclose, communicate and share actively can better integrate into the virtual world by using social media and obtain social support, thus alleviating loneliness. Contrariwise, loneliness increases. Thus, the following hypothesis is proposed:

Hypothesis 2: Self-disclosure can moderate the relationship between social media use and older adults' loneliness.

Considering the findings collectively, a theoretical model is shown in Fig. 1, which explores the influence of social media use on older adults' loneliness and the moderating effect of self-disclosure.

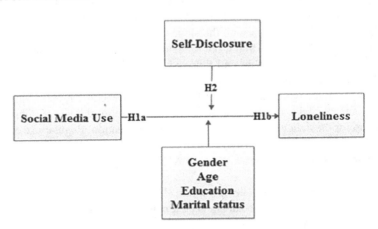

Fig. 1. Theoretical model.

3   Research Method

3.1   Participants and Procedure

The world health organization (WHO) defines those as above 60 years older in developing countries as older adults, so the sample in this study is over 60 years old. Meanwhile, the background of our study is in the context of WeChat usage. So, for the sample selection, we recruited participants who self-identify as using WeChat, and are over 60. Considering that WeChat is the primary way for college students to contact their families at present, we adopt the method of random sampling. Firstly, we send the questionnaire to students, and then the students send the questionnaire to their families who meet the requirements. At the same time, we also used the snowball sampling method. We set a clear prompt in the questionnaire, and after the submission of the questionnaire, which states "if you know any eligible participants around you, please help by forwarding this survey". Finally, all questionnaires will be paid once completed. This questionnaire began from 2019.12.15 and ran until 2019.12.30 for a total of two weeks. In the end, we obtained 337 questionnaires in this study. After eliminating the non-conforming questionnaires, we collected 308 valid questionnaires.

3.2 Measures

All variables were adapted from prior studies. (1) WeChat use was adapted from LaRose et al. [47], Ellison et al. [48] and have nine items. (2) Loneliness was adapted from Russell [49, 50] with seven items. (3) Self-Disclosure was adapted from Miller et al. [51] and Schouten et al. [52] with nine items. (4) Control variables. The four core control variables are gender, age, education, marital status based on Coelho et al. [28], Hawkley and Cacioppo [27], Hawkley and Cacioppo [21]. The complete questionnaire is in Appendix A.

3.3 Data Analysis

The data analysis method implemented multiple stratified linear regression. We analyzed WeChat use and how it affected older adults' loneliness and the moderating effect of self-disclosure, controlled for variables of gender, age, education, marital status.

4 Results

4.1 Sample Description

Detailed demographics are represented in Table 1. The proportion of genders is relatively balanced (male, 52.60%; female, 47.40%). The samples involved in this study are all over 60 years old, and the proportion between 60 and 70 years old is the largest, accounting for about 70.13%. In comparison, other older groups are less than 30%. This is consistent with the distribution of the number of current Internet users of the elderly population. For education, the overall educational level of the older adults is relatively low, mainly concentrated in primary school graduate, junior high school graduate, high school graduate or higher vocational education, accounting for about 76.29%, while the proportion of other groups is only 23.71%. In addition, marital status is mainly married (75.65%), partial divorce (14.94%), widowed (5.19%) and separation (4.22%).

Table 1. Demographic characteristics

Demographic characteristic	n (%)
Gender	
Male	162(52.60)
Female	146(47.40)
Age	
60–65	109(35.39)
66–70	77(25.00)
71–75	69(22.40)
76–80	47(15.26)
80+	6(1.95)
Education	
Less than primary school diploma	34(11.04)
Primary school graduate	78(25.32)
Junior high school graduate	65(21.10)
High school graduate or higher vocational education	92(29.87)
Junior college degree or 4-year college degree	27(8.77)
More than 4-year college degree	12(3.90)
Marital status	
Married	233(75.65)
Separated	13(4.22)
Divorced	46(14.94)
Widowed	16(5.19)

4.2 Reasons for Using Social Media

Figure 2 shows the main reasons that participants use social media (WeChat). The main reason for its use being to connect with family and friends. Secondly, in order to obtain information, such as moments and relevant official accounts information. Thirdly, some older adults are trying to make friends via the WeChat platforms scan, shake and chat, and people nearby which all connect two strangers. Besides, older adults utilize some services, such as paying & receiving money, mini programs and so on. Even for leisure and entertainment, such as games shopping.

4.3 Testing the Hypotheses

First, we conduct a correlation analysis to determine whether there is a significant correlation between the variables. The results are shown in Table 2. We found that most variables are significantly correlated, that can provide a basis for further linear regression analysis. In addition, the overall correlation level is relatively low from the correlation coefficient. We can exclude multicollinearity between variables preliminarily, so as not to disturb the results of the regression analysis.

This study conducted multivariate linear regression analysis by SPSS and used the least square method (OLS) to fit the data, as shown in Table 3. We built three models.

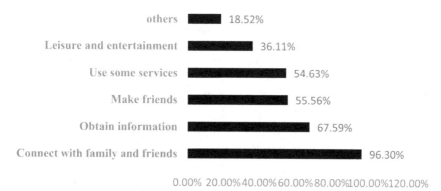

Fig. 2. Reasons for using WeChat

Table 2. Correlation results.

	1	2	3	4
1 Loneliness	1			
2 Whether to use social media	−0.360**	1		
3 The frequency of using social media	−0.149	−0.018	1	
4 Self-Disclosure	−0.461**	0.099**	0.327**	1

n = 308, **p < 0.01.

Model 1 contains only control variables, model 2 introduces independent variables on the basis of model 1, and model 3 introduces an interaction term on the basis of model 2. For model 1: $R^2 = 0.006$, $F_{308} = 1.166$. For model 2: $R^2 = 0.724$, it indicates that the explanatory variable has an interpretation degree of 72.4% to the explained variable, so the interpretation degree is high and fitting degree is good. $F_{308} = 187.175$ indicates that the model as a whole is significant. Model 3 has a similar result ($R^2 = 0.924$, $F_{308} = 164.752$). In addition, All VIF are less than 10, indicating that there is no multicollinearity between variables.

In H1a, we believe that WeChat use can alleviate loneliness compared with older adults who do not use WeChat. From model 2 in Table 3, the results showed a significant negative correlation (B = −0.042, P = 0.010 < 0.05). It indicates using WeChat can reduce the loneliness of older adults by about 0.042 units under the 5% significant level and controlled for gender, age, education, and marital status, further illustrating WeChat use can alleviate older adults' loneliness to a certain extent, so H1a was supported.

H1b holds that regular use of WeChat may alleviate the loneliness of older adults. From model 3 in Table 3, although there was a negative correlation between regular use of WeChat and loneliness, the results were not significant (B = −0.109, P = 0.357 > 0.05). This indicates that there was no direct relationship between regular use of WeChat and older adults' loneliness, so H1b was not supported.

H2 holds that self-disclosure has a moderating effect. From model 3 in Table 3, the interaction term between regular use of WeChat with self-disclosed has a significant negative correlation with the loneliness of older adults (B = −0.121, P = 0.000 < 0.05). This indicates that self-disclosure has a positive moderating effect on the relationship between regular use of WeChat and older adults' loneliness, that means if older adults are good at self-disclosure in WeChat, regular use of WeChat can alleviate loneliness to some extent, H2 was supported.

Table 3. Multiple linear regression analyses results

	Model 1	Model 2	Model 3
Gender	0.135	0.005	0.009
Age	0.112	−0.007	−0.002
Education	−0.035	−0.003	−0.001
Marital status	0.084	−0.015	−0.016
Whether to use SM	–	−0.042*	−0.058*
Frequency of using SM	–	−0.109	− 0.097
Frequency of using SM*Self-Disclosure	–	–	−0.121**
R-squared	0.006	0.724	0.924
F	1.166	187.175**	164.752**

n = 308, **p < 0.01, *p < 0.05.

5 Discussion

With the increasing proportion of the elderly population in China, the mental health of older adults is not only related to their health but also social stability and development. Loneliness has a significant impact on the physical and mental health of older adults and even leads to severe consequences. It is very vital to intervene and adjust the loneliness of older adults [53]. WeChat, as an increasingly popular social media platform for older adults, can break through the limitation of time and space and make up for the lack of social needs due to physical dysfunction. Older adults can find a sense of belonging among family and friends [54]. It is imperative to explore whether it has an intervention effect on older adults' loneliness. Through a questionnaire survey, this study aims to explore the influence of WeChat on older adults' loneliness and the moderating effect of self-disclosure.

The results showed that WeChat use was negatively correlated with older adults' loneliness, that means WeChat use could alleviate the loneliness of older adults compared with those who did not use WeChat, which was consistent with previous studies [16, 37, 38]. This indicates that older adults can indeed reduce loneliness to a certain extent by using WeChat. WeChat, as a circle of acquaintances, is more reliable concerning users compared with other relatively unfamiliar virtual social environments. So, users are more willing to disclose their thoughts, feeling and emotions, indicating that close social relationships are more effective at alleviating loneliness to a certain extent [38]. In addition, we did not find a direct relationship between the regular use of WeChat and older adults' loneliness. However, we found that self-disclosure has a positive moderating effect, that is, regular use of WeChat can alleviate older adults' loneliness if they are willing to disclose their status, exchange ideas and troubles in WeChat. Previous research has shown that venting negative thoughts and emotions online can bring feelings of relief and liberation [26], especially when we obtain encouragement by other users, this kind of emotional support might lead to a feeling of being socially integrated and reduce loneliness [39]. These seem to imply that the quality of WeChat use is more important than the quantity to reduce older adults' loneliness [21], non-social and ineffective social networks use can lead to depression and stress [55]. Active self-disclosure has a positive influence on happiness, relieving pressure and reducing loneliness.

However, most studies have focused on the influence of social media on loneliness in western contexts such as Facebook and Twitter. Relevant research about Chinese social media, especially the role WeChat may have on older adults' loneliness, is not in-depth and specific enough. Based on this, this study explores the influence of WeChat on older adults' loneliness and the moderating effect of self-disclosure, which can enrich the shortcomings of existing studies, and expand the theory of older adults' loneliness, further providing some references for relevant studies. In addition, the research results have some practical significance for the intervention mechanism of loneliness of older adults, and it is worth paying attention to WeChat use in a high-quality way to alleviate older adults' loneliness. We think it is necessary to: (1) improve WeChat skills of older adults. Intergenerational learning is considered to be an effective way at present, that young people guide, participate and transfer relevant knowledge and skills to older adults both online and offline [56, 57]. At the same time, intergenerational learning can reduce social isolation, relieve anxiety and enhance confidence [58]. Besides this, training is also considered as an effective way to improve WeChat skills for older adults. In recent years, libraries, product developers and communities have launched WeChat user manuals, training classes and online courses for older adults [59, 60]. So, we can see that the media literacy of older adults has been improved as a whole. (2) Enhance the experience of WeChat use for older adults. The elderly hope to be as proficient in WeChat as the young for making friends, chatting, entertainment, games, etc., but many are not good at most functions within WeChat. The Internet should be conscious of the needs of older adults, highlighting and creating convenient operation of the service functions frequently used alongside key services of older adults, so they can fully integrate into the online social environment and enhance their sense of experience.

Finally, there are some deficiencies. First of all, the data used in our study are cross-sectional data, whether WeChat use has a persistent impact on older adults' loneliness needs to be further verified with time-series data, which will have some real significance. Secondly, our samples are mostly between 60 and 70 years older, most of whom have just retired and are still connected with the society. Those who are older are more likely to be lonely and should special attention. Finally, self-disclosure in this study only is an expression of online disclosure, and whether offline self-disclosure has different effects also needs further exploration. The research on older adults' loneliness is a continuous process, which needs the attention of scholars and the society.

Appendix

Questionnaire

1. What is your gender?

o Female

o Male

2. What is your age?

o 60-64

o 65-69

o 70-74

o 75-79

o 》 80

3. Education

o Grade school or private school

o Junior high school

o High school/technical secondary school

o University (including junior college)

o above

4. Marital status

o Married

o Separated

o Divorced

o Widowed

5. Whether WeChat was used in the past week?

o Yes

o No

6. How often do you use WeChat in a day?

o Rarely

o Sometimes

o Often

o Always

7. What is/are your purpose(s) for using WeChat?

o Connect with family/friends

o Getting to know some friends

o Getting information

o Using some services

o Leisure and entertainment

o Other

8. According to your real situation, please tell us how often you conduct the following actions in WeChat :

	Never (1)	Rarely (2)	Sometimes (3)	Often (4)	Always (5)
• How often do you normally post your personal feelings and state?					
• How often do you normally post your worries and fears?					
• How often do you normally post your private problems?					
• How often do you normally communicate your personal feelings and state?					
• How often do you normally communicate your worries and fears?					
• How often do you normally communicate your private problems?					
• How often do you normally comment others' personal feelings and state?					
• How often do you normally comment others' worries and fears?					
• How often do you normally comment others' private problems?					

9. According to your real situation, please tell us how often you conduct the following actions in WeChat :

	Never (1)	Rarely (2)	Sometimes (3)	Often (4)	Always (5)
• How often do you feel unhappy doing so many things alone?					
• How often do you feel you have nobody to talk to?					
• How often do you feel you cannot tolerate being so alone?					
• How often do you feel as if nobody really understands you?					
• How often do you feel you are unable to reach out and communicate with those around you?					
• How often do you feel starved for company?					
• How often do you feel it is difficult for you to make friends?					

References

1. Sina. https://tech.sina.com.cn/d/n/2019-06-19/doc-ihytcitk6214106.shtml. Accessed 21 Dec 2020
2. National bureau of statistics of the People's Republic of China. http://data.stats.gov.cn. Accessed 16 Jan 2020
3. Cattan, M., White, M., Bond, J., et al.: Preventing social isolation and loneliness among older people: a systematic review of health promotion interventions. Ageing Soc. **25**, 41–67 (2005)
4. Grenade, L., Boldy, D.: Social isolation and loneliness among older people: issues and future challenges in community and residential settings. Aust. Health Rev. **32**(3), 468–478 (2008)

5. Weiss, R.S.: Loneliness: The Experience of Emotional and Social Isolation. MIT Press, Cambridge (1973)
6. Ernst, J.M., Cacioppo, J.T.: Lonely hearts: psychological perspectives on loneliness. Appl. Prev. Psychol. **8**(1), 1–22 (1999)
7. Wu, G.T., Zhang, M.Q., Ni, G.H.: Changes in loneliness among elderly people and its effect factors: a latent transition analysis. Psychol. sinica **50**(9), 1061–1070 (2018)
8. Masi, C.M., Chen, H.Y., Hawkley, L.C., et al.: A meta-analysis of interventions to reduce loneliness christopher. Pers. Soc. Psychol. Rev. **15**(3), 54–56 (2011)
9. Findlay, R.A.: Interventions to reduce social isolation amongst older people: where is the evidence? Ageing Soc. **23**(5), 647–658 (2003)
10. Dickens, A., Richards, S., Greaves, C., Campbell, J.: Interventions targeting social isolation in older people: a systematic review. BMC Publ. Health **11**(1), 647 (2011)
11. Cohen, M.J., Perach, R.: Interventions for alleviating loneliness among older persons: a critical review. Am. J. health Promot. **29**(3), e109–e125 (2015)
12. Sohu. http://www.sohu.com/a/313683341_355029. Accessed 11 Jan 2020
13. Rubin, A.M., Perse, E.M.: Audience activity and soap opera involvement a uses and effects investigation. Hum. Commun. Res. **14**(2), 246–268 (1987)
14. Kraut, R., Kiesler, S., Boneva, B., et al.: Internet paradox revisited. J. Soc. Issues **58**, 49–74 (2002)
15. Vally, Z., D'Souza, C.G.: Abstinence from social media use, subjective well-being, stress, and loneliness. Perspect. Psychiatr. Care **55**(4), 752–759 (2019)
16. Pittman, M., Reich, B.: Social media and loneliness: why an Instagram picture may be worth more than a thousand Twitter words. Comput. Hum. Behav. **62**, 155–167 (2016)
17. Yang, C.C.: Instagram use, loneliness, and social comparison orientation: interact and browse on social media, but don't compare. Cyberpsychol. Behav. Soc. Netw. **19**(12), 703–708 (2016)
18. Wright, K.B., Rosenberg, J., Egbert, N., et al.: Communication comeptence, social support and depression among college students: a model of Facebook and face-to-face support network influence. J. Health Commun. **18**, 41–57 (2013)
19. Bevan, J.L., Gomez, R., Sparks, L.: Disclousures about important life events on Facebook, Relationships with stress and quality of life. Comput. Hum. Behav. **39**, 246–253 (2014)
20. Wang, K., Frison, E., Eggermont, S., et al.: Active public Facebook use and adolescents' feelings of loneliness: evidence for a curvilinear relationship. J. Adolesc. **67**, 35–44 (2018)
21. Karsay, K., Schmuck, D., Matthes, J., Stevic, A.: Longitudinal effects of excessive smartphone use on stress and loneliness: the moderating role of self-disclosure. Cyberpsychol. Behav. Soc. Netw. **22**(11), 706–713 (2019)
22. Aarts, S.: Social media and loneliness among community-dwelling older adults. Int. J. Geriatr. Psychiatry **33**(3), 554–555 (2018)
23. Ko, H.C., Kuo, F.Y.: Can blogging enhance subjective well-being through self-disclosure? CyberPsychol. Behav. **12**, 75–79 (2009)
24. Chen, H.T., Li, X.: The contribution of mobile social media to social capital and psychological well-being: examining the role of communicative use, friending and self-disclosure. Comput. Hum. Behav. **75**, 958–965 (2017)
25. Wei, M.F., Russell, D.W., Zakalik, R.A.: Adult attachment, social self-efficacy, self-disclosure, loneliness, and subsequent depression for freshman college students: a longitudinal study. J. Couns. Psychol. **52**(4), 602–614 (2005)
26. Zhang, R.: The stress-buffering effect of self-disclosure on Facebook: an examination of stressful life events, social support, and mental health among college students. Comput. Hum. Behav. **75**, 527–537 (2017)
27. Hawkley, L.C., Cacioppo, J.T.: Loneliness matters: a theoretical and empirical review of consequences and mechanisms. Ann. Behav. Med. **40**(2), 218–227 (2010)

28. Coelho, J., Rito, F., Duarte, C.: "You, me & TV" - fighting social isolation of older adults with Facebook, TV and multimodality. Int. J. Hum Comput Stud. **98**, 38–50 (2007)
29. Davis, M.H., Kraus, L.A.: Social contact, loneliness, and mass-media use - a test of 2 hypotheses. J. Appl. Soc. Psychol. **19**(13), 1100–1124 (1989)
30. Quan-Haase, A., Young, A.L.: Uses and gratifications of social media: a comparison of Facebook and instant messaging. Bull. Sci. Technol. Soc. **30**(5), 350–361 (2010)
31. Skues, J.L., Williams, B., Wise, L.: The effects of personality traits, self-esteem, loneliness, and narcissism on Facebook use among university students. Comput. Hum. Behav. **28**(6), 2414–2419 (2012)
32. Lee, E.J., Jang, J.W.: Not so imaginary interpersonal contact with public figures on social network sites: how affiliative tendency moderates its effects. Commun. Res. **40**(1), 27–51 (2011)
33. Pittman, M., Tefertiller, A.: With or without you: connected viewing and co-viewing Twitter activity for traditional appointment and asynchronous broadcast television models. First Monday **20**(7), 13–24 (2015)
34. Silva, F., Scortegagna, A.S., Bertoletti, D.M.: Carolina a: Facebook as a social support environment for older adults. UNIVERSITAS Psychol. **17**(3), 1–11 (2018)
35. Jung, E.H., Sundar, S.S.: Status update: gratifications derived from Facebook affordances by older adults. New Media Soc. **20**(11), 4135–4154 (2018)
36. Lee, C.S., Ma, L.: News sharing in social media: the effect of gratifications and prior experience. Comput. Hum. Behav. **28**(2), 331–339 (2012)
37. Thomas, L., Orme, E., Kerrigan, F.: Student loneliness: the role of social media through life transitions. Comput. Educ. **146**, 103754 (2020)
38. Sohn, Y., Woo, S., Jo, D., et al.: The role of the quality of college-based relationship on social media in college-to-work transition of Korean college students: the longitudinal examination of intimacy on social media, social capital, and loneliness. Jpn. Psychol. Res. **61**(4), 236–248 (2019)
39. Valkenburg, P.M., Peter, J.: Online communication and adolescent well-being: testing the stimulation versus the displacement hypothesis. J. Comput.-Mediated Commun. **12**, 1169–1182 (2007)
40. Brunell, A.B.: Self-disclosure. In: Baumeister, R.F., Vohs, K.D. (eds.) Encyclopedia of Social Psychology. SAGE publications, Inc., Thousand Oaks (2007)
41. Huang, H.Y.: Examining the beneficial effects of individual's self-disclosure on the social network site. Comput. Hum. Behav. **57**, 122–132 (2016)
42. Collins, N.L., Miller, L.C.: Self-disclosure and liking: a meta-analytic review. Psychol. Bull. **116**(3), 457–475 (1994)
43. Kim, J., Dindia, K.: Online self-disclosure: a review of research. In: Wright, K.B., Webb, L.M., (eds.) Computer-Mediated Communication in Personal Relationships. New York (2011)
44. Solano, C.H., Batten, P.G., Parish, E.A.: Loneliness and patterns of self-disclosure. J. Pers. Soc. Psychol. **43**(3), 524–531 (1982)
45. Berg, J.H., Peplau, L.A.: Loneliness - the relationship of self-disclosure and androgyny. Pers. Soc. Psychol. Bull. **8**(4), 624–630 (1982)
46. Vaclavikova, I., Dikaczova, S.: The manifestations of self-disclosure on social media and their relation to self-esteem and the feeling of loneliness among young people. AD Alta-J. Interdisc. Res. **8**(2), 295–297 (2018)
47. LaRose, R., Lin, C.A., Eastin, M.S.: Unregulated internet usage: addiction, habit, or deficient self-regulation? Media Psychol. **5**, 225–253 (2003)
48. Ellison, N.B., Steinfield, C., Lampe, C.: The benefits of Facebook "friends:" social capital and college students' use of online social network sites. J. Comput.-Mediated Commun. **12**(4), 1143–1168 (2007)

49. Russell, D.W.: The measurement of loneliness. In: Peplau, L.A., Perlman, D. (eds.) Loneliness. A Sourcebook of Current Theory, Research and Therapy. Wiley, New York (1982)
50. Russell, D.: UCLA loneliness scale (version 3): reliability, validity, and factor structure. J. Pers. Assess. **66**(1), 20–40 (1996)
51. Miller, L.C., Berg, J.H., Archer, R.L.: Openers: individuals who elicit intimate self-disclosure. J. Pers. Soc. Psychol. **44**, 1234–1244 (1983)
52. Schouten, A.P., Valkenburg, P.M., Peter, J.: Precursors and underlying processes of adolescents' online self-disclosure: developing and testing an "Internet-attribute-perception" model. Media Psychol. **10**, 292–315 (2007)
53. Song, S.J., Song, X.K., Zhao, Y,X., Zhu, Q.H.: The Mitigating effect of internet use on older adults' loneliness: an empirical lesson from CHARLS Data. Libr. Inf. **01**, 63–69 (2019)
54. Tencent. https://mp.weixin.qq.com. Accessed 18 Jan 2020
55. Wendorf, J.E., Yang, F.: Benefits of a negative post: effects of computer-mediated venting on relationship maintenance. Comput. Hum. Behav. **52**, 271–277 (2015)
56. Silverstein, M., Cong, Z., Li, S.Z.: Intergenerational transfers and living arrangements of older people in rural China: consequences for psychological well-being. J. Gerontol. Ser. B-Psychol. Sci. Soc. Sci. **61**(5), S256–S266 (2006)
57. Klamma, R., Lehrstuhl, I.V., Rwth, A., et al.: ACIS: intergenerational community learning supported by a hypermedia afghan sites and monuments database. In: 5th IEEE International Conference on Advanced Learning Technologies, pp. 108–112. Taiwan (2005)
58. Lee, O.E.K., Kim, D.H.: Bridging the digital divide for older adults via intergenerational mentor-Up. Res. Soc. Work Pract. **29**(7), 786–795 (2019)
59. Chen, k.: An encounter between the aged and new media: analyzing the media life under the perspective of positive aging-based on the research of new media classroom in Hefei. Anhui University (2017)
60. Li, S.X., Zhao, Y.X.: An exploration on the media literacy of digital immigrants under the new media environment: based on the grounded theory analysis of smartphone application. Libr. Inf. Serv. **60**(17), 94–102 (2016)

How to Beautify the Elderly?: A Study on the Facial Preference of Senior Citizens

Weiwei Zhang⑩, Yuankun Li, and Jihong Jeung(✉)

Tsinghua University, Beijing, China
zww19@mails.tsinghua.edu.cn, jihong95@tsinghua.edu.cn

Abstract. Selfie is gaining popularity among the senior citizens, but for them using the "beauty" function is not very friendly. In this research, we intended to figure out the facial feature about what senior people care most and to build a prototype for the beautification application. This paper presents two studies: an online survey about senior citizens' behavior on taking photos and a qualitative study on senior citizens' aesthetics preference of faces. By analyzing the data we collected from the studies above, we find how the elderly think and behave are quite different from the traditional assumption. A simple beautification system is built based on the style GAN (Generative Adversarial Network) algorithm according to our conclusions. These results may provide a reference for future designs for beautification products.

Keywords: Senior citizens · Selfie · Aesthetic · GAN

1 Introduction

The word "Selfie" was voted the most popular word in the Oxford Dictionary in 2013, and it has been confirmed that it was first used on an Australian forum and then became widely known. Selfie means users use smartphones to take pictures of themselves [1]. Some of them share their photos on social network sites, where users can communicate and interact with others by commenting or liking them. The selfie has gradually become a part of young people's lives. It is enjoyable for them to use smartphones as their main tool for taking, beautifying and sharing selfies photos [2]. There are plenty of comprehensive and sophisticated smartphone apps that could satisfy their needs. For example, in most selfie apps, reshaping faces, putting on makeup and adding decorative stickers has been achieved perfectly [3]. There is also plenty of social software like Instagram that encourages users to post selfies for more attention and comments. Therefore people take selfies more and more frequently. The more selfies they post out, the more attention they tend to get [4].

There are a lot of studies that focus on young people's behavior of selfie and social relationships [5], but few focus on senior people. Senior people are

Supported by organization the Future Lab at Tsinghua University.

© Springer Nature Switzerland AG 2020

Q. Gao and J. Zhou (Eds.): HCII 2020, LNCS 12209, pp. 146–160, 2020.
https://doi.org/10.1007/978-3-030-50232-4_11

also a part of this technological society, and the desire to learn how to use smart devices such as smartphones. They also want to learn taking selfies [6]. From senior citizens' perspective, taking selfies means not only taking photos but also connections between them and the younger generation, especially their grandchildren. In this study, 127 online survey were used to investigate the selfie-taking behavior of the elderly, usage of photo-taking apps and problems in the process of selfie-taking.

As a popular function, beauty (portrait photo beautification) on a smartphone has been attached to too much attention by users. The aesthetic standard of cosmetic tools on the market is mainly focused on young people. Although beautification apps that are designed for young people have satisfied most users, there is little such product for senior people. One reason to explain that maybe the beauty needs of senior people are not being addressed, or there are not many databases devoted to facial portraits of senior people. We wanted to summarize and propose some of the aesthetic criteria for senior people, so we conducted in-depth interviews with 17 users over the age of 50+ to understand their aesthetic standards and preferences for senior people.

Analyzing data collected from the above studies, a simple senior citizens preference model can be derived. Based on this model, a style generative adversarial net (Style-GAN) was implemented to build a beautification prototype. Instead of directly editing or reshaping origin photos, we generate new landscaping photos based on origin ones by mixing details from two different style photos. In this study, we developed a program to modify photos, transforming origin faces to certain faces mainly focusing on some features.

2   Related Work

2.1   Selfie Behavior and Social Network

Selfie is popular among young people and can reflect a person's behavior and state of mind [7]. There are a lot of researches have analyzed selfie as an important activity for young people to show themselves on social networks. It even shows that selfie has huge effects on merchandise brands [8]. Selfies vary greatly from group to group, especially from men to women. Research shows that women take and share selfies more frequently than men do [9], and younger generations taking selfies more frequently than older generations do [10]. Women have a greater tendency to share their selfies on social networks and compare with others [11]. Judite Gonçalves and others put forward a concept of SAI (Selfie Aging Index), by recording the elderly selfie portrait to observe their health level [12]. Selfie can also show a certain degree of personality [7]. A lot of researches has focused on the younger generation because it is easier for young people to access the Internet and smart devices. Our study wanted to focus on the older population, specifically those over 50.

2.2 Photo Modification

Modifying facial photos is always an interesting and challenging problem in computer vision. A multi-resolution dynamic model using machine learning [13] was published in 2011 to modify faces to different ages. They adopt a high-resolution grammatical face model to account for the large variations of the facial structures and augment it with age and hair features. For every input image, using the Markov process, they first infer the graph representation and then sample the graph structures over various age groups following the learned dynamics model [13]. This method successfully simulated faces under different ages. However, when put different structures together, this method may generate strange faces. Different facial structures may not compatible.

In the past ten years [14–18], with the continuous improvement of hardware, deep learning technology has been widely used, and computer vision has also achieved breakthrough innovation and development. With the help of Generative Adversarial Nets (GAN) [19], we can use any latent code to generate facial images more naturally. In order to generate high-quality photos, progressive growth of GAN (PGGAN) [20] generates images from low-resolution images progressively to high-resolution images. To change images' style, a style based GAN [21,22] known as style GAN can help generate mix-style images.

The secret of GAN is to randomly generate a z vector, and transform it into latent space. This latent code with the dimension of 18×512 decides every information of the image that is about to generate. Scientists were not satisfied with playing with random latent code, but getting interested in finding latent code of any given images, in other words, to project any given images to latent space. In 2017, an image encoder [23] which implemented with stochastic clipping was published. This encoder can transfer any human face image to a latent space. It explored how an 18×512 dimension latent space can decide the style and quality of images. And it also provided ideas for future work in computer vision.

In this paper, we focus on how to beautify the elderly's faces. We see beautification as a process of reconstructing images, adding the details we want and deleting the details we do not need. We applied GAN technologies to specifically senior people's faces. Detail will be explained in the Study 3 session. We used a diagram to show the flow of the studies (Fig. 1).

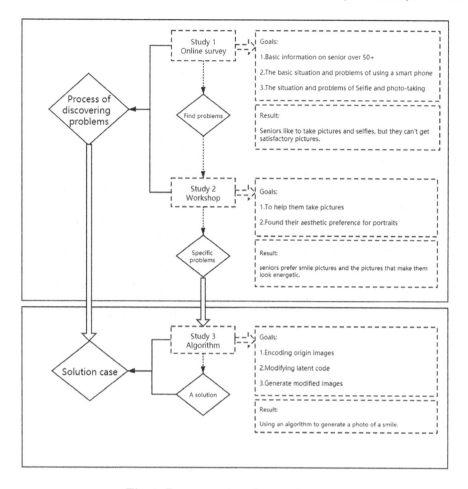

Fig. 1. Demonstration of research process

3 Study 1: Investigation of Selfie and Photo Beautification on Senior Citizens

3.1 Participants and Procedure

Since one of our goals is to find out senior people's behavior, it is more efficient to get information from people who were familiar with advanced technologies. Therefore, we conducted a continuous online survey to collect senior citizens' behavior data. Our target population of the survey was Internet users, including web users and smartphone users. We designed our questionnaire from the following perspectives: (1) Basic information. (2) Usage of taking selfies. (3) Usage of beautification functions. There were mainly three types of questions in the survey: (1) Multiple-choice questions. (2) Multiple answers questions. (3) Ranking questions. This online survey started from 18th November 2019 to

18th January 2020. In order to make questionnaire participants as diverse as possible, we invited senior communities in both Beijing (north of China) and Nanjing (south of China) to help us fill the questionnaire. Questions in the survey were designed easy to understand for senior people to make sure the data we collect as accurately as possible.

3.2   Results

After two months, we have collected 127 online surveys detailing the usage of mobile phones by senior people over the age of 50, focused on problems with the selfie process and face beautification. The survey was completed by 34 people under the age of 50 and 93 people over the age of 50. Over half (50.56%) of the participants were aged between 50 and 60 years old. 76.38% of the participants lived in small cities and villages. 70% of the participants live with their spouses. 89.76% of the participants have used smartphones for more than three years. Watching TV (73.23%), playing mobile phones including browse news and watch the video (69.29%), exercising (62.2%) and chatting with others online (47.24%) are their main interests in daily life. The main functions of using a smartphone are listed in order: chatting, browse news, taking photos (including selfies), and other recreational activities (Fig. 2).

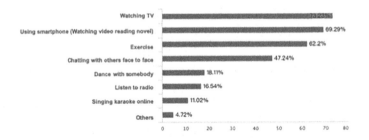

Fig. 2. Favorite activities

In our survey, using a smartphone to take selfies and beautification are the main points. 87.41% of the participants said they know how to take a selfie with their smartphone, while 57.48% said they were skilled at using the selfie function. However, only 37% of participants said they enjoy taking selfies, and more than half (53.54%) of the participants did not have a clear preference. When asked why they didn't like selfies, the primary reason (43.31%) they offered was that selfie photos were not beautiful enough, in other words, they did not know how to take beautiful selfies. The next two reasons were not liking selfies and not knowing why they were taking selfies (Fig. 3).

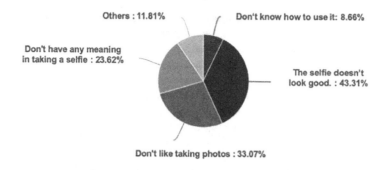

Fig. 3. The reason why they don't like selfie

When asked what was problems with taking selfies on mobile phones, the inability to understand the function of the buttons (34.65%), the shaking of the hands (33.07%) and the inability to see the screen clearly (25.98%) were the three main problems. Others, such as being unable to lift an arm or being unable to find a button, also affected participants' selfie-taking behavior (Fig. 4). Here we find that the two biggest problems affecting people taking selfies come from the use of cell phone selfies and physical reasons. More than half of the participants (53.54%) wanted to record their current state when they took a Selfie.

When it came to using photos for beautifying faces, 63.78% of the participants said they had at least used beautification function once. The majority (76.48%) of participants chose to use the phone's built-in beauty feature rather than the beautification applications. 60.63% of the participants were satisfied with the effect of the beauty camera, while 39.37% were not satisfied. The main causes of dissatisfaction with beauty camera were unnatural effect (53.54%), complex function (40.94%), and the beautified photos by applications did not meet their own aesthetic (27.56%) demands. From the participants' perspectives, the beauty features they liked were adjusting the light, adjusting the angle, removing the messy background, removing the wrinkles and optimizing the face (Fig. 5).

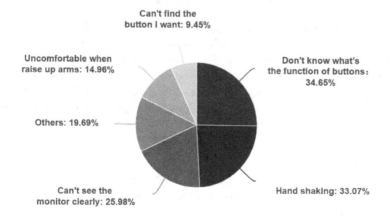

Fig. 4. Problems on taking selfie

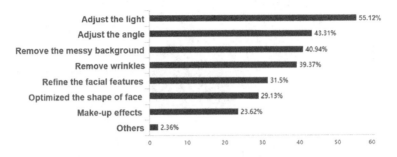

Fig. 5. Beautification function they want on selfie

3.3 Discussion

From this survey, we can conclude that senior people have a huge need for shooting, especially taking selfies. They desire to be skilled in taking photos so that it would be much more convenient to record their lives, perhaps because older people are worried about the deterioration of their memories. Another reason is that they want to get closer to young generations and have more topics with them. But for them, aside from the problems of using smartphone software, there are some physical problems that young people may not imagine. Shoulder or hand tremors may not allow them to hold cell phones for a long time to look for good angles and light. In order to get a good selfie, they need post-production beautification. Most photo beautification software is designed for young people, complex functions and according to young people's aesthetic standards. Senior people need beauty tools that are functionally easy to use and meet their aesthetic needs. Unfortunately, senior people's demands, as special demands from young people, are ignored. Therefore, in order to have a deeper understanding of senior people's aesthetic preferences, we held workshops to make face-to-face conversations with senior generations. Details will be discussed in the Study 2 session.

4 Study 2: Facial Aesthetic Preference of Senior Citizens

According to the online survey in study 1, we have a basic understanding of senior people's behavior about using cell phones to take selfies and beautifying their faces, but their satisfaction and aesthetic preferences were still not clear. Thus, we held two workshops on the theme of "Mobile photo studio - Finding Your Beauty". These two workshops are study2a and study2b. The process is the same for both workshops, but the difference is the participants were different, as we'll explain in more detail below.

4.1 Participants

We've invited 16 (8 males, 8 females, mean = 65, SD = 5.07) senior people. 10 (P1–P10) seniors in workshop1 (study2a) and others (from P11–P16) in workshop2 (study2b). The participants were all retired and all of them had at least three years of experience of using smartphones. The main objective of this workshop was to learn what kind of angle in portrait photos were preferred by the elderly and what their needs about the beautification of the face were (Table 1).

Table 1. Summary of study 2 participates

No	Age	Gender	Years on use of smartphone	Selfie frequency	Beautification frequency
P1	74	M	3–5 years	Almost don't	Don't use
P2	60	F	3–5 years	In common	Don't use
P3	67	F	3–5 years	In common	In common
P4	65	M	3–5 years	Almost don't	Less
P5	65	M	5–10 years	Less	Less
P6	64	M	5–10 years	Less	Don't use
P7	60	F	3–5 years	In common	Less
P8	61	F	5–10 years	Less	Don't use
P9	65	F	Over 10 years	Less	Don't use
P10	68	M	3–5 years	Don't use	Don't use
P11	58	F	5–10 years	In common	Less
P12	65	F	Over 10 years	In common	In common
P13	62	M	5–10 years	Don't use	Less
P14	63	M	5–10 years	Less	Less
P15	68	M	3–5 years	Less	Less
P16	65	M	Over 10 years	In common	Don't use

4.2 Procedure

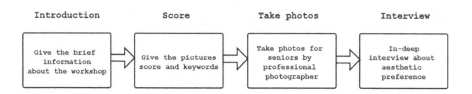

Fig. 6. Workshop procedure

The full process of the workshop can be found at Fig. 6. At beginning we gave them a brief introduction about our workshop, then we showed 30 pictures of senior people's faces we have taken before, we asked them to rate the pictures on a scale from point 1 to point 5, 1 represented the least photo you like, 5 represented the most photo you like and so on. We also let them write down some keywords to briefly explain the reason for the score they gave. Throughout the grading process, volunteers offered help and answered questions around the senior people.

After the scoring section, we invited a professional photographer to take photos for them, In workshop1 we just took pictures from different angles, but in workshop2 we took pictures from different angles, distance and different smile emotions for seniors.

Each person took about 7 photos and then rated their portraits on a scale from point 1 to point 5 by themselves. When senior people rated their own portraits, we also let them briefly explain their aesthetic standards. After that, we had a 10–15 minute in-depth interview to ask them more specifically about smartphones and selfies. In the end, we help them to print out their favorite photos as souvenirs for them. Some of the workshop's documented photos can be found at Fig. 7.

Fig. 7. Workshop pictures

4.3 Results

We calculated the average scores of which respondents in both two workshops rated themselves. The total average score was 4.10 (Fig. 8). Male respondents tended to rate themselves' photos around 4.00 which were lower than the total average, while female respondents tended to give 4.12 points to their photos which were a little bit higher than the total average score.

We also made a peer review of the rating score, to let respondents rate other's photos. The total average score was around 3.84 points. The total average score of male respondents rated all portraits was around 3.49 points, while female respondents gave around 4.23 points (Fig. 9). We also did a work of calculating the gender-portraits cross score. The results showed male respondents gave around 3.23 points to male portraits while female respondents gave around 3.91, and male respondents gave around 3.54 points to female portraits while female respondents gave around 4.29 points.

When we try to let them write down keywords, they provided words that are not analytically relevant, such as a large number of photos rated as "just so" which is not technically a valid word. We need to ask a lot of questions to get an effective comment as the light is good, the accessory looks good, etc. However,

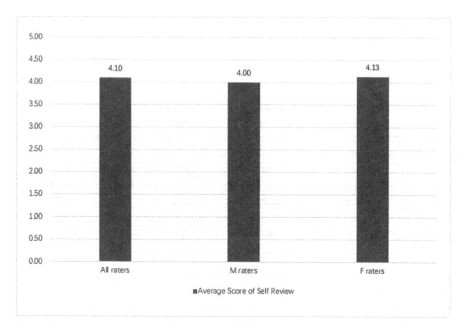

Fig. 8. Average score of which people rated themselves

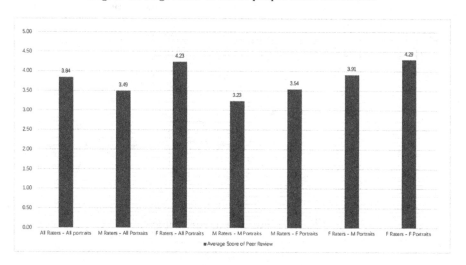

Fig. 9. Average score of peer review

we have concluded that some elderly people prefer to take photos from a positive angle, which means they like happiness selfie pictures. In our workshop 2, 6 out of 7 respondents rated over mark 4 to photos of faces with a smile. 2 raters gave 5 points (highest score) to smile images. Only one elderly person rated 1 point.

The reason he gave why he rated the lowest score has nothing to do with smiles but not satisfied with poses.

4.4 Discussion

Through study 1 and 2, we can find that the seniors are very interested in taking photos, they also have a unique aesthetic preference for selfies, in the angle, lighting, take photos at a distance with young people have similar requirements. But in the facial expression requirements for the portrait photos, we found that "look lively", "smile nice" such as this words are often mentioned by the seniors. Normal beauty features can adjust lighting or angles, but few cameras focus on how to make an senior person smile. After all, senior people don't usually smile when taking pictures without a professional photographer guiding them. So we used an algorithm in study 3 to make the senior people smile.

5   Study 3: Beautification Realization

Using conclusion from study 2, we know that to beautify faces of senior people is 1) to remove age spot such as wrinkles from faces and 2) to add suitable smile to faces. The structure of algorithm is shown in Fig. 10. Original images (I) represents the given image we need to be modified, trained model (m) represents the smile model we used; latent code (w′) represents vector that is derived from encoding I; new latent code (v′) represents latent code of output image; generated image (I′) represents the final image we get (Fig. 10).

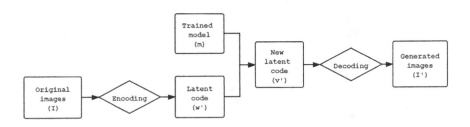

Fig. 10. Different types of photos.

5.1 Encoding Origin Images

We used photos taken by ourselves with SONY ILCE-7M2. Each photo had a resolution of 6000 pixels by 4000 pixels (Fig. 11(A). We first select human faces from each photo and down sampled them to 1024 pixels to 1024 pixels, making sure all faces were right in the middle of the photos (Fig. 11(B)).

To encode aligned photos, we applied style-GAN encoder [23]. The encoder uses gradient descent to optimize latent code w′. Perceptual Loss represents the difference between true image and generated image, which is a value to judge the quality of latent code w'. In our study, we keep the final loss score around 80.

We then generate an image (Fig. 11(C)) using w'. We did a little survey to ask people which one is better based on their aesthetic. 100% of respondents prefer regenerated photos rather than origin photos. The most reasons they gave were people in regenerated photos had less wrinkles and age spots. It shows that it is better to keep images' final loss not to 0.

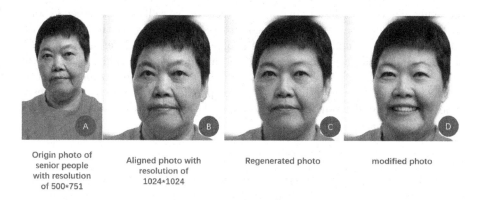

| Origin photo of senior people with resolution of 500*751 | Aligned photo with resolution of 1024*1024 | Regenerated photo | modified photo |

Fig. 11. Different types of photos.

5.2 Modifying Latent Code

In order to change the style of faces, for example, make people smile, we need to modify the latent code. The latent code has a dimension of 18×512. The first 8 dimensions of vector decides hairstyle, shape of the face and some other details of faces. Therefore, the key to change the style of human faces is to change the first 8 dimensions of the latent code.

As shown in Fig. 11(C) and Fig. 11(D), a feature of the smile is added to the image. To do that, we used a smile model trained by style-GAN, using a dataset of FFHQ, a dataset including 70000 human faces. Then we mix the first 8 dimensions vector of our latent code with the smiling model, to get a new latent code (Fig. 12). The image generated with this new vector is the final image we need.

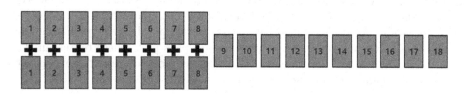

Fig. 12. Latent code modification

6 General Discussion

6.1 Conclusion

Through our survey and in-depth research in the workshop, we found that seniors need to take photos and selfies, they are eager to record their memories, especially when traveling. But there are obstacles to using smart devices. Many senior people don't have enough storage on their smartphones, which makes them worry that taking photos. There are also physical reasons why they use their phones to take selfies, such as shoulder pain and hand tremors, as well as poor screen vision, which is a problem for many senior people. We also found that the aesthetic of selfie portraits of the elderly and young people are also very different. They will obviously prefer pictures that are energetic and bring a pleasant mood like a picture of a smile, a picture of a twinkle in the eyes. In order to remove some wrinkles and age spots from images of senior people's faces, it is better to keep the loss of generated latent code bigger than 0. The less loss we set, the more wrinkles will remain.

6.2 Limitation

This study has potential limitations. The conclusions in this paper are based on online surveys and workshops we held. They are therefore subject to biases due to data limitations and other factors. (1) In our online survey, there are only 39 male respondents out of all 127 respondents. An unequal number of respondents may have influenced our analysis and conclusion. Meanwhile a total number of 127 respondents is still not big enough. (2) In our workshop 1, we interviewed 10 seniors, and in workshop 2, another 7 seniors involved. The number of senior people is limited. (3) Questions in surveys and interviews were some general questions. In order to understand the elderly's needs thoroughly, we need to design our questions more in detail and cover more aspects. (4) Style-GAN has already satisfied our goal to beautify human faces. However, the processing time is not fast enough.

6.3 Future Works

Many different interviews, tests, and experiments have been left for the future due to time, geography and other limitations. Future work concerns a deeper analysis of the particular needs of the elderly and new proposals to try different aspects. We intend to design an interactive mobile application for the elderly so that the elderly would not be worried about too many buttons and complex operation. And with authorized users, the data collected by this mobile application could help us understand senior people's preferences better. In the future, we will also explore the aesthetic preferences of older adults for portrait photographs using neuroscience methods such as eye-tracking and fNIRS.

Acknowledge. This work is supported by NO. 20197010002, Tsinghua University Research Funding. We would like to thank professor Jihong Jeung, Jiabei Jiang and Yuhao Huang for their help and support.

References

1. Oxford Dictionaries (2013). https://en.oxforddictionaries.com/definition/selfie. Selfie
2. Katz, J.E., Crocker, E.T.: Selfies and photo messaging as visual conversation: reports from the United States, United Kingdom, and China. Int. J. Commun. 9(1), 1861–1872 (2015)
3. Chae, J.: Virtual makeover: selfie-taking and social media use increase selfie-editing frequency through social comparison. Comput. Hum. Behav. 66, 370–376 (2017)
4. Kim, E., Lee, J.A., Sung, Y., et al.: Predicting selfie-posting behavior on social networking sites: an extension of theory of planned behavior. Comput. Hum. Behav. 62, 116–123 (2016)
5. Dhir, A., Kaur, P., Lonka, K., Nieminen, M.: Why do adolescents untag photos on Facebook? Comput. Hum. Behav. 55, 1106–1115 (2016)
6. Pew Internet: Social media update 2013 (2013). http://www.pewinternet.org/2013/12/30/social-media-update-2013/
7. Qiu, L., Lu, J., Yang, S., et al.: What does your selfie say about you? Comput. Hum. Behav. 52, 443–449 (2015)
8. Hartmann, J., Heitmann, M., Schamp, C., et al.: The Power of Brand Selfies in Consumer-Generated Brand Images. Social Science Electronic Publishing (2019)
9. Cao, Y., O'Halloran, K.: Learning human photo shooting patterns from large-scale community photo collections. Multimedia Tools Appl. 74(24), 11499–11516 (2015)
10. Dhir, A., Pallesen, S., Torsheim, T., et al.: Do age and gender differences exist in selfie-related behaviours? Comput. Hum. Behav. 63, 549–555 (2016)
11. Manago, A.M., Graham, M.B., Greenfield, P.M., et al.: Self-presentation and gender on MySpace. J. Appl. Dev. Psychol. 29(6), 446–458 (2008)
12. Judite, G., Isabel, G.M., Miguel, F., et al.: Selfie aging index: an index for the self-assessment of healthy and active aging. Front. Med. 4, 236 (2017)
13. Suo, J.L., Min, F., Zhu, S.C., et al.: A multi-resolution dynamic model for face aging simulation. In: 2007 IEEE Computer Society Conference on Computer Vision and Pattern Recognition (CVPR 2007), 18–23 June 2007, Minneapolis, Minnesota, USA. IEEE (2007)
14. Krizhevsky, A., Sutskever, I., Hinton, G.: ImageNet classification with deep convolutional neural networks. In: Advances in Neural Information Processing Systems, vol. 25, no. 2 (2012)
15. Girshick, R., Donahue, J., Darrell, T., Malik, J.: Rich feature hierarchies for accurate object detection and semantic segmentation. In: Proceedings of the IEEE Computer Society Conference on Computer Vision and Pattern Recognition (2013). https://doi.org/10.1109/CVPR.2014.81
16. Ren, S., He, K., Girshick, R., Sun, J.: Faster R-CNN: towards real-time object detection with region proposal networks, pp. 1–10 (2016)
17. Redmon, J., Farhadi, A.: YOLO9000: better, faster, stronger, pp. 6517-6525 (2017). https://doi.org/10.1109/CVPR.2017.690
18. Redmon, J., Farhadi, A.: YOLOv3: an incremental improvement (2018)
19. Goodfellow, I.J., et al.: Generative adversarial networks. In: Advances in Neural Information Processing Systems (2014)
20. Karras, T., Aila, T., Laine, S., et al.: Progressive growing of GANs for improved quality, stability, and variation (2017)
21. Karras, T., Laine, S., Aila, T.: A style-based generator architecture for generative adversarial networks, pp. 4396–4405 (2019). https://doi.org/10.1109/CVPR.2019.00453

22. Karras, T., Laine, S., Aittala, M., Hellsten, J., Lehtinen, J., Aila, T.: Analyzing and improving the image quality of StyleGAN (2019)
23. Lipton, Z.C., Tripathi, S.: Precise recovery of latent vectors from generative adversarial networks (2017)

Technology Acceptance and Societal Impact

Technologies and Images of Older Women

María Silveria Agulló-Tomás$^{(\boxtimes)}$ and Vanessa Zorrilla-Muñoz$^{(\boxtimes)}$

Department of Social Analysis, Universidad Carlos III de Madrid,
University Institute of Gender Studies, 28903 Getafe, Spain
msat@polsoc.uc3m.es, vzorrill@ing.uc3m.es

Abstract. This study is focused on indicators of participation and favourable perception about life in women over 50 years, which are positively associated with technology dispositive aids, social images and identity. Furthermore, stereotypes and image of older women are concepts more negative for older women in comparison to older men. This includes the idea of how technology and cyber-technology have some impact on the positive mobility of older women related to aspects such as participation, perception of life and social and self-perceived image. This chapter aims to explore such dimension in Spain. In addition, the chapter refers to the use of technological devices for functional support (e.g. Tele-care and alarm devices, electric wheelchairs, buggies and scooters). In any case, the main use of devices could be explained because older women manifest a greater need for them and also because they have vital positive attitude and perceptions towards an "ikigai" (oriental concept referring to these concepts) more positive to address the problems. All of this justifies the unmet demand for technology and devices used to support older people, particularly women. This mixed picture also shows the need to improve the social image and further research (from a gender, tecno-feminist and socio-spatial perspectives) in the applicability of systems that seek greater functional mobility of a more active aging, better images and an improvement in the quality of life and a reduction of the digital divide for older women.

Keywords: Technology · Older people · Images · Gender · Participation · Mobility · Cybertechnology

1 Introduction

Technological support for the older people influences both their physical adaptation for better aging and at the psychosocial level - in their social image and identity. The socio-gerontological studies on quality of life reveal that certain everyday life activities (e.g., leisure, care, or volunteering, among others), as well as the favorable perception about life itself, positively influence the quality of life. Besides, the thesis which argued activity as a core for well aging has been followed by classics authors from the 50s to nowadays. According to the criteria of the United Nations Human Development Index [1], a better quality of life is related to health issues, which is directly affecting the unstoppable increase in the life expectancy of people. In general, this phenomenon is more noticeable in older women, which also includes Spain population.

© Springer Nature Switzerland AG 2020
Q. Gao and J. Zhou (Eds.): HCII 2020, LNCS 12209, pp. 163–175, 2020.
https://doi.org/10.1007/978-3-030-50232-4_12

Some recent Spanish sociodemographic and health studies and researches are focused in the paradigm of ageing and increase of life expectancy of people [2], the impact of quality of life and 'ikigai' [3] better ageing and active ageing [4], aspects that are intimate linked to better caring [5], images in ageing [6, 7] and also, the perception about life and participation, wellbeing [8, 9] which itself positively influence the quality of life. Consistently with the gender perspective applied in this study, there is a need to retake some of the most recent trends, such as 'cyber-feminism' and 'techno-feminism'. Although, there is no consensus in the definition [10–14], both concepts reflect the importance of study technology with gender and intergenerational perspective.

Therefore, this chapter is in the line of various authors who demand a more practical 'techno-feminism' - still considered within the psycho-sociological theories most critical - addressing the digital divide [15] and gender. Because technology has mainly been dominated in the past by men, this perspective continues regardless of age. From another perspective, the digital divide is getting shorter growing [16], because they appear the first generation of older people who do know certain technological tools or demanding use [16, 17]. Thus, the accused use of digital networks and technological resources can be a path or key tool for inter-gender equality and inclusion, but not only - as they say from the 'cyber-feminism' that emphasize the main road [18], but leaving out generations of older women. In this sense, the many benefits of ICT in rural, where societies appear disconnected [19] are not visible or. Specifically, in the case of older women seems to be a worse contact with technological resources [20] and are more disconnected digitally than urban women. A priori, the greater digital divide is perceived by territory or socio-spatial dimension [21].

To all this, studies of images and representations of older people have been increasing in recent decades [22–30]. However, research with a gender perspective applied to the study of images or representations on this vital stage is more recent and scarce. In short, images and representations continue to be more stereotyped - usually negatively - on older people in networks, where their appearance often being biased or forced. Thus, it would be of interest - with the theoretical review of feminist currents necessary for theme of this chapter - a said virtual Ethnographic - in this case, images and discourses/words/tweets about older women. It seems to be going from an image stereotyped portrayal of women in networks and technologies, a more modern and 'cyber-feminist' from the studies of science and technology [31] and leaving room for the adults and older women. These currents, with the accent on networks, complement and reach profiles that feminism of the first and second waves did not convince younger - not older - or not address issues that are of recent news and new, and not so new technologies. In sum, and from any gender perspective, there is a need to create new spaces - virtual or not, rural or urban -, new/classical (traditional) technologies - e.g., for dependency, training, or leisure - adapted for the older persons, especially women.

2   Objectives and Methods

This chapter aims to answer the following questions: How technology and cyber-technology have some impact on the positive mobility of older women? Moreover, how cyber-technology has an impact on aspects such as participation, perception of life, and image? How all of them are related?

For the first objective, statistical data are obtained from the Survey of Health, Ageing and Retirement in Europe (SHARE) database[1], specifically from waves 4 (W4, 2011) and 6 (W6, 2015). The methodology applied for the descriptive analysis compiles the following: 1). sociodemographic data that are compared by the statistical analysis of Mean, Standard Deviation, t-Student, and pK Wallis; b) descriptive statistics analysis for self-perceived live variables and participation includes Mean, Standard Deviation and Pearson. The analysis is performed by the software STATA IC. A resume of technical data is presented in Table 1.

Table 1. Technical data of statistical analysis.

Geographical score	Spain
Information collection	Macro-questionnaire SHARE
Population selected	Women and Men in Spain (>50 years)
Sample size calculated (N)	9247 persons (women and men)
Stratified procedure	Classification in relation to functional mobility
Analysis tool	Software STATA IC

For the second objective, qualitative methodology is utilized based on the testimonies of experts and older people. More precisely, data correspond to the ENCAGE-CM Programme (2016–2019), where 60 documents – six Discussion Groups and 54 in-depth – are evaluated in 2017 in the Autonomous Region of Madrid in four contexts: Civil Society Organizations (CSO henceforth), Firms, Institutions and Professionals and ENVACES Project. The following codes were used to the search of discourses: 'image' (social representations); 'funcfisico' (physical functions); 'care' (aspects related to the provision/receiving of care); 'technologic'; 'health'; 'psychologic factors'; 'participation'; 'gestion'; 'future'; 'identity'.

3   Results

For the first analysis, the sample selected considers that the mean for women and men is 69.52 years. The results reveal that Spanish women have fewer functional limitations – or no mobility limitations – despite they suffer more chronic diseases [32] and have a greater tendency to depression than their male peers (see Table 2).

The second analysis (Table 3) reports a high significance level between selected variables related to the items self-perceived life, participation in activities, and the variable of no mobility limitations.

Also, data of the macro-questionnaire identifies some devices into the typical use, for example, devices which are designed to provide functional support, such as telecare and alarm devices, electric wheelchairs, buggies, and scooters.

---

[1] http://www.share-project.org/home0.html.

Table 2. Older women and men according to some sociodemographic variables of the study and some descriptive statistics.

Sociodemographic variables		Total (N = 9247) [Med. ± SD]	Women (nw = 5081) [Med. ± SD]	Men (nm = 4166) [Med. ± SD]	t-Student (p)	p KW
		[N (%)]	[N (%)]	[N (%)]		
Gender	Women	5081 (49.51)	5081 (100)	–	NA	NA
	Man	4166 (42.24)	–	4166 (100)	NA	NA
Age		69,52 ± 0,111	69,52 ± 0,156	69,52 ± 0,158	0.0342 (0.4864)	0.346 (0.5562)
No mobility limitations (mobility)		2.097 ± 0.029	2.551 ± 0.042	1.544 ± 0.039	−17.05 (1)	296.937 (0.0001)
Euro depression scale		2.651 ± 0.028	3.235 ± 0.039	1.938 ± 0.035	−24.02 (1)	553.083 (0.0001)
Number of chronic diseases		1.937 ± 0.017	2.059 ± 0.023	1.788 ± 0.023	−8.12 (1)	56.777 (0.0001)

Note: *t-Student (p)* = *t-Student test* (probability); *p KW* = *Kruskal-Wallis test probability*. Scales used: No mobility limitations = 1 to 11 (where 11 indicate no limitations and 1 indicate very severe limitations); Euro depression scale = 0 (not depressed) to 12 (very depressed); Number of chronic diseases = minimum 0 and maximum 10.

The qualitative analysis is divided into 3 parts: 'Technologies, mobility and participation'; 'Barrier-free mobility and safety with the support of technology'; 'Technologies and mobility, psychosocial support and images'.

3.1 Technologies, Mobility and Participation

From the speeches analyzed, and consistency with quantitative data commented, the participation of older people increases mobility and reduces the use of assistive technology devices. Besides, experts/interviewees and older people themselves, it also prevents social isolation, enhance social relations with other elders and members of other generations and therefore have a better social image and is supposed to help to better self-esteem, self-image, and "ikigai".

[…] *I can not participate in the dining room for my problem. In fact, pans can not lift or catch a lot of dishes, but I do the reception. And then I do several days a week, two hours each person.* […] D62, VC_20170418, older person

[…] *That's what I say, as I can move, it seems that it will be able to because I have friends my age who can not move from the pain they have, I do not have. So how come not a quick thing ... because the years pass, I already have 74, or which are not few.* [...] D72, VF_20170427, older woman

Table 3. Statistical analysis for the items participation, self-perceived life and no mobility limitations.

Item	Scale used	Media ± SD	Pearson (related to "no mobility limitations)
Variables related to self perceived life			
Age prevent for doing things (ac014)	Often, sometimes, rarely or never	2.158 ± 0.115	0.4365**
Out of control (ac015)		2.910 ± 0.010	0.3691**
Feel left out of things (ac016)		3.300 ± 0.009	0.3008**
Do the things you want to do (ac017)		2.014 ± 0.010	−0.2997**
Family responsibilities prevent (ac018)		3.063 ± 0.011	−0.0235*
Shortage of money stops (ac019)		2.401 ± 0.011	0.0435**
Look forward to each day (ac020)		1.671 ± 0.008	−0.3314**
Life has meaning (ac021)		1.583 ± 0.008	−0.3371**
Look back on life with happiness (ac022)		1.755 ± 0.009	−0.1227**
Feel full of energy (ac023)		2.008 ± 0.009	−0.5440**
Full of opportunities (ac024)		2.138 ± 0.009	−0.3384**
Future looks good (ac025)		2.212 ± 0.010	−0.3978**
Variables of participation			
How often done/voluntary/charity work the last 12 months (ac036_1)		0.142 ± 0.006	0.0656**
How often attended and educational or training course the last 12 months (ac036_4)		0.150 ± 0.007	0.0857**

(continued)

Table 3. (*continued*)

Item	Scale used	Media ± SD	Pearson (related to "no mobility limitations)
How often go to a sport/social/other kind of club the last 12 months (ac036_5)		0.255 ± 0.008	0.1200**
How often taken part in a political/community related organization the last 12 months (ac036_7)		0.070 ± 0.004	0.0548**
How often read books, magazines or newspaper the last 13 months (ac036_8)		0.779 ± 0.011	0.1795**
No mobility limitations (mobility)	11 to 1 (where 11 indicate no limitations and 1 indicate very severe limitations)	8.902 ± 0.030	NA

** $p < 0,01$, * $p < 0,05$

[…] *I will not be able to this because the leg does not answer me, I can hardly stand up […] Much, much, much active. Because it is going… one of the reasons that … that helps us because if you do not if you're on television around, you eat the jar.* […] D77, VF_20170424, older woman

In some cases, there is a rejection of technological support - for example, wheelchair -. Whether through ignorance and think they can not handle or negative social image representing related to a negative view of disability, both physical and sensory at this age, but also an even pejorative image of disability at any stage of life. Moreover, although the technological devices use is rejected, the imperative is also shown to remain necessary in certain physical conditions.

[…] *I have a spinal injury, then that limits me quite […] I have to be very active to keep going well. Because obviously, it is clear … when I see them in wheelchairs with computers … buah, it gives me something, really.* […] D1, GD_170424, older woman

[…] *In my home, there are people who can walk, but sit in a chair since breakfast until lunchtime. At lunchtime rise, they go to the dining room and then do not move. What happens? That one day they will not move at all, because if you do not move … The less you have, the less you do.* […] D1, GD_170424, older woman

[…] *because there are people that indeed there to get her wheelchair, they can not go themselves […] because people maybe say "Well, I like … I'm like I walk, I have a wheelchair for someone else to go with time, that is, I take that person and simultaneously serves me support the wheelchair".* […] D7, EP_EPQ_170424, expert

3.2 Barrier-Free Mobility and Safety with the Support of Technology

The first step to improve mobility is to reduce barriers. In this regard, speeches analyzed show that global safety is nowadays a basic point unresolved in the existence. This is an unresolved issue for decades. Unless, there are high advances and adaptability and, accessibility programs increased during the last years. Nevertheless, it still does not reach all residential, rural or urban contexts, especially rural but also in certain urban neighborhoods and residences.

[...] *Well, then there are huge barriers in society, cities and other pose, they good, have learned to live with them and sometimes not see them, but really when they are prevented is when already.* [...] D13, EP_INS_170711, expert

[...] *barriers exist and are evident as declines greater autonomy, but the clear desire is to maintain this autonomy, and our policies - the network of primary and such assistance - are to follow keeping as much as possible that people stay in their homes.* [...] D13, EP_INS_170711, expert

[...] *there are hundreds of older people living in buildings that cannot go to Aunt street, well I came upset were some data that is not now say the percentage is not botch but a brutal data, people more alone than not left his home because there were no adequate elevators, because he had no power and mobility are good because almost going to say we left but I cannot call it.* [...] EP, OSC_170512, expert

Sometimes this means that some of the adaptations, in particular, those carried out in the homes of older people, involve a loss of individuality towards improving their safety.

[...] *The sense of security, see, I think it's essential. In other words, with a feeling of "I will spend some" say that whatever we focus to survival and over, right? It is in that sense in which the residence understands, right? Many of the people who come are of you say, "Well, I do not dare to be alone in the bathroom of my house because it is that at any time I can fall, I can pass something and others, do not ? So I have to sacrifice some privacy to security. Yes, it is a basic need, right? It would be below this. Maybe the problem is how to reconcile the need for security to not to lose too much individuality, is it not? In privacy, decisiveness...* [...] D8, EPQ_20170721, expert

3.3 Technologies, Psychosocial Support and Images

In the analysis, speeches are drawn about safety as it also increases participation. It is a technology that incorporates not only the mobility varies, but goes further and refers to the virtual support, mental or psychosocial, which is also necessary. Those interviewed refer to it as a way to stay connected every day and as a means to learn, although it is also observed much misinformation on the subject.

[...] *if they are sure of the environment, if well with staff, if they are physically fit because they will be much better for all, will participate more, they'll be happier, they'll be more, well, happier with families* [...] D18, EP_INST_ 170404, expert

[...] *Well, say "Grandma likes too much her mobile, she feels now as young people, she is always connecting to the mobile" because it was a ... the computer will not, because things of the computer me solve them all, but this yes because... running around because they get up and I already are sending the photo of the girl how she is dressed to school*

[…] I am more awkward in a matter of technology, but for which I think for example, you're linked to my son, they talk to me, I talk to them, I say, send me … […] D90, VF_20170424, older woman

[…] Too much computer time, which… too much TV time. For as I can not move. […] one thing to read a test and another thing is to inform through both television and computer information, in order to be more informed about society. […] D61, VC_20170418, older woman

Although there is still a clear intergenerational gap in this regard, the elderly - especially men, due to their higher level of studies or other factors differentiated by gender elements - are increasing their use, as seen in previous speeches. Faced with misinformation appear speeches commenting on the need to carry out more activities on the use of devices that encourage older people to participate socially.

[…] New technologies, yes, that we've been doing. Yes, we try to approach things that are more or less novel. Themes emotions, try to talk about these situations, channeling power … […] D12, EP_INS_170607, expert

[…] they are introducing more and more activities and workshop. These activities are more aimed at equipping them to turn instrument on all communication. Especially, activities are focused on new technologies, use of mobile phones, the Internet, so it is taking much into that … to that level […] D16, EP_INS_20170324, expert

[…] our seniors are going to be major centers of Madrid, older people residences in the community to teach, give a talk to the elders, some workshops to explain that we can draw from this device that is a lot. From what I've learned and usually did not know, I had to ask my grandson, "I hear this does not work, give me this and that …" and so on the computer; Of course if I do what they have already learned it in that sense can be more independent or autonomous. […] that older to enter ICT and such which is older and there are many elderly who really want to get into ICT want to learn how to use tablet is going to really encourage is that other needs are demanding the biggest […] D31, EP_OSC_20170615, expert

[…] to the phone we find it hard because it's new. What compels me is what I force myself for my needs. So, I usually used the computer and the phone… […] Internet is very interesting. I use Internet and the phone only to my basic needs. […] These force me to be more active. […] D62, VC_20170418, older person

Moreover, we would highlight the resources to help mobility and how technology can help improve mobility, active aging, and perception of the quality of life, such as assistive devices and technological support should modify their design. Also, they emphasize the need for human care in addition to technical support and vice versa. Some speeches confirm this:

[…] I have difficulty commute, it seems that I lack muscle strength, which I develop here very well, within an order. But if I go out to the street and I have to take such a crutch elbow because it offers more security than a stick. […] I'll end with … because I move … I can hardly walk, then … And that's all that's what … […] So, I'm fine here, the fact that I am alone and have difficulty commute because … I can walk, that is, I can walk yet, but … but … but no doubt I'm like in a golden cage. […] D62, VC_20170418, older woman

[...] *I always live with Dolores* - Spanish name to a lot of pain -. *But it has already gotten used so that as it does not exist, all my entertainment avoid my pain ... [...] and make some movement to place you and what and not how many, but I avoid while I'm entertaining, not worry about them so much, that I have restricted medication because, as eighty percent ...* [...] D118, VF_20170607, older person

[...] *Well, one not, which is the only that is here in a wheelchair, has a great mind, but has a lot of difficulties, but it has a lot of encouragement and has plenty of support ... Here are some nurses [...] When they went away I grabbed a chair, I grabbed the other ... "mom you'll fall, you stay there still sit down", and that influences a lot too. But of course, it is that you have ... you must to be positive in life.* [...] D77, VF_20170424, older woman

From the perspective of the image and social representations, showing speeches appear as, from the technological experience; it can help improve self-image and social image.

Well, I think it's enriched and make the person feel more useful, I see it going well. [...] has a computer [...] We are putting little things, maybe you take a picture, "what is this?" Or you put a letter: "Is this letter" ... or a word a letter, and lack. "? At this point ... this word Which letter would fit" All that we are saying is the computer, they are slowly doing [...] I, for me, I think. that they would meet, because the other way all day so ... it makes ... are not useless, and so they are, for that, they have something to do and they are not so useless as they [...] are thought. D7: EP_EPQ_170724, expert

[...] *or you discover new technologies a priori, being a spectator, think is unattainable, still you see characters that are easy or that involves some effort. Then, it is to have the illusion of having something new to do, right?* [...] D12: EP_INS_170617, expert

[...] *I have my mobile, I have my computer ... because it is that when I stopped working, I did not mean you stay there computer and there you stay. No, I followed as far as possible, keeping the intellectual level I could.* [...] D97_VC_RSC_20170517, older woman

4   Some Proposals and Conclusions

According to the first objective, it concludes that variables related to items participation and self-perceived life are connected to no mobility limitations. As in other studies, it must accompany this data with an ethnographic observational analysis and evaluation of the use of technological devices on resources - videos and photos - of virtual and real, both women and men. To this end, the ENCAGEM-CM Program covers an objective study based on these aspects. In general, this program will focus on images of older women - covering the diversity of aging, the representations on the woman herself, and stereotypes, among others -.

Moreover, the increased use of devices by older women can be interpreted as who needs it most, as they have a greater functional problem. In contrast, it can also be understood that they are more likely to use because they have a better attitude, positivity, and perform more activities than their peers, men. In this connection, there is still a digital divide and, therefore, the need to shorten. Considered within the context of older people still seem further away, is less studied, the relationship between gender/feminism and aging/old age has also been poorly treated - for example, include some recent studies, such as Agulló-Tomás and colleagues [33–35] - but no longer needed. In any case, note that the digital feminism or cyber-feminism - especially in his more optimistic and utopian current – it can also help older to be more connected. At the same time, it can leave out older to reach the technological integration and perpetuate the patriarchal dominance – which would be the more current dystopian or negative and, in our case the virtual older women also accentuate inequality -. In short, if older people fail to connect or use advanced technological devices or, even if they do, they still perceived the inter-gender inequality - for example, because of the level of training -. The gap seems still difficult to even shorten with advances continuous robotics, usability and ergonomics based on the person. At the same time, it seems that technological integration does not perpetuate the patriarchal dominance - that would be the most dystopian or negative current and, in our case of older women also accentuated virtual inequality.

While buildings can be adapted, the concept of wheelchair is a robust design, which is not adapted to the needs of people, because their use is a sign of reduced mobility and, therefore, decreases motivation for participation activities. The redesign could be address to optimize wheelchairs and canes as exoskeleton systems. It could facilitate the integration the principle of Ergonomics – based on the person and not on the machine - and current models of care based on comprehensive care person. From this perspective, the need for programs to improve technical aids and also the social image of them - more tailored, modern, new designs, among others - seems imposed on the like usability and aesthetics.

Undoubtedly, technological aids and, in general, ICTs are positively perceived as security [36, 37] which also help to avoid social isolation and depression in elderly [38, 39]. Of course, the design of new ICT must be based on the universal concept of ergonomics - the person, while taking into account the demands and needs -. Design should be based on the inclusion of most people experience itself [40]. Following this approach, the devices could help improve self-image and social image.

These practices have to be customized, individual arrangements and tailored to the current needs of individuals; and assistive devices for people who need assistance show the care with technology as an exercise constant readjustment attention focused on the uniqueness of each person [41, 42]. However, these individual needs can be added according to groups and socio-demographic variables: whether they are men or women, from rural or urban spaces, etc. That is, the psychosocial, psychological, and technological approach should go hand in hand.

The contributions of technology - whether to support greater mobility, to interact and increase networks, for better health care or for leisure - to a more diverse and positive image of older people also seem clear. Particularly for women whose images are still more stereotyped and suffer more ageism concerning them. Also striking is the increase in programs and workshops for all this, although they are still rare - for example, as mentioned in the workshop speech.

Moreover, older women remain invisible in the awards and achievements through his career, for example, as in the case of leadership [43]. Even more, concerning technology use, because its use is conceived more approximate to a negative connotation on the frailty of old age, rather than positive, on professional skills. Some recent authors discuss the presence of feminism in the online networks and specifically analyze 'hashtags' [44], but older people remain invisible. Other authors have studied in detail a large sample of tweets, for example, on older [45], but there is no perceived gender or techno-feminist perspective. Therefore, the relationship between technologies, feminism/gender, older people, and images is still in need of evaluation and more research against sexism and ageism at this vital stage, from a necessary but also novel interrelation.

5 Fundings and Grants

This work is part of different projects: QASP (Quality of life, Ageing in Sweden, Spain, and Portugal) research project and has-been funded by the Institute of Health Carlos III, Intramural Strategical Action in Health AESI 2018, Ref: PI18CIII /00046. https://qaspre search.wixsite.com, ENCAGE-CM (2016-2019), "Active Ageing, Quality of Life and Gender", Comunidad de Madrid, Fondo Social Europeo), CM/FSE, ref. S2015/HUM-3367, https://encage-cm.es, ENVACES "The construction of Active Aging in Spain: Self-Assessment, Determinants and Expectations of Quality of Life", MINECO/FEDER/UE, Ref. CSO2015-64115-R and ENCAGEM-CM (2020–2021) "Active Ageing, Quality of Life and Gender. Promoting a positive image of old age and ageing against ageism", Ref. H2019/HUM-5698.

References

1. United Nations. The Human Development Index (2019). http://hdr.undp.org/en/content/human-development-index-hdi
2. Abellán García, A., Ayala García, A., Pérez Díaz, J., Pujol Rodríguez, R.: Un perfil de las personas mayores en España. In: 2018 Indicadores estadísticos básicos, Madrid, Informes Envejecimiento en red n 17, 34 (2018)
3. Agulló-Tomás, M.S., Zorrilla-Muñoz, V.I.: Activity and Older European Women (2020). https://qaspresearch.wixsite.com/blog/home/ikigai-activity-and-older-european-women
4. Fernández-Mayoralas, G., et al.: El papel del género en el buen envejecer. Una revisión sistemática desde la perspectiva científica. Prisma Soc. (21), 149–176 (2018)
5. Agulló-Tomás, M.S.: Mujeres, cuidados y bienestar social: el apoyo informal a la infancia y a la vejez. Instituto de la Mujer, Madrid (2002). ISBN: 84–7799-973-2. Re-edición virtual (2015) http://www.inmujer.gob.es/publicacioneselectronicas/documentacion/Documentos/DE1470.pdf
6. Agulló-Tomás, M.S.: Estereotipos y actitudes sociales en el entorno del envejecimiento". Presentación de comunicación en "VI Congreso Nacional de Psicología Social. San Sebastián, UPV (1997)
7. Agulló-Tomás, M.S.: Identidad y representaciones sociales: conceptos, imágenes y construcción psicosocial de las 'vejeces'. págs. 621–696, en Mayores, actividad y trabajo en el proceso de envejecimiento y jubilación: una aproximación psico-sociológica. Madrid: IMSERSO, Ministerio de Trabajo y AA.SS. (Tesis Doctoral máxima calificación. Y premio Investigación "IMSERSO 2000"). ISBN: 84-8446-036-3 y publicación CD por UCM: 84-669-1214-2 (2001). Re-edición virtual (2012). http://www.imserso.es/imserso_01/documentacion/publicaciones/colecciones/informacion_publicacion/index.htm?id=422
8. Kite, M.E., Stockdale, G.D., Whitley Jr., B.E., Johnson, B.T.: Attitudes toward younger and older adults: an updated meta-analytic review. J. Soc. Issues 61(2), 241–266 (2005)

9. Castellano Fuentes, C.L.: Análisis de la relación entre las actitudes hacia la vejez y el enve-jecimiento y los índices de bienestar en una muestra de personas mayores. Revista Española de Geriatría y Gerontología. **49**(3), 108–114 (2014)
10. Núñez Puente, S.: From cyberfeminism to technofeminism: from an essentialist perspective to social cyberfeminism in certain feminist practices in Spain. In Women's Studies International Forum, vol. 31, no. 6, pp. 434–440. Pergamon (2008)
11. Wajcman, J.: Technocapitalism meets technofeminism: women and technology in a wireless world. Labour Ind. J. Soc. Econ. Rel. Work **16**(3), 7–20 (2006)
12. Wajcman, J. Gender and work: a technofeminist analysis. In: Handbook of Gender, Work and Organization, pp. 263–275 (2011)
13. Paasonen, S.: Revisiting cyberfeminism. Communications **36**(3), 335–352 (2001)
14. Sikka, T. Technofeminism and ecofeminism: an analysis of geoengineering research. Ecofeminism in Dialogue (2017)
15. Miró, M., Peracaula, J.: Anàlisi de la utilització de les noves tecnologies a l'àmbit de la gerontologia. In: Forum: Revista d'Informació i Investigació, no. 1, pp. 74–76 (1995)
16. Delello, J.A., McWhorter, R.R.Y.: Reducing the digital divide: connecting older adults to iPad technology. J. Appl. Gerontol. **36**(1), 3–28 (2015)
17. Friemel, T.N.: The digital divide has grown old: determinants of a digital divide among seniors. New Media Soc. **18**(2), 313–331 (2014). https://doi.org/10.1177/1461444814538648
18. Romero Sánchez, A.: La utopía postfeminista: del ciberfeminismo al tecnofeminismo. Cuadernos del Ateneo (2014)
19. Welser, H.T., Khan, M.L., Dickard, M.: Digital remediation: social support and online learning communities can help offset rural digital inequality. Inf. Commun. Soc. **22**(5), 717–723 (2019)
20. Zorrilla-Muñoz, V., Agulló-Tomás, M.S., García-Sedano, T.: Análisis socio-ergonómico en la agricultura. Evaluación del sector oleico desde una perspectiva de género y envejecimiento. ITEA, información técnica económica agraria: revista de la Asociación Interprofesional para el Desarrollo Agrario (AIDA) **115**(1), 83–104 (2019)
21. Agulló-Tomás, M.S., Zorrilla-Muñoz, V., Gómez-Díaz, M.V., Criado, B.: Liderazgo, envejec-imiento y género. In: Alonso, A., Langle, T. (eds.) The Time is Now. Feminist Leadership in a New Era. Published by "Red Global de Cátedras UNESCO en Género y por la Organización de las Naciones Unidas para la Educación, la Ciencia y la Cultura", pp. 112–122 (2019). ISBN 978-950-9379-50. https://catunescomujer.org/globalnetwork/es/articulos/la-hora-del-liderazgo-feminista-nueva-publicacion-de-la-red-global-de-catedras-unesco-en-genero/
22. Featherstone, M.Y., Hepwoth, M.: Changing images of retirement: an analysis of representa-tions of ageing in the popular magazine Retirement Choice. In: Bromles, D.B. (ed.) Geron-tology: Social and Behavioral Perspectives. Croom Helm/British Society of Gerontology, Londres (1984)
23. Crespo, E.: Representaciones sociales y actitudes: una visión periférica. In: Fernandez Vil-lanueva, C., Torregrosa, J.R., Burillo, F.J., Munné, Y.F. (eds.) Cuestiones de Psicología Social. Ed. Complutense, Madrid (1991)
24. Bailey, W.T.: The image of middle-aged and older women in magazine advertisements. Educ. Gerontol. Int. J. **19**(2), 97–103 (1993)
25. Agulló-Tomás, M.S: En tercer plano. Estereotipos, cine y mujeres mayores. In: Muñoz, B. (ed.) Medios de comunicación, mujeres y cambio cultural. CAM, Madrid Chapter 9, pp. 245–276 (2001). http://e-archivo.uc3m.es/handle/10016/18952
26. Blanca Mena, M.J., Sánchez Palacios, C., Trianes, M.V.: Cuestionario de evaluación de estereotipos negativos hacia la vejez. Revista Multidisc. de Gerontología **15**(4), 212–220 (2005)
27. Abrams, D., Vauclair, C.M., Swift, H.: Predictors of attitudes to age across Europe. Depart-ment for Work and Pensions. Research Report No. 735 (2011). http://research.dwp.gov.uk/asd/asd5/rrs-index.asp

28. Bustillos-López, A.Y., Fernández-Ballesteros, R.: Efecto de los estereotipos acerca de la vejez en la atención a adultos mayores. Salud Pública de México **54**(2), 104 (2012)
29. Barrio, E., (coord.).: Gente VintAGE. Los diversos rostros de la edad. Documento sobre la exposición itinerante del proyecto "Gente Vintage. Envejecer es vivir". SEGG (Sociedad Española de Geriatría y Gerontología), Y Fundación BBK, Madrid (2013). DL: M-17909–2013. http://imagenyenvejecimiento.blogspot.com.es/search/label/gentevintage
30. Fernández-Ballesteros, R., et al.: Assessing aging stereotypes: personal stereotypes, self-stereotypes and self-perception of aging. Psicothema **29**(4), 482–489 (2017)
31. Vertesi, J., Ribes, D.: DigitalSTS: A Field Guide for Science & Technology Studies. Princeton University Press, Princeton (2019)
32. Agulló-Tomás, M.S., Zorrilla-Muñoz, V., Gómez García, M.V.: Investigación y evaluación sobre género/feminismo y envejecimiento/vejez. Prisma Social revista de investigación social **21**, 2–4 (2018). https://revistaprismasocial.es/issue/view/183
33. Cimas, M., Ayala, A., Sanz, B., Agulló-Tomás, M.S., Escobar, A., Forjaz, M.J.: Chronic musculoskeletal pain in European older adults: Cross-national and gender differences. Eur. J. Pain **22**(2), 333–345 (2018)
34. Agulló-Tomás, M.S., Zorrilla-Muñoz, V., Gómez García, M.V.: Género y evaluación de programas de apoyo para cuidadoras/es de mayores. Prisma Social revista de investigación social **21**, 391–415 (2018). https://revistaprismasocial.es/issue/view/183
35. Agulló-Tomás, M.S., Zorrilla-Muñoz, V., Gómez-García, M.V.: Aproximación socio-espacial al envejecimiento ya los programas para cuidadoras/es de mayores. Revista INFAD de Psicología. Int. J. Dev. Educ. Psychol. **2**(1), 211–228 (2019)
36. Petersson, I., Lilja, M.Y., Borell, L.: To feel safe in everyday life at home—a study of older adults after home modifications. Ageing Soc. **32**(5), 791–811 (2019). https://doi.org/10.1017/s0144686x11000614
37. Abascal, J., Barbosa, S.D., Nicolle, C., Zaphiris, P.: Rethinking universal accessibility: a broader approach considering the digital gap. Univ. Access Inf. Soc. **15**(2), 179–182 (2016)
38. Peek, S.T., Wouters, E.J., Van Hoof, J., Luijkx, K.G., Boeije, H.R., Vrijhoef, H.J.: Factors influencing acceptance of technology for aging in place. Int. J. Med. Inf. **83**, 235–348 (2014). https://doi.org/10.1016/j.ijmedinf.2014.01.004
39. Wu, Y., Damnée, S., Kerhervé, H.Y., Rigaud, A.S.: Bridging the digital divide in older adults: a study from an initiative to inform older adults about new technologies. Clin. Interv. Aging **10**, 193–201 (2015). https://doi.org/10.2147/cia.s72399
40. Mannheim, I., et al.: Inclusion of older adults in the research and design of digital technology. Int. J. Environ. Res. Publ. Health **16**(19), 3718 (2019)
41. Winnance, M.: Care and disability. practices of experimenting, tinkering with, and arranging people and technical aids. In: Mol/Moser/Pols, pp. 93–117 (2010)
42. Mol, A., Moser, I., Pols, J. (eds.) Care in Practice. On Tinkering in Clinics, Homes and Farms. Transcript Verlag, Bielefeld (2010)
43. Agulló-Tomás, M.S., Zorrilla-Muñoz, V., Gómez-García, M.V., Criado-Quesada, B.: Liderazgo, envejecimiento y género. In: Alonso, E.A., de Paz, T.L. (eds.) The Time is Now. Feminist Leadership for a New Era, pp. 112–122 (2019). ISBN: 978-950-9379-50
44. Reverter, S.: Medina-Vicent,M. El feminismo en 35 hastag. Editorial Catarata (2020). ISBN: 978-84-9097-905-1
45. Makita, M., Mas-Bleda, A., Stuart, E., Thelwall, M.: Ageing, old age and older adults: a social media analysis of dominant topics and discourses. Ageing Soc., 1–26 (2019)

Digital Inclusion or Digital Divide for Older Immigrants? A Scoping Review

Xin Chen[1(✉)] ⓘ, Britt Östlund[1] ⓘ, and Susanne Frennert[2] ⓘ

[1] KTH Royal Institute of Technology, SE-14 152, Huddinge, Stockholm, Sweden
xinchen3@kth.se
[2] Malmö University, 21 119 Malmö, Sweden

Abstract. The discussion of the digital divide and digital inclusion has extended to older adults. Although knowledge on the digital divide and digital inclusion among native older adults has increased substantially, little is known about the situations of older immigrants in relation to the digital divide. This paper employed the scoping review approach to map the situations and research methods of the digital divide among older immigrants from recent empirical studies. The initial search identified 997 articles, of which 13 articles were selected for this review. The results showed that socioeconomic status, language proficiency, degree of acculturation, level of education, and digital literacy are the most common factors leading to the disparities between native older adults and older immigrants. Although the results showed a narrowing gap as concerns access to the Internet, interventions are needed to reduce the divide among individuals of different ethnicities due to disparities in digital skills and knowledge. The included studies applied quantitative, qualitative, and mixed-method approaches. The homogeneity of the findings of some included studies implied the need to develop more methods and models to study the digital divide among older immigrants. This review suggested that future research incorporate ethnic characteristics in the research design to provide in-depth knowledge about the ethnic group. This knowledge could potentially be utilized for future interventions aimed at narrowing the remaining gap of the digital divide.

Keywords: Older immigrant · Digitalization · Digital divide · Digital inclusion

1 Introduction

Population aging in developed countries has been a significant challenge to societies. At the same time, it also drives innovation in products and services for active and healthy aging [1, 2]. In parallel, with the trend of globalization and the international migration movement, a large number of international migrants, who possess various backgrounds and motivations, have migrated to many developed areas [3, 4]. Accompanied by the growth in international migration, one significant trend is the increase in the proportion of older migrants [3, 5]. Although migration studies and aging studies are well-established research fields, the particular and heterogeneous groups who hold intersectional identities have not drawn much attention until recently. The age factor adds more heterogeneities

© Springer Nature Switzerland AG 2020
Q. Gao and J. Zhou (Eds.): HCII 2020, LNCS 12209, pp. 176–190, 2020.
https://doi.org/10.1007/978-3-030-50232-4_13

to this group, which has challenged the ability of authorities to study the group and to provide resources and assistance to this group of people and to maintain equalities, particularly compared with the native older adults in accessing healthcare and welfare resources. Some older immigrants can be invisible in society and experience more difficulties in utilizing the public services from the healthcare system than the native older adults or other immigrant groups with a higher socioeconomic status [6–8].

This review aims at exploring digital divide and digital inclusion among older immigrants in digitalizing societies as well as the methodologies applied for the research in the field. A scoping review was applied to investigate the empirical studies considering the digital inclusion or digital divide of older immigrants who were users of digital technologies. The article emphasizes the methodologies used for involving older immigrants, and the findings relate to digital inclusion or the digital divide, as well as the authors' own interpretations.

1.1 Participating in Digitalizing Society

It is an inevitable trend that our daily lives have been redefined and reconstructed by a myriad of digital technologies that have become an indivisible component of older adults' lives [9]. For some older adults, the development of digitalization creates new opportunities to access more information and resources, yet it also endangers other older adults' situations and widens the inequalities between the "haves" and "have-nots" [5, 10, 11]. The increasing trend of digitalization as a way to participate in social activity and to access social welfare can reduce the differences among or, in the opposite direction, create more social exclusion between native older adults and the older immigrants [12]. It is essential to understand the older adults as the users of digital tools and the Internet, which determine whether an individual is integrated into the digitalizing society or left behind [13, 14]. In a society characterized by rapid technical and digital transformation, it is necessary to understand sources of exclusion in order to provide meaningful insights to guide the direction of digitalization to ensure it is able to encompass all individuals.

1.2 Digital Divide and Digital Inclusion

Digital divide and digital inclusion are well-discussed topics with the rapid development of ICT and the increased rate of Internet usage since the 1990s [14]. The original definition of the digital divide discusses the divergence of access to the Internet that creates disparities among developed and less developed countries, between the information-rich and information-poor in a society, and between the "those who do and do not, use the panoply of digital resources" [12]. In this review, we focused on the digital divide and digital inclusion of older adults within countries.

The digital divide includes inequalities in material means to access the Internet, which is defined as first-level digital divide [12, 15]. Disparities also exist in the level of digital skills and knowledge, the utilization of social resources and the richness of social networks, which is defined as second-level digital divide [14, 16–20]. From the perspectives of older adults [21], the "grey digital divide" leads to greater inequalities when it comes to distributing information and resources that not only influence social participation and social networking [22] but also relate to health and wellbeing [23]. From the immigrant's perspective, the characteristics associated with migration experiences create more difficulties for them to be involved in the trend of digitization in the host counties [21].

1.3 Digital Inclusion

Digital inclusion is frequently used as a political initiative to bridge the digital divide by providing support to improve access to the Internet. Older adults are always identified to be the target for initiatives aimed at digital inclusion, no matter how the older adults feel about this [11]. Digital inclusion should not only try to address the "first-level digital divide" of connections but also solve the "second-level digital divide," which concerns digital skills [20, 23].

Recent studies on digital inclusion started investigating disadvantageous groups throughout the population and suggested the need for more knowledge about older adults' situations of the digital divide and digital inclusion [10, 21, 23, 24]. Only a few studies addressed digital exclusion as a component of social exclusion among older adults, among which fewer concerns were put on the older immigrants.

2 Method

In order to gain an overview of existing knowledge and understanding of the digital divide and digital inclusion among older immigrants, a scoping review was conducted to clarify the essential factors and identify the research gaps in the existing studies. The scoping review method has been used to identify all available literature that provides comprehensive coverage on definitions, methods, and findings regardless of the study designs [25, 26]. This review followed Arksey and O'Malley's methodological framework of conducting scoping reviews, which includes five stages: identify the research question, identify relevant studies, study selection, charting the data and collating, summarizing and reporting the results [25].

2.1 Identifying the Research Questions

The review concerned older immigrants' positions in participating in the digitalizing society, namely, digital inclusion or digital divide. It was necessary to clarify the meanings of these concepts from current studies and to identify the relevant factors that guide intervention and further research. The following research questions were formulated to guide the search for articles.

Q1. What do the digital divide and digital inclusion mean to older immigrants in the studies?
Q2. What are the key factors that contribute to the digital divide and digital inclusion among older immigrants?
Q3. What are the research methods used in the current studies?

In this review, we consider older immigrants to be older adults residing in countries other than the country they were born in. This term is applied to all older immigrants, regardless of the length of residence in the foreign country or the purpose of migration.

2.2 Identifying Relevant Studies

Seven electronic databases, including EBSCO, PubMed, Science Direct, Scopus, Taylor & Francis Online, Web of Science, and Wiley Online Library, were searched to identify the relevant studies, which encompassed most of the peer-reviewed publications in this specific research field.

The keywords that guided the search could be categorized into three groups, namely (1) "Aging" and "elderly" and synonyms, (2) "migration" and "immigrants" and synonyms, (3) "digital divide" and "digital inclusion" and synonyms. The authors used Boolean connectors (AND/OR) to combine the keyword in the group and to connect different groups.

Although the topic of digital divide has been extensively discussed, the research interest concerning the digital divide among immigrant groups has not been recognized until recent years. Thus, this scoping review limited its search to the articles published in peer-review journals between January 1, 2015, and October 31, 2019, with the main focus on older immigrants' use of digital tools and the Internet with perspectives from the digital divide and digital inclusion. The review identified and retrieved the bibliographic details and abstracts of the articles from the databases if these contained the selected terms and phrases in the titles, abstracts, and keywords.

2.3 Study Selection

For the selection of studies, the authors developed inclusion criteria and exclusion criteria of studies and three steps to screen the articles. First of all, the authors imported all the studies from the initial search into Endnote and removed the duplicate articles and the article types book chapter, book review, editorial, review, commentary and conference paper. All the authors then read through the titles and the abstracts to decide whether the articles met the inclusion and exclusion criteria as well as the purpose of this review. Lastly, the authors retrieved and reviewed the full text of the remaining articles and decided whether the articles could be included for synthesis.

Inclusion Criteria

The review included articles written in English and published in peer-reviewed journals with full-text availability in the electronic databases. The articles should be based on empirical studies with a primary focus on the digital divide and digital inclusion among older immigrants. In this review, the definition of old was not defined by a specific age that identified a person as "an older adult." It all depended on how the articles described the older adults based on the local social environment.

Exclusion Criteria

The language of the article was limited to English because of the additional time and expenditure that would be required to include articles in all possible languages. This review excluded book chapters, book reviews, and editorial, commentary and perspective articles. The review also excluded the articles published by non-peer-reviewed sources. The authors also excluded articles that were not based on empirical studies. Articles were eliminated if they did not relate to the key concepts of the review, or if the article was a systematic review or meta-analysis.

2.4 Charting the Data

Relevant data in each study was abstracted and organized into a standardized form for answering the research questions. This form contained the following information:

1. Study characteristics: author names, year of publication, and the location of the study.
2. Methods: the methodology, the study design, and the participants.
3. Factors: identified digital inclusion or the digital divide in the study.
4. Outcome: The empirical findings and the conclusion of the study related to the purposes of this review.

2.5 Collating, Summarizing and Reporting the Results

With the data in charted form, the authors then carried out a thematic analysis to sort, present, and compare the articles, which helped identify the research gaps in the included existing literature [27].

3 Results

The initial search was performed on November 14, 2019. The initial search identified a total of 997 publications, which were found on Taylor & Francis Online (n = 445), Wiley Online Library (n = 281), Science Direct (n = 217), Web of Science (n = 25), Scopus (n = 19), and EBSCO (n = 4). After removing the duplicate articles (n = 30), we screened through the titles, abstracts, and keywords according to the inclusion and exclusion criteria and the research questions. We identified 65 articles that were relevant to the purposes of this review and continued to review the full text. The authors read through the full texts of these articles and identified 13 articles that were finally included for further analysis (see Fig. 1).

3.1 Country of Experiment and Study Sample

The included publications provided studies of the situations of a variety of older immigrants in relation to the increasingly digitalizing environments in five countries, which consisted of Australia [28–30], Canada [31, 32], Israel [33, 34], Spain [35], and the United States [36–40]. Three studies focused on older immigrants of Chinese [31, 32], Irish [28], and Punjabi [32] origin. Two articles studied immigrants and Arabs in Israel in comparison with Israeli-born Jews [33, 34]. Three studies did not explicitly mention the ethnic background, instead stating the partnering organizations working with older immigrants [30, 35, 37]. The other six articles focused on older immigrants living in ethnically diverse areas or selected from a population-based survey [29, 36, 38–40]. The study samples of older immigrants in the articles from the U.S. typically referred to the Hispanic group [36–40], and none of the studies separated and studied a specific ethnicity from this group. We summarized the samples of participants, which can be found in Table 1.

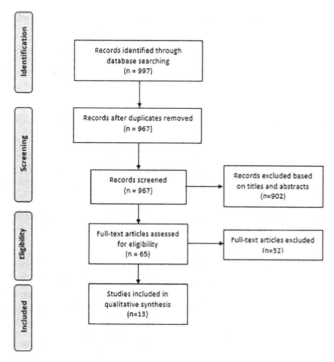

Fig. 1. PRISMA flow diagram for articles selection

3.2 Methodology and Study Design

The 13 included empirical studies employed various methodologies and research designs to investigate the situation of older immigrants in relation to the digital divide in an era of increasing digitalization of society. As shown in Table 1, four publications used qualitative methods, including observation and in-depth interviews, survey and semi-structured interviews, rating scales, and focus group interviews. Two employed mixed-method approaches that started with quantitative questionnaires and continued with focus group interviews. The remaining seven studies used national population-based survey data to examine the differences among different older immigrant groups and between the native older adults and older immigrants.

3.3 Digital Inclusion or Digital Divide?

All the included publications noted the potential influence of the rapid development of digitalization and continuous migration of public information and services online, and in particular how this might influence one of the potentially most vulnerable components of the society, older immigrants, who might experience difficulties with the trend. Several studies examined, from different angles, the general conditions of older immigrants in a society based on extensive national survey data to provide a big picture. The other studies collaborated with organizations to reach the older immigrants in which the findings were firmly related to the living context and the research settings. Overall, older immigrants

Table 1. Results of the methodology employed by the included articles

Author & Year	Methodology	Research design	Sample & Sample size
Ballantyne and Burke 2017	Qualitative	Survey and semi-structured interview	Irish. Survey: 44; semi-structured interview: 16
Bjarnadottir, Millery, Fleck, and Bakken 2016	Quantitative	Survey	Hispanic: 1045
Breunig and McCarthy 2019	Quantitative	National survey	The general population, longitudinal data 2006–2015
Ferreira, Sayago, and Blat 2017	Qualitative	Ethnography: observation and interview	Mixed Ethnic groups: 202
Golub, Satterfield, Serritella, Singh, and Phillips 2019	Mixed method	Questionnaire and focus group interview	Mixed ethnic groups. Survey: 308. Two focus group interviews: 12 and an unspecified number of participants
Lissitsa and Chachashvili-Bolotin 2015	Quantitative	National survey	Israeli-born Jews, Immigrants, and Arabs, Longitudinal data, 12068 older respondents
Lissitsa and Chachashvili-Bolotin 2016	Quantitative	National survey	Israeli-born Jews, Immigrants, and Arabs, Longitudinal data, 12068 older respondents
Massey, Langellier, Sentell, and Manganello 2017	Quantitative	National survey	General population: 15249
Millard, Baldassar, and Wilding 2018	Qualitative	Ethnography: observation and interview	Mixed Ethnic groups: 8 older adults; 4 staffs and 4 informal supporters
Neves, Franz, Munteanu, and Baecker 2018	Qualitative	Scale and semi-structured interview	Chinese: 5
Nguyen, Mosadeghi, and Almario 2017	Quantitative	National survey	General population: 42935
Zibrik et al. 2015	Mix method	Questionnaire and focus group interview	Survey: 895, Interview: Chinese (27), Punjabi (28)

(continued)

Table 1. (*continued*)

Author & Year	Methodology	Research design	Sample & Sample size
Zhao, Yang, and Wong 2018	Quantitative	National survey	Mixed ethnic groups: 1852

showed increasing rates of accessing digital tools and the Internet in the wake of rapid digitalization developments. However, the included studies demonstrated different and unique situations faced by older immigrants under different scenarios and different stages of life.

Digital Inclusion

Older immigrants are often depicted as being excluded from the rapid social development due to many negative factors that might not represent the real picture of their lives. In the included studies, some of the older immigrants utilized the capability of digital technologies to both connect with the host society and to restore contact with their homeland [28]. It was not a simple task for the older immigrant to get to the "right side" of the divide, but some of the older adults have successfully bridged the divide by themselves, and some accomplished this task with assistance from the researchers or the staffs.

Ballantyne and Burke [28] investigated the concept of the meaning of home among older Irish immigrants at different life stages, together with the adoption of new digital technology. The feeling of nostalgia, the desire to connect to Ireland physically or virtually, and the desire to remain in contact with family had driven the older Irish people to take up a range of different digital technologies that ultimately made the participants bridge the digital divide and to be included in different communities.

Ferreira, Sayago, and Blat [35] highlighted another example, concerning an educational intervention that started with teaching older adults to use tablets and Internet browsers to access information online. The participants ended up taking a step forward to change this one-sided communication by producing and sharing videos with friends and relatives. This led to better digital skills and increased the feeling of being socially included.

In the study conducted by Millard, Baldassar, and Wilding [30], the researchers observed and interviewed older immigrants participating in a social learning initiative aimed at helping the immigrants to overcome the cultural and language barriers of using the Internet. The participants not only enjoyed engaging in the social and dynamic learning environment, but they also benefited from being connected digitally (i.e., access to social services, connecting with their social networks) and enjoyed gaining autonomy and becoming empowered in the macrosocial environment.

Neves, Franz, Munteanu, and Baecker [31] investigated the different dimensions and outcomes of the adoption process of new tablet software among a group of institutionalized oldest-old (80+ years) persons. Although the adoption process was difficult and complicated, most of the oldest-old participants reported an increase in social connectedness and a reduction in loneliness. Among the oldest-old group, when the technology self-efficacy was not proved, social, cultural, attitudinal factors and usability factors were more critical in this scenario.

The above studies demonstrated cases in which older immigrants were continuously being included in the digitalizing society, from the younger older adults to the oldest old, from a passive information taker to a positive content creator, from increasing family connections to expanding social networks. Except for the last article [31], the older immigrants adopted a commonly available technology, which was neither specially designed for older adults nor for the specific ethnicity.

Digital Divide

When considering the digital divide, age is the most commonly mentioned factor that separates the younger generations from the old. However, the digital divide also exists in the same age group between different ethnicities as well as in the same ethnic group. The researchers examined and compared the level of digital divide in different user scenarios. In Table 2, we categorized the articles into the abovementioned two groups, namely first-level digital divide (the access to technology/Internet) and second-level digital divide (the digital skills to use the technology).

As shown in Table 2, three studies concluded that access to the Internet was the reason behind the digital divide among older immigrants [29, 33, 34]. Four studies stated that their samples expressed difficulties in using the technology and in finding the relevant information online [36, 38–40]. The remaining two studies [32, 37] showed a hybrid of first-level and second-level digital divides.

For the first-level digital divide, three studies agreed that age, income level, education, language proficiency, and health conditions were the most significant factors that disconnected the older adults [29, 33, 34]. One study stressed that individuals residing in rural and remote areas had a higher chance of being excluded [29]. In addition, two Israeli studies [33, 34] stated that traditional cultures could have negative impacts on Internet adoption, which was agreed on by another included article [32]. Two studies stated that both levels of the digital divide persisted in the same diverse communities [32, 37]. The participants considered the devices to be too expensive for their income level [32, 37]. In addition, some participants considered they could not afford the monthly fee for broadband or cellular data [37]. Meanwhile, their counterparts in the same communities expressed a low level of trust as concerns Internet information and mobile applications and high expectations of receiving public-funded training that could increase digital literacy [32, 37].

Six of the nine studies that explored online information-seeking behaviors studied the use of eHealth or smartphone applications [32, 36–40]. These showed an increasing trend of being connected to the digitalizing society even within the older immigrant groups of lower socioeconomic status. However, in contrast to the narrowing first-level digital divide, the older immigrants now faced new challenges from the second-level digital divide, which were related to insufficient digital skills and lack of appropriate online resources.

In the included articles, language proficiency and eHealth literacy were the two major risk factors behind the second-level digital divide in using the Internet for seeking health-related information. Language proficiency was the most significant barrier for older adults to utilize the Internet effectively [32, 36–38, 40]. The older immigrants tend to

Table 2. Results of the digital divide and the purpose of using

Author & Year	Immigrant ethnicity	Dominant ethnicity/control group	Purpose of using	Digital divide level
Bjarnadottir, Millery, Fleck, and Bakken 2016	Foreign-born Hispanics	Non-Hispanic White	Explore online health information seeking pattern	Second
Breunig and McCarthy 2019	Mixed	Non-Hispanic White	Low expenditure and low expenditure share of telecommunication	First
Golub, Satterfield, Serritella, Singh, and Phillips 2019	Mixed	Non-Hispanic White	Test the effect of smart transport application among disadvantageous community members	First & Second
Lissitsa and Chachashvili-Bolotin 2015	Immigrants and Arabs	Israeli-born Jews	The pattern of Internet use and the adoption rate	First
Lissitsa and Chachashvili-Bolotin 2016	Immigrants and Arabs	Israeli-born Jews	Internet use and life satisfaction	First
Massey, Langellier, Sentell, and Manganello 2017	Foreign-born Hispanics	Non-Hispanic White	Low percentage of seeking online health information	Second
Nguyen, Mosadeghi, and Almario 2017	Mixed	Non-Hispanic White	Low percentage of seeking online health information	Second
Zibrik et al. 2015	Chinese and Punjabi	Non-Hispanic White	Low e-health uptake & low digital literacy	First & Second
Zhao, Yang, and Wong 2018	Mixed	Non-Hispanic White	Low E-health engagement and health information seeking	Second

use more interpersonal communication with healthcare professionals in the communities instead of seeking health information online [38, 40]. From the specific purpose of using eHealth, the disparity of eHealth literacy hindered the older immigrants from utilizing the available online resources, created barriers to contact with healthcare professionals, and reduced the uptake of eHealth and health information seeking [32, 36, 38–40].

4 Discussion

With years of debate concerning the grey digital divide [21] in the fast-developing digitalizing society, the discussion has now extended to cover the older adults with migration experience who are often considered to be excluded or isolated from, or lagging behind in, social developments. This review included the most recent research projects from the last five years that put the focus on these diverse groups of people. The results of the reviews showed the complexities and the difficulties in performing the studies among various ethnicities and social contexts, which created heterogeneities among different ethnicities and even within the same ethnicity. It is necessary to extend the discussion further into specific ethnic groups in order to understand how ethnic traits and cultural preferences come to play in the digital divide among older persons.

For older immigrants, the digital divide has meant being isolated from digitalizing society, which negatively influences social networks and access to online and offline resources [41, 42]. In terms of access to the Internet, the differences in the digital divide between the older immigrants and the native older adults are getting smaller. Many older immigrants have also developed unique patterns that help them to be included in society through digital technologies [28, 35]. However, this review showed that older immigrants are not yet ready to bridge the divide considering the significant disparity in language proficiency and eHealth literacy, as well as the amount of available online resources. In the reviewed studies, it was necessary for the public service providers and the policymakers to consider such disparities and provide information in a different language. This review also revealed that the use of the Internet created a virtual community and enabled older immigrants to be included in a different manner [28]. The prior studies also suggested that the use of the Internet could enable older immigrants to restore their connection with their home countries and to participate in the virtual community, which helped compensate for their difficulties in the host country [43, 44]. It is evident that further research needs to reconsider and conceptualize the meaning of the digital divide and digital inclusion in relation to older immigrants along with the development of digitalization.

The included studies demonstrated various factors that were associated with the digital divide, among which age, socioeconomic status, language proficiency, degree of acculturation, level of education, and digital literacy were the most common factors related to older immigrants. The findings were in line with the prior literature that blended the older adults' use of technology and migratory experience [41]. The results showed a mixed picture when taking family members and cultural norms into consideration. Some studies had shown the negative influences of cultural norms that led to a high dependency among older adults on their children [32–34]. Prior literature demonstrated the positive influence of children in facilitating and motivating the use of the Internet and new media [45–48]. The different views concerning the children's influence originated from the interactions between generations, which also stressed the discrepancies among different ethnic groups.

Age-related impairment entailed a potential risk for older immigrants to abandon the use of technologies with the increase of age [39]. This raises the expectations for the hardware producers and software producers to develop devices and software that could be used by older people with disabilities associated with advanced age. In sum, we need more effort from the stakeholders to collaborate closely to gain more knowledge about the challenges faced by different older immigrants in order to overcome the digital divide. Besides the advancement and technology iteration, the drivers of adopting and implementing the Internet and other digital technologies played a significant role in encouraging older immigrants' presence in the digitalizing society. It is worth noting that it is necessary to understand the motivations at both the individual level and group level in order to help the older immigrant to bridge the divide. Understanding these motivations could lead to a more practical approach, which could improve digital literacy and increase the probability of being digitally and socially included [30, 31, 35, 37].

The researchers chose the quantitative approach, qualitative approach, or mixed methods. Different research methods provided meaningful insights from different perspectives to improve knowledge about older immigrants. From the quantitative studies, the audience could gain a general idea of the conditions of older immigrants. The quantitative data could also help the researchers see the connections between different variables, identify and generalize, and compare the trend from a large amount of data. On the other hand, the quantitative method was not sufficient to provide an in-depth understanding that could be translated into specific needs for further development. From the findings of quantitative studies, age, socioeconomic status, language proficiency, degree of acculturation, level of education, and digital literacy were identified as most likely to contribute to the situation of digital divide and digital inclusion. Most of the studies used extensive scale surveys that compared older immigrants with native older adults. This oversimplifies the variables that ignore intersectionality behind the different backgrounds and life experiences [49, 50]. For this perspective, qualitative studies placed more value on the trajectory before and after migration, which could provide more information that was firmly related to specific ethnicities and cultural preferences. It also clarified the detailed challenges in older immigrants' daily life. The knowledge could be utilized for developing culturally tailored products and services. The mixed-method approach that integrated the realist perspective and the interpretive perspective seemed to be flexible to fit in the research that encompassed aging, migration, and digital divide [51]. The recent discussion had not integrated the diverse opinions toward mixed-method, especially on how and when to integrate qualitative and quantitative methods for research purposes [51].

5 Conclusion

The digital divide has been a constant discussion in public and academia for years. This review demonstrated the older immigrants' position in the digital divide and their natural disadvantages to being on the "right side" of the digital divide in comparison with their younger counterparts or with native older adults. The disadvantages derived from many aspects that were subjected to life experiences and the living environment. The most common factors were age, socioeconomic status, language proficiency, degree of acculturation, level of educational, and digital literacy. Although much of the evidence showed that older immigrants were gradually crossing the digital divide of access, the divide still remained due to the disparities in digital skills and knowledge to use technologies.

Not all of the articles included cultural factors, which also played a significant role, especially in gaining new knowledge to understand the process of technology adoption and to assist the design that helps bridge the divide. The review found homogeneous findings among studies from different countries, which indicated the need to discuss the methodologies in the future. While taking into account the complexity and difficulties of conducting such research, we still need to put more effort into developing more methods and models that could investigate the situation of the digital divide among different ethnicities and also engage people from different cultural backgrounds.

References

1. Essén, A., Östlund, B.: Laggards as innovators? old users as designers of new services & service systems. Int. J. Des. 5(3), 89–98 (2011)
2. Schulz, R., Wahl, H.W., Matthews, J.T., De Vito Dabbs, A., Beach, S.R., Czaja, S.J.: Advancing the aging and technology agenda in gerontology. Gerontologist 55(5), 724–734 (2015)
3. Castles, S., de Haas, H., Miller, M.J.: The Age of Migration: International Population Movements in the Modern World, 5th edn. Palgrave Macmillan Ltd., New York (2014)
4. IOM: World Migration Report 2018. International Organization for Migration, Geneva, Switzerland (2017)
5. Hooyman, N.R., Kiyak, H.A.: Social Gerontology: A Multidisciplinary Perspective, 10th edn. Pearson Education, New York (2014)
6. Castañeda, H., Holmes, S.M., Madrigal, D., Young, M.-E.D., Beyeler, N., Quesada, J.: Immigration as a social determinant of health. Ann. Rev. Publ. Health 36, 375–392 (2015)
7. Derose, K.P., Escarce, J.J., Lurie, N.: Immigrants and health care: Sources of vulnerability. Health Aff. 26(5), 1258–1268 (2007)
8. Sarría-Santamera, A., Hijas-Gómez, A.I., Carmona, R., Gimeno-Feliú, L.A.: A systematic review of the use of health services by immigrants and native populations. Publ. Health Rev. 37(1), 28 (2016)
9. Selwyn, N., Gorard, S., Furlong, J., Madden, L.: Older adults' use of information and communications technology in everyday life. Ageing Soc. 23(5), 561–582 (2003)
10. Mihelj, S., Leguina, A., Downey, J.: Culture is digital: cultural participation, diversity and the digital divide. New Media Soc. 21(7), 1465–1485 (2019)
11. Kania-Lundholm, M., Torres, S.: The divide within: older active ICT users position themselves against different "Others". J. Aging Stud. 35, 26–36 (2015)
12. Norris, P.: Digital Divide: Civic Engagement, Information Poverty, and the Internet Worldwide. Cambridge University Press, Cambridge (2001)
13. Östlund, B., Olander, E., Jonsson, O., Frennert, S.: STS-inspired design to meet the challenges of modern aging. Welfare technology as a tool to promote user driven innovations or another way to keep older users hostage? Technol. Forecast. Soc. Change. 93, 82–90 (2015)
14. van Dijk, J.A.G.M.: The deepening divide: inequality in the information society. SAGE Publications Inc, Thousand Oaks (2005)
15. Van Dijk, J., Hacker, K.: The digital divide as a complex and dynamic phenomenon. Inf. Soc. 19(4), 315–326 (2003)
16. Helsper, E.J.: A corresponding fields model for the links between social and digital exclusion. Commun. Theory. 22(4), 403–426 (2012)
17. Helsper, E.J.: Digital Inclusion: An Analysis of Social Disadvantage and the Information Society (2008)
18. van Deursen, A.J.A.M., Courtois, C., van Dijk, J.A.G.M.: Internet skills, sources of support, and benefiting from internet use. Int. J. Hum. Comput. Interact. 30(4), 278–290 (2014)

19. van Deursen, A., van Dijk, J.: Internet skills and the digital divide. New Media Soc. **13**(6), 893–911 (2011)
20. Hargittai, E.: Second-level digital divide: differences in people's online skills. Charlest. Advis. **7**(4), (2002)
21. Millward, P.: The "grey digital divide": perception, exclusion and barriers of access to the internet for older people. First Monday **8**(7), (2003)
22. Kuoppamäki, S.-M.: Digital participation in service environments among senior electricity consumers in Finland. Technol. Soc. **55**, 111–118 (2018)
23. Friemel, T.N.: The digital divide has grown old: determinants of a digital divide among seniors. New Media Soc. **18**(2), 313–331 (2016)
24. Van Regenmortel, S., De Donder, L., Dury, S., Smetcoren, A.-S., De Witte, N., Verté, D.: Social exclusion in later life: a systematic review of the literature. J. Popul. Ageing. **12**(1), 131–132 (2019)
25. Arksey, H., O'Malley, L.: Scoping studies: towards a methodological framework. Int. J. Soc. Res. Methodol. Theory Pract. **8**(1), 19–32 (2005)
26. Colquhoun, H.L.: Scoping reviews: time for clarity in definition, methods, and reporting. J. Clin. Epidemiol. **67**(12), 1291–1294 (2014)
27. Aronson, J.: A pragmatic view of thematic analysis. Qual. Rep. **2**(1), 4–5 (1994)
28. Ballantyne, G., Burke, L.: "People live in their heads a lot": polymedia, life course, and meanings of home among Melbourne's older Irish community. Transnatl. Soc. Rev. **7**(1), 10–24 (2017)
29. Breunig, R., McCarthy, O.: Household telecommunications expenditure in Australia. Telecommun. Policy **44**(1), 101837 (2019)
30. Millard, A., Baldassar, L., Wilding, R.: The significance of digital citizenship in the well-being of older migrants. Publ. Health **158**(SI), 144–148 (2018)
31. Neves, B.B., Franz, R.L., Munteanu, C., Baecker, R.: Adoption and feasibility of a communication app to enhance social connectedness amongst frail institutionalized oldest old: an embedded case study. Inf. Commun. Soc. **21**(11), 1681–1699 (2018)
32. Zibrik, L., Khan, S., Bangar, N., Stacy, E., Novak Lauscher, H., Ho, K.: Patient and community centered eHealth: Exploring eHealth barriers and facilitators for chronic disease self-management within British Columbia's immigrant Chinese and Punjabi seniors. Health Policy Technol. **4**(4), 348–356 (2015)
33. Lissitsa, S., Chachashvili-Bolotin, S.: Life satisfaction in the internet age – Changes in the past decade. Comput. Human Behav. **54**, 197–206 (2016)
34. Lissitsa, S., Chachashvili-Bolotin, S.: Does the wind of change blow in late adulthood? adoption of ICT by senior citizens during the past decade. Poetics **52**, 44–63 (2015)
35. Ferreira, S.M., Sayago, S., Blat, J.: Older people's production and appropriation of digital videos: an ethnographic study. Behav. Inf. Technol. **36**(6), 557–574 (2017)
36. Bjarnadottir, R.I., Millery, M., Fleck, E., Bakken, S.: Correlates of online health information-seeking behaviors in a low-income Hispanic community. Inf. Health Soc. Care. **41**(4), 341–349 (2016)
37. Golub, A., Satterfield, V., Serritella, M., Singh, J., Phillips, S.: Assessing the barriers to equity in smart mobility systems: a case study of Portland, Oregon. Case Stud. Transp. Policy **7**(4), 689–697 (2019)
38. Massey, P.M., Langellier, B.A., Sentell, T., Manganello, J.: Nativity and language preference as drivers of health information seeking: examining differences and trends from a U.S. population-based survey. Ethn. Health **22**(6), 596–609 (2017)
39. Nguyen, A., Mosadeghi, S., Almario, C.V.: Persistent digital divide in access to and use of the Internet as a resource for health information: Results from a California population-based study. Int. J. Med. Inf. **103**, 49–54 (2017)

40. Zhao, X., Yang, B., Wong, C.W.: Analyzing trend for U.S. Immigrants' e-health engagement from 2008 to 2013. Health Commun. **34**(11), 1–11 (2018)

41. Chang, J., McAllister, C., McCaslin, R.: Correlates of and barriers to, internet use among older adults. J. Gerontol. Soc. Work. **58**(1), 66–85 (2015)

42. Liu, X., Cook, G., Cattan, M.: Support networks for Chinese older immigrants accessing English health and social care services: the concept of Bridge People. Heal. Soc. Care Commun. **25**(2), 667–677 (2017)

43. Makarova, N., Brand, T., Brunings-Kuppe, C., Pohlabeln, H., Luttmann, S.: Comparative analysis of premature mortality among urban immigrants in Bremen, Germany: a retrospective register-based linkage study. BMJ Open **6**(3), e007875 (2016)

44. Andonian, L.C.: Meanings and experiences associated with computer use of older immigrant adults of lower socioeconomic status. Can. J. Occup. Ther. **85**(2), 146–157 (2018)

45. Dekker, R., Engbersen, G., Faber, M.: The use of online media in migration networks. Popul. Space Place. **22**(6), 539–551 (2016)

46. Hsu, Y.-L.: A Chinese response to the aging society. Gerontechnology **14**(4), 187–190 (2016)

47. Rompaey, V.Van, Roe, K., Struys, K.: Children's influence on internet access at home: adoption and use in the family context. Inf. Commun. Soc. **5**(2), 189–206 (2002)

48. Hasan, H., Linger, H.: Enhancing the wellbeing of the elderly: social use of digital technologies in aged care. Educ. Gerontol. **42**(11), 749–757 (2016)

49. Torres, S.: Ethnicity, race and care in older age: what can a social justice framework offer? In: Westwood, S.O. (ed.) Ageing, diversity and equality : social justice perspectives, pp. 167–180. Routledge (2019)

50. Koehn, S., Neysmith, S., Kobayashi, K., Khamisa, H.: Revealing the shape of knowledge using an intersectionality lens: results of a scoping review on the health and health care of ethnocultural minority older adults. Ageing Soc. **33**(3), 437–464 (2013)

51. Yardley, L., Bishop, F.L.: Using mixed methods in health research: benefits and challenges. Br. J. Health Psychol. **20**(1), 1–4 (2015)

Expectations and Sensemaking: Older People and Care Robots

Susanne Frennert[(⊠)]

Internet of Things and People Research Center, Department of Computer Science and Media Technology, Malmö University, Malmö, Sweden
susanne.frennert@mau.se

Abstract. We do not yet know how the robotization of eldercare will unfold, but one thing is clear: technology mediates human practices and experiences [1]. As such, care robots will co-shape the actions of care givers and older people and influence the perceptions and experiences of old age. The robotization of eldercare means that it is essential for developers, policy makers, and researchers to become increasingly aware of the intertwined and implicit expectations that older people impose on care robots. This paper both zooms in towards older people's individual expectations and zooms out towards expectation configurations at a group level and the expectation imagery of care robots in future eldercare.

Keywords: Care robots · Sensemaking · Individual expectations · Expectation configurations · Expectation imagery · Older people

1 Introduction

The adoption of technology has been extensively studied [2–4], and several models to describe technology adoption have been generated and verified [5–7]. However, technology does not only enter our life as digital or physical devices but also as technological visions [8]. As such, older people do not only deal with care robots themselves but also the promises, worries, and hopes in regard to care robots. These expectations give them an idea of what care robots are and whether they will fit into their everyday practices and habits. However, these prior conceptions and judgements may change during actual and repeated encounters with and usage of care robots. Sensemaking, in regard to technology mediation, is an interpretive process [9]. While some care robots may rearticulate existing norms, others may foster new understandings. For example, consider the robotic cats that have transformed the idea of dementia care, which used to be kept free of animals to avoid allergies, and opened up the possibility of having robotic animal companions. These robotic cats have fostered new configurations of engagement and responsibility [10]. Patients can engage, interact, and communicate with the robotic cats and thereby feel more relaxed and comfortable, while care professionals take on the responsibility of keeping the cats' batteries charged at all times [10]. However, the robotic transformation of eldercare practices has not been without concern. Sharkey and Sharkey [11] warn that this development may lead to deception, infantilization, and reduced human contact. To

© Springer Nature Switzerland AG 2020
Q. Gao and J. Zhou (Eds.): HCII 2020, LNCS 12209, pp. 191–206, 2020.
https://doi.org/10.1007/978-3-030-50232-4_14

date, little attention has been paid to older people's sensemaking and interpretation of such innovations as care robots [12]. Traditionally, the older age group is often excluded from product development, even though demographics have shown that people 65 and older constitute the fastest growing segment in most developed societies [13, 14].

Shishehgar et al.'s [15] systematic review of how robotic technology can help older people suggests eight problems areas that have been widely addressed in robotic research. These problem areas are: (1) social isolation, (2) dependent living, (3) physical and cognitive impairment, (4) mobility problems, (5) poor health monitoring, (6) lack of recreation, (7) reminding problems, and (8) fall problems. From this review, it is evident that most research on robotic technology for older people has focused on its physical and psychological deficiencies and the risks of falls, social isolation, and poor health among older people [16, 17]. Theoretically, this research is based on the "medical model" of aging. This kind of research is of course beneficial in developing technologies to address aging impairments and rehabilitation. At the same time, this theoretical framework ignores the fact that the lived experiences of older people are embedded in society and culture [18, 19]. Therefore, this model limits our understanding of how older people cope with aging in their everyday life. Furthermore, undertaking robotic research only through the lens of biomedicine poses the risk of portraying older people as a problem for society due to, for example, increased healthcare costs, which, in turn, may result in negative stereotypes of older people and aging [20]. From a social constructivist perspective, robotic research may play a role in the societal attitudes towards older people and the formulation of the understanding of aging [21] by framing older people and aging as a problem and robotic technologies as a solution [17].

In regard to the expectations imposed on care robots by older people and professional care givers, Johansson-Pajala et al.'s [22] focus group study with 24 older individuals shows that the participants changed from initially negative attitudes towards care robots to more positive attitudes during the focused discussions. This result demonstrates how an increased knowledge and understanding of what robots could do for older people changed the participants' perceptions of care robots. Likewise, Lee and Coughlin's [23] literature review identifies 10 factors that determine older people's adoption of technology: value, usability, affordability, accessibility, technical support, social support, emotional support, independence, experience, and confidence. These findings indicate that technology adoption is essentially a sociotechnical activity that involves cultural norms reinforced by interaction and communication between humans and humans and also humans and technology in complex infrastructures and social settings.

Nymberg et al. [24] conducted a focus group interview with 15 older individuals on their beliefs, attitudes, and experiences of eHealth services and describe the participants' ambivalence towards the use of eHealth in primary care. Feenberg [25] also discusses the ambivalence of technology, which is often due to conceptual problems in regards to the word "technology". According to Feenberg, "technology" is an ambitious word that broadly encompasses idea systems, technical artefacts, projects, and initiatives [26]. As such, different people may interpret the word differently and draw different meanings from the concept [25]. The same can be said of the words "care robots". Feenberg highlights that the boundaries for technical artefacts is never clear and that technical artefacts are never neutral, since their social and technical goals are reached through a power struggle among the actors involved in the design process [25]. Furthermore, the domestication process in which people make sense of a technology and choose to adopt it is a dual one, in which the technology as well as the people may change [2]. However, before a technology becomes meaningful and understandable to individual people, their expectations affect their readiness to engage with it [27]. In van Lente's [28] words, "expectation statements are not only representations of something that does not exist, they do something: advising, showing direction, creating obligation" – that is, expectations are performative [29]. Thus, it is important to understand how older people make sense of care robots and what their expectations of care robots are.

1.1 Expectations

In this paper, expectations are understood to be comprised of three different layers: individual expectations, expectation configurations, and expectation imagery.

Individual expectations, in this paper, refer to the older person's lived experience of aging and his/her belief regarding certain intentions, goals, and hopes in relation to care robots. Individual expectations affect the individual's actions and choices [30] when it comes to the technology in question [31]. However, an individual is not an isolated island but rather interconnected with other people and technologies.

Expectation configurations, in this paper, refer to the assumptions and understandings among a group of individuals of the role of care robots in society, in relation to a specific end user group (i.e. the older participants) [32]. Orlikowski and Gash [32] refer to these as "technological frames". They are understood as cognitive structures at a group level, that is, expectations that are shared among groups of individuals. The expectations at the group level can be either shared between different stakeholder groups or diametrical towards a certain technology [33].

Expectation imagery, in this paper, refers to the narratives and worldviews assigned by the participants to future care robots. These worldviews and narratives are often seen as crucial in the development of new technologies [9]. Expectation imagery constitutes the believed promises of a certain future technology. Expectation imagery has the power to challenge normative societal views of previously marginalized groups. However, gender studies and social gerontology have shown that new technologies often maintain the normative societal views and stereotypes of gender and older people [34–37].

These different layers of expectation are complex and interconnected [38]. How older people's expectations of care robots are viewed and understood may have practical implications for both the development of care robots and their introduction to older people. Too often a product is developed first, and then, if older users are involved in the process, they are usually given only a passive role in evaluating the usability and acceptability of the predesigned product [39, 40]. As past research has shown, typically, older users only become involved post-implementation, once it has been recognized that the use or the outcome of the product has become problematic or has had unexpected consequences [4, 41]. The adoption of care robots will most certainly depend on them being able to fit the end users' expectations and their everyday lifestyles. In order to estimate how older people will (or will not) adopt care robots, we need to start by investigating their interpretations and expectations of the robots (Fig. 1).

(a)

(b)

Fig. 1. (a) The HOBBIT robot (b) The Giraff robot

2 Research Design

This paper builds on a multiple case study carried out within three EU-funded research projects: HOBBIT [42], GiraffPlus [43], and INBOTS [44]. In two of the projects (HOBBIT and GiraffPlus), empirical studies were carried out over a long period of time during which the care robots were developed and deployed in the domestic environment of older people. The remaining project (INBOTS) focused on older people's expectations without them having any experience with the robots. In total, 150 people above the age of 70 participated in the multiple case study.

This multiple explorative case study used participatory design. During the continuous analysis, both empirical and theoretical materials were considered side by side (i.e. abductive reasoning) [45–48]. The study was conducted as part of a larger research project. The unit of analysis in the study was older people's sensemaking and expectations of care robots, comprising individual expectations, expectation configurations, and expectation imagery.

The analysis and interpretation of the emerging findings has been presented to and discussed with the end users themselves. The studies were reviewed by the Ethical Boards in Lund and Stockholm, Sweden. The participants were informed that their participation was voluntary and that they could withdraw at any time without having to explain why.

2.1 Data Collection

The multiple case study builds on data collected from focus groups, workshops, observations, and in-depth interviews in the lab and at the participants' homes [42, 43, 49–54]. Initially, all available research on care robots and older people was reviewed [55]. At a later stage in the analysis, all literature on welfare technologies in eldercare was reviewed as well [56]. In the focus groups, fears and hopes concerning care robots were identified.

Furthermore, barriers and enablers to the adoption of a care robot were identified [52, 54] during workshops and focus groups with older people. In the workshops, we used hands-on activities such as "attention cards" to depict the alternative actions the robot could take [57]. The attention cards were used to identify the participants' expectations in regard to the range of tasks, goals, and activities that the care robots would be able to fulfil. Field notes were taken during the focus groups and workshops. The field notes were analysed with a focus on sensemaking and expectations, specifically, expectation configurations and expectation imagery. In addition to the focus groups and workshops, interviews were also conducted in order to gain an understanding of older people's interpretations and individual expectations of care robots. The interview approach was used to allow prospective users to speak freely and express their own feelings and beliefs in regard to care robots [58]. In contrast to focus groups and workshops, the main advantage of in-depth interviews was that they made it possible to understand the views of individual respondents and build a higher degree of trust between the respondents and the researcher, which would hopefully increase the quality of the data [59]. In addition to the above-mentioned methods, observations were made as the participants tried out the care robots both in the lab and in their own homes [60]. As such, the focus of the analysis was the end users' sensemaking and expectations in regard to their interactions with the care robots.

This qualitative study generated a much larger amount of material than what is presented in this article. All data were produced in a specific sociocultural context, which is considered in the analysis. The few selected quotes primarily serve as illustrations of the most important findings in regard to older people's sensemaking and expectations of care robots.

3 Results

Care robots are a technology in the making; therefore, the results mostly depend on the participants' former experiences with technology and their interpretations of the technological vision of care robots (Table 1). However, some of the participants had actual and repeated encounters with and usage of care robots (the HOBBIT robot and the Giraff robot) over a period of 3–18 months. The quotes provided by the participants in this section have been anonymized to protect their privacy. However, the participants' encounters with and usage of the care robots are detailed for clarity. For individual expectations, one comprehensive theme was identified: Who are care robots for? Two core themes were identified in the expectation configurations: the belief in customized care and the fear of loss of control. One comprehensive theme, timeliness, emerged from the analysis of expectation imagery.

Table 1. Subthemes and themes

	Subthemes	Theme
Individual expectations	• lack of resources: financial, skills, interest • lack of need • curiosity • keeping up with technology • helping others	Who are care robots for?
Expectation configurations	• dignity • safety around the clock • cognitive stimuli • social stimuli and contact with other people	Belief in customized care
	• surveillance • dependency • lack of human-to-human contact • false safety	Fear of loss of control
Expectation imagery	• cost effectiveness • improved working conditions • flexible time and place	Timeliness

3.1 Individual Expectations: Who Are Care Robots for?

As with other people, what was most valuable to the older participants was the feeling that they mattered – that they were important and significant in their own and others' lives. This was frequently expressed when they talked about taking care of grandchildren and volunteering in various organizations. They participated in research activities for the same reason: it was one way of attaining meaning in life. As research participants, they could immerse themselves in the latest technological developments and share their knowledge of growing old. They believed that their participation would be beneficial for other older people who might be in need of robots. However, they themselves did not identify as users of care robots. The reasons for this were manifold, with lack of need being the main reason mentioned by most of the participants.

> *I do not need a care robot. I try to do most of the things at home myself, or I ask my children or neighbours to help me. I am unsure what kind of robot I would need, or if I want one.* (82-year-old man with no experience of care robots, in-depth interview)

It appears as if the participants did not perceive of themselves as needing a care robot. Although some of them could see the potential benefits of having a robot, none expressed a specific desire or need for one. Similarly, the participants who had actual and repeated encounters with and usage of care robots (HOBBIT and Giraff) expressed that the robots did not meet a specific need, but they had tried them to see if they could fulfil any unknown functions, out of curiosity. However, although curiosity was not characterized as a specific need, it could be interpreted as one. Exploration and investigation are necessary for the acquisition of new skills and knowledge.

The robot does not help me but having it at home has been fun. I have had many visitors who like to see the robot, and I am one of the few who actually have had the opportunity to live with a care robot. (76-year-old lady who had the HOBBIT robot at home for 3 months, in-depth interview)

Although the participant in the extract above did not believe that she needed a robot, she also expressed that the care robot had had a positive impact on her life. The idea of needing a care robot seemingly felt like a threat to the participants' notion of self. On the other hand, however, participants who had actual experiences of having a care robot at home mentioned the mediated effects of having more visitors and a novel thing to explore and study.

Care robots were perceived by many participants as expensive gadgets that would not be available through the welfare system but only as a consumer product. This, in turn, raised questions about the equality of healthcare. As one of the participants said,

Having a care robot is only for rich people... a poor pensioner, like me, will not be able to afford a care robot... it's actually somehow hard to make the pension last till the end of the month. I can't afford a new computer or a new smartphone, how would I be able to afford a care robot? (89-year-old lady with prior knowledge but no actual experience of care robots, in-depth interview)

The lack of financial resources was perceived as a barrier for the participants to imagine care robots as a part of their future. Another barrier was that some participants did not feel confident of their ability to handle a care robot. Many of them had had former experiences with technologies that were too difficult to handle, which made them feel stupid. Consequently, care robots were seen as something for others but not for them.

Regarding the question of individual expectations – the participants' lived experience of aging and their conceived intentions, goals, and hopes in relation to care robots – the findings suggest that the participants did not believe that a care robot would fit in or be necessary in their current everyday lifestyle. When trying to make sense of care robots, they did not identify themselves as users of care robots. For some participants, this was because they did not perceive a need for one, while others lacked the financial resources they believed would be needed, and yet others thought they lacked the skills and knowledge they imagined to be necessary. The participants who had actual experiences of having a care robot at home did not acknowledge a specific need that the robots met. Nonetheless, the results have shown that the robots did have a positive impact on the participants' everyday life, including increased social interaction and the opportunity to explore and learn something new. This, however, does not necessarily have to do with the care robots themselves, but rather with being part of a research project and being able to try out something that others find interesting at home. This effect may wear off in the long term when care robots are no longer a novelty.

3.2 Expectation Configurations: Belief in Customized Care and Fear of Loss of Control

We have chosen to refer to the shared assumptions and understanding of care robots among the workshop and focus group participants as expectation configurations. As with all new technology [25], care robots evoked both hope and fear. The development of care robots was often seen in a conflicting light, both as a positive change towards greater customized care and as a negative movement away from the previously valued human-to-human interaction and social inclusion to a robotized scenario of healthcare in which people are no longer in control.

Belief in Customized Care
For many of the participants, care robots sparked hope. Perceived dignity was extremely important, and the participants talked about care robots as a way to maintain dignity. The participants expressed this through different examples, as illustrated by the following excerpts:

I would rather be dependent on a care robot than having different home care personnel coming to my house to help me visit the bathroom or take a shower... it is intimidating... yeah, at least the robot is just a machine and not an unknown person. (92-year-old lady, workshop)

A care robot is available all the time; it does not need to rest, eat, or go on vacation. One does not have to wait for someone to have time to help one out because the robot will always be ready. (78-year-old man, focus group)

If the robot knows a person's habits, it would be able to support him/her in the way he/she wants, not how other people think the person needs to be taken care of. (86-year-old lady, focus group)

The participants' remarks centred on how people in need of care could be independent thanks to care robots care robots instead of having to rely on home care personnel or other people. In this regard, care robots were viewed as a positive development, enabling a sense of security and flexibility in care. The fact that care robots can enable safety around the clock by monitoring falls, recognizing patterns, and reminding users about medication was commonly highlighted as beneficial not only to the person in need of care but also to relatives and care organizations.

Some participants mentioned that care robots could be used for social interaction and as cognitive stimuli:

A robot may be programmed and learn by itself what its user finds interesting... I think as such it may have interesting conversations with its user... yeah, many older people are isolated, homebound, and lonely. For them, a care robot can provide social interactions and cognitive stimuli. (87-year-old lady, focus group)

Robots may increase social interactions if they can remind their users about relatives' birthdays and other important occasions. It is easy to forget birthdays, and sometimes the time just flies by, and I won't get round to keeping in contact with my friends. If I had a robot and it constantly reminded me about birthdays and keeping better contact with friends, I might get the push I most certainly need. (79-year-old man, focus group)

Having a robotic companion who can talk to older people and make them more active is a good idea. Many older people spend all their time in front of the TV – they do not use their brain; they just passively watch the TV. (81-year-old lady, workshop)

It is interesting to note that in the comments above, the participants regarded other old people as socially isolated, lonely, and in need of cognitive stimuli. As such, their comments reflect negative stereotypes of older people [61]. Only a few of the older participants highlighted that they themselves may benefit from a care robot. However, the overall impression was that care robots could provide more customized care for older people.

Fear of Loss of Control

Another theme in the expectation configurations that was as comprehensive as the belief in customized care was the fear of loss of control. These two contradictory themes showed the ambivalence in how older people made sense of and interpreted care robots.

The fear of loss of control underlined the participants' anxiety about care robots. The fear was driven more by their interpretations of care robots and loss of control than by evidence of actual loss of control. The public debates on access to information, privacy, surveillance, and moral values were frequently referred to (e.g. Cambridge Analytica, Edward Snowden, or the Social Credit System in China) [62]. The rapid progress towards artificial intelligence in decision-making and the robotization of care scared the participants. Their reactions were inclined towards maintaining what they were already familiar with. Several of the participants described their own use of technology as very basic (e.g. making phone calls, sending text messages and emails, heating food in the microwave, and using services such as Netflix), with frequent references to the belief that new technologies have a negative impact on social interactions and lead to an isolated and paralysing lifestyle.

Today people do not talk to one another; they just look at their screens. They do not acknowledge their surroundings or other people. (89-year-old lady, workshop)

In the past, you always said hello to your neighbours or talked to people if you were in a queue or met them on the street. Nowadays, people are just immersed in their smartphones or have headphones plugged in... sometimes I feel invisible; no one acknowledges me... not even my children or grandchildren when they visit. They are just busy checking their phones every minute or so. They are not engaged in the discussions... they are always interrupted by notifications from their phones. (93-year-old man, focus group)

The change from the past to the current situation in regard to increased technology usage was often seen as a regressive development in the context of human-to-human interaction and moral behaviour. Similarly, care robots were perceived as reducing human-to-human contact:

> *I'm not sure about care robots replacing home care personnel... is it good for the people who need home care? I don't believe so... my neighbour has a lot of home care, and it is actually the only people she meets; she can't leave her house, and she needs a lot of help. Every day she is looking forward to meeting the home care personnel to get help and have a chat. I don't think that a care robot would give her the same kind of care and companionship... it seems so mechanic and cold to have robots looking after people in need of help and social contact... if something goes wrong with the robot, what should one do? Will anyone react? What kind of surveillance data do care robots collect?... yeah, yeah, I think the robot needs to collect a lot of data in order to be able to react to a person's wishes and needs, but then the older people need to be watched all the time... and someone needs to react if something happens... but there will be a lot of data collected if everyone who has home care uses care robots instead. How should this data be analysed? Who decides when a robot or a human is needed?... does the user decide, or is it depending on how the data is analysed...who analyses the data? (80-year-old lady, focus group)*

Like many participants, this 80-year-old lady conveyed in this quote the interpretation that care robots might replace home care personnel and thereby transform "kindhearted" eldercare into impersonal and mechanical care practices. Another issue that was frequently raised during the workshops and focus groups was the massive amount of data that would be collected and who would have access to it.

On the question of expectation configurations – the older participants' assumptions about and understanding of care robots' role in society – the findings suggest that care robots appeared to be both appealing and intimidating. This ambivalence and anxiety prompted moral debates about care robots and the role they would play in eldercare. For the participants, care robots were seen as a means to customized care but also as a threat to human-to-human relation, self-management, and control.

3.3   Expectation Imagery: Timeliness

In spite of the discomfort and ambivalence noted in the expectation configurations, the participants' expectation imagery reveals that care robots were acknowledged as a part of future eldercare. The participants seemed to rationalize the fears of loss of control and invasion of privacy with the belief that future legislation would protect them as citizens (i.e. the General Data Protection Regulation) when discussing the future of care robots. The participants argued that robots had already entered hospitals and eldercare practices (e.g. robotic companions, transportation robots, and surgery robots) as well as ordinary homes (e.g. vacuum cleaner and lawnmower robots). As such, robots had already initiated new practices that could not be abandoned or ignored.

> *Robots are already here; my daughter has a lawnmower robot, and my son has a vacuum cleaner robot. They just love their robots and talk about them as if they*

were their pets, with a name and all... they will never abandon them... yeah, maybe getting new ones if they break. Of course, we will also have care robots... there are not enough care personnel to take care of older people. (84-year-old man, focus group)

It's not only in domestic places that robots have entered, but also at hospitals. I have seen robots transporting beds together with a nurse, and my neighbour had surgery done by a robot named da Vinci, I think. He said the surgery robot had shortened the queues for surgery. The robot is effective and keeps the waiting time for surgery down. (79-year-old lady, focus group)

We are just at the beginning of a new revolution... in just a few years, a lot of things have changed... shop assistants have been replaced by machines; bank assistants have been replaced by a digital app; more and more services are replaced by machines... in healthcare, there needs to be a change soon... the costs are sky-rocketing, and care professionals are leaving without anyone wanting to take their place. (87-year-old man, in-depth interview)

Almost all participants shared the same expectation imagery. Their arguments for this narrative were that robots already existed in some practices, and the eldercare sector needed to adapt in order to manage the increasing healthcare costs due to the aging population and the lack of care personnel. The narrative and worldview portrayed by these older participants seemed to coincide with the political initiatives and policies for the increased digitalization of the healthcare sector in Sweden [63]. In this regard, it can be argued that the political discourse surrounding digitalization and robotization had shaped the way the older participants thought about future healthcare; they used the same rhetorical arguments and concluded that care robots in eldercare were just in time to solve the problems of the aging population and the shrinking workforce.

4 Discussion

This paper has examined older people's expectations and interpretations of care robots. It both zooms in towards individual expectations and zooms out towards expectation configurations and expectation imagery at a group level. Zooming in towards individual expectations, the findings reveal that older people disassociated themselves from care robots. They did not see a need for one: *a care robot is not for me; it is not something I need.* This finding reinforces the results of previous studies on new technology, robots, and older people [36, 37, 64–66]. Even though the participants did not perceive of themselves as care robot users, they were still interested in participating in the multiple case study. They found it meaningful to participate and believed that their input mattered for the developers, researchers, and other older people who might need a robot. They also participated out of curiosity and willingness to learn more about care robots.

It is interesting to note that even though the participants disassociated themselves from care robots, they did associate care robots with other older people, future eldercare, and a means for customized care. Zooming out from individual expectations towards expectation configurations, the findings reveal two comprehensive themes: the belief in customized care and the fear of loss of control. These two contradictory themes reflect the unease and ambivalence in how older people made sense of and interpreted care robots. Expectation configurations at a group level can at any time be a challenge and a facilitator for change. As mentioned in the introduction, Johansson-Pajala et al. [22] concluded from their focus group study that an increased knowledge and understanding of what care robots could do for older people changed the participants' perceptions of the robots from negative to more positive. Hypothetically, this result may imply that the participants' individual negative expectations were challenges that changed at a group level due to the sense of "we-ness" in the group – a "we-ness" that stems from being in a group of participants and researchers and sharing their beliefs and attitudes.

Within the field of Science and Technology Studies the concept of interpretive flexibility is used to refer to the fact that a certain technology can have different meanings and interpretations in different groups [67]. These meanings and interpretations may reach a closure, in which the different groups reach the same understanding and usage of the technology. Closure may also occur if its alternatives withdraw from the market [67]. However, the understanding and use of a technology at a group level is never stable. Closure is thus dynamic, since new groups of stakeholders may reintroduce interpretive flexibility, or new features of the technology may reintroduce interpretive flexibility among the current groups of end users (e.g. [68]).

The narrative shared by most of the older participants regarding care robots in the future of eldercare was that they were just in time. The three main arguments for this were: (1) robots had already entered everyday life and brought about changes in practices that could not be undone or reversed; (2) the aging population raised the costs for the welfare system, and care robots could be an effective solution to this problem; and (3) there were not enough healthcare professionals, so robots were needed to do some of the care work. These three arguments framed the reasons for the development of care robots, and the understanding among the participants was that care robots would be part of future eldercare. These narratives are not unfamiliar to readers, as they are also heavily forged and propagated by the media and, in some cases, also by researchers. While the participants shared the expectation imagery and expectation configurations about care robots, at an individual level, they consciously differentiated themselves from being care robot users: they generalized other older people but not themselves as being prospective care robot users. As such, care robots expressed a symbolic value that they did not associate with themselves or with who they wanted to be. However, the general understanding (expectation configurations and expectation imagery) was that care robots would be part of future care. As such, they were expected to be used both by care professionals and care givers in the future.

4.1 Limitations

The people who participated in the in-depth interviews, focus groups, workshops, and the testing of care robots did so because of curiosity and time availability. As such, the study used convenience sampling. To be able to participate, the participants had to be healthy, up to date, and mobile enough to travel to the research sites and have enough energy to spend hours with other participants and the research team. Furthermore, they needed to have the spare time and the confidence in partaking in discussions and testing care robots. In sum, it can be concluded that the participants were generally healthy, active, and knowledgeable, while people with dementia, mild cognitive impairments, immobility, and severe illnesses in particular were not represented in the participant sample. One could argue that these participants do not fit the target group that care robots are intended for. However, it has been suggested that new technologies should be introduced before older people begin to suffer from poor health, immobility, or cognitive decline [69]. The problem is that if older people such as this study's participants do not feel that they need a care robot, they will not readily adopt one in their current state of health. Neither do we know if they will adopt one should their state of health and activity decrease.

5 Conclusion

Predicting the future of care robots is almost impossible. This paper has described the participants' narrative of future care robots as timely enablers to solve the challenges of the aging population, the shortage of care workers, and increased healthcare costs for the society. At the same time, there were tensions and ambivalence at a group level towards care robots in current eldercare. Care robots were perceived both as facilitators of customized care and as a threat of loss of control in a person's life and care situation. In terms of individual expectations and interpretations of care robots, it was clear that most participants did not see a fit between the care robots and themselves. Taking a more universal approach [70] and trying to innovate and develop (care) robots that would appeal to all people regardless of age, ability, and situation may be a way forward for the robotization of eldercare. At any rate, care robots need to be used in order to have the intended positive benefits as expressed in the expectation imagery for the future of care robots.

Acknowledgements. I would like to thank all the senior volunteers, Professor Britt Östlund & Associate Professor Håkan Eftring, the GiraffPlus team and the HOBBIT team who worked together to make this happen. The research on which this paper is based on was partially funded the EC under FP7-ICT-288146 Hobbit, FP7-ICT-288173 GiraffPlus and INBOTS (grant agreement no 780073) and by the Knowledge Foundation through the Internet of Things and People research profile.

References

1. Verbeek, P.-P.: Materializing morality: design ethics and technological mediation. Sci. Technol. Human Values **31**(3), 361–380 (2006)
2. Lie, M., Sørensen, K.H.: Making Technology Our Own?: Domesticating Technology Into Everyday Life. Scandinavian University Press North America, Boston (1996)
3. Silverstone, R., Hirsch, E.: Consuming Technologies. Psychology Press, London (1994)
4. Kohlbacher, F., Herstatt, C.: The Silver Market Phenomenon: Business Opportunities in an Era of Demographic Change. Springer, Heidelberg (2008). https://doi.org/10.1007/978-3-540-75331-5

5. Davis, F.D.: A technology acceptance model for empirically testing new end-user information systems: theory and results. Massachusetts Institute of Technology (1985)
6. Rogers, E.M.: Diffusion of Innovations. Free Press, New York (1995)
7. Silverstone, R., et al.: Design and the domestication of ICTs: technical change and everyday life. In: Communication by Design. The politics of Information and Communication Technologies, pp. 44–74 (1996)
8. Kudina, O., Verbeek, P.-P.: Ethics from within: Google Glass, the Collingridge dilemma, and the mediated value of privacy. Sci. Technol. Human Values **44**(2), 291–314 (2019)
9. Borup, M., et al.: The sociology of expectations in science and technology. Technol. Anal. Strateg. Manag. **18**(3–4), 285–298 (2006)
10. Gustafsson, C., Svanberg, C., Müllersdorf, M.: Using a robotic cat in dementia care: a pilot study. J. Gerontol. Nurs. **41**(10), 46–56 (2015)
11. Sharkey, A., Sharkey, N.: Granny and the robots: ethical issues in robot care for the elderly. Ethics Inf. Technol. **14**(1), 27–40 (2012)
12. Bemelmans, R., et al.: Socially assistive robots in elderly care: a systematic review into effects and effectiveness. J. Am. Med. Dir. Assoc. **13**(2), 114–120 (2012). e1
13. Fukuda, R.: Gerontechnology for a super-aged society. In: Kohlbacher, F., Herstatt, C. (eds.) The Silver Market Phenomenon, pp. 79–89. Springer, Heidelberg (2011). https://doi.org/10.1007/978-3-642-14338-0_6
14. Lesnoff-Caravaglia, G.: Gerontechnology: Growing Old in a Technological Society. Charles C Thomas Publisher, Limited, Springfield (2007)
15. Shishehgar, M., Kerr, D., Blake, J.: A systematic review of research into how robotic technology can help older people. Smart Health **7**, 1–18 (2018)
16. Bedaf, S., et al.: A multi-perspective evaluation of a service robot for seniors: the voice of different stakeholders. Disabil. Rehabil. Assist. Technol. **13**(6), 592–599 (2018)
17. Jia, W.: Elderly attitudes towards service robot appearance. In: DEStech Transactions on Computer Science and Engineering (itme) (2017)
18. Calasanti, T.: Theorizing age relations. In: The Need for Theory: Critical Approaches to Social Gerontology, pp. 199–218 (2003)
19. Haraway, D., Manifesto, A.C.: Science, technology, and socialist-feminism in the late twentieth century. In: Simians, Cyborgs and Women: The Reinvention of Nature, pp. 149–181. Routledge, New York (1991)
20. Katz, S.: Disciplining Old Age: The Formation of Gerontological Knowledge. University of Virginia Press, Charlottesville (1996)
21. Fenge, L.A.: J. Soc. Welfare Family Law. **23**(4), 427–439 (2001)
22. Johansson-Pajala, R.-M., et al.: Improved knowledge changes the mindset: older adults' perceptions of care robots. In: Zhou, J., Salvendy, G. (eds.) HCII 2019. LNCS, vol. 11592, pp. 212–227. Springer, Cham (2019). https://doi.org/10.1007/978-3-030-22012-9_16
23. Lee, C., Coughlin, J.F.: PERSPECTIVE: older adults' adoption of technology: an integrated approach to identifying determinants and barriers. J. Prod. Innov. Manag. **32**(5), 747–759 (2015)
24. Nymberg, V.M., et al.: 'Having to learn this so late in our lives…' Swedish elderly patients' beliefs, experiences, attitudes and expectations of e-health in primary health care. Scand. J. Prim. Health Care **37**(1), 41–52 (2019)
25. Feenberg, A.: The ambivalence of technology. Sociol. Perspect. **33**(1), 35–50 (1990)
26. MacKenzie, D., Wajcman, J.: The Social Shaping of Technology. Open University Press, Buckingham (1999)
27. Greenhalgh, T., et al.: What matters to older people with assisted living needs? A phenomenological analysis of the use and non-use of telehealth and telecare. Soc. Sci. Med. **93**, 86–94 (2013)

28. Van Lente, H.: Promising technology: the dynamics of expectations in technological developments (1995)
29. Latour, B.: 10 "Where are the missing masses? The sociology of a fewmundane artifacts" (1992)
30. Bandura, A.: Self-efficacy: toward a unifying theory of behavioral change. Psychol. Rev. **84**(2), 191 (1977)
31. Davis, F.D.: User acceptance of information technology: system characteristics, user perceptions and behavioral impacts. Int. J. Man Mach. Stud. **38**(3), 475–487 (1993)
32. Orlikowski, W.J., Gash, D.C.: Technological frames: making sense of information technology in organizations. ACM Trans. Inf. Syst. (TOIS) **12**(2), 174–207 (1994)
33. Jorgensen, U., Sorensen, O.H.: Arenas of development-a space populated by actor-worlds, artefacts, and surprises. Technol. Anal. Strateg. Manag. **11**(3), 409–429 (1999)
34. Rightler-McDaniels, J.L., Hendrickson, E.M.: Hoes and hashtags: constructions of gender and race in trending topics. Soc. Semiot. **24**(2), 175–190 (2014)
35. Shapiro, E.: Gender Circuits: Bodies and Identities in a Technological Age. Routledge, New York (2010)
36. Neven, L.: 'But obviously not for me': robots, laboratories and the defiant identity of elder test users. Sociol. Health Illn. **32**(2), 335–347 (2010)
37. Oudshoorn, N., Neven, L., Stienstra, M.: How diversity gets lost: age and gender in design practices of information and communication technologies. J. Women Aging **28**(2), 170–185 (2016)
38. Siren, A., et al.: The promise of assistive technology in institutionalized old age care: economic efficiency, improved working conditions, and better quality of care? Disabil. Rehabil. Assist. Technol. 1–7 (2019)
39. Newell, A., Arnott, J., Carmichael, A., Morgan, M.: Methodologies for involving older adults in the design process. In: Stephanidis, C. (ed.) UAHCI 2007. LNCS, vol. 4554, pp. 982–989. Springer, Heidelberg (2007). https://doi.org/10.1007/978-3-540-73279-2_110
40. Rodeschini, G.: Gerotechnology: a new kind of care for aging? An analysis of the relationship between older people and technology. Nurs. Health Sci. **13**(4), 521–528 (2011)
41. Lehoux, P.: The Problem of Health Technology: Policy Implications for Modern Health Care Systems. Routledge, New York (2006)
42. Bajones, M., et al.: Hobbit: providing fall detection and prevention for the elderly in the real world. J. Robot. **2018** (2018). 20 p
43. Coradeschi, S., et al.: GiraffPlus: A system for monitoring activities and physiological parameters and promoting social interaction for elderly. In: Zdzisław S.H., Juliusz, L., Mroczek, T., Wtorek, J. (eds.) Human-Computer Systems Interaction: Backgrounds and Applications 3. AISC, vol. 300, pp. 261–271. Springer, Cham (2014). https://doi.org/10.1007/978-3-319-08491-6_22
44. Pons, José L. (ed.): INBOTS 2018. BB, vol. 25. Springer, Cham (2020). https://doi.org/10.1007/978-3-030-24074-5
45. Cross, N.: Designerly ways of knowing. Des. Stud. **3**(4), 221–227 (1982)
46. Dorst, K.: Design problems and design paradoxes. Des. Issues **22**(3), 4–17 (2006)
47. Dorst, K.: The nature of design thinking. In: Design Thinking Research Symposium. DAB Documents (2010)
48. Martin, R., Martin, R.L.: The Design of Business: Why Design Thinking is the Next Competitive Advantage. Harvard Business Press, Boston (2009)
49. Frennert, S.A., Forsberg, A., Östlund, B.: Elderly people's perceptions of a telehealthcare system: relative advantage, compatibility, complexity and observability. J. Technol. Hum. Serv. **31**(3), 218–237 (2013)
50. Östlund, B., et al.: Intermediate Evaluation Report for the Project GiraffPlus. EU: s Seventh Framework Programme (2013)

51. Pripfl, J., et al.: Results of a real world trial with a mobile social service robot for older adults. In: 2016 11th ACM/IEEE International Conference on Human-Robot Interaction (HRI). IEEE (2016)
52. Frennert, S., Eftring, H., Östlund, B.: Older people's involvement in the development of a social assistive robot. In: Herrmann, G., Pearson, Martin J., Lenz, A., Bremner, P., Spiers, A., Leonards, U. (eds.) ICSR 2013. LNCS (LNAI), vol. 8239, pp. 8–18. Springer, Cham (2013). https://doi.org/10.1007/978-3-319-02675-6_2
53. Eftring, H., Frennert, S.: Designing a social and assistive robot for seniors. Zeitschrift für Gerontologie und Geriatrie 49(4), 274–281 (2016)
54. Frennert, S., Östlund, B.: How do older people think and feel about robots in health-and elderly care? In: Pons, José L. (ed.) INBOTS 2018. BB, vol. 25, pp. 167–174. Springer, Cham (2020). https://doi.org/10.1007/978-3-030-24074-5_28
55. Frennert, S., Östlund, B.: Seven matters of concern of social robots and older people. Int. J. Social Robot. 6(2), 299–310 (2014)
56. Frennert, S., Östlund, B.: Narrative review: welare technologies in eldercare. Nordic J. Sci. Technol. Stud. 6(1), 21–34 (2018)
57. Frennert, S., Eftring, H., Ostlund, B.: Using attention cards to facilitate active participation in eliciting old adults' requirements for assistive robots. In: 2013 IEEE RO-MAN. IEEE (2013)
58. Bradley, J.: Methodological issues and practices in qualitative research. Library Q. 63, 431–449 (1993)
59. Lazar, J., Feng, J.H., Hochheiser, H.: Research Methods in Human-Computer Interaction. Wiley, London (2010)
60. Frennert, S.: Older people meet robots. Three case studies on the domestication of robots in everyday life. Dissertation, Department of Design Sciences, Faculty of Engineering, Lund University, Lund (2016)
61. Robinson, T., Gustafson, B., Popovich, M.: Perceptions of negative stereotypes of older people in magazine advertisements: comparing the perceptions of older adults and college students. Ageing Soc. 28(2), 233–251 (2008)
62. Gritzalis, D., et al.: History of information: the case of privacy and security in social media. In: Proceedings of the History of Information Conference (2014)
63. Wickström, G., Regner, Å., Micko, L.: Vision eHealth 2025 - common starting points for digitization in social services and health and medical care, M.o.H.a.S. Affairs, Stockholm (2017)
64. Sourbati, M.: 'It could be useful, but not for me at the moment': older people, internet access and e-public service provision. New Media Soc. 11(7), 1083–1100 (2009)
65. Waycott, J., et al.: Not for me: older adults choosing not to participate in a social isolation intervention. In: Proceedings of the 2016 CHI Conference on Human Factors in Computing Systems. ACM (2016)
66. Young, R., et al.: "Willing but unwilling": attitudinal barriers to adoption of home-based health information technology among older adults. Health Inform. J. 20(2), 127–135 (2014)
67. Bijker, W.E., Huges, T.P., Trevor, P.: Social Construction of Technological Systems. MIT Press, Cambridge (2012)
68. Peine, A., Van Cooten, V., Neven, L.: Rejuvenating design: bikes, batteries, and older adopters in the diffusion of e-bikes. Sci. Technol. Human Values 42(3), 429–459 (2017)
69. Vaportzis, E., Giatsi Clausen, M., Gow, A.J.: Older adults perceptions of technology and barriers to interacting with tablet computers: a focus group study. Front. Psychol. 8, 1687 (2017)
70. Meyer, A., Rose, D.H.: Universal design for individual differences. Educ. Leadersh. 58(3), 39–43 (2000)

The Impact of the Relationship and Family Status in Retirement Age on Women's Incorporation of Technical Devices in Their Everyday Life

Alina Gales[1]([envelope]) and Eugène Loos[2]

[1] TUM School of Governance, Technical University of Munich, Arcisstraße 21,
80333 Munich, Germany
alina.gales@tum.de

[2] Utrecht University School of Governance, Bijlhouwerstraat 6,
3511 ZC Utrecht, The Netherlands
e.f.loos@uu.nl

Abstract. Older people and specifically women at retirement age are typically not associated with technological competence. However, some of them are avid users and little is known about the ways they incorporate technical devices in their everyday life. In this study, we depict how women's relationship and family status at retirement age have an influence on their technology usage. Having interviewed women between 65 and 75 years old, we describe three types of lifestyles where our analysis follows the women's approach to technical devices. The 'GrandMother' focusses on her family and local community, the 'Half Couple' emphasizes her husband and marriage and the 'Independent' concentrates on herself. Generally, the smart phone is used as an extension of their personal lifestyle and routines of everyday life: the GrandMothers direct their digital technology usage inwards, the Independents outwards and the Half Couples are split between those who use it sideways or not at all. For the GrandMothers, their technical devices are a facilitator of their daily duties and existing ties whereas the Independents have a strong self-motivated interest to use social media as an entertainment platform and as an extension of their interests. For the Half Couples, their mobile phones are either nice to have or simply unnecessary. Our study adds to the limited literature on older women's technology usage and presents an understanding of how technologies are incorporated in a certain life phase.

Keywords: Age · Aging studies · Older adults · Later life · Smartphones · Digitalization · Digitization · Elderly life · Qualitative interviews · Digital practice · Human-computer-interaction

1 Introduction

Looking critically at older women and their positioning in society, it is easy to fall into the trap of only highlighting women's problems and portraying these older women

© Springer Nature Switzerland AG 2020
Q. Gao and J. Zhou (Eds.): HCII 2020, LNCS 12209, pp. 207–225, 2020.
https://doi.org/10.1007/978-3-030-50232-4_15

as a burden for society [1]. Older women's situations are not automatically negative – however, they are quickly labeled "invisible" [2, p. 158] and "the other" [2, p. 159]. On the contrary, they are better at "social networks and social support" [1, p. 438] than men. What is more, Gibson [1] notes that especially for women, the setbacks they apparently face as soon as they are considered older, in terms of their health, their income and their housing situation, have always been there throughout their lifetime and does not just appear when entering retirement phase. Hence, "we run the risk of reinventing and reinforcing a self-concept and a societal concept of old women as a dependent group with little to offer society and much to demand" [1, p. 435]. In this study, the authors' focus is on women's sole conditions, circumstances and positions – and not in contrast to men, which is in line with Gibson's recommendation [1].

Whenever older people and technology are the topic of a conversation, there is usually a belittling of their skills and knowledge and easily some form of stereotyping, presenting older women as incompetent. Loe [3] argues that there is not enough emphasis on older people's actual capabilities and usage of technologies: "we do not have a sense of how elders creatively utilize, reject, and make sense of a wide array of old and new technologies in their lives" [3, p. 320] – which is especially true for older women [3]. Our article aims at fixing this gap to some extent. While most of the research on older people and technology focuses on how they use it for utilitarian reasons, some researchers call for the highlighting of how older people give a sense, connotation and significance to technologies [3], which will be addressed here.

The goal of this study conducted in Germany in 2018 is to highlight how women's relationship and family status at retirement age influence their incorporation of technical devices in everyday life. This is especially relevant because while in 2017, 21% of the population in Germany was aged 65 or older, the number will rise: presumably 27% of Germans will be 65 years old or older by 2030 [4].

In this article, age in society, age and technology as well as anocriticism [5] are presented in a literature and theoretical review. Then, the sample's cluster of our empirical study on older women's relationship and family status influencing their incorporation of technical devices in their everyday life is thoroughly presented. A method section follows on how the qualitative in-depth interviews were conducted and analyzed. After presenting the results, a connection is made back to the aforementioned literature and theory presented, followed by the study's implications and overall conclusion. Altogether, where younger and middle-aged women's technology use has been extensively analyzed, this study helps to fill the gap of research on how older retired women "utilize and ascribe meaning to technologies into their day-to-day lives" [3, p. 321]. We are therefore wondering: How do women's relationship and family status at retirement age influence their incorporation of technical devices in everyday life?

In this article, we refer to the study's participant group as 'older women' which is only meant to be descriptive because of the relevant age category and not discriminatory.

2 Literature and Theoretical Review

2.1 Age in Society

Age is a factor that we all carry with us, there is no escaping or rejection. Age is a social category held by every human being and as such is heavily loaded with assumptions, prejudices and associations. Self-identity is age influenced, as a person's age determines, to some extent, someone's body posture and looks. In Western society, the individual's aging of the body is a place of judgment, especially in connection with sexuality [6, 7]. The physical becomes part of others' perception of oneself and ultimately influences one's own identity construction [8]. This identity creation stems from society and is man-made because, naturally, aging is the most human process every individual encounters. Depending on an individual's lifespan, they enter all age stages, from young to middle to old, one after the other [9]. However, in the Western society of the 21st century, age is a cultural category connected to certain associations for each stage of life and primarily linked to decline when it is an opponent to youth [10].

With life expectancy continuously rising in Europe [11], it is no surprise that there are anticipations from society towards older people to be capable of handling their life by themselves with hardly any need from other people. As Rozanova [12, p. 380] states: "as 'successfully aging' stereotypes are connected to the notion that individual choices and attitudes play a role in aging well, they may possibly serve as further justification for giving increasing responsibility for their wellbeing to the old persons themselves. The larger social, institutional, and cultural issues that underlie economic and health inequalities among older persons […] constrain older adults' lifestyle choices". See [13–15] for more information on this point. This is also frequently visualized on websites for older people, where often pictures of the elderly present them as youthful, healthy, active and social with others [15], which also rings true for print media and television [16].

2.2 Age and Technology

Technologies can play a crucial role in older people's lives, as they help them to "maintain social networks, intellectual growth and participation, and physical wellbeing" [3, p. 320]. Hence, technologies can foster their general happiness and let them work on their cognitive, emotional, and physical abilities [3]. Older people have become more and more digitally active: The D21-Digital-Index of 2016 [17, p. 8] shows that people in Germany older than 60 have steadily increased their Internet usage in the last couple of years. Instant messaging services such as WhatsApp are the most commonly used communication forms on Internet providing devices in the age group of people aged 60 years or older, and social networks such as Facebook are used by a fifth of people in their 60s [17, p. 15]. Melenhorst, Rogers and Bouwhuis [18] had a look at older (aged 65 to 80) people's motivation to use traditional communication (in person or via telephone) versus e-mail communication. They found that it is necessary for older people to see a benefit in using a device and keep being motivated to do so. No apparent necessity or no understanding for digital technologies explains the lack of interest by older people [18]. That is something we would like to address with this study because for seniors, their chances of using digital technologies largely depend on a cost-benefit analysis. For older people specifically, their capability of skillful usage is a crucial factor, too [19].

In this age group, benefits of digital technology can include enjoyments [20] and functions or content they could not receive otherwise or not as fast, such as family pictures, for example [21]. Costs contain the acquisition of new skills [20], "learning and relearning of a product" [19, p. 89] as well as "effort, frustration, time taken away from enjoyable activities, and monetary costs" [21, p. 13]. Moreover, digital technologies need to fit into the older people's lifestyle and daily routines [20].

What is of interest for this study is that digital technologies for enjoyment, such as digital games [22], might function for older women as a distraction from their husband's passing [20]. Indeed, it has been found that older women who have experienced widowhood inherit strong ties to family and friends [1] and older people use digital technologies for social connectedness [20]. Therefore, it is important to ensure older people's connection to society by granting them access to (technology related) information [23, 24]. Bouwhuis [25] confirms that usually older people think of their activities with a main focus on social relationships and that they need the telephone to schedule meet-ups and appointments. This has become more and more important due to the younger generation moving away from the place they grew up in, creating a spatial distance [25]. The importance of social activities within older people's lives is backed by a longitudinal study conducted by Hultsch, Hertzog, Small and Dixon [26]. They find that older women integrate more social activities into their lives than older men. Also, in contrast to men, women do not decrease their social activities while getting older. They keep their close social contacts across time [27].

A common classification of older people is the term "digital immigrants" in contrast to the "digital natives" term, both coined by Prensky [28]. It is a widespread practice to divide generations by their media usage in childhood and teenage years, arguing that media is an influencing and socializing factor for each generation [29]. For example, the interviewed women born between 1943 and 1953 belong to "a generation of the household revolution (born 1939–1948)" and "a generation of technological spread (born 1949–1963)" [30, p. 494]. These differences in technology generations are made with regards to the technologies people grew up with during their so-called formative period, between 15 to 25 years old [31]. However, not only the generational background but also individual experiences have an impact on someone's technology usage [32]. Which media do they own, how do they use them, what kind of meaning do they ascribe to them and how do they identify with them [30]? With respect to the aforementioned division between digital immigrants and digital natives, Jandura and Karnowski [29] question this, as, to them, these wordings have developed from vernacular terms to taken for granted ones instead of scientifically proven expressions. The authors argue that a medium's role is not as ground-breaking in defining a generation as oftentimes assumed and that there are rather differences in media usage because of class affiliation [29]. This viewpoint is underlined by Ball, Francis, Huang, Kadylak, Cotten and Rikard [33] who find older people to be the most dispersed in their digital technology usage. They also find evidence that older people dislike the increasingly common consumption of digital technology in personal gatherings and situations whereas simultaneously they see it as a practical tool to connect with closed ones living farther away [33]. See also

Bennett, Maton and Kervin [34], Helsper and Eynon [35] and Loos [14] for a further critical discussion of the distinction between digital immigrants and digital natives.

Taken together, technologies can function for women of a certain age in two ways: they can "provide a respite from loneliness and boredom, and/or intensify these emotions. They can symbolize mortality and life, stimulation or stasis, isolation or connection, and continuity and change" [3, p. 328]. Nonetheless, in contrast to industrial technologies, "digital technologies, based on brain rather than brawn, on networks rather than hierarchy, herald a new relationship between women and machines" [36, p. 291]. An example comes from Ivan and Hebblethwaite [37] who take a closer look at grandmothers' experiences of Facebook in family communication. They find that grandmothers are willing to use Facebook in order to maintain a relationship with their grandchildren who live far away from them and get informed about their daily lives [37]. Here, grandmothers use social media and video chats to socialize and communicate with relatives [37], although, generally, the telephone is their preferred medium of choice [37].

2.3 Anocriticism

As we are looking at women of a certain age, the social categories gender and age and their connected historical development are of relevance. The combined contemplation of gender and age stems from the 1960s and 1970s when two research interests worked in parallel: feminist studies focused on gender-based disadvantages where social gerontologists examined aging as a social problem [1]. Ultimately, this led "to the emergence of the double jeopardy approach to the analysis of being old and female" [1, p. 434] as, apparently, aging is especially a problem for and of old women [1]. Therefore, Maierhofer [38] asks scholars to examine how age identities are defined by society.

Anocriticism was coined by Maierhofer [5] who classified the need to have a closer look at the differences between how age is perceived by older people and how it is defined by society. She argued that "the feminist concept that individual identity, both in literature and society, is culturally constructed and tied to race, class, and gender can be extended to the notion of age" [5, p. 130], which is why this approach should be taken into consideration. Maierhofer [5] criticizes that there are certain stereotypes for old and female people in society that are exclusively held for them and that are neither questioned nor changed. These stereotypes describe older women as "self-effacing, easy-to-handle, and uncomplaining" [5, p. 132]. Furthermore, she proclaims that age is socially constructed and, similar to gender, not stuck to someone objectively [34]. Moreover, age is an individual perception and, in relation to technology, there are differences in usage and points of view within generations, not only from one generation to the other [36]. This is why Ratzenböck [39, p. 67] recommends anocriticism as a supportive concept to analyze the permanent "interplay of continuity and change" throughout one's course of life because it is an "interpretational lens that emphasizes the individuality of older women's experiences".

3 Methods

3.1 Sample

Individual qualitative in-depth interviews and observations on technology with twenty retired women born between 1943 and 1953 living in the Southwest of Germany were conducted. At the time of the interview, all women were between 65 and 75 years old to make sure none of them was employed, as a job can give you access to technology, which we wanted to exclude as a factor. All interviewees live in the same region in the southwest of Germany to ensure a similar usage and comprehension of language as well as a comparable social environment.

For this cluster, the following statistics can be found:

In comparison to 2015, people aged 60 to 69 gained 4 percentage points from 65% to 69% and people older than 70 gained 6 percentage points from 30% to 36% in the D21-Digital-Index, which indicates the level of digitalization in society [17, p. 8]. 51% of people aged 60 to 69 use smartphones and 25% of people aged 70 or older. Furthermore, 53% of people in their 60s use notebooks and laptops, whereas it is 18% for people aged 70 or older. The least usage in these two age groups is of desktop computers (38% by people in their 60s and 33% by people aged 70 years or older) as well as tablet PCs (19% by people in their 60s and 17% by people aged 70 years or older). Above that, people aged 60 years or older are the strongest users of mobile phones (older version of smart phones): 49% of people in their 60s and 64% of people aged 70 years or older [17, p. 8]. The Internet usage of people in Germany decreases with age: people aged 60 to 69 years old in Germany use the Internet 1 h and 37 min daily and people aged 70 years or older use the Internet 34 min on a daily basis [17, p. 13]. Generally, when combining the categories of access, usage, competence and openness to and of digitalization, it can be found that this index decreases with age: The D21-Digital-Index census of 2016 [17, p. 25] assigns a Digital-Index of 39% to people in their 60 s and of 24% to people older than 70, which gives the latter a score that is half as strong as the average German citizen.

The participants of this study can be assigned to the D21-Digital Index's group of the so-called *outside skeptics* who have the lowest level of digitalization in comparison to other groups [17, p. 28]. On average, they are 66 years old and female with a low educational background. Furthermore, they are mostly not employed and have a below-average income. Their digital competence is almost non-existent and they are hardly open to digitalization. Technology for them is oftentimes "electro-mechanical equipment" [30, p. 494] and this age group has more difficulties than younger people born after 1960 with "multi-layered interfaces" of software driven technologies [30, p. 494].

3.2 Generational Allocation

It should be noted here that the following descriptions and titling of generations are the terms mostly and preferably used in Germany. In other countries or languages, the names for these generations might be different. As German participants are interviewed for this study, the German terms are chosen and translated: 'War Children' for the German word 'Kriegskinder' and 'People of 1968' for the German label '68er'.

War Children

The interviewed women are partly from the age group called 'War Children', born between 1930 and 1945. Therefore, they were born during World War II and/or raised during and have lived in post-war time [40]. As this generation has been confronted with skepticism about their potential traumas leading to failed recognition of possible suffering [40], the interviewed women might also have restraints talking about their opinion and their thoughts, as they might not be used to opening up. Their focal point was to function in order to make up for the absent parents – the working mother and the missing father – and to not talk about their feelings [41]. This generation was perceived as a silent one, not speaking as much about their experiences during the war as the public dealt with this topic [42]. Although the experience of war can be seen as a significantly crucial event in life, psychotherapy has not produced a considerable body of work on that topic – silencing this generation's experiences even more [42]. War Children are confronted with their pain especially when they get older and they usually do not see a therapist [41] nor do they speak about their anxieties [40]. Although they grew up in silence about the war and people's feelings, War Children confront themselves with their emotions related to the war time when getting older [43]. The reasons could be that one can only keep such emotions and thoughts to themselves for so long – they have to free themselves from such burden sooner or later [42]. Also, after retirement, not being mainly occupied with their job, these people seek an understanding of their history and that of their families [41].

Studies show that women born in Germany around 1940 are not in a good mental health state: they are socially isolated and missed out on developing a concept of self on their own [44]. It is no surprise that interviews with War Children show how they longed for safety in their life – in their partners, in their living situation and in their jobs [45]. More precisely: people born in 1945 have a higher chance of falling prey to psychosomatic diseases in later life than those born in 1935 [46].

People of 1968

Another generational group of the interviewed women stem from the so-called 1968 era in Germany. In the 1960s in Germany, people grew up in a post war mentality of a conservative morality with strong rules and strictly defined roles in society [47]. At the end of the 1960s, young people, mostly below the age of 30, cut off this system by proclaiming self-realization, free thinking, anti-authoritarian education, free choice of profession and living arrangements as well as an open-minded sexuality and emancipation [47]. Next to this apparently liberating lifestyle, the people actively trying to change the political status quo were also blamed for a rising wave of "political extremism and terrorism" [48, p. 168] in connection with a worldwide protest mentality with demonstrations across the globe [48]. Also, this cohort paved the way for a more open communication with regards to the private as well as the political – with people talking rather freely in the following years surrounding 1968 [48]. In current times, women born in Germany around 1950 are in a much better mental state than the women born during war time: they can critically assess their marriage, they are busy maintaining some form of independence and have developed and kept their own standards [44].

Many women involved in this transformative phase questioned the supremacy of men and fought for feminism, not accepting the subordination of females any longer.

In those days, the patriarchy – a "system of social structures and practices in which men dominate, oppress and exploit women" [49, p. 214] – in all aspects of life had been analyzed and criticized by female scholars. In contrast to the former rather silent generation, the women of 1968 started conversations about their inner thoughts and problems, which they had not been used to before [50]. Their sociohistorical wave has been labeled as the second German women's movement and became fruitful due to women's increasing professional qualification, higher education and economical self-confidence. Even though these women were not necessarily politically aligned, they shared the goal of a better social positioning for women. For the first time, these women did not focus on other people but solely on themselves [51]. At the end of the 1960s, more and more mothers were working and women expressed interests in their professions and not only justifying their decision to work with the need for money. In the following years, women gained more and more self-confidence in the professional sector. In the 1980s, it became normal for women to be mothers and housewives as well as workers [51].

3.3 Interviews and Analysis

Some of the interviewees were approached by the interviewer personally and through a snowball system, more and more people joined the sample. This proved to be valuable in numerous ways: Especially with the participants the interviewer knew personally, it was possible to note the things and people they talked and did not talk about. As the participants were interviewed in their homes, the setting was not as staged as an interview situation in an unfamiliar environment the interviewees actively had to go to. Also, the women showed the interviewer the places their device of choice usually is, so the shown usage of it was as close to their actual handling of it as possible. With the interviewer stemming from the same region, a conversation in dialect was feasible, additionally supporting a casual and freely spoken chat.

The interviews lasted between 20 min and 95 min. After conducting the interviews at the participants' respective homes, they were transcribed and the relevant statements were translated to English, word by word. To ensure anonymity, the names of the participants in the results section are hidden behind the letter A followed by an allocated number. The interviewer's name is protected with 'A0'.

We applied Braun and Clarke's [52] thematic analysis approach of "identifying, analyzing and reporting patterns (themes) within data" [52, p. 79] in order to "code for a quite specific research question" [52, p. 84]: How do women's relationship and family status at retirement age influence their incorporation of technical devices in everyday life? Here, coding aims to detect repeatedly mentioned themes, showcasing the interviewees' statements, attitudes and comprehensions [52]. We were interested in understanding the contextual reasons for their prepositions. Then, we created coding maps, which helped us in deciphering the relationship and connections between our data and our codes. In our analysis, we wanted to highlight the women's family situation in relation to their digital technology usage. The participants' words signifying the three types of women presented in the results below were chosen in order to answer the research question. Eventually, we linked our findings to the literature and theory depicted above [52].

4 Results

4.1 Introduction

Within the analysis, three types of women at retirement age are presented. The three categories were established depending on the women's focus in life, which is comprised of their relationship and family situation. The analysis follows the women's approach to technical devices in their everyday life with respect to the corresponding typologies, namely the 'GrandMother', the 'Half Couple' and the 'Independent'. The GrandMother's focus in life is her family and local community, the Half Couple emphasizes her husband and marriage and the Independent concentrates on herself. These various possibilities of daily attention seem to have an influence on the women's approach to digital technology in their everyday life. Of course, these typologies do not define the women solely but are valuable classifications of the women's everyday life in retirement in contrast to the professional life phase where the job takes up most of people's time, mind and focus.

4.2 The GrandMother

The name GrandMother highlights both the responsibilities and duties they still have for their grandchildren and children albeit grown up. It is also representative of their caring for the hometown's society that they join in social clubs and support with charitable time and effort. They are all in their first marriage and have at least one child and at least one grandchild. Their identity is that of a matriarch: They are not only or merely focused on their husband but have an umbrella function in which they are strongly involved in their overall family's lives: of the children, grandchildren, siblings, siblings' families and possibly parents. Their role can be described as overarching, protective, supportive and involved. They understand their local communities as a point of reference to which they are closely tied as club members, event organizers, donating supporters or politicians. Their engagement goes even beyond their immediate family and extends to the local community. Similarly to how they care for their relatives, these women embrace a comparable role with their neighbors and village kinship and additionally take on voluntary work. Therefore, in contrast to the Half Couples, their non-independence is not just connected to their husbands (and his status or steps in work and life) but more to the family as a whole. Usually, their family members live either in the same house or at least close by, often just walking distance away. They have fulfilled the role of the family's caretaker since giving birth and have grown into the matriarchal position over the years. Generationally, most of them are rather older and allocated to the 'War Children'.

Their personality is mainly led by caretaking but can also be described with ease, comfort, self-possession, calmness, self-assurance and even casualness, which is transferred to their digital technology usage:

A0: And how are you feeling when it is so easy to you [to use technology]?

A6: How I'm feeling about it? Good! (laughs) no, yes

A0: Yes, yes

A6: I also try out some things! Something I have always done, that I tried it out, if it works

They are happy with what they know and what they can do with their technical devices, using it mainly as a way to connect with their social group:

A13: It [smart phone] can do a lot! It can do a lot, I am well served with it

A0: Do you see it as an enrichment since you have it?

A13: Yes, I like it a lot.

The GrandMothers' connection through digital technology is directed inwards: to their family, community and existing ties. Furthermore, the husband's competence with smart phones and other technologies does not play a role or is even of notice, he might be the point of initial access though. Talking to and observing the GrandMothers shows how the above description of their personality is represented in their usage of digital technology, as they appear content with it however strong or almost non-existent their actual usage, just as they rest within their way of life and their strong connection to nearby social ties:

A3: I feel, what I want to know, that I know and what is there, I cannot say that I am falling behind, I can't say that, just that I am not really occupied with the computer and such, that is basically all, but so ...

If they own and make use of technical devices, it is a connection to and facilitation of their existing ties as well as some hobbies here and there, hence an inwards direction:

A13: WhatsApp. Yes, you see, I always see, you can look yourself, I don't have it for too long now, you see, then they texted me, the neighbor: "I have saved your number, saved it for good", "Hello [name interviewee], now the...", yes, so, good and then when I, then I always take a look, if something came in [...] and [name granddaughter], she always texts me, you know, my little grandchild, she always texts and then I say: "[name granddaughter], come downstairs, it's only a couple of steps" but no, she has to text it.

Just as the women's children and grandchildren represent their focus in life, they are also the women's access to digital technologies and their main go-to point of help in case of problems with their devices. These women embody matriarchal structures by keeping the family close and together. Their role is to make the family system work and they are strongly involved in most of the family members' lives – with the help of smart phones:

A6: Okay, we have, how can I say, from the private side and, yes [of course], it is only private. And then the children [means grandchildren], they have, they play soccer, both of them and we are in groups together [means WhatsApp group chats], so that we know, when the dates are and we share our calendars all around, so that everyone knows, when the other [...], where everyone shares their appointments [...], texting or as in our group [means family WhatsApp group chat] with the, setting up appointments or when something is happening, right, that, yes [...] yes, because, we also, for example, because we pick him [means grandson] up at school, if school finishes early and then he has to text me, so that we can pick him up earlier [...] or when something is going on, he wants that to eat.

4.3 The Half Couple

The Half Couple segment identifies as one half of their marriage in the manner in which they bring up their partner consistently and across topics as their point of reference. It seems as if the Half Couples involve their husband in most of their thought forming processes. Whether these women have children or not, their identity is mainly formed by being one half of a couple and not necessarily a matriarch – at least that is how they present themselves. They frequently refer to their husband not only when talking about the time they were still working but also particularly since both of their retirements. Their other tasks in life were directed at having their husband's back and providing a strong support system. The role of their children and possible grandchildren is different from the GrandMothers, as they do not interact on a daily basis; the children more or less live their own life and the Half Couple women might support them here and there. The local community is not as crucial to them as it is for the GrandMothers because some of the Half Couple women moved depending on their husband's job. What also unites the Half Couples is that they subordinated their career and life mainly to the husband's, with children being a factor, too but the initial and strongest impact came through marriage and the husband's profession. This meant that the women had to step back in their own career. In some cases, the women worked for and in their husband's business, therefore performing as a team even in their working life. This does not mean that they are not aware of their supportive and strong role, as they seem to take pride in their work-related accomplishments. Generation-wise, they all stem from the 'People of 1968'.

With these women regularly referring to their husband across topics, they also mention them when talking about their access to digital technology:

A10: And I often got a used-up computer from the [husband's company's] office, when they got some new ones, when they, when the volume wasn't right for the office or I don't know what, right

Plus, they connect to others through their husband's digital technology usage:

A8: But I ruffle against the computer and cell phone. The laptop, it's always with us on vacation, my husband always says: "come, just a little bit", but, ugh.

A0: But do you take the laptop with you on vacation?

A8: He's always working on it, he's always in touch with several friends and they share with each other …

A0: So you're connected through him?

A8: Yes, right, or now the daughter is in [name country], she constantly sends photos and then he responds via e-mail, well, alright (laughs)

They are basically relying on their husband's technological competence:

A7: I was never interested, already from the beginning, that's what it is and then I always thought "oh well, he does it"

Here, the relation to technical devices is just as well an extension of circumstances and roles the women and their husbands share anyways in their daily life, with the man as the main point of reference:

A0: And do you think you're missing out on something when you, because you don't have WhatsApp or a computer?

A7: No, no, no. [name husband] just made that last night, tomorrow we are having a voucher, where we go out to eat, in [name region] and he prepared the navigation system

A0: So you're happy that he

A7: Absolutely, that he's still up-to-date

The reference is independent of the husband's actual competence and usage of digital technologies:

A5: I don't know, I can't really justify it, why I am against it in that way and fight against it, so, I don't know. Because my husband actually also isn't interested in such things, maybe [that's why].

In some cases, the Half Couple women know more than their husband when it comes to the computer and smart phones and they also highlight it – again, in contrast to the GrandMothers, where all of them are also in long marriages but the husband is not mentioned when talking about digital technology:

A10: Around us, people we know and friends and so, they are all sick and recently so many died and somehow, my husband says "stop with all this shit [talking about the computer and smart phone], come, we go for a ride with the bike, come on, let's have a good time!" or something like that (laughs), that's the intention for me.

Younger family members such as children are not the main reason to own a technical device, they might grant them access to it, though. The Half Couples who do own and use a smart phone stay in touch with the family through it, but it is also used to stay connected to friends and hobbies:

A18: We are also in other, we are also in other social clubs and so on and there, we are committed to nature conservancy and elsewhere and then it's very convenient, of course, right, to inform each other.

In contrast to the GrandMothers, where digital technologies are needed because of their responsibilities and obligations and different from the Independents, where technical devices are vital for entertainment reasons, for the Half Couple women, both of these aspects – the duties and the activities – are mainly directed at and fulfilled by their husbands in real life, perfectly so in the analog world. Plus, their social ties are oftentimes met in couple formations. Therefore, for one part of these women, digital technologies and their benefits seem nice to have, while the other part says that they do not need them and are indifferent about them.

4.4 The Independent

These women are categorized under the Independents label because all of them are independent in multifarious ways: They are not in an active marriage (they are single, divorced, widowed, separated or in a long-distance relationship), their daily life does not evolve around their children and grandchildren (if they even have any), they live alone, and they stand financially on their own two feet because they mostly have worked full-time in well paid jobs in which they actively made career choices on their own. Moreover, most of them particularly mention traveling as a recurring hobby, much more so than the GrandMothers and Half Couples, although they do not necessarily have someone to travel with or to, which makes them even independent in their hobbies. Generally, their personality can be described as self-confident and strong, with a substantial sense of self-fulfillment. Altogether, they take their life into their own hands. Age-wise, they are spread across both the 'War Children' and the 'People of 1968' generations.

All of that leads to the explanation of their digital technology usage, which for them is a connection to the outside world: to family and friends but also to people who share similar interests and who they join in fulfilling them, such as travel or sports groups they would not know privately from their existing social ties:

A1: Yes, when we go hiking, we have an app on the smart phone and the smart phone app, two. One is for seniors till 50 years old and the others are, well, the others are, we actually have, I even have three. One is for seniors up to 50 years old, that's in the area around [name city]. The other one is for [name city], 50 + , they are all younger than me.

The Independents' access to digital technology is self-motivated:

A15: I bought the iPad on my own, the laptop, no, the smart phone I bought on my own

as is the usage:

A12: I just bought a new smart phone

A0: Really? Which one?

A12: The iPhone 8. Yes and I have everything, now I'm advertising Apple, the iPad, the iPhone and the iMac, yes, and then, well it goes, when I take a photo here, it is on everything, yes.

or it might be initiated by family members but they have to deal with it by themselves in a steady learning process:

A0: And who thought you all of this?

A17: Well myself!

In case of problems, they mostly contact external experts, whereas GrandMothers and Half Couple women would contact family members:

A1: I bought it myself, then it was broken, it is six months old now, then I went to [name city] in the repairing store, there is somebody in [name city] and they have, I can from home, when there's a mistake, I can write to them and they can from home, repair it from there, right

In contrast to the GrandMothers, where digital technologies are directed inwards, and different from the Half Couples, who see their husband as a sparring partner, the Independents direct their social media usage outwards:

A15: [in retirement] I was utterly afraid, that I become depressed, that I become depressed but that wasn't the case. I was able to so many interests, yes, and it turned out that I never have time, never! And that's still the case. And in the last couple of years, what I do a lot, do a lot, I travel. Six years ago my partner died and for those six years I am constantly on the go. And so, so you have to, you have to go with the times and then you can't, that you say "oh well, I don't care about it, I don't want anything to do with technology, I don't want to have this and I don't want to have that", no, that is wrong. You have to go with the times. And yes, therefore I, of course I also have that, a smart phone, I have an iPad and that, I have a laptop and I'm online.

It is used for entertainment reasons:

A9: Yes, yes, I sometimes play games on it but only Majong. Or when you sit here in the evenings and there's something with music like "ah, why…?" then I look it up

as an information source:

A12: I read a lot, read a lot on the Internet, for example American politics, so, Huffing Post, HuffPost, and Politico, and I have it all at one glance, the breaking news, on the smart phone and then you're informed.

and to facilitate communication to people that are not part of their everyday life:

A15: And the iPad, I bought it to be able to phone my sister in the USA and my siblings in general, that is just a fabulous thing, you can phone someone on FaceTime and you see each other, that's fantastic!

5 Discussion

Having interviewed German women aged 65 to 75 years old about their incorporation of technologies into their everyday life, we find that digital technologies such as smart phones, laptops and notebooks function as an extension of the women's day-to-day lifestyle. As stated before, it was our goal to provide answers to the request of showcasing older women's assimilation to technologies [3], which we catered to by presenting the typologies and their respective approach to and usage of technologies. Apparently, there is a strong connection between the women's relationship status and family set-up and the role of technologies.

We link to the aforementioned cost-benefit analysis older people make use of when deciding on digital technologies [18]. For the three types we found, there seem to be different reasons: For the GrandMothers, the benefits include a quicker communication to their close circle [37] and therefore, digital technologies are incorporated into their existing family systems, as exemplified by Nap, de Koort and IJsselstein [20]. For the Independents, the advantages of previously out of reach content [21] as well as enjoyments [20] outweigh costs, as they can now connect to societal offers more easily. This rings especially true to them, as there is no husband in the household [1] and not all family and friends live close by [25]. For the Half Couples, however, it is twofold: some make use of digital technologies when they are granted access through their husband, some just rely on their husband's competence, while others do not use any because the husband does not either and it seems like a waste of time and energy, as proposed by McLaughlin, Gandy, Allaire and Whitlock [21] and Sharit, Czaja, Perdomo and Lee [19]. In either case, with the Half Couples, the cost-benefit analysis is made in dependence to the husband. Altogether, we align with the argument made by Ball, Francis, Huang, Kadylak, Cotten and Rikard [33] that older people are dispersed in their digital technology usage. Our study backs parts of Loe's [3] assumption that such usage can function as a nice distraction of lonesomeness, which is the case for the Independents.

Within each of the three typologies, the women seem to be in charge of cultivating social relationships, which has been found in other studies, too [1]. Here, it is either family related, as with the GrandMothers, which has been found by Ratzenböck in her interview studies with older women [32], or it is friends-focused, as with the Half Couples, and additionally aimed at hobbies, as with the Independents. Also in line with what has been stated before [1], the women's lifestyle since their retirement has not fundamentally changed compared to their situation before, with regards to their financial independence, for example. Rather, the women's day-to-day life has been slightly altered, as they do not need to go to work anymore – but the duties in their private life have not changed that much and might have been amplified. This is where we link our findings to the presented generations of the 'War Children' and the 'People of 1968'.

When we take a look at the generational allocation of the three typologies, we find the Independents to not necessarily be tied to a year of birth, as, age-wise, they are dispersed across the two generations of the 'War Children' and 'People of 1968'. In contrast, the GrandMothers are rather older and mainly stem from the 'War Children' generation, whereas the Half Couples are rather younger, with all of them assigned to 'People of 1968'. With the women's lifestyle not necessarily in contrast to their employed life phase, we find the reason for why the 'War Children' women are connected to the GrandMothers in how they were raised. They grew up with a mentality of women as the main caretaker of the household and might therefore focus on their family and extended network of closed ones. Digital technology functions as a facilitator of their communication stream here. In contrast to that are the Half Couples, who all stem from the 'People of 1968'. The reason for those women could also be in their upbringing. They experienced a shift from women's duties in family matters to relationships at eye level and therefore concentrate on their partnerships and their friends. That is why digital technologies are used laterally here. With the Independents, however, there is no definitive generational classification, as they are dispersed across both the 'War Children' and the 'People of 1968'. We argue that the relationship status as non-partnered and the family status that is kept to minimum responsibilities have such a strong impact here that they overtake the generational influence. Apparently, the role of digital technology is the strongest facilitator for external connections here in comparison to the GrandMothers and Half Couples. Altogether, we find the generational background to be prominent when digital technologies function as an internal and lateral connection to people as with the GrandMothers and Half Couples, respectively, but to be not as relevant when digital technologies are mainly used for external connections as with the Independents.

As coined by Maierhofer [5, 38], anocriticism asks for a plurality in age identities and how those various versions of self are constructed especially in old age. We find this approach to be adoptable to our findings because the three typologies presented show, on the one hand, how older women are perceived by society depending on their gender when we listen to the GrandMothers and Half Couples describe how they are expected to perform and have grown into the roles of the typical caretaker and classic wife type, respectively. On the other hand, however, the Independents show how older women can just as well see themselves as self-confident, self-sufficient and autonomous individuals, independent of their age. Taken together, we find a strong connection between the older women's focus in life – their family, their husband or themselves – and their approach to digital technology.

6 Conclusions, Limitations and Implications for Future Research

In our research question we ask: How do women's relationship and family status at retirement age influence their incorporation of technical devices in everyday life? We conclude that for retired women in Germany, new technologies play a role with their value depending on the women's focus in life: whether it is their family and community, their husbands or themselves. Generally, the smart phone is used as an extension of their personal lifestyle and routines of everyday life. It can be concluded that the GrandMothers direct their digital technology usage inwards, the Independents outwards and the Half Couples are split between those who use it sideways or not at all. For the GrandMothers, their technical devices are a facilitator of their daily duties and existing ties, whereas the

Independents have a strong self-motivated interest in using social media as an entertainment platform and as an extension of their interests. For the Half Couples, their mobile phones are either nice to have or simply unnecessary. The GrandMothers have a rather neutral, self-evident appraisal for digital technology, while the Independents highlight the benefits and the Half Couples either evaluate it indifferently or negatively.

Apparently, older women's realities and identities are manifold and it is crucial to keep in mind that an active life just does not stop with retirement. On the contrary, women's duties that have kept them busy next to their former job can become intensified in older age.

What should be kept in mind is that our study additionally shows how in older age one's former education and career can still have an influence on technology usage. As women in this age group usually have not had a high education nor a high position in their previous job, new digital technologies should be created that consider different usage skills. Also, society in general and younger people specifically, as they usually are the go-to point for older people when it comes to new technologies, should be aware of these different competencies people bring to the table. Our study focused on women aged 65 to 75 years old living in Germany. It would be interesting to find other researchers looking at this age group in different countries to see whether other factors such as nationality play a role, too. Moreover, a comparison to men in the same age group would be another way to fill some of our study's limitations.

Acknowledgement. This article is part of Alina Gales' dissertation at the Technical University of Munich in Munich, Germany. Alina Gales is supported by the Friedrich-Ebert-Foundation as a PhD scholarship holder.

References

1. Gibson, D.: Broken down by age and gender: "The problem of old women" redefined. Gender Soc. **10**, 433–448 (1996). http://www.jstor.org/stable/189680. https://doi.org/10.1177/089124396010004005
2. Krekula, C.: The intersection of age and gender: reworking gender theory and social gerontology. Curr. Soc. **55**, 155–171 (2007). https://doi.org/10.1177/0011392107073299
3. Loe, M.: Doing it my way: old women, technology and wellbeing. Soc. Health Illness **32**, 319–334 (2010). https://doi.org/10.1111/j.1467-9566.2009.01220.x
4. McKinsey Global Institute: The future of women at work. Transitions in the age of automation (2019). https://www.mckinsey.com/featured-insights/gender-equality/the-future-of-women-at-work-transitions-in-the-age-of-automation
5. Maierhofer, R.: American studies growing old. In: Kettemann, B., Marko, G. (eds.) Crossing Borders. Interdisciplinary Intercultural Interaction, vol. 15, pp. 255–268. Gunter Narr Verlag, Tübingen (1999)
6. Berdychevsky, L., Nimrod, G.: Sex as leisure in later life: a netnographic approach. Leisure Sci. **39**(3), 224–243 (2017)
7. Gewirtz-Meydan, A., Hafford-Letchfield, T., Benyamini, Y., Phelan, A., Jackson, J., Ayalon, L.: Ageism and sexuality. In: Ayalon, L., Tesch-Römer, C. (eds.) Contemporary Perspectives on Ageism. IPA, vol. 19, pp. 149–162. Springer, Cham (2018). https://doi.org/10.1007/978-3-319-73820-8_10

8. González, C.: Age-graded sexualities: the struggles of our ageing body. Sex. Cult. **11**(4), 31–47 (2007). https://doi.org/10.1007/s12119-007-9011-9
9. North, M.S., Fiske, S.T.: A prescriptive intergenerational-tension ageism scale: succession, identity, and consumption (SIC). Psychol. Assess. **25**, 706–713 (2013). https://doi.org/10.1037/a0032367
10. Gullette, M.M.: Aged by Culture. University of Chicago Press, Chicago (2004)
11. World Health Organization: WHO: Number of people over 60 years set to double by 2050; major societal changes required. World Health Organization, 30 September 2015. http://www.who.int/mediacentre/news/releases/2015/older-persons-day/en/
12. Rozanova, J.: Discourse of successful aging in the Globe & Mail: insights from critical gerontology. J. Aging Stud. **24**(4), 213–222 (2010). https://doi.org/10.1016/j.jaging.2010.05.001
13. Mosberg Iversen, S.: Not without my kitties: the old woman in casual games. In: Paper presented at the Foundation of Digital Games, at Pacific Grove, CA, June 2015. https://www.researchgate.net/profile/Sara_Iversen/publication/281447662_Not_without_my_kitties_The_old_woman_in_casual_games/links/55e823d808ae65b63899707c/Not-without-my-kitties-The-old-woman-in-casual-games.pdf
14. Loos, E.F.: Designing for dynamic diversity: representing various senior citizens in digital information sources. Observatorio (OBS*) J. **7**(1), 21–45 (2012)
15. Loos, E.F., et al.: Ageing well?: A cross-country analysis of the way older people are visually represented on websites of organizations for older people. J. Comp. Res. Anthropol. Sociol. **8**(2), 63–83 (2017)
16. Loos, E., Ivan, L.: Visual ageism in the media. In: Ayalon, L., Tesch-Römer, C. (eds.) Contemporary Perspectives on Ageism. IPA, vol. 19, pp. 163–176. Springer, Cham (2018). https://doi.org/10.1007/978-3-319-73820-8_11
17. Initiative D21 e.V.: Jährliches Lagebild zur Digitalen Gesellschaft [Annual report of the digital society] (2016). https://initiatived21.de/publikationen/d21-diital-index-2016/
18. Melenhorst, A.-S., Rogers, W.A., Bouwhuis, D.G.: Older adults' motivated choice for technological innovation: evidence for benefit-driven selectivity. Psychol. Aging **21**, 190–195 (2006). https://doi.org/10.1037/0882-7974.21.1.190
19. Sharit, J., Czaja, S.J., Perdomo, D., Lee, C.C.: A cost-benefit analysis methodology for assessing product adoption by older user populations. Appl. Ergon. **35**, 81–92 (2004). https://doi.org/10.1016/j.apergo.2003.12.003
20. Nap, H.H., de Kort, Y.A., Ijsselsteijn, W.A.: Senior gamers: preferences, motivations and needs. Gerontechnology **8**, 247–262 (2009). https://doi.org/10.4017/gt.2009.08.04.003.00
21. McLaughlin, A., Gandy, M., Allaire, J., Whitlock, L.: Putting fun into video games for older adults. Ergon. Des. Q. Hum. Fact. Appl. **20**(2), 13–22 (2012). https://doi.org/10.1177/1064804611435654
22. Loos, E., Zonneveld, A.: Silver gaming: serious fun for seniors? In: Zhou, J., Salvendy, G. (eds.) ITAP 2016. LNCS, vol. 9755, pp. 330–341. Springer, Cham (2016). https://doi.org/10.1007/978-3-319-39949-2_32
23. Loos, E.F.: Senior citizens: digital immigrants in their own country? Observatorio **6**(1), 1–23 (2012)
24. Loos, E.F.: De oudere: een digitale immigrant in eigen land? Een verkenning naar toegankelijke informatievoorziening. [Older people: Digital Immigrants in their own country? Exploring accessible information delivery, inaugural lecture]. Boom Lemma, The Hague (2010)
25. Bouwhuis, D.G.: Parts of life: configuring equipment to individual lifestyle. Ergonomics **43**, 908–919 (2000). https://doi.org/10.1080/001401300409107
26. Hultsch, D.F., Hertzog, C., Small, B.J., Dixon, R.A.: Use it or lose it: engaged lifestyle as a buffer of cognitive decline in aging? Psychol. Aging **14**, 245–263 (1999). https://doi.org/10.1037/0882-7974.14.2.245

27. Smith, J., Baltes, P.B.: Differential psychological ageing: profiles of the old and very old. Ageing Soc. **13**, 551–587 (1993). https://doi.org/10.1017/S0144686X00001367
28. Prensky, M.: Digital natives, digital immigrants part 1. On Horiz. **9**(5), 1–6 (2001)
29. Jandura, O., Karnowski, V.: Digital Natives vs. Digital Immigrants – fruchtbares empirisches Konzept für die Kommunikationswissenschaft oder populärwissenschaftliche Fiktion? [Digital natives vs. digital immigrants – fruitful empirical concept for communication science or popular science fiction?]. Publizistik, **60**(1), 63–79 (2015). https://doi.org/10.1007/s11616-014-0221-5
30. Sackmann, R., Winkler, O.: Technology generations revisited: the internet generation. Gerontechnology **11**(4), 493–503 (2013). https://doi.org/10.4017/gt.2013.11.4.002.00
31. Van de Goor, A.G., Becker, H.A.: Technology Generations in the Netherlands: A Sociological Analysis. Shaker Publishing, Maastricht (2000)
32. Ratzenböck, B.: Everyday life interactions of women 60+ with ICTs: creations of meaning and negotiations of identity. In: Zhou, J., Salvendy, G. (eds.) ITAP 2017. LNCS, vol. 10297, pp. 25–37. Springer, Cham (2017). https://doi.org/10.1007/978-3-319-58530-7_3
33. Ball, C., Francis, J., Huang, K.-T., Kadylak, T., Cotten, S.R., Rikard, R.V.: The physical–digital divide: exploring the social gap between digital natives and physical natives. J. Appl. Gerontol. **38**(8), 1167–1184 (2019). https://doi.org/10.1177/0733464817732518
34. Bennett, S., Maton, K., Kervin, L.: The 'digital natives' debate: a critical review of the evidence. Br. J. Educ. Technol. **39**(5), 775–786 (2008)
35. Helsper, E.J., Eynon, R.: Digital natives: where is the evidence? Br. Educ. Res. J. **36**(3), 503–520 (2010)
36. Wajcman, J.: From women and technology to gendered technoscience. Inf. Commun. Soc. **10**, 287–298 (2007). https://doi.org/10.1080/13691180701409770
37. Ivan, L., Hebblethwaite, S.: Grannies on the net: GrandMothers' experiences of Facebook in family communication. Rom. J. Commun. Public Relat. **18**(1), 11–25 (2016). https://doi.org/10.21018/rjcpr.2016.1.199
38. Maierhofer, R.: An anocritical reading of American culture: the old woman as the New American hero. J. Aging Humanit. Arts **1–2**, 23–33 (2007). https://doi.org/10.1080/193256 10701410890
39. Ratzenböck, B.: Examining the experiences of older women with ICTs. Interrelations of generation-specific media practices and individual media biographies. Nordicom Rev. **37**, 57–70 (2016). https://doi.org/10.1515/nor-2016-0023
40. Jachertz, N., Jachertz, A.: Kriegskinder: Erst im Alter wird oft das Ausmaß der Traumatisierungen sichtbar [War children: Only in old age does the extent of trauma often become visible]. Deutsches Ärzteblatt International **110**(14), A656–A658 (2013). https://www.aerzteblatt.de/archiv/136946/Kriegskinder-Erst-im-Alter-wird-oft-das-Ausmass-der-Traumatisierungen-sichtbar
41. Hinrichsen, P.: Kriegskinder ohne Väter: Ein persönlicher Bericht [War children without fathers: a personal report]. Bildung und Erziehung **60**, 465–480 (2007). https://doi.org/10.7788/bue.2007.60.4.465
42. Ermann, M.: Wir Kriegskinder [Us war children]. Forum der Psychoanalyse **20**, 226–239 (2004). https://doi.org/10.1007/s00451-004-0196-3
43. Hagenberg-Miliu, E.: Unheiliger Berg: Das Bonner Aloisiuskolleg der Jesuiten und die Aufarbeitung des Missbrauchsskandals [Übersetzung: Unholy mountain: The Bonn Aloisiuskolleg of the Jesuits and the processing of the abuse scandal]. Kohlhammer Verlag, Stuttgart (2014)
44. Fooken, I.: "Späte Einsichten" bei "späten Trennungen": plötzlicher Konsensbruch, trügerische Konsens-Illusion oder langjähriger Dissens? Subjektive Repräsentationen biografischer Verlaufsmuster und seelische Gesundheit im zeitgeschichtlichen Kontext ["Late insights" in "late separations": sudden consensus break, deceptive consensus illusion or long-term dissent? Subjective representations of biographical patterns and mental health in a historical context]. Zeitschrift für Familienforschung **16**(3), 289–304 (2004)

45. Lamparter, U., Holstein, C., Thießen, M., Wierling, D., Wiegand-Grefe, S., Möller, B.: 65 Jahre später [65 years later]. Forum der Psychoanalyse **26**, 365–387 (2010). https://doi.org/10.1007/s00451-010-0053-5

46. Hiltl, M., Bielmeier, P., Krumm, B., Franz, M., Schepank, H., Lieberz, K.: Die seelische Gesundheit ehemaliger Kriegskinder [The mental health of former war children]. In: Lieberz, K., Franz, M., Schepank, H. (eds.) Seelische Gesundheit im Langzeitverlauf – Die Mannheimer Kohortenstudie [Mental health in the long term – The Mannheim cohort study], pp. 135–144. Springer, Berlin (2011). https://doi.org/10.1007/978-3-642-13057-1_14

47. Mair, B., Stetter, J.: Wenn 68er 68 werden [When 68er turn 68]. GDI Impuls **3**, 104–107 (2013). https://www-wiso-net-de.eaccess.ub.tum.de/document/GDI__7B884427AD0F4F5D37F508882E0378A2

48. Häberlen, J.C.: Review of the book 1968 und die 68er: Ereignisse, Wirkungen und Kontroversen in der Bundesrepublik [1968 and the 68ers: Happenings, impacts and controversies in the Federal Republic], by G. Dworok & C. Weißmann]. Ger. Hist. **32**(1), 168–171. https://doi.org/10.1093/gerhis/ght085

49. Walby, S.: Theorising patriarchy. Sociology **23**(2), 213–234 (1989). https://doi.org/10.1177/0038038589023002004

50. Schaeffer-Hegel, B.: Sozialistische Eminenzen','Busen-Attacken' und 'Weiberrat' – geschlechterpolitische Impulse von 1968 ['Socialist eminences', 'breast-attacks' and 'women's council' - gender political impulses of 1968]. Neue Soziale Bewegungen **21**(3) (2008). https://doi.org/10.1515/fjsb-2008-0309

51. Onnen-Isemann, C., Bollmann, V.: Studienbuch Gender & Diversity. Eine Einführung in Fragestellungen, Theorien und Methoden [Studybook gender & diversity. An introduction to questions, theories and methods]. In: Nitschke, P., Onnen-Isemann, C. (eds.) Aktuelle Probleme moderner Gesellschaften [Contemporary problems of modern societies]. Peter Lang Internationaler Verlag der Wissenschaften, Frankfurt am Main (2010)

52. Braun, V., Clarke, V.: Using thematic analysis in psychology. Qual. Res. Psychol. **3**(2), 77–101 (2006). https://doi.org/10.1191/1478088706qp063oa

Understanding the Influence of AI Voice Technology on Visually Impaired Elders' Psychological Well-Being: An Affordance Perspective

Jie Gu[1], Xiaolun Wang[2], Xinlin Yao[2], and Anan Hu[3]([✉])

[1] Shanghai Academy of Social Sciences, Shanghai 200235, China
gujie@sass.org.cn
[2] Nanjing University of Science and Technology, Nanjing 210094, China
[3] Fudan University, Shanghai 200433, China
huanan@fudan.edu.cn

Abstract. The prevalence of visual impairment increases with age and has become a big threat that causes elders' depression and social isolation. While digital technology is believed to be a solution for social inclusion, the challenge is that visually impaired elders (VIEs hereafter) lack the visual capability to use digital products. Thanks to the innovation of AI voice technology, VIEs are able to connect to the digital world with their speaking and hearing functions. Drawing on the framework of technology affordance, this paper is among the first to examine the effect of AI voice technology on VIEs' psychological well-being. Our findings show that VIEs recognize functional affordance (i.e., human-likeness, interactivity, personalization and sourceness) and emotional attachment (i.e., flow state, intimacy, companionship, and trust) in their using of AI voice technology. Results also reveal a virtuous cycle between functional affordance and emotional attachment. More importantly, functional affordance and emotional attachment are found to positively influence VIEs' psychological well-being. The findings not only have theoretical implications but inform the design of AI voice technology to tailor VIEs' needs.

Keywords: Visually impaired elders · AI voice technology · Technology affordance · Psychological well-being

1 Introduction

The world is getting aging. It was predicted that the global 60-year or over ages population would be around 2 billion by 2050 [1]. In China, the number of elderly citizens over the age of 65 is estimated to reach 500 million by 2050 (United Nations. Department of Economic and Social Affairs, 2017). Faced with the rapid expansion of the aged population, it has become a global issue to protect the physical and psychological well-being of the elders [2]. One possible approach is introducing new digital technologies

© Springer Nature Switzerland AG 2020
Q. Gao and J. Zhou (Eds.): HCII 2020, LNCS 12209, pp. 226–240, 2020.
https://doi.org/10.1007/978-3-030-50232-4_16

to enrich and facilitate the elderly's life. Nowadays, more and more elderly people have begun to adopt and employ new digital technologies in their daily life. The number of active elderly users in WeChat (the most popular social media in China) has exceeded 61 million last year [3], and there were over 41 million elder game players, according to the official report [4]. With such a large number of elderly users, prior studies have found empirical evidence that elderly users' adoption of digital technologies can increase their sense of independence and improve their psychological well-being [5–7].

However, these benefits cannot be enjoyed by visually impaired elders (noted as VIEs hereafter) because visual input is the prerequisite of using new digital technologies such as the Internet and smartphones. According to a 2019 report issued by the World Health Organization, the majority among the 1.3 billion visually impaired people around the world are elders over 60 [8]. VIEs bear the double burden of visual loss and age-related cognitive loss [9], which cut off their connections to the digital world.

Thanks to the innovation of artificial intelligence (AI) voice technology, VIEs now have a way to interact with digital products via their speaking and hearing functions instead of sight-demanding writing and reading. Various applications based on AI voice technology have emerged in the new era, such as voice assistants in smartphones (e.g., SIRI, Google Assistant), smart speakers at home (e.g., Tmall Genie), and so on. The development of AI voice technology enables VIEs to search for information and perform daily activities actively. For example, it is convenient for VIEs to make phone calls through AI voice products. Furthermore, AI voice technology makes the dream of smart home into reality. VIEs can manipulate all the electronic devices (e.g., television, air conditioner) that are connected to the AI voice products through voice recognition. Figure 1 shows that AI voice products can connect almost all electronic devices.

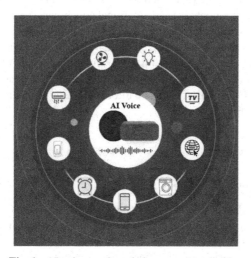

Fig. 1. AI voice products help connect everything

Undoubtedly, with the development of AI voice technology, it has brought more and more convenience for VIE's daily life. However, most digital devices that integrate AI voice technology, such as smartphones with virtual voice assistants and smart speakers, are not specifically designed for VIEs. In practice, marketers have begun to design AI voice products for the elderly population as well as early childhood population [10, 11]. However, the VIEs who can benefit most in using AI voice products are neglected due to a small population size. Therefore, although the core of AI voice technology is to offer voice-based modality, we still know little about what the specific aspects of AI voice technology are valuable in improving VIEs' psychological well-being and how the effect is achieved. The deficit in current understanding makes it difficult to tailor the AI voice technology to visually impaired elderly users.

Under the circumstance, this paper aims to conduct an in-depth investigation of what affordances offered by AI voice technology and how these affordances influence VIEs' psychological well-being. Three research questions were proposed.

1. How do visually impaired elderly users evaluate the technological affordances of the AI voice products in usage?
2. How do visually impaired elderly users evaluate their emotional relationship with the AI voice products in usage?
3. Do the technological affordances and VIEs' emotional attachment improve VIEs' psychological well-being, and how?

A semi-structured interview is used to gain an in-depth insight into VIEs' use of AI voice technology. We choose the smart speaker as the targeted AI voice product because its functional features suit the VIEs' need for use. The final interview size is 5. Considering the small case sample (i.e., VIEs who adopt AI voice products), our interviewee sample is acceptable for exploratory analysis. The qualitative results show that VIEs recognize different aspects of functional affordances (i.e., human-likeness, interactivity, personalization and sourceness) and emotional attachment (i.e., flow state, intimacy, companionship, and trust) in their use of the smart speaker. Results also reveal a virtuous cycle between functional affordance and emotional attachment. More importantly, functional affordance and emotional attachment positively influence VIEs' psychological well-being. Our findings can help enhance our theoretical understanding of the role of AI voice technology. Our findings also help inform the design of technological functions that are tailored to VIEs' needs.

2   Literature Review

2.1   Digital Divide for the Elders

OECD describes the digital divide as "the gap between individuals, households, businesses, and geographic areas at different socioeconomic levels with regard to both their opportunities to access information and communication technologies and their use of the Internet for a wide variety of activities" [12]. As information technology becomes increasingly pervasive, there is an alarming concern that those without access to digital technologies or have no capability to use them may be highly disadvantaged [13]. Of particular concern is the lack of access to digital technologies for older people. In today's information-intensive world, the digital divide for the elders expands the gap between the elderly population and the younger generations and makes elders feel left behind by society.

The digital divide for the elderly population, or known as the "grey divide", have attracted the attention of both researchers and policymakers. Previous studies find that introducing digital technologies to the elderly population help to improve the elders' psychological well-being and life satisfaction [14–16]. For example, Chen et al. (2016) show that elders' access to the Internet and computer reduce elders' depression [14]. Chopik (2016) and Hage et al. (2016) found that the use of online social networks significantly decreases elders' perception of social isolation [15, 16]. Researchers also found that playing digital games helps to improve elders' mental and cognitive ability [7].

Most of the previous studies only emphasize the effect of with vs. without digital technologies on elders [2, 13]. However, whether the elderly can benefit from digital technologies goes beyond mere digital access. Previous studies describe the digital divide according to a two-level model [2]. The first level is the inequality of digital access. Beyond the divide of access, what is more important is the second level, which focuses on the limitation of elders' motivation and capability to use the technology product. Most times, it is not because elders have no chance to know about new technology or cannot bear the economic cost. In fact, it is the limitation of their physical conditions that prevent them from benefiting from the functional affordances and emotional supports offered by new technology.

To bridge the grey divide for social inclusion, it is important to conduct an in-depth investigation of how physical barriers limit their capability and the introduction of new technologies can overcome the barriers. Among various physical barriers, visual impairment is one important factor. Visual impairment cut off the possibility for VIEs to adopt digital technologies independently as most technologies require visual input and visual interaction [9]. Given the fast penetration of digital products into elders' daily life, VIEs seem to be highly isolated.

2.2 Studies About Visual Impairment

A commonly-accepted fact is that the prevalence of visual impairment increases with age. The World Health Organization estimates that approximately 1.3 billion people live with visual impairment, the majority of which are elders [8]. According to a recent report issued by Royal National Institute of Blind People, one in nine people aged 60-over years and one in five people aged 75-over years are living with total sight loss [17].

Previous research showed that visual impairment is negatively associated with psychological well-being, especially for elderly people [9, 18]. To improve visually impaired people's life satisfaction and psychological well-being, researchers have paid attention to the effect of a series of external factors on the visual impaired people's life status. Of particular attention is social support [18, 19]. Living with the visually impaired conditions often entails relying on family members and friends for help with instrumental tasks and emotional companionship [18]. Many studies showed that social support and social networking increase visually impaired people's happiness and decrease their feeling of isolation [18, 19]. However, some studies propose a different view. Recent findings show that social support leads to a series of negative effect, including the decrease of self-efficacy and independence [18]. The main reason for the negative effect is that providers of support often lack an understanding of both the functional and psychological impact of visual loss. For example, the providers of support sometimes underestimate visually impaired people's capability and ignore their pursuit of psychological independence. The lack of understanding can lead to the providers of support adopting an overprotective attitude to the visually impaired, which undermines their life confidence and independence. In addition, social support for visually impaired people often lacks reciprocity [18]. The unbalanced exchange between providers and recipients of support leads to a feeling of depression or a decrease of self-efficacy [18, 19]. In such a non-reciprocal exchange, the visually impaired may give up some of their non-instrumental needs in order to not bother others.

2.3   Research Gap and the Purpose of this Study

The two streams of literature laid the foundation for our understanding of the subjects of this study (i.e., the visually impaired elderly). The digital divide for the elderly has become an important topic in various domains, including sociology, information systems, and design science. Beyond the divide of digital access, what is more important is to understand the factors that limit elders' capability to use digital technology. Many previous studies have focused on the effects of cognitive decline on elders' technology use. Nevertheless, another physiological barrier, visual impairment, has not been fully studied.

In this paper, the related research on visual impairment is also reviewed. Recent studies imply that the mere provision of social support without fully understanding visually impaired people's capability and need for independence will be detrimental to their psychological well-being. In today's technology-intensive world, a common understanding is that by analyzing user data, digital technology provides in-depth insights of users' need and offer real-time, personalized feedback. While digital technology has been widely applied to assist the disadvantaged, no existing studies have analyzed the application of digital technology into the population of visually impaired elders. This is understandable because most digital products require visual input. However, the VIEs simply do not have the prerequisites for using information technology.

With the prevalence of AI voice technology, the VIEs now have a chance to connect to the digital world by adopting the new technology that uses voice-based interaction. Some popular AI voice products, such as smart speakers, require an initial setup using a smartphone or a computer. After that, the product can be used by voice. These AI voice products require the minimum level of visual input and digital literacy. For this reason, these AI voice products are ideal for VIEs to use.

Drawing on the conclusions that the grey divide is beyond mere adoption of new technology, this study adopts an affordance-based perspective to form an in-depth understanding of VIEs' specific usage patterns of the AI voice technology. IS researchers define "technology affordance" as the opportunities for action provided to a user by a computerized system [20]. Previous literature has proposed two types of technology affordance. The first one is *functional affordance,* that means a functional capability offered by the technology to perform instrumental actions [21]. The second one is *emotional affordance,* that means an emotional feeling that is facilitated by the technology [22].

The current study aims to explore what specific functional affordances and emotional affordances are offered by the AI voice technology, and how they affect VIEs' psychological well-beings. Previous literature defines psychological well-being as the positive functioning in terms of purposeful engagement in life, the realization of personal talents and capacities, and enlightened self-knowledge [23]. To gain a comprehensive understanding of psychological well-being, Ryff (2014) proposed a model of psychological well-being that contains six components [23]: (1) the extent to which people felt their lives had purpose and direction (purpose in life); (2) whether they viewed themselves to be living in accord with their willingness (autonomy); (3) the extent to which they were making use of their personal talents and potential (personal growth); (4) how well they were managing their life situations (environmental mastery); (5) the depth of connection they had in ties with significant others (positive relationships), and (6) the knowledge and acceptance they had of themselves, including awareness of personal limitations (self-acceptance).

3 Research Design

3.1 Method

This paper employs a semi-structured interview to collect data. The semi-structured interview is a qualitative method suitable for studying research questions about the elderly population [24]. Compared with a structured questionnaire, semi-structured interview provides deeper insights on VIEs' usage of AI voice technology. The subjects in this study were visually impaired elders who are unable to read the text and may feel difficulty in comprehending survey questions. By contrast, interviewees in a semi-structured interview are encouraged to talk about their experiences with the AI voice technology in an open way. Moreover, Researchers can adjust the interview questions based on interviewees' feedback so that interviewees can understand them.

The smart speaker is chosen as the targeted AI voice product because the use of this product requires the minimum level of visual input. In contrast, the smartphone voice assistant is often used in parallel with visual interactions with the device. After a smart speaker is configured, users first use the awake words, often the brand name of the product, to activate the product. Then, users can ask the smart speaker to perform tasks such as checking the time, making phone calls, reading a story etc. For example, a user can awake the Xiaomi AI smart speaker by calling "Xiaoai", followed by a question "what is the time now?" or a demanding instruction "please read The Romance of The Three Kingdoms". Smart speakers can be easily configured to adapt the home for the elders. Once the smart speaker connects household electronics, users can even call it to control the light or operate the air conditioner. Although smart speakers are not vision-demanding, they are not personalized for VIEs. In the academic field, how VIEs use the AI voice products and how this type of product can be improved to better serve this vulnerable group are still open questions to be answered.

3.2 Procedure and Interviewees

The research objects are VIEs who have adopted the smart speaker. Other criteria for inclusion were the absence of cognitive or hearing deficits that could interfere with VIEs' usage of AI voice technology.

To recruit interviewees, we try two different ways. First, we recruited four confederates to use their social connections to find and invite VIEs who use a smart speaker. Second, with the permission of a major hospital in Anhui, we visited the ophthalmology clinic of the hospital to search for suitable interviewees. Those who were willing to participate in the interview were also encouraged to invite their visually impaired elderly friends who use smart speakers.

Recruitment for this study was completed in November 2019. Nine potential participants were identified at the very first stage, but four of them dropped for different reasons. Specifically, two VIEs own an AI voice product at home but their families rather than themselves use it. The other two VIEs were patients in the ophthalmology clinic. They dropped due to the conflict in time schedule.

At this stage, a total of five VIEs participated in our interview. Among the five interviewees, four were interviewed in a face-to-face way. One interviewee (VIE4) was nominated by another interviewee (VIE 3). As the interviewee (VIE4) moved to another city, her interview was conducted through telephone. All interviews last for around 40 min. Among them, two (VIE 1 & 2) authorized our access to their dialogue with the smart speaker that was textually recorded in the app. Each interview received 100 RMB as reward (around 7 US dollars) (Table 1).

Table 1. Demographic summary

ID	Age gender	Education	City	Cause and severity of visual impairment	Brand (firm) of smart speaker	Length of time of usage	Ways of interview
VIE1	62 female	Technical secondary school	Anhui	Retinitis pigmentosa/blind	Xiaomi AI (Xiaomi)	12 months	Face-to-face
VIE2	66 male	Technical secondary school	Anhui	Failure of glaucoma surgery/severally visually impaired	Xiaoya AI (Ximalaya)	3 months	Face-to-face
VIE3	65 female	Junior college	Shanghai	Age-related macular degeneration/severally visually impaired	Tianmaojingling (Alibaba)	3 months	Face-to-face
VIE4	59 female	College	Hunan	Age-related macular degeneration/severally visually impaired	Tianmaojingling (Alibaba)	6 months	Telephone
VIE5	62 male	Junior college	Anhui	Glaucoma/moderately visually impaired	Xiaomi AI (Xiaomi)	4 months	Face-to-face

3.3 Interview Questions

The questions are organized into four parts, each with several sub-themes that guide the interview. Exemplary questions for the themes were presented in parentheses. Instead of just posing these questions, oral descriptions were given to make the questions understandable. Interviewees were told that details about their usage were encouraged rather than just give a simple answer.

(1) **The living conditions of the interviewees** (*What are the causes for your visual impairment? Could you assess your current eyesight? What daily activities do you do on your own/need others' assistance? For the activities you cannot accomplish on your own, who do you turn to for help? Do you always get timely feedback when you need help?*)

(2) **Functional usage of the AI voice product** (*How long have you been using the product? How often do you use it? Does the product understand exactly what you mean? Does the product give the right feedback? Is it yourself or the product dominate your use? Do you think this product is more like a machine or a human?*)

(3) **Emotional feeling of the AI voice product** (*Do you feel emotional connections with the product? Do you feel that the product is an intimate part in your life? Do you feel less lonely with the product?*)

(4) **Psychological well-being** (*What are the changes the product brings to your daily life? Specifically, how do the functions of the smart speaker and your emotional connections with it influence your perceived autonomy/self-acceptance/purpose in life/environmental mastery/relationship with your intimate others/personal growth?*)

4 Results

4.1 General Usage Pattern

The smart speaker has been an important part of interviewees' daily life. All interviewees indicated that they use the smart speaker every day, showing a high level of involvement. Interviewees stated that they used to try different voice commands to check what the smart speaker can/cannot do. This implies an exploratory pattern in VIEs' use of the smart speaker.

"I have used my 'Xiaoai' (i.e., the name of Xiaomi smart speaker) for one year. I use it every day. It has a lot of different functions, but the use is very simple. You just need to tell 'Xiaoai' what you need. My daughter showed how to use it for me for just one time. All other alternative functions were explored by myself. (VIE 1)".

"The smart speaker is an indispensable part in my life. Every morning I wake up, the first thing I do is to ask it to check the time and weather. My son connects it to my TV. Instead of groping for the remote controller, now I can simply ask the smart speaker to control the TV (VIE 3)".

Consistent with literature [25], reverse intergenerational influence is important for VIEs' use of a smart speaker. Among the five interviewees, four got the smart speaker as a gift from their children. One interviewee (VIE4) was recommended by a friend (VIE3) and then asked her child to buy a smart speaker for her. Although all interviewees reported the ease of use, they also reported that assistance from their children is necessary.

"The smart speaker is a birthday gift from my daughter. My daughter told me that if I face difficulty in using it, she can help me with an app installed on her phone. Once when I asked the smart speaker to read a novel for me, it told me that I need to pay for that novel. I tended to my daughter. She bought the novel and some other content I was interested in." (VIE 3).

"There was a time when the smart speaker did not respond to my calling. My son checked this problem for me and found that it was because of my bad WiFi connection. He helped me to resolve the problem." (VIE 2).

4.2   The Technological Affordance Offered by the Smart Speaker

The qualitative results show that VIEs recognize different aspects of functional affordance (i.e., human-likeness, interactivity, personalization, and sourceness) and emotional attachment (i.e., flow state, intimacy, companionship, and trust) in their using of the smart speaker.

Functional Affordance
Human-likeness refers to the extent to which a non-human device is perceived as human rather than a machine [26]. It is an important factor in the design of socially interactive robot and human-robot interaction [27]. Our results show that the smart speaker offers an affordance of human-likeness for VIEs.

"I like the voice of the smart speaker. It sounds like a young girl." (VIE 2).

"Sometimes, I ask challenging questions. For example, I asked the smart speaker, 'Do you have a boyfriend?' Her answer was, 'I am too shy to answer the question.' The human-like answer made me laugh." (VIE 4).

Interactivity refers to both interaction and activity [21]. Results show that VIEs perceived the communication with the smart speaker as an interactive "conversation". VIEs also stated that instead of passively receiving the information, they could take active actions at any time on an ongoing basis.

"The smart speaker is responsive to my needs. Most times, the smart speaker directly gives me what I need. When it cannot offer the service, it still gives a response to explain. For example, when I ask it to broadcast a classic song, but it does not have it, it will respond by saying, 'Sorry I cannot find the song for you. Do you want to listen to another song such as…'. I really like the two-way communication." (VIE 5).

Personalization refers to the capability to understand users' specific preferences and then offer personalized services that cater to users' needs [28]. Interviewees reported that the smart speaker could understand them and recommend content that is just what they need.

"I have to say that technology is amazing. I let the smart speaker read a novel for me. Next time when I activated it, it directedly asked me, 'Do you want to listen to some new novels?'. The amazing thing here is that what it recommended was just what I wanted to listen to at that moment." (VIE 1).

"The thing bothers many other visually impaired people and me is that, we do not have the ability to explore new things...Sometimes, when I want to 'listen to' a book, I really have no idea what new books are available. I do not know what I need...The good thing is that the smart speaker acts as an agency for me. It knows what I like and helps me to find the content that suits me" (VIE 3).

Sourceness refers to the perception of who is attributed as the source of the communication [21]. Results implied that interviewees the smart speaker empowers users with a feeling of control and sourceness.

"I like the question-and-answer design. I also like the design that allows me to activate or pause its actions. It gives me a feeling that I am the source of all its actions." (VIE 3).

"I am a receiver of information for a long time...(interviewers ask about the use of radio and TV)... Yes, you are right. I do have the chance to learn information from TV or radio. But still, the information is poured on me. But now I have choices. I used to ask the smart speaker to read news for me. It makes me feel so good when I can tell my child what is happening around the world. I can be the one who gives information." (VIE 1).

Emotional Attachment

Flow state defines a sense of immersion when users experience a device [21]. Results showed a high level of involvement in VIEs' using of the smart speakers. Qualitative evidences also implied that a flow state is achieved.

"I used to feel that time goes so slow because I have nothing do to. Now things changed. I can listen to news, novels or songs. Time flies when I use the smart speaker." (VIE 2).

"My daughter cannot believe it when she finds that I stay late in the night in using the smart speaker. I often ask the smart speaker to read books for me. The plot is so attractive that I totally forget the time." (VIE 4).

Companionship depicts the feeling that someone is to be with [29]. Interviewees indicated that the time spent with the smart speaker makes them less lonely.

"My child works in Shanghai. My sister takes care of my living. I call my child every night but in the daytime I sometimes feel lonely. I do not what to bother my friends at such a time. But with the smart speaker, I can do a lot of things. It gives me a feeling that I am not alone." (VIE 1).

Intimacy refers to a feeling of closeness and emotional bonding [30]. With the prevalence of digital technology, intimacy has been extended to describe the close human-technology interaction. Results show that an intimate relationship is built between VIEs and the smart speaker.

> *"I now call my 'Xiaoai' as my younger daughter. 'Xiaoai' is clever and considerate. When my daughter calls me, I make jokes to tell her that 'let me pause my talk with your younger sister first.'" (VIE 1).*

> *"It is now an indispensable part of my life. It not only offers instrumental help but gives me emotional closeness.'" (VIE 2).*

Trust refers to a belief of the ability and benevolence of the device [21]. Results showed that VIEs believe that the smart speaker is capable of offering valuable information and cares about their needs.

> *"(Interviewers ask the question, 'do you trust the smart speaker in its ability to serve you?'). Smart speaker is smart. With regard to trust, I do believe that it is smart enough to give the right information." (VIE 5).*

A Virtuous Cycle Between Functional Affordance and Emotional Attachment
The qualitative results also implied a virtuous cycle between functional affordance and emotional attachment. First, the functional affordances of human-likeness, interactivity, and personalization promote the formation of VIEs' emotional attachment with smart speakers. Specifically, the affordance of human-likeness (e.g., human-like female voice and the human-like answers to challenging questions) increases VIEs' feeling of intimacy and trust. The affordance of interactivity (i.e., responsiveness, reciprocal and continency) increases VIEs' feeling of companionship and the feeling of flow state. The affordance of personalization (i.e., tailoring content according to historical records) increases VIEs' feeling of intimacy, flow state, and trust.

Second, VIEs' emotional attachment with smart speakers increases their tolerance of the technological flows. For example, several VIEs stated that sometimes smart speakers cannot comprehend their voice commands and are not able to give them the responses (i.e., low in interactivity). However, their emotional closeness (e.g., intimacy and trust) make them interpret the flaws as "dull" rather than "useless". As a result, their evaluation of the smart speakers does not get down because of the flaws.

Due to space limitations, we did not provide corresponding evidence for each above finding one by one. Only a few exemplary pieces were reported as below.

Human-likeness → **trust:** *"…it explains things in a considerate and peaceful tone. The tone gives me a sense of trustworthiness." (VIE 3).*

Intimacy → *tolerance of functional flaws: "I now call my 'Xiaoai' as my younger daughter (**intimacy**)…Most times, it can give quick responses. But sometimes it is a little bit **dull** and misunderstands my meaning." (VIE 1) (Fig. 2).*

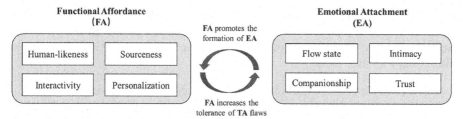

Fig. 2. A virtuous cycle between functional affordance and emotional attachment

4.3 The Effect on VIEs' Psychological Well-Being

Empirical evidence showed that overall life satisfaction and happiness were improved with the use of the smart speaker. Interview questions were delicately designed to guide VIEs to recall their status in the six aspects after the adoption of the smart speaker. To make interview questions understandable, we explain the six components with plain words instead of throwing out theoretical definitions. For example, with regard to environmental mastery, we asked interviewees about their experience with the smart speaker that may improve or hinder their adaptation to the living environment. With regard to personal growth, we asked interviewees to recall what valuable knowledge or capability they have got with the use of the smart speaker.

Our findings indicate that functional affordance and emotional attachment impose different effects on different aspects of psychological well-being. Specifically, the affordance of sourceness directly improves VIEs' feeling of autonomy, environmental mastery and is beneficial to VIEs' positive relationship with their social connections.

> "...It gives me a feeling that I am the source of all its actions (*sourceness*)...It gives me a sense of control (*autonomy*)... My son connects it to my TV. Instead of groping for the remote controller, now I can simply ask the smart speaker to control the TV (*environmental mastery*)" (VIE 3).

> "I love poems... Now I can ask the smart speaker to read and explain poems for me anytime, upon my requests (*sourceness*)... It is not only me that benefits... Now I can learn poems from the smart speaker and teach my granddaughter. It is a happy time (*positive relationship*)." (VIE 1).

The affordance of interactivity and personalization improve VIEs' purpose in life and personal growth.

> "Sometimes, I ask the smart speaker to read poems written by a specific poet (*interactivity*). Most often, it recommends new poems based on my preferences (*personalization*). I often spend one hour to listen to poems every afternoon. I have things to do rather than just sit on the sofa to listen to the TV program for the whole day (*purpose in life*). Now I can recite dozens of poems. I think my memory is better than before (*personal growth*)." (VIE 1).

In aspects of emotional attachment, VIEs' feeling of intimacy and companionship improve their self-acceptance and are positively associated with their positive relationship. However, the flow state is found to be negatively associated with their intimate relationship with their family.

*"My second daughter conforms me a lot (**intimacy**)...I often spend one hour to listen to poems every afternoon (**companionship**)... now my life becomes more fulfilling. It reduces my over-relying on my daughter (**positive relationship**)." (VIE 1).*

"The smart speaker is installed in my bedroom. I often close the door and spend time listening to the program until very late. My child sometimes complains that I become addicted. My mother who lives with me also complains that I am isolated from the families." (VIE 3).

5   Discussion and Future Direction

The advent of AI voice technology is making it easy to adapt the home for VIEs and help them to remain independence. In addition to the instrument tasks that can be completed with the assistance of AI voice technology. The effect of this innovative technology on users' psychological well-being is understudied.

Drawing on the framework of technology affordance, this paper is among the first to examine the effect of AI voice technology on VIEs' psychological well-being. Our findings show that VIEs recognize functional affordance (i.e., human-likeness, interactivity, personalization, and sourceness) and emotional attachment (i.e., flow state, intimacy, companionship, and trust) in their using of AI voice technology. Results also reveal a virtuous cycle between functional affordance and emotional attachment. More importantly, functional affordance and emotional attachment are found to positively influence VIEs' psychological well-being. The findings not only have theoretical implications but inform the design of AI voice technology to tailor VIEs' needs.

Our findings are concluded in Fig. 3.

The findings of this paper are novel and important. Comparing to examine the effect of the sheer presence of AI voice technology on VIEs' perceptions, this study is the first to offer a comprehensive and detailed understanding of how AI voice technology works to influence VIEs and further improve their psychological well-being. This study not only explored the technological affordances of AI voice technology and the emotional attachment but also reveals the virtuous cycle between the technological affordance and emotional attachment, which creates an enhanced influence beyond their independent effects. Our findings also inform the design of future AI voice products that are more suitable for VIEs' functional and emotional needs.

A few limitations exist in this study that guides the directions that our further efforts will focus on. First, due to time limit, the conclusions are derived from a small sample size. Our ongoing effort is devoted to recruiting more participants to achieve more robust findings. Second, in addition to a qualitative interview, future research will conduct a quantitative analysis of the interactive dialogues being recorded in the app. Third, we found that intergenerational communication is important for both the adoption and

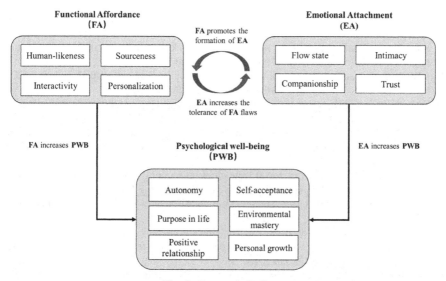

Fig. 3. Research findings

continuous use of AI voice technology. Although intergenerational support is necessary and important, the intervention in VIEs' digital interaction may cause discontinuous usage. A valuable direction is to examine the intergenerational effect on VIEs' use of AI voice technology.

References

1. World population ageing 2009: United Nations, New York (2010)
2. Friemel, T.N.: The digital divide has grown old: Determinants of a digital divide among seniors. New Media Soc. **18**(2), 313–331 (2016)
3. Tecent Technology: Over 61 million elderly users on WeChat, the elderly also live a smart life. https://tech.qq.com/a/20181016/013129.htm. Accessed 30 Dec 2019
4. Sohu News. Playing Games is not for young people. More than 40 million elderly players over the age of 50 in the United States. https://www.sohu.com/a/81181091_352928. Accessed 17 Jan 2020
5. Adams, N., Stubbs, D., et al.: Psychological barriers to Internet usage among older adults in the UK. Med. Inform. Internet Med. **30**(1), 3–17 (2005)
6. Wang, X., Gu, J., Hu, A., Ling, H.: Impact of online social media communication and offline geographical distance on elder users' intergenerational isolation: from technology affordance perspective. In: Zhou, J., Salvendy, G. (eds.) ITAP 2018. LNCS, vol. 10926, pp. 547–559. Springer, Cham (2018). https://doi.org/10.1007/978-3-319-92034-4_41
7. Wang, X., Yao, X., Gu, J.: Attraction and addiction factors of online games on older adults: a qualitative study. In: Zhou, J., Salvendy, G. (eds.) HCII 2019. LNCS, vol. 11593, pp. 256–266. Springer, Cham (2019). https://doi.org/10.1007/978-3-030-22015-0_20
8. World Health Organization: Blindness and vision impairment. https://www.who.int/news-room/fact-sheets/detail/blindness-and-visual-impairment#targetText=Globally%2C%20it%20is%20estimated%20that,people%20are%20blind%20(1). Accessed 28 Jan 2020
9. Pinquart, M., Pfeiffer, J.P.: Psychological well-being in visually impaired and unimpaired individuals: a meta-analysis. Br. J. Visual Impairment **29**(1), 27–45 (2011)

10. IFeng: Artificial intelligence voice speaker becomes necessary for the elderly. http://kr.ifeng. com/a/20181009/6932192_0.shtml. Accessed 18 Jan 2020
11. Sohu News: Finally I don't have to worry about my kids being unaccompanied at home!. http://www.sohu.com/a/309644691_469307. Accessed 18 Jan 2020
12. OECD: Understanding the Digital Divide. OECD Digital Economy Papers, no. 49. OECD Publishing, Paris (2001). https://doi.org/10.1787/236405667766
13. Wei, K.K., Teo, H.H., Chan, H.C., Tan, B.C.: Conceptualizing and testing a social cognitive model of the digital divide. Inf. Syst. Res. **22**(1), 170–187 (2011)
14. Chen, Y.R.R., Schulz, P.J.: The effect of information communication technology interventions on reducing social isolation in the elderly: a systematic review. J. Med. Internet Res. **18**(1), 1–11 (2016)
15. Chopik, W.J.: The benefits of social technology use among older adults are mediated by reduced loneliness. Cyberpsychology Behav. Soc. Networking **19**(9), 551–556 (2016)
16. Hage, E., et al.: The dual impact of online communication on older adults' social connectivity. Inf. Technol. People **29**(1), 31–50 (2016)
17. Royal National Institute of Blind People: How technology can help older people with sight issues. https://www.abilitynet.org.uk/news-blogs/how-technology-can-help-older-peo ple-sight-issues. Accessed 28 Jan 2020
18. Cimarolli, V.R., Boerner, K.: Social support and well-being in adults who are visually impaired. J. Vis. Impairment Blindness **99**(9), 521–534 (2005)
19. Kef, S., Hox, J.J., Habekothe, H.T.: Social networks of visually impaired and blind adolescents. Structure and effect on well-being. Soc. Networks **22**(1), 73–91 (2000)
20. Bloomfield, B.P., Latham, Y., Vurdubakis, T.: Bodies, technologies and action possibilities: when is an affordance? Sociology **44**(3), 415–433 (2010)
21. Sundar, S.S. The MAIN Model: A Heuristic Approach to Understanding Technology Effects on Credibility, pp. 73–100. MacArthur Foundation Digital Media and Learning Initiative (2008)
22. Bell, G., Brooke, T., Churchill, E., & Paulos, E.: Intimate ubiquitous computing. In: Proceedings UbiComp Workshop, pp. 3–6 (2003)
23. Ryff, C.D.: Psychological well-being revisited: advances in the science and practice of eudaimonia. Psychother. Psychosom. **83**(1), 10–28 (2014)
24. Yao, X., Wang, X., Gu, J., Zhao, Y.C.A.: A qualitative investigation on miscommunication of everyday health information between older parents and adult children. In: Zhou, J., Salvendy, G. (eds.) HCII 2019. LNCS, vol. 11593, pp. 109–121. Springer, Cham (2019). https://doi. org/10.1007/978-3-030-22015-0_9
25. Magsamen-Conrad, K., Upadhyaya, S., Joa, C.Y., Dowd, J.: Bridging the divide: using UTAUT to predict multigenerational tablet adoption practices. Comput. Hum. Behav. **50**, 186–196 (2015)
26. Baird, A., Jørgensen, S.H., Parada-Cabaleiro, E., Cummins, N., Hantke, S., Schuller, B.: The perception of vocal traits in synthesized voices: age, gender, and human likeness. J. Audio Eng. Soc. **66**(4), 277–285 (2018)
27. Fink, J.: Anthropomorphism and human likeness in the design of robots and human-robot interaction. In: Ge, S.S., Khatib, O., Cabibihan, J.-J., Simmons, R., Williams, M.-A. (eds.) ICSR 2012. LNCS (LNAI), vol. 7621, pp. 199–208. Springer, Heidelberg (2012). https://doi. org/10.1007/978-3-642-34103-8_20
28. Sundar, S.S., Marathe, S.S.: Personalization versus customization: the importance of agency, privacy, and power usage. Hum. Commun. Res. **36**(3), 298–322 (2010)
29. Bickmore, T., Picard, R.: Establishing and maintaining long-term human–computer relation- ships. ACM Trans. Comput. Hum. Interact. **12**(2), 293–327 (2005)
30. Bickmore, T.W., Caruso, L., Clough-Gorr, K., Heeren, T.: It's just like you talk to a friend relational agents for older adults. Interact. Comput. **17**(6), 711–735 (2005)

A Study on Technology Anxiety Among Different Ages and Genders

Yu-Chen Hsieh[1(✉)], Wang-Chin Tsai[2], and Yu-Chi Hsia[1]

[1] Department of Industrial Design, National Yunlin University of Science and Technology,
Yunlin, Taiwan
chester.3d@gmail.com
[2] Department of Creative Design, National Yunlin University of Science and Technology,
Yunlin, Taiwan
wangwang@gmail.com

Abstract. The internet and mobile phones have become the main communication tools of modern people. Users often unconsciously develop the habit of staring at their mobile phones and processing and focusing on a large number of messages at any given time. This habit causes a lot of anxiety for users. This study explores the causes of technology addiction and technology anxiety through the literature in an attempt to understand the main methods of relieving technology addiction and anxiety. The research uses online surveys to investigate the mobile phone usage behavior of users of different ages and genders, and its correlation to technology anxiety. The survey respondents total 204 smartphone users, ages ranging from 18 to 60 years old. We discovered the main time periods of smartphone use, the purpose of smartphone use, and the tendencies of mobile phone addiction and anxiety. Comparing the causes of mobile phone usage anxiety between different genders and age groups, we find the following: (1) The test subjects' demand for secondary functions of mobile phones have exceeded the demand for basic call functions. Mobile phones have already become the primary tool for socializing and gathering information from the outside world; (2) There is a difference in technology anxiety among different age; groups: those 31 to 40 years old, show the strongest levels of addiction; those 21 to 30 years old, display the highest levels of anxiety; (3) Women's addiction awareness and feelings of anxiety are greater than men's; (4) Users unaware of technology anxiety will underestimate their sense of dependence on mobile phones.

The results of this research can provide researchers with an understanding of the technology dependence levels of users of different ages and genders, including their smart phone usage habits, and the main causes of anxiety. Referencing this information can assist in the development of countermeasures aimed at alleviating the effects of technology related anxiety.

Keywords: Mobile phone · Technology anxiety · Technology addiction

1 Introduction

According to the "GLOBAL DIGITAL REPORT 2019" [10], there are 5.11 billion mobile users in the world, with more than two-thirds of the world's population owning

© Springer Nature Switzerland AG 2020
Q. Gao and J. Zhou (Eds.): HCII 2020, LNCS 12209, pp. 241–254, 2020.
https://doi.org/10.1007/978-3-030-50232-4_17

a smart mobile device. With the advent of smart mobile devices, people's demand for mobile phones has changed, and at the same time, the overuse of mobile devices has greatly influenced people's lives, thus creating something known as "technological anxiety". Excessive use of smartphones not only fails to satisfy, it interferes with individual behavior and social interactions, and can possibly lead to disturbing feelings, depression, or anxiety [9]. This study hopes to understand the usage habits of today's smart phone users and to explore the main differences between mobile device users of different ages and genders in terms of technology addiction and anxiety.

2   Literature

2.1   "Technology Anxiety," a Product of the Digital Age

Along with the rapid development of technology and the speed of information travel, we humans have undergone a significant change in the way we live. Although technology has brought progress, people have not had enough time to adapt. Overreliance on the internet, smart phones, mobile devices and other tech products has created psychological side effects, which affects self-awareness, and leads to anxiety. American doctor of psychology Taylor [22] calls this persistent unpleasant state of mind "Disconnectivity Anxiety." He believes that it is due to technology, equipment, or other reasons. At present, many studies have confirmed that using technology indeed leads to restlessness, with instances of technological anxiety rapidly increasing. Some scholars believe that the invention of smartphones is akin to a large-scale, lethal weapon. The negative impact of people's over-reliance on smartphones was demonstrated by Cheever et al. [3] when they confirmed that mobile phone separation can cause anxiety, and excessive dependence on smart devices can lead to increased anxiety.

2.2   Causes of Technology Anxiety

The internet already plays an important role in everyday life, meeting our communication and social entertainment needs. Furthermore, the development of the Internet of Things has allowed internet technology to infiltrate our lives even more. Wireless-connected and wearable tech have long since made it impossible for us to escape from the online world. We understand the consequences of improper use of technology, however, we cannot escape the control of the internet. Therefore, this study seeks to summarize the causes of technology anxiety: the practicality of technology, Internet addiction, and FOMO (Fear-of-missing-out).

The Practicality of Technology. People's attempt to adapt to the changing times has given rise to a growing dependence on and demand for the internet [12], and the stress of daily life has long-term negative effects on a user's mental health [2].

Internet Addiction. Even though the development of the internet and the network bring a level of convenience to life, the situation of "technology addiction" may lead to "technology anxiety". Young [24] concluded that internet addicts display the following: compulsive and uncontrollable Internet use, loss of interest in interpersonal relationships, with the internet taking up most of their time, an inability to detach themselves from it, etc.

Fear-of-Missing-Out Symptom. Fear-of-missing-out symptom is a term coined in the United States, and is given the acronym FOMO (Fear of Missing Out). Strictly speaking, FOMO is not a symptom, but a psychological phenomenon where one fears missing out on rewarding or pleasurable experiences. People worry about missing a message, which causes them to feel uneasy and anxious [17].

Personal Data Breach. In the context of advanced information, the issues of personal data and the right to privacy have been challenged. The right to privacy and the insecurity caused by the disclosure of personal information can affect the attitude and behavior of young people using Facebook [14].

2.3   The Impact of Technology Anxiety

There is no doubt that technology is now deeply rooted in people's minds. The use of technology has led to dependence and even addiction. In fact, the plagues of civilized technological society have brought about countless changes to our lives. While depending on smart mobile phones, one should understand the influence of technology, and the resulting effects of technology anxiety as are listed below.

The Creation of Negative Emotions. Modern people can no longer avoid the use of technology. According to research, for moderate and heavy daily mobile device users, smartphone separation causes anxiety, and the level of anxiety increases over time [3]. The negative emotions generated by users due to technology anxiety include: worry, anxiety, worry, fear, anger, frustration, etc.

Physiological Effect. Improper use of technology will affect a user's physiological status. In addition to causing negative emotions, users will show signs of muscle soreness, increased heart rate, increased blood pressure, holding one's breath, not breathing while using messaging software on their smart device, and instances of phantom vibration syndrome. These unique civilized diseases show the result of excessive dependence on technology and media [5].

Distraction, Difficulty Focusing. Technology consultant and writer Linda Stone has coined the term "continuous partial attention," which describes the phenomenon where a person pays attention to a variety of devices at the same time [21]. Nowadays, people have many types of smart devices. They have become accustomed to receiving a variety of real-time sensory stimuli, but are unconscious of the diminishing ability to "focus." When one is distracted, their ability to make sound judgments declines, and their productivity decreases.

It has been confirmed that excessive use of media indeed changes the user's health and mental state. Over dependence on technology coupled with a lack of self-control affects our decision making ability, and decreases work productivity and academic performance [8, 19]. Therefore, the purpose of this research includes discovering the modes and methods of alleviating technology anxiety, and considering how to utilize digital media without being hijacked by or addicted to it, so that technology anxiety ceases to be an obstacle to people using digital technology.

2.4 Mobile Phone Anxiety

Improper use of technology can actually cause user frustration and anxiety. Anxiety caused by over a dependence on technology and the use of smartphones is strong correlated to how one uses social media [3, 7, 16]. Constantly being disturbed by excess information affects a user's emotions and quality of life, and may also be a major cause of a users' technology related anxiety. The causes of mobile phone induced technology anxiety are listed below.

Poor Message Feedback Methods. The emergence of e-mail and instant messaging software has accelerated user interaction. Consequently, it has also reduced people's waiting time tolerance for messages, and has created a phenomenon known as "read-but-no-reply" syndrome. Waiting leads to speculation, uneasiness, and other feelings, which may lead to technology anxiety [6].

Purpose of Using Smartphones. The purpose of using a mobile phones, and the target of one's communication may all be factors which lead to technology anxiety. Lenhart et al. [13] have found the following: women are shown to use mobile phones more compulsively than men, and women rely more on mobile phones than men; teenager cellphone induced anxiety is possibly a result of social network interpersonal pressures [20]. A user's dependence on mobile phones, the internet, and community are all key factors in the generation of technology related anxiety. If one's work situation demands high levels of stressful communication, it will have an effect on an employee's personal life and the pressure and negative emotions associated with user interaction will increase [4].

A User's Innate Anxiety Level. Depending on a user's gender, age, personal characteristics, dependence on smart phones, etc., their level of anxiety will vary. However, the more a user is dependent on technology, the greater their level of technology anxiety will be.

The Commercialization of User Data. Smart phones provide a variety of benefits, but in the era of big data, user preferences, shopping habits, usage frequency, and other data are the kinds of information that modern companies are seeking. With the commercialization of personal data, the outflow of data may jeopardize a users' finances and personal safety, and lead to other problems. This influences a user's satisfaction level [23].

3 Methods

In order to understand the correlation between the public's current use of smartphones and technology anxiety, a questionnaire was used to understand the behavior, frequency, and impact on a user's physical and mental state when using their smartphone. The survey was conducted using an online questionnaire form.

3.1 Questionnaire Test Subjects

Covering the ages of 18 to 60 years old, the researchers divided the test subjects into five groups: younger than 20 years old, 21 to 30 years old, 31 to 40 years old, 41 to 50 years old, and 51 and above. Respondents were required to have at least one year of smartphone experience, and totaled 204 subjects. Of these, 89 were males and 115 were females. The age distribution of the test subjects is shown in Table 1.

Table 1. Age distribution of subjects

Age group	20 and under	21–31	31–40	41–50	51 and over
Number of subjects	41	48	39	32	44

3.2 Questionnaire Design

The questionnaire covers four aspects: (1) experience with smartphone use; (2) experience with technology addiction; (3) causes of technology anxiety; (4) awareness of technology anxiety; questions related to mobile phone addiction and anxiety use the Smartphone Addiction Scale (SAS) designed by Kwon [11], and are measured with a seven-point Likert scale.

4 Results

Research results were analyzed based on the four main aspects of the questionnaire: (1) experience with smartphone use; (2) experience with technology addiction; (3) causes of technology anxiety; (4) awareness of technology anxiety. Researchers used narrative statistics to understand user experience and technology anxiety, and used ANOVA to conduct deeper analysis of experiences of technology addiction and causes of technology anxiety.

4.1 Overview of Mobile Phone Use

Most of the test subjects have used mobile phones for more than 4–6 years (47%); with Android OS (55%) and iOS (44%) being their two primary operating systems; According to the statistical results of "the number of hours that the test subjects used their mobile phones at work/school days," we see that most users used smartphones between 2 to 4 h per day: those who used smartphones less than 2 h, 22%; less than 3 h, 25%; and less than 4 h, 16%. The statistical results show that the test subjects use their mobile phones longer on holidays than on weekdays. The first three statistical results (Fig. 1) from the "primary period when subjects use their mobile phones" show the following: 1–2 h (18%), moments of free time (18%), evenings between 19:00–22:00 (16%), which shows that night time is when the subject uses their mobile phones the most.

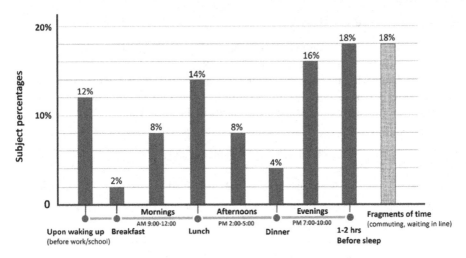

Fig. 1. The primary time period when subjects use their mobile phones

According to the statistical results related to "primary mobile phone activities", the top three activities among the 204 subjects were as follows: instant messaging (91%), search for information (82%), taking pictures/videos (78%), with phone calls only accounting for 42%. This indicates that among the test subjects' mobile phone activities, secondary feature activity exceeds that of the original calling function of mobile phones (Fig. 2).

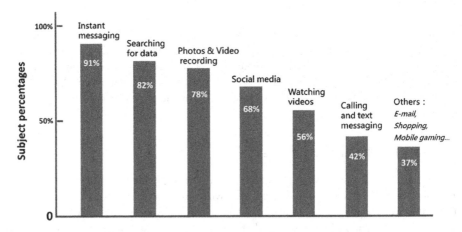

Fig. 2. Test subjects' primary mobile phone activities

4.2 Statistics of Technology Anxiety Awareness

From the statistical results of "Technology anxiety awareness" (see Fig. 3), we can see that the participants generally believe that they should cut down on the number of hours they use their mobile phones, and the attitude of using mobile phones should be reduced.

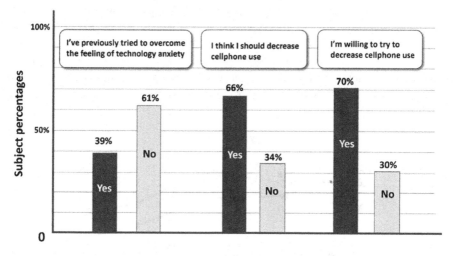

Fig. 3. Subjects' awareness of technology anxiety 1

Although the average respondent is consciousness of their need to reduce mobile phone usage, from the narrative results in Fig. 4, it is found that most of them cannot truly achieve a "reduction in smartphone use" due to reasons such as personal desires, schoolwork, work responsibilities, and more.

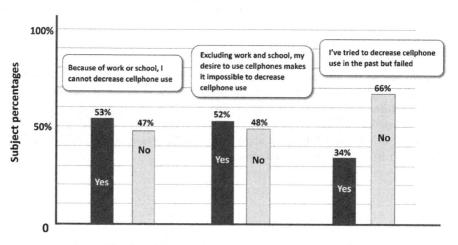

Fig. 4. Subjects' awareness of technology anxiety 2

4.3 Analysis of Technology Anxiety Among Different Age Groups

Analysis of the degree of technology anxiety among all ages from the facet scores of "technology addiction" and "technology anxiety" can be seen in Fig. 5. As seen in Fig. 5, the facet scores of technology addiction are ranked from highest to lowest: 31–40 years old > 21–30 years old > below 20 years old > 41–50 years old > 51 years and older; facet scores of technology anxiety in descending order are: 21–30 years old > 31–40 years old > under 20 years old > 41–50 years old > 51 years old. Looking at the above results, we found: the scores of technology addiction and technology anxiety among the three age groups of 20 and under, 21–30 and 31–40, are higher; while the scores of technology addiction and technology anxiety for the two test subject age groups of 41–50 years old, and 51 above were lower.

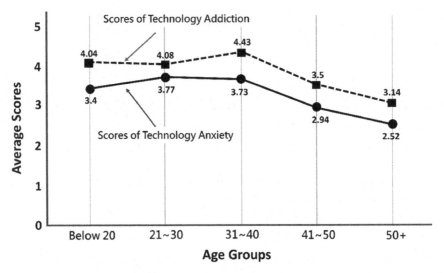

Fig. 5. Technology anxiety scores among age groups

According to the results of one-way ANOVA analysis, the researchers found that the scores of eight questions for technology anxiety (from a total of 10 questions) show significant differences among different age groups. Those questions and the statistical results are listed as Table 2.

The researchers then follow up applying Scheffe's post-hoc test to verify which groups differ from others, the results are shown in Table 3.

Table 2. One-way ANOVA analysis for technology anxiety among different age groups

Causes showing significant difference	F value	P
I feel anxious even without using mobile phone instant messaging software	4.485	.002[*]
I do not play mobile games, I will feel anxious	5.744	.000[*]
If I miss ongoing conversations among peers on social media, I will feel anxious	4.913	.001[*]
If I miss the latest news, I will feel anxious	4.771	.001[*]
Potential personal data leaking causes me to feel anxious	7.031	.000[*]
Having a low battery makes me feel anxious	6.747	.000[*]
If mobile phone does not have internet access, I will feel anxious	7.311	.000[*]
When I do not know how to use a mobile phone function, I will feel anxious	2.897	.023[*]

*p < 0.05 is significant.

Table 3. Post-hoc test for comparing technology anxiety among different age groups

Causes showing significant difference	Age groups with significant differences
I feel anxious even without using mobile phone instant messaging software	• 21–30, and 51 and older (p = .023) • 31–40, and 51 and older (p = .028)
I do not play mobile games, I will feel anxious	• Under 20, and 51 and older (p = .026) • 21–30, and 51 and older (p = .001)
If I miss ongoing conversations among peers on social media, I will feel anxious	• 21–30, and 41–50 (p = .029) • 21–30, and 51 and older (p = .028)
If I miss the latest news, I will feel anxious	• 21–30, and 51 and older (p = .034) • 31–40, and 51 and older (p = .031)
Potential personal data leaking causes me to feel anxious	• Under 20, and 51 and older (p = .010) • 21–30, and 51 and older (p = .000) • 31–40, and 51 and older (p = .003)
Having a low battery makes me feel anxious	• Under 20, and 51 and older (p = .026) • 21–30, and 51 and older (p = .001) • 31–40, and 51 and older (p = .002)
If mobile phone does not have internet access, I will feel anxious	• Under 20, and 51 and older (p = .011) • 21–30, and 51 and older (p = .000) • 31–40, and 51 and older (p = .003)
When I do not know how to use a mobile phone function, I will feel anxious	• Groups with no significant difference

*p < 0.05 is significant

4.4 Analysis of Technology Anxiety Among Different Genders

Comparing the anxiety and addiction scores derived from the males and females' answers (Fig. 6), we found that females have higher scores than males for technology addiction and technology anxiety, thus, it is speculated that females are more likely than males to have addiction and anxiety when using mobile phones.

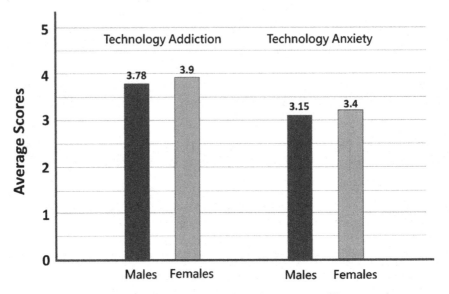

Fig. 6. Scores of technology anxiety and addiction among different genders

5   Discussions

5.1   Mobile Phone Usage Habits

Secondary Phone Functions have Surpassed the Basic Call Functions. Survey results from the interviews on mobile phone usage (Fig. 1) show that the subjects used instant messaging software, social media, watched videos, searched for data, and took pictures and videos more frequently than they made phone calls. And four of these five activities are all internet dependent functions, showing that users' internet requirements have surpassed the basic call and text messaging requirements of mobile phones. At the same time, it verifies the literature that mentions users' dependence on and demand for internet is growing in an effort to adapt to the changing times [12].

Users' Inability to Reduce Mobile Phone Usage. The results of the survey on technology anxiety self-awareness showed that the subjects generally believed that the time spent using the mobile phone should be reduced, however, they failed to try or reduce the use of the mobile phone because of other factors. In fact, users are concerned about the use of smart phones and technology anxiety, but because of factors in modern use (the nature of work, keeping in contact with others) and individual addiction to mobile phones, they cannot reduce cellphone use. As a result, although users do not know how long they use their smartphones, and they know that they are "overusing their phones," still, they are not able to effectively improve the situation, resulting in users becoming increasingly dependent on smartphones.

5.2 Examination of Anxiety Levels Among Different Groups

Differences of Technology Anxiety Among Age Groups

31 to 40 - Year-Olds have the Highest Tech Addiction Scores. Comparing the scores of those experiencing technology addiction among each age group, we can order the addiction level from highest to lowest as follows: 31–40 years old, 21–30 years old > 20 years old and below > 41–50 years old > 51 and older > 31–40 years old, with the 31–40 - year-old age group scoring the highest in terms of technology anxiety. The 31–40 age group is a digital immigrant [18]. Digital immigrants refer to those living in a generation prior to the advent of computers, and who are used to writing and reading on paper. However, because of the digital revolution and the development of the Internet, this group of digital immigrants have been "forced" to respond to technological advances: speed and density of information exchange has changed their pace of life, and the hours spent using technology and smart phones has increased dramatically compared to the past. This causes them to feel anxious about the progress of technology [1]. Therefore, this study speculates that those between 31–40 years old are the group most intensely affected by technology addiction.

21 to 30 - Year-Olds Are the Group With the Highest Levels of Technology Anxiety. Scores of technology anxiety, ranked from highest to lowest, are as follows: 21–30 years old > 31–40 years old > under 20 years old > 41–50 years old > 51 and older, with the 21–30 - year-old age group scoring the highest in terms of technology anxiety. The 21–30 - year-olds belong to digital natives. Digital natives were born into a digital age. Compared to digital immigrants, they are more adapted to a technology-filled life. However, as the hours of technology use increases, so does the level of anxiety.

Addiction and Anxiety of Younger Ages Are Greater than Those of Middle-Aged and Senior Citizens. The results of the study show that scores of anxiety and addiction for those under 20 years old, 21–30 years old, and 31–40 years old are higher; and scores for those 41–50 years old, and 51 and above are lower. This study speculates that the groups of those under 20 years of age, 21–30 years of age, and 31–40 years of age show similar amounts of anxiety. Because young people use mobile phones for longer hours and have higher anxiety, so it is inferred that addiction is a factor that causes technology anxiety. The questionnaire results verified the literatures' findings that excessive use of smart phones will cause user addiction [16], thus increasing the likelihood that users will develop technology anxiety.

Differences of Technology Anxiety Among Genders. Results of the survey supports findings from the literature showing that women were more anxious about using mobile phones than men [12]. Literature and experimental results verify that women's sense of technology anxiety is higher than men's. This study speculates that for women, the factors that cause technology anxiety are derived from the end-goal of their mobile phone usage (e.g., maintaining relationship with friends, FOMO mindset, competitive mentality of mobile games, and pressure from work-related communication). Thus, by reducing the use of mobile phones, women can reduce anxiety. For men, using smart phones is a way to alleviate stress, such as playing games to relieve anxiety. This verifies the literature, which states: playing video games increases anxiety among girls, but is beneficial for boys [15]. Thus, the result of reducing cellphone usage among males is an increase in anxiety. It is speculated that male technology anxiety originates from mobile phone addiction.

6   Conclusions

In order to understand the current mobile phone habits and technology anxiety among the general public, this study used a questionnaire to survey 204 users and analyzed the average test subject's attitudes towards the use of cellphones and their attitudes regarding technology anxiety. The specific contributions of the research are described below.

6.1   31 to 40 Year-Olds Show the Strongest Feelings of Technology Addiction

Those 31 to 40 years old belong to the group known as digital immigrants. They have the highest contrast with the frequency of mobile phone use when comparing past and modern usage habits. Because of this, they show the highest addiction scores.

6.2   21 to 30 Year-Old Show the Highest Levels of Anxiety

Those in the 21 to 30 age group are considered digital natives. For them, the use of smart phones has become an important issue of everyday life. Therefore, whenever something happens to their smartphone, they become anxious very easily. This group shows the strongest tendency of technology anxiety.

6.3   Women's Anxiety and Addiction to Mobile Phones Are Stronger Than Men's

Women are more dependent on smartphones than men, so they are more addicted to and anxious about using mobile phones than men. Women's anxiety comes from the pressure of using the mobile phone; men's anxiety comes from their addiction to mobile phones.

Our research results found that users of different genders and ages have different anxiety and addiction levels when using mobile phones. The younger the user, the greater the level of anxiety. Women show greater levels of anxiety and addiction than men. Most users hope to reduce the amount of time they use mobile phones, however, because of work or academic pressure, they fail to do so. Future research or mobile phone interface designers can focus on how to give assistance to those of different age groups and either gender as they use their mobile phones. This should help users be more flexible in controlling the frequency and duration of their cellphone use, while helping them implement the appropriate methods to reduce mobile phone related anxiety.

References

1. Bozionelos, N.: Computer anxiety: relationship with computer experience and prevalence. Comput. Hum. Behav. **17**(2), 213–224 (2001)
2. Charles, S.T., Piazza, J.R., Mogle, J., Sliwinski, M.J., Almeida, D.M.: The wear and tear of daily stressors on mental health. Psychol. Sci. **24**(5), 733–741 (2013)
3. Cheever, N.A., Rosen, L.D., Carrier, L.M., Chavez, A.: Out of sight is not out of mind: the impact of restricting wireless mobile device use on anxiety levels among low, moderate and high users. Comput. Hum. Behav. **37**(Suppl. C), 290–297 (2014). https://doi.org/10.1016/j.chb.2014.05.002
4. Cheng, H.W.: The relationship between employees' perceived job flexibility and work-life balance: the moderating effect of work-related communication technologies use during non-work hours. Master's thesis, National Sun Yat-sen University, Kaohsiung, Taiwan (2017). Available from National Digital Library of Theses and Dissertations in Taiwan. https://hdl.handle.net/11296/8yr4f5. Accessed 20 Dec 2019
5. Clayton, R.B., Leshner, G., Almond, A.: The extended iSelf the impact of iPhone separation on cognition, emotion, and physiology. J. Comput. Mediat. Comun. **20**(2), 119–135 (2015)
6. Cowan, D.: Message sent, received but no instant reply: how does that make you feel? The Conversation (2019). https://theconversation.com/message-sent-received-but-no-instant-reply-how-does-that-make-you-feel-101110. Accessed 20 Dec 2019
7. Dobrean, A., Păsărelu, C.-R.: Impact of social media on social anxiety: a systematic review. In: New Developments in Anxiety Disorders. InTech (2016)
8. Duke, É., Montag, C.: Smartphone addiction, daily interruptions and self-reported productivity. Addictive Behaviors Reports **6**(Suppl. C), 90–95 (2017). https://doi.org/10.1016/j.abrep.2017.07.002
9. Elhai, J.D., Levine, J.C., Dvorak, R.D., Hall, B.J.: Fear of missing out, need for touch, anxiety and depression are related to problematic smartphone use. Comput. Hum. Behav. **63**, 509–516 (2016)
10. Global Digital Report (2019). https://wearesocial.com/global-digital-report-2019. Accessed 20 Dec 2019
11. Kwon, M., Kim, D.J., Cho, H., Yang, S.: The smartphone addiction scale: development and validation of a short version for adolescents. PLoS ONE **8**(12), e83558 (2013). https://doi.org/10.1371/journal.pone.0083558
12. Lee, Y.-K., Chang, C.-T., Lin, Y., Cheng, Z.-H.: The dark side of smartphone usage: psychological traits, compulsive behavior and technostress. Comput. Hum. Behav. **31**(Suppl. C), 373–383 (2014). https://doi.org/10.1016/j.chb.2013.10.047
13. Lenhart, A., Purcell, K., Smith, A., Zickuhr, K.: Social media and young adults. Pew Internet & American Life Project (2010). Accessed 30 Nov 2014
14. Liu, C., Ang, R.P., Lwin, M.O.: Influences of narcissism and parental mediation on adolescents' textual and visual personal information disclosure in Facebook. Comput. Hum. Behav. **58**(Suppl. C), 82–88 (2016). https://doi.org/10.1016/j.chb.2015.12.060
15. Ohannessian, C.M.: Video game play and anxiety during late adolescence: the moderating effects of gender and social context. J. Affect. Disord. **226**, 216–219 (2018)
16. Oulasvirta, A., Rattenbury, T., Ma, L., Raita, E.: Habits make smartphone use more pervasive. Pers. Ubiquit. Comput. **16**(1), 105–114 (2012)
17. Przybylski, A.K., Murayama, K., DeHaan, C.R., Gladwell, V.: Motivational, emotional, and behavioral correlates of fear of missing out. Comput. Hum. Behav. **29**(4), 1841–1848 (2013). https://doi.org/10.1016/j.chb.2013.02.014
18. Prensky, M.: From on the Horizon, vol. 9, no. 5, pp. 1–6. MCB University Press (2001)

19. Samaha, M., Hawi, N.S.: Relationships among smartphone addiction, stress, academic performance, and satisfaction with life. Comput. Hum. Behav. **57**(Suppl. C), 321–325 (2016). https://doi.org/10.1016/j.chb.2015.12.045
20. Shapiro, L.A.S., Margolin, G.: Growing up wired: social networking sites and adolescent psychosocial development. Clin. Child. Fam. Psychol. Rev. **17**(1), 1–18 (2014)
21. Stone, L.: Continuous Partial Attention. Lindastont.net (1998). https://lindastone.net/qa/continuous-partial-attention/. Accessed 20 Dec 2019
22. Taylor, J.: Re: technology: disconnectivity anxiety do you freak out when you lose your mobile phone signal? [Web blog message], 27 July 2009. https://www.psychologytoday.com/blog/the-power-prime/200907/technologydisconnectivity-anxiety
23. Wixom, B.H., Todd, P.A.: A theoretical integration of user satisfaction and technology acceptance. Inf. Syst. Res. **16**(1), 85–102 (2005)
24. Young, K.S.: Cognitive behavior therapy with internet addicts: treatment outcomes and implications. CyberPsychol. Behav. **10**(5), 671–679 (2007). https://doi.org/10.1089/cpb.2007.9971. ISSN 1094-9313

To Do or Not to Do: How Socio-demographic Characteristics of Older Adults Are Associated with Online Activities

Joerg Leukel[1]([⊠]), Barbara Schehl[1], and Vijayan Sugumaran[2]

[1] Faculty of Business, Economics and Social Sciences,
University of Hohenheim, 70599 Stuttgart, Germany
{joerg.leukel,barbara.schehl}@uni-hohenheim.de
[2] Department of Decision and Information Sciences,
Oakland University, Rochester, MI 48309, USA
sugumara@oakland.edu

Abstract. Older adults use the Internet for a broad range of purposes including interpersonal communication, errands, and leisure. Although barriers towards physical access to the digital world have diminished, relevant subgroups of older adults still lack the digital skills required for diverse online activities. While understanding this second-level digital divide is an active field of research, the results of previous studies are less conclusive in the factors that explain whether one belongs to the group of users or nonusers. We posit that the accumulation of knowledge from empirical quantitative studies is undermined by considerable heterogeneity in the reporting of logistic regression analysis, for which we provide evidence in the extant literature. We then explore the usefulness of socio-demographic characteristics in explaining various online activities. Our results (1) highlight different roles of education and living arrangement in explaining informational, social, and instrumental online activities, and (2) underscore the need to provide contextualized information when conducting logistic regression analysis. Taken together, our findings contribute to understanding differentiated online activities in older adults and provide methodological guidance for future studies.

Keywords: Cross-sectional data · Digital divide · Internet use · Logistic regression analysis · Older adults · Online activities · Survey · Technology adoption

1 Introduction

The Internet plays an increasingly important role in the daily lives of many older adults [1]. For instance, in the European Union, the share of adults aged 55+ using the Internet every day has risen from 23% in 2010 to 37% in 2017 [2]. This increase is complemented by major changes of the activities performed online [3]. The main activities in the past were surfing the web and e-mailing, but the range of activities has broadened by including social networking, shopping, and entertainment [4]. Internet use offers potential to

© Springer Nature Switzerland AG 2020
Q. Gao and J. Zhou (Eds.): HCII 2020, LNCS 12209, pp. 255–268, 2020.
https://doi.org/10.1007/978-3-030-50232-4_18

mitigate some of the consequences of aging. Results of longitudinal studies suggest that being online can help reduce the feeling of loneliness [5], prevent isolation through facilitating social ties across distances [6], and help in maintaining cognitive functioning [7] and psychological well-being [8]. Further, online services can assist older adults in leisure activities [9] and health-related information needs [10]. Therefore, digital divide research has shifted from identifying barriers towards physical Internet access (first-level digital divide) to understanding why some older adults perform various online activities and why others do not (second-level digital divide).

A frequently used approach in digital divide research collects quantitative data from a sample of older adults and then examines the role of individual characteristics in explaining whether one belongs to the group of users or nonusers, respectively. This examination can be accomplished by logistic regression analysis, which estimates the parameters of a logistic function for a binary (dichotomous) dependent variable. Accordingly, users will be coded as 1 and nonusers will be coded as 0. The model's explanatory quality can then be defined as the percentage of observations mapped onto the correct group. This approach has been adopted for explaining older adults' general Internet use [11–13] as well as specific online activities such as e-mailing, general information search, health-related information search, banking, and shopping [14, 15].

Comparing the results of previous studies is difficult because of different sets of explanatory variables being tested as well as heterogeneity in the analysis and reporting of results. Many studies do not discuss the explanatory quality of their regression models. Moreover, many studies solely base their findings on thresholds for levels of statistical significance rather than reporting exact p-values complemented by confidence intervals for the strength of associations. These deficits undermine the ability to compare, appraise, and integrate the results of previous studies, which is essential for building cumulative knowledge from single quantitative studies. Against this backdrop, our research aims at enhancing the understanding of online activities among older adults by demonstrating how contextualized information can aid the interpretation of results from logistic regression in this domain.

Specifically, we address the following research question: *What is the role of socio-demographic characteristics in explaining whether older adults perform various online activities?* To answer this question, we first examine the current state of reporting logistic regression in the older adults' second-level digital divide literature. This examination relies upon reporting guidelines for logistic regression analysis, which have been articulated for research in the tradition of null-hypothesis significance testing (NHST) in fields such as biology [16] and epidemiology [17]. To show how these guidelines can be applied, we present an empirical study that assesses the role of gender, age, education, subjective health, and living arrangement in explaining eight online activities, grouped into informational, social, and instrumental activities. This study analyzes primary survey data, which we collected in the summer of 2017 from older adults (65 +) in Germany ($N = 1,079$).

2   Current State of Reporting Logistic Regression Analysis

Understanding Internet use in older adults is a multi-disciplinary field of research. We focus on empirical studies that used logistic regression analysis to examine how individual characteristics impact the probability of belonging to the group of users vís-a-vís nonusers. We first define a set of reporting criteria, which we derived from recommendations for reporting results of NHST and adapted to the domain.

Correlations Among Independent Variables (IV): Because high correlations between two or more IVs can lead to unstable estimates of coefficients, correlations should be inspected prior to building a regression model. This phenomenon is referred to as multicollinearity. High correlations might suggest that one IV is redundant as it can be explained by the other IV. Multicollinearity can be detected by calculating the Variance Inflation Factor (VIF) for each IV, for which cut-offs have been proposed [18]. There can be reasons to maintain IVs with high VIF, for instance, if the variable is a control, while the variable hypothesized to be a factor does not have a high VIF.

Explained Variance: In linear regression models, r-squared (R2) is a familiar measure for the explanatory power, defined as the share of variance in the DV explained by the model. Therefore, this measure can range between zero and one, with higher values suggesting better explanations. For logistic regression, different counterparts have been proposed such as Nagelkerke's pseudo R2. Interpreting such measures should take into account that values of pseudo R2 are often low and, thus, readers familiar with linear regression might be skeptical about the model's explanatory power [19].

Percentage Correct: Given the difficulties in interpreting pseudo-R2 measures, the explanatory quality can be directly assessed by a comparison of observed values (i.e., participants' answers) to predicted values (i.e., calculated by the logistic function) [19]. Overall, the percentage correct should be (much) greater than 50%, thus exceeding the performance of a random classifier. Moreover, percentages correct can be calculated for each response category such that we know how well the model predicts membership in the user and nonuser categories.

Exact p-values: Much of NHST builds on the p-value measure by assigning statistical significance to a test result (e.g., about an association) if the p-value falls below a threshold, namely, $p < .05$. The role of p-values has been a subject of debate since their emergence, and misconceptions and misinterpretations can still be observed [20, 21]. In short, a p-value does not indicate the strength of an association, does not describe the probability of the null-hypothesis being true, and smaller p-values do not provide stronger support for the association [22]. Moreover, p-values are contingent upon the sample size such that even marginal associations will become "statistically significant" in large samples. Although alternative approaches to the reliance upon p-values have been proposed, interpretation of test results can be facilitated by reporting exact p-values instead of using common but somewhat arbitrary thresholds.

Confidence Intervals (CI): While logistic regression provides a measure for the strength of the association between IV and DV, the resulting odds-ratio (OR) is only an estimation for the sample under study. Therefore, it is very unlikely that a given OR will be the same for another sample. ORs can be contextualized by reporting their confidence interval. For instance, a 95% confidence interval is defined as the range of values that will cover the true value of OR for 95% of samples that can be drawn. This information can aid in interpreting the results with respect to the domain [19]. A relatively wide CI could suggest that the practical meaning of an association can be very different (ranging from negligible to important). If the CI is rather narrow, we might have more clarity about the degree to which differences in the IV (e.g., gender) will impact the probability of belonging to the user (or nonuser) group.

For our review of previous research, we considered studies that met the following requirements: DV is Internet use; socio-demographic characteristics included in the set of IVs; cross-sectional data collected within the past ten years; logistic regression analysis; results published in a refereed journal. Eventually, we identified eleven articles from the literature. Table 1 presents sample sizes, years of data collection, and the fulfillment of reporting criteria that we discussed above.

None of the studies reports on correlations among IVs or assesses whether multicollinearity was present. Five studies use pseudo-R^2 to measure the explanatory power, with values ranging from .20 [23], .25 [13], .34 [24], and .39/.42 [11] to .64 [25]. Percentage correct is available from only one study: the model presented by Friemel et al. correctly predicted group membership for about 84.2% of the observations (DV: general Internet use) [25]. While five studies report exact p-values, six studies omit this information but categorize the level of statistical significance by thresholds such as $p < .05$, $p < .01$, and $p < .001$. Confidence intervals are available from six studies, while three studies report the standard error (SE) for each OR. In principle, CIs can be calculated from SEs but this calculation must be undertaken by the reader. Moreover, SEs cannot be directly interpreted with respect to the domain, which is unlike CIs.

Table 1. Sample characteristics and statistics reported in previous studies.

Study	N	Year	Correlations	R2	Percentage correct	Exact p-values	CI
Choi and DiNitto [26]	6,680	2011	No	No	No	Yes	Yes
Friemel [25]	1,103	2009	No	Yes	Yes	No	No[a]
Gell et al. [14]	7,609	2011	No	No	No	No	Yes
Hong and Cho [15]	1,950	2011–12	No	No	No	No	Yes
Keränen et al. [27]	794	2015	No	No	No	Yes	Yes
König et al. [11]	61,202	2015	No	Yes	No	No	No[a]
Lesauskatie et al. [12]	375	2017	No	No	No	Yes	Yes
Seifert et al. [23]	1,212	2016	No	Yes	No	Yes	No
Seifert et al. [24]	1,299	2016	Some	Yes	No	Yes	Yes
Siren and Knudsen [13]	3,269	2014	No	Yes	No	No	No[a]
Yoon et al. [28]	17,704	2012	No	No	No	No	Yes
	Frequency:		0	5	1	5	6

Note. CI = Confidence interval; $R2$ = Pseudo r-squared (explained variance).
[a] Standard errors reported instead of CI.

Overall, previous studies on the second-level digital divide in older adults exhibit few common reporting practices. The fulfillment of reporting recommendations is still low. This finding similarly applies to measures of explanatory quality, exact p-values, and indicators for the strength and reliability of associations. Given that percentage correct is a likely intuitive measure, it is surprising that only one of eleven studies reports percentage correct to highlight the quality of explanation. In summary, our discussion of previous studies suggests that the provision of contextualized information from logistic regression analysis is in a premature state. Therefore, we seek to demonstrate how this information can facilitate the interpretation of regression results when we examine a broad set of online activities in older adults.

3   Method

We approach older adults' online activities through the lens of van Dijk's *resources and appropriation theory of the diffusion, acceptance and adoption of new technologies* [29, 30]. This theory describes a mechanism that relies upon categorical inequalities between groups of people in society. These inequalities lead to unequal distribution of resources, which then causes unequal access to technologies. The main categorical inequalities relate to socio-demographic characteristics such as age, gender, and health. Each inequality can be described by at least one dominating group versus one subordinated group, e.g., younger versus older and men versus women. The quantity and quality of resources available to an individual will be determined by their belonging to certain groups. In the context of online activities, resources include having a device with Internet access (material), cognitive abilities (mental), and support in use (social). Because the theory explains individual differences in the use of digital technologies, it is adequate for studying Internet use in general [25, 31] and differentiated online activities in particular [32]. We focus on a core set of groups in society defined by differences in gender (men vs. women), age (young vs. old), education (high vs. low), health (good vs. poor), and living arrangement (living together vs. alone). The present study (1) considers socio-demographic factors but not psychometric factors and (2) examines Internet use vs. nonuse but not frequency of Internet use. For these two reasons, the present study distinguishes from our previous study on differentiated Internet use in older adults [33].

3.1   Participants

We analyzed data from a survey, which we conducted in the summer of 2017. This survey targeted all older adults (65+) living in three districts of a city with around 260,000 inhabitants in Germany. The city administration and a municipal provider of geriatric care were involved in the conduct of the survey. A questionnaire was sent out by mail to 6,170 individuals registered in one of the three districts. Considering that 100 addresses turned out to be invalid, the 1,302 responses received account for a response rate of 21.5%. This rate is similar to prior surveys that used posted self-administered questionnaires targeted at older adults [34]. For the present study, we defined a subsample including participants, who answered all questions on online activities and socio-demographic variables ($N =$

1,079; no missing values). With respect to gender and age distributions, our subsample did not differ from the city's population of older adults [35]. Our subsample exhibited a greater share of participants holding a college or university degree (14.9% vs. 6.5%) and a smaller share of participants reporting no high school education (1.2% vs. 6.1%).

3.2 Measurements

Online Activity: Our dependent variables were based on questions about the frequency of various online activities. In the present study, we considered three informational, three social, and two instrumental online activities. *Informational online activities* were defined as follows: "searching for information on the Internet (e.g., using Google)", "using the Internet to inform myself about events in the city", and "viewing pictures and videos". *Social online activities* were listed as follows: "writing e-mails", "sending pictures and videos", and "writing comments and reviews". *Instrumental online activities* included "using banking services on the Internet (online banking)", and "purchasing on the Internet (online shopping)". Because the survey administered a five-point ordinal frequency scale (daily, weekly, monthly, fewer, never), we recoded the responses into a dichotomous variable, with 0 representing "never", and 1 otherwise. Therefore, each of our eight dependent variables differentiated users (who perform an online activity) and nonusers (who do not perform that online activity).

Socio-Demographic Variables: *Gender* was coded as female (0) or male (1). *Age* was calculated from the year of birth. *Education* had three levels: low for primary and lower secondary education, medium for upper secondary education and vocational training, and high for academic education. The values were derived from a question that offered nine answer options specific to the education system of Germany. *Subjective health* was a self-reported measure about one's individual health [36]. We administered a five-point rating scale (1 = very bad, 2 = rather bad, 3 = moderate, 4 = rather good, and 5 = very good). *Living together* was coded as a dichotomous variable, with 1 for those who were living in a household of two or more persons, and 0 otherwise.

3.3 Data Analysis Plan

Our study set out to examine the association between older adults' socio-demographic characteristics and their performance of various online activities. For this purpose, we first conducted descriptive analyses and then assessed correlations between study variables (for which we used the Spearman's correlation test because none of the metric variables was normally distributed). We examined the role of socio-demographic variables in explaining online activities by using logistic regression. We tested the assumptions of logistic regression but there were no deviations. For each regression model, we report explained variance and the percentages correct (per category and total). For the independent variables, we present the exact p-value, OR, and 95% CI. The OR states how the probability of the user category changes for one-unit increase in the independent variable ($OR > 1$ for positive changes, $OR < 1$ for negative changes). All analyses were conducted using IBM SPSS Statistics 25. The significance level was 5%.

4 Results

4.1 Data Screening

Table 2 presents descriptive statistics. Our sample was balanced in terms of gender. The average age was 75.28 years ($SD = 7.07$). Every second respondent had education at a medium level, and academic education was reported by every seventh participant. Good health was indicated by one-half ($M = 3.48$, $SD = 0.89$, on a 1–5 scale). More than two-thirds lived together. The most prevalent online activities were the three informational activities and writing e-mails (each reported by more than half of the participants), followed by sending pictures/videos (43.7%), shopping (37.4%), banking (23.8%), and writing comments/reviews (22.5%).

Table 2. Socio-demographics and online activities ($N = 1{,}079$).

Variable	Scale	%	Variable	Scale	%
Gender	Female	49.0	Information search	User	58.7
	Male	51.0		Nonuser	41.3
Age[a]	65–69	27.3	Information search: events	User	51.9
	70–74	21.5		Nonuser	48.1
	75–79	25.1	Viewing pictures/videos	User	54.1
	80+	26.0		Nonuser	45.9
Education	Low	35.1	Writing e-mails	User	52.8
	Medium	50.0		Nonuser	47.2
	High	14.9	Sending pictures/videos	User	43.7
Subjective health	Very bad	2.2		Nonuser	56.3
	Rather bad	9.6	Writing comments/reviews	User	22.5
	Neutral	37.3		Nonuser	77.5
	Rather good	39.9	Banking	User	23.8
	Very good	10.9		Nonuser	76.2
Living together	Yes	71.1	Shopping	User	37.4
	No	28.9		Nonuser	62.6

[a] We report percentages for age groups (note that age was a metric variable).

In the next step of our data screening, we assessed correlations among the study variables (Table 3). Correlations between the five socio-demographic variables were very weak to weak (absolute coefficients between 0.07 and 0.29). Subsequently, we found that multicollinearity was not present in our data, as shown by VIFs ranging between 1.10 and 1.16, which is below a conservative cut-off of 2.5 [37]. Table 3 shows that online search was positively correlated with being male and younger, reporting higher education and better health, and living together ($p < .001$, weak to average strengths of correlations). The results were similar for the other online activities (not tabulated). Finally, correlations between the eight online activities ranged from weak to strong, providing support for our differentiation of online activities and their categorization into informational, social, and instrumental activities.

Table 3. Correlations of socio-demographic variables and information search ($N = 1,079$).

Variable			1.	2.	3.	4.	5.
1.	Gender						
2.	Age (years)	r_s	−.070				
		p	.021				
3.	Education	r_s p	.236	−.191			
			<.001	<.001			
4.	Subjective health	r_s p	.079	−.293	.189		
			.010	<.001	<.001		
5.	Living together	r_s	.209	−.224	.152	.122	
		p	<.001	<.001	<.001	<.001	
6.	Information search	r_s p	.238	−.424	.297	.269	.208
			<.001	<.001	<.001	<.001	<.001

Note. Spearman's rank correlations (2-tailed). Gender: 0 = female, 1 = male. Education: 1 = low, 2 = medium, 3 = high. Living together: 0 = no, 1 = yes. Subjective health: from very bad (1) to very good (5). Information search: 0 = nonuser, 1 = user.

4.2 Logistic Regression Analyses

Tables 4, 5 and 6 show the results of our logistic regression analyses, grouped into informational, social, and instrumental online activities. To first demonstrate how the results can be interpreted, we refer to information search (Table 4).

The probability of information search was 129% greater for men than for women ($OR = 2.29$). Each one-year higher age reduced the probability by 11% ($OR = 0.89$). Education was associated with use, showing an increase of the probability by 46% for medium levels and 636% for high levels, respectively. We note that the 95% CI for high education was rather wide, which suggests that high education can have a strong but highly varied association when replicating our study. Each one-unit higher rating of subjective health increased the probability by 39%. Participants who lived together with someone had improved odds of information search by 42%. The model correctly identified four out of five users and three out of five nonusers, respectively. These results amount to percentage correct of 71.9%, while the model explained 36.6% of the variance in information search. Considering all three informational online activities, the pattern of results was very similar, except for living together, which was not associated with informing about city events ($p = .169$).

With respect to social online activities, Table 5 shows that participants who were men and younger, indicated high levels of education, and reported better health were

Table 4. Logistic regression analyses for informational online activities ($N = 1,079$).

Variable	Scale	Information search			City events			Viewing pictures/videos		
		OR	95% CI	p	OR	95% CI	p	OR	95% CI	p
Gender[a]	Male	2.29	1.70–3.08	<.001	1.80	1.36–2.38	<.001	1.96	1.38–2.60	<.001
Age	Years	0.89	0.86–0.91	<.001	0.90	0.88–0.92	<.001	0.89	0.87–0.91	<.001
Education[b]	Medium	1.46	1.08–1.98	.014	1.44	1.07–1.93	.015	1.48	1.09–1.99	.011
	High	7.36	3.97–13.65	<.001	4.67	2.85–7.64	<.001	4.10	2.48–6.76	<.001
Subj. health[c]	1–5	1.39	1.17–1.65	<.001	1.27	1.08–1.49	.004	1.24	1.05–1.46	.010
Living together	Yes	1.42	1.03–1.95	.032	1.24	0.91–1.69	.169	1.55	1.13–2.12	.006
Correct: Users		79.9%			72.9%			76.4%		
Correct: Nonusers		60.5%			67.2%			65.3%		
Correct: Total		71.9%			70.2%			71.3%		
Pseudo R2 (Nagelkerke's)		.366			.282			.316		

Note. OR = odds ratio.
[a] Reference is female. [b] Reference is low. [c] Variable ranges from very bad (1) to very good (5).

Table 5. Logistic regression analyses for social online activities ($N = 1,079$).

Variable	Scale	Writing e-mails			Sending pictures/videos			Writing comments/reviews		
		OR	95% CI	p	OR	95% CI	p	OR	95% CI	p
Gender[a]	Male	1.76	1.33–2.34	<.001	1.56	1.17–2.07	.002	1.57	1.14–2.17	.006
Age	Years	0.89	0.87–0.91	<.001	0.88	0.86–0.90	<.001	0.90	0.87–0.92	<.001
Education[b]	Medium	1.16	0.86–1.56	.330	1.14	0.84–1.55	.407	1.18	0.82–1.17	.374
	High	4.30	2.59–7.16	<.001	2.36	1.51–3.69	<.001	2.76	1.75–4.36	<.001
Subj. health[c]	1–5	1.38	1.17–1.63	<.001	1.44	1.22–1.70	<.001	1.26	1.04–1.52	.019
Living together	Yes	1.11	0.81–1.52	.515	1.39	1.01–1.91	.046	1.12	0.76–1.64	.568
Correct: Users		73.2%			65.0%			17.7%		
Correct: Nonusers		65.6%			75.2%			96.2%		
Correct: Total		69.6%			70.7%			78.5%		
Pseudo R2 (Nagelkerke's)		.304			.297			.204		

Note. OR = odds ratio.
[a] Reference is female. [b] Reference is low. [c] Variable ranges from very bad (1) to very good (5).

more likely to belong to the user group. Contrary to the results for information online activities, medium levels of education were not associated with social online activities, and the odds ratios for high levels were also smaller. While living together was associated

Table 6. Logistic regression analyses for instrumental online activities ($N = 1,079$).

Variable	Scale	Banking			Shopping		
		OR	95% CI	p	OR	95% CI	p
Gender[a]	Male	2.43	1.76–3.37	<.001	1.87	1.41–2.49	<.001
Age	Years	0.93	0.90–0.95	<.001	0.91	0.89–0.93	<.001
Education[b]	Medium	1.14	0.79–1.64	.493	1.33	0.97–1.83	.074
	High	3.17	2.02–4.97	<.001	3.23	2.09–5.01	<.001
Subjective health[c]	1–5	1.31	1.09–1.58	.005	1.44	1.22–1.71	<.001
Living together	Yes	1.26	0.86–1.84	.241	1.58	1.13–2.20	.007
Correct: Users		23.0%			51.2%		
Correct: Nonusers		95.6%			86.1%		
Correct: Total		78.3%			73.0%		
Pseudo R2 (Nagelkerke's)		.216			.263		

Note. OR = odds ratio.
[a] Reference is female. [b] Reference is low. [c] Variable ranges from very bad (1) to very good (5).

with sending pictures/videos, the 95% CI was rather wide (1.01–1.91), and the p-value was only slightly below the level of significance ($p = .046$). Therefore, the OR must be interpreted with great caution and related to the large size of our sample. The most interesting result from Table 5 is the low percentage correct of users in the model for writing comments/reviews (17.7%). In other words, while the model was very effective in identifying nonusers (96.2%), its accuracy for users was worse than even chance.

Perusal of Table 6 shows that banking and shopping were associated with being men and younger age as well as reporting high levels of education and better health, respectively. In addition, shopping was associated with living together. However, the model for banking failed in the identification of users (percentage correct of 23.0%), and the model for shopping performed only slightly better than even chance (51.2%).

5   Discussion

5.1   Summary of Findings

This study examined the role of socio-demographic characteristics in explaining whether older adults belong to the group of Internet users or nonusers, respectively. Using logistic regression analysis, we found that those who were men and younger, possessed higher education, and perceived better health had higher odds for various informational, social, and instrumental online activities. Living together with someone enhanced the probability of four out of eight online activities. Across all online activities, we observed nuanced differences in the strengths of associations. We also found that two regression models failed to achieve sufficient explanatory quality as shown by low percentages correct for the user group. Our research highlights the need to include contextualized information when reporting results of logistic regression. In summary, we provide evidence that the adoption of reporting guidelines can help avoid pitfalls in developing logistic regression models and, ultimately, interpreting models of the second-level digital divide in older adults.

5.2 Limitations

Our study has the following limitations. First, our logistic regression analyses used cross-sectional data, which does not allow us making causal inferences of the phenomena. Therefore, longitudinal studies including intervention studies are required to assess cohort effects and provide stronger support for the tested associations. Second, while we considered eight online activities covering a broad range of activities, our study did not examine participation in social networking sites. Third, our convenient sample was drawn from a specific city in Germany; hence, the results may not necessarily be generalized to older adults living in rural areas or other regions.

5.3 Implications

Our study results have several implications for future research. First, researchers can apply the reporting criteria that we adapted to the domain of digital divide in older adults. We suggest to always report percentages correct (for each group), effect sizes, exact p-values, and confidence intervals, and test for multicollinearity, because this information is essential for assessing the validity, reliability, and usefulness of logistic regression analysis. Much less emphasis should be put on thresholds for p-values but test results should always be related to sample sizes, statistical power, and the *practical* significance of results. For this purpose, effect size measures should be translated back to the digital divide domain. As our review of the extant literature shows, heterogeneity in reporting is still prevalent. The proposed actions by researchers can be implemented immediately to promote uniformity and comparability of research results.

Second, our study results demonstrate that barriers towards the accumulation of knowledge about the digital divide in older adults continue to exist. While the literature review by Hunsaker and Hargittai identified barriers due to diversity in the measurement of explanatory variables and Internet use [3], we focus on the statistical analysis and reporting. Providing contextualized information when conducting logistic regression analysis can facilitate the accumulation of knowledge. The pace of the required changes can be amplified within the academic ecosystem by journals that develop reporting standards, and editors and reviewers that reward the adoption of such standards. This new practice will enable the comparison and integration of results from single studies, and in the long run, allow for meta-analysis. Overall, we believe that these efforts will help in building and validating digital divide theory, which can then provide rationale for the development of interventions and policies targeted at the digital inclusion of older adults.

Third, our testing of propositions derived from van Dijk's resources and appropriation theory provides the foundation for examining further online activities. For instance, social networks and messaging services attain increasing relevance for the group of older adults [5, 38], and thus the role of socio-demographics in explaining their use and nonuse requires investigation. Moreover, additional categorical inequalities in society should be examined for a broader range of online activities including the use of specific online services.

Finally, our findings are also relevant for practice as they help identify subgroups who do not perform online activities. For instance, developers and providers can tailor their services to the needs of specific groups of older adults, e.g., by designing responsive and barrier-free interfaces that adapt to individual capabilities in cognition, vision, and motor function [39, 40]. In addition, understanding the predictors of online activities can assist decision-makers in devising legislation and interventions aimed at older adults. To ensure digital inclusion of older adults, they must be considered as an important customer group for online activities and services. Thus, factors that mitigate or promote social exclusion from the digital world should be taken into account [41].

Acknowledgments. The work by Joerg Leukel and Barbara Schehl has been supported by the Federal Ministry of Education and Research, Germany, under grant 16SV7438K. The work by Vijayan Sugumaran has been partially supported by a 2019 School of Business Administration Spring/Summer Research Fellowship at Oakland University. We thank Susanne Wallrafen (Sozial-Holding der Stadt Mönchengladbach GmbH) for her support in conducting the survey.

References

1. Loos, E., Haddon, L., Mante-Meijer, E. (eds.): Generational Use of New Media. Ashgate, Farnham (2012)
2. European Commission: Media use in the European Union. Autumn 2017. https://doi.org/10.2775/116707
3. Hunsaker, A., Hargittai, E.: A review of Internet use among older adults. New Media Soc. **20**, 3937–3954 (2018)
4. Vroman, K.G., Arthanat, S., Lysack, C.: Who over 65 is online? Older adults' dispositions toward information communication technology. Comput. Human Behav. **43**, 156–166 (2015)
5. Szabo, A., Allen, J., Stephens, C., Alpass, F.: Longitudinal analysis of the relationship between purposes of internet use and well-being among older adults. Gerontologist **59**, 58–68 (2019)
6. Sinclair, T.J., Grieve, R.: Facebook as a source of social connectedness in older adults. Comput. Human Behav. **66**, 363–369 (2017)
7. Berner, J., et al.: Maintaining cognitive function with internet use: a two-country, six-year longitudinal study. Int. Psychogeriatr. **31**, 929–936 (2019)
8. Quintana, D., Cervantes, A., Sáez, Y., Isasi, P.: Internet use and psychological well-being at advanced age: Evidence from the English longitudinal study of aging. Int. J. Environ. Res. Public Health **15**(3), 480 (2018)
9. Schehl, B.: Outdoor activity among older adults: exploring the role of informational Internet use. Educ. Gerontol. **46**, 36–45 (2020)
10. Shim, H., Ailshire, J., Zelinski, E., Crimmins, E.: The health and retirement study: analysis of associations between use of the internet for health information and use of health services at multiple time points. J. Med. Internet Res. **20**, e200 (2018)
11. König, R., Seifert, A., Doh, M.: Internet use among older Europeans: an analysis based on SHARE data. Univers. Access Inf. **17**, 621–633 (2018)
12. Lesauskaitė, V., Damulevičienė, G., Knašienė, J., Kazanavičius, E., Liutkevičius, A., Janavičiūtė, A.: Older adults – potential users of technologies. Medicina **55**(6), 253 (2019)

13. Siren, A., Knudsen, S.G.: Older adults and emerging digital service delivery: a mixed methods study on information and communications technology use, skills, and attitudes. J. Aging Soc. Policy **29**, 35–50 (2017)
14. Gell, N.M., Rosenberg, D.E., Demiris, G., LaCroix, A.Z., Patel, K.V.: Patterns of technology use among older adults with and without disabilities. Gerontologist **55**, 412–421 (2013)
15. Hong, Y.A., Cho, J.: Has the digital health divide widened? Trends of health-related Internet use among older adults from 2003 to 2011. J. Gerontol. B Psychol. Sci. Soc. Sci. **72**, 856–863 (2017)
16. Nakagawa, S., Cuthill, I.C.: Effect size, confidence interval and statistical significance: a practical guide for biologists. Biol. Rev. Camb. Philos. Soc. **82**, 591–605 (2007)
17. Greenland, S., et al.: Statistical tests, p values, confidence intervals, and power: a guide to misinterpretations. Eur. J. Epidemiol. **31**, 337–350 (2016)
18. Ryan, T.P.: Modern Regression Methods. Wiley, Hoboken (2008)
19. Hosmer, D.W., Lemeshow, S.: Applied Logistic Regression. Wiley, Hoboken (2000)
20. Cohen, J.: The earth is round (p < 05). Am. Psychol. **49**, 997–1003 (1994)
21. McShane, B.B., Gal, D.: Blinding us to the obvious? The effect of statistical training on the evaluation of evidence. Manag. Sci. **62**, 1707–1718 (2016)
22. Wasserstein, R.L., Lazar, N.A.: The ASA statement on p-values: context, process, and purpose. Am. Stat. **70**, 129–133 (2016)
23. Seifert, A., Doh, M., Wahl, H.-W.: They also do it: Internet use by older adults living in residential care facilities. Educ. Gerontol. **43**, 451–461 (2017)
24. Seifert, A., Wahl, H.-W.: Young at heart and online? Subjective age and internet use in two Swiss survey studies. Educ. Gerontol. **44**, 139–147 (2018)
25. Friemel, T.N.: The digital divide has grown old: determinants of a digital divide among seniors. New Media Soc. **18**, 313–331 (2016)
26. Choi, N.G., DiNitto, D.M.: Internet use among older adults: association with health needs, psychological capital, and social capital. J. Med. Internet Res. **15**, e97 (2013)
27. Keränen, N.S., et al.: Use of information and communication technologies among older people with and without frailty: a population-based survey. J. Med. Internet Res. **19**(2), e29 (2017)
28. Yoon, H., Jang, Y., Vaughan, P.W., Garcia, M.: Older adults' Internet use for health information: Digital divide by race/ethnicity and socioeconomic status. J. Appl. Gerontol. **39**, 105–110 (2020)
29. van Dijk, J.A.: The Deepening Divide. Inequality in the Information Society. SAGE, Thousand Oaks (2005)
30. van Dijk, J.A.: Digital divide research, achievements and shortcomings. The digital divide in the twenty-first century. Poetics **34**, 221–235 (2006)
31. Hargittai, E., Piper, A.M., Morris, M.R.: From Internet access to Internet skills: digital inequality among older adults. Univers. Access Inf. **27**, 325 (2018)
32. Correa, T.: Digital skills and social media use: how Internet skills are related to different types of Facebook use among 'digital natives'. Inf. Commun. Soc. **19**, 1095–1107 (2016)
33. Schehl, B., Leukel, J., Sugumaran, V.: Understanding differentiated internet use in older adults: a study of informational, social, and instrumental online activities. Comput. Human Behav. **97**, 222–230 (2019)
34. Palonen, M., Kaunonen, M., Åstedt-Kurki, P.: Exploring how to increase response rates to surveys of older people. Nurse Res. **23**, 15–19 (2016)
35. IT.NRW: Landesdatenbank NRW. Kommunalprofil Mönchengladbach (2017). https://www.landesdatenbank.nrw.de
36. Idler, E.L., Benyamini, Y.: Self-rated health and mortality: a review of twenty-seven community studies. J. Health Soc. Behav. **38**, 21 (1997)
37. Allison, P.D.: Multiple Regression: A Primer. SAGE, London (1999)

38. Smith, A., Anderson, M.: Social media use in 2018. https://www.pewinternet.org/2018/03/01/social-media-use-in-2018/

39. Calhoun, D., Lee, S.B.: Computer usage and cognitive capability of older adults: Analysis of data from the health and retirement study. Educ. Gerontol. **45**, 22–33 (2019)

40. Czaja, S.J., Boot, W.R., Charness, N., Rogers, W.A.: Designing for Older Adults: Principles and Creative Human Factors Approaches. CRC Press, Boca Raton (2019)

41. Seifert, A., Hofer, M., Rössel, J.: Older adults' perceived sense of social exclusion from the digital world. Educ. Gerontol. **44**, 775–785 (2018)

Understanding the Exclusion Issues of Mobility-as-a-Service (Maas): The Potential Problems of Older Travellers' Involvement

Yuanjun Li[✉], Sharon Cook, and Andrew May

Loughborough Design School, Leicestershire, UK
y.li5@slboro.ac.uk

Abstract. A series of pilots and studies of Mobility-as-a-Service have launched out in recent years, but services are generally recognized as still at the early stage of development, whether in terms of its concept, the level of urban construction and the acceptance of travellers. According to the earlier explorative study of MaaS in a workshop in the UK, the result referred to the lack of consensus among stakeholders and the mismatch of value propositions between service providers and users. This leads to the early market not fully considering the requirements of the different group of travellers, especially for the older people. Therefore, this study reviewed previous literature and summarized the logic relation of the relevant factors, in order to provide the evidence for future sustainable development of MaaS on the aspect of increasing older travellers' social participation.

Keywords: Mobility-as-a-Service · Service development · Design for the elderly

1 Introduction

Mobility-as-a-Service (MaaS) is an emerging concept in the field of transportation in recent years. It was firstly proposed by Hietanen (2014) and has developed fast since then. Various pilots around the world are paving the way for exploring the transformation of future transport eco-system, while the definition of MaaS concept itself has also experiencing continuous development. According to the early proposal of MaaS, it refers to the integration of different transports and information from both private and public sectors (Hietanene 2014; Datson 2016; Hilgert et al. 2016), which is expected to become an alternative choice for people to travel rather than owning a car (Melis et al. 2016, 2018). It can be expected to relieve the traffic congestion on urban road and increase the efficiency of transport system (EI Zarwi et al. 2017; Wong et al. 2018). By using MaaS, users can obtain a seamless travel experience with higher added value and lower price (Melis et al. 2016), and have more flexibility to meet their individual lifestyle (Atkins 2015; Hilgert et al. 2016).

Based on a digital platform (Jittrapirom et al. 2017; Li and Voege 2017), MaaS is shown to have the younger generations (Jittrapirom et al. 2018) and the people who used to take multi-modal transports (Jittrapirom et al. 2018; Ho et al. 2018; Alonso-González

© Springer Nature Switzerland AG 2020
Q. Gao and J. Zhou (Eds.): HCII 2020, LNCS 12209, pp. 269–287, 2020.
https://doi.org/10.1007/978-3-030-50232-4_19

et al. 2017) as the early adopters. However, since there are few MaaS service that have been launched yet, the evidence is limited about the acceptance level of different user groups (Ho et al. 2018). For the older travellers - who are predicted to be less likely using MaaS (Jittrapirom et al. 2018), they are probably to have difficulties with interface interaction due to certain physical functions decrease, and the challenges they face to do with changing their original routine life. Since it will require cognitive and affective efforts of them in undertaking a journey (Stradlling 2006; Lyons et al. 2019), commenters suggest that MaaS will intentionally nudging people's behaviour (Smith et al. 2018), it's worthy to consider whether this innovation is responsible (Stilgoe et al. 2013; Lyons et al. 2019; Pangbourne et al. 2018) – so that will not hurt the trust of customers or cause unnecessary exclusion. Therefore, this paper firstly reviews several key concepts discussed in previous literature about older travellers' behaviour to clarify the logic ration of the relevant influencing factors. Then, it collects the viewpoints of MaaS stakeholders to analyse the storyline that contribute to the potential exclusion of older travellers.

Through literature review, this paper firstly observed the conflicting points of current older people's travel pattern with the expected vision proposed by MaaS, found a series of uncertainties caused by the lack of evidence and knowledges which could make the older people getting excluded from the new service. On this basis, an explorative study focused on the stakeholders in MaaS eco-system is organised to understand whether this situation is actually happen, will happen in the future, and what is the reason for it. Finally, combined with the literature and the data obtained, insights are proposed for later service iteration of MaaS, in order to increase older travellers' involvement.

2 Dimensions to Understand MaaS's Impacts on Mobility

2.1 Individual Mobility and Urban Mobility

According to Suen and Mitchell (2000), "mobility" means having transport services going where and when one wants to travel, being informed about the services, knowing how to use them, being able to use them; and having the means to pay for them. But as mobility itself is ambiguous to define, a popular way to assess it, is by trip rate (Alsnih and Hensher 2003), while the trips basically refer to the original end-to-end journey undertaking with activities or specific purpose.

In literature, mobility is often understood as Individual Mobility and Urban Mobility. Individual Mobility relates to one's specific ability, such as walking, grasping, climbing stairs and etc. To a broader concept, it could also reflect in the movement outdoors and the use of transportation, for example accessing shops, services and facilities in the community and participating in social and cultural activities (WHO 2015; Rantanen 2013); Urban Mobility, refers to the number of personal kilometres travelled per annum, is predicted to be tripled in 2010–2050, and accounts for the proportion of 64% of total mobility. It indicates that if current trends continue, the transport system will breakdown (Lerner and Van Audenhove 2012). Given this, MaaS was proposed as not only a new service, but the reconstruction of supply chain (Kamargianni and Matyas 2017) to reshape urban transport eco-system with disruptive innovation (Matyas and Kamergianni 2017) and encourage travellers to change their original travel pattern to achieve the sustainable goal.

However, Individual Mobility may not share the same purpose as Urban Mobility, especially during the transformation period that people may not have developed with the fixed travel habits. Travellers are required to adapt to the new service to match personal demand, while the service also need to learn from travellers' changing preference to iterate service. But from current situation, the process of mutual learning has not been taken seriously due to the lack of experience, knowledge and research framework.

2.2 Older Travellers' Requirements of Mobility

Maslow (1954)'s Hierarchy of Needs (Fig. 1) explains that each need must be satisfied at a lower level before they progress to higher (McLeod 2007). Relate to this CATAPULT (2015) refined this model specifically to travellers' needs (Fig. 2).

Fig. 1. Maslow's hierarchy of needs (McLeod 2007)

Fig. 2. Hierarchy of traveller needs (CATAPULT 2015)

It indicates that travellers should get a pleasant experience during the journey first and then could possibly achieve the ideal lifestyle. ICF - The International Classification of Functioning, Disability and Health (Broome et al. 2009) believes that activities and participation are the basis of healthy life, while the UK and WHO (World Health Organization) also highlight the significance of independent and free travel in aging-friendly society in the policies (Shrestha et al. 2017), as it is the way to realize self-worth. However, limited by the use of private car and public transports, some older travellers would be gradually isolated from society (Engels and Liu 2011) that directly affect their quality of life (QoL) (Marin-Lamellet and Haustein 2015).

When growing older, people might have less transport options available, for example, the car use decreases after the aged of 55 (Mollenkopf and Kaspar 2005), and the travel distance would also decrease according to retirement (Bakaba and Ortlepp 2010). There are a large number of studies show that the majority of older users are relying on personal transport (Buehler and Nobis 2010; Newbold et al. 2005; Alsnih and Hensher 2003), many researches hence focused on the topics such as safer driving of senior drivers (Li et al. 2003; Lyman et al. 2002; Whelan et al. 2006) and travel mode conversion from driving to taking public transport (Kockelman 1997), but haven't go further to explore the relationship of their lifestyle (Lu et al. 2016; Stradling 2006; Lyons et al. 2019) or its reflection on overall travel pattern (Goulias 2000; Doherty 2000). As shown in Fig. 3, studying older travellers' regiments of mobility requires an understanding of their living environment and value proposition. These factors constitute the context in which older travellers are placed and determine how they act and plan their daily lives, and are reflected in individual's preference of activities which will determine their travel behaviour in specific scenario.

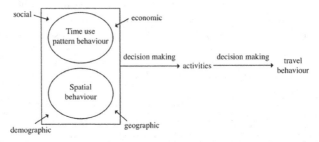

Fig. 3. Context diagram of travel pattern

In the trend of integrated transportation such as MaaS, relevant studies have not yet subdivided the research objects according to individual factors (Giesecke et al. 2016), nor have much quantitative research data been collected (Caiati et al. 2017). Due to the constraints of the early market, the existing results are mainly based on a small population of mostly younger generation within the limited experimental time and geographical area, the result might be not generalizable of the larger public. Start-ups like to develop business for young people because the lower entry of acceptance (Li et al. 2019), while the difficulties of investigating older travellers are, firstly, older people today are more flexible and active than before (Shrestha et al. 2017), and their behaviour characteristics are diverse (Marin-Lamellet and Haustein 2015; Caiati et al. 2017; Buehler and Nobis 2010) with a certain degree of unpredictability (Lu et al. 2010). In addition, the existing studies usually make the fuzzy boundary of the older and the disabled, and misunderstand they are homogenous group (Marin-Lamellet and Haustein 2015). There are services specifically designed for the disabled in the market, but few are designed for the older people (Priestley and Rabiee 2002).

2.3 Influencing Factors

In previous studies, the influencing factors of older people's mobility could be summarized from two aspects: objective and subjective. The former refers to the factors that individual could not control or are unchangeable in short-term, for example the personal factors and living environment. The latter is built on objective conditions, where people can have flexible choices.

Objective Factors. Webber et al. (2010) concluded 5 fundamental categories of key determinants (cognitive, psychosocial, physical, environmental, and financial) of elderly mobility (Fig. 4), with influences of gender, culture, and biography surrounding the entire cone.

Webber highlighted the interrelationships among different determinants because of the linked dimensions. These factors would bring a combined influence on people's mobility and reflect in their travel behaviour. For example, family members would have

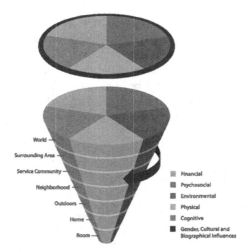

Fig. 4. Conical model of the theoretical framework for mobility in older adults (Webber et al. 2010)

similar life-space (annotated on left of conical model), but due to differences in gender or biography, the overall influence would occur on 5 fundamental determinants, so that we can witness the different travel behaviour of family members. But this model missing the important dimension of interpersonal relationship. In this example, the travel behaviour will also be influenced by familial responsibility and household labour division. Just as if the one who has the responsibility to take the children out to school, he/she will drive more frequently; if the elderly has other drivers in family, he/she would take public transports less.

Subjective Factors. Travel behaviour" refers to both time-use pattern and spatial features of travel and activities, while travel demands are subjectively determined by personal pursuit (or human desire) and their households (Goulias 2000; Timmermans and Zhang 2009). For this reason, activity-based travel demand modelling has become widely used in practice (Hildebrand 2003; Jovicic 2001; Rasouli and Timmermans 2014), and further implies to a decision framework, in which travel decisions are components of a broader activity scheduling decision (Ben-Akiva and Bowman 1998).

In other words, travel demand and related decision making process also embody people's motivation of travel. Factors such as survival, social contact and ego gratification (Ben-Akiva and Bowman 1998) would positively promote people traveling to activities. On the contrary, the aged may negatively impact on their motivation by the concerning the low perceived safety (Haustein and Siren 2015), fear of falling (Mänty et al. 2009), unfamiliar applied technology (Holzinger et al. 2007), navigational problems (Alsnih and Hensher 2003) and other reasons, would reduce travel motivation then further lead to isolation and loneliness of older people.

Moreover, referring to Research Model UTAUT2, which integrates multiple models of user acceptance theory, it illustrates that, except for main determents, Behaviour Intention (BI) is also effected by contingencies from moderators that would amplify or constrain the effects of core determinants, for example, age, gender and experience

(Arenas-Gáitan et al. 2015). These factors work in delicate synergy and apply to individual's behaviour. However, most of the current studies intend to explore the impacts of MaaS on travellers' performance, such as the preference on transport modes and service packages, rather than the synergistic effects of the above factors. If looking at the whole storyline of travellers' behaviour, can it be considered that the current research trend focuses more on the users' performance in the service and lacks data on the potential influencing factors of behaviour, and this leads to some of the consequences observed cannot be well explained.

2.4 Trip-Chain

Another dimension often discussed in previous literature is the "trip-chain", which provides an perspective that puts trips on timeline to help understand how individuals plan their travel routine. This may involve some other factors, such as traveller's choice in a particular scenario or an emergency situation. These are the performance that people would have in real situation, which may be deviated from their previous plan or what they think they should do.

Trips are driven by the purpose of activities which reflect traveller's value and attitude towards personal and social goals. The logistical efficiency of travel is an increasingly important factor for people to consider their trip plan (Su et al. 2009), and thus the trip chain has become more common in everyone's daily travel (McGuckin et al. 2005).

The most used word to define "trip chain" is "stop" (Kitamura 1985). Then the "trip" refers to: "The movement which carries an individual between his home and a stop or between temporally consecutive stop" (Lee et al. 2002). On this basis, "a set of consecutive trips which begin and end at an individual's home or work place" is known as a "tour" (McGuckin et al. 2004). If a tour is composed of more than two stops, it also defined as an "trip chain" (Su et al. 2009).

About the home-based trip chain per day (the start and end points are home), the complexity of travel doesn't decrease too much from the younger to the older travellers, and even has an increase with age 50–54 (Fig. 5). The reason might because as the work trips are not included, the home-based trips are more depend on trip chain to achieve. Figure 6 shows the modes used in trip chain by age, which illustrates self-driving is the most significant factor for trip chain's flexibility, while people have stable demands on public transport chains and car passenger chains, and this demands are not effected by age. It further explains the accessibility on public transport modes and network for older people would matter most for their quality of life.

Research found older travellers would not get benefits from the trip chain with higher logistical efficiency (Su 2008), and tend to have easier tour types. Their preferences on tours like the trip sequences, destination choices and time arrangement are normally limited by reduced mobility. Other factors like gender and life cycle (McGuckin et al. 2005), income and household composition (Noland and Thomas 2007) would also influence travellers' trip chain behaviour. In comparison, older travellers are shown to have shorter trips in a tour, but prefer more than one tour a day (Schmöcker et al. 2010). The complex trip-chain planning can be difficult for older people (Schmöcker et al. 2010).

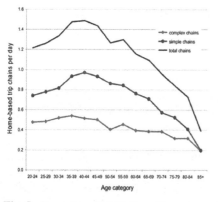

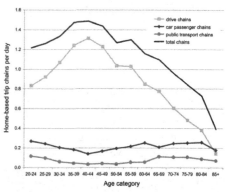

Fig. 5. Percentage distribution of home-based trip-chains by age and complexity (Hensher 2007)

Fig. 6. Average home-based trip-chains per day by age and mode (Hensher 2007)

2.5 Contradiction Points

Intelligent transport has created better conditions for urban sustainability, advocating to reduce automobile travel and increasing collaborative operation. According to the result of UbiGo 6-month trial, the new business model has shown initial success in reducing private car ownership (Sochor et al. 2014) by transforming the concept of "transport" to "accessibility". With the support of ICT, the physical accessibility can be replaced by other options so that the travel plan is more flexible (Van Wee et al. 2013).

But these advantages may bring about barriers for older travellers, such as the interaction mode with digital platform and the impacts on their original travel behaviour. Research showed the low utilization of smart phone among older people (IET 2015) and their reluctance to accept it because of the poor understanding of the benefits (Holzinger et al. 2007). On another aspects, ICT could result in the reorganization of activities (Van Wee et al. 2013). It is recognized as the capability to support more complex trips and trip-chains, as well as multi-tasking during the journey (Van Wee et al. 2013). Parallel activities can reduce the disutility of trips and further affects user experience (Van Wee et al. 2013). However, as the older people prefer the simple travel pattern and are less require of the value on time efficiency (Su et al. 2009), this advantage are not so attractive as to persuade them to overcome the existing difficulties to adopt a new service. In this development trend, the identity of travellers will also change, for example, from "driver" to "passenger". By then, the use of public transport shall increase, with the advent of new forms of transport tools and infrastructures. However, there are few researches to prove that the older people is willing to accept this transformation actively. To turn to public transport, for the people who has long-term dependency on driving, this might be a challenge to their original lifestyle and habits, and can also induce to their exclusion from the new service.

3   The Value Proposition of MaaS Stakeholders

Having an overview of the literature, the integrated resources relate to MaaS seemed to be limited. Both stakeholders and academia are exploring the opportunities of the emerging concept, but the difficulty and opportunities are coexistence. There is limited evidence of users' requirements based ethnographic differences, and most studies tended to be pilot tests and evaluations involving comparison of data between younger and older generations, but do not show a practical recommendation of approaches to increase the involvement of various user groups.

For the perspective of MaaS stakeholders, their different extent of understanding leads to different market penetration. Service operators have their own interpretation, consideration and strategies of MaaS market, which leads to diverse types of service offerings and system architecture. Because of the uncertainties, it's difficult to define and verify the potential exclusion issues mentioned above. Without knowing what the specific problem are, the risk of service exclusion will not be effectively minimized through afterwards service iteration. Therefore, this exploratory study involved and collected the data of a workshop in 2016, hold by IMPART (The Intelligent Mobility Partnership – Midlands Competence Centre of Excellence), brought together industry, the public sectors, academia and NGOs for 54 participants to discuss the topic about how to better understand MaaS by taking users at the centre of proposition.

The study was divided in to 4 steps (Fig. 7), and the data aimed to answer the following questions.

Fig. 7. Methodology of study

- What do MaaS stakeholders focus attention to?
- What do they think about older people using MaaS?
- What is the value proposition of MaaS stakeholders?
- How to understand older travellers are ignored?

The presentation in workshop can help to quickly narrow down the scope of topics and locate current market's interests. Then in group discussion which focus on older travellers' involvement issues, the perspectives from different stakeholders can provide an overall point of view and locate the current knowledge gap. On this basis, a follow-up interview was designed for this study to deeply explore problem and consensus obtained in the workshop.

3.1   Identity of Participation

Referring to the literature review of the actors defined in MaaS system (CATAPULT 2015; Li et al. 2019), participants' composition of the workshop can be roughly divided into the nine categories (Transport Operator 4%, MaaS Provider 2%, Data Provider 4%, Manufacturer 5%, Business and Consultancy 11%, User 2%, Local Authorities 7%, Research Association 24% and Academia 41%), and eight of them delivered a detailed presentation, including three designers, two MaaS providers, one Data Provider, one User and one other interest identity. It is necessary to highlight that a participant's characteristic is defined above by the company or organization she/he belongs to, which might not represent individual's intention. In addition, a single participant may take more than one characteristics, so this statistic can only be referred to as an reference to understand the reason of some results coming out.

3.2 What Do Stakeholders Focus Attention to? - Workshop Presentation

The viewpoints raised by presentation are refined into key words and phrases, and the number counted here is the times one viewpoint being raised rather than the times single words being mentioned.

Key points are generally classified into 5 groups by its content. The higher number of mentions refers to this topic is currently being paid more attention to (Table 1).

Table 1. Data conclusion arranged by contents - key words of workshop presentation.

Design for MaaS (21)	Consider for users (9)
Take users' requirements at centre (4)	Empathy needs (4)
To think wider (4)	Travel modal shift (2)
Understand human(customer) behaviour (4)	Hidden disabilities (1)
Identify pain-points (2)	Safety and security (1)
Co-design (2)	Save time and money (1)
Application of design thinking (2)	
Understand users' motivation (1)	
Service form (18)	**Service content (20)**
Integration and collaboration (8)	Journey plan (4)
Multi-modal transport (2)	End-to-end journey (4)
Personalized service (2)	User experience (3)
App-based service (2)	Access on-demand (2)
Interface interaction (1)	Plan B (2)
Personal data collection (1)	IoT (Internet of Things) (2)
Service package (1)	Easy payment (1)
Virtual journey (1)	Before and After experience (1)
	Car sharing and recruiting (1)
Others (3)	**Sustainable business (2)**
	Additional revenue (1)

In Table 1, stakeholders' knowledge of service content is relatively more clear than their understanding about users. From this, the following hypotheses can be made.

- The exploration and development of MaaS service is more based on technology or enterprises' development strategy rather than data collected from user investigation.
- Their understanding of the user's value proposition is not based on an understanding of the users' requirements.

If you arrange the same data under the criteria of identities (actors) of MaaS system defined by CATAPULT (2015), the data collection would tell a different story (Table 2).

Table 2. Data collection arranged by actor identities– key words of workshop presentation.

Transport Operators (22)	Data Providers (23)
Integration and collaboration (8)	Integration and collaboration (8)
Journey plan (4)	Journey plan (4)
Travel modal shifts (2)	User experience (3)
IoT (Internet of Things) (2)	Plan B (2)
Sustainable business (2)	App-based service (2)
Safety and security (1)	Safety and security (1)
Save time and money (1)	Interface interaction (1)
Car sharing and recruiting (1)	Personal data collection (1)
Additional revenue (1)	Additional revenue (1)
Users/Customers (28)	MaaS Providers (34)
Journey plan (4)	Integration and collaboration (8)
End-to-end journey (4)	Take users' requirements at center (4)
User experience (3)	To think wider (4)
Travel modal shifts (2)	Journey plan (4)
Eliminate pain-points (2)	Eliminate pain-points (2)
Multi-modal transport (2)	Co-design (2)
Access on-demand (2)	Application of design thinking (2)
IoT (Internet of Things) (2)	Sustainable business (2)
Plan B (2)	App-based service (2)
Car sharing and recruiting (1)	Understand users' motivation (1)
Virtual journey (1)	Service package (1)
Easy payment (1)	Save time and money (1)
Hidden disabilities (1)	Additional revenue (1)
Before and After experience (1)	

The different classification of the same key words means this item could be seen in different perspective according to value propositions. On the initial phase of developing a new business model, it's natural for actors to pay most of the attention on some certain aspects, such as the system operation and construction, which might indicate that the responsibilities of actors are not yet clearly defined: the discussion of travellers' requirements have not yet found a clear direction. In the presentations, participants aware the differentiated needs of traveller groups (e.g. children and older generation), but the current conditions seemed to be unable to support them to refine the service offerings as the service capability has not fully developed.

3.3   What Do They Think About Older People Using MaaS?- Workshop Group Discussion

In order to obtain the specific data to tackle this question, the study collected and analysed the data from two of the focused groups which specifically discussed the older travellers' related issues. It was an open discussion, the content is guided to focus on the problems of older travellers' involvement in MaaS. All the topics discussed were recorded on paper for later organization.

The data were generally divided in to two layers, the general questions about MaaS and the concerns related to older travellers.

General Question. The general questions are literally covering the following aspects, Concept, Requirements, and Operation (Fig. 8).

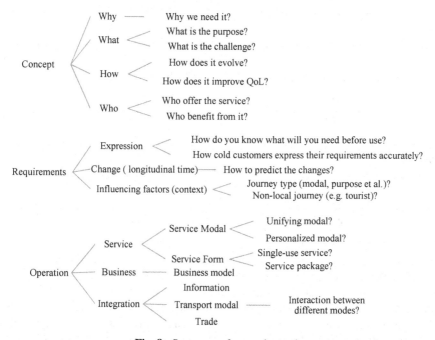

Fig. 8. Summary of general questions

Referring participants' statement, it can understood that the emergence of MaaS is driven by the development of new technologies, rather than human requirements. Stakeholders are thinking of "What can we do with this technology?" before being concerned with travellers' inconvenience and requirements in real environment. It might lead to the consequence that, firstly, considering the uncertainty about its potential possibilities, the outline of concept would be unlikely to be defined in the short term. Secondly, the new technology based services would probably challenge peoples' existing habits and thinking model. It can also be observed from the discussion that the exploration of MaaS and users' requirements in both market and academia are not carried out simultaneously at the early development stage-which results in the gap between understanding and practice. Therefore, the directions of future research for designers need to concentrate more on users themselves and their requirements to seek for the breakthrough points in order to positively connect their demands with technologies.

Older Travellers-Related Questions. Questions relate to older travellers are gathered around 3 themes, Motivation, Challenges and Implication (Fig. 9).

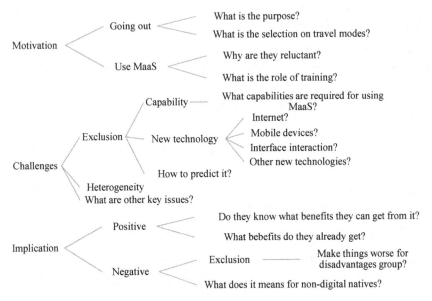

Fig. 9. Summary of older travellers-related questions

Older travellers' related questions can be regarded as the extension of general questions rather than a separated research area. The context for older travellers is more complicated because they have to overcome the reluctance of "going out" and "use new service"- the double obstacle, while the most of the topics here haven't been clearly clarified yet as they are ended with a question mark. In addition, it's unclear whether the new service will affect the older people more positively or negatively. Without this data, service providers will have a hard time persuading older people to attempt adopting it.

Consensus Acquired. In the open discussion – each group presented the results of the discussion to the other groups to exchange ideas, the participants have generally reached a consensus on some of the issues. Firstly, traveller's pain-points should be the basis to shape service performance. The touch-points should respond to traveller's pain-points and either reduce the difficulties or improve the original experience. Through understanding travellers' pain-points, service providers can obtain the evidence to set up the scenario and characteristics of touch-points in service design.

Secondly, systematic integrative thinking is needed in the MaaS eco-system. It contains two aspects, one is to the collaboration of different organizations, such as real-time information, easy payment and multi-modal transport; the other refers to the systematic service, which not only covering the cooperation of all the service channels, but is also reflected on the connection of difference experience phases, for example, the "pre-" and "after-" trip experience are equally important with "during-" trip experience for travellers' overall satisfaction.

Compared to the definition of MaaS actors summarized by CATAPULT in 2015 - "Traveller Needs and UK Capability Study", participants in this workshop have updated the understanding of the identity of MaaS actors and universally agreed that the same person could be classified into different categories simultaneously according to specific scenario, for example, Uber drivers who are both service provider and user. This is due to the characteristic of service logic which highlights the value co-creation, where operators are mainly taking the role of organizing available resources rather than direct offer services.

A question which was raised during discussion is "Are the journeys all necessary?". Virtual trips could release people from the trips of "what need to do" to "What want to do". Take older travellers as example, such "need to do" activities as go to hospital or regular shopping could be replaced by online operation. Therefore, MaaS can help people to get flexibility to reschedule their daily routine, which is agreed to bring benefits to their quality of life (QoL).

Summary. The proposition discussed in this exploration study is about whether the older travellers' requirements have been considered on early development stage of MaaS. It has to clarify that, "whether it has been considered" is not the same as "whether do they actually engaged" and can't be regarded as the direct evidence to judge the level of inclusiveness of MaaS service. But the neglect of users' needs in service development will inevitably lead to a certain degree of exclusion or difficulties for some users.

There are two ways to improve inclusiveness. One is to decrease the level of task demands to make it being easier adopted by wider audience (e.g. UbiGo Call Services for older people), another needs to provide necessary support to users' original capabilities to encourage higher involvement (e.g. mobility scooter). The former one is more likely to take the market-oriented perspective that roughly filters the user group that the service aims to include, while the latter depends on the individual's willingness, which is inclined to be the subjective behaviour that largely influenced by personal factors, such as emotion. However, these factors are difficult to collect and measure. In addition, most empirical studies relies on self-report measures instead of behavioral data, which leads to the lower data accuracy (Scharkow 2016), especially with older people who have the age-related changes in cognitive and communication functions, which will also impact on the result of self-report (Knäuper et al. 2016). For these reasons above, future research on this topic should look forward to appropriate methods to investigate the expanded user experience timeline and ensure data accuracy and reliability.

3.4 What Is the Value Proposition of Stakeholders? – Follow-up Interview

To further explore the different stakeholders' value proposition and their understanding of older travellers' involvement issues, semi-structured interviews were used to multiple perspectives. The 4 participants in this step are all from the workshop and have different identities. They were asked to develop the answer of the remaining questions from previous discussion and help us think more and deeply.

- Transport solution Specialist– Transport Provider
- Service Design Specialist – Service Designer
- Research Fellow - Academia
- Product Manager – Vehicle Manufacturer

Through content analysis, the interviews showed that the neglect of older travellers' requirements in current market is a recognized fact, and most of the stakeholders are already aware of the issue and have the willingness to involve older travellers in their service through later iteration. However but due to the lack of knowledge and resource, pilots and trials that have been promoted so far are mainly "testing the water" to seek the possibility for further cooperation, and this process take time. They mentioned the importance of including older people participating in the design process to improve service inclusion as nobody would know their requirements better than themselves. However, there are limited experience could be referred to.

The stakeholders expect the new service can be user-centred and also business-oriented to ensure the continuous development, but have not found an approach to satisfy both sides. From the perspective of market, private and public enterprises are offering various service characteristics, which are just "fragments" and haven't come into integrated system. The uncertainty of future market of MaaS would be vital for the promotion of MaaS among older travellers, it might need to add other actors participating in the system to bridge the service delivery, for example, the NGOs and government.

3.5 How to Understand Older Travellers Are Ignored? – Understanding and Discussion

The Gap Between Knowledge and Application. The various dimensions that affect an individual's mobility have been relatively well-discussed in previous literatures. The influencing factors of mobility can affect every aspect of travel experience, and the influence is not limited within trips, but the associated life as well. The complexity of the study of MaaS lies in the fact that experience evaluation involves both "service" and "trip" covering physical and psychological dimensions. As shown in the Fig. 10, experience is divided into 4 themes, the characteristics discussed in each theme are different.

However, as the stakeholders in the workshop discussed, the current condition cannot support the personalized service offerings of each traveller segmentation. The existing theories and data are accessible, but what is missing is the method to apply them reasonably. In follow-up interviews, participants mentioned the different design for older and younger generations should not only be reflected by the service offerings, but also in the methods applied to do New Service Development (NSD). Stakeholders should learn to explore the real needs of different groups and make sustainable development to meet users' changing demands.

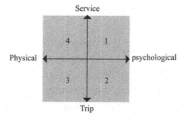

Fig. 10. 4 themes of MaaS experience

Fostering Travel Behaviour. As discussed in the literature review, the development route that MaaS proposed for future transports is to some extent contrary to existing travel pattern of older people. There needs to be an appropriate plan to ensure that travellers' behaviour and service can develop simultaneously in a dynamic balance. The service should help users fit into the new service system mode while guiding the behaviour change, apply technology flexible and leave enough room for service innovation.

Market Competition. Market competition in the future would occur among strategic alliances. Because of the trend of multi-modal collaboration, individual transport system should not only consider their own operating manner, but also the way to coordinate with others. On this basis, the competitiveness would also depend on one system's flexibility and coordinate ability. As for the elder market, choosing service partners that meet the requirements of older travelers can improve the service attractiveness, but the key is to figure out what do they really need and in what approach to cooperate to keep them engaged.

Data Sharing. Although data sharing remains a challenge for MaaS integration, but from a customer perspective, desired data could help them make decisions. More data items mean more choices. Stakeholders would establish cooperative relationships according to the database they respectively have with the intention of providing seamless travel experience. On this basis, it can be understand as the data and collaboration of different stakeholders that work together on building the market in older travellers mind.

4   Conclusion

This paper indicates the concern that the emerging concept of MaaS might have ignored some specific groups' requirements in the business-driven market environment. For older travellers, the travel behaviour proposed by MaaS may cause new barriers, which not only occur in human-computer interaction or physical environment, but also affect the elderly's travel planning, the choice of activities to participate in, and even have an impacts on the quality of life. Previous studies have provided a relatively comprehensive understanding of travel characteristics of the older people, but in the context of new services, new dimensions have emerged which need to be further explored. The older travellers have to learn about how to adapt to the new travel logic while overcoming the travel difficulties they used to have. Based the global aging trend, this service, designed for the younger generations, is not benefitting those who do already, and will increasingly, really need it.

The explorative study described in this paper verified the potential exclusion issues caused by MaaS and showed a lack of deeper understanding among stakeholders on the current MaaS development stage. Furthermore, given the lack of previous experience and evidence, the direction of future iterations cannot be clearly defined.

In the view of this, this paper suggests that stakeholders in the system should consider the different requirements of various groups and open their thoughts through a revised design process, instead of sticking to the conventional thinking in the current context. Operators should make plans to ensure that the travellers and transport service can learn from each other and develop in the same pace, and strengthen communication among different stakeholders to coordinate value propositions, in order to realize the sustainability goal of urban transport system by iterating the service with the user-centred perspective.

References

Alonso-González, M.J., van Oort, N., Oded, C., Hoogendoorn, S.: Urban demand responsive transport in the mobility as a service ecosystem: its role and potential market share (2017)

Alsnih, R., Hensher, D.A.: The mobility and accessibility expectations of seniors in an aging population. Transp. Res. Part A: Policy Pract. **37**(10), 903–916 (2003)

Arenas-Gaitán, J., Peral-Peral, B., Ramon-Jeronimo, M.A.: Elderly and internet banking: an application of UTAUT2. J. Internet Bank. Commer. **20**(1), 1–23 (1970)

Atkins: Journeys of the future. Introducing Mobility as a Service (2015). https://www.atkinsglobal.com/~/media/Files/A/Atkins-Corporate/uk-and-europe/uk-thought -leadership/reports/Journeys of the future_300315.pdf

Bakaba, J.E., Ortlepp, J.: Belange von Senioren zur Verbesserung der Verkehrssicherheit/For considerating elderly's interests by improving road traffic safety. Zeitschrift für Verkehrssicherheit **56**(1) (2010)

Ben-Akiva, M.E., Bowman, J.L.: Activity based travel demand model systems. In: Marcotte, P., Nguyen, S. (eds.) Equilibrium and Advanced Transportation Modelling. CRT, pp. 27–46. Springer, Boston (1998). https://doi.org/10.1007/978-1-4615-5757-9_2

Broome, K., McKenna, K., Fleming, J., Worrall, L.: Bus use and older people: a literature review applying the Person–Environment–Occupation model in macro practice. Scand. J. Occup. Ther. **16**(1), 3–12 (2009)

Buehler, R., Nobis, C.: Travel behaviour in aging societies: comparison of Germany and the United States. Transp. R. Rec.: J. Transp. Res. Board **2182**, 62–70 (2010)

Caiati, V., Feneri, A.M., Rasouli, S., Timmermans, H.J.P.: Innovations in urban mobility and travel demand analysis: mobility as a service context. In: Proceedings BIVEC-GIBET Transport Research Days 2017, Liège, Belgium, pp. 492–503 (2017)

CATAPULT: Traveller Needs and UK Capability Study (2015). https://ts.catapult.org.uk/wp-con tent/uploads/2016/04/Traveller-Needs-Study-1.pdf

Datson, J.: Mobility as a service: exploring the opportunity for mobility as a service in the UK (2016)

Doherty, S.T.: An activity scheduling process approach to understanding travel behaviour. In: 79th Annual Meeting of the Transportation Research Board, Washington, DC, January 2000

El Zarwi, F., Vij, A., Walker, J.L.: A discrete choice framework for modeling and forecasting the adoption and diffusion of new transportation services. Transp. Res. Part C: Emerg. Technol. **79**, 207–223 (2017)

Engels, B., Liu, G.J.: Social exclusion, location and transport disadvantage amongst non-driving seniors in a Melbourne municipality, Australia. J. Transp. Geogr. **19**(4), 984–996 (2011)

Giesecke, R., Surakka, T., Hakonen, M.: Conceptualising mobility as a service. In: 2016 Eleventh International Conference on Ecological Vehicles and Renewable Energies (EVER), pp. 1–11. IEEE, April 2016

Goulias, K.G.: Traveller behaviour and values research for human-centered transportation systems. Transportation in the New Millennium: State of the Art and Future Directions, Perspectives from Transportation Research Board Standing Committees. Transportation Research Board, Washington, DC (2000)

Haustein, S., Siren, A.: Older people's mobility: segments, factors, trends. Transp. Rev. **35**(4), 466–487 (2015)

Hensher, D.A.: Some insights into the key influences on trip-chaining activity and public transport use of seniors and the elderly. Int. J. Sustain. Transp. **1**(1), 53–68 (2007)

Hietanen, S.: "Mobility as a Service" – the new transport model? ITS & Transport Management Supplement. Eurotransport **12**(2), 2–4 (2014)

Hildebrand, E.D.: Dimensions in elderly travel behaviour: a simplified activity-based model using lifestyle clusters. Transportation **30**(3), 285–306 (2003)

Hilgert, T., Kagerbauer, M., Schuster, T., Becker, C.: Optimization of individual travel behavior through customized mobility services and their effects on travel demand and transportation systems. Transp. Res. Procedia **19**, 58–69 (2016)

Ho, C.Q., Hensher, D.A., Mulley, C., Wong, Y.Z.: Potential uptake and willingness-to-pay for mobility as a service (MaaS): a stated choice study. Transp. Res. Part A: Policy Pract. **117**, 302–318 (2018)

Holzinger, A., Searle, G., Nischelwitzer, A.: On some aspects of improving mobile applications for the elderly. In: Stephanidis, C. (ed.) UAHCI 2007. LNCS, vol. 4554, pp. 923–932. Springer, Heidelberg (2007). https://doi.org/10.1007/978-3-540-73279-2_103. https://pdfs.semanticscho lar.org/b01e/13938c1199393852801f580017936e7b656e.pdf

Jittrapirom, P., Caiati, V., Feneri, A.M., Ebrahimigharehbaghi, S., Alonso González, M.J., Narayan, J.: Mobility as a service: a critical review of definitions, assessments of schemes, and key challenges (2017)

Jittrapirom, P., Marchau, V., van der Heijden, R., Meurs, H.: Future implementation of mobility as a service (MaaS): results of an international Delphi study. Travel Behav. Soc. (2018)

Jovicic, G.: Activity based travel demand modelling. Danmarks Transp. Skn (2001)

Kamargianni, M., Matyas, M.: The business ecosystem of mobility-as-a-service. In: Transportation Research Board, vol. 96 (2017)

Knäuper, B., Carrière, K., Chamandy, M., Xu, Z., Schwarz, N., Rosen, N.O.: How aging affects self-reports. Eur. J. Ageing **13**(2), 185–193 (2016)

Kockelman, K.: Travel behavior as function of accessibility, land use mixing, and land use balance: evidence from San Francisco Bay Area. Transp. Res. Rec.: J. Transp. Res. Board **1607**, 116–125 (1997)

Lee, M.S., Chung, J.H., McNally, M.G.: An empirical investigation of the underlying behavioral processes of trip chaining (2002)

Lerner, W., Van Audenhove, F.J.: The future of urban mobility: towards networked, multimodal cities in 2050. Public Transp. Int.-Engl. Ed. **61**(2), 14 (2012)

Li, Y., Voege, T.: Mobility as a service (MaaS): challenges of implementation and policy required. J. Transp. Technol. **7**(2), 95–106 (2017)

Li, Y., May, A., Cook, S.: Mobility-as-a-service: a critical review and the generalized multi-modal transport experience. In: Rau, P.-L.P. (ed.) HCII 2019. LNCS, vol. 11577, pp. 186–206. Springer, Cham (2019). https://doi.org/10.1007/978-3-030-22580-3_15

Lu, J., Hung, K., Wang, L., Schuett, M.A., Hu, L.: Do perceptions of time affect outbound-travel motivations and intention? An investigation among Chinese seniors. Tour. Manag. **53**, 1–12 (2016)

Lyman, S., Ferguson, S.A., Braver, E.R., Williams, A.F.: Older driver involvements in police reported crashes and fatal crashes: trends and projections. Injury prevention **8**(2), 116–120 (2002)

Lyons, G., Hammond, P., Mackay, K.: The importance of user perspective in the evolution of MaaS. Transp. Res. Part A: Policy Pract. **121**, 22–36 (2019)

Mänty, M., et al.: Outdoor and indoor falls as predictors of mobility limitation in older women. Age Ageing **38**(6), 757–761 (2009)

Marin-Lamellet, C., Haustein, S.: Managing the safe mobility of older road users: how to cope with their diversity? J. Transp. Health **2**(1), 22–31 (2015)

Matyas, M., Kamargianni, M.: A holistic overview of the mobility as a service ecosystem. In: Transportation Research Conference, Gyor, Hungary, pp. 30–31, March 2017

McGuckin, N., Zmud, J., Nakamoto, Y.: Trip-chaining trends in the United States: understanding travel behavior for policy making. Transp. Res. Rec.: J. Transp. Res. Board **1917**, 199–204 (2005)

McLeod, S.: Maslow's hierarchy of needs (2007). http://www.simplypsychology.org/maslow.html

Melis, A., Mirri, S., Prandi, C., Prandini, M., Salomoni, P., Callegati, F.: Integrating personalized and accessible itineraries in MaaS ecosystems through microservices. Mob. Netw. Appl. **23**(1), 167–176 (2018)

Melis, A., Prandini, M., Sartori, L., Callegati, F.: Public transportation, IoT, trust and urban habits. In: Bagnoli, F., et al. (eds.) INSCI 2016. LNCS, vol. 9934, pp. 318–325. Springer, Cham (2016). https://doi.org/10.1007/978-3-319-45982-0_27

Mollenkopf, H., Kaspar, R.: Ageing in rural areas of East and West Germany: increasing similarities and remaining differences. Eur. J. Ageing **2**(2), 120–130 (2005)

Newbold, K.B., Scott, D.M., Spinney, J.E., Kanaroglou, P., Páez, A.: Travel behaviour within Canada's older population: a cohort analysis. J. Transp. Geogr. **13**(4), 340–351 (2005)

Noland, R.B., Thomas, J.V.: Multivariate analysis of trip-chaining behaviour. Environ. Plan. **34**(6), 953–970 (2007)

Pangbourne, K., Stead, D., Mladenović, M., Milakis, D.: The case of mobility as a service: a critical reflection on challenges for urban transport and mobility governance. In: Governance of the Smart Mobility Transition, pp. 33–48 (2018)

Patrício, L., Fisk, R.P., Falcão e Cunha, J., Constantine, L.: Multilevel service design: from customer value constellation to service experience blueprinting. J. Serv. Res. **14**(2), 180–200 (2011)

Priestley, M., Rabiee, P.: Same difference? Older people's organisations and disability issues. Disabil. Soc. **17**(6), 597–611 (2002)

Rantanen, T.: Promoting mobility in older people. J. Prev. Med. Public Health **46**(Suppl 1), S50 (2013)

Rasouli, S., Timmermans, H.: Activity-based models of travel demand: promises, progress and prospects. Int. J. Urban Sci. **18**(1), 31–60 (2014)

Scharkow, M.: The accuracy of self-reported internet use—a validation study using client log data. Commun. Methods Meas. **10**(1), 13–27 (2016)

Schmöcker, J.D., Su, F., Noland, R.B.: An analysis of trip chaining among older London residents. Transportation **37**(1), 105–123 (2010)

Shrestha, B.P., Millonig, A., Hounsell, N.B., Mcdonald, M.: Review of public transport needs of older people in European context. J. Popul. Ageing **10**(4), 343–361 (2017)

Siren, A., Haustein, S.: Baby boomers' mobility patterns and preferences: what are the implications for future transport? Transp. Policy **29**, 136–144 (2013)

Smith, G., Sochor, J., Karlsson, I.M.: Mobility as a service: development scenarios and implications for public transport. Res. Transp. Econ. **69**, 592–599 (2018)

Sochor, J.L., Strömberg, H., Karlsson, M.: Travellers' motives for adopting a new, innovative travel service: insights from the UbiGo field operational test in Gothenburg, Sweden. In: 21st World Congress on Intelligent Transport Systems, Detroit, 7–11 September 2014 (2014)

Stilgoe, J., Owen, R., Macnaghten, P.: Developing a framework for responsible innovation. Res. Policy **42**(9), 1568–1580 (2013)

Stradling, S.: Moving around: some aspects of the psychology of transport. In: Foresight Intelligent Infrastructure Systems Project (2006)

Su, F.: Understanding and satisfying older people's travel demand. Doctoral dissertation, Department of Civil and Environmental Engineering, Imperial College London (2008)

Suen, S.L., Mitchell, C.G.B.: Accessible transportation and mobility. In: Transportation in the New Millennium (2000)

The Institution of Engineering and Technology (IET): Meeting the needs of older and disabled travellers (2015). http://www.theiet.org/factfiles/transport/age-pop-page.cfm?type=pdf

Timmermans, H.J., Zhang, J.: Modelling household activity travel behaviour: examples of state of the art modeling approaches and research agenda. Transp. Res. Part B: Methodol. **43**(2), 187–190 (2009)

Van Wee, B., Geurs, K., Chorus, C.: Information, communication, travel behaviour and accessibility. J. Transp. Land Use **6**(3), 1–16 (2013)

Webber, S.C., Porter, M.M., Menec, V.H.: Mobility in older adults: a comprehensive framework. Gerontologist **50**(4), 443–450 (2010)

Whelan, M., Langford, J., Oxley, J., Koppel, S., Charlton, J.: The elderly and mobility: a review of the literature. Monash University Accident Research Centre (2006)

Wong, Y.Z., Hensher, D.A., Mulley, C.: Emerging transport technologies and the modal efficiency framework: a case for mobility as a service (MaaS) (2018)

World Health Organization: World Report on Ageing and Health. World Health Organization, Geneva (2015)

Intergenerational Communication in Traditional and Virtual Bulgarian Families

Lilia Raycheva$^{(\boxtimes)}$, Mariyan Tomov, and Neli Velinova

The St. Kliment Ohridski Sofia University, Sofia, Bulgaria
lraycheva@yahoo.com, mariyan.d.tomov@gmail.com,
nelikdkd@gmail.com

Abstract. Mobility and migration processes through transnational borders outline the new dimensions of the modern world. The countless possibilities to work and study abroad are among the main reasons for the younger generations in Bulgaria to leave their country and their family, relatives and friends. The newly formed virtual family form composed of a married or unmarried couple, a family with children (narrowly) and their ancestors (broadly) where single, several or all members of the family unit do not live in the same household faces immense challenges.

Despite the contemporary seamless and timely communication possibilities, the paper seeks to answer two research questions: Does the intergenerational divide deepen in the virtual family over time? How the communication is changing in the virtual family compared with the traditional one? Thus the aim of the study is to measure the generational divide in the communications between virtual and traditional families. A comparative analysis of in-depth face-to-face and Skype interviews with respondents from virtual and traditional families has been conducted. The results and conclusions indicate that the different daily routine and lifestyle of the family members could alienate them. Intergenerational divide between younger and older members is detected both in virtual and traditional family. This reduces the effectiveness of the interactive communication between the family members, especially with regard to older people when they live apart.

Keywords: Virtual family · Traditional family · Intergenerational divide · Ageing

1 Introduction

The process of digitization is among the main milestones tracing the dimensions of humankind's transformations in the 21st century. Today these transformations are catalyzed by the intense development of the communication technologies. As positive as their impact might be on progress in all areas of life, it is no less true that they pose challenges for the social stratification of society in terms of age [1].

Institutional attention for the ageing population began to appear in the last decade of the 20th century. The UN *Principles for Older Persons* (Resolution 46/91) are grouped under five themes: independence, participation, care, self-fulfillment and dignity. The

© Springer Nature Switzerland AG 2020
Q. Gao and J. Zhou (Eds.): HCII 2020, LNCS 12209, pp. 288–300, 2020.
https://doi.org/10.1007/978-3-030-50232-4_20

Madrid International Plan of Action on Ageing (MIPAA) and the *Political Declaration,* adopted by the Second World Assembly on Ageing in April 2002 [2], are still among the global guiding documents that have a priority focus on the areas of the rights of older adults and their well-being in a supportive environment.

Demographic imbalances, such as population decrease and ageing stronly impact the workforce developments. Thus they create problems for the macro-fiscal stability and sustainability of all social systems - the labor market, the retirement methods and pension plans, the healthcare arrangements, the social assistance and long-term care order, the education classification, etc. The rise of the proportion of retired and older people over the next few decades is considered to be one of the greatest challenges to the economic and social system of the EU [3].

Mobility and migration processes through transnational borders draw the new dimensions of the modern world. The countless possibilities to work and study abroad are among the main reasons for the younger generations in Bulgaria to leave their country and their family, relatives and friends seeking for a better life.

The development of Human-computer interaction (HCI) and free movement across the national borders facilitate some virtual relationships to develop into long-distance relationships [4]. In this sense, at macro level, the Oxford Dictionary uses the definition "virtual community" described as a "community of people sharing common interests, ideas and feelings on the Internet". Therefore, at micro level (family), the term "virtual family" may be used.

According to Tomov [5] the newly formed virtual family form composed of a married or unmarried couple, a family with children (narrowly) and their ancestors (broadly) where single, several or all members of the family unit do not live in the same household faces immense challenges.

HCI eases to maintain family relations and therefore creates mediatized or virtual ways of communication and living. The emergence of the Internet has changed the balance between communication and spatial distance, promising to put into action what Marshall McLuhan [6] predicted, and Manuel Castells [7] called the "space of streams" where communication is a function regardless of the place. Along with the spatial distance, the time concept should be considered as well. This correlates with the frequency, the duration of communication and in many cases reflects the quality of relationship between members of the family. Personal motivation and feelings of absence, loneliness, self-isolation are among the major factors motivating the personal contact with the closest people. The intergenerational divide between younger and older participants in the new HCI environment has important implications on contemporary communication processes as well. "Intergenerational contact has the potential to reduce the prevalence of ageism and significantly improve the mental and physical health of younger and older persons" [8]. Although the communication is not a universal substitute of the physical contact or "remedy", it could "mild" the negative feelings, but in some cases may intensify them. This corresponds with Fortunati's [9] statement that the ideal form of communication is the personal interaction, despite the prospects of future scenarios related to the new technological developments that might change the way of interaction between relatives especially with regard to older people.

2 Methodology

The aim of the research is to measure some of the parameters of the generational divide in the communication between virtual and traditional families. When studying the topic in detail we came out to two research questions, which are not sufficiently addressed in the literature: Does the intergenerational divide deepen in the virtual family over time? How the communication is changing in the virtual family compared with the traditional one? In order to answer these questions, in-depth interviews were conducted to explore the nature of liaison between family members who maintain personal communication and those not living together, herein defined as "virtual families". Questionnaires included also problematic discourses related to the older adults – their accessibility to urban environment; their working capacity and opportunities to stay active beyond retirement; the way they communicate with younger relatives; and the intergenerational divide.

Sampling included a total of 40 (N = 40) respondents. The first group of interviewees represents families (parents, their children or grandchildren) who stick to interpersonal communication (N = 20), while the second (N = 20) portrays families who maintain remote communication (virtual families) via mobile phone, social networks and communication applications. Methodology follows the theory of Duncombe and Marsden [10], according to which a distinguishing feature of distant communication is the presence of many emotional aspects, which are often unclear and confused. In case of further analysis these aspects require a qualitative research.

The questionnaire consists of 15 basic questions and 5 supplementary ones such as place of birth of the interviewees, their gender, age and place of residence. Basic questions are structured as follows: four open, eleven closed (one of which is dichotomous – offering two possible answers) and two semi-open ones. In addition, respondents were asked clarifying questions. This approach broadens the spectrum of knowledge, eliminates some weaknesses of the structured interview method; predisposes the more introverted respondents to share further about communication with relatives and about challenges facing the older adults in Bulgaria.

Interviews were conducted in person, in a convenient place and at a time appropriate for the respondents. Given the long distance, the financial constraints of the study and the deadlines set, part of the interviews took place via Skype. The online connection was conducted with microphones and cameras switched on, which helped to increase intimacy, sense of closeness and trust between the interviewers and interviewees.

Given the intimate nature of the questions, the survey guaranteed the anonymity of the respondents, observing the ethical standards and the Code of Ethics of the Bulgarian Sociological Association [11]. This further helped to achieve greater openness, honesty and desire with which the interviewees shared their feelings and emotions. The mutation in the voice intonation, the spontaneously bursting in tears and the uncontrolled gestures betrayed their hidden anguish from the rare physical encounters with relatives and loved ones. In addition to the emotionally releasing effect, in the course of the interview respondents often reflected on topics and problems related to their communication with the older adults which they had never discussed before in their everyday life.

The selection of interviewees was random, including friends, acquaintances and colleagues. They were also the initial mediators in the recruitment of the next interviewees. Use of the mediated sampling method has aided their recruitment, providing greater diversity and confidentiality than the standard snowball sampling. Due to the combinability of the selection, some of the weaknesses of the indirect and snowball sampling, mainly related to the representativeness, were avoided.

It also encompasses, without attempting to distinguish between the generations, the two main groups forming the family, namely, parents with their children and grandparents with their grandchildren. In the study the groups are distributed relatively evenly.

In addition, the methodology includes age differentiation covering groups between the age of 19 and 35 years, on the one hand, and older adults over 60 years of age. Starting age of 19 was applied for two main reasons:

(1) At the age of eighteen or nineteen, the secondary education level shall be completed. In their desire to pursue higher educational degree, some prospective students leave the household they shared with their parents and siblings, to continue their education in another city, and often choose the prospect of studying abroad.
(2) After completing their secondary education, these young people have reached the legal age, have accumulated life experience and are able to discuss freely topics related to their family, communication and feelings from a distance. At this age individuals have reached the age of majority, have accumulated life experience and are able to freely discuss topics related to their family, communication and feelings from a distance.

In the survey also participated older adults over the age of 60, living in Bulgaria. Age is linked to the ageing process, which can be crucial for any individual as it involves major changes. These changes are work-related (retirement), as well as family, societal, physiological and health related changes, which require adjustments to perceptions and structuring of life. In addition to that, the purpose of the age differentiation was to determine whether the older adults possess the necessary computer literacy and access to the new technologies. And also - to determine whether there is an intergenerational divide in communication between family members who maintain an interpersonal relationship and those who are separated (live in different cities or countries).

In addition, the study follows the concept of the so-called virtual family, which represents an alternative family form consisting of married or unmarried couple, a family with children (in the narrow sense) and their grandparents (in the broader sense) where one, several or all members of the family unit do not live in the same household [5]. It is characteristic of them that they share daily challenges, exchange ideas and feelings remotely through the new ICTs.

The questions raised in the survey also highlight future scenarios related to new technological developments that will change the mode of communication and interaction between relatives, especially with regard to the aged ones.

3 Results

All members of the surveyed families living together prefer to interact in person. When they are separated in everyday life or for longer periods of time, most of them communicate over the phone, as well as via social networks (in particular, Facebook and Messenger) and other applications such as Viber and Skype. The key to choosing a medium of communication, according to Miller & Madianou, is to consider each medium as a structure of opportunity [12]. This has also been historically confirmed when consumers wishing to communicate remotely had access to one or two media, such as the letter and recorded voice on audio tape sent by mail.

This study, focused on the communication among the members of the Bulgarian family not living together, confirms this thesis. Here is what two of the interviewees shared:

When microphone and camera are switched on in Viber I can fully sense my child's moods and feelings. This way I feel able to support him and to empathize to his emotions.

On the phone, through Viber app, I communicate when I want to quickly hear from my mom or dad living abroad. Usually I use Facebook when the message I want to leave is not so urgent and does not require an immediate response. I use e-mail only for business communication – almost never when communicating with my relatives.

Duration of Communication. The majority of the interviewed families living together (93%) talk to each other for more than 30 min a day, with topics being discussed ranging from health (64%) to leisure (64%), then work/study (57%), finance (21%) and games and sports (14%). The total sum of the percentages exceeds 100 as respondents indicated more than one conversation topic.

Among the family members not living together the percentage ratio is almost the same with only the topic about financial situation that is viewed in a different way. In families who live together, this is very often an issue leading to subsequent conflicts and disagreements, while in families not living together this topic is more about worrying about the financial situation of the other family members. Additionally, current political or social events in the county or in the city where family members located are also discussed.

An interesting fact is that there are still per cent of the interviewed families who live together, but have answered that they were talking to their relatives between 5 and 15 min a day. Mostly they explain:

We have nothing to say to each other.

This is an example of a typical generation divide where young family members feel that they have no common topics to discuss with older adults and, accordingly, do not want to communicate with them, claiming that they have nothing to learn from them or share with them.

One of the interviewees stated:

My parents are stubborn and I avoid communicating with them very often because they do not understand me. They have old fashioned understanding of life, they always are the right party to the dispute, and they do not enter their children's shoes.

Another respondent declared:

When we have nothing to share with my mother or my father we resort to discussing the weather forecast – how cold it is outside, that I have to wear my jacket when I go out, and that I have to be careful not to forget my umbrella because it is raining outside and I will be soaked to the bone.

Weather information is sometimes, as interviewees admitted, a "lifeline", especially when topics are exhausted and there is no other curiosity to share.

Compared to family members living together, the conversation duration among family members not living together is much shorter. Exactly 44% of them say that they talk about 30 min a day. For 39% of the interviewed family members not living together that duration is even shorter – up to 5 min a day. Between 5 and 15 min is the conversation for 17% of people who do not live together (Fig. 1).

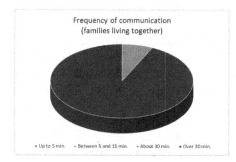 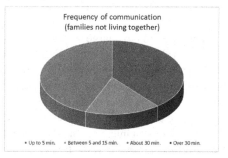

Fig. 1. Frequency of communication

Emotionality. In the present study emotionality is considered as maintaining the stability of the relationship between relatives and intimate partners. On the one hand, it is at the root of the motivation to start communication, and on the other, the persistence in communication and experiencing emotionality promotes empathy and interest (in the absence of perseverance and empathy, the closest family members may feel lonely and abandoned). According to Stoyanova, positive-oriented emotions confirm the confidence that people are loved. Communication with a loved one brings joy and is an immanent characteristic of emotional acceptance [13].

An interesting fact is that 29% of the interviewed family members living together said that they always openly express their emotional state when talking to their relatives. 7% claimed that rarely express their emotions openly and the remaining 64% stated that in most cases they show openly and naturally what they feel. This indicates that although they live together, communicate on a daily basis and share a common home and emotions, the majority of the members of one family are in fact rarely fully honest and natural when communicating with each other. However, none of them answered that they never express their feelings honestly, while among families not living together 17% said that they never express their emotions honestly. Only 11% were categorical that they always show what they care about, but the same percentage (11%) answered that they rarely show their emotional state openly. Similarly to the families living together more than half of those who do not live together express their emotional state most often during a conversation (61%) (Fig. 2).

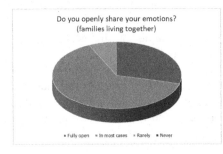
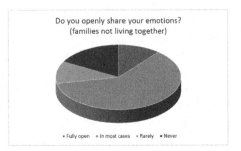

Fig. 2. Emotionality of communication

This situation to a large extent suggests the question to what extent and how family members value communication as meaningful, sincere and comprehensive. The paradox is that people living together confess that they have more secrets and taboo topics with their loved ones than those who do not share a roof over their heads. The question arises whether the idea of daily communication overlaps with the idea of a short and synthesized conversation that lasts a maximum of 30 min by phone or via Viber. Perhaps the ideas of communication and understanding diverge here. Or due to the fact that they live together under one roof, family members actually have to hide more things from each other than when communicating virtually with their loved ones who are far from them. It is better to further investigate this issue in another study.

Generational Divide. More than half of the family members living together believe that between the representatives of the youngest and the oldest in the family the so-called generational divide does not exist (57%). The opposite is the opinion of 36% who believe that the generational divide is more likely to exist. Fewer, only 7%, said that they sometimes feel this generational divide. Another 7%, however, are adamant that it exists. According to the younger representatives who responded in this way, and who still coexist with their parents, there is a perception that the behavior of adults is old-fashioned and conservative and therefore does not correspond with their view of life and the world.

A respondent shared:

My father has a rigid mindset and far-left political beliefs that do not correspond with my democratic understandings. My mother, for her part, grew up in a time where she did not have the opportunity to get a good education and did not travel much around the world. Although I am grateful that she raised me and gave me the opportunity to get a college degree, her ideas about life are limited and at odds with mine, which predetermines the generational divide between us. This characterizes the communication with my parents, when there is any such, and the answers to their questions are reduced to short answers like "Yes" and "No".

A 25-year-old's impressions of communicating with her mother were:

My mother is often annoying and asks me questions for my personal life that I do not consider appropriate. But I attribute them to her worry whether everything is okay with me, especially when we haven't heard from each other in a while.

The dependence-independence between the mother and her children, the attempt to enter the personal space and the encounter of resistance in the opposite side to make it happen also cause the conversations not to proceed smoothly, despite the preliminary desire of both parties. Generally, in families not living together, the generational divide could also be due to the different socio-economic environment and dynamics of life, the multidimensional perception and interpretation of reality, as well as the sense of apathy.

In comparison, the percentage of representatives of families not living together, who consider that there is no generational divide between the youngest and the oldest family member is higher (61%). This may be due to the fact that they do not actually live with their relatives and do not have to face daily the differences in communication and perception of the world. And it may also be due to the existing nostalgia and the idealization of the loved ones who are far from the particular person. Nevertheless, 28% of the interviewed families not living together consider that there is a generational divide and 11% stated that they could not say so (Fig. 3).

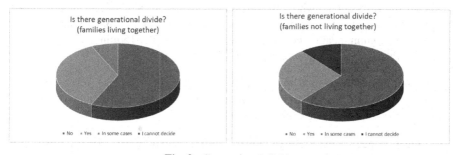

Fig. 3. Generational divide

Almost all respondents from both types of families (93%) believe that the generational divide can be overcome through more communication, greater tolerance for one another more time spent together, more conversations and games with younger members of the family. Only 7% claim that this generational divide will always exist and there is nothing to be done about it.

One of the respondents, a man 65 years old, stated:

Generational divide could be only overcome by constant conversations, conversations and conversations again. Whether there is a problem, a hesitation, a situation to solve, the most important is to keep a lively dialogue with children. Otherwise, the generational divide will deepen enormously.

Work, Integration and Health of the Older Adults. Half of all respondents from both types of families (50%) were of the opinion that older adults should continue to work after retirement. As a motive for this understanding, they pointed out the fact that in this way people will be more motivated, engaged and will feel better. Another 36% considered that it is a decision that depends on the individual himself, on the situation he/she is in, and on whether he/she feels comfortable, etc. Only 14% stated firmly that the older adults should not work after retirement. It is interesting to note that these answers were given by young family members, and the motive they pointed out was that after retirement, people are less able to work and get tired easily (Fig. 4).

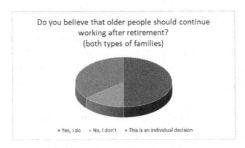

Fig. 4. Work after retirement

7% of the respondents who gave this answer are those who openly acknowledge the generational divide in communication between them and their older relatives, with average daily communication between them in the range of 5–15 min.

One of the interviewees, a woman of 70, shared:

After retirement, it is good to give yourself a well-deserved rest, to pay more attention to your grandchildren, to help your children, as well as to receive a fair pension for the work done over the years.

As the average pension in Bulgaria is not high (less than EUR 200) [14], this is also among the reasons that some older people are economically forced to continue working.

A 76 years old man pointed out that working for him is also a way to break away from the banality of everyday life. He also stated:

My pension and that of my wife are not enough, so I continue to work, albeit a low-skilled job as a janitor in a parking lot.

Asked whether older adults are socially integrated, a total of 79% of all families in the sample answered "to a small extent", 7% were fully categorical that the older generation is not integrated in the modern society. Other 7% stated that all depends on the individuals. And only 7% considered that the older adults in the country are largely socially integrated.

51% of all respondents from both types of families believe that information and communication technologies have a positive effect on the health of the older adults, because, thanks to the media and information on the internet, people are more informed and aware of different health services, technologies and innovations that would help them as long as they have the necessary resources for that. 14% strongly agree that information and communication technologies do not in any way help elderly with regard to their health. Another 14% consider that communication technologies help raise awareness of the health status of the older adults, but only of those living in big cities. 7% of the respondents are of the opinion that the elderly are failing to take advantage of information and communication technologies and are not fully informed on important for them issues. Another 7% state that technologies had impact on them, however not positive, but by offering various advertising products and services that aim not to cure them but for a commercial purpose. The survey also reflects the opinion of 7% seniors who rely on health TV shows or specialized newspapers (such as the *Third Age*) for appropriate information (Fig. 5).

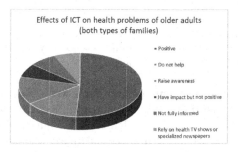

Fig. 5. Effects on health problems

One of the 65 years old respondents stated:

I read in Third Age what is recommended for tone, for a healthy heart or for what to take to keep my blood pressure normal.

In connection with the development of the new technologies, the survey also contains a non-standard question regarding the presence of a robot prototype of someone's relative, with whom one could share daily experiences and everyday needs. When asked whether this robot could substitute the person whose prototype it is, 57% of the family members living together responded that this could happen, but to a small extent. 36% claimed categorically that no talk about substitution could take place and only 7% stated that they could not judge.

Compared to family members living together, only 33% of the family members not living together stated that such a robot-prototype could substitute to a small extent their loved one in their everyday life. 55% were adamant that a robot would not substitute a loved one, 7% stated that they could not judge and another 5% were of the opinion that such a robot to a great extent could substitute the physical contact with a loved one (Fig. 6).

It is interesting to note that the percentage of people not living together who would not substitute their close relative with a robot-prototype is higher than among the family members living together. The sense of nostalgia and the idealization of relatives who are far from the other family members can also intervene here.

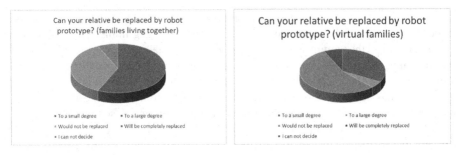

Fig. 6. Robot-prototype as a substitute

The overall result from the both types of families shows a rather important conclusion, namely that modern representatives of families do not completely reject the idea of a robot-prototype to substitute their loved ones.

Conclusions, Limitations and Implications for Future Research. The results in answering the research question: Does the intergenerational divide deepen in the virtual family over time? indicate that the different daily routine and lifestyle of the family members could alienate them. The distance and time of separation further intensifies this feeling. Everyday experiences, emotions, problems and worries often exclude the involvement of the virtual family. Although virtual relationships and virtual family are extremely complex phenomena, availability of relatively frequent and qualified communication often turns out to be vital for the survival of the family structure and for preservation of the relationship.

Due to some study time constraints the results in the current paper could not fully measure whether the intergenerational divide deepen in the virtual family over time. This problematic issue should be studied further over a longer period in future research.

Despite these limitations, the answers of the respondents support more completely the second research question: How the communication is changing in the virtual family compared with the traditional one? One of the conclusions is that with the development of new modern technologies family members, whether living or not together, are less able to find themselves in a situation where they cannot communicate with each other. Communication tools are constantly increasing their capacity in every aspect. Communication becomes a matter of specific attitude and desire, of choice of means and of a recipient.

Besides, among the family members not living together is observed the fact that there are almost no taboo topics and people share almost any emotions, regardless of distance and whether they communicate more via social networks or over the phone. Even more, sometimes in families living together, there is a larger generational divide and restraint of emotions than with the families not living together. Cohabitation together does not always lead to a closer relationship and more trust and commitment to the other. On the other hand, the different lifestyles of family members lead rather to their alienation. Daily experiences, emotions, dating, problems and anxieties often preclude the involvement of relatives, and sharing is not specific to them or is limited by the reasoning mostly of young people that adults will not understand them as they have spent most of their lifespan at another time.

On the other hand, the question arises whether a short remote conversation of 30 min a day on average could completely displace daily communication with loved ones. The fact that some family members do not live together with the others allows them to do things that they rarely share when communicating with each other. This raises the question of whether these things are becoming taboo topics in their perception or they simply do not find it necessary to share them. For example, topics that children avoid discussing with their parents often affect their privacy, thus trying to prevent any interference in it and gain personal freedom. As a consequence, the question arises as to what extent virtual and real communication is subject to comparison and to what extent the expectations for both are the same.

The difference in views on life and the world between the youngest and the oldest in one family can be clarified through more communication, insight into the problems of the other and compromises on both sides. This is the opinion of most of the interviewed family members. Few of them believe that such an abyss exists and much less that it is a problem that interferes with daily communication. The idea of a robot-prototype of someone's relative to substitute the real person in everyday communication, sharing experiences and providing assistance, albeit to a small extent, is accepted by the members of both types of families. In modern society there are almost no family members who do not have and do not use communication and information technologies on a daily basis. As they get used to them, people expect more and more new technologies to hit the market, and stereotypes about communication and the means to use them, more and more to improve. Communication tools, which in the past were only found in fantasy novels, are now not only a reality but also an integral part of people's daily lives. The idea of robots entering our daily lives for a long time is not associated with negative evaluation only. The extent to which technologies are moving in this direction changes the attitudes of society making it ready to accept this idea.

At the same time, remote communication between family members is dynamically dependent on the constant internal and external changes of the environment – cultural, technological, corporative, which determines the need of further in-depth research in this relatively new scientific field.

Acknowledgements. The paper has been developed within the framework of COST Action CA16226 *Indoor Living Space Improvement: Smart Habitat for the Elderly* (SHELD-ON) of the European Commission, supported by the research projects KP-06-COST/5-18/06/2019 and KP-06-M35/4-18/12/2019 of the National Scientific Fund of Bulgaria and the Program *Young Scientists and Post Docs* of the Bulgarian Ministry of Education and Science.

References

1. Raycheva, L., Velinova, N.: Reappraising the intellectual debate on ageing in a digital environment. In: Zhou, J., Salvendy, G. (eds.) HCII 2019. LNCS, vol. 11592, pp. 300–312. Springer, Cham (2019). https://doi.org/10.1007/978-3-030-22012-9_22

 2. United Nations: The United Nations Principles for Older Persons (1991). http://www.olderp eoplewales.com/en/about/un-principles.aspx
 3. United Nations: Madrid International Plan of Action on Ageing (2014). http://www.unescap. org/resources/madrid-international-plan-action-ageing
 4. Sánchez, L., Goldani, A.: The changing shape of ties in European families: profiles and intentions of LAT couples. Presented at Population and Association of America 2012, in Session 56: Non-marital and Diverse Family Forms (2012)
 5. Tomov, M.: Human-computer interaction (HCI) between "virtual family" members: a Bulgarian case. In: Meiselwitz, G. (ed.) HCII 2019. LNCS, vol. 11579, pp. 54–67. Springer, Cham (2019). https://doi.org/10.1007/978-3-030-21905-5_5
 6. McLuhan, M.: The Gutenberg Galaxy. University of Toronto Press, Toronto (1962)
 7. Castells, M.: The Rise of the Network Society, 2nd edn. Oxford Blackwell, Oxford (2000)
 8. Loos, E., de la Hera, T., Simons, M., Gevers, D.: Setting up and conducting the co-design of an intergenerational digital game: a state-of-the-art literature review. In: Zhou, J., Salvendy, G. (eds.) HCII 2019. LNCS, vol. 11592, pp. 56–69. Springer, Cham (2019). https://doi.org/ 10.1007/978-3-030-22012-9_5
 9. Fortunati, L.: Is body to body communication still the prototype? Inf. Soc. **21**(1), 53–61 (2005)
10. Duncombe, J., Marsden, D.: Love and intimacy: the gender division of emotion and 'emotion work': a neglected aspect of sociological discussion of heterosexual relationships. Sociology **27**(2), 221–241 (1993). https://doi.org/10.1177/0038038593027002003
11. Bulgarian Sociologist Association: Code of Ethics (2004). http://bsa-bg.eu/bsa1/wp-content/ uploads/2018/07/ethical_code.pdf
12. Miller, D., Madianou, M.: Migration and New Media: Transnational Families and Polymedia. Routledge, New York (2011)
13. Stoyanova, D.: Conceptual and technological approaches to parental education in the context of positive-oriented family upbringing. Sci. Pap. Univ. Ruse **51**(6.2), 129–133 (2012)
14. National Social Security Institute: Pensions statistical bulletin as of 30 June 2019 (2019). https://www.nssi.bg/images/bg/about/statisticsandanalysis/statistics/pensii/STATB2 2019.pdf

The Relationship Between Social Participation and Internet Addiction in Older Persons

Javiera Rosell[(✉)] and Alvaro Vergés

Escuela de Psicología, Pontificia Universidad Católica de Chile, Santiago, Chile
{jerosell,ajverges}@uc.cl

Abstract. The addiction to technology of older persons is an emerging field, because the literature tends to focus only on the benefits of the use of technology in this age group. Along with this, there is interest in how participation improves the quality of life of older persons. In this context, the present study aims to examine the association between the level of participation of older individuals and their addictive behaviors to Internet, including lack of control and emotional deregulation. All this, considering the social influence for the use of the Internet as a mediator of this relationship. For this, 151 older Internet users answered a set of questions about internet addiction, level of participation, and social influence for the use of technology. A structural equation modeling was carried out to evaluate the mediation model. The results show that the level of participation is indirectly associated with the two dimensions of Internet addiction, via the social influence that promotes the use of technology. This has important implications in the development of interventions that encourage Internet use in older persons, decreasing addictive behaviors that could emerge as the use of technology becomes more common.

Keywords: Internet addiction · Older persons · Social participation

1 Introduction

The negative consequences of Information and Communication Technologies (ICT) use, such as addictive behaviors, have been less explored than its benefits. However, these should also be considered for a complete understanding of the impact of ICT on people's well-being [1]. Along with this, the evaluation of technology addiction has been carried out predominantly in the young population. For this reason, there is a lack of evidence regarding what happens with older persons. This aspect is relevant, since, although the extension of the use of ICT is higher in young people than in the population over 60 years, the literature points to a growing motivation for the use of ICT by this age group [2].

In general, addiction to technology is evaluated by analyzing the interference and mismatch caused by its use in the activities of the person's daily life [3]. It has been established that ICT use becomes addictive and pathological when it generates dependence, reflected, for example, in loss of control or its use to cope with stress or unpleasant feelings [4].

© Springer Nature Switzerland AG 2020
Q. Gao and J. Zhou (Eds.): HCII 2020, LNCS 12209, pp. 301–311, 2020.
https://doi.org/10.1007/978-3-030-50232-4_21

In this context, there is an interest in Internet use as a strategy to cope with stress and how this can be transformed into an addiction to technology [5]. This discussion is relevant from a gerontological perspective, where an issue of concern is the different strategies to cope with aging and its changes.

Furthermore, the active and healthy aging, proposed by the World Health Organization [6, 7], highlights the link of the participation of older persons with their well-being. In this sense, the active participation of older persons improves well-being in old age, reducing the probability of impairment and dependence.

ICT use has been found to increase social contact and decrease loneliness in older persons. This is one of the main benefits of the use of technology by this age group [8–10]. Some authors state that the positive effects found in some studies that evaluate the impact of the use of technology in older persons are due to the socialization with the group participating in the intervention rather than the use of ICT itself, although this is an aspect that should be further explored [9].

Also, the Unified Theory of Acceptance and Use of Technology (UTAUT) [11] raises social influence as a fundamental dimension that facilitates the use of technological devices. This model has also been tested with older persons, where the social influence factor acts as a significant predictor of the use of technology [12]. Along with this, several studies have identified social influence as a fundamental factor for an older person to decide to use technology; this includes family, friends, and organizations [13]

The impact of ICT use on the psychological well-being of older persons has also been studied. For instance, ICT use decreases depressive symptomatology or suicidal ideation [14–16] and increases life satisfaction [17]. However, the literature that assesses the relationship of the psychological well-being of older people with the use of ICT has paid less attention to potential harmful aspects, focusing more on the benefits of this use [1]. Therefore, the exploration of the negative aspects of the use of technology in this age group is necessary.

To understand these negative aspects, such as internet addiction, it is crucial to include motivations of use. This will provide information to understand why the person continues to be contacted despite the adverse effects [18]. From this perspective, the compensatory model proposes an alternative understanding of the concept of technology addiction. Its purpose is to explore the reasons for using ICT, with the purpose to explain the use of the Internet as a mean to escape or regulate negative moods [5].

Thus, compensatory behaviors through Internet use can bring positive or negative results. One of the negative consequences is addiction, generated by the level of compensation and use that is required to alleviate negative emotional states [5]. In this sense, it has been argued that the time connected to the Internet is not in itself an indicator of problematic use, although they are variables that correlate strongly [19]. In contrast, the concern for social acceptance has been found to be a factor that predisposes to higher addictive Internet behaviors [20]. At this point, it is important to clarify the difference between addiction to the Internet and addiction on the Internet, because, in this last case, the person uses technology to conduct an addictive behavior (e.g., gambling), beyond the use of technology itself, so the Internet use is just a means for other typo of addiction [21].

Concerning psychological well-being, the literature describes negative consequences of the use of technology associated with addictive behaviors such as less social skills, self-motivation, empathy, and depression [22]. A study with young people found that the use of ICT to avoid negative feelings was associated with worse levels of mental health [18]. This is related to the increase in psychological vulnerability that occurs with all types of addiction, including the problematic use of the Internet [23].

Similarly, a study with young Smartphone users found a positive association between problematic use of the device with anxious symptomatology [24]. However, the frequency of use was negatively related to depressive symptomatology; that is, those who used more the device had lower symptoms of depression. The authors consider two theories regarding the inverse relationship of Smartphone use with depressive symptomatology, the first one related to the lower Smartphone use of people with depression, and the second one involving the greater distraction of emotional depressive contents as a result of the device use.

Regarding life satisfaction, the impulsive behaviors in the use of ICT turn into a lower level of life satisfaction, predominantly in male users [25].

In this context, the present study aims to describe the association between the level of participation of older individuals and their addictive behaviors toward the Internet, including a lack of control and emotional deregulation. All this, considering the social influence for the use of the Internet as a mediator of this relationship.

We hypothesized that social participation and social influence increases Internet use in older persons, which can favor addictive behaviors such as lack of control and emotional deregulation. The literature highlights social influence as a predictor of technology use [11, 13, 26] and suggests that ICT use can reduce the feeling of loneliness and increase social contact. We sought to provide inputs to understand more clearly the link between the use of the Internet in older persons and its negative consequences, which in turn could promote interventions that favor a good use of the Internet in the older population.

2 Methodology

2.1 Sample and Procedures

The sample was composed of 151 Internet users over 60 years without cognitive impairment. Sociodemographic information like gender and education level was collected.

The exclusion criterion was time disorientation of the participant because it is an indicator sensitive to cognitive impairment [27].

Participants were recruited through email, social networks, and organizations for older persons. Instruments were applied online (Google Forms) or on paper, where all participants had to accept voluntary participation in the study through the informed consent approved by the Institutional Ethics Committee.

2.2 Measures

Level of Participation. This was assessed through 6 questions about participation in different activities such as sports, culture, neighborhood association, and senior clubs.

Also, this question had the option of adding another type of activity in which the person participates. From this, a variable was created with the sum of the different activities. Higher scores indicate that the person participates in more different activities.

Social Influence. This was evaluated through 3 items of the Unified Theory of Accepting and Use of Technology (UTAUT), which has a Likert response format between 1 (strongly disagree) and 7 (strongly agree), for example, "people who are important to me think that I should use the internet" [11]. The original version of the items is in English and has not been formally validated in Spanish. However, a translation has been used for its evaluation in the Chilean population, where the measurement model showed factor loadings over 0.5 in all items and a Cronbach's Alpha of .96 [28]. The items used were based on this translation. Also, only the word "internet" was used instead of "mobile internet," as it is a more comprehensive concept of different ICT.

Internet Addiction. This was evaluated through the Internet Addiction Test (IAT) validated in Chile [29], including 10 items with a 6-point Likert type response between 0 (not applicable) and 5 (always), for example, "How often do you realize that you stay connected on the Internet longer than you planned?" or "How often do you lose hours of sleep by being connected late at night?". This questionnaire has a structure with two factors: loss of control and an emotional deregulation factor. The loss of control factor includes items about the neglect of daily life activities because of the connection and difficulties to stop the connection when it is required (for example, when it is time to sleep). The emotional regulation factor includes items about psychological discomfort associated with the interruption of internet use or the use of Internet to cope with unpleasant thoughts. For data analysis, the categories "frequently", "almost always" and "always" were collapsed. So, the analysis was carried out with only 4 categories in these items.

2.3 Data Analysis

The evaluation of the mediation model was carried out through a structural equation model (SEM), where the participation level was a predictor of the two dimensions of internet addiction, mediated by social influence. For this, the measurement model was evaluated to verify that the dimensions had robust indicators in this sample. Also, the structural model was established to evaluate the relationship between the variables. This procedure allows describing the direct association between participation and the two dimensions of addiction to Internet and also the indirect effect through social influence.

The WLSMV estimator was used because it is appropriate for the study with ordinal items [30]. The CFI, TLI, RMSEA, and SRMR indexes were considered to assess model fit, with cut-off values higher than .95 for the first two and lower than .08 for the last two [31, 32].

The structural equation model was performed with Mplus 8 [33]. The rest of the analyses were performed with R 3.6.1.

3   Results

3.1   Sample Characteristics

The final sample was composed of 76.8% of females. The average age was 69.6 years ($SD = 6.6$), with a range between 60 and 92 years. The predominant educational level was university studies (25%) and postgraduate studies (14.5%). However, 19% of the participants did not have a complete primary education.

The average participation in different activities was 2.37 ($SD = 1.42$), with a range between 0 and 7 activities. Table 1 shows the frequencies and percentages of participation in different activities.

Table 1. Percentage of older persons who reported participating in activities

Activity	N (%)
Senior clubs	68 (45.03)
Neighborhood association	60 (39.74)
Culture	56 (37.09)
Sports	54 (35.76)
Religion	52 (34.44)
Politics	11 (7.28)

3.2   Addiction to Internet

Being connected to the Internet more than the expected time is one of the addictive behaviors that was reported most frequently among older participants, since 40% reported that it happens frequently, almost always or always.

On the other hand, getting angry, shouting, or getting irritated when they are interrupted while online is one of the addictive behaviors reported less frequently, where 67% said it happens rarely.

Table 2 shows the percentages of response by category in each of the items related to addiction to Internet.

3.3   Relationship Between Participation and Addiction to Technology with Social Influence as Mediator

For the initial mediation model, all the loadings were over .3 in their respective dimensions but not all fit indices were in the acceptable range $\chi^2 (72) = 184.219, p < .01$, CFI $= .98$, TLI $= .975$, RMSEA $= .102$, SRMR $= .062$. After this, the modification indices were evaluated, which suggested a high correlation between item 3 of IAT (emotional deregulation factor) and items 1 and 6 of IAT (loss of control factor). To improve the fit of the model, the cross-loading of item 3 on the two factors of the IAT was included. However, this yielded an improper solution (i.e., negative residual variance).

Table 2. Percentage of response by category in items of addiction to internet

	Does not apply	Rarely	Occasionally	Frequently, almost always or always
How often do you realize that you stay connected on the Internet longer than you planned?	21.2	17.2	21.2	40.4
How often do you neglect household chores to spend more time online?	31.1	31.1	29.1	8.6
How often do you fear that life without internet would be boring, empty and sad?	36.4	34.4	13.9	15.2
How often do you get angry, scream, or get irritated if someone interrupts you while online?	43.7	44.4	7.9	4.0
How often do you lose sleep because of being connected until late at night?	44.4	31.8	12.6	11.3
How often do you find yourself saying "just a couple more minutes" when connected?	37.1	28.5	21.2	13.2
How often do you try to reduce the time you spend on the internet and fail?	40.4	37.1	16.6	6.0
How often do you choose to spend more time online instead of dating other people?	49.7	32.5	13.2	4.6
How often do you feel depressed, cranky or nervous when you are not connected to the internet, and do you feel better when you connect again?	55.0	36.4	5.3	3.3

For this reason, item 3 was eliminated from the IAT, achieving an adequate model fit: $\chi 2$ (60) = 115.977, $p < .01$, CFI = .99, TLI = .987, RMSEA = .079, SRMR = .053. All paths were significant, except for the direct relationship between participation and loss of control ($\beta = .11, p = .14$) and the direct relationship between participation and emotional deregulation ($\beta = .07, p = .40$) (see Fig. 1).

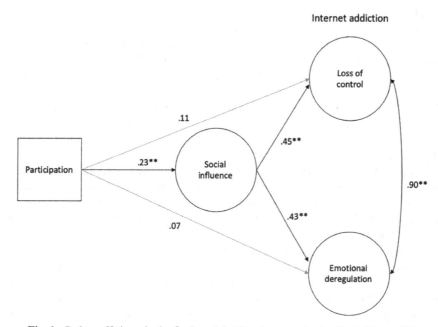

Fig. 1. Path coefficients in the final model. All values are standardized. **p < .001

Moreover, social influence significantly mediated the association of participation with loss of control (indirect effect: $\beta = .10, p = .014$). The same applies to the association between participation and emotional deregulation, which was mediated by social influence (indirect effect: $\beta = .098, p = .014$).

4 Discussion

It is necessary to generate comprehensive models that explain the influence of the use of technology in older persons, especially regarding their psychological well-being. While there has been progress in the generation of evidence in this area, many studies continue to focus only on the beneficial aspects of the use of technology, neglecting the negative dimension that may impact the psychological well-being of older persons. In this sense, the results of the present study provide evidence regarding technology addiction in older persons and the factors that favor it.

Results show the importance of participation in the use of Internet among older persons, because it correlates with social contact and, therefore, social influence for Internet use. However, it was observed that this is associated with addictive behaviors, with more lack of control over the connection, for example, spending more time online than was planned or neglecting the responsibilities in daily life activities. Similarly, participation and, in turn, social influence, was also associated with emotional deregulation in internet use, for example, feeling irritable if someone interrupts or prevents from getting online. Also, emotional deregulation includes the use of Internet to forget unpleasant thought, which could explain why people stayed connected despite negative consequences (for example, fewer hours of sleep).

It is essential to analyze why people remain connected despite negative consequences to understand internet addiction [5]. The results of the present study allow hypothesizing that the great social influence produced by contact with others through participation, drives the person to stay connected more than the desired time, even neglecting their commitments or duties.

It can be hypothesized that higher participation and more social influence also imply greater online socialization, allowing the person to feel less lonely due to the maintenance of contact with their friends and family [8, 9]. However, it must be ensured that this connection does not involve addictive Internet behavior.

Along with this, the increase in participation in different activities favors social influence to stay connected and therefore increases the desire of the person to be accepted and recognized by their peers if they use technology. This concern for social acceptance has been described as an aspect that is associated with higher addictive behaviors in the use of technology [20].

In this sense, it is essential to be able to generate interventions where older people can be educated in a satisfactory use of the Internet, and that this does not become a factor that leads to emotional deregulation or lack of impulse control when connected. This is especially relevant because it has been shown that the use of technology can favor the psychological well-being of older persons through the decrease in depressive symptomatology or the increase in life satisfaction [16, 17]. However, it seems that not all ways of staying connected are suitable for this psychological well-being.

Thus, the present study goes beyond the positive aspects of the use of technology in older persons. Therefore, results are a contribution to overcoming the bias that technology is good in itself [1].

As far as we know, this is one of the first studies that discuss the issue of addiction to technology in older persons, proposing a model that advances our understanding of this phenomenon. These aspects can be useful in digital literacy interventions for older persons, where information and tools for less addictive ways of using the Internet should be considered.

However, some limitations of the current study should be noted, mainly regarding sample size and its composition with a large number of people with a high educational level. However, it should be considered that the educational level of older people is associated with greater use of technology [34]. Besides, the cross-sectional design does not allow establishing causality among the variables included in the model.

In turn, future research should consider the different activities that the person can perform online. This would make it possible to determine whether contact with others is one of the main goals that older people have when connecting to the Internet. In this way, new explanatory models can be generated where online contact with others is included as a reason to explain the addiction to technology.

Acknowledgments.. This work was supported by the Comisión Nacional de Investigación Científica y Tecnológica de Chile - CONICYT-PFCHA/Doctorado Nacional/2017-21170060 and the Fund for Innovation and Competitiveness (FIC) of the Chilean Ministry for the Economy Development and Tourism, through the Millennium Scientific Initiative under "grant number IS130005".

References

1. Dickinson, A., Gregor, P.: Computer use has no demonstrated impact on the well-being of older adults. Int. J. Hum Comput Stud. **64**, 744–753 (2006). https://doi.org/10.1016/j.ijhcs.2006.03.001
2. Wagner, N., Hassanein, K., Head, M.: Computer use by older adults: a multi-disciplinary review. Comput. Hum. Behav. **26**, 870–882 (2010). https://doi.org/10.1016/j.chb.2010.03.029
3. Beranuy Fargues, M., Chamarro Lusar, A., Graner Jordania, C., Carbonell Sánchez, X.: Validacion de dos escalas breves para evaluar la adiccion a internet y el abuso de movil. Psicothema. **21**, 480–485 (2009). https://doi.org/10.1016/S1001-7844(10)60008-9
4. Chamarro, A., et al.: El cuestionario de experiencias relacionadas con los videojuegos (CERV): Un instrumento para detectar el uso problemático de videojuegos en adolescentes españoles. Adicciones **26**, 303–311 (2014). https://doi.org/10.20882/adicciones.31
5. Kardefelt-Winther, D.: Computers in human behavior a conceptual and methodological critique of internet addiction research: towards a model of compensatory internet use. Comput. Hum. Behav. **31**, 351–354 (2014). https://doi.org/10.1016/j.chb.2013.10.059
6. World Health Organization: World Report On Ageing And Health. World Health Organization, Geneva (2015)
7. World Health Organization: Active Ageing: A Policy Framework., Spain (2002)
8. Berg, T., Winterton, R., Petersen, M., Warburton, J.: Although we're isolated, we're not really isolated: the value of information and communication technology for older people in rural Australia. Aust. J. Ageing. **36**, 313–317 (2017). https://doi.org/10.1111/ajag.12449
9. Chen, Y.-R.R., Schulz, P.J.: The effect of information communication technology interventions on reducing social isolation in the elderly: a systematic review. J. Med. Internet Res. **18**, 1–11 (2016). https://doi.org/10.2196/jmir.4596
10. Heo, J., Chun, S., Lee, S., Lee, K.H., Kim, J.: Internet use and well-being in older adults. Cyberpsychology, Behav. Soc. Netw. **18**, 268–272 (2015). https://doi.org/10.1089/cyber.2014.0549
11. Venkatesh, V., Morris, M.G., Davis, G.B., Davis, F.D.: User acceptance of information technology: toward a unified view. MIS Q. **27**, 425–478 (2003)
12. Macedo, I.M.: Predicting the acceptance and use of information and communication technology by older adults: an empirical examination of the revised UTAUT2. Comput. Hum. Behav. **75**, 935–948 (2017). https://doi.org/10.1016/j.chb.2017.06.013
13. Tsertsidis, A., Kolkowska, E., Hedström, K.: Factors influencing seniors' acceptance of technology for ageing in place in the post-implementation stage: a literature review. Int. J. Med. Inf. **129**, 324–333 (2019). https://doi.org/10.1016/j.ijmedinf.2019.06.027
14. Cotten, S.R., Ford, G., Ford, S., Hale, T.M.: Internet use and depression among retired older adults in the United States: a longitudinal analysis. J. Gerontol. Ser. B Psychol. Sci. Soc. Sci. **69**, 763–771 (2014). https://doi.org/10.1093/geronb/gbu018

15. Cotten, S.R., Ford, G., Ford, S., Hale, T.M.: Internet use and depression among older adults. Comput. Hum. Behav. **28**, 496–499 (2012). https://doi.org/10.1016/j.chb.2011.10.021

16. Jun, H.J., Kim, M.-Y.: What accounts for the relationship between internet use and suicidal ideation of korean older adults? a mediation analysis. J. Gerontol. Ser. B. Psychol. Sci. Soc. Sci. **72**, 846–855 (2017). https://doi.org/10.1093/geronb/gbw163

17. Lifshitz, R., Nimrod, G., Bachner, Y.G.: Internet use and well-being in later life: a functional approach. Aging Ment. Health **22**, 85–91 (2016). https://doi.org/10.1080/13607863.2016.123 2370

18. Panova, T., Lleras, A.: Avoidance or boredom: negative mental health outcomes associated with use of information and communication technologies depend on users' motivations. Comput. Hum. Behav. **58**, 249–258 (2016). https://doi.org/10.1016/j.chb.2015.12.062

19. Carbonell, X., Chamarro, A., Griffiths, M., Oberst, U., Cladellas, R., Talarn, A.: Problematic internet and cell phone use in Spanish teenagers and young students. An. Psicol. **28**, 789–796 (2012). https://doi.org/10.6018/analesps.28.3.156061

20. Seo, D.B., Ray, S.: Habit and addiction in the use of social networking sites: their nature, antecedents, and consequences. Comput. Hum. Behav. **99**, 109–125 (2019). https://doi.org/10.1016/j.chb.2019.05.018

21. Widyanto, L., Griffiths, M.: Internet addiction: a critical review. Int. J. Ment. Health Addict. **4**, 31–51 (2006). https://doi.org/10.1007/s11469-006-9009-9

22. Scott, D.A., Valley, B., Simecka, B.A.: Mental health concerns in the digital age. Int. J. Ment. Health Addict. **15**(3), 604–613 (2016). https://doi.org/10.1007/s11469-016-9684-0

23. Griffiths, M.: A components model of addiction within a biopsychosocil framework. J. Subst. Use. **10**, 191–197 (2005). https://doi.org/10.1080/14659890500114359

24. Elhai, J., Levine, J., Dvorak, R., Hall, B.: Fear of missing out, need for touch, anxiety and depression are related to problematic smartphone use. Comput. Hum. Behav. **63**, 509–516 (2016). https://doi.org/10.1016/j.chb.2016.05.079

25. Dhir, A., Chen, S., Nieminen, M.: Psychometric validation of the compulsive internet use scale: relationship with adolescents' demographics, ICT accessibility, and problematic ICT use. Soc. Sci. Comput. Rev. **34**, 197–214 (2016). https://doi.org/10.1177/0894439315572575

26. Peek, S.T.M., Wouters, E.J.M., van Hoof, J., Luijkx, K.G., Boeije, H.R., Vrijhoef, H.J.M.: Factors influencing acceptance of technology for aging in place: a systematic review. Int. J. Med. Inf. **83**, 235–248 (2014). https://doi.org/10.1016/j.ijmedinf.2014.01.004

27. O'Keeffe, E., Mukhtar, O., O'Keeffe, S.T.: Orientation to time as a guide to the presence and severity of cognitive impairment in older hospital patients. J. Neurol. Neurosurg. Psychiatry **82**, 500–504 (2011). https://doi.org/10.1136/jnnp.2010.214817

28. Ramírez-Correa, P., Grandón, E., Painén-Aravena, G.: Efectos de los rasgos de personalidad en el uso de las tecnologías de información. Multidiscip. Bus. Rev. **10**, 19–26 (2017)

29. Hernández Contreras, C., Rivera Ottenberger, D.: Adaptación Transcultural y Evaluación de las Estructuras Factoriales del Test de Adicción a Internet en Chile: Desarrollo de una Versión Abreviada. Rev. Iberoam. Diagnóstico y Evaluación **49**, 143–155 (2018). https://doi.org/10.21865/RIDEP49.4.12

30. Hoyle, R.H.: Handbook of Structural Equation Modeling. The Guilford Press, New York (2012)

31. Hu, L.T., Bentler, P.M.: Cutoff criteria for fit indexes in covariance structure analysis: conventional criteria versus new alternatives. Struct. Equ. Model. A Multidiscip. J. **6**, 1–55 (1999). https://doi.org/10.1080/10705519909540118

32. MacCallum, R.C., Browne, M.W., Sugawara, H.M.: Power analysis and determination of sample size for covariance structure modeling. Psychol. Methods **1**, 130–149 (1996). https://doi.org/10.1037/1082-989X.1.2.130

33. Muthén, L., Muthén, B.: Mplus User's Guide (2017)
34. Quintana, D., Cervantes, A., Sáez, Y., Isasi, P.: Internet use and psychological well-being at advanced age : evidence from the english longitudinal study of aging. Int. J. Environ. Res. Publ. Health **15**(3), 480 (2018). https://doi.org/10.3390/ijerph15030480

Age and the City: The Case of Smart Mobility

Maria Sourbati$^{(\boxtimes)}$ (iD)

School of Media, University of Brighton, Brighton, UK
m.sourbati@brighton.ac.uk

Abstract. This article investigates social inclusion from the perspective of smart mobility and transport, which are core aspects of smart city policy. More specifically, it discusses older people's mobility practice in smart city environments as a phenomenon at the intersection of age, digital ICT and data. Drawing on mobility studies, communications and critical data studies the article uses the following questions to frame its analysis of inclusive smart transport services from the perspective of old and advanced age: How transport (and) mobility practices interact with mobile ICT use in smart cities? What do we know about the transport mobilities of older people? What do we know about the mobile media and ICT practices of older people? After introducing the concepts of smart city and smart mobility the article discusses these questions through literature review, secondary data, and examples from public transportation services in the city of London, one of Europe's principal 'smart' cities. The analysis highlights age-bias in inherited transport system, gaps in available data about older people's mobility practices and their media and ICT use, and opportunities for more inclusive (and sustainable) smart transport.

Keywords: Age · Data · Older people · Smart city · Smart mobility · Social inclusion

1 Introduction: Smart Cities and Smart Transport

Cities are both physical and conceptual realms. Key functions in city systems such as transportation, communication, education and policing comprise built, material and digital environments including green spaces, transport networks and Wi-Fi infrastructure, [1, 2]. The 'smart city' concept first emerged under initiatives by global tech companies such as CISCO https://blogs.cisco.com/tag/smart-cities and IBM and has been proposed as digital upgrades to the built city and its institutions. According to IBM, a smart city 'makes optimal use of all the interconnected information available today to better understand and control its operations and optimise the use of limited resources' [3]. The concept of smart city entails 'the use of intelligent solutions' for infrastructure, energy, housing, mobility, services, and security, 'based on integrated sensor technology, connectivity, data analytics, and independently functional value-added processes' [4] (p. 25). This kind of 'smart city' ideas and practices can be seen to 'apply technologies to cities' [2] (p. 45).

© Springer Nature Switzerland AG 2020
Q. Gao and J. Zhou (Eds.): HCII 2020, LNCS 12209, pp. 312–326, 2020.
https://doi.org/10.1007/978-3-030-50232-4_22

Smart city solutions apply big data to urban governance [5] as a new way to understand and address urban problems in which 'ICT is merged with traditional infrastructures, coordinated and integrated using new digital technologies' [6] (p. 481). This is a techno-centric model, where an analysis of social, spatial, transport and environmental data, generated through communications systems and integrated into the structures of the city can provide a general understanding of the living conditions in these cities [1] (p. 32). Resonating this perspective the European Commission sees the advantages of smart cities laying in making the traditional city systems and services more efficient with the use of digital ICT 'for the benefit of [city's] inhabitants and businesses' [7]. Internationally, smart cities are widely considered as the new engine for economic and social growth supported by digital, networked ICTs [8].

Smart mobility is a core element of smart city initiatives. Enabled by networked communications smart mobility and transport can be understood as a convergence of movement in the physical space and in data flow. In an urban setting the application of networked ICT capability in existing mobility systems, including sensors in public roads and parks, IoT solutions built into public and private transportation modes such as buses and cars, and citizens' use of networked ICT, generates millions of data points, which can be processed to create insights that help improve mobility. The potential of smart mobility to improve quality of life, sustainability and economic opportunities through digital support for connected mobility in cities is increasingly recognized in public policy, both in Europe and internationally [7]. According to Gassmann, Böhm and Palmié [4] (p. 40) smart mobility pursues the following core objectives: sustainable, innovative, and secure transportation systems; access to diverse transportation modes; good availability in the entire city; inclusion of nonmotorized transportation; integration of ICT in transportation systems.

From an 'end-user' perspective – this of the citizens—the smartphone becomes an essential technology in the smart city. The smartphone becomes 'the platform for reinventing smart cities from the bottom up' [9] (p. xiv). Described as 'computers on wheels' [10] smartphones can transform moving vehicles, means of transport and movement in urban spaces. A familiar, to many, example of innovative applications of smartphone data is the sharing of rides in cars. 'Carpooling' was launched as a successful commercial service in 2016 by Uber's ride sharing option *Uberpool* and became commercial success in cities across the world.

Policy and industry attention on smart mobility has been technology-centric and uneven. As demonstrated in Behrendt's study [11] (pp. 1–16) despite the potentially ground-breaking social, environmental and sustainability impacts of smart mobility applications, only those modes of transport mobility that are smart/intelligent/networked and engage with data – especially the car and related IoT – gain visibility and become major policy focus areas with associated funding. Important considerations of environment and sustainability [11] of place more broadly, relating to the communities, neighbourhoods, spaces and networks in which we live, and of social inclusion [12] are left out.

Today, within a broader context of converging 'mega-trends' [13] in population ageing, urbanisation and digitalisation the needs of older city residents are beginning to receive some acknowledgement across Europe as an area of smart city outcomes [7].

In the UK, ageing and mobility are seen by government as 'Industrial Strategy Grand Challenges', representing an urgent case for change – yet to be addressed by stakeholders [14]. In this socio-economic context the digital ICT capabilities of older groups and the growing diversity of ageing urban populations is an important conversation, which this article aims to introduce. The research questions are: How transport (and) mobility practices interact with mobile ICT use in smart cities? What do we know about the transport mobilities of older people? What do we know about the mobile media and ICT practices of older people? The remaining of this article is structured as follows: The following section introduces the concepts of (smart) mobility and transport. Then the article introduces a framework for the analysis of older people's mobility in the city that highlights the role of digital data and of mobile ICT use as a capability for smart transport mobility. The article goes on to discuss examples from smart transport applications in London, one of Europe's principal 'smart' cities, illustrating tensions between their potential to create a more socially inclusive transport system for all ages and prevailing age-discriminatory bias in inherited transport systems and in digital data datasets. The final section summarises main threads of this discussion and highlights areas requiring further engagement with in research and policy practice.

2 Mobility

The concept of mobility can be used to refer to peoples' movements outdoors, to access desired places, activities and people or simply to move around. It can be destination dependent and destination independent. Mobility is often considered 'as a prerequisite for citizens to have independence and participate in activities, access services, and form social relations' [15] (p. 2). Transport mobilities are resource-dependent and embedded into their material conditions, including policy and space [1] (p. 33). Following Levin [15] (p. 3) mobility involves not merely moving bodies in the transport system but 'desires, abilities, and resources, which are only partly observable and may be investigated indirectly by observing their manifestations' (see also [16, 17]).

Drawing on disability and capability models [18] mobility practices can be understood as an integration of personal and environmental components: A 'person-environment relationship' [19] of transport mobility comprises the physical and the built environment, the social/cultural and the institutional/regulatory systems [20]. The affordability, e.g. of public transport, information devices, and understanding how to use them are important components of access to mobility and social inclusion [16, 17] bringing in the dimension of social, technological infrastructures of digital data and networks. In light of this, an urban road environment can be considered as 'a system with human presence' [1] (p. 31) on which demographic trends, such as population ageing, and development in digital technology is having an effect.

Framing transport (and) mobility as person-environment, interactive and resource-dependent practices allows for a better appreciation of the role of public policy in shaping access to those systems. Complexes of social mobility practice such as working, shopping, visiting friends and family are connected to infrastructural arrangements across space and time [21] (e.g. routes, destinations, shelters, data infrastructures) in ways that cannot be controlled by individuals alone. The policy, the design, the spatial, the personal and the social elements of transport mobility therefore must be seen as interconnected.

2.1 Older People's Transport Mobility

In terms of their broadly similar general mobility patterns older people travel less than younger people, considering all modes of travel, and replace driving a private car, after retirement, by walking or the use of public transport [22]. Public transport and walking are the most recurring mode of transport among older people in cities in Europe [1, 23] A Reliance on public transport, especially busses, and walking, is a practice older people share in common with other socially disadvantaged groups, namely the poorer groups and younger people aged under 21, who are less likely to own cars [22] (p. 64). These options hardly ever appear to be able to fully satisfy their mobility needs. According to research in the UK one third of older adults report unmet travel needs in relation to pursuing leisure activities or visiting friends and family [14, 24].

Lack of voice in transport policy is another common characteristic between the older and the younger (and the poorer) groups alike whose transport practices remain 'at the margins of transport planning' [15] (p. 2). A study prepared for the UK Department for transport found that pedestrians are rarely included in transport system appraisals. There appears to be no legal requirement for this effectively creating an appraisal process that does not encourage walking and values pedestrians less than other road users: The study report cites 'a built-in assumption that walking tends to be carried out by people at much lower incomes' [25] (p. 5). The transport mobility practices of older populations require further attention from a social and cultural inclusion perspective that would account for large differences due to gender, sex, ethnicity, cultural norms [26] as well as individual's health and skills, and the growing heterogeneity of hyper-diverse city populations – but this is a discussion outside the scope of this paper.

3   Smart Mobility, Transport, Data Networks

Smart mobility has been descriptively defined, as alluded to in the introduction of this article, as the converging of the digital ICT and traditional transportation (see also [27]). In a broader sense 'smart' transport refers to the use of digital technologies to improve transport by improving access to information about any aspect of the journey, including destination and pickup points, booking and payment systems, timetable etc. [28]. Smart transport solutions include a range of services, from transport journey updates accessed on the web or through an app, to smart buses and autonomous vehicles. Journey planning information such as real time public transport and traffic updates (e.g. www.tfl.gov.uk) and demand responsive smart technology services [28] use real time data from vehicle and passenger movement. In the first category, information, provided by the service provider to passengers, can be used to help plan all aspects of their prescheduled journey: route, ticket purchase, signalling the driver and navigation around the trip. Transport operators in the second category are responding to client travel requests, to accommodate mobility needs through flexible routes, e.g. dial a bus ride, carpool services, and provide information. These services can improve access to transport for people who are less mobile and less able to stand for long (for example at a bus stop). Smart mobility systems comprise vehicle technology; intelligent transport systems (e.g. traffic management); data; new mobility services [29].

A more socially-oriented analysis can expand on the conceptualisations of mobility as a person-environment relationship [40, 48] to include digital environments, and as practice [15] to incorporate practices of data generation, registration and use. Following [30] smart mobility relies on digital networks, in addition to mobile physical objects and people, and involves data collection and analysis at scale [31] and can be conceptualised as a data-driven service. From this perspective, as digital data can be understood as shaping people's opportunities for (transport) mobility. The potential of smart transport services to meet the travel and mobility needs of citizens, is therefore constrained by the data to use to design and run smart transport – and shaped by ways these data are being looked at and used. We must therefore develop awareness not only of the data available as e.g. evidence for policy *but also* the data *not* available [12] and the 'gaps cracks and silences' in data [32] as both have consequences in the design of smart services. Data biases are endemic in research on smart ICT and older people and may result from the technologies available (including software and research instruments) to sample selection and respondent recruitment systems, research design and methods [33] (p. 7). Consequently, a 'lack' of digital data is an indication of power asymmetries in access to networked media devices, in connectivity required to generate and display the data, such as home or mobile internet, but also in biased research agendas and instruments can reinforce the exclusion of those without access to the data for analysis, manipulation and (re)presentation, or of those whose data does not get collected or used [12]. These bias both originate in and reproduce an age-discriminatory culture through generational approaches that frame new technologies as the domain of younger groups.

4   Mobile Communications, Older People and the Smartphone

Following Campbell [34] (p. 9) the term 'mobile communication technology' can be used to refer to 'devices and services that supported mediated social connectivity while the user is in physical motion'. In light of the previous discussion mobile ICTs can further be understood as resources for transport mobility (for example using a journey planning application; buying paying for transport fares; using an online travel navigator while driving) and for walking in the city (for example, using a map). In the context of smart city systems mobile media use has profound social consequences of ongoing datafication 'not only means of communication but increasingly also [as a means] of generating data'. [35] (p. 387) Intelligent transport can be seen to typify this shift towards data-enabled services [12]: ICT capability and data becomes intrinsic to social institutions such as public transport systems, and practices, including participation in leisure and cultural activities.

Older groups are especially disadvantaged in this respect. Research into the use of smart mobile ICTs by older people is both limited and fragmented [33] (p. 12). Older people have been most commonly considered a minority in digital communications systems, in terms of both access and use of ICT. Although age remains a main demographic factor with regards to inequality of digital access, skills and ICT use alongside income and education [36] differences in engagement with media technologies are not usefully explained as generationally located, i.e. by birth cohort [37] (p. 2). In countries with high internet diffusion rates older groups have been the fastest growing user groups of smart technology. In 2017 internet use figures among 64- to 74- year old adults were counting 70% or over in one in three EU member states. New smartphone users today are mostly older people. Where available, data confirms that older individuals tend to rely more on mobile Internet access than a landline connection (e.g.[38]; Pew Research Center in [39]) Across the EU in 2019 52% of adults aged 55 to 75 were using mobile devices to access the internet on the move with figures ranging from 85% in Sweden and Norway to 28% in Italy [38]. However, there are also segments of older demographics who are not using digital media devices such as computers, tablets and smartphones. As indicated in these figures there is currently a variation in mobile internet usage among older groups across Europe. Importantly, there are also significant intra-group differences in smartphone usage. Rosales and Fernández-Ardévol [39] triangulated qualitative interviews, smartphone tracking and survey data demonstrating how the currently limited (i.e. less intensive use compared to other generations) usage of smartphones by older people is at the same time diverse: They see three categories of older mobile phone users, the basic, the proficient and the advanced and highlight the importance of research that accounts for the significance of diversity in the media practices of older groups. Proficient users for example 'often have extensive experience with digital technologies' and have adopted smartphones as part of their digital media use (62). Citing Kitchin [40] Rosales and Fernández-Ardévol call for attention to '[d]ata granularity … in order to take into account the different ways in which older people, as a minority in the digital world, use digital media, and therefore better incorporate their uses into intelligent systems' [39] (p. 63).

Age-biased data stock can potentially have a far- reaching consequences for social inclusion in a smart city environment where data trails generated by mobile connectivity are creating new digital tools for research, for example social media use proxies used to map city areas and deploy city services. Writing about the reliance of social media by local governments Zook [5] notes how the use of geosocial media networks and geo-tagging data and metrics derived from them can provide useful insight and policy direction. At the same time there is a risk of solidifying existing inequalities between citizens. The following section uses the example of a physical infrastructure (traffic lights) and a digital infrastructure (journey planning and map apps) to illustrate some of the tensions, gaps, age bias and opportunities related to the use of digital data in transport and mobility in the city.

5   Smart Mobility for All? Pedestrian Walking Speeds in the Built and Digital Environment

This section discusses the example of transport infrastructure (pedestrian crossings) and journey planning applications and online maps to navigate the city of London. London has led developments in smart transport and in all age-inclusive transport, with measures such as free bus passes for all its residents of a pensionable age (65+) and free children's travel on busses and in the city's underground and over-ground train system, and Transport for London corporation's (www.TFL.gov.uk) free journey planning app, live transport updates available on screens in city bus stop network.

Walking Speed Values, Pedestrian Crossing Lights and Digital Journey Planners.
The case of pedestrian crossing lights, that regulates traffic flow in cities in the UK
and internationally, is a characteristic example of measurement that uses demographic
information data that are no longer representative inadequate provision in city and
transport mobility. The current value of pedestrian speed used in the UK road traffic
control system and internationally, comprising roads and traffic lights is 1.2 m per
second (ms)/75 m per minute/4.5 km per hour [25] (p. 5). This value, and the systems
built on this basis, both built/material and many popular digital apps use to calculate
average pedestrian speed that originates in the mid-twentieth century (early 1960s) [23]
a time when the average age of the population was much lower and traffic was many
times lighter and less complex.[1] Older people today travel more than their peers did
20–25 years ago, with everyday trip rates higher and activities outside the home being
more common [41]. However most pedestrians over 65 are unable to cross the road in
time at traffic lights, and the walking speed of 76% of men and 85% of women over
65 is slower than the assumed normal walking speed of 1.2 m/s [42]. The length of
time before traffic lights turn green implicitly favours vehicles rather than pedestrians
[22] (p. 67). The average pedestrian walking speed value corresponds to competent
walking for adults under 65 years of age. The typical values of pedestrian walking
speed are: 0.84 m/s (ms) for people over of the age 65 to 80, and 0.55 for people aged
80+. In light of this average walking speed standard the 1.2 ms value used in pedestrian
crossing and live maps is more often than not inadequate for older pedestrians.[2] The
current assumed walking speed at 1.2 ms is higher than what can be achieved by a
significant and growing proportion of the population, particularly the older people. As
a consequence most pedestrians over 65 are unable to cross the road in time at traffic
lights with the walking speed of 76% of men and 85% of women over 65 being slower
than the assumed normal walking speed of 1.2 m/s [42]. Smart technologies, e.g. as
trialled by TfL to detect the number of pedestrians and vary the time they have to cross
a road, can be used to address this age bias.

---

[1] This situation is not unique to transport but characterises most urban infrastructure that was built
during the post WW2 era and was designed for a younger society.

[2] Most of the data have been captured from movement of pedestrians actually walking and crossing
the roads (excluding all others) [25] (p. 6).

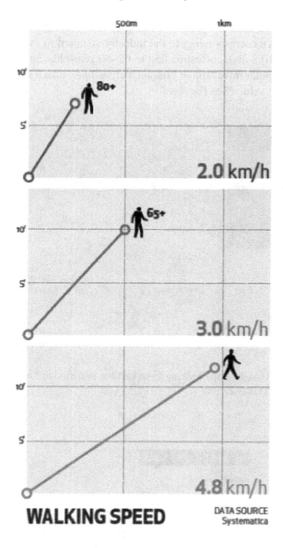

Image source: Arup et al. 2015, p.50

Digital Navigation Apps. To illustrate the use of average walking speed values by the three most popular city navigation and journey planning applications we used the example of a walk from London's Waterloo station to the London Bridge station (1.8 km walking distance). The figures below show how long it takes to walk from London Waterloo station to London Bridge station according to *Google maps* (Fig. 1) *Transport for London* journey planner (Figs. 2, 3, 4, 5) and *Citymapper* (Fig. 6) *Google maps* use the same standard value of 1.2 ms as the default for their walking speed internationally (see here for an example from India). By contrast *Transport for London*'s journey planer

(TfL.gov.uk) includes three options of walking speed values (See Figs. 2, 3, 4 & 5): The average (1.2 ms), corresponding to the industry standard of average adult up to 65 year-olds, the slow (0.8 ms), corresponding to 65–80 year-olds, and the fast, at 1.4 ms. The second most popular travel app in London, *Citymapper*, uses a similar value to TfL's 'fast' walking speed value (See Fig. 6).

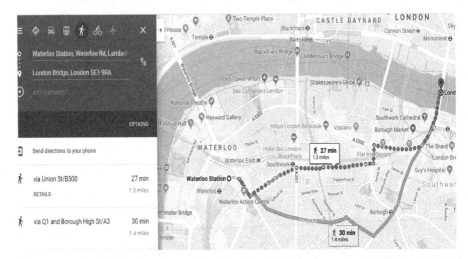

Fig. 1. According to Google maps walking from London Waterloo to London Bridge (selected option of 1.8 km walk) takes 27 min

Fig. 2. TfL journey planner options include public transport, cycling and walking at different speeds

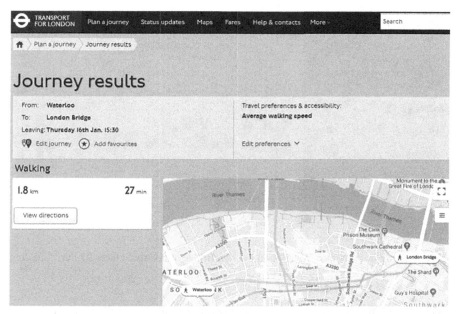

Fig. 3. Walking from London Waterloo to London Bridge at average speed takes 27 min according to the TfL journey planner

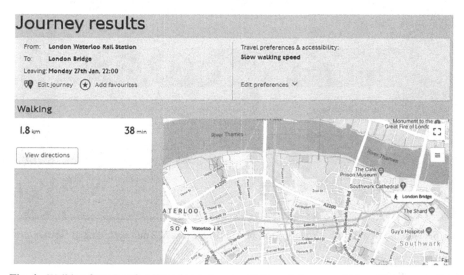

Fig. 4. Walking from London Waterloo to London Bridge at slow speed takes 38 min according to the TfL journey planner

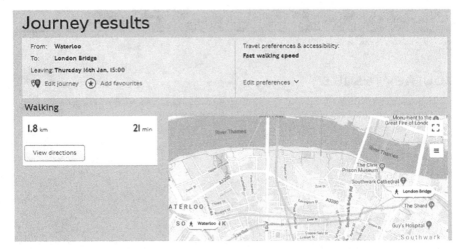

Fig. 5. Walking from London Waterloo to London Bridge at fast speed takes 21 min according to the TfL journey planner

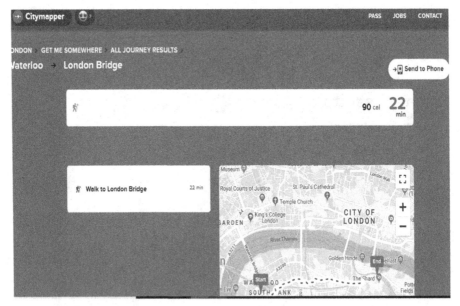

Fig. 6. Walking from London Waterloo to London Bridge takes 22 min according to *Citymapper*

5.1 Age Bias

Hundreds of new apps have helped to make people's journeys more efficient. Travel information plays an important facilitating role in mobility practice: Research has found the more mobile older adults attribute their higher levels of mobility to carefully pre-planning their trips by using information [43]. Travel information can be used to plan a forthcoming journey, allowing individuals to choose between different modes and routes. Travel information can encourage people to choose a different mode to their usual one, especially important for reducing habitual or default car trips [41] (pp. 26–27). Lack of travel information can be a key barrier to getting out and about for older people.

Age-biased average walking speeds in journey planning apps persist at the intercession of digital ICT, data, mobility. As critical social gerontology and studies of media technology have demonstrated age bias discriminating against older people are a relationship of cultural assumptions in the design of a service [26] of available data sets, [39] of common misconceptions surrounding generational use of ICT used widely in public and policy debates [44], promoting the perception that generation alone is the most significant variable in explaining engagement with digital media [45].

Un-noticed and not acted upon these deeply entrenched assumptions and cultures reproduced in data bias and in the design of transport apps may discourage walking or using public transport with effects on public health, the environment as well as inclusion: The data bias of the apps, particularly about the wider lived experiences of older groups, and other excluded and disadvantaged populations, 'feed into a wider subjective sense that these experiences are undervalued or [un]acknowledged, which ultimately exacerbate feelings of inadequacy, vulnerability and frustration' [46] (p. 181).

6   Concluding Remarks: Age, Inclusive Mobility, and the Smart City

What does the example of default pedestrian speed values show us? Smart city systems combine physical, digital and data infrastructures, and cultural bias, such as those surrounding age, may operate across these: The mundane example of pedestrian speed values used in traffic lights as well as in digital maps and journey planners demonstrates both this bias (in maps, journey planners and light) as well as how smart transport solutions can create more inclusive places in the city (e.g. TfL). The example of pedestrian walking values also demonstrates the significance and social consequences of the embedding of cultural assumptions and values in city infrastructures (such as traffic control) and digital transport applications (such as route planners), for example in further discouraging walking or the use of environmentally sustainable transport such as buses. Referring back to the research questions 'how transport (and) mobility practices interact with mobile ICT use in smart cities?' and 'what do we know about the transport mobilities of older people?' this article used to frame its investigation of smart mobility and/in old age: Mobility is both resource-dependent (as transport research has demonstrated) as well as a resource for citizenship (freedom of movement). Therefore an understanding of the consequences of those resource-dependent practices and their implications for inclusion and citizenship requires an understanding of the social relations, particularly the power relations that mutually constitute the production, distribution and exchange of resources (see [2]). The preceding discussion highlighted the role of digital data trails generated though media use (such as the mobile telephone/smartphone) as well as through IoT (for example smart train payment systems, smart traffic lights) and both are areas that require attention in research into age relations. Data-driven mobility can be shaped by partial datasets, e.g. those combining health data relating to medical conditions, poor health and vulnerability associated with old age. These data are generated by ICT systems, both by the end-user (though use of smarty mobile phones) and embedded into systems (IoT). As Mosco [2] (p. 19) contents, it is therefore 'essential to consider the implications for cities [and their citizens] of communication systems that are almost seamlessly integrated into the structures of everyday life.' To those who have an interest in age relations and communications it comes as no surprise that ICT-based solutions are age-discriminating) – once we take into account what do we (not) know about the mobile media and ICT practices of older people (see e.g. [39]).

On a more broad level we need new conceptualisations of smart city and its domains and dimensions, away from technology-centric models and motivations of urban betterment largely driven by technology advocates [5] to reflect the messiness of the city and its politics and enable more refined taxonomies of smart city aspects [47]. A more inclusive, and sustainable, conceptualisation of smart cities entails more inclusive thinking around smart places [1], mobilities [11] and publics [48] for the city to have more agency in these debates. These discussions are expected to grow in importance given the trends in urbanisation, ageing and datafication. As cities incorporate significant changes in forms of mobility into their (infra)structures, diversity remains core normative value of social inclusion in digital design [26, 49]. An age-inclusive environment for pedestrians and public transport users will enhance mobility as well as have clear public health and the environmental benefits.[3] This paper therefore extends the proposition for alternative conceptions of smart cities and smart citizenship [50] that bring age-relations to the centre of critical investigations of ICT, data and socio-economic justice.

References

1. Arup, Help Age International, Intel, Systematica.: Shaping Ageing Cities. 10 European Case Studies. Arup, Help Age International, Intel, Systematica (2015)
2. Mosco, V.: The Smart City in a Digital World. Emerald Publishing Limited, Bingley (2019)
3. Dirks, S., Keeling, M.: A vision of smarter cities: How cities can lead the way into a prosperous and sustainable future. IBM Global Business Services Executive Report IBM Institute for Busines Value (2009)
4. Gassmann, O., Böhm, J., Palmié, M.: Smart Cities : Introducing Digital Innovation to Cities. Emerald Publishing Limited, Bingley (2019)
5. Zook, M.: Crowd-sourcing the smart city: Using big geosocial media metrics in urban governance. Big Data Soc. **4**, 205395171769438 (2017). https://doi.org/10.1177/205395171769 4384
6. Batty, M., Axhausen, K.W., Giannotti, F., et al.: Smart cities of the future. Eur. Phys. J. Spec. Top. **214**, 481–518 (2012). https://doi.org/10.1140/epjst/e2012-01703-3
7. European Commission (EC): Smart Cities - Smart Living| Digital Single Market. https://ec.europa.eu/digital-single-market/en/policies/smart-cities
8. Rjab, A. Ben, Mellouli, S.: Smart cities in the era of artificial intelligence and internet of things: literature review from 1990 to 2017. In: ACM International Conference Proceeding Series. Association for Computing Machinery (2018). https://doi.org/10.1145/3209281.320 9380

---

[3] A growing body of evidence has been highlighting the role of walking, cycling and the use of public transport contribute to better health and wellbeing and sustainability outcomes [51].

9. Townsend, A.M.: Smart Cities: Big Data, Civic Hackers, and the Quest for a New Utopia. W. W. Norton & Company, New York (2013)

10. Rajamanickam, V.: Rethinking urban mobility systems through data intelligence. Freight-Waves (2019). https://www.freightwaves.com/news/rethinking-urban-mobility-systems-through-data-intelligence

11. Behrendt, F.: Cycling the smart and Sustainable City: analyzing EC policy documents on internet of things, mobility and transport, and smart cities. Sustainability 11, 763 (2019). https://doi.org/10.3390/su11030763

12. Sourbati, M., Behrendt, F.: Smart Mobility, Age, and Data Justice. New Media Soc (2020). https://doi.org/10.1177/1461444820902682

13. Price Waterhouse Coopers (pwc): Five Megatrends And Their Implications for Global Defense & Security. PWC (2016)

14. Centre for Ageing Better: Ageing and mobility: a grand challenge. London (2019)

15. Levin, L.: How may public transport influence the practice of everyday life among younger and older people and how may their practices influence public transport? Soc. Sci. 8 (2019). https://doi.org/10.3390/socsci8030096

16. Smith, A.E.: Ageing in Urban Neighbourhoods: Place Attachment and Social Exclusion. Policy Press, Bristol (2009)

17. Smith, A.E.: Ageing in Urban Neighbourhoods. Bristol University Press, Bristol (2018)

18. Sourbati, M.: Disabling communications? a capabilities perspective on media access, social inclusion and communication policy. Media Cult. Soc. 34 (2012). https://doi.org/10.1177/0163443712442702

19. Iwarsson, S., Ståhl, A.: Accessibility, usability and universal design - positioning and definition of concepts describing person-environment relationships. Disabil. Rehabil. 25, 57–66 (2003). https://doi.org/10.1080/dre.25.2.57.66

20. Wennberg, H.: Walking in old age: a year-round perspective on accessibility in the outdoor environment and effects of measures taken. Bulletin. 247, University of Lunt Publications (2009). https://lup.lub.lu.se/search/publication/1494608

21. Shove, E., Watson, M., Spurling, N.: Conceptualizing connections. Eur. J. Soc. Theory 18, 274–287 (2015). https://doi.org/10.1177/1368431015579964

22. Foresight.: Future of Mobility: A time of unprecedented change in the transport system. Government Office for Science (2019)

23. LaPlante, J., Kaeser, T.P.: A history of pedestrian signal walking speed assumptions. In: 3rd Urban Street Symposium: Uptown, Downtown, or Small Town: Designing Urban Streets That Work, 24–27 June 2007, Seattle, Washington (2007)

24. Luiu, C., Tight, M., Burrow, M.: The unmet travel needs of the older population: a review of the literature. Transp. Rev. 37, 488–506 (2017). https://doi.org/10.1080/01441647.2016.1252447

25. Crabtree, M., Lodge, S., Emmerson, P.: A review of pedestrian walking speeds and time needed to cross the road (2014)

26. Sourbati, M., Loos, E.F.: Interfacing age: diversity and (in)visibility in digital public service. J. Digit. Media Policy 10, 275–293 (2019). https://doi.org/10.1386/jdmp_00003_1

27. Albino, V., Berardi, U., Dangelico, R.M.: Smart cities: definitions, dimensions, performance, and initiatives. J. Urban Technol. 22, 3–21 (2015). https://doi.org/10.1080/10630732.2014.942092

28. Behrendt, F., Hancox, A., Huber, J., Murray, L., Sourbati, M.: Intelligent transport solutions for social inclusion (ITSSI) (2017)

29. Jeekel, H.: Social sustainability and smart mobility: exploring the relationship. Transp. Res. Procedia. 25, 4296–4310 (2017)

30. Elliott, A., Urry, J.: Mobile Lives. Routledge, Abingdon (2010)

31. Behrendt, F.: Why cycling matters for smart cities. internet of bicycles for intelligent transport. J. Transp. Geogr. **56**, 157–164 (2016). https://doi.org/10.1016/J.JTRANGEO.2016.08.018

32. Thornham, H., Gómez Cruz, E.: Not just a number? NEETs, data and datalogical systems. Inf. Commun. Soc. **21**, 306–321 (2018). https://doi.org/10.1080/1369118X.2017.1279204

33. Fernández-Ardèvol, M., et al.: Methodological strategies to understand smartphone practices for social connectedness in later life (2019). https://doi.org/10.1007/978-3-030-22015-0_4

34. Campbell, S.W.: Mobile media and communication: a new field, or just a new journal? Mobile Media Commun. **1**, 8–13 (2013). https://doi.org/10.1177/2050157912459495

35. Breiter, A., Hepp, A.: The complexity of datafication: putting digital traces in context. In: Hepp, A., Breiter, A., Hasebrink, U. (eds.) Communicative Figurations. TCSCR, pp. 387–405. Springer, Cham (2018). https://doi.org/10.1007/978-3-319-65584-0_16

36. Dutton, W.H., Reisdorf, B.C.: Cultural divides and digital inequalities: attitudes shaping internet and social media divides. Inf. Commun. Soc. 1–21 (2017). https://doi.org/10.1080/1369118X.2017.1353640

37. Gilleard, C., Jones, I., Higgs, P.: Connectivity in later life: the declining age divide in mobile cell phone ownership. Sociol. Res. Online. **20** (2015). https://doi.org/10.5153/sro.3552

38. Eurostat: Eurostat - Tables, Graphs and Maps Interface (TGM) table. https://ec.europa.eu/eurostat/tgm/refreshTableAction.do;jsessionid=i4TkHKAVCZNDE3xtM3ooppZbioeBTZDfAOzWMGirFLhurELs829g!272774262?tab=table&plugin=1&pcode=tin00083&language=en

39. Rosales, A., Fernández-Ardèvol, M.: Smartphone usage diversity among older people (2019). https://doi.org/10.1007/978-3-030-06076-3_4

40. Kitchin, R.: The Data Revolution: Big Data, Open Data, Data Infrastructures & amp Their Consequences. 1st edn. SAGE Publications Ltd, London (2014). EC1Y 1SP

41. Ormerod, M., Newton, M.R., Phillips, J., Musselwhite, A.C., Mcgee, S., Russell, R.: How can transport provision and associated built environment infrastructure be enhanced and developed to support the mobility needs of individuals as they age ? Future of an ageing population : evidence review. Government Office for Science (2015)

42. Asher, L., Aresu, M., Falaschetti, E., Mindell, J.: Most older pedestrians are unable to cross the road in time: a cross-sectional study. Age Ageing **41**, 690–694 (2012). https://doi.org/10.1093/ageing/afs076

43. Lindsay, S., Jackson, D., Schofield, G., Olivier, P.: Engaging older people using participatory design. In: Proceedings of the 2012 ACM Annual Conference on Human Factors in Computing Systems CHI 2012, p. 1199. ACM Press, New York (2012)

44. Sourbati, M.: When ageism goes digital. Ageing-Equal (2018)

45. Helsper, E.J., Eynon, R.: Digital natives: where is the evidence? Br. Edu. Res. J. **36**, 503–520 (2010). https://doi.org/10.1080/01411920902989227

46. Thornham, H.: Algorithmic vulnerabilities and the datalogical: Early motherhood and tracking-as-care regimes. Convergence Int. J. Res. New Media Technol. **25**, 171–185 (2019). https://doi.org/10.1177/1354856519835772

47. Doody, L.: Smarter London: The role of city government for a digital future. LSE Cities. London School of Economics (2019)

48. Cowley, R., Joss, S., Dayot, Y.: The smart city and its publics: insights from across six UK cities. Urban Res. Pract. **11**, 53–77 (2018). https://doi.org/10.1080/17535069.2017.1293150

49. Loos, E.F.: Designing for dynamic diversity: Representing various senior citizens in digital information sources. Observatorio (OBS*). 7 (2013). https://doi.org/10.15847/obsobs712013639

50. Cardullo, P., Kitchin, R.: Smart urbanism and smart citizenship: the neoliberal logic of 'citizen-focused' smart cities in Europe. Environ. Plann. C: Polit. Space **37**, 813–830 (2019). https://doi.org/10.1177/0263774X18806508

51. Public Health England (PHE): Cycling and walking for individual and population health benefits (2018)

The Effects of Increasing Degree of Unreliable Automation on Older Adults' Performance

Claire Textor[(✉)] and Richard Pak[(✉)]

Clemson University, Clemson, SC 29634, USA
ctextor@g.clemson.edu

Abstract. Automated technology may help older adults maintain an independent lifestyle (e.g., Mynatt et al. 2004; Labonnote and Høyland 2017). For example, domestic robots could help older adults remain in their homes longer, or cars with semi-autonomous safety technology can help older adults maintain their ability to drive. However, as older adults interact with technology that is more automated (i.e., automation is higher in stage and degree), they may become more subject to the negative effects when that technology fails. This concept of reaping greater benefits of higher degrees of automation that is reliable but suffering catastrophic performance consequences when it is unreliable has been termed the lumberjack effect and has been well documented among younger adults (Endsley and Kiris 1995; Onnasch et al. 2013; Rovira et al. 2017). The cause of this effect is that frequent interaction with reliable, high level automation induces a complacency or disengagement with the task (becoming out of the loop). Thus, when that automation fails, the user has been out of the loop (Endsley and Kiris 1995) and is thus unprepared to resume the task. As older adults have reduced cognitive abilities, they may be even more subject to the lumberjack effect. The purpose of the current study was to examine the presence and magnitude of the lumberjack effect in older adults as it has not yet been documented in the literature. Older and younger adults interacted with various degrees of automation. We replicated the finding that performance was negatively affected on unreliable trials of automation compared to reliable trials for both age groups (i.e., the lumberjack effect). However, these effects did not appear to be more pronounced in older adults. These results are the first to show that the lumberjack effect previously observed in younger adults is equally pronounced in older adults. However, what aspect of aging cognition was the source of this similar lumberjack effect is still an empirical question.

Keywords: Degree of automation · Older adults · Working memory

1 Introduction

Automated technology may be a key resource for enabling older adults to maintain independence (e.g., Mynatt et al. 2004; Labonnote and Høyland 2017). Even though the positive effects of using automation have been well documented (Nof 2009; Manzey et al. 2011; Morrow et al. 2005), there is comparatively less research examining older adult's performance with it (McBride et al. 2011; Sanchez et al. 2014).

© Springer Nature Switzerland AG 2020
Q. Gao and J. Zhou (Eds.): HCII 2020, LNCS 12209, pp. 327–340, 2020.
https://doi.org/10.1007/978-3-030-50232-4_23

One effect of reliable automation is that while it can alleviate users from highly working memory-intensive tasks (e.g., complex decision making), the tradeoff is that when the automation malfunctions, the operator is left to diagnose a problem in a situation that they have not been attending to ("out of the loop" phenomenon; OOTL) (Endsley and Kiris 1995). This partially explains a phenomenon known as the lumberjack effect (Onnasch et al. 2014). The lumberjack effect is the observation that when lower levels of automation fail, the consequences are less severe because the operator is still relatively engaged in the task (they are more "in the loop"). However, with higher level automation, they are more OOTL and thus, much less able to recover when automation fails. Given that higher levels of automation are likely to be more beneficial to older adults (because it supports age-related declines in working memory), older adults may be more subject to the lumberjack effect than other age groups.

1.1 Types and Levels of Automation

While automation can take many forms (e.g., robots, software) it can be conceptually described by type and level. Type of automation refers to one of four categories which are defined by the stage of human information processing being supported: (1) information acquisition; (2) information analysis; (3) decision and action selection; (4) action implementation (Parasuraman et al. 2000). Level of automation (LOA) refers to how much of the human's task is being replaced by the machine (Parasuraman et al. 2000). Each type exists on a continuum from levels of low to high automation. The combination of type and level is referred to as the degree of automation (DOA) (Parasuraman et al. 2000). The degree increases along with the level and type of automation as a linear relationship. Prior research has shown abrupt performance consequences between information automation (types 1 and 2) and decision automation (types 3 and 4) (Rovira et al. 2007). Thus, we will discuss the major differences that distinguish the two broad classes of automation.

Information automation serves to apprise the operator of their surrounding environment. It is responsible for taking raw sensor data and transmitting information in a way that is useful for task completion. Even though the additional processing may alleviate the requirement for attentional selection, the user is naturally more in-the-loop compared to tasks using higher-level automation. The operator is still required to complete and carry out decision making tasks.

The purpose of decision automation is to present the operator with options on how to carry out the task at hand based on information from the environment. It goes further than lower level automation by devising actionable options for the operator to carry out. With higher level automation, more of the cognitive components of the task are alleviated. However, since the operator is less involved in the decision making and selection process, they are naturally more vulnerable to OOTL effects. The primary differentiation between the two broad classes of automation are that the first primary support perceptual demands of the task while the latter primary support working memory requirements of the task.

1.2 Automation and the Lumberjack Effect

Despite the benefits of reliable high-level automation, there are also potential negative effects (Bainbridge 1983). Operators who are OOTL for an extended period may experience skill degradation, loss of situation awareness, and increased complacency (Parasuraman et al. 2000; Wickens 1992). These consequences are only detrimental to performance when the automation fails and the operator must resume the task. Importantly, the level of the automation (i.e., amount of the task being assumed by automation) determines the consequences of failures such that failures of low-level automation may be of low magnitude while failures of high-level require cognitive effort for users to get back "in-the-loop." For example, malfunctions of a voice dictation system (a low-level system), which automates the well-learned skill of typing, merely requires users to resume typing, whereas failures of lane-keeping automation in a car (a high-level system) require operators to recognize the vehicles speed, location in the roadway, and proximity to potential hazards in order to safely take-over manual control of the vehicle. This rapid switch from automated operation to manual control can lead to a sharp decline in task performance.

The paradoxical notion that high-level automation is helpful when it is reliable but extremely detrimental to human performance when it is unreliable defines the lumberjack effect. The main source of the lumberjack effect seems to be the unique cognitive properties of higher-levels of automation, which supports more working memory-intensive tasks. Given age-related declines in working memory capacity, it is reasonable that individuals with diminished working memory capacity, such as older adults, may exhibit a stronger lumberjack effect.

1.3 Possible Negative Effects of Unreliable Automation in Older Adults

Automation can be particularly beneficial to older adults who may experience age-related declines in many physical and cognitive abilities (e.g., Salthouse 1994; Salthouse 1996; Dobbs and Rule 1990; Rybash et al. 1995). Given that the source of the lumberjack effect seems to be tied to combination of increased automation (and the working memory reducing effects associated), studies using varying degrees of automation should show a relatively large lumberjack effect in older adults—because of their reduced ability to resume a previously automated task (due to age-related declines in working memory). However, this has not been the case in previous literature. Pak et al. (2016) found that when automation was reliable, older adults' performance was enhanced. However, they did not observe the performance decrement when automation failed, as was expected. That is, they did not seem to observe a lumberjack effect in older adults.

There are some possible reasons that this study did not show a lumberjack effect, despite it being a well-supported phenomenon. First, Pak et al. (2016) only used two levels of automation (information analysis, medium decision). Recall that high level automation alleviates working memory demands more than lower levels. By using a moderate level of automation, participants may have been able to easily recover from automation failure. Implementing a higher level of decision automation may increase OOTL effects, thus illustrating an increased lumberjack effect. Second, the authors held workload constant at a low level so participants might have been able to easily recover from failure without the use of automation, therefore, we would not expect to see a lumberjack effect. Third, this task was carried out in a military domain which may not be familiar to many civilians. Performance could have been affected by the relative novelty of the domain if it was distracting or disorienting. If participants were not comfortable interacting with the system, they might have been more inclined to rely on their own manual control as opposed to the automation.

For the present study, we used a similar task but implemented unique components to investigate how the lumberjack effect manifests in older adults. First, the most significant aspect of our study compared to Pak et al. (2016) is that we include a condition with an even higher level of automation (high decision). We expect that this higher degree will take the participant even more OOTL, thus inducing the lumberjack effect. Second, we are manipulating workload, unlike Pak et al. (2016) who kept workload consistent throughout. We suspect that low task workload (not enough working memory demand on the participant) may have been one reason they did not observe a lumberjack effect. Manipulating workload and increasing DOA should allow us to more precisely control/manipulate the working memory demand of the task. Third, in contrast to other studies (Rovira et al. 2007, 2017; Pak et al. 2016), we are utilizing a more conventional, civilian task domain. We predict that civilian participants might not have been accustomed to looking at a terrain or had previous knowledge of UAVs. This could have led to confusion and a lower likelihood of utilizing the automation aid. We anticipate that the use of taxis instead of UAVs will clear up any distraction or disorientation that may have resulted from the previous task domain.

The purpose of this research is to examine how the lumberjack effect manifests in older adults. Given that high-level automation is working memory alleviating and that older adults tend to have reduced working memory capacities, the consequences of unreliable automation may be even greater. Based on findings from Rovira et al. (2017), we hypothesize that older adults will exhibit a greater lumberjack effect than younger adults. That is, we expect older adults to suffer significantly greater performance decrements when the automation fails compared to younger adults. This is a direct consequence of older adults reduced working memory capacity (Salthouse 1994), and the fact that task resumption with failed high-level automation is a working memory-intensive task.

2   Method

2.1   Participants

Forty-three community-dwelling older adults (22 females; mean age 72.2, SD = 3.37) were recruited and compensated $20 for their time. Forty-four college students (29 females; mean age 18.8, SD = 1.39) were recruited from the Clemson University participant pool and compensated with course credit in exchange for their participation. Data from 4 participants were excluded from analyses (3 older adults and 1 younger adult) because their performance was lower than the requisite score of 85% on the math portion of the working memory task.

2.2 Materials

Equipment. PC-compatible (Windows 7) computers running at 3.2 GHz with 4 GB of RAM was used with a 19-inch LCD monitor set at a resolution of 1024 × 1280 pixels. Participants sat approximately 18 inches from the monitor, using a mouse (on the preferred side) and a keyboard.

Taxi Dispatching Task. The task was adapted from previous studies (Rovira et al. 2007, 2017; Pak et al. 2017). The task screen was split into four parts: a street map with a grid overlay (right), a target input area which contained automated assistance (left), and a communication module (upper left). The map display depicted customers (green boxes C1 to C6 for high workload; C1 to C3 for low workload), taxis (red boxes T1 to T6 for high workload; T1 to T3 for low workload), one headquarters (orange box labeled HQ) and three extraneous boxes (yellow boxes B1 to B3). The primary task was to observe the map and dispatch the taxi/customer pairing which were closest in proximity to one another. If two sets of customers and taxis were equidistant from each other, the pair closest to HQ took priority.

Participants dispatched taxis by selecting a customer and taxi from the target input area. To assist participants in the task, three conditions were created: a lower level information analysis automation aid (Fig. 1), a medium-level decision automation aid (Fig. 2), and a high-level decision automation aid (Fig. 3). For the information analysis automation condition, a dispatching selection chart provided an unordered list of the distances from customer to taxi and customer to HQ. The list relieved the operator from having to manually calculate the distances between each taxi and customer. However, the level was still considered low because the list of distances was unordered. The operator was still required to visually search through all the numbers and retain the lowest value in working memory while comparing it to all other values in the list. This particular task could be effortful for the operator to complete. The medium-decision automation condition calculated the distances and provided the closest three customer/taxi pairs to the participant in an ordered list. This alleviated working memory demand by reducing the number of options and ordering them from best to worst. The medium-decision automation was considered a comparatively higher DOA because the task it completed was more complex and the automation took over more of the task than the information automation. The participant was not given the distances, but they could choose to "view distance calculations", "select best" or disregard the automation. The high-decision automation performed the same task as the medium-decision automation except it presented the top choice instead of the top three. This is considered the highest level of decision automation because it only provided the participant with one option. For each condition, the next trial began if the participant either selected or did not select a pair within the allotted amount of time.

A secondary task was included because the effects of automation on performance and complacency are most often seen in multitasking situations (Parasuraman and Manzey 2010). For this communications task, participants were instructed to monitor the communications panel (upper left) looking for a particular call sign which appeared every 6 s. If the specified call sign appeared, they are required to click the "ANSWER" button. This secondary task was performed during each block, there was no single task condition.

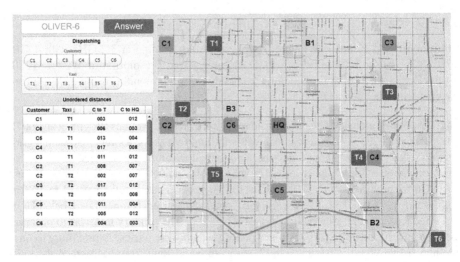

Fig. 1. Information analysis automation, high workload. All taxi (T) and customer (C) distances are calculated and presented in an unordered list. (Color figure online)

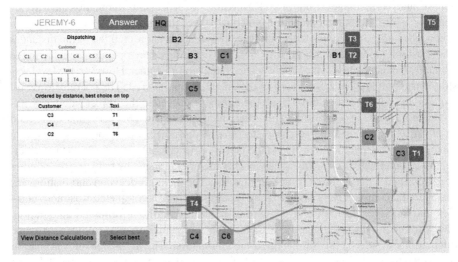

Fig. 2. Medium-decision automation, high workload. All taxi to customer distances are calculated and the top three are put in order and presented to the participant. (Color figure online)

Working Memory. Working memory span was measured using the automated operation span task (Aospan), a computerized version of the operation span memory task (Unsworth et al. 2007). The Aospan was chosen because it is a highly reliable measure and automated so there was little need for researcher intervention while participants were in the lab. The Aospan asks participants to complete simple math problems while remembering the order of letters that are being presented to them between each problem.

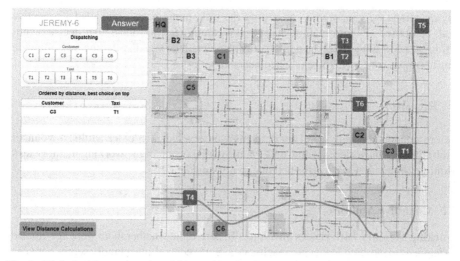

Fig. 3. High-decision automation, high workload. All taxi to customer distances are calculated and the top choice is presented to the participant. (Color figure online)

2.3 Procedure

The experiment used a 3 (degree of automation: information analysis, medium-decision, high-decision) × 2 (workload: low, high) × 2 (age: younger, older) mixed-factorial design. Participants completed six blocks of 50 trials each totaling 300 trials. The automation reliability was set at 80% (Wickens and Dixon 2007), therefore, in each block, 10 trials provided incorrect assistance. For the information analysis automation conditions, the display showed incorrect distances between customers and taxis. For the medium-decision automation conditions, the best three pairings were incorrect. For the high-decision automation conditions, the single option presented to the participant was incorrect. There were no automation failures before the 10th trial to establish trust in the automation (Wickens et al. 2002). The subsequent automation errors were randomly distributed among the remaining trials for each block. The participant continued to the next trial once they submitted their pairing or after 13 s elapsed or 20 for older adults (Pak et al. 2016), whichever comes first. Each block contained either information analysis, medium-decision, or high-decision automation and blocks was randomized for each participant. Workload was manipulated by the number of pairs of taxis and customers presented on the screen, three pairs for low workload and six pairs for high (Rovira et al. 2017).

    The main dependent variable was task performance, a.k.a decision accuracy, which was calculated as a ratio of how many trials each participant chose the correct answer compared to the total number of trials. Participants were run in groups of up to 5 at a time on individual computers with partitions between each person to avoid potential distractions. Participants signed the informed consent and immediately completed the working memory task outlined above. Once each participant completed these tests, they were shown instructions for using the taxi dispatching simulator. They were told that automation was present for all the conditions but that it was not perfectly reliable. Once any questions were answered concerning the task, participants completed 12 practice trials composed of 4 information analysis, 4 medium-decision, and 4 high-decision conditions at a low workload. The participants completed the taxi dispatching task allowing for short breaks between blocks when necessary.

3 Results

Before conducting analyses, 4 participants were excluded (3 older adults, 1 younger adult) because they scored below 85% on the math portion of the working memory test. Multiple imputation was performed due to missing data.

3.1 Cognitive Abilities

Working Memory Differences and Age. To determine whether there were age-related differences in working memory capacity, we compared working memory scores between the younger and older adults. Working memory capacity was quantified using the OSPAN task. Scores were calculated by first identifying each set of perfectly recalled letter strings and summing the number of letters in those strings producing scores between 0 and 75. We performed outlier analyses and no scores were excluded. Consistent with the widespread literature, there was a significant effect for age on working memory score, $t(83) = 2.743$, $p = 0.008$, with younger adults (M = 33.70, SD = 19.153) demonstrating higher working memory capacity scores compared to older adults (M = 23.00, SD = 16.346). The following analysis compares performance between younger and older adults to determine if older adults exhibit a greater performance decrement with unreliable automation compared to younger adults (i.e. the lumberjack effect).

3.2 Taxi Dispatching Task

Working Memory and Dispatching Task Decision Accuracy. Regression analyses were first conducted to investigate whether working memory capacity significantly predicted decision accuracy across degrees of automation. If older adults exhibit a greater lumberjack effect as we hypothesized, working memory should be a significant predictor of decision accuracy. The results showed that working memory capacity was not a significant predictor for decision accuracy in the information analysis automation and medium decision automation conditions for younger or older adults. However, working memory was a significant predictor of performance in the high decision automation conditions for younger adults ($R^2 = 0.349$, $F(1,41) = 5.688$, $p = 0.022$). This was not significant for older adults ($p > 0.05$) which indicates that working memory was not predictive of decision accuracy.

To address our hypothesis, we conducted analyses to assess performance across reliability conditions. The rationale is that when the automation is reliable, both younger and older adults should show performance benefits with increasing (reliable) automation. However, the key comparison is performance as a function of age group with unreliable automation.

Working Memory and Dispatching Task Decision Accuracy. Decision accuracy (performance) was assessed by conducting a 2 (age group: younger or older) × 3 (degree of automation: information or medium decision or high decision) × 2 (workload: low or high) × 2 (reliability: reliable or unreliable) repeated measures ANOVA. There was not a significant 4-way interaction ($F(2,80) = 0.230, p = 0.795, \eta_p^2 = 0.006$). However, there was a significant 3-way interaction between DOA, workload, and reliability ($F(2,80) = 35.627, p < 0.001, \eta_p^2 = 0.471$). The interesting finding here was that there were no age differences in the magnitude of performance benefit or decrement by age (the nonsignificance of age group). This is not supportive of our hypothesis that older adults would exhibit a greater lumberjack effect. The sources for the 3-way interaction outlined below.

The source of the 3-way interaction, as shown in Figs. 4 and 5, was a significant 2-way interaction between DOA and workload between reliable ($F(1,81) = 41.943, p < 0.001, \eta_p^2 = 0.509$) and unreliable conditions ($F(2, 81) = 7.193, p = 0.001, \eta_p^2 = .151$). For unreliable trials (Fig. 4), when workload was low, participants performed better at low DOA (M = 0.719, SD = 0.198) compared to high DOA (M = 0.636, SD = 0.271). When workload was high, however, performance didn't change from low (M = 0.547, SD = 0.189) to high DOA (M = 0.569, SD = 0.028). For reliable conditions (Fig. 5) when workload was low, performance was significantly improved using high DOA (M = 0.873, SD = 0.084) compared to low DOA (M = 0.686, SD = 0.166). When workload was high (Fig. 2), however, there were no differences between low (M = 0.733, SD = 0.192) and high (M = 0.755, SD = 0.154) DOA. These results show that low workload conditions were impacted in opposite directions with increasing DOA depending on reliability. Specifically, for low workload conditions, decision accuracy decreased with unreliable automation and increased with reliable automation. Performance under high workload was not significantly impacted by increasing DOA for unreliable or reliable conditions.

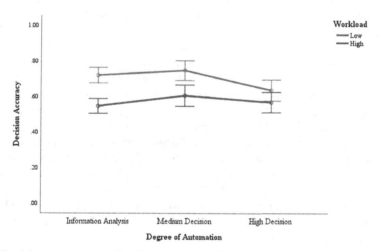

Fig. 4. Decision accuracy as a function of degree of automation and workload for unreliable conditions.

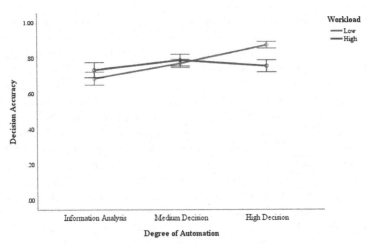

Fig. 5. Decision accuracy as a function of degree of automation and workload for reliable conditions.

Since the previous analyses demonstrated that performance did not significantly vary between younger and older adults, we conducted the following analyses collapsed across age groups. Performance was significantly lower during unreliable trials using information analysis ($t(83) = 7.027$, $p = 0.001$), medium decision ($t(83) = 3.353$, $p = 0.005$), and high decision automation ($t(83) = 5.897$, $p < 0.001$). This indicates performance was better using reliable automation at each DOA compared to unreliable automation.

In order to investigate the presence of the lumberjack effect, we next conducted analyses to understand the changes in performance across DOA comparing reliable and unreliable conditions. To remind the reader, one manifestation of the lumberjack effect is a consistent performance benefit with increasing levels of automation, but also an increasing performance penalty with increasing levels of automation. Thus, the lumberjack effect should appear as a greater difference between reliable and unreliable trials as the level of automation increases. To directly compare the performance benefits and consequences of reliable versus unreliable automation, we conducted an analysis only on the lowest and highest LOA conditions. A lumberjack effect should appear as an interaction between reliability and LOA. Specifically, performance with reliable automation should increase while performance with unreliable automation should decrease across degrees of automation. A repeated measures ANOVA was conducted. Results, shown in Fig. 6, indicated a significant interaction between reliability and degree of automation collapsed across age and workload ($F(1,82) = 12.496$, $p = .001$, $\eta_p^2 = 0.132$). However, this analysis only showed a performance improvement with increasing reliable level of automation ($t(82) = 4.510$, $p < 0.001$), not a performance decrement with increasing unreliable LOA ($t(82) = 1.303$, $p = 0.196$).

We suspected that the above results were due to the analyses being collapsed across workload conditions. This study included a higher workload condition in order to induce a lumberjack effect that was not observed in Pak et al. 2016. Higher workload should

The Effects of Increasing Degree of Unreliable Automation   337

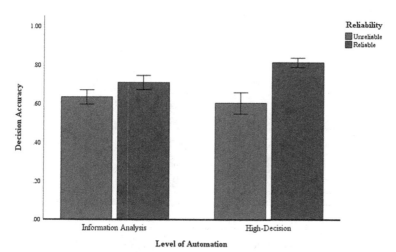

Fig. 6. Decision accuracy as a function of level of automation and reliability collapsed across workload.

make participants more susceptible to OOTL effects, thus inducing the lumberjack effect. Analyzing only high workload conditions, there was not a significant interaction between LOA and reliability ($F(1,82) < .001$, p = .995, $\eta_p^2 < 0.001$ as shown in Fig. 7. The fact that there was no significant change in performance with increasing LOA for reliable automation shows that higher-level automation was neither beneficial nor detrimental under high workload. However, there was a significant interaction between level of automation and reliability when we isolated low workload conditions ($F(1,82) = 50.080$, $p < 0.001$, $\eta_p^2 = 0.379$ (Fig. 8). Performance improved with increasing reliable automation ($t(82) = 8.785$, $p < 0.001$) and diminished with unreliable automation ($t(82) = 2.963$, $p = 0.004$). Figure 8 illustrates a lumberjack effect.

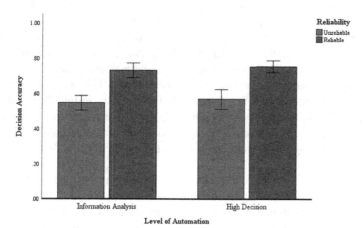

Fig. 7. Decision accuracy as a function of level of automation and reliability for high workload conditions.

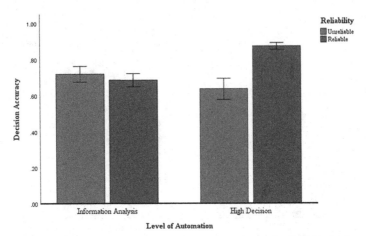

Fig. 8. Decision accuracy as a function of level of automation and reliability for low workload conditions.

4 Discussion

The purpose of the current study was to investigate how the lumberjack effect manifested in younger adults compared to older adults. We hypothesized that because of age-related differences in working memory capacity, older adults would exhibit an enhanced lumberjack effect compared to younger adults. That is, we expected older adults to show a greater performance decrement at the highest degree of unreliable automation compared to younger adults.

The results did not support our hypothesis that older adults would exhibit a greater lumberjack effect than younger adults even though there were significant differences in working memory capacity between groups. The idea behind the lumberjack effect is that performance improves with increasing degree of automation but declines under failure (Onnasch et al. 2014). In other words, the performance gap between reliable and unreliable conditions should be wider using high-level automation compared to low-level. Although both age groups exhibited the lumberjack effect under low workload, it was not significantly more pronounced in older adults. This was evidenced by the non-significance of age in the 4-way interaction. However, the results showed that under low workload, the performance decrement using unreliable automation increased from low to high degrees of automation, demonstrating the lumberjack effect. This study shows that both younger and older adults exhibited a lumberjack effect, but they were not differentiated by age.

The finding that performance did not change under high workload conditions across reliability conditions does not support the findings in Rovira et al. (2017). They found a performance decrement under high workload conditions using unreliable automation. We suspect that these discrepancies were due to differences in our sample populations. Their sample involved cadets performing a similar task to ours using a UAV simulator. Participants may have been more comfortable completing the task in that particular domain because of their experience at a military institution. Our findings showed no significant differences in performance across LOA indicating that the high workload made the task too difficult for our sample of participants. Pak et al. (2016) did not observe a lumberjack effect under the same level of workload. However, we suspect that we were able to observe a lumberjack effect because we used a higher degree of automation which is necessary to induce OOTL effects (Parasuraman et al. 2000). In summary, implementing higher workload did not have the intended effect on performance but the addition of a higher degree of a higher DOA condition did produce a lumberjack effect.

The lumberjack effect has been documented in other studies using younger adults (Rovira et al. 2017) but this is the first study to observe its presence in older adults. We hypothesized that older adults would exhibit a greater performance decrement compared to younger adults because of their reduced working memory capacity. While our older adults did indeed have reduced working memory compared to younger adults, they were not more detrimentally affected. This suggests that the source of the lumberjack effect observed in other studies may have causes other than working memory. These results are consistent with an earlier study with younger adults only (Rovira et al. 2016), that compared high and low working memory individuals' performance with increasing levels of automation. They also found that the magnitude of performance decrement with unreliable automation did not increase between low and high working memory participants.

4.1 Future Directions

The results of this study reinforce previous findings about the detrimental effects of using imperfect automation on performance. Further research should be done to investigate the relationship between age-related changes in cognitive abilities and performance with various levels of imperfect automation. Additionally, more work should clarify the causes of age-related differences with automation, specifically pinpointing the cognitive sources, such as attentional control.

References

Bainbridge, L.: Ironies of automation. Automatica **19**(6), 775–779 (1983)

Dobbs, A.R., Rule, B.G.: Adult age differences in working memory. Psychol. Aging **4**, 500–503 (1990)

Endsley, M.R., Kiris, E.O.: The out-of-the-loop performance problem and level of control in automation. Hum. Factors **37**(2), 387–394 (1995)

Labonnote, L., Høyland, K.: Smart home technologies that support independent living: Challenges and opportunities for the building industry – a systematic mapping study. Intell. Buildings Int. **9**(1), 40–63 (2017)

Manzey, D., Luz, M., Mueller, S., Dietz, A., Meixensberger, J., Strauss, G.: Automation in surgery: the impact of navigation-control assistance on performance, workload, situation awareness, and acquisition of surgical skills. Hum. Factors **53**, 544–599 (2011)

McBride, S.E., Rogers, W.A., Fisk, A.D.: Understanding the effect of workload on automation use for younger and older adults. Hum. Factors **53**(6), 672–686 (2011)

Morrow, D., North, R., Wickens, C.D.: Reducing and mitigating human error in medicine. Rev. Hum. Factors Ergon. 1(1), 254–296 (2005)

Mynatt, E.D., Melenhorst, A.S., Fisk, A.D., Rogers, W.A.: Aware technologies for aging in place: understanding user needs and attitudes. IEEE Pervasive Comput. 3(2), 36–41 (2004)

Nof, S.Y. (ed.): Springer Handbook of Automation. Springer, New York (2009). https://doi.org/10.1007/978-3-540-78831-7

Onnasch, L., Wickens, C.D., Li, H., Manzey, D.H.: Human performance consequences of stages and levels of automation: An integrated meta-analysis. Hum. Factors J. Hum. Factors Ergon. Soc. 56(3), 476–488 (2014)

Pak, R., McLaughlin, A.C., Leidheiser, W., Rovira, E.: The effect of individual differences in working memory in older adults on performance with different degrees of automated technology. Ergonomics 60(4), 518–532 (2016)

Parasuraman, R., Manzey, D.H.: Complacency and bias in human use of automation: an attentional integration. Hum. Factors 52(3), 381–410 (2010)

Parasuraman, R., Sheridan, T.B., Wickens, C.D.: A model for types and levels of human interaction with automation. IEEE Trans. Syst. Man Cybern. Part A Syst. Hum. 30(3), 286–297 (2000)

Rovira, E., McGarry, K., Parasuraman, R.: Effects of imperfect automation on decision making in a simulated command and control task. Hum. Factors J. Hum. Factors Ergon. Soc. 49(1), 76–87 (2007)

Rovira, E., Pak, R., McLaughlin, A.: Effects of individual differences in working memory on performance and trust with various degrees of automation. Theor. Issues Ergon. Sci. 18(6), 573–591 (2017)

Rybash, J.M., Roodin, P.A., Hoyer, W.J.: Adult Development and Aging, 3rd edn. Brown & Benchmark, Dubuque (1995)

Salthouse, T.A.: The aging of working memory. Neuropsychology 8, 535–543 (1994)

Salthouse, T.A.: General and specific speed mediation of adult age differences in memory. J. Gerontol. Psychol. Sci. 51B(1), 30–42 (1996)

Sanchez, J., Rogers, W.A., Fisk, A.D., Rovira, E.: Understanding reliance on automation: effects of error type, error distribution, age and experience. Theor. Issues Ergon. Sci. 15, 134–160 (2014)

Wickens, C.D., Dixon, S.R.: The benefits of imperfect diagnostic automation: a synthesis of the literature. Theor. Issues Ergon. Sci. 8(3), 201–212 (2007)

Wickens, C.D., Hellenberg, J., Xu, X.: Pilot maneuver choice and workload in free flight. Hum. Factors 44(2), 171–188 (2002)

Wickens, C.D.: Engineering Psychology and Human Performance, vol. 2nd. Harper Collins, Scranton (1992)

Unsworth, N., Engle, R.W.: The nature of individual differences in working memory capacity: active maintenance in primary memory controlled search from secondary memory. Psychol. Rev. 114(1), 104–132 (2007)

Older People as Digital Newcomers: From Evidence to Intervention Proposal

Milica Vukelic$^{(\boxtimes)}$ ⓘ, Svetlana Cizmic ⓘ, Dunja Jankovic ⓘ, Branislava Vidanovic ⓘ, and Ivana B. Petrovic ⓘ

Department of Psychology, Faculty of Philosophy, University of Belgrade,
Cika Ljubina 18-20, 11000 Belgrade, Serbia
`{mbvukeli,ipetrovi}@f.bg.ac.rs, svetlana.cizmic@sbb.rs,`
`dunja.jankovic55@gmail.com, branislavavidanovic@gmail.com`

Abstract. The aims of this mixed-method study were to analyze: older adults' computer proficiency in relation to intelligence, personality traits and attitudes towards computers (Study 1); intention to use online services in relation to attitudes towards computers (Study 2); enabling factors of using digital devices (Study 3). The goal of the overall study was to propose the intervention that would support older people as digital newcomers. The main findings were that: attitude towards computer was the strongest predictor of older adults' computer proficiency (Study 1); perceived ease of use proved to be a significant predictor of intention to use electronic services (Study 2), and most important finding from the qualitative research was that family and friends, especially peers, were older adults' most preferred source of support in acquiring new IT skills (Study 3). On the long run, advocating for involving older people in designing digital tools should be imperative. It is important to develop a self-sustainable program that would, at first, fully engage all the relevant stakeholders: municipality and social care officials, Red Cross professionals and volunteers, social clubs and spaces for seniors, IT and user experience experts, psychologists, producers and retailers of devices, family and friends. Brief focused train the trainer program based on the needs of older people would be the core of the intervention. Sustainability wise, based on identifying and supporting the most skilled ones, older people should be empowered to run the program themselves with stakeholders' occasional support.

Keywords: Digital newcomers · Older people · Serbia

1 Introduction

The number of people aged 60 years and over has almost doubled in 2017 (962 million) compared to 1980 (382 million) [1]. UN expects that by 2050 the number of persons over the age of 60 will get close to 2.1 billion. Following this prediction, in 2050, older people will account for 35% of the population in Europe. Life expectancy increased dramatically over the last 150 years, from 30 to 65, and it continually grows [2, 3]. According to some estimates, life expectancy will exceed 100 years before 2100 [2].

© Springer Nature Switzerland AG 2020
Q. Gao and J. Zhou (Eds.): HCII 2020, LNCS 12209, pp. 341–350, 2020.
https://doi.org/10.1007/978-3-030-50232-4_24

As Neves and Vetere [4] noted, new technologies could have a crucial role in meeting the needs and interests of older people. New technology could help older people to expand their social support through better communication with family and friends [5, 6]. Also, it could help older people to gain important health information, to compensate for memory lapses and cognitive decline, as well as to explore additional resources related to fun and leisure. The use of new technologies, such as e-banking and online shopping, is closely related to the wide range of services that are almost imperative in the modern world. The service sector relies heavily on technology solutions, viewing it as a competitive advantage, but without paying proper attention to older users. Taking into the account the rising number of older employees in the global workforce [7], and the fact that training methods heavily rely on technology-based instruction [8], the acceptance and adjustment of new technology to older users is imperative.

Even though the acceptance and usage of new technology have increased, older people are still less prone to keep pace with digital development. Usually they are dropping out with age. Consequently, the conceptualization of older/old age is, apart from other frameworks, also shaped in relation to technological context as being 'too old' for adjusting to new technology [4].

The cognitive and physical changes that come with aging tend to become more noticeable around the age of 65 [8]. However, many researchers found that the main obstacle for older people to embrace ICT is not related to skill deficits, but rather to negative attitudes [9]. Personality dimensions could improve the acceptance of technology, with the most significant predictors being extraversion, openness to experiences, and emotional stability [10]. Nevertheless, in a number of studies [11–13], attitude toward computers stood out as the most significant predictor for their use. In the study of Rosenthal [14] where she analyzed obstacles and factors that influence some older women to accept computers and to become 'computer literate', nearly half of the women (48%) reported being anxious or stressed when beginning to learn how to use a computer. Based on being perceived as anxious when facing new technologies, older people are usually considered as 'technophobic'. However, as Lee et al. [6] pointed out, this is usually dispelled when benefits of adoption of new technology are more prominent then potential costs.

The term older adult is defined in different ways [15]. Whether some adult would be treated as older highly depends on the context in which the observation is made [15]. In the workplace context, the term older adult generally refers to workers over 50. At the same time, employees over 50 are the age group whose labor participation is among the most scrutinized. For example, the share of employees aged 50 years and older has risen from 24% to 31% over a period of 10 years, 2005–2015 [7], but still there is a need to rise their labour participation. As Lee et al. [6] stated, researchers divide seniors into following stages: the young-old (65–74), the old-old (75–85), and the oldest-old (85 years and beyond). The group of 50–64 years of age is considered as pre-seniors or pre-retirees, and they are also sometimes included in the analyses of constraints of using technological devices among seniors [6].

ICT design for older people was until recently perceived as something on the outskirt of the designing trends [16]. The concept of 'inclusive design' [16], as well as 'gerontechnology' [17] has emerged as a strong trend aiming at embracing the needs of older users and overcoming the 'digital divide' [17] between generations. Thus understanding the needs, capabilities and experiences of older people is crucial in developing successful inclusive design [17].

The aims of this study were to: 1). analyze middle-aged and older adults' computer proficiency taking into the account intelligence, personality traits and attitudes towards computers (Study 1); 2). analyze middle-aged and older adults' intention to use online services in relation to their attitudes towards computers on the example of online payment (Study 2); 3). explore enabling factors of using digital devices among older people (Study 3). The overall aim of the paper was to propose a way to better introduce and integrate older people to the digital world as digital newcomers.

2 Study 1

2.1 Sample and Procedure

The sample comprised of 120 persons. The average age was 63 years (57% women), 78% of respondents were above the 55 years, with the majority of them having high school diploma (42%). Respondents filled out paper-and-pencil tests and scales. The participation was voluntary, anonymous and not remunerated.

2.2 Instruments

Cognitive Abilities. Cognitive abilities were assessed using the nonverbal general intellectual ability test BEG-SERIES [18]. The test consists of two sub-tests: the matrices and the combining shapes test. The reliability of the matrices test, determined by the Spearman-Brown method was .88, and by the test-retest method .76. The reliability of the combining shapes test predicted by the Spearman-Brown formula was .86, and the test-retest reliability was .89. The combining shapes test is mostly saturated with the perceptual reasoning factor, while the matrices are most saturated by the "G" factor. The test is suitable for older people as well as for the people with a lower educational level [18].

Personality Traits. Personality traits were assessed using the Big Five Inventory [19]. The BFI consists of 44 items rated on a five-point Likert scale (from 1 – completely disagree, to 5 – completely agree). Three dimensions previously shown to be relevant for the research of older people and ICT adoption and usage were included in this research, i.e. Openness to experiences (10 items), Extraversion (8 items) and Neuroticism (8 items).

Attitude Toward Computers. Attitude toward computers was assessed using the Computer Attitude Measure for Young Students (CAMYS) [20]. CAMYS was originally intended to evaluate the attitudes of students, age from 10 to 13. However, the primary goal of CAMYS authors was to use the instrument to evaluate attitudes of respondents with limited or no experience in working on a computer. Therefore it was suitable for use with older respondents. This questionnaire covers three dimensions: perceived ease of use, affect toward computers and perceived usefulness, 12 items in total (four items for each factor), each accompanied by five-point Likert scale (from 1 – completely disagree, to 5 – completely agree).

Computer Proficiency. The Computer Proficiency Questionnaire (CPQ) [21] was used to assess computer proficiency. It consists of six subscales covering different activities with a computer, such as using a printer and the Internet, or using a computer for entertainment. For the purposes of this research, a shorter version of the questionnaire (CPQ-12) was used. It consisted of 12 items (2 items for each subscale). Respondents rated their performance on a five-point scale from 1 – never tried, to 5 – being completely successful in the activity.

2.3   Results and Discussion

Table 1 summarizes the descriptive statistics and correlation analysis. Computer proficiency was positively and significantly correlated with general ability, neuroticism, openness to experience and computer attitudes. The strongest correlation was found between computer proficiency and computer attitude, while there was no significant correlation between extraversion and computer proficiency.

A three-stage hierarchical multiple regression was conducted with computer proficiency as a criterion variable. Sociodemographic variables (gender, age and education) were entered at step one of the regression to control for these differences. The intelligence and personality dimensions were entered at step two, and, finally computer attitude at step three. The hierarchical multiple regression revealed that at step one, sociodemographic variables contributed significantly to the regression model, $F(3,114) = 14.02, p < .01$ and accounted for 27% of the variation in computer proficiency. Introducing the intelligence and personality variables explained an additional 18.4% of variation in computer

Table 1. Descriptive statistics for cognitive abilities, personality traits, attitudes toward computer and computer proficiency and correlation of computer proficiency with remaining variables.

	M	SD	Matrices test	Combining shapes	Extraversion	Neuroticism	Openness	Computer attitude
Matrices	11.77	4.47						
Combining shapes	9.63	3.41						
Extraversion	28.48	4.48						
Neuroticism	23.03	5.18						
Openness to experience	36.50	4.61						
Computer attitude	42.26	12.42						
Computer proficiency	40.30	13.44	.35**	.52**	.01	−.24**	.30**	.74**

$**p < .01; *p < .05$

proficiency $F_{Change}(5,109) = 7.33, p < .001$. Adding computer attitude to the regression model explained additional 31% of the variation in computer proficiency $F_{Change}(1, 108) = 139.598, p < .001$. When all six independent variables (apart from sociodemographic ones) were included in stage 3 of the regression model, it was shown that only the following predictors remained significant; i.e. combining shapes (*beta* = .217, $p < .01$), openness to experiences (*beta* = .135, $p < .05$) and the attitude toward computers, as the strongest of the remaining significant predictors (*beta* = .621, $p < .01$).

Another hierarchical multiple regression analysis was conducted with computer proficiency as a criterion variable and different dimensions of attitudes - perceived ease of use, affect toward computers and perceived usefulness as predictors. Sociodemographic variables (gender, age and education) were entered at step one of the regression (as in the first model). The perceived ease of use, affect toward computers and perceived usefulness were entered at step two. Sociodemographic variables contributed significantly to the regression model, $F(3,114) = 14.03, p < .01$ and accounted for 27% of the variation in computer proficiency. Introducing the attitudes dimensions explained additional 44.2% of variation in computer proficiency $F_{Change}(3,111) = 56.86, p < .001$. Nevertheless, not all dimensions of attitudes were significant. Namely, it was shown that most significant predictors were perceived ease of use (*beta* = .396, $p < .00$) and affect toward computers (*beta* = .222, $p < .05$).

3   Study 2

3.1   Sample and Procedure

The sample comprised of 86 adults (62% women); their average age was 62 years, while 91% of respondents were above the age of 55 years. Respondents filled out a questionnaire in paper-and-pencil form. The participation was voluntary, anonymous and not remunerated.

3.2   Instruments

Attitude Toward Computers. Attitude toward computers was assessed using the Computer Attitude Measure for Young Students (CAMYS) [20].

Intention to Use the Electronic Payment of Bills. Intention for electronic bill payment was assessed using a 3-item scale from the study of Lian and Yen [22], which was initially developed for assessing drivers and barriers to online shopping. The items were adapted for the electronic payment of bills; examples of items were: I intend to pay bills electronically in the future; I predict I would pay bills electronically in the future; I intend to continue paying bills electronically.

3.3   Results and Discussion

Table 2 summarizes the descriptive statistics and correlation analysis. As can be seen from Table 2, computer attitude is strongly and positively correlated with the intention to use electronic bill payment.

Table 2. Intention for electronic bill payment and attitude toward computers: descriptive statistics and intercorrelations.

	M	SD	Intention to use electronic bill payment
Intention for electronic bill payment	9.01	3.71	
Computer attitude	41.40	10.84	.69**

$**p < .01; *p < .05$

A hierarchical multiple regression analysis was conducted with the intention to pay bills electronically as a criterion variable and different dimensions of attitudes toward the computer, i.e. perceived ease of use, affect toward computers and perceived usefulness as predictors. Sociodemographic variables (i.e. gender and age) were entered at step one of the regression, as in the previous study. The perceived ease of use, affect toward computers and perceived usefulness were entered at step two. Sociodemographic variables did not contribute significantly to the regression model, $F(2,83) = 0.819, p = .444$. Introducing the dimensions of attitudes in step 2 explained additional 48.2% of variation in the intention to pay bills electronically $F_{Change}(3,80) = 25.764, p < .001$. When all three dimensions of attitude towards computer were included in step 2, it was shown that only perceived ease of use remained a significant predictor (*beta* $= .459, p < .00$).

4   Study 3

4.1   Sample and Procedure

The qualitative sample encompassed 30 adults, age 56 years and older (average age was 65 years). Data were collected using semi-structured interviews. The research participation was voluntary, anonymous and not remunerated.

4.2   Instruments

The semi-structured interview covered attitudes toward using digital devices (desktop computers, laptops, smartphones and tablets), and drivers and barriers for their usage.

4.3   Results and Discussion

Digital devices are mainly used for fun (interests and hobbies), communications (especially with family and friends living abroad) and following news. Main drivers are social pressure as everyone uses them and ease of doing things (as research participants put it: "Information is easily accessible and you do not have to try hard to collect them"; "It is faster and easier and relaxing for the brain"). Usage of various digital devices is more easily spread among those that started using computers at work. Having close support, such as family members and friends, on one side, and a learning buddy on the other, are powerful drivers in mastering new electronic devices and software. One of the strongest barriers to using online services is the wish of older people to maintain social contacts in person while using traditional services.

Main identified barriers were related to lack of skills. Using digital devices is sometimes perceived "as a waste of time", mainly because older users are not skilled enough, and it takes them more time to do something. One of the barriers related to acquiring IT skills is fear of failure. Likewise, the process of mastering skills brings problems as usually younger, informal trainers (i.e. family members, friends and colleagues) easily get impatient if they have to repeat instructions, to quote one respondent: "If I forget how to do something and ask again, they get annoyed". Concerning lack of skills and knowledge about devices, there is also widespread fear of damaging the device, "making a mess", or as one of the participants said, "If I spoil something, I get frustrated, and I am not able to touch it for several days". Poor command of English (as it is a foreign language), presents a significant barrier for truly embracing the digital world.

5 Overall Discussion and Intervention Proposal

Attitude towards computer was the strongest predictor of computer proficiency of older people (Study 1). Analyzing intention to use electronic services, i.e. electronic payment, only one dimension of attitude towards computers - perceived ease of use proved to be a significant predictor (Study 2). Most important findings from the qualitative research (Study 3) were: 1). desktop computers' main advantages for older users are large screen and keyboard; external mouse was easier for use than laptop touchpad; 2). main benefits of using laptops for older users were their portability (as for smartphones), and screen size (larger than on smart phones); 3). smartphones are strongly preferred as portable, more intuitive and easier to use (on the other hand, the smaller size of the touch screen and consequently smaller touch targets make it easier for older users to make mistakes).

In line with previous research, family and friends are older persons' most preferred source of support in acquiring new IT skills, not just because of their availability and as an impulse for highly valued social interaction with close ones [23], but also as a self-confidence building mechanism, especially for those that are more anxious [24]. The conclusion that the attitude towards digital devices turns out to be the strongest predictor of users' digital proficiency supports Wolfson, Cavanagh and Kraiger's [8] recommendation about the need for motivating and developing self-efficacy as part of training for older people. As peer education is already a widespread mechanism for acquiring IT skills among older people, the trainers should give them some additional understanding that would help pass the acquired knowledge to their older friends. Trainers should also encourage them to take part in coaching older friends. The future research should further explore, and later on evaluate, appropriate contents and training methods, as well as effects of different trainers (e.g. peer trainers or professional trainers) on computer proficiency of older training participants. Apart from that future research should explore the motivation of older people for taking part in IT skills training.

Problems that older people still encounter in using various digital tools prove that designers still rely on stereotypes about older users [25]. Though proposals about involving older persons into developing new IT tools right from the beginning could be found in the literature for quite some time [26], there is still a strong need to advocate for this.

Qualitative findings are in line with findings of the change in cognitive capacities of older people that point to the need to tailor IT training of older people according to their capabilities [8].

Based on presented findings and the literature review, we propose an intervention that would enable older people to rely more heavily on ICT devices, mainly on a tablet as an adequate device for older people. One of the important long-term aims of the intervention should be advocating for involving older people in designing digital tools, both devices and programs. In order to be sustainable, this intervention should engage the relevant stakeholders: municipality officials, social care officials, Red Cross professionals and volunteers, social clubs and spaces for older people, IT and user experience experts, psychologists, producers and retailers of tablets, family of older people and their friends (both peers and younger).

Municipality officials, social care officials, Red Cross professionals and volunteers should support the program and enable all the needed resources (people, devices, training equipment, space). IT experts, user experience experts and psychologists should provide the expert knowledge base for the training, as well as setting tablets for older users. Family and friends of older people should be the trainers and first line of motivators and supporters.

The core of the intervention entails designing the training for older people and two levels of train the trainer program: 1. Train the trainer program for older persons' family and friends, and 2. Train the trainer program for older persons that would be 'focal points' and those that would spread digital literacy among older peers. It is important to stress that, as family members and younger friends belong to the so-called "sandwich" generation that has to deal with numerous pressures, the training itself should be brief. It is of utmost importance to provide online tools and support and to stress the importance of specific issues of motivating older people to learn and to use digital tools. The training should also cover giving instructions and feedback to older people in line with their cognitive and motor functioning. For the long-term sustainability of the program, senior experts for spreading digital literacy among older peers should function as 'focal points'. Senior focal persons should be active participants at social spaces for older people, both offline and online.

The proposed intervention may seem too complex and demanding. We should be aware that we live in the world of constant IT innovations. Under these circumstances, people of all ages are a sort of digital newcomers that have to keep pace with the constant development of new technologies. Older people will always be in a specially challenging position in this never-ending story. As an adequate response, it is important to develop a self-sustainable system of training through social spaces for older people, with, occasional support of relevant stakeholders.

References

1. United Nations: World Population Ageing 2017 - Highlights (ST/ESA/SER.A/397). Department of Economic and Social Affairs, Population Division (2017)
2. Bloom, D.E., Canning, D., Fink, G: Population aging and economic growth Working Paper 32. The World Bank, Commission on growth and development (2008)

3. Prettner, K., Canning, D.: Increasing life expectancy and optimal retirement in general equilibrium. Econ. Theor. **56**(1), 191–217 (2014). https://doi.org/10.1007/s00199-013-0776-9
4. Neves, B.B., Vetere, F.: Ageing and emerging digital technologies. Ageing Dig. Technol. 1–14 (2019). https://doi.org/10.1007/978-981-13-3693-5_1
5. Charness, N., Boot, W.R.: Aging and information technology use. Assoc. Psychol. Sci. **18**(5), 253–258 (2009). https://doi.org/10.1111/j.1467-8721.2009.01647.x
6. Lee, B., Chen, Y., Hewitt, L.: Age differences in constraints encountered by seniors in their use of computers and the internet. Comput. Hum. Behav. **27**(3), 1231–1273 (2011). https://doi.org/10.1016/j.chb.2011.01.003
7. Eurofound (2017), Sixth European Working Conditions Survey – Overview report (2017 update), Publications Office of the European Union, Luxembourg (2017)
8. Wolfson, N.E., Cavanagh, T.M., Kraiger, K.: Older adults and technology-based instruction: Optimizing learning outcomes and transfer. Acad. Manag. Learn. Educ. **13**(1), 26–44 (2014). https://doi.org/10.5465/amle.2012.0056
9. Heinz, M.: Exploring predictors of technology adoption among older adults. Unpublished graduate thesis, Graduate Iowa State University Capstones (2013)
10. Correa, T., Hinsley, A.W., de Zúñiga, G.H.: Who interacts on the Web? the intersection of users' personality and social media use. Comput. Hum. Behav. **26**(2), 247–253 (2010). https://doi.org/10.1016/j.chb.2009.09.003
11. Czaja, S.J., et al.: Factors predicting the use of technology: Findings from the center for research and education on aging and technology enhancement (CREATE). Psychol. Aging **21**(2) (2006). https://doi.org/10.1037/0882-7974.21.2.333
12. Mitzner, T.L., et al.: Older adults talk technology: technology usage and attitudes. Comput. Hum. Behav. **26**(6) (2010). https://doi.org/10.1016/j.chb.2010.06.020
13. Vroman, K.G., Arthanat, S., Lysack, C.: "Who over 65 is online?" older adults' dispositions toward information communication technology. Comput. Hum. Behav. **43**, 156–166 (2015). https://doi.org/10.1016/j.chb.2014.10.018
14. Rosenthal, R.L.: Older computer-literate women: their motivations, obstacles, and paths to success. Educ. Gerontol. **34**(7), 610–626 (2008). https://doi.org/10.1080/03601270801949427
15. Wagner, N., Hassanein, K., Head, M.. Computer use by older adults: a multi-disciplinary review. Comput. Hum. Behav. **26**(5), 870–882 (2010). https://doi.org/10.1016/j.chb.2010.03.029
16. Lim, C.S.C.: Designing inclusive ICT products for older users: taking into account the technology generation effect. J. Eng. Des. **21**(2–3), 189–206 (2010). https://doi.org/10.1080/09544820903317001
17. Charness, N., Boot, W.R.: Aging and information technology use: potential and barriers. Curr. Dir. Psychol. Sci. **18**(5), 253–258 (2009)
18. Bukvic, A., Stajnberger, I.: BEG Serija [BEG series]. Centar za primenjenu psihologiju, Beograd (1984)
19. John, O.P., Srivastava, S.: The Big-Five trait taxonomy: history, measurement, and theoretical perspective. In: Pervin, L.A., John, O.P. (eds.) Handbook of Personality: Theory and Research, pp. 102–138. Guilford Press, New York (1999)
20. Teo, T., Noyes, J.: Development and validation of a computer attitude measure for young students (CAMYS). Comput. Hum. Behav. **24**(6), 2659–2667 (2008). https://doi.org/10.1016/j.chb.2008.03.006
21. Boot, W.R., Charnes, N., Czaja, S.J., Sharit, J., Rogers, W.A., Fisk, A.D.: Computer proficiency questionnaire: assessing low and high computer proficient seniors. Gerontol. **55**(3), 404–411 (2015)

22. Lian, J.W., Yen, D.C.: Online shopping drivers and barriers for older adults: age and gender differences. Comput. Hum. Behav. **37**, 133–143 (2014). https://doi.org/10.1016/j.chb.2014.04.028

23. Kurniawan, S.: Older people and mobile phones: a multi-method investigation. Int. J. Hum. Comput. Stud. **66**(12), 889–901 (2008). https://doi.org/10.1016/j.ijhcs.2008.03.002

24. Page, T.: Touchscreen mobile devices and older adults: a usability study. Int. J. Hum. Fac. Ergonomics **3**(1), 65–85 (2014). https://doi.org/10.1504/IJHFE.2014.062550

25. Eisma, R., Dickinson, A., Goodman, J., Syme, A., Tiwari, L., Newell, A.F.: Early user involvement in the development of information technology-related products for older people. Univ. Access Inf. Soc. **3**(2), 131–140 (2004). https://doi.org/10.1007/s10209-004-0092-z

26. Essén, A., Östlund, B.: Laggards as innovators? old users as designers of new services & service systems. Int. J. Des. **5**(3), 89–98 (2011)

Understanding Older Adults' Vulnerability and Reactions to Telecommunication Fraud: The Effects of Personality and Cognition

Honglian Xiang[1], Jia Zhou[2(✉)], and Bingjun Xie[3]

[1] Department of Industrial Engineering, Chongqing
University, Chongqing, People's Republic of China
xianghonglian18@gmail.com
[2] School of Management Science and Real Estate, Chongqing
University, Chongqing, People's Republic of China
zhoujia07@gmail.com
[3] Chongqing Chuanyi Automation Co. Ltd., Chongqing, People's Republic of China

Abstract. Older adults are one of the high-risk groups vulnerable to telecommunication fraud, but little is known about what strategies will be taken by them to fight telecommunication fraud and what the underlying rationales are behind their reactions. Therefore, this study examined it through three phases. In phase 1, sixty older adults participated in a face-to-face survey of possible influence of personality and cognition. Then, they judged the authenticity of messages they have read on a real phone and were interviewed. Phase 2 is an online questionnaire survey to identify two more factors to enrich the results of phase 1. Phase 3 is a text analysis of 120 supreme court verdicts. The results reveal individual differences in anti-fraud strategies and show that older adults adopted different strategies to address potential telecom fraud. Particularly, older adults with lower need for cognition (NFC) were more likely to adopt extremely conservative strategies.

Keywords: Scams and frauds · Older adults · Telecommunication · Anti-fraud strategies · Need for cognition · Individual difference

1 Introduction

Telecommunication fraud is a prevalent and costly societal problem, to which countless older adults fall victim. In the United States, 67% of fraud perpetrators used telecommunication to reach potential scam victims [1] and have targeted scams at particular age groups [2]. Particularly, the loss caused by telephone fraud, which is a highly efficient means for fraud perpetrators to victimize a large number of people [3], was $9.5 billion in 2016 [4]. In China, the loss caused by telecommunication fraud was $16.7 billion, and 70% of Chinese victims were seniors. Some victims even lost their lives because of being swindled. It is obvious that telecommunication fraud crime has threatened the quality of seniors' lives.

© Springer Nature Switzerland AG 2020
Q. Gao and J. Zhou (Eds.): HCII 2020, LNCS 12209, pp. 351–363, 2020.
https://doi.org/10.1007/978-3-030-50232-4_25

Many actions have been taken to fight telecommunication fraud under the premise that people report scams and frauds. In the United States, people can use the "Do Not Call Registry" to stop unwanted calls and report scams and frauds to organizations, such as the Federal Trade Commission, the Internet Crime Complaint Center, and the Ripoff Report. In China, the government, collaborating with telecom operators and banks, has established provincial and city-level anti-fraud centers to remind people of potential fraud through warning text messages. However, these efforts are not effective if people do not even cast suspicion/doubt on the content of possible fraud. Older adults are still vulnerable to becoming victims of scams and frauds.

Anti-fraud actions are usually macro-level policies and services that do not tailor to individuals. It is obvious that the last protection against fraud is always individuals, whose reactions to potential fraud are crucial. However, there is limited research on individual differences in anti-fraud strategies. Therefore, this study aims to explore the following questions. (i) What kind of strategies will be taken by older adults to fight against SMS fraud? (ii) What factors influence the vulnerability and reactions of older adults to SMS fraud and general telecommunication fraud? (iii) What are the tricks of telecommunication fraudsters in China?

2 Literature Review

Over long periods of time, many studies investigated why certain individuals are vulnerable to fraud, and loneliness, self-control, interpersonal trust, and the need for cognition (NFC) were found to be influential.

2.1 Loneliness

Loneliness has the positive impact on vulnerability to telecommunication fraud among older adults, particularly for telemarketing fraud. Older adults who feel lonelier and socially isolated are more willing to interact with telemarketers [6, 7], and received more weekly telemarketing calls and consistently lost more money, which increased their chance of being telemarketing fraud victims [5]. The need for social contact of lonely older adults may increase willingness to communicate with strangers [8], however they might not realize an offender's aims and the fact that their relationship is one-sided [9]. Besides, older adults' attitudes and behaviors toward telemarketing fraud can be influenced by parasocial relationships and pseudo-friendships with marketers [10]. Wagner [7] noted that loneliness increases the willingness to listen to and the tendency to engage in pseudo-friendships or parasocial relationships with marketers, which increases the probability that they adapt their beliefs to what marketers tell them and results in fraud victimization eventually.

2.2 Self-control

A variety of victimizations (e.g., homicide victimization and violent victimization) have been found to be associated with self-control [11–13]. Meanwhile, the self-control effect may vary depending on the type of victimization. Pratt, Turanovic, Fox, and Wright [14] divided victimization into direct-contact victimization (e.g., violent victimization and theft) and noncontact victimization (e.g., fraud, stalking, and cyber victimization) and found that the effect of self-control is significantly stronger when predicting noncontact forms of victimization. Unlike many other types of victimization, noncontact victimization requires a high degree of cooperation between the victim and the offender. Low self-control significantly increased the likelihood of fraud victimization [15]. Low self-control individuals will be more likely to behave in ways that elevate their exposure to fraud victimization [16], for example, directly engaging the fraudster by providing personal information over the telephone [15]. It can be assumed that self-control will have a great impact on the telecommunication fraud victimization of older adults.

2.3 Interpersonal Trust

The role of interpersonal trust in cooperative relationships is of fundamental importance [17]. Many researchers have found that attitudes, purchase intentions, and purchase behavior can be influenced by interpersonal trust. A consumer with higher interpersonal trust can address the seller successfully regardless of the potential negative consequences [18]. E-consumers who are low on interpersonal trust are less likely to shop on the Web due to their heightened concerns with Web security [19]. Alternatively, Hung, Li, and Tse [20] focused on the Chinese online community and found that interpersonal trust enhances a user's engagement with an online community and his or her intentions to act on fellow users' suggestions. Interpersonal trust may play an important role in telecommunication fraud because telecommunication fraud requires a very high degree of cooperation between the victim and the offender.

2.4 Need for Cognition

The effect of NFC on decision-making was investigated [21, 22]. Specifically, individuals with high NFC tend to exert more effort and exhibit higher decision quality when performing complex judgment tasks, while those who with low NFC are less likely to engage in careful information-processing and are more likely to be influenced by simple cues. Das et al. [19] found that NFC is the only trait that has a strong, direct effect on information-seeking behavior on the Web. Fraud judgment requires individuals to expend sensible cognitive effort in identifying relevant fraud risk factors, evaluating them, and integrating a series of judgments to form overall judgments. In the financial field, individuals with high NFC enjoy thinking more deeply and engaging in more developed thought processes for complex cognitive tasks, such as fraud risk assessments, compared to those with low NFC [21]. These individuals demonstrated that NFC was quite important in fraud risk assessment. However, the effect of NFC on older adults' anti-fraud strategies has been rarely investigated. It can be assumed that NFC will play a role in older adults' judgment related to telecommunication fraud.

2.5 Other Factors on Telecommunication Fraud Victimization

The effects of educational background and social isolation on telemarketing fraud vulnerability among older adults were investigated. Empirically, less-educated adults (e.g., those with less than a high school education) are more likely to become victims of consumer and telemarketing fraud than more educated adults [5], while those who possess a bachelor's degree or higher are less likely [8]. However, Gross [23] found that most older victims of telemarketing fraud tended to be married and well-educated. In addition, Lee and Geistfeld [8] found that social isolation increases older adults' risk of telemarketing fraud victimization by prompting them to seek social interaction from telemarketers. However, Reiboldt and Vogel [24] found that social isolation did not increase the chance of the potential victimization of older adults. The conflict in the results should be further investigated. Thus, in this study, the influence of demographic factors on older adults' anti-fraud strategies for telecommunication fraud was investigated.

3   Methodology

This study consists of three phases (shown in Fig. 1). Phase 1 aimed to explore what strategies will be taken by older adults and what factors would affect the judgments of the elderly related to telecommunication fraud. Phase 2 aimed to investigate two more factors to enrich the results of phase 1. Then, in phase 3, the fraud types and strategies taken by fraudsters were investigated.

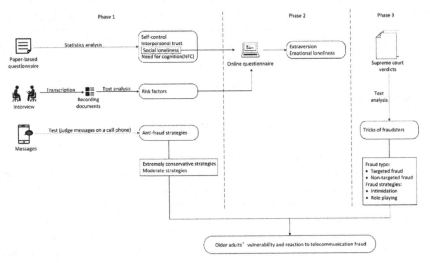

Fig. 1. The conceptual framework of this study.

3.1   Phase 1

There were 60 participants involved in this phase, including 11 males and 49 females, and their ages ranged from 60 to 88 years old (mean age = 63.78, SD = 6.13). All participants were recruited from Chongqing, China, and they belonged to various socio-economic backgrounds: older adults with higher-education; those who have not graduated from primary school; older adults with good financial situation; and who with poor economic position.

Questionnaire Survey. The questionnaire was made up of two parts. The first part collected participants' demographic information (e.g., age, educational background, living status, income, fraud experience and experience using technology products). The second part contained widely used scales to measure participants' cognition and personality (shown in Table 1).

Table 1. Different scales used in this study.

Instrument	Number of items	Source
Social loneliness scale	5	[25]
Self-control scale	24	[26]
Interpersonal trust	4	[19]
NFC	18	[27]

Social loneliness was first considered because telecommunication fraud is more relevant to social activities. It can be assumed that social loneliness may be more important in older adults' anti-fraud strategies related to telecommunication fraud. The social loneliness scale was adopted from DiTommaso, Brannen, and Best [25] for two reasons: (i) the items is fewer compared to other scales, which makes it easier for older adults to keep patient, and (ii) the reliability was relatively high. The interpersonal trust scale, in which the items were high reliable and fewer, was adopted from Das et al. [19].

There were 51 items in the questionnaire totally. All scales were translated into Chinese and then back-translated. The questionnaire was tested on two retired professors (aged 72 and 81, respectively) of Chongqing University. Corrections were made to the questionnaire based on the comments received from the pretest before it was administered to the participants.

Test. A test simulated SMS fraud was conducted to observe judgment performance. First, 13 short messages were made up by the researchers. Among them, eight messages were fraud messages that included six types of fraud (e.g., role playing, telemarketing, promotion and winning), and the rest were distractors. The authenticity of each message has been first assessed by an expert group with retired professors from Chongqing University, two retired officials, three college students, and two middle-aged adults were invited. The results were then synthesized by the experimenter. All messages were presented on a real phone to simulate SMS fraud.

Second, participants' subjective ratings and objective response behaviors were recorded. They were first required to give a score on the message they read (1 through 5, 1 = he lowest credibility, 5 = the highest credibility). Then, their responding actions (e.g., whether they called back the phishing or real phone number or tapped the phishing or real link in the messages) were observed. Their behaviors are the criteria of judgment when their subjective ratings were not consistent with their objective responses. For example, if a participant gave a true message 5 points while she or he chose not to tap the link in the message, then the final judgment is that she or he did not trust the message. If a participant gave a message 1 point and she or he chose to call back the real number in the message, then the final judgment is that she or he does trust the message. Two older adults were recruited for a pretest. Corrections based on the comments received from the pretest were made to the test before administering it to the participants.

Interview. A five-minute interview was conducted to explore the risk factors of the messages, which mainly contained two questions: "What factor makes you give such a score and take such actions toward the message?" and "Please talk about the fraud experience you got through or heard." The participants' comments were recorded through the voice recorder, transcribed, and analyzed through NVIVO 11.

3.2   Phase 2

Inspired by the results of phase 1, a 20-item questionnaire was constructed to investigate the effects of emotional loneliness and extraversion. Ten items adapted from DiTommaso, Brannen, and Best [25] were used to measure emotional loneliness. Eight items adapted from Eysenck, H. J. and Eysenck, S. B. G. [28] were used to measure extraversion. All items were back-translated. There were two reverse items to check reliability. Most of older adults are not interested in filling out online questionnaires in China. Some of them are not familiar with the internet tools (e.g., smart phones and computers), and others are not willing to spend their limited energy to conduct the survey. Besides, many seniors are reluctant to admit that they have been deceived. While their grandchildren who can easily get accessed to the online survey may know their grandparents well. They can objectively conduct the survey by themselves or through interviewing their grandparents the items of the online questionnaires directly. Due to that, the questionnaire was changed to a third-person perspective from the first-person perspective, such as "My grandparents feel alone when they are with us." and "Are your grandparents lively people?", and distributed among college students online. One hundred twenty-seven questionnaires were collected. Among them, 121 questionnaires were valid.

3.3   Phase 3

This phase investigated the fraudster's characteristics and the strategies taken by them. To achieve that, supreme court verdicts about telecommunication fraud were analyzed. First, more than 150 verdict papers about telecommunication fraud were found by combing key words (e.g., older adults and telecommunication fraud) from the largest open platform for court verdict documents in China, "China Judgments Online", which covers all types of cases and posted more than 30 million verdict papers with detailed description. Then, the verdict papers without older adult victimizations were removed, finally, 120 supreme court verdict papers were selected and analyzed through NVIVO 11. The fraud type committed by fraudsters and the strategies taken by the fraudsters were determined.

4 Results and Discussion

4.1 Successful Judgment Rate

The participants could correctly judge eight messages out of 13 messages on average, with the error rate of 38.5%. Eleven factors (i.e., gender, age, health status, educational background, income level, living status, social loneliness, interpersonal trust, self-control, NFC, and fraud experience) were analyzed by one-way ANOVA. The results (shown in Table 2) showed that participants who had a higher education, higher income, lived alone, and had lower interpersonal trust performed better in judging the authenticity of messages. Consistently, Das et al. [19] found participants who had lower interpersonal trust had more security concerns.

Table 2. The effects of education, income, living status and interpersonal trust on judgment success rate.

	SS	df	MS	F	p
Education	2.740	3	0.913	4.264	0.009
Income	2.602	3	0.867	4.005	0.012
Living status	1.613	1	1.613	7.132	0.010
Interpersonal trust	4.622	9	0.514	2.540	0.017

Participants who lived alone had lower judgment success rates. One possible reason is that people who lived alone are always in the absence of guardians, which increases the chance of being deceived. The results support the assumption of the routine activity theory [29]. However, participants who felt social loneliness did not perform worse than those who did not. People who lived alone may not necessarily feel social loneliness if they have more social activities and contacts with others. It is necessary to distinguish two types of loneliness: the social loneliness and the emotional loneliness that plays an important role in loneliness [30]. Noteworthy, people who had richer fraud experience did not perform better in fraud detection than those who had not. The possible reasons may be that (i) the major fraud type that participants previously encountered is face-to-face fraud, so their knowledge derived from the face-to-face fraud might not transfer to the SMS fraud in this study, and (ii) telecommunication fraud is complex, various and mutated, and the content and methods of telecommunication fraud are always changing, which weakens the role of previous fraud experience in fraud detection.

4.2 Strategies to Fight Against SMS Fraud

To dig into their judgment patterns, two types of judgment were defined in this study: J1 represents judging the true message as fraud; and J2 represents judging the fraud message as true. Participants are more capable of identifying fraud messages than true messages ($t = 12.802$, $p = 0.000$), and the rate of successfully identifying fraud messages

(M = 0.828, SD = 0.266) was 107% higher than that of true messages (M = 0.243, SD = 0.233). Specifically, participants with a higher education level tended to make J1 (F = 3.001, p = 0.038), while participants with a lower education level, lower income, and higher interpersonal trust tended to make J2 (shown in Table 3).

Table 3. The effect of education, income, interpersonal trust and living status on J2.

	SS	df	MS	F	p
Education	3.775	3	1.258	6.632	0.001
Income	3.442	3	1.147	5.862	0.001
Interpersonal trust	4.315	9	0.479	2.377	0.025

Furthermore, although their J1 accuracy was 100%, there were 14 participants who rated all of the messages as fraud messages, without considering the possibility of true messages. Such an extremely conservative strategy was compared to the moderate strategy, which was used by the remaining 46 participants to judge messages depending on content. Fourteen out of the 46 participants who had the lowest J1 accuracy were chosen for comparison. An independent sample T-test was conducted. Participants with higher education, higher income, and lower need for cognition were more likely to take extremely conservative strategies (shown in Table 4).

Table 4. The difference between J1 and J2.

	t	df	p	Diff%
Education	4.877	26	0.000	74%
Income	2.855	26	0.009	25%
NFC	−2.227	26	0.035	12%

Note. Diff% means percentage difference, Diff% = (M1 − M2)/[(M1 + M2)/2]

People with higher need for cognition are more willing to carry out cognitive thinking activities. Thus, they are more likely to judge the authenticity of messages through cognitive thinking. The traditional way to combat fraud is teaching older adults about fraud cases, which loses its effectiveness when the fraud type is not the same. The results indicated that the need for cognition had an impact on the anti-fraud strategies taken by older adults. Training older adults to form the habit of cognitive thinking is a good way to fight against fraud. This method may be more effective than the traditional ones (e.g., teaching older adults fraud cases) because it focuses on aspects of cognition.

4.3 Rationales of Judging Fraud or True Messages

To understand why participants judged certain messages as fraud or true messages, their comments in the interview were analyzed. As shown in Table 6, most participants are cautious to receive benefits, such as huge discounts or free of charge. Chinese people are educated from childhood that nothing worth having is cheap, such as the Chinese saying goes "There is no free lunch in the world". Such education will increase the psychological alertness of participants, which will make participants more careful when dealing with messages with "some kind of benefits" (Table 5).

Table 5. The risk factors of fraud messages.

Risk factors	Portion
Promising some kind of benefits (e.g., huge discount)	24/50
Free of charge	22/50
The process of the event being done was not consistent with my understanding	22/50
The message gave the specific operation orders (e.g., transferring money, given phone numbers to call)	12/50
The message contained a URL	15/50
The message was sent by a wrong phone number	6/50

Note. The portion used "a/b" to demonstrate that "b" participants chose to evaluate and "a" participants mentioned the words.

In contrast, Table 6 indicated that the certain Chinese seniors tended to trust messages sent by official institutions or some authority institutions. One possible reason is that Chinese people are told that they should trust in authority institutions, such as government departments, from their childhood. In the interviews, when asked why they trusted one of the messages, some participants said, "The government will not deceive us"; this is same as the findings of Liang [31].

Table 6. The reasons why participants think the message is not fraud.

Reasons	Portion
The message was sent by an official institution or authority institution (e.g., government department)	13/36
The message was related to real life (e.g., pay phone bill)	4/36

Note. The portion used "a/b" to demonstrate that "b" participants chose to evaluate and "a" participants mentioned the words.

4.4 Effects of Emotional Loneliness and Extraversion

One-way ANOVA and independent sample T-test were conducted to investigate the effects of emotional loneliness and extraversion. The results showed a marginal effect ($F = 3.74$, $p = 0.12$) of emotional loneliness on judgment related to telecommunication fraud, which indicated that older adults are easier to be targeted by telecommunication fraudsters when they feel less emotional loneliness. This is quite different from what Alves and Wilson [5] found, which demonstrated that loneliness had great effects on older adults' trust. One possible reason is that the research object of Alves and Wilson [5] was American older adults' trust, while this study focuses on how Chinese older adults judge a fraud message or call. The conflict in the results showed that cultural difference has a great impact on judgment related to telecommunication fraud.

In addition, a significant effect (F = 0.97, p = 0.002) of extraversion showed that older adults who are more extroverted are easier to be aimed by fraudsters. One possible reason is that older adults who are more extroverted may have more social activities and get access to more diverse people, which increases their opportunity of being a potential telecommunication fraud victim. This finding is consistent with the routine activity theory [29].

4.5   Tricks of Fraudsters

Two types of fraud were identified from supreme court verdicts: targeted fraud (i.e. fraudsters know a lot about their victims) and non-targeted fraud (fraudsters know nothing about their victims). Compared to the non-targeted fraud, targeted fraud was used most by the fraudsters, accounting for 64% of all fraud cases, and which made more serious economic losses. With increasing anti-fraud laws or products launched, personal information is more difficult to get. It can be predicted that fraudsters are more likely to first conduct non-targeted fraud to get more personal information and then conduct targeted fraud.

Table 7. Different roles played by fraudsters.

Item		Percentage (accounts for the all cases)
Fraud type	Targeted fraud	64%
	Non-targeted fraud	36%
Strategies	Intimidation	18%
	Telemarketing promotion	23%
	Role playing	59%
Roles	Family members	27%
	Relatives	9%
	Professional experts	27%
	Government officials	37%

The most widely used fraud strategy taken by fraudsters was role playing. Fraudsters were more likely to play a variety of different roles (shown in Table 7). Among them, the most frequent roles played were government officials (e.g., police department, supreme court), which shows that Chinese seniors were affected heavily by authority, while the older adults from the US did not care about authority as much as Chinese older adults. A possible reason for this finding may be that traditional Chinese culture, which told people the government has great power and is always reliable, had a great impact on older adults. In addition, the fraudsters created scenes corresponding to the different roles they played, which makes it more difficult for older adults to judge the authenticity of messages or incoming calls.

5 General Discussion

There are three main findings of this study. First, older adults will take different strategies to fight telecommunication fraud. Traditional ways to fight fraud were by means of fraud experience or fraud cases they acquired. This study found that the discussed method may be not appropriate for older adults. In this study, certain older adults took extremely conservative strategies (i.e., trust nothing or nobody) to avoid being victims of telecommunication fraud, while others took moderate strategies. Specifically, participants with higher education and income were more likely to take extremely conservative strategies. The existing anti-fraud systems and laws focus on teaching older adults about prior fraud cases without considering their individual differences. It is not appropriate to teach older adults the same strategies (e.g., teaching older adults about same fraud cases). Individual difference should be considered in preventing fraud.

Second, this study found that need for cognition (NFC) plays an important role in anti-fraud strategies taken by older adults. Older adults with lower NFC prefer to take extremely conservative strategies. One possible reason is that older adults with lower NFC are less willing to carry out cognitive thinking activities. Hence, they preferred to think all messages were fraud instead of taking risks. Training older adults to form the habit of cognitive thinking may be a good way to fight fraud. Moreover, this method may be more effective than traditional ones (e.g., teaching older adults fraud cases) because it focuses on the aspects of cognition.

Third, fraudsters are more likely to first take a non-targeted fraud strategy to get more personal information and then take a precise strategy to commit telecommunication fraud. Role playing was the most frequently taken strategy by telecommunication fraudsters. Specifically, government officials were the most "popular" roles, showing that Chinese older adults are influenced heavily by authority.

6 Conclusion and Future Work

This study investigated older adults' reactions to telecommunication fraud. Through a three-phase experiment, their anti-fraud strategies, their vulnerability, and the tricks played by fraudsters were examined. Older adults who lived alone and had higher interpersonal trust were more vulnerable to fraud messages. In contrast, whether older adults feel social and emotional lonely or whether they were exposed to general fraud did not help them successfully identify the authenticity of messages. Individual differences in anti-fraud strategies were found. Older adults with higher education, income, and lower need for cognition (NFC) were more likely to take extremely conservative strategies.

This finding calls for the need to tailor anti-fraud training programs to non-homogeneous older adults.

The limitations of this study and future work should be noted. (i) The telecommunication fraud type only considered the message, which is not representative; more telecommunication fraud types (e.g., phone call fraud) should be involved. (ii) Only Chinese older adults are involved, and cultural difference might apply to results in other countries (e.g., the degree of trust in the government). (iii) The gender of participants was not balanced, and more male participants should be investigated. (iv) The survey in phase 2 conducted among colleges rather than older adults may bias the results, and may lack of generality. (v) This study is exploratory and should be further investigated.

Acknowledgment. This work was supported by funding from Chongqing Municipal Natural Science Foundation (cstc2016jcyjA0406) and the National Natural Science Foundation of China (Grants no. 71661167006).

References

1. National Consumers League: Telemarketing scams, January–December 2004. http://www.fraud.org/telemarketing/2004-telemarketing%20scams.pdf. Accessed 19 Feb 2018
2. National Consumers League. Scammers targeting their victims by age group, says National Consumers League's Fraud Center (2012). https://www.nclnet.org/scammers_targeting_their_victims_by_age_group_says_national_consumers_league_rsquo_s_fraud_center. Accessed 27 May 2020
3. Johnson, K.D.: Financial crimes against the elderly. US Department of Justice, Office of Community Oriented Policing Services (2004). http://citeseerx.ist.psu.edu/viewdoc/download;jsessionid=3F220FD69925296F7AFBF59560199A6B?doi=10.1.1.531.309&rep=rep1&type=pdf. Accessed 27 May 2020
4. Kok, K.F.: Truecaller insights special report: An estimated 22.1M Americans lost $9.5B in phone scams last year. Truecaller (2017). https://truecaller.blog/2017/04/19/truecaller-us-spam-report-2017/. Accessed 27 May 2020
5. Alves, L.M., Steve, R.W.: The effects of loneliness on telemarketing fraud vulnerability among older adults. J. Elder Abuse Neglect **20**(1), 63–85 (2008)
6. Cross, C.: 'They're very lonely': understanding the fraud victimisation of seniors. Int. J. Crime Justice Soc. Democr. **5**(4), 60 (2016)
7. Wagner, J.: The role of social factors in explaining consumer fraud victimization of the elderly (2017)
8. Lee, J., Geistfeld, L.V.: Elderly consumers' receptiveness to telemarketing fraud. J. Public Policy Mark. **18**(2), 208–217 (1999)
9. Waddell, F.E.: Consumer research and programs for the elderly-the forgotten dimension. J. Consum. Aff. **9**(2), 164–175 (1975)
10. Lim, C.M., Kim, Y.-K.: Older consumers' Tv home shopping: loneliness, parasocial interaction, and perceived convenience. Psychol. Mark. **28**(8), 763–780 (2011)
11. Forde, D.R., Kennedy, L.W.: Risky lifestyles, routine activities, and the General Theory of Crime. Justice Q. **14**, 265–294 (1997)
12. Schreck, C.J.: Criminal victimization and low self-control: an extension and test of a general theory of crime. Justice Q. **16**, 633–654 (1999)
13. Schreck, C.J., Stewart, E.A., Osgood, D.W.: A reappraisal of the overlap of violent offenders and victims. Criminol. Interdiscip. J. **46**(4), 871–906 (2008)

14. Pratt, T.C., Turanovic, J.J., Fox, K.A., Wright, K.A.: Self-control and victimization: a meta-analysis. Criminology **52**(1), 87–116 (2014)
15. Holtfreter, K., Reisig, M.D., Pratt, T.C.: Low self-control, routine activities, and fraud victimization. Criminology **46**(1), 189–220 (2008)
16. Holtfreter, K., Reisig, M.D., Leeper Piquero, N., Piquero, A.R.: Low self-control and fraud: offending, victimization, and their overlap. Crim. Justice Behav. **37**(2), 188–203 (2010)
17. Smith, K.G., Carroll, S.J., Ashford, S.J.: Intra- and interorganizational cooperation: toward a research agenda. Acad. Manag. J. **38**(1), 7–23 (1995)
18. McKnight, D.H., Chervany, N.L.: What trust means in e-commerce customer relationships: an interdisciplinary conceptual typology. Int. J. Electron. Commer. **6**(2), 35–59 (2001)
19. Das, S., Echambadi, R., McCardle, M., Luckett, M.: The effect of interpersonal trust, need for cognition, and social loneliness on shopping, information seeking and surfing on the Web. Mark. Lett. **14**(3), 185–202 (2003)
20. Hung, K., Li, S.Y., Tse, D.K.: Interpersonal trust and platform credibility in a Chinese multibrand online community. J. Advert. **40**(3), 99–112 (2011)
21. Trongmateerut, P.: The impact of assessment procedures and need for cognition on fraud risk assessments (2011). https://research.libraries.wsu.edu/xmlui/handle/2376/2847. Accessed 27 May 2020
22. Venkatraman, M.P., Marlino, D., Kardes, F.R., Sklar, K.B.: Effects of individual difference variables on responses to factual and evaluative ads. Adv. Consum. Res. **17**(1), 761 (1990)
23. Gross, E.A.: Elderly victims of telemarketing fraud: demographic, social, and psychological factors in victimization and willingness to report. University of Southern California, Los Angeles, California (2001)
24. Reiboldt, W., Vogel, R.: A critical analysis of telemarketing fraud in a gated senior community. J. Elder Abuse Neglect **13**(4), 21–38 (2001)
25. DiTommaso, E., Brannen, C., Best, L.A.: Measurement and validity characteristics of the short version of the social and emotional loneliness scale for adults. Educ. Psychol. Measur. **64**(1), 99–119 (2004)
26. Grasmick, H.G., Tittle, C.R., Bursik, R.J., Arneklev, B.J.: Testing the core empirical implications of Gottfredson and Hirschi's general theory of crime. J. Res. Crime Delinq. **30**(1), 5–29 (1993)
27. Cacioppo, J.T., Petty, R.E., Feinstein, J.A., Jarvis, W.B.G.: Dispositional differences in cognitive motivation: the life and times of individuals varying in need for cognition. Psychol. Bull. **119**(2), 197–253 (1996)
28. Eysenck, H.J., Eysenck, S.B.G.: Manual of the Eysenck Personality Questionnaire: (EPQ-R Adult). EdITS/Educational and Industrial Testing Service, San Diego, California (1994)
29. Miró, F.: Routine activity theory. In: Michalos, A.C. (ed.) The Encyclopedia of Theoretical Criminology. Springer, New York (2014)
30. Russell, D., Cutrona, C.E., Rose, J., Yurko, K.: Social and emotional loneliness: an examination of Weiss's typology of loneliness. J. Pers. Soc. Psychol. **46**(6), 1313–1321 (1984)
31. Liang, Y.: Trust in Chinese Government and Quality of Life (QOL) of Sichuan earthquake survivors: does trust in government help to promote QOL? Soc. Indic. Res. **127**(2), 541–564 (2016)

Internet Use and Loneliness Among Older Adults: The Moderating Role of Self-perceptions of Ageing

Wenqian Xu[1]([✉]) and Hanna Köttl[2]

[1] Division Ageing and Social Change, Linköping University, Norrköping, Sweden
wenqian.xu@liu.se
[2] Faculty of Social Sciences, Bar-Ilan University, Ramat Gan, Israel
kottl.hanna@biu.ac.il

Abstract. Loneliness in advanced age has become one of the societal concerns considering its detrimental effects on physical and mental health of older people. Information and communication technologies show the potential to prevent or tackle loneliness and social isolation among older people. Given a percentage of the older population feeling lonely, loneliness in older age has been increasingly recognized as a stereotype about older people and ageing which shapes self-perceptions of ageing. This cross-sectional study aims to investigate the interaction between older people's Internet use and the level of loneliness, as well as introduce the important role that self-perceptions of ageing may play in this association. The analyses were performed on data of community-dwelling older adults aged 65+ years from the German Ageing Survey. Findings from this study have shown that older people's greater Internet use was significantly associated with a lower level of loneliness; meanwhile, positive self-perceptions of ageing were correlated with a lower degree of loneliness. Additionally, self-perceptions of ageing (in the aspect of personal competence) moderate the relationship between Internet use and loneliness among older people. This paper allows insight into the important moderating role of positive self-perceptions of ageing in the relationship between older people's Internet use and the level of loneliness. This moderating effect hence contributes to the beneficial implications of frequent Internet use on preventing or reducing the level of loneliness. Given the global context of overwhelming facilitation of digital technologies across sectors and vulnerable social groups, it is of significance to empower older adults with negative self-perceptions of ageing to ensure they gain benefits from technological advances, as well as to challenge the prevalent stereotypes about older people and ageing in societies.

Keywords: Digital technology · Image of ageing · Internet use · Loneliness · Older people · Self-perceptions of ageing · Social contact · Stereotypes · Survey data

1 Introduction

In recent years loneliness in older age has become a societal concern considering its detrimental effects on physical and mental health [1]. Loneliness is conceptualized as

© Springer Nature Switzerland AG 2020
Q. Gao and J. Zhou (Eds.): HCII 2020, LNCS 12209, pp. 364–381, 2020.
https://doi.org/10.1007/978-3-030-50232-4_26

an index of social well-being and is relevant to the feeling of missing an intimate relationship (emotional loneliness) or missing a wider social network (social loneliness) [2–4]. The present article considers loneliness consisting of two dimensions, social and emotional. Previous studies found that the feeling of loneliness was associated with depression [5], cognitive decline [6], elevated systolic blood pressure [7] and coronary heart conditions [8]. Moreover, loneliness was found as a contributor to reduced well-being, social isolation and exclusion [9, 10]. Based on various country-level surveys loneliness was found to be alarmingly prevalent among older adults [11, 12]. Several longitudinal studies have demonstrated how the prevalence of loneliness among older people remains relatively constant at different time points [13, 14], however, across the individual's lifespan, loneliness is not constant but becomes volatile in older age [15]. Their findings give prominence to the significance of exploring factors that prevent and reduce older people's feeling of loneliness.

Various attempts have been made to prevent or tackle loneliness, including older people-targeted interventions [10, 16]. Increasing attention has been paid to the effects of older people's technology use on reducing the feeling of loneliness and supporting daily activities [17]. Meaningful social interactions of older adults play a significant role in decreasing the level of loneliness [18]. Computer-mediated communication (CMC) technologies have offered affordances for older people in fostering daily interactions and maintaining social contact [19], such as the Internet. A body of evidence showed the positive correlation between more Internet use and lower degrees of loneliness [20–22]; meanwhile, some studies show that extensive online communication may increase the feeling of loneliness due to a potential reduction of real-life relationships [23, 24].

In order to shed further light on the Internet and its potential to decrease loneliness in older adults, the present study adds a new dimension, the role of self-perceptions of ageing, into the discussion. As previously argued, loneliness has been a major concern associated with old age and growing older [25–27]. Likewise, loneliness has appeared to be one of many stereotypes about older people and ageing. Evidence shows that reported level of loneliness was significantly associated with stereotypes and expectations about loneliness in old age [28]. Individuals who believed that loneliness is an unavoidable by-product of older age experienced more loneliness in later life. Additionally, self-perceptions of one's own health has been proven to be associated with social loneliness [21]. In this respect, self-perceptions may play a major role in explaining the occurrence and degree of loneliness in later life.

Accordingly, this paper attempts to: (1) investigate the effects of Internet use for social contact on loneliness in a sample of community-dwelling older adults in Germany; (2) examine the interaction between self-perceptions of ageing and loneliness in community-dwelling older individuals; and (3) investigate the possible role of self-perceptions of ageing as a moderator that accentuates the positive relationship between Internet use and the level of loneliness.

2 Previous Studies

2.1 Older People's Internet Use and Loneliness

It has been recognized by governments and United Nations that promoting the accessibility of ICTs may help with improving the livelihoods of vulnerable populations, such as children, older people and persons of a lower socioeconomic status [29]. A set of policy initiatives have been introduced to promote ICT developments for older populations at the regional and country levels [30–32]. Older people in many countries have gained greater access to digital technologies, particularly in public sites, given state-subsidized information and communication technology (ICT) provisions and other targeted policies. In practice, public services (e.g., healthcare, education, elderly care) and public information have increasingly become web-based, since the Internet demonstrates its potential in improving the provision of public services. Additionally, older people have been considered as a highly relevant population group for online social services, due to the higher likelihood of physical or mental illness associated with older age [33, 34]. In this respect, Internet use has become crucial to access important digital public services, concerning the vision of making Internet relevant to our daily life (including older people) [35, 36].

Unlike the prevalent stereotypical and negative depictions of older adults as technophobic, unwilling or incapable of learning and using new digital technologies [37, 38], various studies have demonstrated that older individuals are indeed willing and capable of learning and using digital technologies, especially for communication purposes [17]. Evidence shows that older people in an adult education center in Barcelona (Spain) extensively use computer-mediated applications [39]. In terms of older people's online activities, older individuals in England and Wales mostly used computers for word-processing activities (e.g., reading and sending emails) [39], while older people in Japan mostly used online message boards to share stories and memories that reinforce their supportive companionship relationships [40]. Internet potentially improves the wellbeing of older people [33].

The ways in which people interact with Internet may be associated with the levels of loneliness in older age. It has been suggested that the use of Internet facilitates social connections and reduces loneliness in older people [21, 22]. The present paper investigates the relationship between older people's Internet use and their perception of loneliness. Therefore, we propose Hypothesis 1:

H1: Greater Internet use is associated with lower reported levels of loneliness in community-dwelling older adults.

2.2 Loneliness in Older Age and Self-perceptions of Ageing

Being socially isolated or lonely is one of the myths and stereotypes about older people [41]. Likewise, Loneliness was stereotypically associated with the lower status of older people, lack of meaning, and neglect by relatives in Finnish media [42]. This media representation of loneliness potentially contributes to the formation of stereotypes about older people. A literature review suggests that a small proportion of older persons aged between 65 and 79 years reported the experience of loneliness; while the prevalence of loneliness is higher among the oldest-old members of society (those age 80 and older) [43, 44]. Even though growing older is often equated with increasing loneliness, this phenomenon does not occur due to age per se, but rather because ageing adults are more likely to experience losses [45], both social and physical.

In respect to potential ageing-related social losses, Weeks [46] argued that loneliness may result from the losses that obstruct the acquisition of desired relationships and the maintenance of existing relationships, given that the possibility of experiencing losses rises as people age. Likewise, Routasalo and Pitkala [47] suggest that widowhood and the loss of a close friend are risk factors of loneliness over the lifespan. Regarding physical losses, hearing loss was mentioned as a cause of isolation, anxiety and depression [48]. Similarly, sensory losses such as hearing or visual impairments may result in increasing communication difficulties and decreasing socialization [49]. These losses contribute to the likelihood of loneliness [50, 51]. In respect to a potential reduction of personal competence in older age, older people are often stereotypically portrayed as incompetent in societies. It was found that older people's self-perception of personal competence was related with their social engagement in paid work and voluntary work [52]. Given that loneliness is entangled with potential loss during the ageing process, self-perceptions of ageing serve as a measurement of the extent that people of advanced age perceive these losses.

Self-perceptions of ageing (SPA) refer to a person's subjective views (positive or negative) on the aspects of ageing; SPA represents societal views on ageing that are internalized throughout the life course [53]. Evidence suggests that SPA are associated with specific health outcomes, affecting functioning wellbeing and longevity [54–57]. Specifically, positive self-perceptions of ageing may contribute to better health and wellbeing. According to the Stereotype Embodiment Theory, stereotypes and prejudice are internalized over the life course and shape people's perceptions and attitudes towards their experience of ageing. These stereotypes are eventually taken over from the surrounding environment by younger people and become self-definitions and internalized stereotypes as they age. Hence, ageing-related (sometimes ageist) messages may eventually be embodied, affecting health, wellbeing and functioning in later life [58]. Based on a meta-analysis and systematic literature review, it was found that negative stereotypes impair people's performance in a stereotype-consistent manner [59]. As such, it may contribute to older people withdrawing from meaningful social activities and a higher likelihood of feeling lonely.

Since there are many stereotypes of older people and ageing, a longitudinal study was conducted to investigate the relationship between expectations of loneliness in old age and actual self-reported loneliness. The results showed that expectations about loneliness in old age were significantly associated with reported loneliness eight years later [28]. Likewise, another study showed that the positive expectations about ageing were associated with new friendships two years later, including close friendships [60]. In this respect, the stereotypes of ageing at the individual level potentially are associated with the degrees of loneliness in older age.

Both self-perceptions of ageing and the experience of loneliness seem to be cross-culturally differentiated. This present study focuses on a sample of community-dwelling older people in Germany and investigates the potential association between self-perceptions of ageing and the reported loneliness among older people. It may contribute to our understanding of this underexplored domain and provide practical measures to prevent or tackle loneliness among older people.

We expect that older people's positive self-perceptions of ageing are related to lower degrees of loneliness. Therefore, we propose Hypothesis 2:

H2: Positive self-perceptions of ageing are associated with lower reported levels of loneliness in older adults.

2.3 Self-perceptions of Ageing as a Possible Moderator in the Relationship Between Older People's Internet Use and Loneliness

Self-perceptions of ageing may serve as a potential moderator in the relationship between Internet use and the degrees of loneliness in later life. Following the reasoning of the Stereotype Embodiment Theory, individuals perceiving their ageing more positively are more likely to have positive perceptions of being socially connected or feel less lonely. Older people's greater Internet use may effectively decrease the feeling of loneliness, especially if older individuals possess positive self-perceptions of ageing. Considering the role of a moderator affecting the strength of the relation between an independent variable and a dependent variable, the basic moderation effect refers to "an interaction between a focal independent variable and a factor that specifies the appropriate conditions for its operation" [61]. Hence, older people's self-perceptions of ageing are expected to moderate the correlation between Internet use and loneliness in older age. Specifically, we expect that having more positive self-perceptions of ageing strengthens the effect of Internet use on decreasing the feeling of loneliness. Due to data availability, three aspects of self-perceptions of ageing are considered, including personal competence, physical loss and social loss. Therefore, we suggest Hypothesis 3:

H3a: Older people's positive self-perceptions of ageing in personal competence accentuates the effects of digital technology use on the feeling of loneliness.
H3b: Older people's positive self-perceptions of ageing in physical loss accentuates the effects of digital technology use on the feeling of loneliness.
H3c: Older people's positive self-perceptions of ageing in social loss accentuates the effects of digital technology use on the feeling of loneliness.

As the self-perceptions of ageing are potentially transitory, it may accentuate the negative interaction between higher Internet use and loneliness. This paper may contribute to developing interventions to reduce older people's feeling of loneliness in the global context of technological facilitation.

3 Method

3.1 Respondents

This study utilized the German Ageing Survey (DEAS) [62] conducted by the Research Data Centre of Gerontology (DZA). The Survey is nation-wide and representative cohort-sequential, and it resulted in cross-sectional samples with longitudinal samples of community-dwelling people aged 40 and older. The main goal of the DEAS study is to provide insight into middle-aged and older Germans' living conditions, targeting both individual developments over time and social change [62]. The first sample was randomly drawn in 1996 using a national probability sampling technique and applying stratified sampling by age, gender, and region (East and West Germany). Wave 2 followed in 2002, Wave 3 in 2008, Wave 4 in 2011 (panel survey), Wave 5 in 2014 and Wave 6 in 2017 (n = 6626). Additional panel assessments were performed in Waves 2, 3, 5 and 6. Respondents participated in a 90-min face-to-face interview and filled in a paper-pencil questionnaire, at each measurement point. Before the interview, written informed consent was given by respondents. Please note that an ethical statement was not necessary under the German Research Foundation Guidelines (Deutsche Forschungsgemeinschaft, DFG).

This study derived cross-sectional data from Wave 6 which includes the latest data on older adult's Internet use. In 2017, 5,617 study participants completed the drop-off questionnaire. An online version of the drop-off questionnaire was first introduced in this wave. Among those who filled in the drop-off questionnaire, 1,001 people participated online, and the rest, 4,607 respondents, filled in the paper-pencil version. Those using the online drop-off questionnaire were more likely to be male, younger, healthier, of higher-level education and income, and living in west Germany. As this study focuses on web-use, 4252 (75,8%) stated to have access to Internet, while 1164 (20,8%) had no access. Those respondents without access were significantly older (F $=$ 13,00; p $=$ 0,000; [$-15,47$; 14,02]), female $\chi 2 = 81,76$, df $= 1$, p $= 0,000$) and from East Germany ($\chi 2 = 100,82$, df $= 1$, p $= 0,000$). Those without Internet access were also more likely to be depressed (F $= 8,04$; p $= 0,000$; [$-2,15$; 1,21]) functionally impaired (F $= 238,40$; p $= 0,000$; [14,11; 17,82]) and had less positive self-perceptions of ageing (F $= 3,84$; p $= 0,000$; [0,24; 0,30]) but were not significantly more lonely (F $= 3,914067$; p $= 0,67$; [$-0,03$; 0,05]).

The respondents included in this study are those aged over 65 years old (65 is the retirement age in Germany for people born before 1947), those who participated in the drop-off questionnaire in 2017 and participants who had access to the Internet (n $=$ 2119).

3.2 Measuring Instruments

Dependent Variable. The de Jong Gierveld Loneliness Scale [63] is an example of a multidimensional measure of loneliness. A shortened version contains six items was used in the questionnaire to indicate the degrees of loneliness. It was proved that the scale is appropriately regarded as bi-dimensional in samples of older people [64], even if the instrument can also be used to indicate a single index of loneliness [65]. It is comprised of three negatively formulated items ("I miss emotional security and warmth", "I miss having people around among which I feel comfortable" and "I often feel rejected") and three positively formulated items ("There are plenty of people I can rely on when I have problems", "There are many people I can trust completely" and "There are enough people I feel close to"). It was measured based on a 4-item Likert scale (1 $=$ "strongly agree", 2 $=$ "agree", 3 $=$ "disagree" and 4 $=$ "strongly disagree"). The three negatively formulated items were recoded, and the mean calculated using the six items. At least three of the four items must contain valid values to calculate the mean. Hence, a higher value indicates a stronger feeling of loneliness. The internal consistency was proved to be acceptable in our sample, given the reliability coefficient of 0.75 (Cronbach's alpha).

Independent Variable. Internet use for social contact was assessed by one question in the questionnaire (How often do you use the web for being in contact with friends and relatives e.g. through e-mail, Facebook, chat, video telephony). Respondents ranked the frequency of Internet use on a 6-item Likert scale from "never" to "daily". The variable was re-coded in a way that higher values represent more frequent Internet use.

As an independent and moderating variable, self-perceptions of ageing (SPA) was assessed using the Age-Cog scales [56, 66, 67]. These subscales capture the individual perception of the ageing-related losses and gains in three aspects. The aspects included in the present study are personal competence (PC), physical loss (PL), and social loss (SL). Each aspect consists of four items. Specifically, PC is measured by four items ("I continue to make plans;" "My capacities are increasing;" "I can still learn new things;" "I can still put my ideas into practice"); PL is measured by four items ("I am less energetic and fit;" "I am less healthy;" "I cannot make up for my physical losses;" "I cannot take as much as before"); SL is measured by four items ("I feel less needed;" "I feel lonely more often;" "I feel less respected;" "I am bored more often"). Respondents rated all items on a four-point Likert scale ranging from (1) strongly agree to (4) strongly disagree. To facilitate the interpretation of the results, the scale PC was re-coded for the analysis. A higher value indicates more positive SPA. The global self-perceptions of ageing score (globSPA) was constructed by aggregating the three perception of ageing subscales and is represented by the mean score. Likewise, a higher value on the aggregated SPA indicates more positive SPA. The internal consistency was proved to be acceptable, given the reliability coefficient of 0.81 (Cronbach's alpha).

Control Variables. Due to the potential impact of some factors on social interactions, several variables were controlled in the analysis, including age, gender, marital status, physical functioning related to everyday activities [5, 7] and depressive symptoms [5, 68]. The SF-36 subscale was used to measure physical functioning. The degree of physical impairment was assessed by evaluating ten daily activities on a scale from 1 to 3. The sum of the items was eventually transferred into the standard 0–100 range. Higher values indicated a better physical functioning. To capture symptoms of depression the 15-item short form of the German translation of the Centre for Epidemiologic Studies Depression (CES-D) Scale was applied. Higher values indicate higher depressive symptoms.

3.3 Statistical Analysis

The descriptive statistics and pairwise correlations were computed. In addition, multiple linear regressions were used to model the relation of the outcome variable (loneliness) to Internet use (Hypothesis 1) and self-perceptions of ageing (Hypothesis 2), controlled by potential confounders. In addition, this study tested whether the interaction between

Internet use and loneliness varies by degree of SPA (Hypothesis 3). The moderation analysis was performed using a regression-based approach [69].

The model assumptions for linear regressions were checked. In the linear regression models, multicollinearity was tested for by applying the variance inflation criterion. The largest variance inflation factor was 1.5; hence, the absence of multicollinearity was assumed. Further, the White test for heteroscedasticity in the error distribution was performed. Regarding the test statistics (with loneliness as an outcome measure: White's general test statistic $= 17{,}70$; $p < .001$), the null hypothesis of homoscedasticity was therefore rejected. Consequently, robust standard errors were used. The normality assumption of the residuals was checked using normal-probability plots, showing that the residuals were approximately normally distributed. The statistical significance was set at $p < .05$. All statistical analyses were performed using SPSS 25.0.

4 Results

4.1 Description of the Sample and Bivariate Correlations

In Wave 6, 3276 participants aged over 65 years (mean age: 74.36 years $\pm$ 6.19 years) replied with either yes or no to the question on Internet access. 47% of those respondents were female and 67.6% were married. The mean score of depressive symptoms in the whole sample was 6.31 ($\pm$5.50; ranging from 0 to 44) and the mean score of physical functioning was 77.89 ($\pm$24.37, ranging from 0 to 100).

All those who reported having access to the Internet (n $= 2119$; 64.7% of the whole sample) constituted the final sample used for analysis (see Table 1).

Bivariate analysis (see Table 2) suggested that higher Internet use was negatively correlated with the feeling of loneliness ($r = -.07$, $p < .01$). while more positive self-perceptions of ageing (globSPA) were moderately correlated with a lesser feeling of loneliness ($r = -.42$, $p < .001$). Hence, these findings are in line with our suggested hypothesis 1 and hypothesis 2. In addition, the feeling of loneliness was significantly associated with gender, region, marital status, physical activity and depression.

4.2 Moderation Analysis

Table 3 shows the result of the moderation analysis. Controlling for potential confounders, the analysis indicated that greater Internet use was associated with a lesser feeling of loneliness ($\beta = -.02$, $p < .01$). Additionally, positive self-perceptions of ageing were significantly associated with lower loneliness scores ($\beta = -.48$, $p < .001$).

Moreover, the higher level of loneliness was significantly associated with age (older age), gender (female), marital status (married), severer depression symptoms and lower physical functioning.

Finally, moderated models of regression analyses were used to test the hypothesis that older people's positive self-perceptions of ageing (in personal competence, physical loss and social loss) moderate the correlation between Internet use and the levels of loneliness. Interaction terms (PC $\times$ Internet use, PL $\times$ Internet use and SL $\times$ Internet use) were included in the regression model. The moderation analysis revealed that the correlation

Table 1. Characteristics (n = 2119) of the sample (community-dwelling older adults over 65 with Internet access)

Variables	N (%)	Mean (Std. Deviation)
Age (in years)	/	72.71 (5.67)
Gender		/
Male	1226 (57.9%)	
Female	893 (42.1%)	
Region		/
West Germany	1507 (71.1%)	
East Germany	612 (28.9%)	
Marital status		/
Married, living together	1584 (74.8%)	
not married	535 (25.2%)	
Physical functioning [a]	/	82.20 (21.54)
Depression [b]	/	5.72 (5.19)
Loneliness [c]	/	1.72 (.51)
Internet use [d]		3.97 (1.73)
Daily	475 (22.4%)	
Several times a week	611 (28.8%)	
Once a week	220 (10.4%)	
Once to three times a month	206 (9.7%)	
Less often	348 (16.4%)	
Never	241 (11.4%)	
GlobSPA [e]	/	2.81 (.42)
Personal competence		2.93 (.54)
Social loss		3.24 (.52)
Physical loss		2.27 (.54)

Note. [a] Higher score indicates better physical status. [b] Higher score indicates higher levels of depression. [c] Loneliness was assessed using a short version [70], ranging from 1 to 4 (higher values reflect higher perceived loneliness). [d] Internet use for social contact was assessed through the question 'How often do you use the web for being in contact with friends and relatives?' Frequency of use was assessed from 1 to 6 (higher values higher use). [e] The aggregated score of the global self-perceptions of ageing (globSPA) was calculated as the mean score of all three subscales. Higher values indicate more positive SPA; The globSPA consists of three subscales: personal competence, physical loss and social loss.

between older people's Internet use and their feeling of loneliness was significantly moderated by the AgeCog subscale personal competence (PC). However, the association between Internet use and loneliness in older age was not moderated by the other two subscales of social loss (SL) and physical loss (PL).

Table 2. Result of Pearson and Chi-square correlation analysis

Variables	Loneliness	Internet use	GlobSPA	Personal competence	Physical loss	Social loss	Age	Gender	Region	Marital status	Depression
Loneliness [a]	1										
Internet use [b]	-.07**	1									
GlobSPA [c]	-.42***	.11***	1								
Personal competence [d]	-.26***	.16***	.79***	1							
Physical loss [e]	-.20***	.08***	.78***	.43***	1						
Social loss [f]	-.51***	.016	.75***	.37***	.39***	1					
Age	.02	-.11***	-.25***	-.24***	-.12***	-.08***	1				
Gender: female [g]	.06*	.01	.01	.01	.02	.00	.06**	1			
Region: east [h]	.10***	-.03	.05*	.04*	.08***	.02	.00	.03	1		
Not married [i]	.09***	.03	.08***	.03*	.02	.14***	.13***	.24***	.01	1	
Depression [j]	.30***	-.05*	-.44***	-.30***	-.36***	-.37***	.11***	.10***	.026	.12***	1
Physical status [k]	-.12***	.079***	.40***	.30***	.43***	.20***	-.25***	-.11***	-.03	-.09***	-.41***

Note: [a] Loneliness was assessed using a short version [70], ranging from 1 to 4 (higher values reflect higher perceived loneliness). [b] Frequency of Internet use was assessed from 1 to 4 (higher values higher use) through the question 'How often do you use the web for being in contact with friends and relatives?'. [c] The aggregated score of globSPA was calculated as the mean score of all three subscales. Higher values indicate more positive SPA. [d] Personal competence subscale of the Age-Cog scales. [e] Physical loss subscale of the Age-Cog scales. [f] Social loss subscale of the Age-Cog scales. [g] Gender: Ref.: Male. [h] Region: Ref.: living in West Germany. [i] Marital status: Ref: married. [j] Higher scores indicate higher levels of depression. [k] Higher scores indicate better physical status. Observations with missing values were dropped for reasons of simplicity (listwise deletion). *** p < 0.001, ** p < 0.01, * p < 0.05.

5   Discussion, Conclusion and Limitations

This paper firstly investigated the relationship between older people's Internet use for social contact and their feeling of loneliness. Given that negative stereotypes and expectations of the inevitability of loneliness in later life have been prevalent, we shed light on self-perceptions of ageing among older people. In this respect, this paper zoomed in on three aspects of self-perceptions of ageing (SPA) (i.e., personal competence, social loss and physical loss) that are often connected to the subjective experiences of loneliness. This research therefore investigated whether older people's self-perceptions of ageing accentuate the positive relationship between Internet use and a lower level of loneliness.

The finding supporting Hypothesis 1 suggested that more frequent Internet use (for social interaction with friends and family) was associated with lower levels of loneliness in community-dwelling Germans over 65. This is consistent with prior studies emphasizing the positive impact of older adults' Internet use on various health-related outcomes including loneliness [22]. The association in our analysis was statistically significant (P-value < 0,01), yet, relatively weak. One explanation could be that some older people might not perceive the Internet as a meaningful tool to stay socially connected. Acknowledging the heterogeneity of older adults, some individuals may prefer ways to keep in touch with friends and relatives other than through Internet, without being necessarily lonelier. Future research may also consider applying a life-course perspective for investigating the seemingly bidirectional association between Internet use and self-perceptions of ageing across generations. While among older adults, Internet use appears to be predominantly promoted as a positive medium to decrease loneliness, in younger adults, extensive media use has been widely discussed as a potential cause for loneliness [71]. A life-course perspective may add value to our understanding that Internet use may have significant implications for all populations.

In response to Hypothesis 2, this study confirmed that older individuals with positive self-perceptions of ageing reported a lower score of loneliness. Considering the formation of personal perceptions of ageing, negative self-perceptions of ageing may result from the internalization of prevalent ageist messages, according to the Stereotype Embodiment Theory. Negative self-perceptions of ageing and ageism appear to be closely connected [72], while ageism, like other forms of discrimination, can lead to the feeling of loneliness [73]. For example, Sutin et al. [74] investigated the longitudinal relationship between perceived discrimination and subsequent loneliness in a representative sample of older Americans. Over a time period of 5 years everyday perceived discrimination was significantly associated with reports of loneliness. The unique focus on positive self-perceptions of ageing in the present paper may incite future in-depth qualitative studies on investigating the reasons why individuals with positive self-perceptions of ageing prevent or reduce loneliness. This study focused on positive self-perceptions of ageing due to its modifiable nature, which lead to the discussion on the next hypothesis.

The result related to Hypothesis 3 indicated that older people's self-perceptions of ageing (merely in the aspect of personal competence) significantly moderated the relationship between their Internet use and experiences of loneliness. This finding underlines the importance of older people's positive perceptions on their individual competencies in reducing the experience of loneliness. Hence, believing in one's personal competencies regardless of age (e.g., making plans, learning new things, putting ideas into practices)

Table 3. Result of moderation analysis

Variables	B (SE)	B (SE)	B (SE)	B (SE)	B (SE)	B (SE)
Age	-.00 (.00)	-.001*** (.18)	-.01** (.00)	-.00* (.00)	-.00* (.00)	
Gender [a]	-.12*** (.02)	-.09*** (.02)	-.11*** (.02)	-.10*** (.02)	-.08*** (.02)	
Region [b]	-1,5*** (0.2)	-.14*** (.02)	-.14*** (.02)	-.15*** (.02)	-.12*** (.02)	
Marital status [c]	.030** (.01)	.030*** (.01)	.03*** (.01)	.03*** (.01)	.01 (.01)	
Depression [d]	.03***(12,07)	.01*** (.00)	.02*** (.00)	.02*** (.00)	.01*** (.00)	
Physical functioning [e]	.00 (-.01)	.00** (.00)	.00 (.00)	.00 (.00)	-.01 (.00)	
Internet use [f]	-.02** (.006)					
GlobSPA [g]	-4.49*** (.03)					
Personal competence [h]		-.21*** (.02)				
Physical loss [i]			-.21*** (.02)	-.15*** (.02)		
Social loss [j]					-.46*** (.02)	
PC x Internet use						-.02* (.01)
PL x Internet use						-.01 (.01)
SL x Internet use						-.01 (.01)
Adjusted R² [b]	.11	.23	.15	.13	.30	.16

Note: [a] 1 Male, 2 Female. [b] 1 Western Germany, 2 Eastern Germany. [c] 1 Married living together, 2 Not married. [d] Higher score indicates a stronger degree of depression. [e] Higher score indicates a better physical status. [f] Have been discriminated against. SWB is the mean of the standardized scores of positive affect and satisfaction with life. [g] The global self-perceptions of ageing score was calculated as the mean score of all three subscales. [h] Higher values indicate more positive SPA. [i] Physical loss subscale of the Age-Cog scales. [j] Physical loss subscale of the Age-Cog scales. Social loss subscale of the Age-Cog scales; observations with missing values were dropped for reasons of simplicity (listwise deletion). *** p < 0.001, ** p < 0.01, * p < 0.05.

increased the chance to benefit from Internet use and therefore decreased older people's experiences of feeling lonely.

The potential interpretation for the moderating role of SPA (in the aspect of personal competence) could be that Internet users with more positive self-perceptions of ageing are better connected with younger generations, often considered as the more tech-savvy population. A systematic literature review and a meta-analysis launched by the World Health Organization has shown that intergenerational contact has the greatest promise in decreasing negative self-perceptions of ageing and ageism [75]. In this respect, future interventions to prevent and reduce older people's loneliness should consider facilitating intergenerational contact.

Surprisingly, the findings did not support H3b and H3c, since older people's perceptions of ageing-related physical and social losses failed to affect the extent to which Internet use interacts with the feeling of loneliness. A possible explanation might be that some older people have a greater acceptance of ageing-related physical and social loss in later life; therefore, these perceptions would not significantly affect their wellbeing and behaviors.

In conclusion, this study advanced our knowledge of Internet use in decreasing the feeling of loneliness in later life, as well as self-perceptions of ageing functioning as a moderator in this relationship. Additionally, it provided insights into a practice issue which is how to effectively decrease loneliness in later life. As SPA are modifiable [76], self-perceptions of ageing interventions for older adults might be effective in reducing feelings of loneliness, especially for those less involved in Internet use.

This paper has several limitations to be addressed. First, it acknowledges that there might be relevant covariates neglected in the present analysis. Second, there might be response bias regarding the Internet use variable, since it is socially expected to use the Internet. Third, the generalization of research findings might be limited for the oldest-old members of society and individuals without access to the Internet.

6   Implications for Future Research

Longitudinal studies can be performed to further investigate the relationship between older people's Internet use and the level of loneliness, and the moderating role of SPA, adjusting for time-constant factors. Additionally, future studies may consider other online activities of older people, given that they are engaged in a diversity of activities that contribute to a lower level of loneliness. Moreover, future research may ensure that the oldest-old members of society are not neglected, considering they are more likely to be living with and affected by loneliness [43]. Future research could also explore the relationship between the level of loneliness and other types of ICT use among older people (e.g., radio, television).

Based on the findings of the present study, it becomes significant to challenge prevalent stereotypes about older people and ageing, especially the stereotypes that conceive older people as an incompetent group. Future intervention studies could provide insights into the role of old age and ageing stereotypes in the context of everyday technology, thus enabling the development of effective methods of improving older people's social participation and wellbeing. In this respect, combatting common ageist assumptions and empowering older people with negative perceptions of ageing may further promote equal access to the benefits Internet technologies promise.

Acknowledgement. This research has received funding from the European Union's Horizon 2020 research and innovation programme under the Marie Skłodowska-Curie grant agreement No 764632.

References

1. Courtin, E., Knapp, M.: Social isolation, loneliness and health in old age: a scoping review (2017). https://doi.org/10.1111/hsc.12311
2. Gierveld, J.D.J., Theo, V.T.: The De Jong Gierveld short scales for emotional and social loneliness: tested on data from 7 countries in the UN generations and gender surveys. Eur. J. Ageing 7, 121–130 (2010). https://doi.org/10.1007/s10433-010-0144-6
3. Dahlberg, L., McKee, K.J.: Correlates of social and emotional loneliness in older people: evidence from an English community study. Aging Ment. Health. 18, 504–514 (2014). https://doi.org/10.1080/13607863.2013.856863
4. Weiss, R.S.: Loneliness: The Experience of Emotional and Social Isolation. The MIT Press, Cambridge (1973)
5. Cacioppo, J.T., Elizabeth, M., Waite, L.J., Hawkley, L.C., Thisted, R.A.: Loneliness as a specific risk factor for depressive symptoms: cross-sectional and longitudinal analyses. Psychol. Aging 21, 140–151 (2006). https://doi.org/10.1037/0882-7974.21.1.140
6. Tilvis, R.S., Kähönen-Väre, M.H., Jolkkonen, J., Valvanne, J., Pitkala, K.H., Strandberg, T.E.: Predictors of cognitive decline and mortality of aged people over a 10-year period. J. Gerontol. Ser. A Biol. Sci. Med. Sci 59, 268–274 (2004). https://doi.org/10.1093/gerona/59.3.M268
7. Hawkley, L.C., Berntson, G.G., Burleson, M.H.: Loneliness in everyday life: cardiovascular activity, psychosocial context, and health behaviors. J. Personal. Soc. Psychol. 85, 105–120 (2003). https://doi.org/10.1037/0022-3514.85.1.105
8. Thurston, R.C., Kubzansky, L.D.: Women, loneliness, and incident coronary heart disease. Psychosom. Med. 71, 836–842 (2009). https://doi.org/10.1097/PSY.0b013e3181b40efc
9. Barbosa Neves, B., Sanders, A., Kokanović, R.: 'It's the worst bloody feeling in the world': experiences of loneliness and social isolation among older people living in care homes. J. Aging Stud. 49, 74–84 (2019). https://doi.org/10.1016/j.jaging.2019.100785
10. Findlay, R.A.: Interventions to reduce social isolation amongst older people: where is the evidence? Ageing Soc. 23, 647–658 (2003). https://doi.org/10.1017/S0144686X03001296
11. Yang, K., Victor, C.: Age and loneliness in 25 European nations. Ageing Soc. 31, 1368–1388 (2011). https://doi.org/10.1017/S0144686X1000139X
12. Drennan, J., et al.: The experience of social and emotional loneliness among older people in Ireland. Ageing Soc. 28, 1113–1132 (2008). https://doi.org/10.1017/S0144686X08007526
13. Dahlberg, L., Agahi, N., Lennartsson, C.: Lonelier than ever? Loneliness of older people over two decades. Arch. Gerontol. Geriatr. 75, 96–103 (2018). https://doi.org/10.1016/j.archger.2017.11.004
14. Victor, C.R., Bowling, A.: A longitudinal analysis of loneliness among older people in Great Britain. J. Psychol. 146, 313–331 (2012). https://doi.org/10.1080/00223980.2011.609572
15. Bath, P., Yang, H., Nicholls, J.: Changes in loneliness and patterns of loneliness among older people. Innov. Aging 2, 480 (2018). https://doi.org/10.1093/geroni/igy023.1794
16. Masi, C.M., Chen, H.-Y., Hawkley, L.C., Cacioppo, J.T.: A meta-analysis of interventions to reduce loneliness. Personal. Soc. Psychol. Rev. 15, 219–266 (2011). https://doi.org/10.1177/1088868310377394

17. Fan, Q.: Utilizing ICT to prevent loneliness and social isolation of the elderly. A literature review. Notebooks Soc. Work **29**, 185–200 (2016). https://doi.org/10.5209/CUTS.51771

18. Hubbard, G., Tester, S., Downs, M.: Meaningful social interactions between older people in institutional care settings. Ageing Soc. **23**, 99–114 (2003). https://doi.org/10.1017/S01446 86X02008991

19. Fuss, B.G., Dorstyn, D., Ward, L.: Computer-mediated communication and social support among community-dwelling older adults: a systematic review of cross-sectional data. Australas. J. Ageing **38**, e103–e113 (2019). https://doi.org/10.1111/ajag.12703

20. Desharnais Bruce, L., Wu, J.S., Lustig, S.L., Rusell, D.W., Nemecek, D.A.: Loneliness in the United States: a 2018 national panel survey of demographic, structural, cognitive, and behavioral characteristics. Am. J. Heal. Promot. **33**, 1123–1133 (2019). https://doi.org/10.1177/0890117119856551

21. Sum, S., Mathews, R.M., Hughes, I., Campbell, A.: Internet use and loneliness in older adults. CyberPsychol. Behav. **11**, 28–211 (2008). https://doi.org/10.1089/cpb.2007.0010

22. Kaspar, R.: Technology and loneliness in old age. Gerontechnology **3**, 42–48 (2004). https://doi.org/10.4017/gt.2004.03.01.007.00

23. Hu, M.: Will online chat help alleviate mood loneliness? CyberPsychol. Behav. **12**, 219–223 (2009). https://doi.org/10.1089/cpb.2008.0134

24. Morahan-Martin, J.: The relationship between loneliness and Internet use and abuse. CyberPsychol. Behav. **2**, 431–439 (1999). https://doi.org/10.1089/cpb.1999.2.431

25. Vozikaki, M., Papadaki, A., Linardakis, M., Philalithis, A.: Loneliness among older European adults: results from the survey of health, aging and retirement in Europe. J. Public Health (Bangkok) **26**, 613–624 (2018). https://doi.org/10.1007/s10389-018-0916-6

26. Cattan, M., Newell, C., Bond, J., White, M.: Alleviating social isolation and loneliness among older people. Int. J. Ment. Health Promot. **5**, 20–30 (2003). https://doi.org/10.1080/14623730.2003.9721909

27. Victor, C.R., et al.: Has loneliness amongst older people increased? An investigation into variations between cohorts. Ageing Soc. **22**, 585–597 (2002). https://doi.org/10.1017/S01 44686X02008784

28. Pikhartova, J., Bowling, A., Victor, C.: Is loneliness in later life a self-fulfilling prophecy? Aging Ment. Health. **20**, 543–549 (2016). https://doi.org/10.1080/13607863.2015.1023767

29. United Nations Department of Economic and Social Affairs: UN E-Government Survey 2018 (2018)

30. Damant, J., Knapp, M., Watters, S., Freddolino, P., Ellis, M., King, D.: The impact of ICT services on perceptions of the quality of life of older people. J. Assist. Technol. **7**, 5–21 (2013). https://doi.org/10.1108/17549451311313183

31. Obi, T., Ishmatova, D., Iwasaki, N.: Promoting ICT innovations for the ageing population in Japan. Int. J. Med. Inform. **82**, e47–e62 (2013). https://doi.org/10.1016/j.ijmedinf.2012.05.004

32. Hur, M.H.: Empowering the elderly population through ICT-based activities: an empirical study of older adults in Korea. Inf. Technol. People. **29**, 318–333 (2016). https://doi.org/10.1108/ITP-03-2015-0052

33. Sourbati, M.: 'It could be useful, but not for me at the moment': older people, internet access and e-public service provision. New Media Soc. **11**, 1083–1100 (2009). https://doi.org/10.1177/1461444809340786

34. Gell, N.M., Rosenberg, D.E., Demiris, G., LaCroix, A.Z., Patel, K.V.: Patterns of technology use among older adults with and without disabilities. Gerontologist **55**, 412–421 (2013). https://doi.org/10.1093/geront/gnt166

35. Loos, E.: Senior citizens: digital immigrants in their own country? Observatorio **6**, 1–23 (2012). https://doi.org/10.15847/obsOBS612012513

36. Sourbati, M., Loos, E.F.: Interfacing age: diversity and (in)visibility in digital public service. J. Digit. Media Policy. **10**, 275–293 (2019). https://doi.org/10.1386/jdmp_00003_1

37. Peine, A., Neven, L.: From intervention to co-constitution: new directions in theorizing about aging and technology. Gerontologist **59**, 15–21 (2019). https://doi.org/10.1093/geront/gny050

38. Fang, M.L., Canham, S.L., Battersby, L., Sixsmith, J., Wada, M., Sixsmith, A.: Exploring privilege in the digital divide: implications for theory, policy, and practice. Gerontologist **59**, e1–e15 (2019). https://doi.org/10.1093/geront/gny037

39. Sayago, S., Sloan, D., Blat, J.: Everyday use of computer-mediated communication tools and its evolution over time: an ethnographical study with older people. Interact. Comput. **23**, 543–554 (2011). https://doi.org/10.1016/j.intcom.2011.06.001

40. Kanayama, T.: Ethnographic research on the experience of Japanese elderly people online. New Media Soc. **5**, 267–288 (2003). https://doi.org/10.1177/1461444803005002007

41. Durick, J., Robertson, T., Brereton, M., Vetere, F., Nansen, B.: Dispelling ageing myths in technology design. In: Proceedings of the 25th Australian Computer-Human Interaction Conference: Augmentation, Application, Innovation, Collaboration, OzCHI 2013. pp. 467–476. Association for Computing Machinery (2013). https://doi.org/10.1145/2541016.2541040

42. Uotila, H., Lumme-Sandt, K., Saarenheimo, M.: Lonely older people as a problem in society-construction in Finnish media. Int. J. Ageing Later Life **5**, 103–130 (2010). https://doi.org/10.3384/ijal.1652-8670.1052103

43. Dykstra, P.: Older adult loneliness: myths and realities. Eur. J. Ageing **6**, 91–100 (2009). https://doi.org/10.1007/s10433-009-0110-3

44. Tijhuis, M.A., De Jong-Gierveld, J., Feskens, E.J., Kromhout, D.: Changes in and factors related to loneliness in older men. The Zutphen Elderly Study. Age Ageing **28**, 491–495 (1999). https://doi.org/10.1093/ageing/28.5.491

45. Jylhä, M.: Old age and loneliness: cross-sectional and longitudinal analyses in the Tampere Longitudinal Study on Aging. Can. J. Aging/La Rev. Can. du Vieil. **23**, 157–168 (2004). https://doi.org/10.1353/cja.2004.0023

46. Weeks, D.J.: A review of loneliness concepts, with particular reference to old age. Int. J. Geriatr. Psychiatry **9**, 345–355 (1994). https://doi.org/10.1002/gps.930090502

47. Routasalo, P., Pitkala, K.H.: Loneliness among older people. Rev. Clin. Gerontol. **13**, 303–311 (2003). https://doi.org/10.1017/S095925980400111X

48. Alpass, F.M., Neville, S.: Loneliness, health and depression in older males. Aging Ment. Health. **7**, 212–216 (2003). https://doi.org/10.1080/1360786031000101193

49. Heine, C., Browning, C.J.: The communication and psychosocial perceptions of older adults with sensory loss: a qualitative study. Ageing Soc. **24**, 113–130 (2004). https://doi.org/10.1017/S0144686X03001491

50. Sung, Y.-K., Li, L., Blake, C., Betz, J., Lin, F.R.: Association of hearing loss and loneliness in older adults. J. Aging Health. **28**, 979–994 (2016). https://doi.org/10.1177/0898264315614570

51. Chen, H.L.: Hearing in the elderly. Relation of hearing loss, loneliness, and self-esteem. J. Gerontol. Nurs. **20**, 22–28 (1994). https://doi.org/10.3928/0098-9134-19940601-07

52. Bowen, C.E., Skirbekk, V.: National stereotypes of older people's competence are related to older adults' participation in paid and volunteer work. J. Gerontol. Ser. B Psychol. Sci. Soc. Sci. **68**, 974–983 (2013). https://doi.org/10.1093/geronb/gbt101

53. Levy, B.R.: Mind matters: cognitive and physical effects of aging self-stereotypes. J. Gerontol. Ser. B Psychol. Sci. Soc. Sci. **58**, 203–211 (2003). https://doi.org/10.1093/geronb/58.4.P203

54. Sargent-Cox, K.A., Anstey, K.J., Luszcz, M.A.: The relationship between change in self-perceptions of aging and physical functioning in older adults. Psychol. Aging **27**, 750–760 (2012). https://doi.org/10.1037/a0027578

55. Moser, C., Spagnoli, J., Santos-Eggimann, B.: Self-perception of aging and vulnerability to adverse outcomes at the age of 65–70 years. J. Gerontol. Ser. B Psychol. Sci. Soc. Sci. **66**, 675–680 (2011). https://doi.org/10.1093/geronb/gbr052

56. Wurm, S., Tesch-Römer, C., Tomasik, M.J.: Longitudinal findings on aging-related cognitions, control beliefs, and health in later life. J. Gerontol. Ser. B Psychol. Sci. Soc. Sci. **62**, 156–164 (2007). https://doi.org/10.1093/geronb/62.3.p156

57. Horowitz, B.P., Chang, P.-F.J.: Promoting well-being and engagement in life through occupational therapy life redesign: a pilot study within adult day programs. Top. Geriatr. Rehabil. **20**, 46–58 (2004)

58. Levy, B.R., Slade, M.D., Kasl, S.V.: Longitudinal benefit of positive self-perceptions of aging on functional health. J. Gerontol. Ser. B Psychol. Sci. Soc. Sci. **57**, 409 (2002). https://doi.org/10.1093/geronb/57.5.p409

59. Schmader, T., Johns, M., Forbes, C.: An integrated process model of stereotype threat effects on performance. Psychol. Rev. **115**, 336–356 (2008). https://doi.org/10.1037/0033-295x.115.2.336

60. Menkin, J.A., Robles, T.F., Gruenewald, T.L., Tanner, E.K., Seeman, T.E.: Positive expectations regarding aging linked to more new friends in later life. J. Gerontol. Ser. B Psychol. Sci. Soc. Sci. **72**, 771–781 (2017). https://doi.org/10.1093/geronb/gbv118

61. Baron, R.M., Kenny, D.A.: The moderator–mediator variable distinction in social psychological research: conceptual, strategic, and statistical considerations. J. Pers. Soc. Psychol. **51**, 1173–1182 (1986)

62. Klaus, D., et al.: Cohort profile: the German ageing survey (DEAS). Int. J. Epidemiol. **46**, 1105–1105g (2017). https://doi.org/10.1093/ije/dyw326

63. De Jong-Gierveld, J., Kamphuls, F.: The development of a Rasch-type loneliness scale. Appl. Psychol. Meas. **9**, 289–299 (1985). https://doi.org/10.1177/014662168500900307

64. Van Baarsen, B., Snijders, T.A., Smit, J.H., Van Duijn, M.A.: Lonely but not alone: emotional isolation and social isolation as two distinct dimensions of loneliness in older people. Educ. Psychol. Meas. **61**, 119–135 (2001). https://doi.org/10.1177/00131640121971103

65. Gierveld, J.D.J., Tilburg, T.V.: A 6-item scale for overall, emotional, and social loneliness: confirmatory tests on survey data. Res. Ageing **28**, 582–598 (2006). https://doi.org/10.1177/0164027506289723

66. Dittmann-Kohli, F., Kohli, M., Künemund, H., Motel, A., Steinleitner, C., Westerhof, G.: Lebenszusammenhänge, Selbst- und Lebenskonzeptionen [Life coherence, self-concept and life design: The conceptualization of the German Aging Survey] (1997)

67. Steverink, N., Westerhof, G.J., Bode, C., Dittmann-Kohli, F.: The personal experience of aging, individual resources, and subjective well-being. J. Gerontol. B Psychol. Sci. Soc. Sci. **56**, 364–373 (2001). https://doi.org/10.1093/geronb/56.6.P364

68. Ayalon, L., Shiovitz-Ezra, S.: The relationship between loneliness and passive death wishes in the second half of life. Int. Psychogeriatr. **23**, 1677–1685 (2011). https://doi.org/10.1017/S1041610211001384

69. Hayes, A.: Introduction to Mediation, Moderation, and Conditional Process Analysis: A Regression-Based Approach. The Guilford Press, New York (2017)

70. Jenny De Jong, G., van Tilburg, T.G.: A 6-item scale for overall, emotional, and social loneliness: confirmatory tests on survey data. Res. Ageing **28**, 582–598 (2006)

71. Nowland, R., Necka, E.A., Cacioppo, J.T.: Loneliness and social Internet use: pathways to reconnection in a digital world? Perspect. Psychol. Sci. **13**, 70–87 (2018). https://doi.org/10.1177/1745691617713052

72. Giasson, H.L., Queen, T.L., Larkina, M., Smith, J.: Age group differences in perceived age discrimination: associations with self-perceptions of aging. Gerontologist **57**, S160–S168 (2017). https://doi.org/10.1093/geront/gnx070

73. Ayalon, L., Tesch-römer, C. (eds.): Contemporary Perspectives on Ageism. Springer, Cham (2018). https://doi.org/10.1007/978-3-319-73820-8

74. Sutin, A.R., Stephan, Y., Carretta, H., Terracciano, A.: Perceived discrimination and physical, cognitive, and emotional health in older adulthood. Am. J. Geriatr. Psychiatry. **23**, 171–179 (2015). https://doi.org/10.1016/j.jagp.2014.03.007

75. Burnes, D., et al.: Interventions to reduce ageism against older adults: a systematic review and meta-analysis. Am. J. Public Health **109**, e1–e9 (2019). https://doi.org/10.2105/AJPH. 2019.305123

76. Beyer, A.-K., Wolff, J.K., Freiberger, E., Wurm, S.: Are self-perceptions of ageing modifiable? Examination of an exercise programme with vs. without a self-perceptions of ageing-intervention for older adults. Psychol. Health. **34**, 661–676 (2019). https://doi.org/10.1080/08870446.2018.1556273

Author Index

Printed in the United States
By Bookmasters